W9-AFK-464

Our poisoned planet

TD
176
.097
1989

JAN 1993

KALAMAZOO VALLEY COMMUNITY COLLEGE
LEARNING RESOURCES CENTER
KALAMAZOO, MICHIGAN   49009

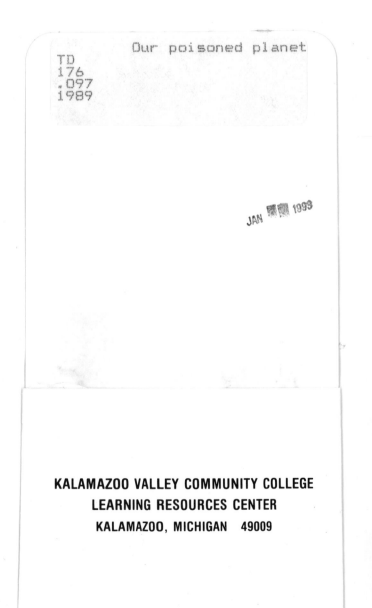

OUR POISONED PLANET:
Can We Save It?

TD
176
.O97
1989

OUR POISONED PLANET:
Can We Save It?

AN EDITORIALS ON FILE BOOK

Editor: Oliver Trager

Facts On File
New York • Oxford • Sydney

WITHDRAWN

KVCC KALAMAZOO VALLEY
COMMUNITY COLLEGE
LIBRARY

NOV 1 2 1990

OUR POISONED PLANET:
Can We Save It?

Published by Facts On File, Inc.
© Copyright 1989 by Facts On File, Inc.

All rights reserved. No part of this book may be reproduced in any form without the permission of the publisher except for reasonably brief extracts used in reviews, which retain their copyrights.

Library of Congress Cataloging-in-Publication Data
Main entry under title:

Our poisoned planet: can we save it?/editor, Oliver Trager
        p. cm.
    Summary: Examines environmental issues through the words and images of the nations leading editorial writers and cartoonists.
    ISBN 0-8160-2249-6 : $24.95
    1. Pollution–Environmental aspects–Juvenile literature. 2. Environmental protection–Juvenile literature. [1. Pollution. 2. Environmental protection.] I. Trager, Oliver.
TD176.097 1989
363.73–dc20

Printed in the United States of America

9 8 7 6 5 4 3 2 1

Contents

Preface

Public attention is focusing on environmental issues as never before. Whether it is the devastating oil spill in Prince William Sound off Valdez, Alaska, or hospital waste washing up on the shores of the East Coast or the drought that has ravished many parts of the U.S., Americans have become painfully aware of the fragile balance between nature and man.

Since the 1960s, doomsayers have been issuing dire prophecies concerning the dangers to our health, natural resources and surroundings posed by the pollution of an industrial society. Despite legislation passed in the 1970s and 1980s to control pollutants spewed into the air, dumped into rivers and lakes, and spread across the land, the nation faces an environmental crisis of potentially catastrophic proportions. As scientific evidence accumulates and public interest mounts, the environmental consequences of the nation's industrial prowess and quest for ever higher living standards and the resultant damage to the environment and our health is clear.

Less clear, however, is whether a national consensus and a will to save the environment actually exist. Even as environmental issues move to the forefront, many, or perhaps most, Americans are unwilling to do without the products and activities — from using laundry detergents to driving family cars — whose manufacture or use create these dangerous contaminants.

Industry argues that health benefits to be gained from pollution control must be counterbalanced by economic considerations. This cost-benefit approach was enthusiastically embraced by the Reagan administration and reflected in its environmental policies. But environmentalists respond that a problem with a cost-benefit approach is the difficulty of assessing the monetary value of human health or the cost of life curtailed.

As the debate over environmental health risks continues into the 1990s, it is this fundamental fact that must be addressed: We have only one Earth on which to live and must necessarily suffer the consequences of defiling it. On the other hand, is the cost of cleaning up past pollution and effectively preventing it in the future worth the price if it means a loss of U.S. competitiveness among other nations that have opted for wealth over environment.

The questions raised in the last two decades are still relevant. Is it wise or possible to try restricting the proliferation of potential environmental damage without regard to cost? Is the Environmental Protection Agency paying enough attention to these hazards? What is the impact of activist environmental groups such as Greenpeace? Are toxic chemical wastes threatening current and future generations? What is the future of the nuclear power industry? Is pollution affecting worldwide weather patterns? What are the consequences of the huge hole in the ozone layer above Antarctica and what caused it?

OUR POISONED PLANET: Can We Save It? takes a look at the environmental issues raging worldwide: Acid rain and the U.S.-Canadian efforts to curb it. Toxic waste and the threats it poses to humanity. Nuclear power: Is it on the way out? Rain forest destruction and its impact on oxygen supply. Greenpeace and the activist environmental movement. Clean water and air and the legislative moves to guarantee them.

As we enter the 1990s and environmental consciousness grows, *OUR POISONED PLANET: Can We Save It?* explains this important issue through the words and images of the nation's leading editorial writers and cartoonists.

September 1989

Oliver Trager

1

Part I: Air & Water Pollution

Air pollution has been tackled with some success in the world's developed countries. Smoke and sulfur pollution have been cut markedly, although auto pollution remains a problem in many urban areas. Simultaneously, however, several countries of Europe and North America are experiencing growing problems with acid rain – whether they cause such problems or suffer from them. And the cities of the Third World, from Bombay to Mexico City, are experiencing air pollution, whether from domestic, industrial or vehicular sources.

Acid rain is now the most controversial form of air pollution in the developed world. Factories spew forth sulfur oxides and nitrogen oxides, which dissolve in rain before returning to earth as sulfuric and nitric acids. In parts of Pennsylvania, the result is a corrosive solvent 1,000 times as acidic as natural rain. Equally to the point, the pollutants are dispersed through the atmosphere until they descend far removed from their point of origin, often in another country.

To date, this phenomenon has been felt most in northern Canada, parts of the U.S., central Europe, and Scandinavia – though Australia and Brazil are noticing early signs of this silent scourge. Thousands of lakes are now lifeless, unable to support fish of any sort.

Preliminary projections suggest that damage could become ten times as severe by the end of the century if not checked. But certain political leaders are reluctant to take action until there is more conclusive evidence. Moreover, since the pollution takes little notice of national frontiers, a solution depends on international agreement – a scarce commodity in environmental affairs. Yet a basic dilemma with acid rain – as with many environmental issues – is that its workings are so complex that we may not be able to afford to wait until we can formulate a 100% correct answer.

In the realm of the automobile, the exhaust-caused smogs of Los Angeles and Tokyo are slowly starting to fade as leaded gasoline is being phased out. Regrettably, they are being replaced by photochemical palls over Melbourne, Ankara and Mexico City. Cars are also the source of well over half the 450,000 tons of lead that are ejected as fine particles over our skies each year.

Photochemical smog, of the kind formed in Los Angeles basin, has had a dramatic impact on the ecosystems of Southern California, causing extensive damage to forests as well as posing a serious health hazard. The smog is composed of a number of chemicals, notable ozone and peroxyacetyl nitrate, both of which are extremely harmful to plants. These substances are formed by the action of strong sunlight on a mixture of nitrogen oxides and hydrocarbons exhausted to the air by vehicles, combustion and industrial processes. The geographical features of Los Angeles serve to promote the formation of such smogs. Wind patterns and the surrounding mountains create conditions for the formation of temperature inversions, trapping air pollution close to the ground. Controls designed to reduce emissions from vehicles and other sources have been introduced with partial success to combat the smog.

Equally serious, there is now a build-up of charcoal-caused smoke over Third World cities such as Lagos, Jakarta, and Calcutta.

Water covers most of the Earth. Yet, astonishingly, little of it is directly usable. Only a small fraction is fresh, and 77.5% of this fresh water is locked up in ice caps and glaciers. Of that tiny fraction of available fresh water, only 3% occurs in the atmosphere, rivers and lakes, the rest being held in underground aquifers.

Although the "usable hydrosphere" contains more water than we are likely to need in the foreseeable future, many problems exist. Primary among these, as is often the case with natural resources, is that water is not evenly distributed around the globe. While many people spend their time fighting floods, others go thirsty. By the year 2000, at least 30 countries will experience scarcity. Water management is the only way to boost both the quantity and quality of our long-term water resource.

Perhaps more than we care to recognize, our lifestyles depend on the availability of fresh water. If, for whatever reason, our taps were to run dry, our household routines would collapse, our health would be at risk, factories would grind to a halt and agriculture would be in dire straits. The entire fabric of our societies could begin to unravel. We may take fresh water for granted at our own peril.

Almost everyone in the U.S. is allowed to use as much water as he or she wants. But the water resources of many areas are also exploited without restraint. In addition, many rivers, especially in the east, are so polluted by industrial chemicals that they can no longer possibly serve as sources of drinking water, while the water of other less polluted rivers is treated at immense cost without any guarantee that it will provide an uncontaminated water supply.

In many places in the U.S. groundwater is already contaminated. In 1982 poisonous industrial chemicals were detected in the groundwater of 35 states. At present, more than 700 chemicals have been detected in U.S. drinking water, 129 of which are considered to be particularly dangerous by the Environmental Protection Agency (EPA). Nonetheless, drinking water is regularly tested for only 14 of these contaminants. One of the reasons for this is that supplies are often from sources near former industrial sites, or sites where hazardous chemicals have been dumped.

It is not just America's groundwater reserves that are being poisoned, but also its surface waters. The Great Lakes, for instance, covering an area of 9,340 square miles, form the largest fresh water reservoir in the world. That ecological system, however, has been irreversibly degraded by human settlements, modern agriculture and industrialization – all on a massive scale.

Environmentalists argue that the limitless faith we put in technology as a means of solving any problem may be unjustified. It may be more than questionable whether technical expertise can ever remove all the undesirable pollutants that have seeped into our groundwater reserves. It is equally questionable, they argue, that purification techniques will enable us to derive from highly contaminated sources, on a sufficient scale, and at an economic price, the pure drinking water that we require.

It follows that, wherever possible, drinking water supplies should be derived from clean and unpolluted water. This means rigorous conservation measures are necessary to protect both our groundwater reserves and our surface waters.

Canada Protests U.S. Inaction on Acid Rain, Pledges Unilateral Effort

The issue of acid rain had become a source of high tension between Canada and the United States by 1984. Canada had sought a joint pledge to reduce by 50% the industrial emissions believed to cause acid rain pollution, but the U.S. had said that further research would be necessary to understand the problem fully before costly pollution-control requirements were tightened. Finally, Canada Feb. 22, 1984 strongly protested the Reagan administration's failure to take steps to control sulfur dioxide emissions, expressing "deep disappointment" with the the U.S. decision "to do nothing." According to a statement issued by the Canadian embassy, "the continued delay in adopting effective abatement measures is not acceptable to Canada. Acid rain is a grave threat unless both countries reduce their emissions now."

Two weeks later, Canada announced that it would unilaterally increase its commitment to reducing acid rain pollution despite the failure of the U.S. to take similar steps. Canada's decision was taken at a meeting in Ottawa between federal Environment Minister Charles Caccia and his ten provincial counterparts. The ministers agreed to reduce sulfur dioxide emissions by 50% by 1994, based on 1980 pollution levels in Canada, estimated at 4.5 million metric tons annually. (Canada had previously pledged a unilateral 25% cut by 1990, with an additional 25% reduction if the U.S. also agreed to cuts its pollution level by 50%.)

"We will proceed independently of the United States in the hope that they will join us at the earliest possible date," Caccia said. He stressed that U.S. cooperation was necessary to prevent the further destruction of lakes and forests on both sides of the border caused principally by industrial emissions from the U.S. Midwest.

Acid rain was widely held to be an acidic deposit of precipitation of sulfur and nitrogen oxides, and other pollutants, emitted into the atmosphere by coal-burning plants. The problem was particularly acute in the Northeast and Canada, thought to be the deposit points of pollutants thrown into the air in the Midwest.

The London Free Press
London, Ont.,
March 9, 1984

Canada's federal and provincial environment ministers have decided not to wait any longer for the United States to come onside in the fight against acid rain. Given the intransigence of the Reagan administration, they made the right decision.

Basically, Canada should do what it can to try to minimize the environmental damage from acid rain caused by emissions from power and industrial plants on this side of the border. It won't be enough to save the lakes and forests of Ontario and Quebec from harm, because so much of the pollution is coming from the northeastern United States, but it's better than postponing further action while waiting for the U.S.

About two years ago, Canada said it would cut sulphur emissions by 25 per cent on its own; Canada also said it would make the target 50 per cent if the U.S. would co-operate and do the same. After extensive lobbying, Canada was getting nowhere with its joint-action strategy — President Ronald Reagan announced an increase in the budget for research on acid rain earlier this year, but didn't allocate any resources for cleanup.

At a meeting in Ottawa this week, the environment ministers decided to move to the 50 per cent reduction target without American participation. "We cut the umbilical cord with the Americans today," said Ontario Environment Minister Andy Brandt.

It had been hoped that Canada's bargaining position would have been strengthened by the offer to double its efforts if the U.S. would help too. But since that obviously hasn't worked, Canada can only hope to set a good example and perhaps embarrass a few people in Washington who are still insisting the case against acid rain hasn't been made.

Winnipeg Free Press
Winnipeg, Man., March 9, 1984

Canada's federal and provincial environment ministers have sent another acid rain signal to U.S. President Reagan but there is no sign that he is listening.

Their announcement of intent to cut by 50 per cent between now and 1994 sulphur dioxide pollution produced in Canada is praiseworthy in its own right. There is little doubt, however, that the main goal of this announcement is to concentrate attention on the fact that the United States is doing virtually nothing about acid rain, which is no respecter of international boundaries.

Sulphur dioxide pollution travels long distances in the upper atmosphere, combines with rain and falls as sulphuric acid. This sulphuric acid is provided to Ontario and Quebec forests and lakes as an unsought gift from U.S. states such as Ohio. It kills trees and it kills fish.

The same unwanted gift is provided to the beautiful New England states, which are experiencing slowed tree growth and silent, empty lakes. Evidence suggests that the phenomenon is being identified in other parts of the United States, where consciousness of the acid rain threat is low.

Mr. Reagan's position on acid rain is crystal clear: he does not care about the damage to either Canadian or American forests and lakes and will do everything in his power to prevent any remedial action.

Canadians must look elsewhere for deliverance. Getting cracking on Canada's own polluting industries is a vital part of any program to save Canadian lakes and forests. Coal-fired power stations in Saskatchewan and nickel smelters in Manitoba and Ontario are examples of contributors to air pollution that must be guided into new methods that radically cut the trash and gas pumped into the air from high chimneys. The only feasible approach is national, for these pollutants tend to be carried away from the immediate area in which they are produced.

Other arguments for a national effort are the cost of such changes, the possible effect on employment, the need to share knowledge of technological solutions and the ease with which a giant industrial corporation could bring pressure to bear on one province or one region trying to negotiate reduced air pollution. Solving the acid rain problem is a national interest of Canada and that justifies a combined effort by all its governments and all its citizens.

In a sense, Canada is announcing the same plan twice. Two years ago, a 50-per-cent cut was declared to be policy but at that time it was presented as a joint deal with the United States. Canada would go ahead with a 25-per-cent cut on its own that would double when the United States announced a plan to cut its sulphur dioxide emissions by 50 per cent. Mr. Reagan tricked this country by pretending concern but dropped the facade in January during his state of the union address which contained provision for a little extra money for more acid rain research, not action.

The government of Canada acknowledged Mr. Reagan's January decision to come out of the closet by sending his government a blunt diplomatic note of protest in February.

That done and this week's announcement of federal-provincial intent made, some questions are appropriate. How much of the 25 per cent goal has been achieved in the past two years? By how much has Canadian government action, at whatever level, reduced the pollutants in the skies shared by Canada and the United States? How do the participating governments plan from now on to reduce Canadian pollution?

Detailed answers to these questions could affect the opinion of influential Americans other than the president who may be wondering what they should do.

Some of them are in the U.S. Senate, whose environment committee has just approved a program to cut sulphur dioxide emissions over the next decade in 31 states east of the Mississippi Basin, which begins just south of here. Domestic factors will decide the fate of that bill on the senate floor, although its passage would be of great advantage to Canada. Canada can help proponents of U.S. action by moving quickly and effectively on a Canadian sulphur dioxide reduction program.

The Toronto Star

Toronto, Ont., March 10, 1984

The decision by Ottawa and the provinces to go it alone in the fight against acid rain was a step in the right direction. We can't wait for the United States to help — the Reagan Administration seems intent on stalling. Half of the acid gas threatening our waters and forests spews out from sources here at home, so there's no point in putting off cleaning up our act.

But our decision to cut acid emissions by 50 per cent over the next decade will only be meaningful if it's backed up by specific action.

We need to put realistic control orders on major polluters such as Ontario Hydro and the large nickel and copper smelters in northern Ontario, Manitoba and Quebec. These controls should take us to the 50 per cent cut, with no extensions or excuses allowed.

But industries that need financial help to meet the necessary controls should be able to get it from government, as loans, on the clear condition that the industries eventually pay the money back. The technology to clean up already exists. It's up to government to make sure that no one gets off the hook by pleading lack of funds.

The Globe and Mail

Toronto, Ont., March 13, 1984

In the miserable little package of excuses with which a number of U.S. politicians have sought to deflect Canadian nagging on the subject of acid rain, we occasionally encounter the suggestion that this is a case of the pot calling the kettle black. Thus, New Hampshire Governor John Sununu's assessment that Canada is doing a "terrible job" on acid rain and using scare tactics to convince Americans to shut down coal-fired generating stations and so create a market for Canadian electrical power.

Governor Sununu insists that Canadian industries produce twice as much acid rain per capita as U.S. sources, a sure sign that Canada is not really serious about solving the problem.

Cutting through the conspiratorial rubbish in the governor's preamble, we come to the legitimate question of how serious Canada really is about acid rain. Certainly serious enough to consider the question worthy of lengthy research, extended discussions with U.S. officials and proposals for a joint attack on the causes.

When the whole thrust of the plan for co-operative effort was bluntly brought to nought by President Ronald Reagan's insistence that research was more urgently needed than action to reduce pollution, Canada was serious enough to lodge a stiff diplomatic protest in Washington — not the kind of action we take lightly.

If all of this still leaves Governor Sununu unconvinced that we are serious, he will probably be equally unimpressed by the sequel: Canada's announcement that it will tackle its end of the problem regardless of whether the United States meets its own obligations or not.

Federal and provincial environment ministers emerged from a meeting with the announcement that they were prepared to embark on a program aimed at cutting sulphur pollution, the acknowledged cause of acid rain, by 50 per cent in the next 10 years. The federal minister, Charles Caccia, said, "We will proceed independently of the United States in the hope that they will join us at the earliest possible date." He added that there were estimates that acid rain was doing $5-billion worth of damage a year in the United States.

It is worth keeping figures like this in mind as we close in on the undeniably high costs of combatting acid rain. If we balk at finding the money, a glance at the debit side of the ledger — where we keep items like the deaths of lakes, the loss of fishing and the threat to Canada's forests — should restore a proper perspective.

We are glad Canada picked up the challenge — not just because the move may encourage the United States to take action, or because we thereby acquire a superior moral position. If a job is worth doing, it is worth doing alone. Of course it is discouraging to realize that the benefits of our effort will be shared by those who think of acid rain as scaremongering; depressing to think how much further down the road we could travel by 1994 with the U.S. as a partner. Yet we are obliged to do what we can.

Too often in Canada we have seen disputes over jurisdiction and responsibility serve as a reason for inaction, even when sanity and justice called out urgently for something to be done. We find insurmountable obstacles to compensating a man wrongly imprisoned for 11 years; we agree that radioactive soil should be removed from neighborhood backyards, but can't agree who should do it or where to take the stuff. So it lies for years.

For long enough now, the battle against acid rain has been stalled. We are proud that Canada is showing the way.

la presse

Montreal, Que., March 9, 1984

Les ministres provinciaux et fédéral de l'Environnement ont eu le courage de leurs opinions en s'entendant pour réduire de moitié d'ici dix ans les émanations sulfureuses qui provoquent les pluies acides. Bien qu'il ne s'agisse que d'une déclaration de principe, la position du Canada est renforcée dans les négociations avec les États-Unis pour trouver une solution continentale à ce problème.

L'engagement sans équivoque du Canada dans cette tâche herculéenne doit dissiper les doutes des Américains quant à la volonté des Canadiens de faire leur part. En effet, la décision d'agir seul signifie plus que jamais qu'il faut élaborer un programme commun entre les deux pays pour essayer d'en minimiser les coûts.

Le Canada s'est engagé dans un projet qui coûtera entre $10 milliards et $20 milliards, soit environ le coût de la Baie James. Les gouvernements supporteront une partie de ces coûts, mais le reste devra être assumé par les industries concernées. Ni les uns, ni les autres ne sont dans une situation financière qui leur permet d'investir des sommes aussi importantes sans sourciller dans des procédés qui ne procureront pas de nouveaux revenus.

D'importantes économies pourront être réalisées si dans chaque cas on n'utilise que la technologie la mieux adaptée. La raffinerie d'Inco à Sudbury, par exemple, devra décider s'il vaut la peine de remplacer une grande partie de son équipement dans l'espoir que l'augmentation de productivité couvrira les coûts additionnels.

Pour faciliter cette tâche, il faudra que les gouvernements veillent à ce que les innovations technologiques deviennent accessibles à tous ceux qui doivent faire un effort. Ce serait, en effet, contraire à l'esprit même de toute l'entreprise si une compagnie arrivait à obtenir un avantage sur ses concurrents grâce à un moyen de dépollution meilleur marché dont elle garderait le secret. La dépollution doit être considérée comme un service public et non comme n'importe quelle autre activité commerciale.

Les discussions avec les États-Unis devront continuer à porter avant tout sur l'adoption d'un programme semblable aux États-Unis. Toutefois, la décision canadienne signifie qu'il faut aussi passer à l'étape suivante et étudier ensemble les meilleurs moyens de diminuer les émanations sulfureuses. Ce n'est pas mettre la charrue devant les boeufs, car une étude commune des moyens est peut-être une bonne façon de convaincre les Américains de suivre l'exemple canadien; et on a tout avantage à jeter les bases d'un développement commun de nouvelles technologies le plus rapidement possible.

Mais la tâche la plus ardue des ministres de l'Environnement ne sera peut-être pas de convaincre les États-Unis à suivre l'exemple canadien. Jusqu'à présent, il ne s'agit que d'une prise de position politique. Il faudra maintenant que les gouvernements élaborent des programmes législatifs et qu'ils obtiennent les crédits nécessaires des parlements. On risque encore de découvrir que l'élimination des pluies acides est une cause populaire quand on en parle en principe, mais qu'elle l'est moins quand il s'agit de payer.

Cela n'enlève rien au mérite des ministres de l'Environnement qui ont fait leur possible pour remettre sur la bonne voie des négociations importantes avec les États-Unis. Cette attitude positive est sans doute le meilleur moyen d'arriver à une solution à l'échelle continentale.

Arkansas Gazette.

Little Rock, AR, March 12, 1984

Canada finally has decided that it can count on no help from the Reagan administration in an effort to reduce acid rain and has decided to strike out alone. At the same time, says Environment Minister Charles Caccia, Canada will leave the door open should the United States have a change of heart. Canada thus has chosen to follow a course of responsibility while President Reagan has kept the United States on a course of irresponsibility.

Strong scientific evidence identifies sulphur dioxide from coal-burning power plants as the principal cause of acid rain that falls on both sides of the eastern border between Canada and the United States. Canada correctly accepts this evidence, but Mr. Reagan continues to call for more studies before taking any remedial action. In the meantime, acid rain causes an estimated $5 billion worth of damage each year to lakes, vegetation and important man-made structures in both countries.

Canada's independent program will have the same aim that its program for American and Canadian co-operation has had all along: to reduce acid rain pollution by 50 per cent in 10 years. Some of Canada's sulphur dioxide drifts across the border to the United States, and a similar pattern is followed by the pollutants from United States plants, most of them in the Ohio River Valley. Until the United States decides to meet its part of the responsibility to reduce acid rain pollutants it will be free-loading on the Canadians. This is the stuff of which good relations are not made.

The Morning News

Wilmington, DE, March 10, 1984

CANADIAN sealers, conceding that international protests have depressed the seal pelt market, say they've suspended indefinitely the hunts in which baby harp seals are clubbed to death. That's one for Canada on the world public relations stage.

Meanwhile, Canadian officials say they will act on their own to combat causes of acid rain, without waiting for the United States to join them.

It might help the U.S. image to hurry to join efforts to curb this costly and widespread pollution. To do so we need to end Reagan administration insistence that more research is needed before positive steps can be taken.

A new study described the other day by the National Clean Air Coalition indicates acid rain is much more uniform through the United States than had been believed. That might help reduce regional factors in the debate and persuade all sections that they would benefit from action and therefore should help pay for it.

AKRON BEACON JOURNAL

Akron, OH, March 5, 1984

OCCASIONALLY an issue stirs so much controversy and debate that it seems to cry out for action. Of late, the problem of acid rain has been sending urgent signals.

Consider what has happened recently. Canada delivered a stern note to the State Department, expressing disapproval with the Reagan administration's inaction on acid rain.

Four years ago, the two countries signed a memorandum of understanding, outlining a plan to cut sulfur dioxide emissions. But little has happened. The Canadians have taken some action, implementing a program to reduce sulfur dioxide emissions 25 percent by the end of the decade.

But the United States has done much less. President Reagan insists the problem needs more study and has been reluctant to sponsor a costly program.

Without the presidential leadership necessary to reconcile differences in Congress, American leaders have been left to bicker among themselves. That was plain at the National Governors Association conference in Washington last week.

The governors generally agree on the need to reduce sulfur dioxide emissions from coal-burning power plants in the Midwest, but differences abound on how to finance the reductions. The association approved a plan that does not include a national fund to assist states, such as Ohio, in installing scrubbers and other equipment to reduce emissions.

States in the Ohio River Valley may be responsible for more than half of the emissions of sulfur dioxide in the country, but that does not translate into funds to control pollution.

Gov. Richard Celeste reminded the governors that acid rain control has a "human impact" in high utility rates, lost jobs and a bleak business climate. But the governors still argued that the polluters should pay — even if they cannot reasonably raise the money.

All of this bickering, of course, postpones action. And that becomes disturbing when scientists tell us, as they did last week, that the forests of the Eastern United States are in serious decline. Scientists are not ready to point specifically to acid rain, but the evidence suggests man-made pollution is the culprit.

What is happening to the environment is serious, complex and not entirely understood. But enough is known about these hazards to warrant action to control emissions from the nation's factories and power plants. Unfortunately, as the need for action grows, our nation's leaders grow further apart, unable to work together or with Canada.

The TENNESSEAN

Nashville, TN, March 10, 1984

THE TVA is doing research on acid rain in some areas of the Appalachians where trees have been dying or are stunted in growth. It has asked Congress for $100,000 for the research in fiscal 1985 and plans to spend $150,000 from electricity revenues.

One spot to be examined is on top of Mount Mitchell in North Carolina. Trees in that area which have a normal life span of up to 400 years have been dying as young as 45 years, according to plant specialists who have inspected the trees. Also tests of rainfall on the mountain have showed acid content 10 to 20 times greater than normal. Large amounts of lead also have been found in the rain samples.

There has been a great deal of discussion about acid rain and the damage it may be causing to forests, lakes and other natural resources throughout the eastern United States. However, little definitive research seems to have been carried out. At least, there doesn't appear to be any conclusive scientific evidence that condemns acid rain or absolves it. As a result, some in government and private industry who don't want to cleanse the atmosphere of acid rain claim they can't do anything until there is more evidence as to the cause of environmental damage. It is time the evidence was provided.

Acid rain is formed from natural rain in combination with sulphuric and other acidic emissions from smokestacks, automobile exhausts and other combustion reactions. Stacks on coal-fired steam plants for generating electricity are among the most abundant producers of acid rain chemicals.

Since TVA operates numerous steam plants which are blamed for much of the acid rain buildup in this region, some may question whether TVA is the right agency for conducting research on the damage caused by acid rain. This would be cause for concern if TVA were a private, profit-making corporation. But as a publicly-owned corporation created to serve the public interest rather than its own, TVA has a mandate, which it usually has carried out faithfully, to take the lead in finding ways to conserve and wisely use natural resources.

TVA ought to be able to come up with some definite answers about the threat posed by acid rain and what to do about it. But the important thing is that the research be carried out as soon as possible before irreversible damage may be done to the nation's forests.

If acid rain is causing trees to die and polluting lakes and streams, this should be conclusively determined as quickly as possible so that those who want to do nothing about the problem will no longer have an excuse for their inaction. But the $250,000 which TVA is planning to put into the project may not be enough to get the job done.

It is also questionable whether TVA consumers should be required to pay for more than half the research when private power companies don't seem to be interested in finding out what damage is being done to the environment by their acid rain. Acid rain is a national problem which needs to be solved by a national effort.

Detroit Free Press

Detroit, MI, March 9, 1984

HALF A decade ago, when the term "acid rain" was just entering the American vocabulary and researchers were sounding the alarm about the sterile, fishless lakes of the Adirondacks, a few voices suggested that empty lakes would turn out to be the least of the troubles caused by long-range transport of airborne sulfates.

The more potentially devastating problem, they suggested, would be the impact on forests. Acid deposition, dry or wet, would leach out nutrients in the thin forest soils, blighting and slowing the growth of trees across the eastern United States. Surely enough, a widespread decline in those forests is currently being documented, with several species suffering simultaneously from a rapid fall-off in the growth rate, loss of foliage, failure to reproduce and premature mortality. An even more advanced form of the malaise is decimating European forests. Scientists, predictably, cannot yet pinpoint the cause. It seems likely it is manmade pollution. It seems possible it is acid rain.

The acid rain debate is still split among those who think further controls on sulfur emissions need to be imposed yesterday, those who think more study is needed, and those who maintain the whole thing is a chimera drummed up by the popular press. It is true that no direct cause-and-effect relationship has been shown between particular sources of sulfur emissions and the damaged lakes and forests. We may never be able to say for certain that the 375,000 tons of sulfur dioxide spit out yearly by Ohio's filthy Gavin power plant are killing the fir trees in Asheville, N.C.

But the circumstantial evidence is that, as a whole, forests and lakes downwind of the country's largest coal-burning utilities are suffering from cumulative, accelerating and possibly irreversible environmental stress. Sulfur emissions are also responsible for the visibility-reducing summer haze that blankets the eastern United States. In high concentrations, they are a health hazard. They are quietly fizzling away at our architectural stone and marble; you can see the long-range consequences of that in Europe, where uncontrolled pollutants are blackening and eroding the monuments of Western civilization.

The circumstantial evidence that sulfur emissions are a major problem has to be considered compelling enough to act upon. But in its final form, the acid rain legislation now working its way through Congress in an election-year burst of concern ought to be flexible, setting emission standards but permitting utilities to decide how best to meet them. It ought to fall hardest on such dirty coal burners as Ohio and Indiana, who use their tolerance for dirty air and their resultant lower energy costs to lure industry away from other states.

It is imperative that Congress allows Michigan credit for the tremendous reduction in sulfur emissions already achieved here. And the concentration on sulfur emissions ought not to overlook the evidence that nitrogen emissions may also play a large role in the damage being done.

But opponents of any controls at all are beginning to sound very much like the Tobacco Institute, arguing that because the precise chemical pathway from cigaret tars to lung cancer has still not been plotted, it's too soon to worry. It is not. If Congress waits much longer for the perfection of the evidence on acid rain, there's a good chance it will not be a study of America's forests and lakes that we'll be conducting, but an autopsy.

The Hartford Courant

Hartford, CT, March 4, 1984

In addition to the ample circumstantial evidence of the damaging effects of acid rain on the environment, new research indicates that Eastern forests are in sharp decline.

Scientists have found that some species of softwood trees are dying and failing to reproduce at high altitudes in the southeastern Appalachian chain — a finding that had previously been limited to the Northeast.

Other studies and a survey by the U.S. Forest Service show a widespread drop in the growth rates of at least half a dozen species of coniferous trees in the East.

The fear of some scientists is that the region's forests are headed for the kind of dramatic decline that is now being experienced in the forests of Central Europe. The prime suspect is man-made pollutants, perhaps in combination with many natural factors.

Of the natural factors, such as climate changes, policy-makers can do little. But they can do something about air pollution from power plants, factories, motor vehicles and other human activities. They can do something about the acid rain, which might not only be damaging forests, but also wiping out aquatic life in ponds and lakes in the East.

Yet neither Congress nor the administration has faced up to the necessity for a program to finally staunch the flow of sulfur dioxide and nitrogen oxides from Midwest industry and power plants, which are believed to be the main source of acid rain.

Even the nation's governors, meeting in Washington this week, could not agree on an acid rain resolution endorsing a specific method for financing acid rain controls.

Perhaps the causal link between acid rain and dying forests cannot be indisputably established, but the evidence is more than sufficient for taking specific action, beyond more research, for curbing acid rain now. By the time the smoking gun is found, the victim — in this case, the forests — might already be dead.

THE SUN

Baltimore, MD, March 4, 1984

The destruction of forests in Europe, Canada and the United States is an environmental nightmare that may be already upon us. There is not yet a scientific consensus on causes — although acid rain is a leading suspect — but agreement grows that forests (probably including Maryland's) are in trouble.

The destruction was first noticed in intensively-monitored West German forests, where 35 percent of trees were damaged or dying by 1983. Signs often are subtle: slowed growth, detected only by examining growth rings. German scientists once believed the main cause was toxic aluminum ions released from the soil by acid rain, primarily from coal-burning power plants. Now they think that while aluminum is part of the problem, there probably are other contributors: heavy metals, for one, and ozone from photochemical smog, generated partly by auto exhausts.

The U.S. problem probably has similar causes, but data are limited. So far, reports of damage have come from Maine, New Hampshire, Vermont, New York, New Jersey, Virginia, Tennessee, North and South Carolina and Georgia. The damage worsens with altitude: Red spruce and Fraser fir are deteriorating and dying on top of North Carolina's Mount Mitchell, where plants have virtually stopped reproducing. Trees at higher altitudes are more likely to be damaged because that is where locally-enerated pollutants tend to concentrate. Conifers — evergreens — are most susceptible, presumably because of their shallow root systems, but deciduous trees are harmed, too.

Apart from the threat to the important forest products industry, widespread loss of forests could upset the whole ecological balance. One predictable result would be widescale destruction — and perhaps extinction — of many animal species.

West German Chancellor Helmut Kohl said last year that it was "five minutes till midnight" on the forest issue. Some polls showed the issue as more important to European voters than deployment of U.S. intermediate range missiles. In July, the West German parliament mandated reduction of acid-rain-causing emissions by 50 percent over 10 years. The United States and Canada need a crash program to quickly identify the causes and extent of their forest destruction — the study shouldn't take more than six months, given the high probability that acid rain is the major cause — and then firm, vigorous action to correct the problem.

As one German scientist said in response to Chancellor Kohl's remark, "It may really be five minutes *after* midnight."

Ontario Announces Acid Rain Crackdown

The Ontario government Dec. 17, 1985 unveiled a program to significantly reduce acid rain by cracking down on emissions of sulfur dioxide. The program called for emissions to be cut to 733,186 tons a year by 1994, a 70% reduction from the 1980 permissible level of 4.6 million tons. The plan targeted Ontario's four largest industrial polluters, who together accounted for about 80% of the province's sulfur dioxide emissions. The companies were: Inco Ltd., that operates nickel-smelting plants in Sudbury, Ontario Hydro, the provincially owned utility which operates a nickel smelter in Sudbury, and Algoma Steel Corp. of Algoma. Inco's facilities were believed to be the largest single source of sulfur dioxide emissions in North America. Earlier in the year, the company had announced a plan to reduce its annual emissions to 358,887 tons by 1994.

The program was presented to the provincial legislature by James Bradley, Ontario's environment minister. Bradley estimated that the program would cost "several hundred million dollars" to implement, with Ontario and the federal government paying for the installation of some pollution-control devices. However, the bulk of the costs were to be borne by the companies themselves. Bradley contended that the program would benefit the United States by cutting acid rain in New Hampshire by about 8%, and added: "The effects of Ontario's acid rain production on U.S. states and other parts of Canada is minimal when compared to the effect U.S. acid rain has had on us." A spokesman for the U.S. Environmental Protection Agency (EPA) Dec. 17 commended Ontario for its "important commitment," but said that it would it be "premature" for the EPA to decide on the need for pollution controls beyond those in the Federal Clean Air Act.

ST. LOUIS POST-DISPATCH

St. Louis, MO, December 27, 1985

The Reagan administration is under new pressure from different directions to change its do-nothing stance on acid rain. The Canadian province of Ontario issued orders requiring sharp cuts in sulfur dioxide emissions, which cause acid rain, and called on the U.S. to reciprocate. Meanwhile seven states and four environmental groups have filed a federal suit in New York seeking to force the Environmental Protection Agency to obey the law, charging that the agency is violating the Clean Air Act by failing to update standards for allowable levels of sulfur oxide pollution, which, when it descends to Earth as acid precipitation, destroys life in streams and lakes and damages forests, crops and buildings.

Canada's longtime concern over acid rain from U.S. sources finally led President Reagan last March to agree to select a special envoy from each country to study the problem. Yet the administration still did nothing even when Drew Lewis, Mr. Reagan's own appointee, later said he would urge the president to begin taking steps to control acid rain. Ontario has now set an example by requiring its four biggest industrial sources of sulfur dioxide — two smelters, a coal-fired power plant and a steel plant — to cut their emissions by more than a third in the next decade.

But since the administration seems impervious to persuasion by diplomacy from across the border or by scientific evidence at home, still another federal court order seems necessary. Such an order is being sought by New York, Connecticut, New Hampshire, Massachusetts, Vermont,

Rhode Island and Minnesota and by the Environmental Defense Fund and three other environmental groups. These plaintiffs complain that, even though the Clean Air Act requires the EPA to revise its standards for allowable sulfur oxide pollution every five years in accordance with the latest scientific data on pollution's effects, the agency has not done so despite its own findings that existing standards endanger human health and fail to curb the environmental damages of acid rain.

How many more suits will be needed? Last summer, as a result of a deadline set by a federal court, the EPA ordered moderate cuts in emissions of coal-fired plants with tall stacks. But more recently the agency proposed regulations that would give such plants the option of balancing excessive emissions from their tall stacks with reduced emissions of the same pollutant from other nearby industrial sources. The EPA's continuing lenient treatment of tall stacks flies in the face of a 1970 congressional ban against tall stacks as an alternative to pollution reduction except in rare cases in which available pollution controls are not sufficient to protect the health of local people.

The Reagan administration's stalling on acid rain is inexcusable either on grounds of evidence of damage or of cost. Damage has now shown up in all parts of the nation. As for cost, a recent draft study by the EPA, the Army Corps of Engineers and the Brookhaven National Laboratory suggests that a control program might pay for itself in reduced damage to building materials alone.

The Globe and Mail

Toronto, Ont., December 19, 1985

While it is not always easy to measure the potential value of a new government program, it might be worth noting for a start that all three parties in the Ontario Legislature applauded Environment Minister James Bradley's announcement of new targets for the reduction of acid rain pollutants. As a rule, only the most innocuous subjects escape partisan treatment.

This is not at all innocuous. It is bold, tough, sweat-and-tears stuff with a hefty price tag; by far the most determined effort the province has yet made to pull the big polluters — notably Inco Ltd. and Ontario Hydro — down to more tolerable levels. It also contains a calculated gamble in the hope that it will be recognized by Washington decision-makers as exemplary, a gesture worthy of reciprocal response.

Mr. Bradley's plan is to cut the acidic air pollution generated in Ontario to a third of 1980 levels by 1994 at a cost of hundreds of millions of dollars in smokestack scrubbers and other pollution-control equipment. Part of the burden is to be shared by the Ontario and federal Governments, but the bulk of it will be borne by the polluting industries.

Four regulations passed under the Environmental Protection Act call upon Ontario Hydro to reduce sulphur dioxide emissions in stages from 450,000 tonnes a year to 175,000; Inco will be required to come down from 1.1 million tonnes to 265,000; Falconbridge Ltd. from 154,000 to 100,000 and Algoma Steel from 285,000 to 125,000 tonnes. Understandably, these industries are not entirely happy about the expense. Inco chairman Charles Baird described the development as "the straw that broke the camel's back."

From south of the border, however, there was a quick return on the investment. Maine's Senator George Mitchell hailed it as a first-rate initiative and declared pointedly that "in one day, the Ontario Government will be doing more to reduce acid rain in this country than the Reagan Administration has done in five years."

Mr. Bradley rammed the message home: "I urge the United States to face up to its responsibilities, as Ontario is doing today, before it is too late. It is imperative that our neighbors now implement stringent pollution standards ..." It may have been said before, but not with the same moral force.

The Toronto Star

Toronto, Ont., December 13, 1985

More than 35 million people live near the Great Lakes. So why are we still sending poison — chemical wastes like dioxins, polychlorinated biphenyls (PCBs) and pesticides — into the water through discharges, leaking waste dumps and the like?

The problem keeps growing faster than our ability to deal with it

These toxic chemicals don't just stay in the water. Through evaporation, they fall back on the land, polluting our crops and livestock. The result is that people living near the Great Lakes have more toxic chemicals in their drinking water and food — even in mothers' milk — than anyone else in North America, according to a new Canada-U.S. study.

What can be done? We need a crackdown on companies that discharge toxic chemicals into the lakes in excess of their operating permits. Dozens of industries on both sides of the border are said to violate the rules. Better enforcement and tougher fines would ensure that, if companies pollute, they pay.

There's also a need for modern waste treatment facilities, as proposed by the Ontario Waste Management Corp. And the Ontario government should establish an ample "superfund" to clean up dangerous pollution dumps.

But in order to know how best to tackle this problem, we need to know more about how contaminants move through the environment and how they affect us: It's worrisome that, according to the study, the complexity of the problem "keeps growing faster than the ability of our institutions to deal with it." Yet in last spring's budget the Mulroney government withdrew funding for a national centre for toxicology research. Federal Environment Minister Tom McMillan should see that the funding is restored.

Each year we hear more horror stories about pollution. Now's the time for governments and industry to change that.

Portland Press Herald

Portland, ME, December 20, 1985

Long impatient with U.S. failure to curb industrial emissions that return to earth as acid rain and snow, Canada's Ontario Province has decided to reduce the pollution even if it must act alone.

The province has directed its four largest industrial producers of sulfur dioxide emissions to reduce them from a current level of 1.9 million metric tons a year to 665,000 metric tons by 1994. Among those affected is the Inco Ltd. smelter in Sudbury, Ontario, the largest source of sulfur dioxide pollution on the North American continent.

The Canadian cutbacks should have a positive effect on Maine. Ontario's environment minister, Jim Bradley, estimates that the emissions reduction mandate, which also affects coal-burning power plants in southern Ontario, will reduce acid rain pollution in northern New England by as much as 8 percent. Given the damaging effects of acid rain on freshwater life in lakes and streams, any reduction will be welcome.

But, as Bradley made clear, the province does not expect its forthright action to be forever one-sided. "The effects of Ontario's acid rain production on U.S. states and other parts of Canada is minimal," he said, "when compared to the effect U.S. acid rain has on us."

Instead of acting to curb industrial sulfur dioxide emissions, however, the United States takes refuge in endless research and studies.

Sen. George J. Mitchell succinctly contrasted Ontario's action with the lack of action in this country when he said the province "has now done more in a single day to reduce acid rain than the Reagan administration has done in five years."

The administration should study that.

The London Free Press

London, Ont., December 19, 1985

Strong regulations to cut sulphur dioxide emissions by Ontario's four major air polluters drastically are a good first step in reducing the acid rain threat to Canada's lakes and forests.

However, wholesale air improvement will only come if action is also taken in the United States and a concentrated effort is made to reduce emissions of nitrogen oxides produced through coal burning and by automobile exhausts.

Still, Ontario deserves praise for its bold initiative in targeting polluters responsible for almost 80 per cent of Ontario's acid rain-causing sulphur dioxide: smelters operated in Sudbury by Inco and Falconbridge, Algoma Steel's iron ore plant at Wawa, and Ontario Hydro's coal-burning generators.

Plans requiring them to cut sulphur dioxide levels by 1994 — from 1980 levels of 1,993,000 tonnes to 665,000 tonnes — are long overdue. That is a reduction of 67 per cent.

Inevitably, the cleanup program will add to production costs which will have to be absorbed in the prices of finished goods and power.

An example is offered by Arvo Niitenberg, Hydro's executive vice-president of operations. He estimates it will mean Hydro spending an extra $1 billion in the next decade, which will add another one per cent to electricity rates. The existing abatement program will require spending about $4 billion by the year 2000 and will add about four per cent to electricity rates by that time.

That's cheap if it means a cleaner environment. Lost income from destroyed forests and polluted lakes clearly would be higher in the long term.

The predictable cries have already started, though. Inco chairman Charles Baird says that Inco will try to meet the new limit but that it will make it harder for the company to compete for international markets. "If you can't compete, you can't exist."

That's too bad, but with renewable resources such as fish and timber and the thousands of jobs that depend on these resources at stake, it's about time the province stopped talking and started acting. Continued subsidization of industry at the cost of resources and the environment has to end sometime.

For those in difficulty, however, Environment Minister James Bradley has promised federal and provincial assistance. Each level of government has set aside $85 million to achieve the emission cuts.

A problem still exists, though. Half the acid rain threatening Canada's outdoors will continue to come from U.S. sources.

Although few serious scientists dispute that trees and lakes are dying and that pollution is at fault, U.S. politicians — in particular President Ronald Reagan — continue to take a wait-and-see attitude and refuse to get tough on polluters.

Ironically, a Louis Harris poll of more than 10,000 Americans last spring showed that awareness of acid rain had soared to 94 per cent from 30 per cent five years ago and that there was strong support for cleanup efforts.

Nonetheless, Republican Senator Robert Stafford of Vermont, chairman of the Senate environment committee, concedes there is only a 50-50 chance that legislation to curb acid rain-causing emissions will win approval in Congress in the coming year.

It can only be hoped that Ontario's actions will strengthen the hand of Canada's acid rain envoy, former premier William Davis, in his continuing efforts to get American action.

Although welcome, Ontario's bold initiative is unlikely to have the desired effects unless the U.S. follows suit. Clearly, the program adds pressure for recriprocal action.

Congress Overrides Reagan Veto of Clean Water Bill

Congress enacted the Clean Water Act Feb. 4, 1987 over President Ronald Reagan's veto. Reagan Jan. 30 called the bill a "budget buster," one "loaded with waste and larded with pork." The president said he knew the bill would be overridden. "But it's time we did the right thing, all of us, regardless of the political fallout," he said. The bill provided $18 billion through 1994 for sewer construction grants and revolving loan funds, plus $2 billion for cleaning up estuaries and toxic "hot spots" and dealing with polluted runoff from farms and urban streets. President Reagan had vetoed an identical measure after Congress adourned in 1986. The same bill was reintroduced in the 100th Congress at the outset, and was passed with overwhelming support by both houses.

The vote override – a two-thirds majority was necessary to override a veto – was cast by the House Feb. 3. The vote was 401-26, with the 26 votes backing Reagan coming from the Republicans. Another 147 Republicans, and 254 Democrats, voted against the President's position. "The American people want us to act," Rep. James Howard (D, N.J.), chairman of the Public Works and Transportation Committee, said. "They want clean water, not excuses and bickering." Rep. Arlan Strangeland (Minn.), who helped shape the bill, said, "This body needs to send a strong message to the president and the American people that this Congress won't tolerate delays in cleaning up American waters."

The Senate override, after which the Clean Water Act became law, was 86 to 14. Sen. John Chafee (R, R.I.), one of the architects of the bill, said the measure was "fiscally responsible and lives up to our national goal of making the nations's waters fishable and swimmable."

"President Reagan said we can't afford the bill," Sen. Quentin Burdick (D, N.D.) said. "We in the the Congress disagree with the president. I believe the American people disagree with the president. The American people want clean water."

Houston Chronicle

Houston, TX
January 20, 1987

President Reagan has lost his battle with Congress over the Clean Water Act. A Lake Houston provision in that bill is just one of many reasons why he is going down to defeat.

Before 1972, local and state governments built most sewage treatment plants. Growth outstripped construction and environmental damage was heavy. Congress stepped in that year with a Clean Water Act and federal money. More plants were built, and the strict environmental rules helped clean up the nation's water.

The inevitable happened, though. Federal funding became addictive. A renewal of the Clean Water Act calling for the expenditure of $18 billion through 1994 was approved by Congress in the closing days of the last session but was vetoed by President Reagan. This session, the House has already voted 406-8 for the same bill, and Senate approval is expected later this week by a similar margin, making another veto useless.

Congressmen like the bill because it provides funds for local improvements that they can point to with pride. For instance, the bill would create a demonstration program for Lake Houston to be administered by the Environmental Protection Agency.

Lake Houston, a primary source of Houston's drinking water, badly needs such attention. Pollution control strategies would be explored, including the feasibility of regional wastewater treatment plants. Rep. Jack Fields, who represents that area, worked hard to get the program included in the bill.

Theoretically, Reagan has a good point that the federal government shouldn't be spending billions it doesn't have to fund projects local and state governments have handled in the past. Practically, as Lake Houston illustrates, it's a lost cause.

The new bill does tip its hat to the president's position. It would phase in state loan programs and phase out federal aid by 1994. That, of course, remains to be seen.

Post-Tribune

Gary, IN, January 29, 1987

Now that his State of the Union address is over, President Reagan must face making a decision on renewing the Clean Water Act, which he has opposed. He should be a good sport and sign the bill; it is supported by a huge majority in Congress and the people want it.

He could, of course, simply withhold his blessing from the legislation by doing nothing within the 10-day period that he has to either sign or veto a bill that Congress has passed. The bill would automatically become law. Last year, he weaseled out of vetoing the popular bill by pocket vetoing it after Congress adjourned.

If he decides to veto the bill this time, Congress will be around to override the veto. That seems likely because the bill passed the House 406-8 Jan. 9 and the Senate 93-6 Jan. 21.

Fifteen years after the first Clean Water Act, many of the nation's waterways are still shamefully polluted. Continuing the cleanup effort and promoting preventive measures are responsibilities that must be met to assure both decent health and living conditions for future generations.

Some $18 billion of the $20 billion authorized by the bill is for grants and loans for municipal sewage treatment plant construction that will be spread out over the next eight years. Indiana would receive $58.4 million. The remaining $2 billion is for special cleanup projects of highly polluted major waterways, including a five-year plan to clean up toxic waste in the Grand Calumet River and the Indiana Harbor and Ship Canal.

Reagan objects to the expense. Congress thinks this is one place spending is needed. Congressmen worked cooperatively to formulate the bill and contain costs. In 1981, Congress agreed to cut the federal share of sewage grants and to gradually turn that program over to state and local governments if the administration would agree to doing it over a 10-year period.

Congress lived up to its part of the bargain on this one. Now it's Reagan's turn.

"FOR OUR NEXT WISH..."

The Burlington Free Press

Burlington, VT, February 11, 1987

Editorials

In overriding President Reagan's veto of the $20 billion clean water bill, lawmakers not only handed him his first defeat of the 100th Congress but also sent a signal to the White House that his final two years as chief executive will not be as smooth as his first six.

That he enjoyed a term and a half as a virtual imperial president perhaps was due more to his popularity than to the inherent appeal of his domestic and foreign policies. Lawmakers on both sides of the aisle were reluctant to oppose a popular president. It may be a commentary on the state of the American electorate that popularity supersedes competence. In the television age, the public gets what it sees on the screen, no more, no less.

While Reagan worries about the cost of cleaning up the nation's waters, Congress and the citizenry are concerned about the consequences of not doing so. With broad bipartisan support and the backing of the people, the clean water bill clearly was something that the president could put aside simply by vetoing it. To say he chose the wrong issue for his first major battle with the new Congress is an understatement. Coming on the heels of the Iranian-Nicaragua arms scandal, the ill-timed veto was bound to raise the hackles of supporters of the clean water bill.

What effect the congressional repudiation of Reagan's veto will have on his other legislative proposals in the coming months is difficult to predict.

Yet one thing is certain: Having succeeded in overriding his veto of the clean water bill, Congress may have acquired the necessary backbone to stand up to the White House when its proposals are in conflict with the views of lawmakers and their constitutents.

The nation's congressmen should be applauded for having the political courage to put the public interest above partisan politics.

THE INDIANAPOLIS STAR

Indianapolis, IN, February 8, 1987

President Reagan does not have an agenda, House Minority Whip Trent Lott said shortly before gearing up for congressional passage of the $20 billion Clean Water Bill.

The Mississippi Republican was wrong

Maybe he just forgot what the Reagan agenda is: cutting the size of government, reducing its burden on the American people and making the nation stronger so that it can defend American freedom and independence.

What upset Lott was the president's opposition to the size of the bill. Mr. Reagan called it budget-busting pork barrel legislation.

Is the president against clean water? No. He is against budget-busting. He is against pork barrel legislation.

Congress could have trimmed the lard out of the bill. But Congress passed it lard and all. The president vetoed it. Congress passed it over his veto.

The president has an agenda all right. High on his agenda is trying to control the size and cost of government.

Congress has an agenda too. High on its agenda is the passage of budget-busting pork barrel legislation.

The Record

Hackensack, NJ, February 5, 1987

Both the Senate and the House of Representatives have voted overwhelmingly to override President Reagan's veto of a $20-billion bill to clean up the nation's rivers, lakes, and seashores. The vote, 401-26 in the House and 86-14 in the Senate, was even more lopsided than supporters had hoped and illustrates just how politically isolated the administration has become.

The isolation is not confined to environmental issues. It extends across the spectrum, from foreign affairs to fiscal policy and social spending. Judging from the polls, Mr. Reagan is still personally popular: Americans still admire his boundless optimism and enjoy his oratorical rhapsodies about "we the people." But politically his capital is exhausted. As the 1986 congressional elections showed, Americans want detente with the Soviet Union, nuclear arms control, and a modest increase in federal spending at home in such areas as aid to education, public transportation, and drug counseling — none of which the Reagan administration is prepared to give them.

They also want vigorous action on the environmental front. Conservatives may sneer at environmentalists as misanthropic nature buffs who prefer the company of snail darters to people. But *everyone* is an environmentalist these days. Everyone wants stringent rules against pollution. Clean water, soil, and air are public concerns and, like public health and public safety, amenable only to public action. Any notion that the private sector can somehow be left to clean up itself is simple-minded right-wing dogma, yet the Reagan administration clings to it stubbornly.

Contrary to the White House characterization, the 1987 Water Quality Act is not a budget-busting pork-barrel bill. Earlier water bills were overly generous when it came to funding new sewerage lines, which only encouraged suburban sprawl by making it possible for developers to build farther and farther afield. But the new bill eliminates that loophole by concentrating its resources more exclusively on new or expanded plants to treat the effluent before it enters rivers and streams and coastal waters. Unlike money for Star Wars or other military toys that add to the deficit while doing little to enhance national security, the clean-water bill is literally an investment in a cleaner and healthier America. In overriding the president's veto, Congress has handed Mr. Reagan a well-deserved rebuff.

THE CHRISTIAN SCIENCE MONITOR

Boston, MA, February 5, 1987

PRESIDENT Reagan's veto of the Clean Water Act and Congress's override of that veto was a confrontation of convenience.

With the outcome never really in doubt, both the White House and the Congress could afford to strike postures they intend to carry through the year. President Reagan's veto was futile. Yet he signaled he could still frustrate congressional initiatives in 1987 that do not have the overwhelming backing of a clean water bill. Congress indicated an eagerness to challenge the President's authority. Republican legislators seek independence from an Iran-wounded White House and an administration reputedly depleted of new ideas. Democrats boast they are "ready to run the government," flush with majorities in both chambers and improved presidential prospects for 1988.

Given this legislative opening round, 1987 looks to be a year of confrontation, apparent and real. Among the key issues: aid to the Nicaragua contras, trade legislation, arms control inducements, health care, and of course the House and Senate inquiries into the Iran arms affair.

Ronald Reagan should not be counted out of the game just yet, however. His ablest Cabinet player, James Baker at Treasury, brought congressional leaders into successful negotiations over the tax bill in 1986, an election year. Now Mr. Baker is in charge of an array of economic maneuvers that involve dollar valuation, trade talks, and legislative proposals. At the moment, international economic affairs is the administration's most vibrant policy area. We could yet see a more bipartisan, consensus-based economic approach in Washington than now seems likely.

Also, Health and Human Services Secretary Otis Bowen has taken the public lead on insurance against catastrophic illness, a legislative comer that could finish in successful compromise.

And some of the more confrontational voices – White House communications director Patrick Buchanan and the Defense Department's Richard Perle – are reported or rumored soon to go.

Nonetheless, the Democratic majority in Congress has begun to attack where it senses vulnerability. In assessments today of how voting for president might go in 1988, Democrats have picked up strength in the Middle West and South, among Roman Catholics, low-income whites, and independents. These are the very constituencies with which the GOP had hoped to forge a new majority. While such voters may not be utterly lost to the Republicans, they are at least looking to see what the Democrats have to offer.

Mr. Reagan opened the year with a rhetorically confrontational State of the Union message, followed by a more temperate economic message. The Congress has responded with its own water-bill gambit and veto override. But the 1987 legislative game has really yet to be played, and the prospect for some significant working together should not be discounted.

Los Angeles Times

Los Angeles, CA, February 6, 1987

When President Reagan vetoed the renewal of the Clean Water Act a second time, he might as well have hung a sign around his neck that said, "Hit Me."

Congress certainly obliged. Pow! House votes 401 to 26. Pow! Senate votes 86 to 14. The successful program to control pollution from sewage and other sources, with a special fund for San Francisco Bay, now is the law. It took a lot of unnecessary high jinks to get there.

This has been one of the more curious episodes in the President's career. Congress approved the bill without a single dissenting vote last fall, and Reagan vetoed it. Congress passed the bill overwhelmingly in January, and Reagan vetoed it, acknowledging at the time that he would be overridden. He denounced the program as full of pork-barrel projects, and offered a $12-billion alternative that contained essentially the same pork

as Congress' $18-billion version, saving money only by ending the program sooner. Then he said that the effort to clean up the nation's waters is "a national priority of the highest order."

Throughout Reagan's career in government, his aides have fought some of their hardest fights in trying to avert the embarrassment of veto overrides. But no effort at all was made this time. And usually when a program that he did not like passed by such overwhelming margins, Reagan would quietly allow it to go into law. Since last fall, Congress has cast a cumulative vote of 1,898 in favor of the Clean Water Act to 60 against.

It is puzzling why Reagan pretended to fight a battle that he could not win and seemed to have no heart for. What is important now, though, is that the nation once again has a strong program on the books for continuing the clean-up of our streams, lakes and estuaries.

Arkansas Gazette.

Little Rock, AR, December 29, 1987

Passage of a tough new Clean Air Act should be a high priority for the 1988 Congress. Clean air for all Americans has been too long delayed.

The original Clean Air Act, passed in 1970, began the great task of cleaning the air. Yet more than 60 cities, including such giants as Los Angeles and Chicago, still fail to meet the standards established by the act. The American Lung Association estimates that 146 million Americans still live in places where air quality is unhealthful much of the time. Those most endangered by air pollution are the very young, the elderly and the chronically ill.

Even though the goal of the original Clean Air Act is far from reached, the rate of progress in cleaning the air has slowed. Levels of some pollutants that were reduced by 20 or 30 per cent over the last decade are now actually increasing.

★ ★ ★

The present administration shows no enthusiasm for cleaning the air, and the big industries that pollute it are waging a terrific battle to block new clean air legislation. But Congress has a duty to enact the legislation. Polluted air does not recognize city or state boundaries; it's a national problem. Truthfully, it's an international problem, as our Canadian friends keep reminding us.

It has been almost two decades since the original Clean Air Act held out the promise of healthful air quality for all. It is time to finish the job.

Minneapolis Star and Tribune

Minneapolis, MN, February 3, 1987

President Reagan vetoed reauthorization of the Clean Water Act on Friday during a slapstick ceremony at which he pretended to toss the bill into the trash. The House of Representatives should ignore Reagan's theatrics when it meets today to consider overriding the veto. By passing the bill over Reagan's objections, lawmakers can demonstrate their seriousness about a concern the president casually dismisses.

Fighting water pollution has been a national priority since the act's initial passage in 1972, when several of the Great Lakes were in danger of becoming lifeless, stinking pools. Both critics and supporters agree that America's waterways are cleaner now than then. But slowly rising pollutant levels continue to threaten fish and plant life in some lakes and rivers. Tons of untreated sewage still contaminate estuaries near coastal cities. And despite tight controls on industrial emissions, highly polluted "toxic hot spots" still exist.

The bill Reagan vetoed Friday — identical to the one he pocket-vetoed after Congress adjourned in November — would plug loopholes in the law. It would reduce runoff pollution from streets and farms that is slowly poisoning many waterways,

bar untreated wastes from oceans and hasten the cleanup of toxic hot spots. Most important, the bill provides an essential $18 billion fund to finish a job lawmakers began long ago: construction of much-needed sewage-treatment plants in America's small cities and towns.

It is the price tag that so alarms the president, who insisted last November that state and local governments should underwrite their own sewage systems. Friday's message was no different: The measure, he complained, was "so loaded with waste and larded with pork that I cannot in conscience sign it."

But where is the waste? The president overlooks the bill's affirmation on two occasions by a nearly unanimous Congress — including scores of staunch fiscal conservatives. He ignores the bill's critical role in fulfilling a federal promise to help finance the prevention of water pollution. And he fails to recognize the reality that the price of breaking that promise will ultimately be higher than keeping it. President Reagan's veto was as fiscally foolish as it was wrong. Lawmakers in both chambers should seize the opportunity to override it this week.

St. Petersburg Times

St. Petersburg, FL, February 7, 1987

Water is a state resource, to be managed for the common interest of all the people. Every candidate in the 1986 governor's race was committed to that principle. Within a few short months, we'll know whether Bob Martinez meant it.

There are five district water management boards, each with nine members. By July 1, the governor will have the opportunity to appoint, reappoint or replace 29 of them, including a majority of each board.

These agencies don't just build dams and drainage canals, which was the extent of water management under old agricultural regimes. They also regulate the pumping and diversion of ground water for virtually everyone's drinking water supplies. And they are responsible for regulating the use of wetlands by agriculture. It's a big job, and a tough one.

There was a time when the South Florida Water Management District contributed to the decline of the Everglades by serving as a front for the ditch-and-drain mania of the U.S. Army Corps of Engineers, the sugar industry and assorted other planters. No longer. Until a few years ago, the Southwest Florida Water Management District — commonly called Swiftmud — was a slave of the cattle, citrus and phosphate interests. Now it is an agency that has everyone's needs at heart. Will that progress continue under the Martinez appointees?

Nothing Martinez does pertaining to the environment or growth management will be as significant as the choices he makes for those 29 thankless positions. He's under some heavy pressure, as it happens, from agricultural interests who contributed generously to his campaign. Darrell McAteer, Swiftmud's chairman in the bad old days, beat an early path to his Tallahassee office door. So perhaps he needs to hear now from his other constituents, those who still expect him to be fair to all Florida.

The situation of one board member in particular may be instructive. She is Mary Kumpe, a prominent conservationist from Sarasota who has served since 1982 on the Swiftmud board, where she played a large role in broadening the agency's attitude. Though it was a Democratic governor, Bob Graham, who appointed her, she thought she had a chance to remain on the board under the new

Republican governor, Bob Martinez. She s a Republican, a circumstance that never seemed to bother Graham.

But not enough of a Republican, perhaps, for Martinez or those who advise him. A well-placed but unofficial source warned Kumpe last week, "Lady, you're out!" The reason, she was told, is that she has been known to support some Democrats, too — among them, Harry Johnston in last year's gubernatorial primary.

The governor's office isn't saying. J. M. "Mac" Stipanovich, Martinez's chief of staff for patronage, commented Friday only that the governor has made no decisions about the district board, other than to renominate Chairman Michael Zagorac of Clearwater, who is president of the business lobby Associated Industries. "All the others are still in review," Stipanovich said. He mentioned hearing "good things" about two other members of the board, but he didn't mention Kumpe.

But Kumpe *is* in trouble, without a doubt. Her own state senator, Sarasota Republican Bob Johnson, said he and "everyone I know" wants her off the board. While Johnson said he hasn't talked to Martinez about it, "there's no question that she's not going to be reappointed.

"She supported Pat Neal (former Democratic senator from Bradenton), she supported Harry Johnston, she did not support any Republican I know of," Johnson said. But isn't it true she supported *him* in his last election? Yes, Johnson conceded, but that was two years ago. (Kumpe says, by the way, that while she's Neal's friend she didn't contribute a dime to his unsuccessful campaign. What if she had?)

Such talk is disappointing coming from a senator of Johnson's reputation. It would be even more disappointing if Martinez yields to such overly partisan influence. The politics of water management are complicated enough already. Board members have the thankless job of balancing the competing interests of farms and cities, of industry and conservation, of the coastal megalopolis that needs water and the rural counties where the wells are. It demands people who are supremely dedicated and objective, qualities that are rarely compatible with indiscriminate partisanship.

THE DAILY OKLAHOMAN

Oklahoma City, OK
February 3, 1987

THE U.S. House of Representatives likely will vote today to override President Reagan's veto of the clean water bill and thereby gain political mileage at his expense.

The expected margin is so great even he conceded defeat while signing his veto message. The Senate probably will take similar action later this week.

Many members of Reagan's own party stood against him on this issue, raising the question why the president would deliberately endure such embarrassment. Before the veto he was offered face-saving alternatives. One GOP lawmaker urged him to sign the bill and take political credit for doing so. Another suggested way out was neither to sign nor veto the bill, letting it become law after 10 days.

Thus, he could make his point without the embarrassment of an override. But Reagan was not inclined to take the easy way out when he feels so strongly about excessive government spending.

The bill, amending the 1972 Clean Water Act, would provide $18 billion through 1994 to state and local governments for construction of sewage treatment plants and another $2 billion for other pollution control programs. It's identical to one passed by Congress last year that became the victim of Reagan's pocket veto.

Congress likes the bill because it can be on the side of the angels by voting to protect the environment and at the same time bring home federal dollars.

Despite efforts to portray Reagan as standing alone against Congress and the American people, the issue is not pollution control or nothing. His substitute proposal would simply have scaled the sewage treatment aid down to $12 billion.

Reagan Pledges Acid Rain Funds

President Ronald Reagan, responding to pressure from Canada, March 18, 1987 renewed his commitment to a US$5 billion (C$6.9 billion) program to fight acid rain. In a 1986 agreement with Canada, the Reagan administration had endorsed a five-year program under which Washington and U.S. industry would each contribute US$2.5 billion (C$3.4 billion) to develop new technologies to burn coal more cleanly. Airborne sulfur dioxide emissions from industrial coal burning were believed to be a primary source of acid rain pollution. Canada charged that at least 60% of the acid rain that was destroying lakes and forests on both sides of the border was being generated in the U.S. Reagan's fiscal 1988 budget sought only US$287 million (C$392 million) for the program, prompting widespread criticism in Canada. (See pp. 4-7, 8-9, 18-19)

In his statement March 18, the president said he would ask the U.S. Congress for the "full amount" of US$2.5 billion, at a rate of US$500 million (C$657 million) a year over five years. Reagan said that his administration in calender year 1988 would target selected coal projects with US$850 million (C$1.1 billion) in federal funding. The US$850 million figure would include the fiscal 1988 and 1989 apropriations (US$500 million each) minus US$150 (C$197 million) for projects that were already being funded by the government. In addition, Reagan called for the creation of a U.S.-Canadian commission to advise the U.S. Energy Department of the allocation of the funds. He also ordered a review of U.S. federal and state regulations on emission controls. The president March 19 appeared to temper his commitment on acid rain. Speaking at his nationally televised news conference, Reagan suggested that he still opposed federal legislation mandating new emission controls.

Canadian Prime Minister Brian Mulroney March 18 praised Reagan's reversal as an "important step." Mulroney March 23 told a conference of North American environmentalists in Quebec City that his policy of "talking – rather than cursing – across the back fence" was "yielding welcome results" on acid rain. Nevertheless, the prime minister admitted that he was not sure he could convince Reagan to agree to a timetable on reducing U.S.- generated pollutants.

The News and Courier

Charleston, SC, March 31, 1987

It must have seemed a good idea when British Labor Party leader Neil Kinnock called for the removal of U.S. cruise missiles and announced a non-nuclear defense policy. It must have seemed a good way to get at Prime Minister Margaret Thatcher. Seeking to ridicule Mrs. Thatcher's support for the United States, NATO and nuclear deterrence, Mr. Kinnock described her in the House of Commons as "Reagan's poodle."

Mr. Kinnock's trip to the United States last autumn opened the eyes of members of his own party to the folly of his endorsement of unilateral nuclear disarmament. Mr. Kinnock's phony appeal to British nationalism failed. The British themselves saw through his clumsy attempt to exploit nuclear fears among the general public while pandering to the lunatic leftwing fringe of the Labor Party.

When he left for the United States last week to mend fences with the administration, he was accompanied by Denis Healey, one of the steadier members of the Labor Party's "shadow" cabinet. The idea, this time, was to show America — and British voters — that Labor's defense policy was not as foolish as it seemed.

Mr. Healey has always been opposed to unilateral nuclear disarmament but Mr. Kinnock has simply changed his tune. He now says that Britain's nuclear disarmament will be accomplished over a period of years and not in a rush. Mr. Kinnock has also promised to build up Britain's nonconventional forces.

Although the visit of Mr. Kinnock and Mr. Healey to Washington caused hardly a ripple here, the Labor leader ran into a storm of criticism upon his return home. His continued endorsement of unilateral nuclear disarmament may have settled the next election before it is held. The Labor Party is now in retreat and another victory for Margaret Thatcher is looming.

The Courier-Journal & TIMES

Louisville, KY, March 24, 1987

WHEN he committed the United States to spend $5 billion on developing clean coal technology, President Reagan must have thought his promise was a public relations ploy to cheer up the Canadians. As well he might, since his chief adviser on the issue was his aide and master PR technician, the recently indicted Mike Deaver.

In any case, Mr. Reagan seems to have dismissed clean coal from his mind after the much publicized agreement with Prime Minister Brian Mulroney last March. The budget he proposed ten months later included only a fraction of the money he had said the federal government would contribute to the five-year research project.

But those pesky Canadians, upset because pollutants from U. S. coal-burning plants contribute to their acid rain problem, didn't forget. Indeed, they have become increasingly restive, raising concerns that the next meeting between Mr. Reagan and Mr. Mulroney in April may not be altogether friendly.

So the President, his memory jogged, changed course last week and said, again, that Washington would put up $2.5 billion to match private research funds. The goal is to reduce sulfur and nitrogen emissions — the sources of acid rain — by developing cleaner methods for burning coal. New England and Canada will realize long-term benefits, but so will high sulfur coal regions in Kentucky and Indiana, which have been hurt by declining demand for "dirty" fuel.

The trouble is that new combustion technologies won't be available soon. The virulent form of pollution known as acid rain will therefore continue to damage lakes and forests unless coal-burning utilities are required to cut emissions drastically in the meantime.

Mr. Reagan is unlikely to push for new controls, in part because he has never really acknowledged that acid rain exists. Many scientists, including some on White House panels, have tried to enlighten him (and several powerful members of Congress), to no avail. The most recent study, by the Environmental Protection Agency, warns that 300 New England lakes are in danger of becoming acidic.

But even if the President remains unmoved by the degradation of U. S. resources, he is at least making good on last year's promise in order to stay on good terms with Canada. Whatever his reason, this research will pay off eventually in a better environment — assuming it doesn't slip Mr. Reagan's mind.

THE ATLANTA CONSTITUTION
Atlanta, GA, March 23, 1987

If left to his own devices, there is no doubt that President Reagan would continue to shrug off air pollution as the natural by-product of trees and other vegetation. For years, the administration evaded the issue of acid rain. When finally forced to act last year, it agreed to a remedial plan, then promptly ignored most of it. Now, pushed into action again by Canadian complaints, the president has promised $2.5 billion for test projects to combat acid rain.

That's great, but Americans should hope that this latest pledge is more than a sop to Canada. While Canadian officials fume like Ohio Valley smokestacks about the poisoned air that blows toward them, the fact is, the administration's obtuse policies also have harmed the United States. The evidence mounts that we urgently need a cleanup.

Example: An Environmental Protection Agency study (as yet unreleased) shows that without stronger acid-rain controls, 300 Northeastern lakes could lose their capacity to neutralize acidity in the next 50 years. Moreover, lakes in the Southeast would start becoming acidic.

What then? A terrible chain-reaction is possible. Consider a recent report by the Izaak Walton League of America. It offers strong evidence that acidified lakes could hamper the reproduction of waterfowl. As acidity rises, the food for ducks (insects, snails and the like) gets scarce. It is highly likely that this limits egg-laying in some species and narrows the chances of survival for ducklings.

Of course, the fish decline in acidified lakes, and this decimation, too, may have a wider effect. Researchers in New York state believe the fish-eating American Bald Eagle faces an indirect threat from acid rain. In other areas, ospreys, diving ducks, loons and mergansers could be at risk.

Along with a cleanup, the nation needs more study of acid rain. That's right, *study*. Unfortunately, the Reagan administration has made this word a synonym for delay It shouldn't be. If the urgency of a cleanup is obvious, countless questions need resolution — especially in the Southeast: What poses the biggest threat to forests of the region, ozone pollution or acid rain? What effects are emissions from Southeastern industries having? While the industrial Midwest has been studied plenty, not enough is known about our own pollution.

Besides the stirrings in the White House, Congress is set to tackle the issue yet again. In the past, regionalism has precluded any agreement. The Midwesterners have opposed strict controls while the New Englanders have pleaded for them. Perhaps this time around, the Southeast can help facilitate an agreement. After all, our lakes and perhaps our forests are at risk; at the same time, we produce our share of poisons.

So the congressional delegations of the Southeast are in a perfect position to forge a compromise that is fair but effective. Hope that they do. Because at bottom, only a strong bill from Congress will give strength and credibility to the president's begrudged promises.

The Kansas City Times
Kansas City, March 30, 1987

President Reagan, of all people, has added a new twist to the acid rain debate. His action may even stimulate a quicker resolution of the problem.

For years, his administration has contended no one knows what causes acid rain. More studies are needed. Costly programs should be stalled. These delaying tactics have rightfully earned the scorn of people concerned about the real effects in this country and in Canada.

But the president has done an about-face. He is now recommending that the government put up $2.5 billion over the next five years, matched by the coal industry, to develop commercial clean-coal technology aimed at reducing sulfur dioxide emissions from power plants.

In essence, even while Reagan keeps saying no one knows what causes acid rain, he is willing to spend billions of dollars trying to curb the one pollutant most closely identified with the dangerous precipitation.

The irony of the shift is not lost on environmentalists. Sure, Reagan's decision to support the clean coal measure involves politics; he's trying to make Canadian officials get off his back. But at least the president is on

the right track by trying to cut emissions of sulfur dioxide.

The National Wildlife Federation correctly promotes the idea that cleaning up the pollutants will save money in the long pull. It recently noted, "One study found that acid rain damage to homes and other structures can cost each resident of some cities as much as $45 annually in added maintenance. However, the solution to acid rain — reducing sulfur dioxide by 10 million tons annually and cutting nitrogen oxide emissions by 4 million tons — would increase monthly electric bills a mere 25 to 50 cents."

By itself, Reagan's recommendation is small comfort to people who have been involved in the battle for a long time. For six years the president has pretty much ignored any work that might have helped resolve this environmental concern. Just think what kind of emission reduction plans could have been followed by now if earlier action had been taken. But it wasn't.

Perhaps it's not too late. The next few years will be important to U.S. efforts to control acid rain, as long as the president keeps his promise and the money is spent on developing ways to more cleanly use coal.

The Salt Lake Tribune
Salt Lake City, UT
March 24, 1987

The Reagan administration's proposed acid rain mitigation plan has to be proof that persistence pays off. After prolonged argument that U.S. polluters were aggravating acid deposition problems in Canada, a position the administration had steadfastly resisted, the White House is proposing a five-year, $2.5 billion program to encourage innovative technology to deal with the problem.

It was a monumental concession to Canada, which has tried persistently but fruitlessly to get the United States to drastically reduce the emissions of sulfur and nitrogen from American industrial plants. Those emissions, which when allowed to react with atmospheric moisture form acid rain, have been wind-driven across the international border and fall indiscriminately on Canadian cities, farms, lakes, rivers and forests.

The Reagan administration, until now, had been unmoved by arguments that these trans-boundary flows were causing millions of dollars in damage in Canada, as well as in the Northeastern United States. Besides causing widespread economic damage in Canada, trans-boundary acid rain has been an aggravating factor in U.S.-Canadian relations.

Contending that there wasn't enough scientific data to support claims about acid rain's destructiveness, the administration adopted a wait-and-see attitude.

Happily, the White House has changed its tune. "We think the Canadian concerns about acid rain are legitimate and parallel our own concerns," is how White House spokesman Marlin Fitzwater explained the change of attitude.

While the new plan will work to eliminate much of the half of the acid rain that falls on Canada that is U.S.-originated, a goodly portion of the United States will benefit from the program.

Much of the pollution that upsets Canadians also falls on the New England and Northeastern states, with the same damaging effects that have occurred in places like Ontario and Quebec.

So, while the administration's proposal won't move the American electrical generating industry, the major source of the pollutants, any closer to the mandatory use of pollution controls the environmentalists seek, it has to be recognized as a significant step by the Reagan administration away from its indefensible, head-in-the-sand, position about the origins and impacts of acid rain.

That has to be regarded as progress, in efforts to preserve the environment, as well as a sagely constructed concession to continuing smooth relations with America's staunchest ally, largest trading partner and very close neighbor.

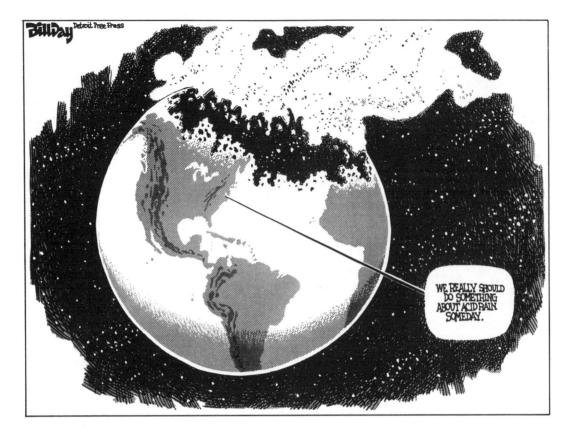

THE DAILY OKLAHOMAN
Oklahoma City, OK, March 30, 1987

OKLAHOMANS may yawn when President Reagan and Prime Minister Brian Mulroney take up the acid rain issue in their annual summit meeting next week.

The long-running controversy may seem too far away from Oklahoma's borders, involving as it does the smoke-emitting factories of the Northeast and Canada's forests. But Sooners are taxpayers and they will have to help bear the cost of whatever federal programs are launched to deal with the acid rain problem. And, as consumers, they also will have to help foot the bill for the expensive anti-pollution equipment industry has installed under Clear Air Act requirements.

The trouble is that even the scientists can't seem to agree on how much, if any, of the damage to forests and lakes, and their wildlife, in Canada can be attributed to the sulfur dioxide emissions from U.S. factories.

The president pledged March 18 to seek $2.5 billion over the next five years to demonstrate innovative pollution-control technologies.

It is ironic, then, that right after the president's announcement scientists advising the Environmental Protection Agency concluded that the agency's data suggest little or no lake acidification is occurring in the Northeast from acid rain.

This reverses initial findings of the EPA staff that about 300 Northeastern lakes and possibly as many as 1,500 will become acidic over the next 50 years if current rates of acidification persist.

Thus, what appeared initially to be ammunition for environmentalists' demands for acid-rain controls has now become support for the arguments of opponents. The scientists' conclusion coincides with claims by the coal and electric utility industries, who insist there is no proof that lakes and streams will suffer substantial and increasing damage if sulfur dioxide emissions from coal-fired power plants continue at current levels.

Despite Reagan's commitment to the $2.5 billion demonstration project, many Canadian and U.S. environmentalists demand tougher action against emissions from coal-fired plants. Some of their congressional friends advocate a 50 percent reduction in sulfur dioxide emissions. The new finding should strengthen Reagan's hand in resisting such overreaction to a problem that cannot be easily pinpointed.

Edmonton Journal
Edmonton, Alta., March 20, 1987

Ronald Reagan's pledge to ask the U.S. Congress for $2.5 billion in funds advances the fight against acid rain.

But it must be kept in perspective. The president did not promise to reduce U.S. industrial emissions; only to search for new ways to burn coal more cleanly. Congressional funding will be sought; it is not guaranteed.

Reagan's pledge is hardly a breakthrough in the campaign to save Canada's lakes and streams. He made the promise last year during his summit meeting with Prime Minister Brian Mulroney. It is only proper that he honor it.

But why has it taken him so long to act? Is it only to avoid political embarrassment when he meets Mulroney next month?

Reagan's renewed pledge is significant only in that it is the first step toward an agreement to cut transboundary air pollution emissions — something Washington seems loath to do, at least where it concerns Canada.

Yet the U.S. has acknowledged that emissions from an Arizona copper smelter have contributed to pollution in Mexico and has signed an emission control pact with that country. Why is the U.S. so worried about industrial pollution crossing its southern border, but not its northern border? The answer is clear: Mexico has a huge copper smelter that spews as much pollution into the U.S. as the Arizona smelter dumps into Mexico. It was in the U.S. interest to deal with the problem quickly.

Not so with Canada though, as Environment Minister Tom McMillan notes, Reagan has come a long way from the days when he blamed "volcanoes and trees and even ducks" for acid rain. Still, McMillan says: "We have not found the Holy Grail. We do not have the... binding commitment we are seeking from the Americans to slash acid-rain causing emissions on the American side of the border."

Canadian pressure may have caused Reagan to renew his pledge to fight acid rain, but the U.S. is still a long way from cleaning up the mess it has made of the world's environment.

𝔇etroit 𝔉ree 𝔓ress

Detroit, MI, March 24, 1987

IF ACID RAIN and its depredations were as visible, say, as a plague of locusts, perhaps the political dithering in the United States over what to do about acid rain — its production and its deleterious effects — could be transformed into action.

It is widely known that the lakes and forests of northeastern Canada are being ravaged by airborne nitrous oxides and sulfur dioxides, which, when they fall to earth in precipitation, acidify bodies of water rendering them unfit to support plant and animal life. What is less often remarked upon is that, to a lesser degree but just as deadly effect, the same fate has befallen lakes in northern Minnesota, Michigan and parts of New England.

Though the research is not yet complete, scientists and environmentalists almost universally agree that the burning of high-sulfur coal in power plants across the Midwest causes the pollution that ends up becoming acid rain. The Canadian government has been negotiating with the United States for almost a decade to get U.S. power industries to clean up and reduce their toxic emissions.

For both political and economic reasons, not much has been done. Michigan managed to clean up its smokestacks in the past decade. As much cannot be said for Missouri, Illinois, Ohio and Indiana. Anti-pollution devices cost a lot of money, especially when power plants have to be retrofitted. That's one set of problems. Another is that of states in which soft-coal mining is a major industry.

Both the power and the coal industries have succeeded so far in stalling action on acid rain. In that, they have had a willing partner in the Reagan administration, in which much jawboning and little actual progress is being made. The federal government has the power under the Interstate Commerce Act and through the Environmental Protection Agency to force power plant operators to install anti-pollution devices in the form of acid-gas scrubbers on offending stacks. The administration and Congress have the responsibility to craft a coherent policy that would establish proper anti-pollution standards for fuel and its burning processes.

In a meeting a year ago with Canadian Prime Minister Brian Mulroney, President Reagan committed this nation to a $5 billion anti-acid rain program — $2.5 billion more than he had originally offered. The fiscal 1988 budget he sent to Congress contained only $350 million, however. Canadians are upset, understandably, at the president's welshing. Their tempers are not much brightened by his offer to return to the original $2.5 billion. Who can blame them?

It is in the interests of people on both sides of the border for the United States to 1) require power plants now emitting the material that becomes acid rain to equip their stacks with anti-pollution equipment to cut back on those emissions in the short term, 2) fund further research into the phenomenon and its prevention, including an exploration of ways to clean high-sulfur fuels before they are burned, and 3) explore a long-term national policy on the use of fossil fuels.

Los Angeles, CA, March 24, 1987

The corrosive impact of acid rain on U.S.-Canada relations finally has persuaded the White House to fulfill promises it made, then reneged on, last March. President Reagan now has agreed to ask Congress for $2.5 billion and business for a like amount to study solutions to emissions that cause acid precipitation. Welcome as the president's belated action is, it doesn't go nearly far enough.

President Reagan hasn't been alone in dragging his feet. Coal-state legislators and utilities have blocked action by challenging environmentalist alarm about acid rain and calling for more studies. Sen. Robert Byrd, D-W. Va., made the outrageous claim this month that acid rain damage is "a crisis that does not exist."

On the contrary, as Canadians and Americans in the Northeast well know, the crisis already has caused extensive damage, and research shows it is harming lakes in the Southeast and the Rocky Mountains.

Scientists also believe acid rain is a serious threat to healthy lungs. The source is no longer a matter of reasonable dispute: Sulfur and nitrogen oxide emissions from power plants and autos are generating precipitation that contaminates the soil, and kills trees and freshwater life.

The Canadians have been irked by what they perceive, quite correctly, as Washington's stubborn unwillingness to do anything about the problem except talk. But, oddly enough, the U.S. has concluded an acid-rain pact with Mexico that could stand as a model for international cooperation.

To reduce sulfur pollution from copper smelters in northern Mexico and Arizona, the two nations have agreed to shut down one unimprovable operation and install devices at another to cut emissions 95 percent.

This narrow agreement points in the right direction but, ultimately, something broader is needed. Acid rain won't go away until Congress passes legislation of the sort pushed last year by California Rep. Henry Waxman. His bill mandated gradual cuts in sulfur and nitrogen emissions from power plants, factories and cars. No amount of studying can substitute for such a measure.

𝔗he 𝔖tar-𝔏edger

Newark, NJ, March 31, 1987

The President has moved to allay environmental concerns of our Canadian neighbor with the assurance that he will ask Congress to approve $2.5 billion over the next five years for projects to combat acid rain. This airborne pollution is an ecological problem that seriously endangers freshwater lakes and forests, killing fish and damaging plant life in the United States and Canada.

The Reagan Administration's proposed funding marks the opening stage in an overdue collaborative effort to attack the virulent sources of acid rain. It represents a commitment made more than a year ago in an agreement worked out by special envoys of both countries to move toward abating the acid rain problem.

In the past, Canada had been critical of the lack of an American commitment in trying to reduce sulfur emissions that are the principal source of acid rain contamination. It is estimated that 50 percent of the acid rain pollution in Canada emanates from American sources, mainly from smokestack industries in the Midwest.

In positive contrast, the government of Canadian Prime Minister Brian Mulroney unilaterally instituted a program last year to fight acid rain pollution. But without a comparable commitment by the United States, it would be impossible even to begin reversing the widespread environmental damage caused by acid rain, given its insidious atmospheric mobility.

Mr. Mulroney, who will meet with President Reagan in Ottawa next month, recently expressed impatience with the White House's proposed spending for acid rain programs in the new federal budget. The Mulroney reservations now have been fully addressed by the new $2.5 billion funding Mr. Reagan has promised he will call on Congress to approve.

However, some environmental groups doubt that the joint program will appreciably reduce sulfur contaminants in the atmosphere in an immediate context because the new spending would be focused on clean coal technology. The latter will have to be widely utilized to attack acid rain sources. But the acid test must be on the basis of effectively reducing levels of sulfur emissions—reductions that would at last begin reversing the long-term deleterious effects of acid rain pollution.

Acid-Rain Report Criticized by Experts

A report by the Reagan administration's National Acid Precipitation Assessment Program Sept. 17, 1987 drew a flurry of criticism from scientific and environmental sources. The report, a midway accounting of a $300 million, 10-year research effort on the acid-rain phenomenon, discounted the problem. Relatively few U.S. lakes and streams had become acidified, it said, and damage to crops, forests and human health was negligible. No "abrupt change in aquatic systems, crops or forests at present levels of air pollution" was likely, it said.

Scientists from areas afflicted by acid rain quickly rejected the report. In Canada, Environment Minister Tom McMillan called it "awkwardly out of step. . .with prevailing scientific judgment on the subject." *Science* magazine Sept. 18 reported that the research effort was generally considered "quite good, perhaps first rate," but presentation of the facts from the study had caused consternation. Eville Gorham of the University of Minnesota, who had monitored lake acidity in the upper Midwest, said the report "seems to be slanted toward making the problem rather minor."

The federal study was also deplored Sept. 29 by the National Audubon Society, which announced it had undertaken its own national survey of the acid-rain problem because of dissatisfaction with government efforts. Peter A. A. Perle, president of the society, said the data on acidity of rainfall used by the administration's report were often years out of date, and the data had been collected in the fall, he said, when acidity was generally at its lowest level. The Reagan administration had persistently maintained that scientific evaluation of the acid-rain problem so far did not justify the high cost of the proposed controls.

THE SACRAMENTO BEE

Sacramento, CA, September 24, 1987

The Reagan administration recently released a major assessment of the national impact of acid rain that it hopes will be taken as the president's last word on the subject. Since he's never had anything sensible to say about it in the past — and this report is no exception — that's probably a mercy. But this certainly won't be the last that the rest of the us are likely to hear about this problem in the years to come.

In keeping with the president's consistent indifference toward the threat that acid rain poses for the environment, this analysis by the National Acid Precipitation Assessment Program strives mightily to present a case that there isn't any problem at all. Or at least a little bit of the report does, the part that the administration expects most people will read. Scientists who contributed to the study complain that their findings documenting the seriousness of the problem appear in the report all right, but not in the executive summary that was distributed to reporters, members of Congress and the public.

Environmentalists argue that Reagan's researchers managed to see only sunshine because they dismissed large bodies of the most recent data concerning the impact of acid rain on leaf growth, and they left out whole areas of study into such things as the damage that's being done to homes and other man-made structures. The authors of the report point out that the methods of calculating these effects aren't yet precise. But the fact that they can't be quantified doesn't mean that the problems don't exist.

In addition, the report doesn't say anything at all about Canada, where a lot of the pollution from U.S. smokestacks falls back to earth as acid rain. Canadian officials, who have been disappointed before by the president's failure to follow through on his promises to help them deal with this problem, are understandably outraged. "Voodoo science," the environment minister calls it.

Even the report's cheery assessment that hardly any of our own lakes and streams are suffering the ill effects of acid rain depends on a little statistical mumbo jumbo. The government analysts simply set the definition of acidic contamination so high that hardly anything qualifies.

This isn't a problem that the president can make go away just by wishful thinking. The rain keeps right on falling. If this administration won't deal with it, somebody else inevitably will have to.

The London Free Press
London, Ont., September 22, 1987

The Reagan administration continues to close its eyes to the acid rain problem. A United States government report, released by the National Acid Precipitation Assessment Program last week, concludes that acid rain has had minimal damage on lakes and streams, has not damaged crops, and cannot be shown to have any detrimental impact on trees.

Such nonsense can only further harden administration resistance to any regulations that would force mid-western industries to reduce sulphur and nitrogen emissions — the cause of acid rain.

In reality, almost all scientific data have established the threat to forests, buildings, lakes and human health from acid rain.

It's impossible not to conclude that the report was based on political considerations more than scientific evidence. The selective use of data proves the point. Tom Brydges, an Environment Canada acid rain expert, told reporters the American study is fairly accurate as far as it goes, but misrepresents the over-all issue by ignoring Canadian data.

For example, many Canadian experts say American emissions probably cause more damage in Canada than the U.S. because they cause most damage down wind. Canadian studies say about half the acid precipitation in Canada originates from American emissions. Geology also plays a role in how susceptible waterways are to acidification. Lakes in the Canadian Shield are more susceptible to acidification, the experts say.

Ironically, the report was issued just as the U.S. was agreeing to a program of reductions in the production of chlorofluorocarbons, blamed for destroying the Earth's ozone layer. It seems strange they can accept ozone damage but not acid rain.

The response from Canada's Environment Minister Tom McMillan that his department will double the $425,000 budget for its acid rain communications program and start a mass-media publicity program to tell Americans about Canada's scientific data is admirable. But it may be futile.

Certainly, Canada must keep up the pressure. However, the U.S. administration appears unwilling to listen.

 **StarPhoenix**

Saskatoon, Sask., September 25, 1987

Canadians have every reason to be surprised and bitterly disappointed by the latest U.S. report on acid rain.

 **S-P Opinion**

The progress of Canadian-American talks aimed at curbing the problem of acid rain which is killing lakes and forests at an alarming rate has never been smooth. But several events last April gave reason to hope a joint effort to reduce sulphur dioxide emissions might be undertaken. U.S. President Ronald Reagan conceded for the first time that American sources are causing half the acid rain precipitation in Eastern Canada. And a team of research scientists from both countries agreed the environment is capable of recovery if reductions are achieved soon.

Last week, however, the National Acid Rain Precipitation Assessment Program (the same agency which formed part of that earlier team) declared acid rain has damaged only a tiny fraction of U.S. lakes, has had no harmful effect on crops and no proven effect on forests and is unlikely to get much worse.

Such an apparent about-face shocked both American and Canadian environmental groups and led Environment Minister Tom McMillan to say the report was out of step with prevailing scientific judgment and the broad public demand for action on the acid rain problem.

Given the Reagan administration's past lack of enthusiasm for pushing meaningful emission reduction programs, this report could bring the effort to a virtual standstill. McMillan can only redouble his lobby with the administration and the American public to convince them Canadians are not imagining things and that the U.S. has a moral obligation to stop destroying this country's environment, even if it persists in turning a blind eye on the death of its own.

The Toronto Star

Toronto, Ont., September 19, 1987

American economist Herbert Stein once remarked that "there is no conservative or liberal economics, just as there is no conservative or liberal chemistry." Science is science, except, of course, when *political science* gets in the way. And, that's exactly what happened to a $300 million U.S. scientific study which says that the causes and consequences of acid rain are still unclear.

The problem was apparently unclear to the Reagan administration's economists as well, but at least they suggested why. In their annual report to Congress this year, the top economic advisers said: "The usual difficulties of assessing environmental risks and internalizing costs are magnified because some costs and benefits occur in another country." In other words, in economic terms U.S. acid rain isn't a major problem as long as it falls on Canada.

The scientists, it seems, took their cue from the economists. By downplaying the evidence of acid rain damage to Canada, the scientists simply assumed the problem away. As one Canadian acid rain expert put it: "If you ignore the examples of the problem, then you are not going to see the problem."

Furious over the report, Environment Minister Tom McMillan called it "voodoo science." In an attempt to deflect the criticism, the head of the study said it was "good science." By giving the U.S. ever more excuses to ignore acid rain, it properly belongs on the "political science" shelf.

The Sun

Vancouver, B.C., September 19, 1987

A United States report says that acid rain has caused minimal damage to lakes, streams, crops, and trees, notwithstanding many other reports that show exactly the opposite. Perhaps this one was done by the same lab that puts out reports saying smoking doesn't harm lungs, that nuclear power is as harmless as sunlight, and that peach pits will cure rheumatism, headaches, and several forms of cancer.

THE DAILY HERALD

Biloxi, MS, September 28, 1987

Tom McMillan, Canada's minister of the environment, has it right.

The Reagan administration's latest report on acid rain is "voodoo science."

The report concludes acid rain is damaging only a handful of lakes in the Northeast and has no demonstrable effect on trees, buildings or crops.

In other words, there's no urgency about reducing acid pollution from Midwestern power plants — a convenient conclusion, since it supports Reagan's determined reluctance to do anything about air pollution.

Where's the voodoo in the science?

Well, the report defines an acidified lake as one with a Ph of 5 (as acid as coffee), and says only 10 percent of Adirondack lakes are acidified.

Independent scientists say that's setting the acid threshold way too high. Aquatic life begins to suffer at a much lower level of acidity, and that at least 20 percent of Adirondack lakes are suffering.

The report further minimizes the damage of acid rain by looking only at U.S. lakes. Weather patterns carry far more Midwestern acid pollution over Canada.

Scientists say the government study simply ignores the growing body of evidence that acid rain damages the health of forests, particularly on mountains.

"We don't know the overall effect (on trees) but to say there is no effect is just not true," one scientist summed up.

It's one thing to acknowledge the damage done by acid rain and then to argue society can't afford the cost of ending it.

To deny the evidence — or subvert science to political ends — is pernicious.

Omaha World-Herald

Omaha, NE, September 22, 1987

Acid rain isn't just an environmental issue. It also has become a domestic political issue in the United States and an excuse for some Canadians to vent anti-American feelings. For that reason, it is perhaps inevitable that some people have condemned a new government report suggesting that acid rain isn't an imminent threat.

The report, prepared by the National Acid Precipitation Assessment Program, concluded that a number of other questions about acid rain can't be answered until research techniques improve, which could take years. That view is heresy to extremists who already know all they care to know about acid rain and are demanding that industry and the taxpayers finance a multibillion-dollar effort to reduce smokestack emissions.

No knowledgeable person on either side of the debate denies that air pollution is unpleasant. Or that it can harm plants and animals. The fact that oxides of sulfur and nitrogen combine with airborne droplets to form acid rain has been documented. So has the fact that oxides of sulfur and nitrogen are among the products of combustion in factories and motor vehicles.

From those facts, some people have jumped to the conclusion that rigid controls are needed immediately on motor vehicles and factories in the Great Lakes region to save Canadian lakes and forests from acid rain. The new study is part of the Reagan administration's effort to provide perspective.

Lawrence Kulp, who directed the study, said the purpose was to bring together the latest scientific information about the subject. He said some of the major questions about acid rain can't be answered at this time.

For example, scientists can't predict where the pollution from a relatively small area will come down. They haven't adequately explained the changes in forest soils. They don't know what the long-term impact of relatively low levels of pollution may be. And, while they can't explain why some high-altitude forests have been damaged, they have no reason to believe that most U.S. forests will show "an abrupt change in health." Kulp said that language refers to the next decade or two.

If human beings are to live in balance with their environment, they must develop the tools to make informed, rational decisions. The Kulp study was part of an effort to do so.

EPA Seeks to Delay Clean-Air Deadlines

The Environmental Protection Agency (EPA) asked Nov. 17, 1987 for a delay in implementing clean-air deadlines on reduction of ozone and carbon monoxide pollution. Some 50 to 60 cities were facing failure to meet a Dec. 31, 1987 deadline for reducing the pollutants below levels designated dangerous to public health. Failure to meet the deadlines called for sanctions on construction of new industrial plants, as a way to avoid increasing the pollution problem. (See pp. 34-37)

The EPA proposed instead to extend the compliance date, allowing a grace period of up to eight years for most of the delinquent metropolitan areas. New plans to attain the standards by 1996 would be required to be submitted by the states involved. The goal would be to reduce the carbon monoxide and hydrocarbon pollution by 3% annually. The plans would be due by the spring of 1990, designed to bring the areas into compliance within three to five years, depending on the extent of the pollution. EPA Administrator Lee Thomas said a ban on new construction still was in the offing for 14 metropolitan areas that had been warned in June of their noncompliance status because of failure to submit adequate plans. The areas included Los Angeles, Cleveland, Chicago and Denver.

The latest EPA plan, which was subject to a 60-day review period, encountered immediate criticism by environmental spokesmen. "The whole point of sanctions has been to stimulate action to clean up pollution," said Richard Ayers, chairman of the National Clean Air Coalition. "If you delay them, you take off that pressure. The states relax, and we go back to drifting."

The Dec. 31 deadline itself was an extension of earlier deadlines. The original deadline had been 1975, but this was extended to Dec. 31, 1982 or to Dec. 31, 1987 for areas with more severe problems. Congress also allowed in 1983 a moratorium on sanctions against the communities that had failed to meet the 1982 deadline but were attempting to implement cleanup plans.

THE ATLANTA CONSTITUTION

Atlanta, GA, November 25, 1987

It's a regulatory free-for-all. Federal law says cities must meet clean-air rules by year's end or face sanctions. But the cities and their respective state governments want new deadlines; they insist that the old rules haven't worked too well. The Environmental Protection Agency (EPA) is sympathetic to their pleas and has said it may relax the deadlines. But Congress is incensed; it wants to know where the EPA found authority to offer such dispensations.

There are two possible outcomes here. If nothing changes, the brouhaha could land with a splat in court as EPA winds up sued for its leniency. Or Congress could get smart, decree a grace period for the states and enact a new clean-air law — one that is tough but more effective. The first course guarantees continued confusion. The second could result in healthier air.

Why change the law? Look at the plight of metro Atlanta. We are among cities that face sanctions on Jan. 1. And yet officials here have worked hard to reduce emissions that cause ozone pollution. In fact, they cut them by 65 percent. When the law was passed a decade ago, most people assumed that such a chop would put our pollution levels within tolerable bounds.

Surprise. Our level of ozone pollution (also known as smog) has hardly budged. Meanwhile, scientists have learned that the production of this poison is vastly more complex than originally thought — a curious interaction of variables such as automobile and industrial vapors, heat, sunlight and wind. Given the trickiness of the problem, the old deadlines now make little sense.

Several remedies have been put before Congress, but Rep. Henry Waxman (D-Calif.) has a particularly sensible idea. His bill would give the states an eight-month grace period. Then they would be held to new rules that acknowledge the wide diversity of smog problems throughout the nation. Cities with a severe problem like Los Angeles would face one standard. Cities with a less serious problem such as Atlanta would face another. The objective here is to fashion an effective law, not a lenient one.

Any new law that Congress passes should push metro Atlanta to try harder. Emissions standards for automobiles could be tightened, as could standards for local factories. The state could encourage use of rapid transit. It could encourage its cities to install synchronized traffic signals (which would reduce vapors from idling engines). Congress could fight air pollution directly, too, by requiring refiners to make gasoline that is less likely to create smog.

Today's bureaucratic brawl serves no one's interest. Congress must excuse itself from the eyeball-gouging and name-calling and — with new rules — find a way to end this mess.

The Miami Herald

Miami, FL, November 21, 1987

THE Environmental Protection Agency wants to extend the Dec. 31 deadline for some 60 cities to meet air-pollution standards. Penalties include factory-construction moratoriums and loss of Federal highway funds and sewage-treatment grants.

Those are drastic measures. But so is the degree of air pollution inflicted on urban residents. Congressional testimony this year cited respiratory ailments as a growing cause of debilitation and death. Those illnesses have a direct connection with polluted air.

In Florida, the rules affect Miami, Hialeah, Tampa, and Jacksonville. The U.S. cities already have received two deadline extensions — totaling 10 years — from Congress. Delaying implementation by another three to five years, which the EPA proposes, simply encourages noncompliant cities and complacent legislatures to do nothing.

Much can be done. The major air polluter is the automobile. One of the worst polluters in Dade County, for example, are vehicles whose catalytic converters, requiring unleaded gasoline, have been dismantled. Reinstituting car inspections, with more attention to catalytic converters and exhaust systems, would help solve the Dade cities' noncompliance problems. Without the EPA's clout to force action soon, this issue will continue to languish.

A viable mass-transit system — one that goes places users need to get to with efficiency and consistency — would reduce auto use considerably. A fatal combination of poor transit systems, low gas-pump prices, *and* the lack of air-quality standards for so many years has allowed cities and residents to disregard the control of auto emissions.

Pending legislation to renew the Clean Air Act addresses, fairly adequately, control of other air-pollution sources such as coal-burning power plants. It also would extend the cities' compliance deadlines yet again.

The EPA should withdraw its deadline-extension proposal and fight the legislators' unwarranted generosity as well. The agency has indicated flexibility if deadlines are imposed — working with cities that show good-faith efforts to comply within a reasonable time. That's as much leniency as should be allowed after a decade of delay.

The Kansas City Times

Kansas City, MO, November 28, 1987

As might be expected, the National Coal Association is upset about possible acid rain control measures pending before Congress. While the concern is understandable, it's also a little shortsighted.

The association trots out the usual suspects. The Clean Air Act has prompted $100 billion in industry spending in the last 15 years; American competitiveness has been reduced; a new report says there is no environmental emergency associated with acid rain; and the National Association of Manufacturers predicts a monumental negative impact from any acid rain control legislation.

The three-page release by the association conveniently ignores the fact that the Clean Air Act has improved the health of millions of Americans. It ignores that the recent acid rain report was produced by a group friendly to the administration's do-nothing approach to the problem. Finally, the coal association tosses around wild figures on how spending money to clean up the environment could "reduce GNP $223 billion, increase the federal budget deficit by $247 billion and cost 862,000 jobs by the year 2000."

Oh, really? Proponents of clean air policies will correctly and gladly point out that if industries have to allocate billions of dollars to improve their manufacturing procedures, they will have to spend the money *on* something—such as hiring environmental engineers and buying new equipment to reduce pollution.

Yes, that actually creates jobs and increases the GNP. There's no use expecting the National Coal Assooication to point out this side of the equation. But it is worth knowing.

Birmingham Post-Herald
*Birmingham, AL
November 25, 1987*

The U.S. Environmental Protection Agency is being criticized by environmentalists and some congressmen for proposing to extend the deadline for cities to achieve air quality standards for smog and carbon monoxide. But it's hard to see what else the EPA could do.

There is no chance that the more than 50 metropolitan areas involved can meet the existing Dec. 31 deadline. Without an extension, the cities would face harsh penalties that include a ban on construction of plants that could be sources of air pollution and the withholding of federal funds for highways, sewers and, ironically, air pollution control. The sanctions would inflict an undue drag on economic activities in the communities.

The pollutants at issue are ozone, which is a major component of smog, and carbon monoxide. Motor vehicle engines are the major source of both.

Limits on ozone and carbon monoxide in the air were established under the Clean Air Act of 1970. The original deadline for compliance was 1975, but that has been extended twice. Most large metropolitan areas still have been unable to meet the standards.

Under EPA's new proposal, states would be given two years to come up with plans designed to meet the standards by 1996. The states could choose their own strategies, but their plans would have to result in at least a 3 percent reduction annually in levels of ozone and carbon monoxide.

Critics claim EPA is not being tough enough. But the fault does not lie with that agency. Congress simply was overly optimistic in 1970 about how long it would take to reduce smog and carbon monoxide. Great strides have been made in removing pollutants from motor vehicle emissions, but squeezing out more, at an acceptable cost, is not easy.

EPA administrator Lee Thomas said his agency's proposed new policy would "move cities steadily toward attainment of the standards" while avoiding the "severe social and economic disruptions, at least in the near term," which the imposition of sanctions could bring.

That makes sense.

THE BLADE

Toledo, OH, November 16, 1987

YOU can't get much more fundamental than clean air. And perhaps not even the heavy hitters at the Heritage Foundation (or any other anti-government think tank) would disagree that the feds should play a role in protecting clean air. But what role? And how?

Congress is dithering around with rewriting the Clean Air Act now on the books, as cities across the country struggle to try to meet Dec. 31 pollution guidelines that probably are unrealistic.

Cities that fail to control smog-producing ozone could have sanctions imposed, such as a ban on new construction. Chicago, Dallas, and Los Angeles are among the cities facing the deadline.

This is plainly silly. The deadlines will have to be extended. There is no discernible debate on that point. What is being debated is what sort of extension should be made and what requirements will be added to or subtracted from current law.

Rep. Henry Waxman of California wants a brief extension and a tougher law, especially with respect to acid rain. That would keep the issue before the public eye in 1988. On the other side are forces who might call themselves more pragmatic and might be called by others environmental obstructionists. These members of Congress want to delay the deadlines — indeed the rewriting of the rules until after the 1988 elections.

Acid rain is a more complex problem than many environmentalists would have us believe, but Mr. Waxman is right. In a campaign in which the nature of the substance that former Arizona Gov. Bruce Babbitt smoked in college or when Pat Robertson's first child was conceived is an issue, clean air ought to be on the national agenda somewhere.

THE ⬛ SUN

Baltimore, MD, November 30, 1987

State environmental officials have entered into a significant agreement with Bethlehem Steel Corp. to lessen the pollutants churned out of its Sparrows Point smokestacks. Over three years the company will spend $15.2 million to eliminate particulates harmful to the air we breathe. However, the state Air Management Administration does not expect metropolitan Baltimore to turn overnight into a nosegay of freshness.

The Sparrows Point plant produces steel and accounts for a payroll of 8,200 workers. The waste from its product is not easily absorbed into the natural environment. The plant has tried unsuccessfully before to clean up its coke oven smokestacks. Now, in its consent agreement with the state, the company agrees to pay $750,000 for past air violations. That is the largest penalty ever in Maryland. Failure to deliver under terms of the agreement could bring further penalties.

The steelmaker agrees to meet federal and state standards on a regular basis, requiring reduction of all the plant's iron oxide, sulfur and toxic emissions. That would eliminate 481 tons of particulates. Though the amount would cut Bethlehem's total emissions by only 15 percent, officials believe it is enough to elevate the quality of air in the surrounding metropolitan area.

Bethlehem Steel hopes to meet air quality standards by modifying smokestacks over its coke ovens by adding scrubbers and other modern devices. In addition to reducing carcinogenic pollutants, the equipment is expected to lessen escape of sulphur dioxide and nitrogen oxide. If so, that could help in lowering damage to creeks and streams caused by acid rain that threaten larger rivers feeding into the Chesapeake Bay.

Maryland environmental officials are quietly negotiating similar agreements with other firms whose power plants pour particulates and other wastes into the environment. But none is as important to overall air quality as Bethlehem Steel. Not since the early 1970s, when Maryland's major utilities signed similar consent agreements, has the state made such headway.

Oil Spill Fouls Monongahela; Pa., W. Va., Ohio Affected

The collapse of an Ashland Oil Co. storage tank spilled nearly a million gallons of diesel fuel into the Monongahela River Jan. 2, 1988 about 30 miles upriver from Pittsburgh, Pa. The accident, one of the largest inland fuel spills in U.S. history, endangered water supplies for thousands of people and businesses and destroyed or jeopardized fish, fowl and other wildlife.

A bank-to-bank oil slick moved quickly downriver, stretching 20 miles in length, forcing communities to shut off water intake valves. The patch was approaching Newell, W. Va. along the Ohio River by Jan. 4. By Jan. 6, Steubenville, Ohio officials detected the smell and taste of oil in their intake system, which was closed down. Pittsburgh itself largely escaped the crisis, drawing water from the Allegheny River above its convergence, downtown, with the Monongahela, to form the Ohio River.

But the oil patch slowed and more or less came to a standstill at Steubenville, solidified by ice and frigid weather. "The water is mostly oil, all the way to the bottom," an Ohio Environmental Protection Agency spokesman said Jan. 8. "We've got some big time water problems," Steubenville council member Tina Grump said. "The river is not moving. The oil slick is stationary, and it's smack on top of our intake valve." The town was closed down except for food and drug stores, medical facilities and gas stations.

The pollution damage and other environmental problems caused by the accident remained to be assessed. At least three class-action suits had been filed against Ashland by Jan. 7. Company officials expressed assurance immediately after the spill that insurance policies would cover the bulk of the costs from the accident. Company Chairman John R. Hull later stressed that coverage was complete despite questions on whether the company had obtained the proper permits for construction of the holding tanks that collapsed. Initial reports on the accident said that the tank was a new one that collapsed the first time it was filled. But it turned out that the container, made from 40-year-old steel, had been moved from a company site in Cleveland and reconstructed at Jefferson Borough outside Pittsburgh along the Monongahela. Normally, the company filled a tank with water to make sure it was strong enough to hold the fuel. This time, only five feet of water was pumped into the 48-foot-high tank to check the welds. When it gave, 3.85 million gallons of oil spewed forth.

THE PLAIN DEALER

Cleveland, OH, January 7, 1988

At this moment, a more than 100-mile long sheen of diesel fuel is heading down the Ohio River at about a mile an hour. For 17 of those miles, the fuel is more than just a thin coating; it is drawn by the current to a greater depth. Water supplies to hundreds of thousands of people have been cut off. Hospital patients have been denied showers. Schools have closed. Swarms of local, state and federal environment and wildlife personnel, as well as the National Guard, have been called in. While fish and wildlife personnel are optimistic—the cold has driven fish to the river's bottom, below the oil—they do not know the long-term ecological impact of the spill.

It is, obviously, much more than the "inconvenience" for which Ashland Oil Co. chairman and CEO John Hall apologized Tuesday. Hall accepted blame, offered to have his company pay for clean-up costs, and acknowledged that Ashland personnel may not have followed proper procedures in constructing and testing the tank that failed Saturday, dumping a million gallons of contamination into the Monongahela River, an Ohio River tributary. His statements went beyond what many businessmen would say following such an event.

Still, there can be no excuse for Ashland's apparent failure to obtain a permit to reassemble the tank near West Elizabeth, Pa., last year. There can be no excuse for the company's total disregard for recommended testing procedures. Surely Ashland engineers knew that a sudden rupture of such a structure—as happened Saturday—could swamp containment dikes designed to keep slower leaks from spreading.

Such spills have happened before, though they've been rare. In Ohio alone, 40,000 tanks, each holding from 660 to millions of gallons of liquid, are subject to federal Clean Water Act regulation. In the vast majority of cases, environmental protections are adequate, even against corporate irresponsibility. But what happened near Pittsburgh last Saturday was the result of a combination of irresponsible actions by Ashland *and* the public authorities charged with enforcing the rules. Why was Ashland not forced to obtain a permit? Where were the public inspectors? Why aren't dikes designed to withstand the sudden collapse of millions of gallons of oil?

As the ooze heads downriver to foul yet another river—the Mississippi—somebody should be looking for some answers.

AKRON BEACON JOURNAL
Akron, OH, January 13, 1988

THE ASHLAND Oil storage tank that collapsed Jan. 2 near Pittsburgh did more than pollute the Ohio River. The incident also stained the notion that the public is adequately protected against such hazards.

The almost million-gallon spill now is working its way downriver, creating water emergencies for communities along the Ohio. Part of the problem is that the cleanup technology was designed for oil spills at sea. A churning river takes the oil too deep to be contained by floating booms and then scooped off the surface. So the oil runs deep, where city water intakes are found.

Back on dry land, suits have been filed against Ashland, which has vowed to pay for the cleanup, and regulation is being questioned, as it should. In Ohio, which may be out $1 million for the spill, state Environmental Protection Agency officials are looking at state laws, and may recommend new rules for inspecting and approving oil storage tanks.

New laws might be justified but in this spill there was an apparent disregard for existing law. Ashland officials admit they never got "written" permission from authorities to begin operating the 40-year-old tank after it was dismantled in Cleveland and reassembled in Pennsylvania. And the tank did not appear to be properly tested before it was filled with oil.

The biggest question mark, however, concerns the dike that was supposed to contain any spill at the site. When the tank, not quite full, collapsed, some 3.8 million gallons of diesel oil was released; 860,000 gallons escaped the holding dike and went into the Monongahela River. Why aren't dikes big enough to contain the largest spill that could be possible at that or any site?

Investigations into the spill are only beginning. The immediate crisis is a long way from being over and long-term damage — to businesses along the river, to fish, wildlife and plants, and to the region's image — may not be known for months.

Perhaps answers will soon come. The public outcry for real environmental protection will only increase in the weeks ahead, as the 20-mile oil slick floats leisurely down one of America's most important inland waterways.

The Pittsburgh
PRESS

Pittsburgh, PA, January 5, 1988

It took decades to clean the polluted Monongahela River. It took hours to foul it again.

In both cases, industry was the culprit.

For a century, heavy industry in the Mon Valley used the river as its own waste sewer. But clean-up efforts finally overcame the years of abuse — until a massive oil spill over the weekend turned back the river's evolutionary clock.

A storage tank collapsed at the Ashland Oil Co.'s tank farm in Floreffe, Jefferson Borough, spilling between 2 million and 3 million gallons of diesel fuel. About 1 million gallons found its way into the Monongahela. The slick that ensued spoiled even the Ohio River.

Still, as massive as the spill is, the effort being expended to contain it thus far has produced less than optimum results.

It would be difficult to accept the renewed pollution even if it had been caused by an unavoidable accident. But the circumstances of this incident — possibly the first of its kind in the nation — make it even more unpalatable than usual.

The tank that collapsed, it turns out, is about 40 years old and was moved to the Floreffe tank field from an Ashland terminal near Cleveland. It appears that such moves are not uncommon in the oil industry and, according to the company, the relocation and age of the tank were noted on applications filed with the Environmental Protection Agency and the county fire marshal's office.

If so, that's about as far as the information was disseminated. Ashland certainly didn't tell anybody about it during the weekend, claiming throughout that the tank was new.

"New," the company explained later after The Pittsburgh Press uncovered the tank's previous life in Cleveland, means new to the location. It doesn't mean "spanking brand new," as Allegheny County Fire Marshal Martin Jacobs said he was told even as fuel oil was gushing into the river at the rate of 250 gallons per minute.

The reason an oil company relocates a tank? It's "a matter of economics," said the man whose company cut it apart in Ohio and reassembled it in Floreffe.

But Ashland's attempt at saving money has caused environmental damage still not determined, threatened aquatic and wildlife along two rivers and fouled water supplies to communities which rely on the river as their primary source. At this point, clean-up costs can't even be calculated.

The "matter of economics" has, indeed, turned into a matter of dire consequence.

Another problem was the confusion over where storm drains were located, and where they would carry the gushing diesel. As much as a two-hour delay occurred before it was realized that the fuel was speeding into the river.

No matter what caused the Floreffe spill — it's possible the tank foundation was undermined by water — the EPA should seek to outlaw matters of "economics" that are in reality nothing more than risky shortcuts on the road to catastrophe.

Pittsburgh, PA, January 10, 1988

Like the oil spill itself, the water crisis in Allegheny County has moved on. The worst is over here, but very real problems have flowed down the Ohio River.

At week's end, Steubenville was overcoming a "catastrophic" situation and Wheeling battled similar threats to its water supplies.

And where from there? The indications are that the diesel oil that spilled into the Monongahela River, and subsequently carried into the Ohio, has the potential for causing water and environmental havoc for hundreds and hundreds of miles.

It was last weekend that the huge tank at the Ashland Oil terminal in Jefferson collapsed, sending a tidal wave of oil over containment dikes and into the Mon. The immediate effect was to produce water-supply emergencies in several suburban areas; Pittsburgh itself was not directly affected since it draws its drinking water from the Allegheny River.

The cleanup effort here, over several days of bitterly cold weather, was impressive in its overall effectiveness and in the many selfless displays of neighborly concern and help for distressed communities.

The mop-up likely will continue for weeks and maybe months to come, even as water intake and distribution systems return to normal. Trapped pockets of oil could still emerge and foul water supplies and shorelines. The long-term effects on fish and fowl remain to be fully assessed and dealt with. The overall cost cannot even be guessed at.

To its credit, Ashland Oil quickly moved to accept financial responsibility. The first damage claims and liability suits already have been filed; it will be years before the Kentucky-based firm settles all the bills.

Meantime, federal, state and local governments need to continue to seek the cause of the tank collapse and how the ensuing spillage might have been better contained. And there's the matter of reaction to river emergencies. Allegheny County Commissioner Chairman Tom Foerster has called the initial response to this oil spill too slow.

Although an accident of this magnitude may be a rarity, the reality of the water crisis that followed has raised questions about whether restraining dikes should be built higher and whether more cleanup equipment should be kept at storage centers where contamination of nearby rivers or residential areas might occur.

A former official of the Ashland Chemical Co. claims dangerous spills and leakages occur more commonly than may be known. In a suit filed in Roanoke, Va., last Thursday, Randolph H. Cunningham says he was fired for his warnings about actual and potential chemical contamination problems at 12 Ashland plants in five Southern states.

For crisis-weary Pittsburghers, that news could not have been comforting.

DESERET NEWS
Salt Lake City, UT
January 8, 1988

If corporate executives still wonder why the public doesn't always have a high opinion of business and industry, let them ponder the sad case of Ashland Oil Co.

Ashland made some particularly unhappy history this week with one of the worst inland oil spills ever in the United States. It also seems to have made history in terms of corporate irresponsibility.

The firm was filling an old tank near Pittsburgh with diesel fuel last Saturday when the tank ruptured, spilling fuel into the nearby Monongahela River.

The upshot was a 110-mile-long oil slick that has imperilled the water supplies of more than one-million Americans and threatened serious environmental damage in Pennsylvania, Ohio, and West Virginia.

Any industrial society needs tanks to hold diesel fuel, oil, gasoline, chlorine, and many other chemicals. Some risk in building and using such tanks is inevitable. But that doesn't excuse Ashland's inept performance.

Just look at the mistakes that Ashland itself has admitted. The tank was a 40-year-old facility that had been taken apart at an Ashland plant in Kentucky, shipped to Pittsburgh, and re-assembled. Company officials failed to obtain the necessary local permits to erect the tank. When it collapsed, the tank was being filled — for the first time at Pittsburgh — with more fuel that it had held before. What's more, the tank had not been tested for leaks or durability in the accepted way — by filling it with water. Instead, only five feet of water were pumped into the 48-foot-high tank before the decision was made that it was safe.

But that's not the full story. Does it really make sense to let fuel tanks be placed so close to a major waterway? Moreover, why didn't the dike around the tank contain all of the spilled fuel and keep it from going into the adjacent Monongahela?

Anyway, the massive spill has prompted a federal investigation and focused attention on the fact that no federal agency has authority to regulate oil storage tanks. Already, there are some calls in Congress for federal regulation of above-ground storage tanks.

Such suggestions are premature at best. One accident doesn't justify sweeping new regulations. But a mishap as bad as this one certainly does warrant vigorous efforts to make sure that industry obeys local laws as well as the canons of common sense.

THE TENNESSEAN
Nashville, TN, January 8, 1988

THE disastrous oil spill that began when a storage tank collapsed and sent a million gallons of diesel fuel into the Monongahela River in Pennsylvania has wreaked heavy damage down the river system.

Along the way, hundreds of thousands faced drinking water shortages, particularly those whose systems take water from the rivers. The extent of damage to wildlife, fish and fowl probably won't be known for some time.

The spill began last Saturday when an Ashland Oil Co., fuel tank collapsed. The 40-year-old tank had been moved from Cleveland last year to be a part of the terminal at West Elizabeth, Pa. Apparently the structural integrity of the tank was enough to pass all inspections, but nevertheless it collapsed as it was being filled. Why is a question yet to be resolved.

A containment dike around the tank held 2.5 million gallons of the spilled fuel, but it couldn't prevent the overflow. The spill is believed to be one of the largest ever to occur in U.S. inland waters, according to the Coast Guard.

Oil spills into rivers are not infrequent, but mostly involve small amounts lost from barges or leaking pipelines. This one was big.

Oil spilled into a river system is much different than oil spilled into oceans which can disperse it fairly rapidly because of so much area. A river is a much smaller body of water and it is moving, which tends to break up oil, making it difficult to scoop up.

The emulsified oil can and does sink, leading to fears that it could contaminate submerged water intake pipes and treatment facilities. Ashland Oil is paying for the cleanup operations, which are overseen by the Environmental Protection Agency. The tough thing is that the cleanup can last months before the river systems can be said to be flushed clean.

In view of the size of the spill, the EPA had better look more closely at tank facilities everywhere, with close examination of containment dikes and ponds at such tank terminal operations. This spill has been very costly in terms of impact on people and on the environment itself. ■

ST. LOUIS POST-DISPATCH
St. Louis, MO, January 7, 1988

The spill of more than a million gallons of oil into the Monongahela River in Pennsylvania is affecting the lives of more than a million people in that and other states downstream. It is not overstating the point to say that anyone whose drinking water is drawn from the Ohio or the Mississippi River below Cairo, Ill., should be concerned about the diesel fuel that spilled from an Ashland Oil Co. storage tank.

But those whose lives could be affected by this spill are not the only ones who should be concerned. The accident should be regarded by all as a reminder of just how vulnerable we are when the technology and ancillary chemicals upon which we have come to depend behave in unexpected and unwelcome ways.

Unexpected, perhaps, but not unpredictable. When safety precautions are not taken, when people become complacent about inherent dangers, accidents become inevitable. In this case, Ashland Oil apparently did not apply for the required permits or conduct standard safety tests before beginning to fill the tank after it was moved and reassembled from its former location in Ohio. The disassembly, shipment and reconstruction of oil storage tanks is routine, we have been told, something that is accomplished time and again without incident. Perhaps so, but past successes obviously are no guarantee of future ones. The need for vigilance cannot be compromised by easy-going familiarity.

That vigilance is all the more necessary when we lack the means to cope with accidents. Here, too, the Ashland spill is instructive. The tools being employed in the effort to get as much of the spilled fuel as possible from the river are simply not up to the task. They were designed with the open seas in mind, not for use on swiftly moving inland streams.

The accident then raises an important question that only now is beginning to receive the attention it deserves. Is it unreasonable to insist that no corporation be allowed to undertake operations involving potentially catastrophic hazards without assuring that the means exist for coping with a worst-case accident and can be quickly brought to work when need arises?

In a few weeks, this accident will disappear from the headlines. In even less time, it will probably recede from public consciousness. The momentary outrage it has sparked will dissipate — much like the outrage over previous abuses of the environment by industry. Here, too, there is a danger in complacency, bred perhaps by the false notion that nature and time heal whatever wounds we inflict on ourselves and on our environment.

The cumulative effects, however, of the injuries are not to be lightly dismissed. From the greenhouse effect and depletion of ozone in the outer atmosphere to the widespread contamination of groundwater with industrial chemicals, evidence mounts that we reap the bitter fruits of our failure to respect the environment. Nature tries to heal, but more and more it requires our cooperation. We can take steps now to mitigate future damage to the Earth, or live — and die — with the consequences.

The Miami Herald
Miami, FL, January 7, 1988

THE MONONGAHELA, the Allegheny, the Ohio, the Mississippi. These great rivers have provided transportation, food and drinking water, inspiration, industrial power, and the means for exploration, income, and shelter since North American Indians first traversed the continent's interior.

The unexplained collapse of a storage tank last Saturday at West Elizabeth, Pa., spilled one million gallons of diesel fuel into the Monongahela 20 miles upriver from where it meets the Allegheny in Pittsburgh. There the rivers converge to make the Ohio, which eventually connects with the Mississippi River. By Tuesday, despite monumental containment efforts, the oil slick stretched 65 miles over the river system.

These rivers attract heavy industries with serious pollution potential, which threatens their other major use by man as a source of potable water. The water for most Pittsburgh residents comes from the Allegheny, which was not contaminated. But the city's western suburbs and communities along the affected segments of the Monongahela and Ohio are still without water.

Emergency measures demonstrate the rivers' importance. Schools were closed and the National Guard mobilized to distribute water. Round-the-clock clean-up crews are working in frigid temperatures. Pennsylvania Gov. Robert P. Casey has sought the help of the Environmental Protection Agency, which must respond all-out.

No one knows how much time or money it will take to clean the spill, the largest ever in the inland United States. This time oil and water are mixing, which means that the rivers' surfaces cannot be scooped clean. Water-intake systems may be contaminated for months. Damage to the river environment may last years.

Urban rivers (including the Miami River, recently contaminated by a sewer-line break) give benefits beyond measure and in return often endure vile abuse. Underground rivers such as the aquifers of South Florida are equally vulnerable and giving. The disaster in Pennsylvania could happen anywhere, but shouldn't any more. Mankind knows better, but still takes these ancient natural gifts too much for granted.

Pittsburgh Post-Gazette
Pittsburgh, PA, January 6, 1988

The oil spill on the Monongahela River demonstrates anew how interdependent everyone in this region is — and the need to change local institutions to reflect that fact.

An oil storage tank collapses in Jefferson Borough and the resulting spill into the Monongahela River affects the water supplies of dozens of communities downstream, not to mention commerce, industry and river transportation and the employment of at least a thousand people. Suddenly artificial municipal boundary lines look insignificant in the face of a regional catastrophe.

And not just municipal boundary lines. Suddenly metropolitan Pittsburgh realizes that there are no connections from one water system to another to allow piping safe water from, say, the Pittsburgh Water Works to the spill-affected areas served by the West Penn, West View, Robinson Township and Western Allegheny water authorities.

It is fortunate that the huge Pittsburgh system will be able to help its neighbors as the new connections are made. (The shoe would have been on the other foot, of course, if the spill had been in the Allegheny River, Pittsburgh's source of water supply.)

But one question is obvious: When for years electric utilities have formed grids to wheel electricity from one network to another when needed, why haven't the water authorities long ago had similar connections? To be sure, Pittsburgh and West Penn were planning such a link in the spring. But how absurd that the first tie between the Pittsburgh and West Penn systems came through fire-hydrant hookups before the emergency speeded up work on a direct pipeline connection in Allentown.

Similarly, the city's Fire Bureau has offered to respond to calls in communities facing a water shortage. Pittsburghers can be pleased with this neighborliness, as they should be with the prompt response of the Public Safety Department under Glenn Cannon in calling out emergency personnel and the city Public Works Department within 10 minutes of the first word of the Ashland Oil Co. spill. Certainly this demonstrates the central importance to the region of Pittsburgh with its resources, a point often overlooked by suburbs fiercely proud of their "independence."

But shouldn't there be an automatic arrangement through which communities everywhere in the county were assured they would be covered if something went wrong with their own emergency systems?

Proof of the importance of regional cooperation is the role played by the county's Emergency Management Agency in coordinating many of the necessary activities in the early hours after the crisis arose. Particular credit should go to county Police Superintendent Robert Kroner, as the emergency management coordinator, along with his deputy, John Kaus. Here again the growing importance of Allegheny County government in addressing problems larger than any one municipality is demonstrated.

The point is that for emergencies, not to mention future economic growth, the people of Allegheny County need to begin thinking beyond their own municipal boundary lines and, indeed, about obliterating some of them. The time is past when it makes sense to raise the false cry of "metropolitanism" anytime useful suggestions are made to reduce duplication of services or to improve their coordination.

Los Angeles Times
Los Angeles, CA, January 7, 1988

Last Saturday a diesel-oil storage tank in western Pennsylvania collapsed, allowing an estimated 1 million gallons of fuel to gush over a surrounding earthen dike and flow into the nearby Monongahela River. By today the oil spill was expected to reach Wheeling, W.Va., 60 miles downstream from its origin. Along its route hundreds of thousands of people who draw their water from the Monongahela have been left looking bleakly at the prospect of days and perhaps weeks of dry taps and increasing discomfort. Businesses have been forced to shut down. Schools have closed. Daily, lines form to draw drinking and cooking water from supplies trucked in by the National Guard.

Is the pollution of the Monongahela and the enormous inconvenience and considerable economic loss that it has caused due to an act of God? Hardly. Is it the result of an unavoidable accident, one of those risks that we accept as part of the price of living in a technologically based society? No. The Monongahela oil spill instead appears to be due solely to one oil-refining company's curious and even cavalier disregard of legally required safety procedures, to say nothing of plain common sense. From all indications, the collapse of the Ashland Oil Co.'s tank resulted from an attempt to carry out an inherently dangerous activity without first meeting routine standards of safety.

John Hall, the chairman of Ashland Oil, acknowledges that his company's officials failed to obtain the necessary local permits to erect the 4-million-gallon oil storage tank near Pittsburgh. He acknowledges that the 40-year-old steel tank, which was recently moved to the Pennsylvania site from Cleveland, had not been tested for leaks or durability in the accepted way—by filling it with water. Instead, only five feet of water were pumped into the 48-foot-high tank before the decision was made that it was safe. When the tank collapsed on Saturday it was being filled for the first time, with more than 3 million gallons of diesel fuel.

"In hindsight," Hall said, "one might question the use of 40-year-old steel. We might have been more persistent in getting our permits. I would have preferred to use water-testing methods" [to check the tank's integrity]. The safety procedures that Hall suggests should have been followed are, of course, precisely those required and intended to obviate the kind of regretful hindsight that he now demonstrates. Hall says that he's sorry for what happened. Still to be explained is what on Earth the Ashland officials could have been thinking of when they so recklessly courted danger.

Clean Water Goal Still Unmet as Pollutants Foul Beaches

The Environmental Protection Agency July 27, 1988 reported that 87% of the nation's municipal sewage plants had met a July 1 deadline requiring removal of at least 85% of the bacteria and pollutants from industrial and household waste. The remaining 13% of sewage systems, some 423 large treatment plants, still had not complied with the deadline, which was set under the Clean Water Act of 1972 and required at least secondary treatment by 1977. Congress subsequently extended the deadline to July 1, 1989. (See pp. 10-13)

Legal action to obtain compliance with the deadline could be taken unless the areas had agreed on a schedule for establishing facilities that were in compliance. The Justice Department filed suit July 27, against the City of San Diego for discharging raw sewage into the Pacific Ocean. On the East Coast at least 34 cities were providing only primary treatment of sewage, which removed only 30% of pollutants and did not neutralize fecal or infectious matter. Of these cities, 22 had established a schedule for compliance. But two of the cities were discharging sewage into coastal waters – Key West, Fla. into the Gulf of Mexico and Gloucester, Mass into the Atalantic Ocean. Boston, Mass. was discharging 485 million gallons of waste daily into Boston Harbor after only primary treatment. Boston was one of those scheduled to build a secondary plant.

In the New York metropolitan area, two sections of the city – Red Hook and North River – did not have secondary treatment facilities, nor did 14 cities in New Jersey.

Beaches in the New York metropolitan area had been blighted recently by pollution from sewage and hospital wastes, including syringes and blood vials. The medical wastes began washing ashore on Long Island beaches July 6 closing more than 10 miles of the shorefront. While the source of the mysterious medical wastes remained unidentified, it continued to reappear throughout most of the month, forcing closings at various sites on Long Island and Staten Island. In New Jersey, sewage wastes forced beach closings in the Asbury Park area south to Avon-by-the-Sea in mid-July. During the summer of 1987, beaches along the New Jersey shore from Atlantic City north to Sandy Hook had been sporadically closed by health and environmental officials because raw sewage and hospital and other waste had been found in coastal waters along beaches.

Omaha World-Herald
Omaha, NE, July 15, 1988

The beaches of Staten Island, Brooklyn and Long Island are among the most pleasant places to be when the concrete of the Big Apple heats up in midsummer, but this year they are also frightening places.

For several weeks, hospital waste, including vials of AIDS-infected blood, has been washing onto the shores. But the worst came Tuesday: A power failure at a treatment plant caused at least 25 million gallons of sewage to gush into New York Harbor, possibly contaminating more of the area's beaches.

Officials said there was little danger of AIDS infection from the water in which the syringes, vials and other debris float with the incoming tide, although the officials closed several beaches. But even on open beaches, the sight of the filthy medical paraphernalia was enough to give pause to many would-be swimmers. Parents, particularly, were keeping their children away from the cooling waters.

New York and New Jersey officials from the communities plagued by medical waste couldn't immediately determine a source but blamed it on illegal dumping. Who would endanger the public by tossing potentially dangerous waste away so carelessly? Health officials in the affected states should track down the culprits and prosecute them.

New York officials said the sewage discharge is an even more significant and immediate health hazard. They closed several beaches while testing for harmful bacteria.

Sewage-contaminated water can cause hepatitis, infections and intestinal disorders, health department officials said, particularly if swimmers and waders swallow the water, which is difficult to avoid doing.

The sewage came from a treatment plant on Staten Island that appeared to have no backup containment system to hold the effluent if a power outage occurred. Such a system should be a minimum requirement for sewage plants that discharge into the nation's waterways. Perhaps New York should strengthen its procedures for monitoring such plants to prevent such spills.

Herald News
Fall River, MA, July 29, 1988

The concern in this region about the pollution of the ocean, to say nothing of tributary streams, is natural and right.

Hereabouts, the stench from Lees River has Swansea residents up in arms, and health authorities have not yet determined its cause.

But this is merely one way in which a general problem affects us locally and regionally.

This summer waste materials and hypodermic needles washed up on the Long Island shore. Then this dangerous debris turned up along the Connecticut and Rhode Island coast lines and in the last couple of weeks has been found on some beaches in this general area.

No one knows as yet precisely where this debris came from. There were allegations that it was caused by New York hospitals dumping waste materials in the ocean. These allegations have not been validated as yet.

The various possibilities are being investigated by police and health authorities, but wherever these materials and objects came from, their presence has caused widespread alarm.

It is certainly true that the wholesale dumping of waste materials in the ocean by New York City should be halted at once. At the same time the federal government should enforce the provisions of the Clean Water Act there or wherever else they are being violated.

Pollution of the ocean with waste materials should be penalized; so should its pollution by individuals who have thrown possibly infected hypodermic into it.

Obviously, laws of this kind are difficult to enforce, but their existence at least provides law enforcement agencies with a threat to hold over the heads of violators.

Waste dumping on land has been against the law for years, but apparently the ocean is not yet out of bounds. As is apparent now, it should be.

The washing up of debris that is certainly unsightly and is possibly a menace to health has occurred on beaches where for generations, if not centuries, Americans have been accustomed to enjoy bathing in the ocean.

Some washed up on the shore at Little Compton where people from here have gone swimming for decades.

This is the way the damage that is being done to our coastal areas in a variety of forms is happening here in our own area.

The remedies for the damage must be as varied as the forms in which the oceans and waterways of the country are being contaminated.

But a start must be made somewhere, somehow, and the most appropriate way is for the public to make clear that it appreciates the danger and insists on its elimination.

WORCESTER TELEGRAM.

Worcester, MA, July 13, 1988

Beachgoers along the New Jersey and Long Island shores have a new kind of red tide to deal with: medical waste in the form of syringes, blood vials, surgical gloves and masks washing up on shore.

Vials of blood thought to be contaminated with the AIDS virus have caused the biggest scare, even though health officials claim the virus is too fragile to pose danger of infection. The risk of contracting hepatitis from such hospital waste is far greater, however.

Few would want to risk contact with trash carrying those diseases or any other. The situation at those beaches is frightening and intolerable. Besides contamination, the chief risks to sunbathers and children playing on the beach are cutting themselves on the vials or puncturing themselves with the needles.

The ugly stuff washing ashore serves as a reminder that the ocean's ability to absorb waste is not limitless. Authorities in Connecticut, New York and New Jersey, as well as the U.S. attorney's office, are trying to determine whether illegal ocean dumping was involved.

New York, for instance, has strict laws regulating incineration of contaminated medical trash, but hospitals generate far more of that kind of refuse than existing incinerators can handle. The sheer volume of this suspicious waste indicates that some of it may have been dumped at high sea.

Even if the disposal was technically proper, it raises serious questions about how far we can tax the waters off the congested Northeast shoreline. Waste that is not dumped from barges flows out of coastal cities and down rivers. Shellfish beds have been closed in record numbers because of pollution.

Even when the debris is dumped hundreds of miles at sea, out beyond the continental shelf, buoyant, nondegradable material refuses to sink. In an angry gesture, the sea regurgitates it back onto the shore.

This latest outrage suggests that the fouling of the beaches is a matter for federal regulation, for the effects of ocean dumping — legal or illegal — affect millions of people. Existing laws and regulations must be enforced and, if necessary, new ones formulated to halt the contamination of coastal waters.

Cleaning up our rivers has cut the amount of sewage flowing into the ocean. It would be tragic if pollution were to be allowed to flow inland from the sea. The current appearance of medical refuse — perhaps the ugliest form of pollution — must trigger immediate action.

BUFFALO EVENING NEWS

Buffalo, NY, July 10, 1988

WHEN POLLUTION is discovered at a toxic waste site, the first question in the minds of nearby residents is, "Will my family's health be affected?" Where such sites are clearly contaminated — and many in Western New York are severely affected — there should be a role for health-related studies to help the public know what it is dealing with.

Such studies could involve epidemiological surveys, health checks on residents and examination of wells in the neighborhood. The state agency properly equipped to do them is the Department of Health.

But the current legal mechanism for starting a health study in the neighborhood of a toxic site does not kick in unless there is "great and imminent peril." This stringent standard so far has limited health monitoring to Love Canal and the FMC site at Middleport, out of 1,047 identified toxic dumps.

A proposed change in the law would greatly expand the role the Health Department could play, without mandating studies that are unwarranted. It would be permissive, allowing the department to intervene without requiring it to at every toxic dump.

Known as the Health Monitoring Bill and pushed by a coalition of environmental and citizen action groups, it would lower the threshold of action to "actual or potential danger" to public health. Health studies would become likely where environmental investigations had shown a threat, such as barrels of toxic chemicals leaking in an area near home wells.

This simple provision is a natural complement to the state's superfund law. The whole point of sealing and cleaning up toxic dumps is to prevent poisons from getting into water, soil and the air, where they could cause harm to people. It only makes sense, then, to check the health and safety of people living close enough so that they may already have been affected.

The bill also has provisions for charging the polluters, where they can be found, with the costs of the health studies, just as they must now pay cleanup costs on the dumps themselves. This provision helps overcome a major obstacle to widespread health studies — the price.

The bill is similar to legislation proposed several years ago by the Health Department itself, but never passed. The new version eliminates a too-encompassing provision that would have had the Health Department doing studies after any toxic spill.

There is still time in this session for this legislation to gain the support it deserves and be passed. Western New York, with its many citizens living near toxic sites, has a special interest in its success.

New York, NY, July 18, 1988

The state law governing the disposal of infectious hospital waste in New York is the statutory equivalent of a burglar alarm that broadcasts the sound of a barking dog.

It is not only toothless, it's dogless.

The law, passed last year, left it to the state Departments of Health and Environmental Conservation to draft the regulations to make it enforceable. Those regulations were supposed to have been in place before the law took effect April 1.

They're not ready yet. That's one reason why, in the wake of the recent discovery that medical wastes had washed up on Long Island beaches, Gov. Mario Cuomo came up with an additional $2 million to create a dog to go with the bark. The money would be used to expedite the paperwork and staff the enforcement effort when the regulations are ready.

But the governor recognizes that's not enough. As it now reads, the law deals only with licensing infectious waste handlers. Those found in violation could lose their permits. Cuomo now wants the Legislature to deem the illegal dumping of dangerous hospital wastes a felony, punishable by up to 10 years in jail and up to $100,000 in fines.

That would really put teeth into the law and, considering the hazard, the Legislature should comply.

Then it will become incumbent on Cuomo and his successors to make sure that they budget enough to support a realistic enforcement effort. The $2 million extra this year won't go very far, considering the breadth of the program outlined by the governor.

The DEC recently initiated a telephone hot line to receive reports of spills in New York waters. That's good. And Cuomo, in addition, has asked it to develop a standing plan to deal with any recurrence of the recent rash of medical waste reports. He should also consider seeking improved labeling of hospital material so that investigators would have a better chance of tracing mishandled medical waste.

The Cuomo administration's new appreciation of the infectious waste menace is laudable. But experience suggests the governor and his budget staff need to shift attitudes and priorities if — over the long term — this new watchdog program's bite is going to be as strong as its bark.

The Star-Ledger

Newark, NJ, July 11, 1988

The Assembly is set to vote today on a controversial bill, narrowly adopted by the Senate, to phase out by 1991 the Ciba-Geigy pipeline discharges into the Atlantic Ocean at Ortley Beach. The issue is over water quality: Just how clean is the effluent coming out of Ciba's pipeline?

The U.S. Environmental Protection Agency (EPA) and the New Jersey Department of Environmental Protection (DEP) have given the Ciba-treated wastewater high marks for purity. State Environmental Commissioner Richard T. Dewling has described the discharges as "not detrimental" to the marine environment three feet from the pipeline, which extends from a half-mile to two-thirds of a mile into the ocean.

The EPA wants to use Ciba's advanced treatment technology to clean up the hazardous wastes at its Toms River "superfund" plant site, a project that will cost the company more than $60 million over the next 10 to 30 years.

The DEP and EPA are opposed to closing the pipeline, which ultimately could shut down one of Ocean County's largest employers.

The Save Our Ocean Committee wants Ciba-Geigy to increase treatment so that its 4 million gallons a day of wastewater can be recycled for further production use. It's a goal all industry is striving to obtain.

But to close the pipeline at an arbitrary point in time is somewhat like throwing the baby out with the bath water. The Ciba purification plant is the best that technology can yield at the moment. It already is far superior to the dozens of sewage treatment plants discharging into the ocean and other New Jersey waterways.

If the Legislature puts the Ciba discharges on a deadline, then all treatment systems should comply to the same standard. Singling out one pipeline is not the solution to ocean pollution.

LEXINGTON HERALD-LEADER

Lexington, KY, July 31, 1988

Something scarier than *Jaws* is chasing ocean swimmers in New York off the beaches: the dreaded discarded hypodermic syringe.

Twice this summer, swimmers have been ordered off New York beaches because intravenous tubing, blood vials and needles washed up onto the beach.

Hospital waste includes such stuff as lab wastes, body parts and disposable medical supplies. Some of it can carry infectious diseases. The rest of it is just plain scary to look at.

The right way to dispose of hospital waste is through incineration at temperatures of 2,000 degrees. But not all hospital waste ends up in an incinerator. The cost of disposing of wastes generated by a 500-bed hospital easily exceeds $120,000 in a year. At that price, there evidently has been some temptation to dump illegally.

Even New York's infamous garbage barge was loaded with some hospital waste, although tests indicate it wasn't dangerous. But how did it get there?

Whether it is a blood vial washing up on a beach in New York, a new landfill in Greenup County or illegal dumping in Kentucky, the nation is facing a real problem with solid waste. We're making more trash all the time, and we're running out of places to put it.

In New Jersey, which has one of the nation's most progressive solid waste laws, citizens are required to compost leaves and separate recyclables such as paper, aluminum and glass from other trash. In spite of all that, New Jersey is worried about landfills that fill up too fast.

Back in Kentucky, Knott County Judge-Executive Homer Sawyer, a self-educated expert on solid waste after shepherding a mandatory garbage pickup system through his county, argues that eventually even rural states such as Kentucky are going to have to go to high-temperature incineration.

Right now, Kentucky is struggling with keeping its trash picked up. But already, another problem looms large: What are we going to do with it once we collect it?

There's some scary stuff in the nation's trash bin. And as some New York swimmers have learned, if it is not disposed of properly, it can resurface — just when you thought it was safe to go back into the water.

The Providence Journal

Providence, RI, July 22, 1988

After littering the beaches and disconcerting the citizens of New Jersey, Connecticut and New York, medical debris has arrived in Rhode Island.

The plastic vials and syringes that washed ashore in Middletown and Little Compton this week have literally brought home to us the reality of this latest insult to the environment.

In some odd ways the medical debris recalls the best-selling novel "Jaws." A number of summers ago people who swam in the ocean had sharks on their minds. This summer it is the possibility of rubbing up against HIV-contaminated syringes. Though it must be stressed that the chances of contracting AIDS, as well as other diseases, from syringes that have been saturated in the ocean's salt water are very slim.

Also, as it was with sharks, the concern about the prevalence of such waste is somewhat exaggerated. Yet it is not unwarranted. Unlike sharks, the syringes have no business being there.

And, of course, the book was fiction; the medical debris is not. Yet it is, at this writing, very much a mystery. Why now? Why hospital waste? It has been suggested that it is a crude, if massive, practical joke, or even a sinister attempt to bring ocean pollution into the public eye. What better way — in these days of the dreaded AIDS disease — to alarm people about the crisis of the seas than to have them swimming in waters with plastic vials from our metropolitan hospitals?

There is concern that the debris is being dumped with sludge in the Atlantic — 106 miles off the southern tip of New Jersey — or, more conceivably, is being dropped closer to shore, illegally, by barges. Governor DiPrete and Atty. Gen. James E. O'Neil have now announced plans to set up investigations into the problem. Yet whatever its explanation, it should serve as a catalyst in bringing about a popular consensus that we can no longer treat the ocean as a dumping ground.

The dangers of such an attitude are clear, and affect everyone whose work, pleasure, or evening meal is tied to the sea. There are many of us who remember going as children to the seaside and spending hours in the ocean without a thought to pollution. Those days are over. Yet so, too, then, should be the days of thinking of the ocean as an immense, incorruptible body of water.

The business of cleaning the seas is not simple, nor is it free from controversy. There are those now who say more legislation is needed, others who claim that good legislation has been passed, but it has been hindered by inactivity on the part of the Environmental Protection Agency. The agency, not surprisingly, disagrees.

Safe, effective systems for the disposal of waste on land must be developed to take the burden away from the ocean. With this development in mind, New Jersey has passed a law banning ocean dumping as of 1991. New York, which each year dumps eight million tons of sludge into the Atlantic, should follow suit. Rhode Island Sens. John H. Chafee and Claiborne Pell and Rep. Claudine Schneider have been in the forefront of congressional attempts to phase out such offshore dumping.

If the public becomes vociferous enough about the importance of a clean ocean, lawmakers and public officials will be forced to act. And then the syringes of the summer of '88 will have served a purpose.

The Boston Globe

Boston, MA, July 12, 1988

Odious medical debris – vials of blood, syringes and hospital waste – has been washing up on beaches on Long Island and other shoreline points in New York. Although some of the debris has been contaminated by AIDS and other pathogens, usually such a spill is more disgusting than dangerous.

What is worrisome is how often large amounts of infectious waste from hospitals and medical laboratories are turning up offshore and on beaches. Dumping must be taking place on a rising scale; rather than washing out to sea in a day's time, the detritus lingers through several days of tidal cycles.

Earlier last week, 120 vials of blood, some of them showing signs of the AIDS virus, came ashore in Bayonne, N.J. About a month ago, similar vials turned up at two other New Jersey seaside beaches. Last summer, hospital waste scared away tens of thousands of beachgoers in New Jersey beach towns.

New York and New Jersey, like Massachusetts, have strong regulations requiring that infectious medical waste be carefully disposed of. The waste must be sterilized or incinerated on site at the hospital or laboratory, or segregated – kept in heavy-duty, red plastic bags – and repacked in leak-proof containers. Massachusetts also tracks the transportation of infectious waste from hospitals to its final destination by monitoring its movement at various checkpoints. "We have a traceable paper trail along the way," said a state health department spokesman – a system that New York and New Jersey are now considering.

Yet Massachusetts hospitals, especially those caring for large numbers of AIDS patients, are worried about how appropriately the waste is handled, despite the regulations. They know that difficulties lie ahead in finding sufficient disposal sites for the enormous amount of infectious waste being produced.

Medical authorities downplay the prospect of contracting AIDS from such waste; though possible, it is highly improbable.

Nevertheless, the dumping of infectious waste is an AIDS complication that will not be easily solved.

The Globe and Mail

Toronto, Ont., July 18, 1988

Water, one of the elements most essential to life on earth, has a wondrous capacity to serve mankind. We drink it, we wash in it, we catch fish in it, cool automobile engines with it, ship cargoes on it, irrigate crops and water lawns with it. We ought to be extremely grateful to water, but we are not.

In the thoughtless exploitation of its capacity to dissolve and dilute, we have choked many bodies of water with the discarded junk we create on land — much of it poisonous. It has long seemed likely that we would seriously overtax the ability of this great resource to withstand that sort of assault. The weekend gave us a preliminary opportunity to view the consequences.

A large section of North America has been going through an intense, debilitating heat wave, and has discovered that just when it turned for blessed relief to oceans, rivers and lakes, some of them were not available. Out of order.

New Yorkers faced a larger horror than most when they sought the comfort of a splash in the Atlantic Ocean. Waiting for them along the beaches of Long Island and Staten Island were the flotsam and jetsam of their collective folly. There were dozens of hypodermic needles, vials of AIDS-contaminated blood and medical waste which is, by law, supposed to be incinerated. Raw sewage had been added to this revolting mix as a result of a power failure at a city waste-treatment plant.

"What right do we have to pollute the beaches like this?" a Long Beach resident asked of no one in particular. "It's a horrible thing that we can't even go in the ocean." Horrible, indeed — and it could be the result of either criminal disregard or misplaced faith in the ocean's ability to make anything we throw at it conveniently disappear.

Toronto residents will look with revulsion on what New Yorkers are doing to the ocean. They may be discussing it as the family sets out for a day at one of Toronto's beaches. They will then find most of the beaches closed by order of the city health department. The water is unfit for swimming because of what we have deposited in it.

River Protection Pact Signed

The U.S. Forest Service entered into a pact with environmentalists and loggers to protect 1,000 miles of rivers in the East and Midwest, it was announced Aug. 14, 1987.

The agreement covered 112 rivers and 301,000 acres of national forest within a quarter of a mile of the banks of the rivers in 11 states.

The areas were to be protected for up to 10 years pending evaluation by the forest service for permanent protection under the Federal Wild and Scenic River Act. Some 7,363 miles of river in the U.S. had been brought under protection of the legislation so far, with another 61,700 miles of rivers identified by a federal survey as potentially eligible for protection.

The agreement was signed by representatives of the U.S. Forest Service, the logging industry and the American Rivers Conservation Council, an environmental group based in Washington, D.C.

The Record

Hackensack, NJ, September 11, 1988

One can't help noticing the flurry of activity at the federal Environmental Protection Agency.

On Aug. 21, the EPA gave special protective designation to New Jersey's two major underground water supplies, the New Jersey Coastal Plan Aquifer, which underlies much of the southern half of the state, and the Northwest New Jersey Aquifer, which is under the state's northwestern quarter.

The agency has had the power to regulate drinking-water supplies since 1974. But in 1984, the EPA announced that it would leave the responsibility to the states, assisting, when asked, with technical support. Now the EPA has changed its mind, getting into the business of aquifer-watching along with the states.

On Aug. 24, the EPA announced its first-ever set of regulations on the management of garbage dumps. The purpose is to stop leakage of chemical poisons into streams and rivers.

On Aug. 31, the EPA announced that it would draw up new rules for tracking the medical wastes that have fouled East Coast beaches this summer and last. Congress asked the EPA to do that two years ago, but the agency deferred to the states.

This is the agency that critics have called an enforcement weakling and the captive of industry? What's going on here? The answer may lie in the calendar, which shows that Election Day is only nine weeks away. Environmentalists among the voters are beginning to look at the records of both sides. You know the rest.

Los Angeles Times

Los Angeles, CA, October 2, 1988

Federal lawmakers from Oregon have taken a significant new direction in the protection of American rivers, just as river conservationists prepare to mark the 20th anniversary of the national Wild and Scenic Rivers Act today. The Oregon delegation has proposed an omnibus law that would grant protection all at once to as many as 45 Oregon streams totaling 1,800 miles.

The omnibus approach is similar to the one used in designating wilderness areas in various states. Congressional delegations from Montana and Washington now are considering possible omnibus legislation for their rivers.

Up to now, river-protection enthusiasts have had to fight mile by mile and stream by stream for incorporation into the national system. Such was the case in the past four years during the successful drive to afford wild-and-scenic status to the Tuolumne, Merced, Kings and Kern rivers in California.

In recent years the fight has been a tough one, in part because of opposition from within the Reagan Administration. Since 1981, 802 miles of river have been incorporated into the system, including more than 400 miles of the four California streams. By comparison, 5,298 miles were added during the Carter Administration, including more than 3,000 miles brought in through the Alaska lands act of 1980. In 1982 the National Park Service identified 1,524 segments of rivers running 61,700 miles in the lower 48 states that had potential for wild or

scenic status. The U.S. Bureau of Land Management currently is studying rivers within its jurisdiction for recommendations.

The rivers program is growing in popularity. Broad coalitions, including both environmentalists and business people, are coming together in many states to support such legislation. One reason is the flexibility afforded by the law. Wild-river stretches normally are reached only by trail. Scenic reaches are accessible by automobile. And areas designated as recreational have even fewer restrictions.

Usually the major threat is dam construction, encouraged by the 1978 Public Utility Regulatory Policies Act that attempted to offset energy shortages with new hydroelectric dams. The law provides for a federal tax subsidy of up to 17% and guarantees the builder a market for the electricity. There has been a rush to build these hydro dams, even though the electricity is not now in demand. The utility act should be amended at the least to eliminate the unnecessary and unwarranted tax break.

The wild-rivers law was passed three years after President Lyndon B. Johnson said in his 1965 State of the Union address that the time had come to "preserve free-flowing stretches of our great scenic rivers, before growth and development make the beauty of the unspoiled waterways a memory." While progress has been made, the full promise of Johnson's words has yet to be fulfilled.

The Oregonian

Portland, OR, March 6, 1988

Sen. Mark Hatfield, R-Ore., deserves broad and deep support as he tries to include for protection in the National Wild and Scenic Rivers System 40 Oregon rivers and segments of streams that are especially prized natural resource gems.

The rivers in Hatfield's bill flow through federal land. That is an important distinction between this effort and any statewide river-protection initiative because states have limited standing in influencing decisions by federal agencies over development practices on federal land.

Hatfield's protected-river candidates have been studied and examined carefully by the U.S. Forest Service and the Bureau of Land Management. They meet all criteria for designation established by the original Wild and Scenic Rivers Act, though not all of the river segments in Oregon that qualify for protection status are included in Hatfield's bill.

The senator conspicuously omitted a segment of the Klamath River that might qualify under a recreational designation, though certainly not as a wild river. That omission is being taken care of in the House, in a separate resolution sponsored by Oregon Reps. Peter DeFazio, D-Ore., and Les AuCoin, D-Ore.

Very little has happened to protect and preserve Oregon's most precious water resources in the 20 years since Congress enacted the wild-rivers act. Hatfield has introduced his Omnibus Oregon Wild and Scenic Rivers Act of 1988 with that in mind.

Only portions of the Owyhee, Snake, Rogue and Illinois rivers, totaling a modest 317 miles, are protected by federal wild and scenic status, and only 73 rivers nationally are on the list.

Hatfield's proposal would add 1,603 miles to the system, bringing protected status to 1,920 miles out of Oregon's estimated 90,000 miles of rivers, streams and tributaries.

Adding the new candidates still would mean that only 2 percent of Oregon's waterways would be protected from damaging development. That makes this a modest proposal, especially considering that it represents Oregon's first comprehensive effort in nearly two decades to protect valued rivers and streams on federal lands.

This protection is needed to stop the erosion, through dam construction, logging and other human development, of valued state resources that future generations can enjoy and that also can become magnets for tourism.

The Hatfield bill is a reasonable response. Little more than half the rivers being designated in the Hatfield measure are to be classified as "wild" — that is, preserved in a natural state with no development allowed. Many of the others are to be classified as "scenic" or "recreational," which would allow some compatible development, but no dams.

ST. LOUIS POST-DISPATCH

St. Louis, MO, September 28, 1988

I do not know much about gods; but I think that the river/Is a strong brown god — sullen, untamed and intractable. These words open T.S. Eliot's poem "The Dry Salvages"; the Mississippi is unnamed, but it is unmistakably the source of the image invoked.

Would Eliot recognize the Mississippi today? Not brown, but a sickly green in parts from chemical wastes pouring into it. Not strong, but anemic, barely able to float barges after a summer of drought. Sullen, surely, but as a beaten child. Untamed still, as flood waters remind us, but not for want of efforts to dam, cut channels and buffer ourselves from every manifestation of its temper. As for intractable — well, pollution might spell the end of that.

The Mississippi has become a sewer. Because of the volume of water it normally carries, few people notice the presence of industrial chemicals or untreated human waste. Only at points where discharge pipes — such as the one at the Sauget sewer — meet the river is the fouling offensively apparent, but most people can live their entire lives in communities along the river and never experience this firsthand. For them, the river is just there — genial most times, pretty from a distance, an attraction only for tourists or the hopelessly sentimental.

But the river is much more than that. Its distress is a matter that should be of grave concern to all who rely on it for drinking water, as many St. Louisans do; for food, as many people would like to do and did until the level of contaminants made fish not fit to eat; for recreation; and for business

(boats can be harmed by industrial wastes; tourists will stay away in droves if the river smells more of solvents than of silt).

The recent visit of the Greenpeace research vessel Beluga called attention to the river's sorry state. One may dismiss the actions of accompanying Greenpeace members as publicity stunts, but the reality that they were trying to focus attention upon won't go away when their boat casts off.

The Sauget sewer *does* discharge industrial chemicals in excess of standards set by the federal government. The Environmental Protection Agency *has* filed suit to force it into compliance. The Metropolitan Sewer District, on the Missouri side of the river, is not as egregiously in violation of EPA rules. Nevertheless, it still allows hundreds of millions of gallons of untreated sewage to spill into the father of waters each year.

National attention was focused this summer on the East Coast as vacations were ruined by foul water and medical waste washing ashore. Midwesterners have no cause to be smug, however. Recreational swimming in the Mississippi has been unthinkable for decades. As for washed-up waste, a walk along the riverfront is enough to deflate any regional pride.

The Mississippi is part of our history and should be a source of national pride. Instead, it has become a disgrace. In this campaign year, we would challenge those seeking office at all levels to speak out on the river's behalf. And those who continue to defile it with industrial wastes we challenge to clean up their act.

The Hartford Courant

Hartford, CT, October 5, 1988

The dramatic shrinkage of what was once the world's fourth-largest lake, in the Soviet Union, is a reminder of the fragility of ecological balance, and of the unintended consequences of what seems to be technological advance.

The Aral Sea lies north of the Iran-Afghan border, in one of the most arid regions of Central Asia. Since 1900, a growing number of irrigation projects have tapped the two rivers feeding the lake. With the water, the Kara-Kum desert has become a major cotton-growing region.

What about the price for such diversion? Almost no fresh water is being added to the lake, whose water level has fallen 40 feet in the past three decades, and its area has shrunk by 40 percent. Only one of the U.S.-Canadian Great Lakes, Superior, is larger than Lake Aral on old maps; but now Lakes Michigan and Huron are larger. Aral has dropped to sixth place among world lakes.

The less obvious result is increasing salinity; most fish species have disappeared from Aral, and with them a whole industry. Toxic salts now invade farmlands; salt-laden dust storms reach for hundreds of miles; drinking-water supplies are threatened.

If the trend continues, Lake Aral could become a lifeless body like the Dead Sea.

The Soviet government has responded by

halting construction of new irrigation canals, ordering repairs of existing canals to reduce seepage, and placing restrictions on water use.

Those are stopgap measures. Some people argue for more engineering: a 1,500-mile network of dams, canals and pumping stations to divert water from two Siberian rivers, far to the north, to replenish Aral.

Apart from the enormous scale of such a project — it would take 10 to 15 years to complete — is the risk of further ecological damage. One American climatologist fears that diverting the Siberian rivers would increase the salinity of the Arctic Sea, whose ice cover would diminish. That could affect the world's climate.

Soviet engineers are hardly alone in tinkering with rivers. The United States has diverted much of the Colorado River's waters, and the climate of parts of Arizona has changed. There are schemes to divert the Columbia River from the Northwest to Southern California, and the waters of the Great Lakes to the desert Southwest.

We can make the desert bloom. In the process, we may create new deserts, destroy fisheries and change the climate of vast regions. The need for caution, and respect for ecological balance, could hardly be more compellingly demonstrated than the shrinking of Lake Aral.

The Des Moines Register

Des Moines, IA, September 4, 1988

The U.S. Army Corps of Engineers is seeking optimum economic efficiency in the hydroelectric power unit it is building on the Savannah River between Georgia and South Carolina. But instead it may waste millions in pursuit of false economy.

Demand for electricity is lower at night than in daylight hours, when the air conditioners and elevators and engines of industry are going full tilt. So hydroelectric power plants can operate what appears to be a perpetual-motion machine, generating power by running water over the dam in the daytime, then using that power at night to lift the water back up behind the dam for recycling.

The difference between the quantity of power generated and consumed is more than offset by the difference in day-night prices.

One problem: The turbines that lift the water back over the dam will in all likelihood chew up fish by the ton. But that doesn't seem to bother the Corps.

Similar reverse turbines were built — at a cost of $100 million — by the Corps at the Harry S Truman Dam in Missouri. In three hours of testing, one of the turbines ground up 2,000 pounds of fish. The turbines were never again operated. Meanwhile the National Wildlife Federation has gone to court to stop the Corps from operating similar turbines in Ludington, Mich.

Undaunted by evidence, the Corps now wants to spend $60 million to put the reverse turbines in the Richard B. Russell hydroelectric project on the Savannah. It, too, would chew up fish. When it does, the Corps promises, it will shut down the turbines. But first it wants to spend $60 million. An injunction sought by the NWF has temporarily blocked the Corps.

What is $60 million? Enough to pay the doctor bills for 62,000 Iowa welfare recipients for a year. Enough to pay for all the maintenance and repair jobs needed in all of Iowa's state parks, with plenty left over to buy more parkland. Enough to buy two Marriott Hotels for downtown Des Moines.

Enough to be worth saving.

BUFFALO EVENING NEWS
Buffalo, NY, July 24, 1988

THE U.S. ARMY Corps of Engineers' decision against further Great Lakes water diversion should help in the Great Lakes states' fight to keep control of this precious international resource.

It is an important initial victory in what is sure to be a series of battles to protect the lakes from possibly devastating raids by thirsty regions to the south and west.

The drought in the Midwest is a calamity. But water from the lakes can do little to make a significant difference to the Mississippi shipping interests that want it, the Corps says. And setting a precedent for diversion could cause incalculable damage.

The Mississippi is the great drain of the nation's midsection. This summer there is not much to drain, and the river is running low. The states along the Mississippi are hurting.

But the Great Lakes drain a completely different section of the North American land mass. They are a separate basin, from which water flows north instead of south. They, too, support industries — and millions of people — in their own natural area. Tampering with the basic paths of water systems as gigantic as these is dangerous in the extreme.

Great Lakes water does not just run unused and unwanted out to sea. It generates electrical power, holds up ships, supports fishing and recreation industries and provides millions of people with drinking water. The lakes are a key support of the whole web of life in the states that border them — and in the most populous parts of Canada as well.

They are also a giant ecosystem, which could prove to be much more fragile than might be readily apparent.

The biggest trouble with letting water out to bolster the Mississippi — even if it could make a difference — is that once this practice is started, the way would be open to more diversion. The West may soon have a larger population than its water sources can support. Ancient aquifers are being overused, and rivers are being used up before they reach areas close to the sea that once depended on them.

The pressures to make the lakes next on the list of water resources to be misused could be great. The lakes area's state governments and members of Congress must not let the process start.

The lakes may look temptingly full to the thirsty Midwest. But they, too, are subject to the whims of nature, which sends their levels rising and falling. If the lakes states allowed them to be tapped, the consequences when their own water was in a low cycle could be devastating.

The lakes are not unaffected, either, by this year's drought. Levels are lower, with lower power generation at Niagara Falls one early warning.

The Corps decision should help fend off the threat of water diversion for a while. But the lakes states and Canada must be ready for further defense of their lifeline. The problems of one region must not be attacked by recklessly endangering another.

LEXINGTON HERALD-LEADER
Lexington, KY, July 12, 1988

The Great Lakes hold more than half of the Surface water in the United States. Water diverted from the lakes would offer only marginal relief to Mississippi traffic at the cost of reducing the lake levels. That would be a short-sighted policy for short-term gains.

In all likelihood, the plan can't be put into effect anyway. It would require the approval of all the states bordering the lakes. And it probably would require the approval of the Canadian government, too.

Still, any idea that has 13 senators behind it has some chance of becoming reality. President Reagan should reject this idea before it gets any more momentum.

The old saying is that everybody talks about the weather, but nobody does anything about it. There's a proposal in Congress now that would do something about the drought in the Mississippi River basin, but it shouldn't get beyond the talking stage.

Thirteen senators have asked President Reagan to order the diversion of water from the Great Lakes into the Mississippi River. This would raise the level of the river by a foot, proponents say, thus easing the shipping bottleneck caused by low water.

That is true. But lowering the level of the Great Lakes to benefit Mississippi River shippers would be a world-class mistake.

DESERET NEWS
Salt Lake City, UT, August 3/4, 1988

Western water users won a big victory a few days ago when federal legal officers concurred that wilderness areas have no rights to water unless Congress specifically grants them.

In a way, the decision is also a victory for environmentalists — though they certainly don't see it that way.

Instead, they fear that unless wilderness areas automatically get such rights, they could be deprived of the water needed to make them viable and enjoyable as more dams are built.

It would be unrealistic to pretend that the environmentalists have no reason to be concerned. There may be times when the U.S. must choose between a wilderness area and a water development project.

But when such problems arise, the decision should be made on a case-by-case basis rather than according to some sweeping rule that automatically favors either wilderness or water over the other. Under such circumstances, surely environmentalists can be expected to win a few and lose a few.

Moreover, environmentalists should not ignore the way that the new federal stance on water rights can help overcome some opposition to the designation of new wilderness areas.

Much of that opposition was based on the fear that setting aside more land for wilderness would mean less water to raise crops and livestock and develop new industries. Such fears prompted the Legislature to adopt in 1986 a resolution opposing any further designation whatsoever of wilderness areas in Utah. But the new federal stance on water rights makes it harder to justify such sweeping opposition to wilderness.

Water and wilderness alike are essential to the future of the West. Instead of constantly being forced to choose between the two, let's strive for both whenever possible.

THE SAGINAW NEWS
Saginaw, MI, August 25, 1988

We've been throwing our garbage into the lakes and the oceans, and they're sick of the insult. They're finally throwing it back in our faces — and on our beaches.

Earlier this summer, used needles, vials of contaminated blood, and other medical refuse washed up on the Atlantic shores. But the Great Lakes were not exempt. Repulsive garbage floated onto the beaches of Lake Erie, too.

No stinking barges go out on Saginaw Bay. Hospitals in Saginaw insist they take great care in disposing of their effluvia. For instance, St. Mary's Medical Center, according to a spokeswoman, follows the guidelines of the state Department of Natural Resources and the Centers for Disease Control in Atlanta. The hospital's waste is incinerated or hauled to approved landfills. St. Mary's tracks the waste and assumes responsibility for its final disposal.

Even with the best efforts, though, a hospital or medical office cannot know for certain where its waste will wind up. Incinerators release gases into the air. Landfills can leak into groundwater. The 200 hospitals in Michigan produce about 50,000 tons of trash a year. That includes up to 5,500 tons a year of "red-bag wastes," infectious materials such as body parts. It is frightening even to think of the implications of the AIDS epidemic.

The vast oceans may seem capable of living with any abuse. The Great Lakes, too, have proved remarkably resilient. Lake Erie once was declared dead from industrial pollution. It lives again.

But let's not keep trying to poison these precious resources.

Michigan, the heart of the Lakes, so dependent on their waters, is one of only six states without specific laws covering medical waste disposal. Federal law does not cover medical garbage.

State officials report no evidence over the past five years of health problems caused by present methods of disposal. That sustains the hospitals' contention that they take care with their hazardous waste.

But the Lake Erie incident, the closing of East Coast beaches, the contamination of harbors, suggests that we've been lucky, too.

This week Gov. James Blanchard asked the DNR and Department of Public Health to recommend new laws and regulations controlling disposal of medical waste. Currently, "The situation is, in effect, unregulated," said J.D. Snyder, a state environmental aide.

A comprehensive law would protect health and disposal workers, the public — and the water. The American Hospital Association itself recommends "model state waste-disposal rules to eliminate confusion and inconsistencies." In fact, Carol McCarthy, the group's president, endorses "protection of oceans from serving as disposal sites for any wastes."

The Great Lakes deserve that protection, too. A dose of regulatory prevention can help preserve their health, and ours.

The Idaho STATESMAN
Boise, ID, September 17, 1988

During this century man has dammed up several Idaho rivers to store water for power and irrigation. The dams benefited man, but wiped out thousands of acres of wildlife habitat.

Now, man has a chance to do something for the benefit of wildlife by replacing some of the habitat that was taken by the dams.

The Northwest Power Planning Council is proposing to spend several million dollars to enhance the wildlife habitat around three Idaho dams — Black Canyon on the Payette River, Anderson Ranch on the South Fork of the Boise River and Palisades on the South Fork of the Snake River.

The proposal stems from the Northwest Power Act's mandate to develop programs to enhance fish and wildlife because of the setbacks they experienced when the federal dams were built on Northwest rivers. Until now, most of the attention had been focused on rehabilitating migratory fish runs.

If the Power Planning Council agrees to the program after public hearings, an estimated $21 million could be spent for land acquisition and the enhancement of wildlife habitat. The annual maintenance cost could run $501,000.

The bill would be footed by customers of the Bonneville Power Administration, which include public and investor-owned utilities and their customers.

The proposal is running into opposition from utilities. Al Wright, executive director of the Pacific Northwest Utilities Conference Committee, said that $21 million is too much to spend. He noted that rehabilitation efforts near certain Oregon dams cost much less than the original price tag.

Rick Applegate, the Power Council's fish and wildlife director, said that a slow approach, perhaps spending $5 million per year, probably would not increase rates for BPA customers.

The estimated $21 million may or may not be too high. The right price tag should be determined through the public hearings and by the Northwest Power Planning Council. Nobody wants to waste money.

But the basic idea of restoring wildlife habitat is a sound one. The people and businesses of the Pacific Northwest have benefited from those dams because of the power and irrigation water they have provided.

The cost of doing something in return for the wildlife should be considered just part of the cost of doing business.

Bush Unveils Clean Air Plan

President George Bush brought forth a clean-air program June 12, 1989, setting goals for major reductions of smog, acid rain and toxic industrial emissions. (See pp. 18-21)

In a speech at the White House, Bush presented proposals for a sweeping revision of the Clean Air Act. Bush's plan would reduce smog in 78 cities currently flunking the federal clean-air standard, cut acid rain by 50% and curb the release of airborne toxic chemicals by industry by 75% to 90%.

No tax increase was attached to Bush's proposed program, which was expected to cost industry $14 billion to $19 billion extra a year, with most of the goals set to be attained by the year 2000. Higher utility rates, perhaps up by more than 2% by the year 2000, were anticipated, as were higher costs to consumers for cars and cleaner fuels.

Cities would be expected to meet federal health standards for ozone, a major factor in smog, and carbon monoxide, another harmful component of vehicle exhaust, by the year 2000. Three of the worst offenders – Los Angeles, Houston and New York – would get a longer deadline, to the year 2010.

The administration hoped to promote a switch to cleaner-burning alternative fuels for motor vehichles. The auto industry would be required to manufacture 500,000 alternative-fueled cars a year beginning in 1995, and one million a year by 1997, to sell in the nine dirtiest metropolitan areas: Los Angeles, Houston, New York City, Milwaukee, Baltimore, Philadelphia, greater Connecticut, San Diego and Chicago.

A goal was set for a 40% cutback in tailpipe emissions of hydrocarbons by 1993 models, and a 30% reduction in nitrogen dioxides. Steps were to be taken to reduce gasoline vapor levels in vehicles and at gas pumps.

The move to alternative fuels, such as methanol, natural gas or ethanol, drew criticism from both industry and environmentalists because none had been commercially tested as yet. The critics pointed out that a focus on pollution reduction by that means was uncertain at this point.

But the administration offered industry some flexibility in meeting the ozone-reduction standards. While the Environmental Protection Agency (EPA) would draft regulations setting "performance standards" for vehicles and gasoline production, the companies would be allowed to propose their own methods for achieving them.

Auto makers also would be permitted to engage in "emissions trading" in which they could use different devices on different models to meet the standards. Oil companies would be allowed "fuel pooling," or using different refining techniques or mixes of oil to meet standards.

President Bush's initiative represented a break with the Reagan administration, which had opposed any attempt to impose antipollution regulation on industry. Efforts to strengthen pollution curbs had been stymied in Congress even longer, since 1977.

In his speech, Bush said, "We've seen enough of this stalemate." "Ours is a rare opportunity to reverse the errors of this generation in the service of the next," he said. "It's time to clear the air."

The plan drew qualified praise from environmental groups, though some wanted stronger air pollution provisions and less discretion for the EPA to determine acceptable risks.

The plan drew some criticism from industry, particularly electric utilities and petroleum. The natural gas industry, which stood to benefit from the emphasis on alternative fuels, praised it.

Bush's plan to combat acid rain also signaled an end to a decade-long dispute over the issue with Canada, which had been insisting on action by the U.S. to prevent the toxic fallout across the border. (See pp. 14-17)

At a White House briefing June 12, William K. Reilly, administrator of the U.S. Environmental Protection Agency, said he had told Canadian Ambassador Derek Burney earlier that day, "We're going to go for the goals Canada wanted."

THE CHRISTIAN SCIENCE MONITOR
*Boston, MA,
June 14, 1989*

WHEN it was launched in 1970, the Clean Air Act was supposed to herald a new age of environmental progress. But that new age has been painfully slow in coming. Though significant progress has been made, clean-air goals have too often been obscured by special-interests lobbying and administrative laxity.

George Bush has now made his bid to blow the politics aside and get on with cleaning up the air. His targets are well chosen: the chemical pollutants that cause acid rain, smog-producing automobile emissions, a range of industrial emissions known to pose serious health hazards. All were targeted in the earlier legislation, but a combination of over-optimistic projections, constantly loosening clean-up deadlines, and poor state-federal cooperation caused governmental efforts to fall short.

Mr. Bush's initiative includes some much-needed specifics such as: a halving of sulphur-dioxide emissions from coal-burning power plants by the turn of the century. Equally important, in William K. Reilly the President has an Environmental Protection Agency chief who appears ready to strengthen the government's enforcement record.

Will it be enough? Many environmental groups, while praising the Bush proposal plan as a start and noting its break from the Reagan era, have doubts about the plan's reliance on industry to choose the methods of cutting back on certain pollutants. When it comes to smog reduction, some critics point out that tighter pollution-control deadlines for carmakers are the most promising option, rather than reliance on new fuels.

As before, industrial concerns – oil, coal, chemicals – are going to mass their forces against stronger pollution standards. Some in Congress will want to toughen the Bush proposals; many, reflecting business interests back home, will try to weaken them.

The environment is unmistakably back on the agenda, and not just in the United States. The European Community is waging its own campaign for cleaner air. As President Bush seems to understand, few policy goals are more important than proving that pollution doesn't have to be tolerated.

THE ARIZONA REPUBLIC
Phoenix, AZ, June 15, 1989

IT may be, as Environmental Protection Agency chief William Reilly boasts, that "the environment won" Tuesday when President Bush unveiled his clean-air plan. Capitol Hill does seem more hospitable than during the Reagan years to stiffening the provisions of the Clean Air Act, last changed in 1977.

But for all the encouraging signs, it remains to be seen whether regional disputes can be resolved, or whether the president's proposals can survive the cost estimates — $14 billion to $18 billion a year.

Even if the sweeping new regulations weather congressional nitpicking, the question of enforcement remains. Under both Republican and Democratic administrations, enforcement of the Clean Air Act has been lax. Congressmen have contrived to have the requirements watered down when home-state industries fell short of established standards. More often than not, compliance has been the result of court orders, not bureaucratic enterprise.

In spite of this, Mr. Bush expresses a desire to "make the 1990s the era for clean air," and that is encouraging. He seems to see the need to restrict coal-burning power plants, mostly in the Midwest, thus lowering sulfur dioxide emissions by 50 percent, or 10 million tons. That should be welcome news in Canada and the Northeast, where oxides of sulfur and nitrogen, falling as acid rain, have destroyed life in lakes and streams and damaged forests.

What is novel is Mr. Bush's free-market approach. Utilities, for example, would be allowed to install smokestack scrubbers or cleaner-burning plants. If they dropped below reduction targets, they could transfer or sell pollution credits to companies falling short of reduction goals.

To speed the cleanup of urban smog in 100 cities, Mr. Bush proposes a series of measures: stricter controls on auto emissions, the mandatory use of alternative fuels (such as Phoenix will begin requiring in October) and requiring automakers to phase in cars that use methanol.

Under Mr. Bush's program, industrial pollution would be cut by 75 percent in 10 years through requirements for "maximum available control technology." In the case of serious public health risks, the EPA would be authorized to take additional steps — a provision that came under immediate fire on grounds that it would give the agency too much discretion.

Mr. Bush's proposals are a good starting point nonetheless. More important than the specifics is the president's environmental commitment, especially after his disappointing performance in the *Exxon Valdez* affair.

The Atlanta Journal
THE ATLANTA CONSTITUTION
Atlanta, GA, June 14, 1989

So bereft of anti-pollution accomplishment were Ronald Reagan's two terms that his successor, George Bush, could have planted a tree on Arbor Day and environmentalists would have counted it an auspicious turn in White House attitudes.

In fact, Mr. Bush has gone considerably beyond such an obligatory nod to the ecology set with the clean-air proposals that he announced Monday. Though his recommendations have their flaws — and America's homegrown Greens were quick and right to identify them — they are far stronger than expected, given the Reagan record and Mr. Bush's own halting performance on environmental issues since he took office.

Most significant, the Bush proposals are of sufficient heft and credibility that they establish the executive branch once again as a key player in upgrading America's air quality. For the past decade, what few clean-air initiatives there were originated on Capitol Hill, only to be stymied there because of regional and special-interest opposition, especially the coal, oil and auto industries. Prospects for positive if not quick action on air-quality legislation are much better because of the improved atmospherics at the White House and in the Senate, too, where Sen. George Mitchell of Maine, an avid environmentalist, has taken over the Democratic leadership from Sen. Robert Byrd of West Virginia, a last-ditch defender of high-sulfur coal.

The Bush plan is strongest in attacking acid rain, surely cause for rejoicing in America's Northeast and in Canada, but Congress will have to fortify his proposals for combating urban smog and toxic air pollutants. To reduce smog, Mr. Bush is banking heavily on methanol as a cleaner-burning alternative to gasoline, yet he failed to follow the recommendation of the Environmental Protection Agency (EPA) for reducing smog-producing emissions by requiring that auto pollution-control systems be operative for 100,000 miles, rather than the current 50,000-mile standard. As for the toxic-gases hazard, such as the accidental release of methyl isocyanate that caused the Bhopal disaster, the Bush plan dallies over the seminal job of identifying noxious chemicals and gives the EPA so much regulatory leeway as to make the administration's standards unclear.

These shortcomings can be fixed in the give-and-take with Congress. The president's newly acquired commitment to clean air will count for a lot there, but it will be even more pivotal in selling the benefits of improved air quality to private industry, to affected unions, to public utilities and to us taxpayers and consumers.

The plain fact is that this effort, if it is to be a serious one, will add billions of dollars a year to the cost of using energy and force millions of Americans to alter their habits, driving and otherwise. Nothing less than a skillful and sincere effort by the president can put across a change of that magnitude; nothing less will do if the nation is to save the lungs of 150 million Americans who currently breathe substandard air.

Omaha World-Herald
Omaha, NE, June 15, 1989

One of the more commendable aspects of President Bush's clean-air initiative is its emphasis on balance. The time has come, as the president said Tuesday at Grand Teton National Park, to end "environmental gridlock" and to get on with the task of reducing acid rain and other forms of air pollution.

No group, as Bush also said, is likely to get everything it wants.

Certainly disagreements will occur as the nation works to end "environmental gridlock." As the president pointed out, some people want him to do more and others believe that he has proposed doing too much too fast. Coal producer groups say too much of the clean-air burden will fall on their industry. Divisions exist between industry and some of the more outspoken environmental activists.

But as Bush indicated, almost everyone agrees on the need for cleaner air. To live on this Earth is to share a duty to treat the planet and its resources responsibly. Polarization can only hurt the effort.

Some people noted the irony of the president's visit to ethanol country at the same time his Environmental Protection Agency director was saying that methanol will be the clean fuel of the future. Ethanol and methanol are natural competitors. Ethanol, an ingredient in Gasohol, is distilled from grain. Methanol, which the EPA says costs less to produce, comes from wood, coal or natural gas.

Bush, following the balanced approach he established a day earlier in his speech discussing his clean-air program, left room during his Nebraska visit for a variety of solutions.

While mentioning methanol and natural gas, he didn't slight ethanol. Referring to the fact that ethanol is made from grain, he said American farmers are going to "help America fill up its tank," providing clean fuel for motorists of the future.

EPA officials said later that Bush hopes ethanol will earn a larger share of the market. University of Nebraska President Ron Roskens, commenting on the president's speech, said: "I think he made a very strong statement with respect to the value of ethanol."

It is good that the White House, under Bush, is moving ahead on these and other environmental matters. The government during the Reagan years held back on some of the things that could have been done to protect and improve the environment, leaving a leadership vacuum that in some cases has been filled by environmental activists. President Bush, with his clean-air initiative, has pointed the government toward its rightful place in dealing with a matter of concern that affects every American.

OHMAN THE OREGONIAN © 1989 BY TRIBUNE

CLEAN AIR

WHAT'S THAT STENCH UPWIND?

COAL

DETROIT

Houston Chronicle

Houston, TX, June 13, 1989

President Bush's speech sets the laudable goal of clean, safe, breathable air. Just as all Americans share that goal, all Americans will wind up paying a heavy price to achieve it.

The president's plan seeks to curb acid rain by requiring coal-burning power plants to install expensive scrubbing equipment or pay for the privilege of polluting. To cut smog in half in 20 years, Bush would require automakers to produce millions of cars that burn methanol instead of gasoline. Industry would have to use the latest technology to reduce toxic chemical emissions.

Bush's speech reverses the policy of the Reagan administration, which tolerated current pollution levels rather than impose limits on economic growth and competition. The Bush approach — which seeks to form a partnership of environmental and industrial interests — is preferable and necessary, but Houstonians should be aware that they will pay a disproportionately heavy price.

Drivers in ozone-plagued Harris County will have to buy the more expensive vehicles and less convenient fuels. Our area's vast petrochemical industry will have to spend more on equipment and charge more for its products, probably losing some competitiveness and jobs along the way.

The president's plan offers some flexibility in reaching its goals, and Bush vows that he will not micromanage industry and the marketplace. However, inefficient micromanagement is traditionally supplied by Congress, which can be expected to do the same during the current overhaul of the 1970 Clean Air Act.

After a drastic recession, Houston is beginning to recover. Sustaining that recovery in the face of strict pollution limits will require all the ingenuity of this area's engineers and all the influence of our representatives in Washington.

The Oregonian

Portland, OR, June 14, 1989

The most important part of the clean-air speeches President Bush delivered this week is not in their details. It is in the the message they send that the president intends to put his weight behind efforts to reduce air pollution instead of blocking them as his predecessor, Ronald Reagan, did for eight years.

Bush proposes action on three fronts — against smog, acid rain and the emission of toxic chemicals from industrial plants.

Instead of prescribing a single cure for each condition, Bush's plan sets goals and deadlines and leaves it up to industries and cities how they choose to meet them.

For example, it would require 107 of the dirtiest electric utility plants to cut their emissions of sulfur dioxide gas by 10 million tons a year, or nearly in half, and of nitrogen oxide by 2 million tons, by the year 2000, with half of that reduction to be achieved by the end of 1995. Those gases that stream from utility smokestacks undergo chemical changes in the atmosphere and fall downwind as the acid rain that kills forests and poisons lakes and streams.

To meet the goals the utilities could adopt various means: Install scrubbers to clean their stack gases; switch to burning low-sulfur coal instead of coal with a high sulfur content; or even buy credits — a sort of license to pollute — from neighboring plants that have more than met their clean-air targets.

Similarly, auto manufacturers would be required to reduce tailpipe emissions and produce some cars that run on alternatives to petroleum, such as alcohol fuels or propane. Industries would be called on to use the best available technology to cut down on the toxic chemicals their processes send into the air.

This approach obviously calls for careful monitoring. Still, it is wise. It takes account of the wide range of costs and conditions that industries and consumers will have to meet in the varied parts of our huge country.

It also can help avoid the regional politics that has stalled clean-air legislation in Congress all through the 1980s. President Reagan was not the only obstacle. Bills to renew and improve the Clean Air Act have pitted high-sulfur coal producers against low-sulfur coal states; the industrial Midwest, where much industrial air pollution originates, against New England states downwind; auto manufacturers against smog-choked cities.

The Bush administration's proposals are far from the only ones on the table. Major clean-air bills are far advanced in both houses of Congress. Even before Bush spoke, their backers were predicting that after many previous failures, strong legislation could pass, perhaps this year.

But Bush's announcement gives the issue visibility and momentum. He set the standard at which laws and industrial policy should aim when he said, "Every American expects and deserves to breathe clean air."

PORTLAND EVENING EXPRESS

Portland, ME, June 13, 1989

President Bush and Senate Majority Leader George J. Mitchell, two men whose Maine backgrounds make them particularly sensitive to the ravages of acid rain, are poised to launch a powerful two-pronged attack against polluters.

It's about time. In a thinly veiled attempt to do nothing, the Reagan administration spent eight years studying the acid rain issue to death.

Now, with Bush in the White House pledged to protect the environment, and Mitchell, long the point man on acid rain legislation, leading the Senate, the time seems ripe for forceful action.

Bush has unveiled an extensive proposal to reduce by half the sulfur dioxide emissions from coal-burning power plants, many in the Midwest. Those emissions, mixed with moisture, travel widely in the atmosphere and fall back to earth as acid rain. Acid rain is blamed for heavy damage to lakes, forests and aquatic life in the Northeast and Canada.

Bush will also give strong new emphasis to reducing automotive emissions that contribute to air pollution. His proposal calls for cars running on non-polluting fuels to be widely used by the end of the century.

Overall, the president's program, it is estimated, will eventually cost as much as $19 billion a year. And that could give it tough sledding in Congress.

Which brings us to Mitchell, a senator who has for years been urging vainly that sulfur dioxide emissions be cut in half. Mitchell is expected to lead the fight for meaningful revision of the Clean Air Act, last changed in 1977, and sulfur dioxide reductions are bound to be in it.

"I can't guarantee the outcome, but I can guarantee a bill will come to the floor," Mitchell said this week.

After eight years of drift, the power to fight acid rain and air pollution seems finally to be in the right hands.

The Charlotte Observer

Charlotte, NC, June 14, 1989

Every American deserves to breathe clean air. And you shouldn't have to drive 2,000 miles here to do it. Environmental gridlock must end.

— George Bush

Those words came as President Bush launched his clean-air campaign not in some smoggy downtown, but amid the beauty of Grand Teton National Park. A public relations gesture? Sure, but one worth making. The debate over acid rain and air pollution is more than a battle between accountants. The national goal ought to be to preserve — to restore — the clean air and natural beauty that are the nation's treasures.

In politics, of course, gestures are sometimes substitutes for policy. But not this time. The president's specific proposals are extensive and serious. They bespeak a willingness to take strong, but prudent, measures to combat urban smog, acid rain and toxic air pollution.

The president called for sharp cuts in pollution emitted by plants burning high-sulfur coal, a major culprit in acid rain. He called for further reductions in the automobile emissions responsible for urban smog and, for high-pollution areas, would require development of cars using alternative fuels that pollute less.

By all appearances, he means to push hard. That's good. And Congress ought to reject parochial arguments that stalled previous clean-up efforts, such as objections from producers of high-sulfur coal.

But there still must be extensive debate over the details, for air pollution is a complex subject scientifically as well as economically. For example, the alternative fuels that the president wants to push on the automobile industry present their own practical and pollution problems. These fuels must be judged not only for the impact on smog and acid rain, but also for their contribution to the greenhouse effect and depletion of the ozone layer. In cars, power plants and elsewhere, the question is not just what looks good, or even what works best in the laboratory, but what will do the best job of getting the nation's air clean and keeping it clean.

What's most encouraging is the evidence that Mr. Bush, unlike the president he served so dutifully, is ready to commit the government's power, money and prestige to cleaning up the air and conserving the nation's marvelous natural heritage. It will be a tough job. We're glad to see the White House back on the right side. It's refreshing to have a president who thinks clean air is worth something and goes out of his way to say creating the national parks was one of America's best ideas.

The Wichita Eagle-Beacon

Wichita, KS, June 14, 1989

ONE way or another, we Americans will have to come up with $14-$19 billion a year to pay for more breathable air if a series of clean-air proposals that President Bush made Monday become law. But pay it we should.

As Mr. Bush noted in making his pitch for a much tougher U.S. Clean Air Act, "Every American expects and deserves to breathe clean air." Right now, the air is foul — even, at times, in Wichita. The national cost: avoidable cancer deaths, aggravated respiratory ailments, damage to structures, destruction of lakes and forests, global warming, etc.

Such problems grew worse during the 1980s. Congress didn't toughen the Clean Air Act in 1982, as it was supposed to. Thus, federal standards for such pollutants as ozone, carbon monoxide, sulfur dioxide and nitrous oxide remain pegged at 1977 levels. Meanwhile, the nation's automobile fleet swelled, new coal-fired power plants came on line and Rust Belt industrial output — and smokestack emissions — again began to grow.

Much of the blame for Congress' inaction on clean air goes to Mr. Bush's predecessor, Ronald Reagan, who considered tougher environmental laws anti-business. Mr. Bush, however, recognizes that cleaner air and a stronger economy "are not mutually exclusive." In calling on "our best minds to turn technology and the power of the marketplace to the advantage of the environment," he offers hope that the present environmental logjam — and cleaner air is far from the only environmental issue needing congressional attention — at last will be broken.

In the light of the Reagan administration's what-me-worry attitude toward U.S. air pollution, Mr. Bush's proposals likely will strike some as draconian. His proposed 10-million-ton-a-year reduction in sulfur dioxide emissions — a major source of acid rain — would raise homeowners' power bills $2 a month in some parts of the country. His proposals to cut auto emissions in half would raise the price of new cars and force older cars out of service. His proposal to slash toxic chemical emissions by three-quarters would force chemical companies to spend millions on new pollution-control technologies. And so the proposals' impact would be felt, all across the American economic spectrum.

Why should Americans assume these additional burdens now, when other economic pressures abound? For their children's and grandchildren's sake. As Mr. Bush says, "Ours is a rare opportunity to reverse the errors of this generation in the service of the next."

The president's willingness to lead the fight for cleaner air dramatically hikes chances that this reversal will come to pass. Congress should get to work on his proposals immediately.

Reilly Confirmed at EPA; Lujan Confirmed at Interior

Interior Secretary Manuel Lujan Jr. and Environmental Protection Agency Administrator William K. Reilly were confirmed to their posts in the Bush administration Feb. 2, 1989 by perfect 100-0 votes.

At a confirmation hearing before the Senate Energy and Natural Resources Committee Jan. 26, Lujan had pledged an environmentally sound stewardship of the nation's lands that would allow careful development of public resources. Lujan said the nation did not have to choose between protection of federal resources and proper development of energy, mineral or other resources on federal lands. He expressed regret that "a line had been drawn" already by environmental groups on the Arctic National Wildlife Refuge. The Reagan administration had sought to open the refuge to oil drilling, and environmental groups were urging President Bush to reverse this recommendation.

"It bothers me we are starting in a confrontational way," Lujan said. He was willing to "sit down and talk" about the issue, he said, although he did not say which side he favored at this point.

The hearing was brief and the senatorial questioning friendly. Only one witness opposed the nomination. He was Michael S. Clark, president of the Environmental Policy Institute, who criticized Lujan's "antienvironment record" while serving 20 years in Congress.

At his confirmation hearings, Reilly told the Senate Environment and Public Works Committee Jan. 31 that, like Interior Secretary-designate Manuel Lujan Jr., he regarded strong environmental protection and strong economic development as fully compatible.

"The kind of economic growth we want is the kind that doesn't shorten our breath or our life," Reilly said.

But Reilly, a professional environmentalist who was president of the Conservation Foundation and the World Wildlife Fund, pledged "aggressive" environmental laws and forceful advocacy of environmental causes within the Bush administration.

THE SACRAMENTO BEE

Sacramento, CA, Februrary 20, 1989

By announcing that he is suspending the Reagan administration's plans for new offshore oil drilling on sections of the California coast, George Bush has partially redeemed an important campaign promise to the Golden State. But it's only a beginning. Even if all California drilling sites were included, as they should have been, there's a lot more the new president has to do if he really means to reverse his predecessor's dismal record of environmental neglect.

It was significant that the new secretary of state, James Baker, devoted his first major foreign policy address to the need to combat the threat that the so-called greenhouse effect poses for the planet. But the only specific program Baker had to offer amounted to little more than a rehash of Reagan's do-nothing proposals. U.S. officials explained that there hadn't been time for the State Department to reverse course since the inauguration.

Bush likewise made the most of his first foreign visit since taking office by using his recent meeting in Ottawa with Canadian Prime Minister Brian Mulroney to announce action against the acid rain problem that has devastated forests, lakes and rivers in both countries. Whereas Reagan always said he needed more time for study, Bush promises to commit more funding to the task and to set new, tougher limits on toxic air pollution and a firm schedule for achieving them. But

as welcome as Bush's support for acid rain control should be on both sides of the border, the new administration isn't ready yet to say when or how much it intends to cut back on emissions from the smokestack industries that are the principal source of the problem.

Incoming Interior Secretary Manuel Lujan may be in the best position to provide an immediate demonstration of the new administration's commitment to reform. He's inherited an office whose integrity has been severely compromised by an extensive series of questionable deals and backdoor policy decisions that were rushed through in the closing hours of the Reagan administration. Among other things, Lujan's predecessor, Donald Hodel, relaxed air pollution standards for offshore oil development, opened the door for coal mining in the national parks and approved a series of land swaps in Alaska aimed at bypassing congressional review of the oil companies' plans for pumping in the Alaska National Wildlife Refuge.

All of those dirty deals can be reversed by Congress or in the courts, but that takes time. It would be a lot better in terms of wiping the Reagan administration's blotted environmental slate clean if the Bush people did it themselves. And it would leave a lot more room for the achievements of the new president to be writ large.

Roanoke Times & World-News

*Roanoke, VA,
February 18, 1989*

WITH THE PRESIDENCY safely won last fall, George Bush abandoned his overheated rhetoric about patriotism, the Pledge of Allegiance, Willie Horton and the American Civil Liberties Union. That's fine.

But also put aside was at least one other prime concern he showed during the campaign. Boston Harbor, which Bush called "the dirtiest harbor in America," gets not a penny in the president's first budget.

That's quite a departure, inasmuch as Congress in 1987 authorized $100 million to improve water quality in the harbor. But with Michael Dukakis defeated — and planning as well to step down as governor of Massachusetts — there's no political mileage for Bush from earmarking money for that allegedly dirtiest of harbors. On that little matter, it's back to business as usual: Ronald Reagan twice vetoed the bill with that $100 million in it, and included no budget funds for harbor cleanup in fiscal 1988 or 1989.

With mock surprise, Paul Levy — executive director of the Massachusetts Water Resources Authority — said: "I thought [Bush] was firmly committed to the Boston Harbor cleanup. We were counting on him to follow up his moral support during the campaign with financial support." David Ryan, comptroller of the federal Environmental Protection Agency, countered that the administration still considers the harbor a significant problem but lacks money to make it a special project.

Granted, Bush's environmental agenda still is fuller than Reagan's. Action has been promised on acid rain and other pollution, offshore oil leases will be postponed, and the budget includes funds for new parks. There's ample reason for EPA chief William K. Reilly to say that Bush's speech and budget "clearly identify the president and the administration with the environment." And outside of Boston, who really cares much about how dirty that harbor is?

We may learn in less than four years. The president should not be surprised if some rival takes another boat ride for the TV cameras in Boston Harbor and uses the setting to denounce pollution. It makes such a nice sound bite. Too bad all of those symbolic gestures had so little to do with what governing is about.

THE DENVER POST

Denver, CO, February 10, 1989

JUST AS A man with strong opinions may be described as obstinate by critics and tough-minded by admirers, one with an open mind may be derided on the one hand as wishy-washy and defended on the other as someone who's willing to listen.

So it is with Manuel Lujan, President Bush's appointee as secretary of the interior. At a news conference in Denver this week, the former congressman from New Mexico depicted himself as a "centrist" who likes to "sit together with groups of people and take their views into consideration."

This may mean Lujan will be able to forge compromises among the various interests affected by Interior Department policies — everyone from Indians to oilmen to visitors to national parks. But his middle-of-the-road approach also could mean he'll be pushed easily to one side or the other, depending on what direction the political winds are blowing.

Regrettably, Lujan's public comments so far have suggested that he's so ill-informed he'll have a tough time even staying on the fence — much less straddling it.

Lujan admitted in his Denver appearance, for example, that he hadn't yet read the report of a cabinet-level committee that reviewed federal firefighting policies in the wake of last summer's conflagrations in Yellowstone National Park. In view of the fact that more than a month passed between his nomination and his swearing-in, such indifference to one of the hottest questions in the West seems inexcusable.

In Washington a week earlier, Lujan was asked about a California desert-protection bill that had just been reintroduced by Sen. Alan Cranston. Instead of saying he wanted to study this complex issue further before taking a stand, or otherwise finessing the question, the new secretary embarrassed himself by charging off into uncharted territory. He said the federal government doesn't have "millions of dollars to buy new land" — which isn't contemplated in the bill at all.

Such appalling ignorance of some of the basic questions that confront the Interior Department might be understandable in an appointee who had just switched agencies. But Lujan spent much of his 20-year tenure in Congress as the ranking Republican on the House Interior Committee.

Certainly he has a right to reserve judgment on many of the tough decisions the secretary must make. Subjects such as offshore oil drilling and the reintroduction of wolves into Yellowstone are both technically complex and emotionally charged. But Lujan's apparent lack of insight is hardly reassuring.

He may be a decent and down-to-earth guy. But the man from Albuquerque looks as ill-prepared for a cabinet post as Dan Quayle is for the vice-presidency. He'll have to put in some heavy "think" time if he expects to survive.

THE TENNESSEAN

Nashville, TN, February 6, 1989

PRESIDENT George Bush's choice to head the federal Environmental Protection Agency, Mr. William Reilly, made a good impression before the Senate Environment and Public Works Committee last week.

He said his chief priority would be reducing acid rain. "Acid rain from our point of view is first out of the box," he told the committee in confirmation hearings. He said he would propose legislation to curb acid rain within a few weeks.

This outlook is a far cry from the EPA's eight years of foot dragging during the Reagan administration. But it will take more than good intentions to get the EPA off its seat and put it to protecting the environment in an effective way.

The EPA has been doing nothing for so long that it may take Mr. Reilly quite a while to get it turned around and headed in the right direction.

One of the first tests of Mr. Reilly's resolve may come in the effort to prevent the Champion International Corp. from continuing to pollute the Pigeon River in East Tennessee from its paper mill in Canton, N.C.

Champion is now threatening to close the plant and throw about 2,000 people out of work instead of cleaning up its wastes. That sounds like an attempt to pressure the EPA into compromising on clean water standards for the Pigeon River.

If Champion gets away with its polluting, Mr. Reilly could just forget about doing much to reduce acid rain. Every big polluting business and industry in the country would start crying about how jobs would be lost if it had to adhere to environmental standards, and the EPA wouldn't be in much position to resist them.

It is ridiculous to say that the nation can't have clean air and clean water and jobs too. But that is the line that the industry sold the Reagan administration, and it is certain the Bush administration will be hearing the same thing. It shouldn't take long to find out if Mr. Reilly is going to stand up to polluting industries. ■

Chicago Tribune

Chicago, IL, February 17, 1989

It is too soon to know whether President Bush's new breeze will be fit to breathe, so those environmentalists who agonized through the Reagan years may be forgiven some wait-and-see skepticism. But the early, consistent signals from the new administration suggest that the President meant his campaign rhetoric, and that those who figured him to be the closet environmentalist on the Reagan team figured him correctly.

The most visible demonstration was Bush's getting down to business on acid rain, first in his budget message declaration that the matter had been studied long enough—a simple but breathtaking break with the Reagan doctrine. There followed his brief meeting with Canadian Prime Minister Brian Mulroney, in which he told all Canadians what they wanted to hear: that he would push for a strengthened Clean Air Act to reduce acid rain pollutants, and would deal with Canada on an acid rain treaty.

No issue has divided our two countries more wrenchingly in recent years; none has been such a lightning rod to the environmental community as the evidence mounted of lakes destroyed, forests scarred, and buildings and monuments defaced by acid rain.

Bush may soon confront another bellwether issue in another meeting with an American neighbor, Brazilian President Jose Sarney. The two are expected to meet during the funeral of Emperor Hirohito in Tokyo, with Bush likely to press Sarney on Brazil's intransigence over the wholesale destruction of the Amazon rainforest—perhaps linking the protection of this vital ecosystem with U.S. help on Brazil's foreign debt.

These are major strokes, but there are smaller ones as well, enough to seem orchestrated to make a point:

● Secretary of State James Baker, in his first diplomatic meeting, joined a 17-nation working group in calling for international action to deal with the threat of global warming—the greenhouse effect. Time, said Baker, will not make the problem go away, and action cannot wait on all the uncertainties being resolved.

● William K. Reilly, the first professional environmentalist named to head the Environmental Protection Agency, said he would carry through Bush's pledge for specific acid rain legislation, and called for deeper cutbacks in the chemicals threatening the ozone layer, faster action on cleaning up toxic waste dumps and better protection for vanishing wetlands.

● New Interior Secretary Manuel Lujan, the most suspect of the bunch for his uninspiring congressional voting record on environmental issues, nevertheless said environmental sensitivity would come first in developing natural resources on U.S. land and allowing offshore oil drilling. He also indicated he may back off on recommendations widely seen as giveaways by former Interior Secretary Donald Hodel, including the bargain-basement sale of Western oil shale property.

All these are litmus causes in the environmental movement. More important, they represent government acknowledgement that the problems exist, or that there is enough evidence to worry about them after years of deferring their reality. And there is an emphasis that most of them are global problems that will demand U.S. leadership toward global solutions.

So far, of course, there are only words. But words can be powerful in setting a tone and direction, in catalyzing a mood and marshaling support. So far, at least, this breeze is blowing in the right direction.

WINSTON-SALEM JOURNAL

Winston-Salem, NC, January 4, 1989

A world suffering multiple afflictions confronts the Bush administration. Most attention has been directed toward foreign policy and economic matters, but the deteriorating condition of the environment may be the biggest time bomb demanding urgent attention. Three major problems cannot be ignored. Population growth, the burning of fossil fuels and deforestation.

As is so often the case in environmental matters, they are interrelated. More people use more energy. In developed countries, the energy is most often in the form of fossil fuels. Their use pollutes, consumes oxygen and emits carbon dioxide with such unfortunate consequences as acid rain and the greenhouse effect. In developing countries, cutting trees for fuel and clearing land for farming and industrialization reduces the ability of the ecosystem to convert carbon dioxide into oxygen. It's the other half of a vicious circle with world altering ramifications.

Of these three big problems, that of fossil fuels is most obviously a top priority for the United States. The other two are largely developing country concerns. There we can help, but can't control. But on fossil fuels we can assume a leadership role. Will we?

George Bush proclaimed himself an environmentalist during the campaign, but little in his resume justifies that self-description. Some feel he sees himself as a latter-day Teddy Roosevelt — setting aside pretty acres where well-to-do hunters and fishers can besport themselves while doing little to confront bedrock environmental problems with the potential for profound economic impact. An aesthetic rather than a scientific environmentalist. Few believe Bush has a bone-deep commitment to reversing life-threatening trends.

As evidence, aside from his record, there is the message he's sent through his appointments. When campaigning, Bush claimed the environment was near the top of his priority list. But Interior, EPA and Energy were not the first appointments he concerned himself with. Nor did he rush to put close personal friends or Washington heavy hitters into those jobs.

It's true that Bush has chosen an unimpeachable environmentalist to head EPA — William Reilly, head of the Conservation Foundation. However, as with several of his other appointments including that of Elizabeth Dole, there may be more political shrewdness than policy substance to the move. Reilly is noted for his diplomatic persuasiveness, but some think him constitutionally ill-suited for a post less concerned with jawboning polluters than jailing them. In addition to appeasing the environmental lobby with Reilly, Bush may have finessed it.

At the minimum, Reilly is certain to be outnumbered on a variety of energy and development topics. Unfortunately, fossil fuel efficiency is generally regarded as synonymous with pain for the petroleum industry, and the Bush administration is closer to constituting an oil cartel than OPEC. Bush himself is a former oil man. Tower at Defense, Mosbacher at Commerce and Baker at State are all Texans whose personal and political fortunes are closely linked to oil. To them can be added Lujan of New Mexico, the new secretary of the interior. He has consistently voted pro-oil on offshore drilling, clean water, development of federal lands and a variety of other touchy environmental issues.

All in all, the records of the administration's personnel suggests that when environmental protection and economic growth are locked in increasingly frequent and divisive tugs of war, the heavyweights of the Bush administration aren't going to be pulling on Reilly's end off the rope.

Yet time is running out on a range of crucial environmental issues. We hear a lot about economic hard choices in regard to the budget, but the hardest choices of all during the next four years could revolve around environmental decisions. If, as seems increasingly likely, the choices come down to the oil industry's prosperity or the planet's posterity, Bush and his people could find themselves having to decide between their own interests and the public's. It isn't going to be easy.

Los Angeles Times

Los Angeles, CA,
February 10, 1989

The United States will not just be a kinder, gentler nation if George Bush diligently pursues the environmental initiatives that he has launched. It will be a cleaner, healthier nation. In the long run that will mean a stronger America both in economic vitality and in moral standing as it seeks solutions to global environmental problems.

Bush's most dramatic announcement is of particular importance to California: his decision to postpone indefinitely a proposed oil-lease sale in federal waters off the Northern California coast and to delay for more study a second lease offering off Southern California beaches. The Reaganites never seemed to grasp the unity of California in opposition to the plan that put a virgin stretch of the North Coast at risk for a minimal amount of oil. In the south the new Administration will take the realistic course of assessing the oil potential against real national energy needs and energy gains from other sources—something that the Reagan Interior Department always refused to do.

The President should be applauded for his other initiatives as well, like support for a new Clean Air Act with a strong acid-rain component. He noted that environmental progress must be achieved without stifling the economy. Certainly. But the Bush Administration at least seems to understand that environmental progress is worth pursuing for its own value, not something to be abandoned any time it conflicts with private exploitation of public resources. This is a welcome and critical change in attitude from the recent past.

The ★ State

Columbia, SC, January 5, 1989

PRESIDENT-ELECT George Bush's choice for director of the Environmental Protection Agency is encouraging evidence that he intends to follow through on a campaign commitment to safeguard this country's environment.

The credentials of Mr. Bush's nominee for secretary of the interior are less impressive. Taken together, however, the nominations suggest that the Bush White House will do more to protect the nation's natural resources than regrettably was the case under the Reagan administration.

William K. Reilly, president of World Wildlife Fund's American affiliate and of the Conservation Foundation, is a first-class pick to succeed South Carolinian Lee Thomas as head of EPA. The selection of retiring Rep. Manuel Lujan Jr. of New Mexico for Interior sends a mixed signal.

Mr. Lujan was an early defender of James Watt, a combative sort who served as President Reagan's first secretary of the interior. He later became a critic of the Watt regime after it approved the lease of 700 acres of New Mexico wilderness for oil and gas development.

Mr. Reilly, a lawyer, has built the Conservation Foundation into one of the most effective and respected environmental organizations in the country. When efforts to clean up abandoned toxic dumps bogged down in litigation, he helped break the impasse by founding Clean Sites, a group that mediates cleanup settlements between polluters and the government.

Mr. Reilly has long evinced an interest in pollution problems abroad, issues like acid rain and the greenhouse effect which are linked so tightly on this continent to U.S. relations with Canada.

In his role with WWF, Mr. Reilly has supported conservation projects in Latin America, Africa and Asia, especially in tropical forests.

Mr. Lujan, a 20-year House member from Albuquerque and the second Hispanic named to the Bush Cabinet, did not endear himself to conservationists by sponsoring a bill in the last session of Congress to permit oil development in the Arctic National Wildlife Refuge in Alaska.

But in a statement when nominated, Mr. Lujan made an earnest effort to defuse whatever wariness environmentalists may have towards him. "If one little piece of our public trust is desecrated," he said, "we all suffer for it."

Deeds, of course, speak far louder than words. Whatever may be the understandable misgivings over the Interior appointment, Mr. Lujan bids fair to be an improvement over Mr. Watt or his successor, Donald Hodel.

Given his past track record, the nomination of Mr. Reilly, at least, bodes well in the Bush years for the precedence of the environment over excessive land development.

Arkansas ★ Gazette

Little Rock, AR, February 7, 1989

Already, the Bush administration signals that it will be a more sympathetic caretaker of the environment than its predecessor. Even before taking office, the new head of the Environmental Protection Agency said last week he intended to offer legislation to curtail acid rain, which the Reagan administration stonewalled for eight years, and to move on other fronts.

But the president's first chance to put resolve behind his promises will be at the Transportation Department, which must decide once more whether to yield to the car makers, as the Reagan administration did repeatedly, and roll back the fuel-efficiency standards of new American cars. A bipartisan group of senators urged the new Transportation secretary, Samuel K. Skinner, last week to allow the standard to rise to 27.5 miles a gallon. A 1975 law would have pushed the standard to 27.5 in 1986, but the Reagan administration has used its discretion each year to hold it to 26.5, as two of the big three American manufacturers requested. Chrysler Corp., which has met the standard, has urged that the higher standard be imposed.

★   ★   ★

The law established the average fuel efficiency that manufacturers must meet for the entire fleet of cars sold on the domestic market. Ford and General Motors say that the higher standard will prevent their making enough large, gas-guzzling cars to suit the American demand.

National, even global, interests should prevail sometimes over the short-term profits of a major industry. This is such an instance, although the health of the automobile industry need not conflict with provident environmental and energy policies. Japanese products have a competitive advantage over American ones because of the higher fuel efficiency of Japanese industry. It is a lesson American industry, particularly car makers, haven't absorbed sufficiently.

Higher fuel efficiency will help control global climate changes, to which greenhouse gases like carbon dioxide from vehicles contribute heavily. It also will reduce dependence on foreign oil.

The Reagan administration's rollback of the efficiency standards for new cars by one mile a gallon is wasting more oil than would be yielded by the areas that are currently off limits in Alaska and off-shore California. The pressures applied to the car makers by the federal law and by the big increases in fuel prices that followed the oil-price shocks of the 'seventies caused the average gasoline usage to rise from 13.1 to 18 miles a gallon between 1973 and 1986. By 1986, that improvement saved more than twice as much oil as the United States imported from the Persian Gulf and more than the total oil output in Alaska.

Saving oil saves oxygen, too. Burning it more efficiently will reduce smog and the greenhouse effect, which occurs when gases like carbon dioxide and methane collect to trap solar heat in the atmosphere.

The Reagan administration studied environmental problems and acted on none of them. This is President Bush's first chance to revoke that terrible legacy of neglect.

Part II: Nuclear Power

Though the vision of cheap nuclear electricity may have faded in the 1980s, many protagonists still believe that nuclear power provides the main hope of the abundant energy they see as critical for future social stability. As oil supplies diminish, they argue, an expanding nuclear industry will prevent the need to make forced changes in our lifestyles – and provide a means for the worldwide improvement of living standards. There are risks, they accept, but these must be traded off against the benefits. During the 1960s and 1970s, energy utilities in the U.S., United Kingdom, Japan, France and the Soviet Union committed huge financial and scientific resources to nuclear development programs. By 1981, more than 250 reactors in 22 countries supplied eight percent of the world's electricity.

But optimistic predictions to the effect that nuclear power would provide 50 percent of the world's electricity by the year 2000 now look unrealistic at best. Outside the ever-dwindling number of countries that still have ambitious nuclear programs, the world's nuclear power industry looks as though it might have reached a dead end. Though the industry could probably live with the disapproval of environmentalists, its most serious problems now are economic. Massive cost over-runs, with U.S. plants proving 5-10 times more expensive than had been projected, have resulted in the largest municipal bond default in U.S. history and have pushed many utilities to the brink of bankruptcy. Inflation and high interest rates have combined with tightening regulations to undermine the economics of nuclear power schemes. Nuclear construction programs have virtually ground to a halt in the U.S., with 100 plants canceled and no new ones ordered since 1977.

But those countries that have declared nuclear moratoriums have not typically done so because of economic problems.

Sweden's reactors were among the safest and most efficient in the world. The real problems are social and political: people simply do not believe that the wider impact of nuclear technology can be controlled. Growing concerns about the environmental risks involved, about the inability of the industry to dispose safely of long-lived radioactive wastes, and about the proliferation of nuclear weaponry, have all contributed to at least temporarily derailing growth in nuclear power.

From its inception, the civil nuclear industry has insisted that nuclear reactors, unlike nuclear weapons, are clean and safe. Indeed, until the early 1980s, the industry refused to acknowledge that radiation from reactors had ever caused a death. In addition to dismissing as remote the chances of a major accident occurring at a reactor, the industry has consistently denied that the health effects of reactor accidents, however serious, could ever compare with the devastation caused by a nuclear bomb.

Minor accidents involving relatively small releases of radioactive material occur all the time at nuclear installations. But what are the risks of a major accident? In 1957, the U.S. Brookhaven National Laboratory put the probability of the most serious accident conceivable occurring in a nuclear plant at less than one per 1 million years of reactor operation. Such an accident would lead to 3,400 deaths, 43,000 injuries and $7 billion worth of damage to property.

By 1974 the WASH 1400 Report, better known as the Rasmussen Report, gave the chance of a major accidental release of radioactive material from a nuclear reactor as one in a one billion years of reactor operation.

Critics say such calculations are highly suspect. As Nobel Laureate Professor Liebe Cavalieri writes, "The case of the Oak Ridge Research Reactor accident is one example of how misleading probability calculations can be. In this accident there were seven sequential failures, each involving redundance of three parallel elements, for a total of 21 failures, the absence of any one of which would have prevented the incident. Three of the seven were personnel failures: an experienced operator threw wrong switches in three separate rooms; another operator failed to report finding any of these errors; and so forth. The others were design or installation errors in a reactor with an outstanding performance record. The probability of the event was calculated to be one in 100 billion billion. The event 'was almost unbelievable,' but it happened. Again, in the complex nuclear reactor accident that occurred in 1970 at the Dresden II reactor, the most generous assessment of the probabilities of the separate events could not raise the overall probability above something like one in a billion billion. Yet, here again, it happened."

Serious accidents have already occurred to nuclear installations, notably at Kyshtym in the Soviet Union in the winter of 1957; at Windscale in Britain in 1957; at Three Mile Island in the United States in 1979; and, in 1986, at Chernobyl in the Soviet Union.

These four serious accidents have occurred within the space of 30 years and seemingly bring into question the Rasmussen Report's official calculations. Indeed, some officials at the U.S. Nuclear Regulatory Commission now estimate the chance of a reactor in the U.S. suffering a core meltdown before the end of the century at 50 percent. This fits with the experience to date. Since the U.S. possesses about a quarter of the world's reactors, we may see several more serious nuclear accidents before the end of the century.

At Chernobyl, the power rose to at least 480 times maximum operating power before the reactor exploded. Should the gas circulatory system in a British advanced gas-cooled reactor fail, followed by a failure to scram, an even more devastating accident than Chernobyl could result within seconds.

Since Chernobyl, it has become increasingly difficult for supporters of nuclear power to maintain the stance that major nuclear accidents are so improbable as not to be not worth worrying about. Instead, there is an acceptance that accidents will occur and the emphasis is now put on ways in which their consequences can be mitigated. As the prestigious science journal *Nature* wrote at the time of Chernobyl, "The important question is not so much how accidents like these can be prevented but how we can live with them safely."

Nuclear Power Industry Beset by Financial Woes; Seabrook Halted

The future of nuclear power in the United States was described as "bleak" in a February 1984 study by the congressional Office of Technology Assessment (OTA). As of April 1984, one hundred plants had been canceled in the past decade alone, and many others were in danger of cancellation because of continuing safety problems and the skyrocketing costs of plant construction. To survive into the 1990s, the OTA report predicted, the commercial nuclear energy industry would have to undergo a radical transformation.

Another blow was dealt to the future of the industry April 18, 1984 when Public Service Co. of New Hampshire stopped all work on both units of the Seabrook nuclear power plant. The utility laid off all but a thousand of the 6,200 workers at the plant, citing "financial pressures" as the reason for the work stoppage. The project had been so over budget and behind schedule that it threatened to throw Public Service into bankruptcy. The company had originally estimated the cost of building both reactors at $900 million, but on March 1 it revised its latest estimate to $9 billion. Public Service said the move would save it and other utilities involved in the project $750,000 per day in building costs. However, interest costs on the $2.5 billion already spent on the project would reportedly continue at about $1 million per day.

As the fifth anniversary of the 1979 Three Mile Island in Pennsylvania passed March 28, it appeared that the financial problems of the industry could cause its demise by 1994. (See pp 82-85)

The Burlington Free Press
Burlington, VT, April 6, 1984

The Seabrook power project in New Hampshire is perhaps a classic example of how not to construct a nuclear-powered generating facility.

Teetering on the edge of bankruptcy as a result of its investment in the plant, the Public Service Company of New Hampshire is desperately seeking help in bailing itself out of its financial bind. Since construction began in 1976, the completion cost of the twin reactor units has jumped from under $1 billion to an estimated $9 billion, representing an 800 percent cost overrun. Finishing just one of the units will cost about $6 billion, according to figures released by the New Hampshire utility. Customers of 53 New England utilities, including seven private and municipal companies in Vermont, will be forced to pay higher electric rates because of the cost overrun. Should Public Service Company be forced into bankruptcy, several other utilities could be ruined.

But the New Hampshire firm now is seeking new lines of credit after its bankers last week said they would not renew an existing arrangement to provide $163 million in credit. If it cannot find new creditors soon, the company may be forced into bankruptcy, according to its auditors. Public Service Company officials believe that they can secure credit. "While the company is in a very serious situation, we remain hopeful that a solution can be reached," said Robert J. Harrison, company president.

Critics are skeptical about that possibility. "It looks to me like Public Service is going to beat the Long Island Lighting Co. to be the first utility to take refuge in Chapter 11," said Robert A. Backus, a Manchester attorney who has represented the Seabrook Anti-Pollution League in its 14-year fight against the construction of the plant. Even if Seabrook 2 is scrapped, utility regulators said consumers will pay the price. "It's going to cost a bundle to someone," said Peter Bradford, chairman of Maine's Public Service Commission and a former member of the federal Nuclear Regulatory Commission. "It's an ongoing fiasco at this point." Some customers in his state could see 20 percent to 30 percent increases in their power bills, he said.

Meeting Wednesday in Warwick, R.I., New England governors heard officials of the New England Power Pool outline a plan to pay for the cost of canceling Seabrook 2 through savings gained in purchasing Canadian hydroelectric power. Gov. Richard A. Snelling, a stanch opponent of the idea, objected that the plan did not deal with the issue of "the feasibility of the Seabrooks." He termed the briefing by the utility group "irrelevant and immaterial." The six governors then decided to hire a consultant to determine the impact of the financial collapse of Public Service Company and failure to finish the plants. "I think it was a cozy deal," he said of the power pool's plan. "The utilities said, 'We'll get together and save one of our own.' "

That Vermont ratepayers should be forced to surrender a portion of the $200 million savings which will be gained by New Englanders through the purchase of Quebec power to bail out Seabrook may be a facile solution to the problem for the utilities. But it imposes an unfair burden on utilities' customers for the mismanagement of construction by officials of Public Service Company. Why should ratepayers now be asked to throw good money after bad in an effort to rescue a firm that apparently made few, if any, efforts to hold down construction costs? Customers of several Vermont utilities which have invested in the plant already have paid a share of the cost of construction. Even if Seabrook 1 is finished, wholesale costs of power would be 20 cents per kilowatt-hour and mean further rate increases for consumers.

Snelling has suggested that Public Service Company officials explore the possibility of abandoning both Seabrook units and building a coal-burning plant on the site. Certainly that might be a more feasible solution to the problem of costs than spending more billions to complete Seabrook 1.

The governor and the state's utility regulators should continue to oppose the use of savings from purchase of Quebec hydropower to finance the construction of the nuclear monstrosity in New Hampshire.

BUFFALO EVENING NEWS
Buffalo, NY, April 15, 1984

NUCLEAR WHITE elephants in the form of incomplete or abandoned power plants today dot the landscape around the country. Of the 48 nuclear plants under construction, perhaps only two dozen will actually go into operation in the foreseeable future. What is the cause of the billion-dollar cost overruns and construction problems that are plaguing the nuclear power industry?

The Nuclear Regulatory Commission, in a 500-page report made at the request of Congress, cites the root cause as a failure of management — both by the builders of the plants and by the NRC itself. The utility companies and those in charge of construction failed to maintain adequate control over all aspects of the projects. But the NRC was guilty of a similar lapse by failing to understand the vast new technological challenges of the nuclear power field and failing to assess the capabilities of the companies to which it issued permits.

The industry as a whole appears to have had a false sense of security because of the experience of utility companies with conventional power plants. Nuclear power actually turned out to be a much more complex matter, with little margin for error. One industry expert said a nuclear plant was comparable to a vast Swiss watch. One glaring example of management failure was the Zimmer plant near Cincinnati. It was 98 percent complete before government regulators discovered serious problems. It is now being converted into a coal-fired plant.

While the immediate outlook for new nuclear plants is not good, the problems cited by the NRC result from inexperience rather than from any basic flaw. And the industry's problems have been accentuated by the slowing demand for all kinds of power and by the lack of public confidence.

Nevertheless, we should not forget that the United States today has 82 operating nuclear power plants. They produce 13 percent of the nation's electrical needs — much of it more efficiently than plants using coal or oil.

There is no real alternative to nuclear power in the long term except coal, and that carries with it serious environmental problems. Thus, nuclear power should not be written off. No new plants have been started in this country since 1978, and no others are likely until perhaps the 1990s, but if management problems are solved, nuclear power may again seem attractive to help meet our gradually rising power needs.

The Dallas Morning News

Dallas, TX, March 14, 1984

AS you will have gathered from a just-concluded series in this newspaper, the Comanche Peak nuclear plant, near Glen Rose, is in some difficulties. Once-unthinkable things are being thought about it: such as that, due to imputed safety problems, it may never open for business.

Laymen — which is to say, 99.999999 percent of us — have a hard time judging these matters. How many of us would know a defective pipe support if we were sitting on it? It's reassuring, then, that the federal Atomic Safety and Licensing Board — whose job it is to know all about such matters — is being endlessly careful about Comanche Peak.

Or is it really that reassuring? It depends. Any reasonable man will concede the need for federal oversight of the nuclear power industry. But not all oversight is good oversight — as seems spectacularly true at Comanche Peak.

All through the building of Comanche Peak, the federal government has continually switched signals. Hardly was the plant under way before the federal pipe supports code got rewritten. This cost the owners (principally Texas Utilities Electric Co.) an extra $400 million.

Literally thousands of new safety requirements flowed from on high after Three Mile Island. More millions of dollars, more delays.

All this notwithstanding, TU never doubted the plant would open — that is, until last December, when the licensing board called into question the general quality of workmanship at the plant. Now TU must defend itself against the complaints of a few former employees.

A fair question is: To what purpose? Protection of the public? Not necessarily. As an American Enterprise Institute study has shown, "It is not possible to say with any certainty that nuclear regulation has increased the level of safety very much over what it would be in the absence of regulation."

Absent congressional guidance, there's no formula even for balancing risk against social benefits. It's mainly guesswork.

AEI suggests that the licensing process would be vastly enhanced if Congress lifted the nuclear industry's legal immunity from damage claims. This would give the industry an enormous incentive to build and operate safely.

How sad that all this perplexity must dog Comanche Peak. First, because Texas Utilities has historically been a reliable and trustworthy energy supplier. Second, because Comanche Peak has become an ideological target: No-growthers just don't trust advanced technology. Third, because this region demonstrably needs nuclear power as a cheaper replacement for crude oil, natural gas and coal.

It's the energy question that gets lost amid all this talk of pipe supports and licenses. Modern civilization runs on a constant flow of affordable energy. That's what Comanche Peak is about. That's why we continue to pull for it.

Boston Sunday Globe

Boston, MA, March 25, 1984

Five years ago next Wednesday a new name – Three Mile Island – catapulted into American consciousness by an accident that should not have happened but did. Through a series of flukes, a nuclear power plant in Pennsylvania collapsed toward disaster, its problems aggravated by inadequately trained personnel who understandably panicked as the system crashed.

Fortunately, no one died, but the episode has become the best known event in American nuclear power history. The lesson the event inspired has been fully learned.

One central message of Three Mile Island was that the people assigned to run nuclear plants were not prepared for their responsibilities. Foreign critics of American utilities were astonished that technicians were left to handle potential dangers that Europeans placed in the hands of more highly trained engineers.

Three Mile Island was probed deeply by a presidential commission under the competent leadership of Dartmouth College's president, John Kemeny. Its recommendations focused on the need for more remote location of future plants, greater standardization of plant equipment, and better training of personnel.

Some of these objectives have been met. While the proposal for a nuclear "academy" like those graduating military officers has come nowhere near implementation, on-the-job training facilities have been improved to equip technicians with realistic test runs similar to accidents like the one at TMI. Control boards have been simplified to reduce extraneous data that might distract operators. While these steps are in the right direction, there is still doubt about whether all operating companies are adequately staffed.

Three Mile Island has become symbolic of the difficulties facing the nuclear power industry today, problems that are more economic than safety-related. Even before TMI, electric utilities had stopped ordering new plants because of the sharp reduction in the growth of demand for electricity. Soaring interest rates played havoc with capital costs for nuclear plants, much higher than those for fossil-fueled plants.

These difficulties led not only to elimination of proposals for new plants but to increasing abandonment of plants already under construction. A plant in Indiana, 97 percent complete, will be converted to a coal-fired facility. A Long Island plant, ready to roll, stands idle while the state of New York evaluates emergency evacuation proposals and questions of how the plant's costs should be borne.

For New Englanders, nuclear disaster can be spelled with a dollar sign. Boston Edison dropped its Pilgrim 2 plant after nearly $400 million had been invested in site and equipment. Seabrook, N.H., has absorbed more than $7 billion for a twin-reactor plant that very probably will be scaled back to completion of only the first reactor. Just last Friday 300 more workers were laid off from a construction force that once numbered 7000.

The problems at Seabrook are typical of those facing the industry all over the country. So far, financial problems have been manageable except in the case of reactors in the state of Washington cancelled at a cost in excess of $2 billion, with more to come.

The future is less promising. Some shareholder utilities may be forced into bankruptcy – which will shift the burden away from corporate managements to those who have bought stocks or bonds in utilities overcommitted to nuclear projects. These problems overshadow successful operations that remain profitable.

In Massachusetts, the most startling manifestation could emerge not in shareholder-owned utilities but among municipal utilities that bought into Seabrook one way or another. One highly competent observer estimates that municipal rates will rise a minimum of 35 percent and, in the worst case, will double because of Seabrook. This will surely provoke a desire for solutions, and sale to private utilities at book value may seem attractive to politicians and public alike. Such decisions should not be made in haste.

Nationally, TMI was a sad event because it helped foreclose the study of other nuclear options that might have been more attractive for everyone. Too many dollars were piled into too many oversized plants in the wrong places. Three Mile Island itself was an enormous commitment for the builder, for the utility company and for the supplier.

Smaller plants using other technologies – notably the simpler gas-cooled reactors built by the British – should have been explored more fully by Americans. With excess capacity in generating facilities and disenchantment bred by TMI, that exploration lies well in the future, at best.

Three Mile Island was America's most spectacular nuclear accident to date and, one hopes, forever. It was only a forerunner of more complex, deeper problems that have not nearly run their course. The nuclear-power industry must confront them.

The Star-Ledger

Newark, NJ, March 26, 1984

It now has been five years since the occurrence of the frightening accident at the Three Mile Island nuclear plant in Pennsylvania, but the incident continues to occupy the attention of regulatory agencies throughout the nation. In many instances, Three Mile Island forced regulators to become more conscious of safety factors at nuclear plants, a development that must be applauded.

A decision by the New Jersey Board of Public Utilities, the state's regulatory agency, also deals with Three Mile Island, and has economic reverberations that could be consequential. The principle it is based on is an unusual one.

The state agency ruled that a local utility, Jersey Central Power & Light Co., must share the blame for the accident in Pennsylvania—and may be penalized for negligence as a result. This blame exists despite the fact that the Pennsylvania plant was operated under contract at the time of the accident by Metropolitan Edison Co. of Reading, Pa.

Both Jersey Central Power and Metropolitan Edison are subsidiaries of General Public Utilities Co., the owner of the Three Mile Island Station. Jersey Central Power has a 25 per cent interest in the station, although it does not manage it.

Because of this financial interest, Jersey Central Power's management "should have known that a problem existed" and must therefore accept a portion of the blame, said Barbara Currran, the president of the New Jersey regulatory agency.

* * *

This position is contrary to the one that usually governs responsibility for corporate mistakes. It is not unusual for one company to have a substantial minority financial interest in another company. Corporations frequently make purchases of the stock of another company that they do not manage but which they think is a good investment. If minority stockholders are to be held responsible for the actions of a company they do not manage, this practice of interlocking holdings will quickly cease.

Certainly there is blame enough at Three Mile Island to be spread throughout the nuclear industry. But whether one company should be held responsible for the management mistakes of another company is quite another matter.

The Board of Public Utilities could punish the New Jersey utility either by forbidding it to pass some of the costs of the accident on to ratepayers, or by ordering the utility to propose new conservation measures to help customers. Given the unusual nature of its decision, the second alternative seems preferable.

Houston Chronicle

Houston, TX, March 23, 1984

Following the 1979 accident at Three Mile Island, that power plant's towers came to symbolize the potential hazard of the nuclear age. Hazardous radiation itself, however, is invisible. Without the concrete reality of a nuclear reactor, radiation's threat to health is difficult for the public to perceive.

The recent contamination of a junkyard in Juarez, Mexico, by the inadvertent dismantling of a stolen cancer therapy device, is a case in point. Experts say it is the worst nuclear spill in North American history, exposing scores of people to harmful radiation hundreds or thousands of times stronger than that received by persons at Three Mile Island. Yet, there was relatively little public reaction, even after hundreds of tons of contaminated — though relatively harmless — steel from Mexico were discovered in Texas.

In the Three Mile Island accident, the possibility of a nuclear explosion or "meltdown," though remote, was genuinely alarming, while actual exposure to radiation was held to a minimum. The contamination of the junkyard just across the border from El Paso, on the other hand, still represents a clear and present danger, though not to U.S. residents.

A comparison of the two incidents conjures up the phrase, "out of sight, out of mind." So it is with the hazards of the nuclear age. It's difficult to fear what cannot be seen, while the presense of a heavily monitored and relatively safe cooling tower can elicit irrational fear, even panic.

AKRON BEACON JOURNAL
Akron, OH, April 14, 1984

THE NUCLEAR Regulatory Commission has produced a remarkable report on the state of the nuclear power industry. Searching for the cause of the industry's construction and design problems, the commission pointed a finger at itself and poor management at utility companies.

The commission admitted that it often was inadequately prepared to decide if a utility applying for a construction permit was capable of building a sound plant. The commission found that some utilities, especially those embarking on their first nuclear plant, often fail to grasp the complexity and attention to detail involved.

In addition, problems in construction frequently went unnoticed. Apparently, too much NRC regulation amounts to paperwork as opposed to actually examining the workmanship. The NRC may be fully capable of understanding what it takes to build a safe and efficient nuclear plant, but it still doesn't have a way of ensuring a well-built plant.

The NRC found that many utilities had jumped in over their heads and were overwhelmed by breakdowns in planning and oversight.

Delays brought a tendency among some managers to view NRC regulations as maximum, not minimum, standards of construction. The NRC found that utilities with a successful record of building nuclear plants usually imposed their own standards, much higher than the NRC's, and had a longer time to construct the plant.

As the report's many recommendations are carefully examined, it would be well to recognize that the NRC has already taken an important step. The report clearly states that building a nuclear power plant is unlike any other construction job. The dangers are plain, and the details are excruciating.

That may seem obvious, and yet many plants, such as the Zimmer plant near Cincinnati, were constructed without proper care. Should the country call on the nuclear industry to meet its electricity needs in the future, and that's not unlikely, it would be best if the utilities and the regulators were properly prepared.

The Virginian-Pilot

Norfolk, VA, March 29, 1984

Yesterday's fifth anniversary of the Three Mile Island incident, nuclear power's worst accident in its quarter-century history, gave no cause for celebration to either the industry or the public it serves.

The industry's fire, since the accident and even before, has been cooled by a long list of problems — growing costs of construction and operation, complexities of plants and equipment, delays in government licensing, concerns about environmental hazards, declines in investment capital, adverse court decisions and on and on. No wonder no new plants have been ordered since 1978. No wonder the industry's death-knell has been sounded by some groups opposed to nuclear power.

But consider: Nuclear power now provides its biggest slice ever of the nation's total electricity pie — 13 percent, according to the Atomic Industrial Forum Inc., an industry group. Although the growth in this percentage since Three Mile Island has been slow, it has been steady.

And consider too: The coal industry, touted as the nation's energy alternative and savior, is hardly enjoying a robust economic outlook. Neither is it without health risks. In an average year roughly 150 coal miners die in accidents and 15,000 suffer disabling injuries. (No one has died from a nuclear-power accident, the industry notes.) Air-pollution risks from coal include respiratory illness, cancer, acid rain and global warming from atmospheric accumulations of carbon dioxide. Many of these same health and environmental risks, incidentally, apply as well to firewood, which, according to some calculations, is producing much more heat for American homes than all our nuclear reactors put together.

None of this is intended to minimize nuclear power's considerable risks and safety defects. But it is intended to point out that nuclear power is safer and cleaner than coal and wood power. And as demand for electricity grows with the economy, as predicted, nuclear power — carefully managed and sensibly regulated — must remain an important factor in the nation's energy equation.

The Kansas City Times

Kansas City, MO, April 23, 1984

Another delay announced in the completion of the Wolf Creek nuclear power plant means bad news if consumers ultimately will pay the bill. Kansas Gas & Electric Co. officials say construction is as much as six weeks behind schedule. Others knowledgeable about the plant, including one Kansas Corporation Commission official, believe that is an optimistic projection.

Even an official of the Kansas Electric Power Cooperative Inc., a minor partner, believes the plant might not be operating fully until October 1985, seven months later than KG&E officials have estimated.

KG&E bases its operating date on having the plant at 50 percent power, while KEPCO officials consider commercial operation as 100 percent power. That difference of opinion is likely to be lost on consumers who must pick up a massive bill one way or the other.

It is certain, however, that the longer the plant is delayed the greater the cost will be — to someone. Thanks to legislative action in Kansas, the Corporation Commission has explicit authority to curb rate increases which it finds are unjustified. It can deny the higher rates and shift the burden of some costs to the shareholders.

Missouri legislators are toying with a bill which proposes to accomplish the same thing in that state. But this legislation was watered down during House passage and now a Senate committee has made it even weaker.

The full Senate must vote to restore some of the original consumer protections if this legislation is going to do any good. Otherwise, construction delays combined with poor regulatory authority could do a rate shock number on electric customers.

DAYTON DAILY NEWS

Dayton, OH, April 11, 1984

The Nuclear Regulatory Agency, at the request of Congress, has taken a long look at the sorry state of the nuclear power industry in the United States and discovered what people have been saying for years: Part of the problem is the NRC.

It's hard to see how an agency designed to cheer on an industry can effectively oversee it, too.

It wasn't until the mini-problems at Ohio's Zimmer nuclear power project escalated into major disasters that the NRC caught on to what people were saying. By that time it was too late to save many of the power plants plagued by the same problem:

The Nuclear Regulatory Agency has made a worthwhile discovery.

Inexperience.

The report, based on case studies of six failed projects, including Zimmer, states that the NRC should have screened utilities' management capabilities before giving them the nuclear go, and should have paid more heed to reported problems. As Zimmer proves, a utility may be the greatest coal-fired plant builder around, but nuclear power generation is a different ball game.

The report says NRC will take care of those failings.

Meanwhile, the Reagan administration is pushing for Congress to remove some of the piles of rules and regulations the nuclear industry is under so it can build plants more efficiently. It would be better to begin by having the NRC prove that it can force utility companies to build nuclear power projects correctly.

The Hartford Courant

Hartford, CT, April 8, 1984

It's all over but the shouting for the Seabrook 2 nuclear power plant.

The Public Service Co. of New Hampshire, the builder and principal shareholder in the plant, is reduced to trying to cut the best deal it can with the other New England utilities to recover some of its losses before it pronounces the project dead.

The remaining questions of note are whether Seabrook 1 will also have to be canceled and whether Public Service will go bankrupt. There is a distinct possibility that both unit 1 and the company will collapse, threatening to take down or seriously damage three or four other utilities that invested too heavily in Seabrook — including United Illuminating Co. of New Haven.

Connecticut's Northeast Utilities is a relatively small shareholder and would not be as hurt by the project's collapse, but, in combination with a bankruptcy, the failure would make it more expensive for NU and every other utility to do business.

Obviously, it is to the disadvantage of all utilities to allow Public Service to go under and they might be willing to join in some reasonable financial scheme to rescue the company. The prerequisite for a plan should be that the principal financial burden fall on company stockholders — who assumed the risk of failure when they invested in utilities — not ratepayers.

There is no easy way out of the financial labyrinth that Public Service got itself into by taking on a project that was always too big for it, and whose cost estimate quickly ballooned to $9 billion — 900 percent of its original size. Surely any effort to save the company should begin by stopping further construction on Seabrook 2 now; the company, whose approval is required to cancel the plant, has stubbornly refused to do so in defiance of the economic facts and the pleas of its partners.

Hundreds of thousands of dollars are being wasted every day to keep building the plant, which isn't going to be finished. This apparently is being done to pressure its out-of-state partners to hand over about $200 million of ratepayers' money to ease its financial burden. That money would be part of the expected savings from a Canadian hydropower project that kicks in sometime in 1987.

New Hampshire law prohibits Public Service from recovering from its ratepayers in the Granite State the losses from a canceled plant. But the New Hampshire Supreme Court could change that situation with a declaratory ruling this spring. In any case, the law was not designed to allow the company to shift the burden on to the ratepayers of other New England states.

There may not be enough time anyway. The company could be out of cash within a few weeks without additional credit lines, according to the company's accounting firm, and, as of now, there is little likelihood of credit lines opening up.

Public Service is no position to be making financial demands on other utilities, implying that it could otherwise sour the Canadian energy deal. As an official from another utility put it, Public Service has to be willing to "compromise, compromise, compromise — even if it means canceling everything and yielding to every demand."

Besides canceling Seabrook 2 now and with no strings attached, it should be poised to cancel Seabrook 1 if the consulting firm asked by the New England governors to assess the project concludes — as others have — that finishing the unit would be a financial disaster all around.

Completion of Seabrook 1, which is about three-quarters built, could take another $3 billion. Where is Public Service, already deep in debt and whose total annual revenues are about $430 million, going to come up with an additional $1 billion for its share?

The longer the company waits before acting to cut its losses, the greater the drain on its partners and the less the chances of winning support from other New England utilities, regulators and politicians for a cooperative effort to throw it a lifeline.

The Boston Herald

Boston, MA, April 20, 1984

ON THE question of whether to abandon Seabrook 1, which is nearly three-quarters completed, the issue comes down to this:

Stop construction now, for good, and what we've got up there on the New Hampshire coastline is a $3.5 billion tomb. Find the financing to finish it and by early 1986 New England will have a $4.1 billion addition to its energy pool.

Close it down now, and the customers of the 16 New England utilities who have a share in it will see their rates increase 10 to 20 percent for at least 15 years to pay for it. Come up with the funds to get it into production and those same customers will at least buy some benefit with their money.

Allow it to stand empty and unproductive, and we'll still have our dependence on imported oil, as well as the possibility of a future restriction or ban on coal-fired power generation because of the steadily-increasing menace of acid rain. Complete it and we'll attack both problems.

Indisputably, the grandiose plan for twin reactors at Seabrook has been the most trouble-plagued and expensive project the northeast has ever been saddled with. Admittedly too, its major partner and builder, the Public Service Co. has been to blame for part of that. But so too has excessive government regulation and oversight at every stage of the project from the first application to the halt in construction.

And so do the environmental zealots and splinter groups whose on-site protests and whose succession of suits, objections and challenges before the courts and federal agencies delayed the project, not for months but for years, and added immensely to its cost. But all the fears they raised, all the unchained dangers they forecast if an accident should occur at Seabrook, were not borne out even at Three Mile Island — where an incident did occur.

Seabrook 1 is nearly 75 percent complete but, critics say, New England doesn't need it — right now. It can get all the energy it requires, at its present rate of consumption, and in a few years hydroelectricity from Quebec will be fed into this region. But we can never again be certain there won't be an oil boycott, a ruinous price hike, or some other misfortune to choke off our supply of foreign oil; nor can we be sure that proven environmental hazards won't one day dictate a prohibition on coal.

In either of those events, or in any other conceivable situation that could diminish our sources and supply of energy, a plant producing clean and relatively cheap power — a Seabrook — would help take us over the hump.

We've gone too far on it, invested too much in it, to turn back now.

Detroit Free Press

Detroit, MI, April 18, 1984

EVERY revelation of the financial problems at Consumers Power makes abandonment of the Midland nuclear plant seem more likely. Consumers is resisting the negotiated settlement offered it by a coalition of state regulators, consumer advocates and industrial customers. But if there were another way to continue the plant, to ensure Consumers' solvency, and to guarantee Midland would come on line with affordable energy, it is doubtful that coalition would ever have come into being.

The utility is asking the state for a rate hike to help finance the completion of the plant, a request that to some degree attempts to shift the blame — to force the state to bear the onus of a bailout or a cancellation of the plant that Consumers couldn't build.

Even if the Public Service Commission granted the request, not much in Midland's history inspires confidence that it could be finished at the currently projected cost and to the satisfaction of federal regulators. A few days ago, Consumers disclosed it may have to spend up to $247 million more than the announced $3.95 billion to ready Unit 2 of the twin-reactor plant. The utility is still correcting soil settlement problems at the site, a massive project whose success remains uncertain.

And even if the plant is completed, approval to operate from the Nuclear Regulatory Commission is not assured. In recent months, Dow Chemical Co. has pulled out of the Midland project, the price of Consumers' stock has fallen, and the utility has faced difficulty in borrowing. These factors represent a hardheaded judgment on the part of investors, lenders and private industry that Consumers cannot get the plant on line within a time frame and at a price that will satisfy either regulators or customers.

Meanwhile, consumer activists have launched a campaign to put on the November ballot a constitutional amendment that would make it impossible for the costs of Midland to be passed onto customers, a proposition that would bankrupt Consumers and strangle other Michigan utilities. We think the proposal is far too rigid and unrealistic, but it will be difficult to defeat at the polls. Abandonment of Midland, with a negotiated cost-sharing among customers, the utility and its contractors, would help take the steam out of the petition campaign or defeat the measure in November.

Consumers Chairman John Selby has suggested the utility will go into bankruptcy court rather than negotiate a settlement and abandonment. But bankruptcy for a major utility is an untested option that could prolong Midland's agonies and force a massive battle over who has the power to set Consumers' rates during the proceeding — again, a delay that will escalate costs at Midland, where interest charges alone amount to $22 million a month.

It is important to note that it was not the enemies of nuclear power that brought Midland to its knees, but the plant's unique problems and the miscalculations of the utility and its contractors. Federal regulators, responding to public concern and the shock of Three Mile Island, did impose costly, retroactive changes. But Detroit Edison faced the same problems at its Fermi plant and that plant is approaching successful completion despite the delays and cost overruns.

The decision on Midland has consequences not only for Consumers and its customers, but for other utilities here, since investors and lenders will watch closely the way the state deals with Consumers. There are obvious risks to abandonment, both in terms of financial impact and the assurance of future power supplies. Those risks still seem preferable to the risks of going ahead with the plant. Until the fate of Midland is settled, it remains by far the biggest financial problem facing Michigan, much more momentous than the controversy over the temporary income tax — which, alas, has probably generated more heat and energy than the Midland plants ever will.

The Washington Post

Washington, DC, April 27, 1984

FOUR NUCLEAR power plants, construction well along, have been cancelled and abandoned so far this year. Four others have slid into limbo, unfinished or finished but not operating. Although these eight are big plants, the delays and cancellations will not create an immediate shortage of electricity. But the pattern here points toward trouble. If Americans don't want nuclear power, perhaps the time has come to decide what kind of power they prefer instead.

With the current rise in industrial production, the demand for electric power is also rising. There's still excess generating capacity available, and scrubbing eight nuclear plants won't plunge the country into darkness tomorrow. But generating plants wear out, and the need to replace some of them is going to get urgent as the decade goes on. Most of the country's power is now generated with coal. Anxieties about acid rain seem to be rising, and, unfortunately, acid rain is the least of the damage that results from the present methods of burning coal. The smoke is toxic, and breathing it kills thousands of people in this country every year.

Nuclear plants are both safer and cleaner than coal. But, caught among rising construction costs, past mistakes and increasingly stringent enforcement of federal safety standards, the utilities are rapidly backing away from nuclear power. The last time a utility ordered a reactor without later cancelling it was in October 1973—just before the first oil crisis arrived, with its warning not to count on oil-fired generators.

Of the four nuclear plants abandoned this year, the extreme example is the Zimmer plant that three Ohio power companies were building near Cincinnati. Suffering from an accumulation of disputes over quality control, it was 97 percent complete by the owners' reckoning when they called it quits, confronted with estimates of another $1 billion or so to meet the Nuclear Regulatory Commission's requirements.

The latest addition to the limbo list is the Seabrook plant in New Hampshire, three-quarters built. Last week, after years of litigation and disputes, the principal owner suspended work there simply because it had run out of cash.

Under these circumstances, no American power company is likely ever again to try to build a nuclear plant with its own money. If Americans think they will need nuclear power in the 1990s, the government is going to have to intervene—and it may well have to build the plants itself. Alternatively, if Americans want to dispense with nuclear power they will need to find ways to burn more coal without driving up the death rates. Ideally those are choices to be made now. But past experience suggests that decisions will come only after the brownouts begin.

Pittsburgh Post-Gazette

Pittsburgh, PA, March 28, 1984

Who would have thought five years after the nuclear accident at Three Mile Island:

• That the damaged Unit 2 would not have been cleaned up and repaired, let alone restored to service?

• That its undamaged twin, Unit 1, also would not have been started up again?

• That (depending upon your point of view) the reputation of nuclear energy could have been so badly damaged in an incident where no one was killed or injured — or that it would have survived so well despite the negative publicity?

Few Pennsylvanians can forget the fear that was engendered five years ago today when a faulty water pump started a series of malfunctions that for a time created dread that the damaged plant might spew deadly radiation across the countryside.

Predictably enough, the incident was cited by groups that had long opposed nuclear power. But nuclear power has continued to grow as a source of energy, with more than 86 power reactors now licensed to operate in 27 states and 31 more scheduled to come on line by the end of 1986.

At the same time, since the Three Mile Island affair no utility has ordered a nuclear plant, and plans for 63 have been canceled. The reason in most cases has been economic. But, undeniably, public apprehension caused by Three Mile Island has increased the cost to utilities of meeting heightened environmental standards and adding back-up systems and extra personnel. A plea of guilty on Feb. 28 by Metropolitan Edison, TMI licensee, to a federal criminal count of falsifying records before the accident hasn't helped the image of nuclear power.

•

As for the Three Mile Island units themselves, progress continues at a snail's pace. As if the tortuous task of investigating and then launching the clean-up weren't enough, there has been the Herculean job of raising the finances.

Gov. Thornburgh deserves continuing credit for devising, in July 1981, a plan for sharing the $765 million cost of the remainder of the $1 billion TMI cleanup, when it became evident that Metropolitan Edison and its parent company, General Public Utilities Nuclear Corp., couldn't finance it by themselves without going bankrupt. The task hasn't been easy; so far about $600 million has been pledged. In fact, there is reason to believe that the reason the governor opposes the restart of undamaged Unit 1 is that he wants, in effect, to hold it hostage until he sees all the money available for cleaning up TMI-2.

GPU Nuclear has come up thus far with $170 million of the $245 million assigned it in the Thornburgh plan. If the state Public Utility Commission allows GPU to shift another $18 million annually from the amortization portion of the rate structure to the cleanup portion, the utility can meet the goal.

Another $90 million has come from the corporation's insurance, plus another $37 million in a settlement with Babcock and Wilcox, manufacturers of the TMI units. The Thornburgh plan ticketed the federal government for $192 million; through the Department of Energy the feds have kicked in $159 million so far.

Pennsylvania taxpayers are committed to a $30 million share; the third $5 million annual installment in the state budget this year. New Jersey's share was $12 million; the first $2 million is coming through the budget process this year.

Unexpected help came from a consortium of Japanese utilities, who agreed to pay $18 million in return for the research information to be gained in the clean-up process.

•

That leaves one big gap — the nation's utilities. Gov. Thornburgh assigned them a $192 million share. The Edison Electric Institute, trade organization for the investor-owned utilities, agreed to take a $150 million share on two conditions: that the Internal Revenue Service would make the contributions tax-deductible and that $100 million would be collected before any money was turned over for the cleanup. The IRS has agreed to the first stipulation. The institute has collected $79 million so far but, as Gov. Thornburgh pointed out recently, thanks to the second stipulation not one dime has yet gone from the utilities into the clean-up fund.

And in the New York Legislature there is a move afoot to try to block a "pass-through" to ratepayers in that state of their utilities' $7.1 million prorated share of the TMI cost. The counterargument that needs to be stressed is that *all* utilities are benefited by the lessons learned at TMI, making their plants that much safer.

The utility industry is fortunate that the damage to its nuclear-power thrust from Three Mile Island hasn't been worse. If there is anybody who should be hastening to make the Thornburgh fiscal plan work and the Three Mile Island cleanup transpire, it should be the utilities. Hasn't five years been long enough?

Nuclear Fuel Plant Leaks Toxic Gas; Technical Training in Question

A gas leak at a Kerr-McGee Corp. uranium-processing plant Jan. 5, 1986 killed a plant employee and caused the brief hospitalization of 26 other plant workers and four local residents. The Gore, Okla. plant, which produced fuel for nuclear power plants, belonged to Sequoyah Fuels Corp., a Kerr-McGee subsidiary. Workers had overloaded a 14-ton storage tank with liquid uranium hexafluoride, a key ingredient of nuclear fuel and weaponry. In an effort to make the excess evaporate, workers then heated the tank. Instead of evaporating, the chemical expanded and burst the tank. Contact with the air's moisture broke the uranium hexafluoride into two chemicals. One of the chemicals was hydrofluoric acid, low in radiation but highly corrosive. It escaped as a cloud of gas that killed the worker, James Harrison, and caused about 100 people to seek hospital examinations or treatment. Strong winds dissipated the gas before further harm could be done.

A federal investigator Jan. 9 said workers involved with the Gore leak had not realized that overfilling the tank and heating it would be dangerous. It was the first official indication that their training had been faulty. The investigator, Richard L. Bengart, led a 19-member team assigned to the accident by the Nuclear Regulatory Commission (NRC). Heating a chemical tank to remove excess was barred by the Department of Energy. Kerr-McGee said its rules also forbade the operation. Safety precautions at the Gore plant had been described as "marginal" by an NRC report issued in September 1985. Other issues surfaced after the accident. The plant had no evacuation plan for nearby residents and local authorities said notification of the leak had been slow.

TULSA WORLD
Tulsa, OK, January 7, 1986

MORE than 1,300 Americans die each year in accidents involving toxic gases. Few get much attention outside the communities where they occur.

Last Saturday's poison-gas accident at the Kerr-McGee nuclear fuel plant near Gore was an exception. The mishap which killed one young workman and injured several others was still in the network news summaries and on the front page of the New York Times two days later.

There is a double standard on industrial safety in America — one standard for industry in general and a second, much higher standard for the nuclear energy industry.

It's not that nuclear power is more dangerous. Measured in deaths and injuries, atomic energy has a far safer record than the energy industry as a whole. But there is a fear of the word "nuclear" that borders on superstition. Maybe it's because the power of the atom was introduced to the world as a horrible weapon and only later converted to peaceful uses.

For whatever reason, Americans have a strange perception about industrial accidents. We sound the alarm at any accident in the nuclear power field while accepting almost casually thousands of accidental deaths in other, more dangerous industries.

THE DAILY OKLAHOMAN
Oklahoma City, OK, January 9, 1986

LOOK for nuclear energy foes to make a major case out of the accidental spill of uranium hexafluoride at the Sequoyah Fuels Corp. processing plant near Gore.

A spokesman for the Kerr-McGee Corp., plant owner, said workers violated company operating rules when they overheated an overloaded chemical container. But he refrained from saying this caused the vessel to rupture, allowing the chemical to escape and separate into two other gases, one of which was "mildly" radioactive.

The anti-nuclear crowd will try to liken the spill to the Karen Silkwood story. That involved the contamination of a worker at Kerr-McGee's now defunct plutonium processing plant at Crescent. Continuing references to her "mysterious" death in a traffic accident keep ignoring the autopsy report, which showed the presence in her blood of Quaalude and alcohol, a potentially lethal combination.

Without minimizing the tragedy of a worker's death in Saturday's accident, it's important to remember this was a chemical spill not unlike others that occur in the chemical industry. A nuclear reactor was not involved.

The Kansas City Times
Kansas City, MO, January 7, 1986

The disaster at an Oklahoma uranium-processing plant, which killed one person, will focus attention again on the ugly side of toxic chemicals. It's important to point out the incident may not be as damning as critics claim, even as doomsayers beat the drums of bad publicity louder against the bedeviled nuclear and chemical industries.

Yes, something went wrong at the Sequoyah Fuels Corporation facility in Gore. Early reports indicate a scale used to weigh tanks malfunctioned, allowing one canister to become too full. The tank eventually cracked, a cloud of uranium hexofluoride gas spread for miles, a worker died and more than 100 persons were treated at hospitals.

Critics are describing this as the worst nuclear-related accident since Three Mile Island in March 1979. But as an investigation continues, several things should be recalled about the chemical and nuclear industries.

The death Saturday was the first, as far as experts could determine, that has occurred at a commercial reactor or at a nuclear fuel processing facility. Overall, chemical firms have the best worker safety record among U.S. manufacturers.

As for the nuclear industry, thousands of pounds of radioactive products, everything from original fuel to waste, are handled every year with very few problems. In fact, most of the people hospitalized in Oklahoma as a result of breathing the gas had been treated and released by Monday.

Yet critics do have a powerful argument remaining: The industries *must* strive to be the safest in the world, simply because the products they handle have so much potential destructive power. A different gust of wind could have made the Oklahoma incident far worse.

Questions remain about that accident: Were appropriate precautions taken? Was the equipment that malfunctioned properly maintained? If upcoming answers indicate guilt can be assigned, then punishment must be dealt out and procedural changes made at the plant. But it makes no sense at this juncture to launch any kind of witch hunt against the chemical or nuclear industries.

AS YOU KNOW – EVER SINCE THE ACCIDENT, WE'VE HAD A PROBLEM HERE WITH CORPORATE GROWTH.

ST. LOUIS POST-DISPATCH

St. Louis, MO, January 12, 1986

Not long ago, *The New Yorker* magazine drew a chilling parallel between industrial disasters, such as the incident at Three Mile Island and the chemical leak at the Union Carbide plant in Bhopal, India, and the possibility of a breakdown in the elaborate systems employed by the Pentagon to guard against an accident that could result in nuclear war. As the magazine pointed out, fail-safe systems were in place at both TMI and Bhopal. Yet accidents occurred that quickly developed a logic of their own. Could the same thing happen in a military setting, thus leading the nation (and the world) to the ultimate catastrophe?

Two recent developments have brought us to reconsider that question. The first was the accident at Kerr-McGee's nuclear reprocessing plant in Oklahoma, in which a worker was killed and more than 100 persons required hospital attention. The second was the Center for Defense Information's release of a compilation of air threat analyses conducted by the Pentagon.

In the case of Kerr-McGee — as with Bhopal, Three Mile Island and the leak at Union Carbide's plant in Institute, W. Va. — a small problem turned quickly into a full-blown emergency. A failure in weighing a cylinder caused it to be overloaded; attempts to empty the container (by unapproved methods) caused it to rupture.

The military's reliance on extensive back-up systems is offered as assurance that the chain reactions that characterized these industrial accidents could not occur where missiles that could kill millions of people are concerned. Yet two distinctions need to be kept in mind. First, the consequence of any disaster involving the accidental launching of a nuclear missile are so enormous that even the smallest element of risk should be unacceptable. Second, the immense number of times in which the defense system is activated increases the chance for that single error or

malfunction that could start the fatal chain reaction.

CDI learned that from 1982 to 1984 there were 9,998 incidents (or nine a day) requiring analysis and consultation among air defense and strategic commands and the Pentagon. Although these were considered low-level threats (unexplained radar sightings, aircraft off course, etc.), in each case decisions had to be made quickly as to whether the situation warranted more attention — and possibly action. In that three-year period, 626 incidents were deemed serious enough for more careful analysis.

So the pressure upon the system is almost constant. Like the fail-safe mechanisms and procedures at chemical or nuclear plants, the military system depends upon accurate instruments, proper interpretation of data and correct response.

What the industrial accidents have taught us is that the human component upon which the systems ultimately rest is not fail-safe, especially in emergencies. Were it otherwise, the workers at Kerr-McGee would not have attempted to heat the cylinder to empty its gases; and those at TMI would not have turned off the emergency core cooling system at the wrong time or deactivated crucial auxiliary water pumps at the critical moment.

No matter how sophisticated, redundant or foolproof the systems that govern the nuclear arsenal, they can be compromised by panic or bad judgment on the part of those who operate them. The Pentagon, of course, says that the chances of that occurring are so slight as to be insignificant. But so was the possibility of a serious accident at Three Mile Island, and at Bhopal, and at Institute, and at Kerr-McGee. We have come to learn that despite the best assurances of industry, accidents can happen; and we had best understand that the same holds true for the military, and act on it.

The Chattanooga Times

Chattanooga, TN, January 11, 1986

Three major accidents in 13 months at facilities operated by two American chemical companies — not to mention thousands of other incidents over the past five years — illustrate the need for even more diligent oversight by the chemical industry and the federal government. Failure to provide such oversight would be trifling with workers' lives, and the lives of those who live near the plants.

The latest incident occurred last weekend at a uranium reprocessing plant in Gore, Okla., when a cylinder containing uranium hexafluoride ruptured. One worker died and 100 others were injured. The accident was less serious than the December 1984 disaster at a Union Carbide chemical plant in Bhopal, India. There, the death toll exceeded 2,000 persons. And at another Union Carbide plant, this one in Institute, W. Va., an accident last August sent 135 persons to the hospital.

Last Saturday's accident occurred after workers at the Sequoyah Fuels Corporation plant, a Kerr-McGee subsidiary, discovered that a cylinder had been accidently overloaded with uranium hexafluoride. The cylinder ruptured while it was being heated, an untested process that is supposed to "vent" the gas. After the rupture, the gas separated into uranyl fluoride, a slightly radioactive substance, and toxic hydrofluoric acid.

The similarities between the Oklahoma incident and those in Bhopal and Institute are striking. All of them involved a storage facility, and instruments that malfunctioned when the chemicals were being transferred. Similarly, the latest incident also occurred on a weekend, when there was less supervision, and involved a relatively new procedure. Finally, a common complaint by emergency officials near all three plants was that they were either unprepared for such an incident or were not notified properly.

Of course, absolute safety in the chemical industry, or any other industry for that matter, is not possible. But the circumstances of the incidents, at least insofar as chemical plants in this country are concerned, suggest 1) the need for a review of inspection procedures for storage tanks, 2) additional training in new or untested procedures, and 3) increased supervision on weekends.

If the chemical industry is unwilling or unable to do that, then the federal government should require it.

Crisis at Chernobyl Nuclear Plant Spreads Radiation, Fear

A serious accident at a nuclear-power plant in the Soviet Ukraine spewed clouds of radiation that eventually spread over other nations in Europe. The mishap, initially veiled in secrecy by Moscow, caused widespread fear and conjecture April 28-30, 1986.

The accident involved the No. 4 reactor in the Chernobyl nuclear plant, located in the town of Pripyat, about 60 miles north of Kiev. Based on Western speculation and unconfirmed reports, were feared thousands of Soviet casualties, mainly due to exposure to high levels of radiation in the accident area. Western experts also speculated that the accident might actually have occurred as early as April 24.

Moscow downplayed the accident while denouncing the West for exaggerating the seriousness of the crisis. The Kremlin rebuffed most Western offers of assistance. The Soviet Union came under strong international condemnation for not initially revealing the accident and for withholding detailed information on the mishap. Western analysts noted that Moscow's secrecy conformed to a policy of not disclosing domestic mishaps. Evidence gathered outside the U.S.S.R. suggested at least one other nuclear accident, with a high loss of life, had occurred in the country at Kyshtym in the Ural Mountains in 1957.

The lack of detailed information prompted mounting speculation in the West. As early as April 28, some nuclear experts surmised that the stricken reactor had sustained at least a partial meltdown of its core. The supposition was prompted by the presence of isotopes and iodine in the Swedish fallout. A melting of the uranium fuel in a damaged reactor would cause the release of such isotopes. In turn, the speculation over a meltdown raised fears, particularly in Europe, of the possible cancers that could result from the radioactive fallout carried on the wind from Chernobyl.

Based on Soviet accounts and Western satellite surveillance, the crisis had appeared to have abated as of May 1.

However, there were new indications that the trouble persisted and might worsen. In a worst-case scenerio, a so-called "China Syndrome," the burning core – a molten slag of graphite, metal and nuclear fuel – could burn through the floor of the reactor building until it contaminated the groundwater under the building.

The plant was located next to the Pripyat River. The river fed into a reservoir that provided water for Kiev and the surrounding region. West German scientists May 8 revealed that they had been approached by Soviet diplomats seeking information on how to battle a core burn-through.

The Soviet news media May 5-8 told of the efforts "under the reactor block" to build dikes and earthworks to shield the waters from the molten core should it burn through. Meanwhile, the burning reactor continued to spread wind-borne radiation over great areas. Low levels of fallout from the accident reached the U.S. West Coast May 5.

Technical experts of the European Community (EC) May 7 recommended a temporary ban on food and animal imports from Eastern Europe that might have been contaminated in the Chernobyl disaster. The ban, to last until May 31, covered the Soviet Union, Poland, Romania, Hungary, Bulgaria, Czechoslovakia and Yugoslavia. Banned products included milk and dairy products, fresh fruit and vegetables, fresh meat, fresh water fish, chicken, horses and mules. The EC action came as Western scientists and economists debated the impact of the accident on Soviet agriculture. Moscow, for the first time, May 5 acknowledged evidence of contamination outside the 18-mile evacuation zone around the nuclear power plant, located in the Ukrainian farm belt.

The Soviet Union partially lifted the veil of secrecy surrounding the Chernobyl nuclear accident May 4-6. Soviet television broadcast the first live footage of the damaged reactor building May 4. The same day, Soviet television and newspapers assailed the Western press for sensationalizing the mishap.

The Oregonian

Portland, OR, May 12, 1986

If the Soviet power reactor at Chernobyl didn't "melt down" in the best China Syndrome fashion, there is little occasion to rejoice, for the accident still proves that serious human and environmental damage can follow other types of nuclear reactor accidents.

An International Atomic Energy Agency official, Morris Rosen, who is leading non-Soviet investigations of the accident, has been quoted as saying that no meltdown of the reactor core occurred and that the fire in the graphite pile that moderates the reactor's has been put out.

This is by no means an end to the problem, because the reactor's fuel, believed to have been nearly exhausted at the time of the accident and hence far less lethal, is still a mass of hot decay elements that will take a long time to cool to a safe level. They are also a potential for another explosion if they contact ground or other water, releasing more lethal doses of radioactivity.

The word "meltdown," which has become a kind of scare word, means that failure of a reactor's coolant materials have permitted its uranium fuel rods to actually melt.

The Argonne National Laboratory in Arco, Idaho, has reported that its April tests of a new kind of reactor encourage convictions that a reactor inherently safe from a meltdown can be built. The reactor uses metal uranium fuel instead of uranium oxide and is cooled with liquid sodium. Physical properties of the fuel will close down the reactor before it can melt, even if all coolant systems are removed, the laboratory has shown in actual "melt-down" tests run on an experimental breeder reactor.

But this solution, while good news to the industry, may be 15 years away from being translated into a commercial power-producing nuclear plant.

Scientists critical of current reactor safety, argue that fully safe reactor technology can be achieved and that current reactors would be safer if the government would only get tougher with nuclear operators.

Meltdown may eventually be removed from the lexicon of scare words, but nuclear energy safety will always be of worldwide concern — not just the responsibility of local officials in a single country.

THE ANN ARBOR NEWS
Ann Arbor, MI, May 15, 1986

You can add the word Chernobyl to the English language as noun, adjective and even verb form. Chernobyl is certain to be one of the most important occurrences of our lifetime.

We have been conditioned over the years to scare talk from politicians about the difficulty of getting the nuclear genie back into the bottle.

Then came "The Day After" as scientists and medical experts described the horrors of nuclear winter.

Now even the faded images of Hiroshima have taken on new meaning with the reality of the Chernobyl nuclear accident and the prospect of scorched agriculture and death by radiation.

It is as sobering an event in human history as the most appalling statistics compiled in humankind's many wars. We have been given a glimpse into a future where our nurturing environment – the air and the soil – is poisoned.

One would think intelligent beings would blanch with fear at that privileged peek into a world-to-come and take immediate steps to ensure that the worst will never come to pass.

But even on his best behavior, man as an intelligent being is always suspect. Dominance, power, lust and greed – or whatever the seven deadly sins pass for these days – often take reason and intelligence hostage. Given a blade, man is just as apt to use it in anger against a neighbor as he is to fell a tree to heat his home.

Missiles explode, cannons roar and rifles crack – these engines of war are recognizable for the noise they make on the killing fields. But radiation is just as certain a killer for all its silence and it does not respect international boundaries.

Chernobyl has given the world and the nuclear power industry pause. What, for example, are they thinking in France where they have sown the countryside with nuclear plants without apparent thought to safe disposal of the wastes these plants generate?

Chernobyl ought to promote discussion of safety standards and emergency evacuation procedures. If ever there were an opportune time for international cooperation in a sensitive area, that time is the present.

The implications of Chernobyl for the nuclear industry and the governments it serves go on and on. In free societies, nuclear power plants are tempting potential targets for terrorists. What is being done in terms of security to protect these facilities?

What is being done to ensure the safe operation of nuclear plants the world over? When the usefulness of nuclear plants is nearly over, what is being done to ensure that decommissioning steps are orderly for the disposal of the deadly wastes?

The near-calamity of Chernobyl and the earth's exposure to nuclear rain ought to persuade world leaders of the folly of nuclear weapons stockpiling. More and better missiles do not buy security or immunity from attack; they do, however, raise the chances of an accident or a misunderstanding. Can't our respective leaders see how Chernobyl *demands* that we cooperate in ending the nuclear arms race?

Perhaps, and this is a big maybe, the glimpses of Armageddon – Hiroshima, Chernobyl, and, to a lesser extent, the Cuban missile crisis standoff – we have received have also blessed us with insight. With insight will also come wisdom and with wisdom, the authority to act in the world's best interest in managing and controlling a power we don't fully understand.

If the use of the atomic nucleus is bigger than we're prepared to handle and if it cannot serve its master without also destroying him, then it should be removed or abandoned. If there is no consensus to reject nuclear power as a source of electricity and heat, then plants must be constructed and maintained with the penultimate in safety precautions.

If nothing else, Chernobyl has reminded us how small our planet really is and how interdependent the world's peoples are. If fallout can cross national boundaries and leap the oceans, why can't the desire for peace and friendly co-existence?

THE BILLINGS GAZETTE
Billings, MT, May 1, 1986

Reality brushed nightmare this week in the Soviet Union.

Apparently some "chemical explosion" triggered a core meltdown at the Chernobyl power plant. Temperatures in the plant reached 4,000 degrees.

The Soviets were silent, at first, then came reports that two had died, with 197 injured. Outsiders estimated the toll may already have reached 2,000.

A ham radio operator in the Netherlands said he had intercepted a call in broken English from a radio operator within the Soviet Union which reported:

● "Many hundreds dead and wounded."

● "We heard heavy explosions ... you can't imagine what's happening here with all the death and fire."

● "Thousands and thousands of people are moving, taking their children and cattle to the south."

● "I heard many dead can't be removed because of the radiation."

Concern spread around the world like the radioactive cloud of dust from the accident.

In Austria, environmental officials advised parents to keep infants indoors, and a specially chartered flight sped to Shlobin, about 100 miles west of the reactor, to evacuate relatives of Austrian steel specialists.

In Poland, the government banned the sale of milk from grass-fed cows and ordered all children to receive iodine solutions at schools and health clinics.

In Sweden, authorities advised people in coastal areas not to drink rainwater and banned the importation of fresh meat, fish and vegetables from the Soviet Union and East bloc countries.

The Greenpeace environmental group said the disaster could cause up to 10,000 cases of cancer in the Soviet Union and up to 4,000 in Sweden over the next few decades.

The group estimated that agriculture would be affected in a 4,000 square mile area around the plant, and farming there was unlikely for several decades.

There are lessons in this.

The first is that this meltdown is a mote in a gnat's eye compared to the consequences of a nuclear war. We must negotiate nuclear weapons reductions — with adequate inspection provisions — so the fate of mankind no longer hangs on a red button.

The second is that we are fortunate to live in America. This week, there was an accident at Exxon refinery. The accident was minuscule in comparison to the Soviet meltdown, but the company, government officials and the media all worked to explain the cause, the correction, and the consequences for Billings residents.

In contrast, a ham radio operator in the Ukraine pleaded for answers from the outside world because his leaders tell him nothing while he watches his countrymen die.

Reality brushed nightmare this week in the Soviet Union.

Minneapolis Star and Tribune

Minneapolis, MN, May 2, 1986

The Des Moines Register

Des Moines, IA, May 3, 1986

The fires of Chernobyl have raised disturbing questions for Americans mindful of some near disasters of our own, presumably safer, nuclear-power plants. Although nuclear power supplies only 13.5 percent of our electricity, the United States has more operating plants — 96 — than any other nation.

The utility companies repeatedly assure the public that the plants are safe; there hasn't been a single radiation death at a commercial nuclear plant in this country. But while the nuclear industry is long on assurance, it is woefully short on insurance.

In case of a disaster, federal law provides that liability is limited to the amount of insurance available, and that now comes to $640 million — $160 million provided by private insurers, plus retroactive assessments of $5 million per operating reactor in case of an accident. If damage claims exceed that amount, according to the law, "Congress will thoroughly review the particular incident and will take whatever action is deemed necessary and appropriate."

A 1982 study by the Sandia National Laboratory said that damages from a worst-case accident involving the Indian Point nuclear plant north of New York City could exceed $300 billion. But under the law, the victims or the taxpayers would foot almost all of the bill. The utilities would pay only a tiny fraction of the damages.

The liability limit was established under the Price-Anderson Act of 1957 because insurance actuaries had no experience upon which to estimate risks and set rates.

Today they have a better fix on the risks. But they still won't write policies to cover realistic damage potential, and the utilities won't operate nuclear plants without the protection of Price-Anderson. So the "temporary" limit, adopted in expectation that it would be needed just long enough to get the industry off the ground, remains in effect almost 30 years later.

Price-Anderson is up for its third renewal. The first two times Congress extended the act, it drew almost no public attention. But in the wake of Chernobyl, the public may indeed question whether victims and taxpayers should bear the risk of a nuclear disaster while those responsible are held only minimally liable.

Chernobyl is labeled "the worst nuclear disaster ever," but who knows what that means? Were two people killed or 2,000? Is the accident so grave that countless Soviet citizens will die in years to come from radiation illness? Or is it merely a mishap, remarkable mainly because no real nuclear disaster has ever occurred?

It could be either; it could be neither. The point is that beyond the Soviet hierarchy, the world's people don't really know and may never know. But they deserve to know. Chernobyl reinforces the truth that humans are a family and the Earth is our house. We have responsibilities to one another that transcend the rooms in that house or conflicts with brothers and sisters. Yet at Chernobyl, the Soviets behaved like the child who realized, halfway through the movie, that he'd left the bathtub filling at home, then kept silent for fear of punishment.

Mikhail Gorbachev made much of his desire for openness in Soviet society and of his campaign to prove the Soviet Union a trustworthy neighbor. But when the chips were melting down, the wall reappeared. Traditional Russian insecurity reasserted itself. Fear of internal dissent and external criticism proved more powerful than the requirement to notify other nations promptly, more powerful than the right of Soviet citizens to be informed. As Flora Lewis points out in a column on this page, it probably was no coincidence that the Soviets turned up a one-time U.S. employee Monday — after the accident but before it became a major story — to denounce Radio Liberty. Within the day, Radio Liberty would become an important source of information on Chernobyl for Soviet citizens.

Now the Soviets are lashing back at what they say are wild rumors circulating in the West of death and destruction at Chernobyl. They seem to find in those rumors confirmation of their vision of a world waiting to pounce on Soviet weakness or failure. That is the wrong lesson. The proper antidote for rumors is more information, not less. Political paranoia and secrecy cannot remove the international black eye the Soviet Union has received at Chernobyl; they only inflame it. If the Soviets learn anything from this episode, let them learn that their nuclear accident could have earned them international sympathy and understanding; that their foolish attempts to contain the news have earned them international scorn.

St. Petersburg Times

St. Petersburg, FL, May 13, 1986

One of the seemingly obvious lessons of Chernobyl is that the four most dangerous words in any language are "it can't happen here." It's what the Russians must have said after Three Mile Island, or Chernobyl would not be the result. Nonetheless, the U.S. nuclear power industry continues to insist that what happened at Chernobyl can't happen here.

But if not, why does federal law strictly limit the industry's liability in the event of just such an accident? Why is there currently a sharp debate in Congress on how much to increase that limit, which is at present a plainly inadequate $640-million?

The reason, of course, is that utility investors and insurance underwriters measure the risk by the cold light of logic, which tells them that there is no such thing under the sun as a guarantee of perfect safety. Technology can fail. Human error can occur. There have been more than a dozen serious accidents in the United States, as recently as one in Ohio last year that threatened to replicate Three Mile Island. The Brown's Ferry reactor at Decatur, Ala., was imperiled in 1975 because a technician using a candle to check for air leaks started a fire that burned out the electrical controls for many of the safety systems. The thought of a candle nearly destroying a nuclear plant should have cured the industry of its hubris, but it did not.

By wild coincidence, the Chernobyl accident occurred two days after two congressional committees acted to increase liability limits applied under the Price-Anderson Act, first enacted in 1957. In setting the limit, originally $500-million, Congress acknowledged that nuclear power would not be feasible if the utility industry had to bear all the potential risk. Today, there is no denying that even $640-million is ridiculously low, but only two days before Chernobyl the Senate Energy and Natural Resources Committee voted 19-1 that $2.4-billion would be enough. That same day, the House Interior and Insular Affairs Committee voted 21-20 to set the limit at $8.2-billion, which outraged the nuclear power industry and prompted a walkout by Republican members to prevent final action on the bill. It is still uncertain, even after Chernobyl, whether Chairman Morris Udall, D-Ariz., has the votes to

retain the higher limit. No further action is expected before May 21.

In the event of a major accident, the U.S. government would pay the damages up to the limit, less private conventional insurance coverage, and recover the money from after-the-fact assessments on all nuclear utilities. Each would be liable to only $20-million under the Senate bill, but to $80-million under the House version.

The utilities complain that the higher limits would ruin them. But $8.2-billion can hardly be called excessive, given the example of the vast tangible damage and the harm yet to be measured that Chernobyl has inflicted. In the United States, there are operating nuclear reactors within a few miles of major population centers. What would be the costs, in evacuation expenses alone, if an accident on the scale of Chernobyl occurred near Miami, New York or Detroit?

Such an accident may be unlikely here, considering that U.S. commercial nuclear power reactors use a different design and are required (unlike the government's own reactors) to have containment structures like that which served its purpose at Three Mile Island. But to say it is unlikely is to beg the question of whether it is impossible.

The United States now has 101 operating reactors, according to the International Atomic Energy Agency, slightly more than a fourth of all those in the world. Nuclear power will not be disinvented, nor should it be. It offers an abundant source of relatively cheap energy which, waste storage problems aside, is also theoretically nonpolluting. What the debate over the Price-Anderson Act points out is that nuclear energy would not be so cheap if it had to shoulder a more realistic burden of potential liability. The Price-Anderson Act is a subsidy in every respect. A higher limit means that nuclear power will cost its customers more and save them less compared to oil, coal and other sources. But it also means that it will save them less compared to energy conservation and to the potential benefits of solar and renewable energy, which have been sadly neglected of late.

Nuclear power is here to stay, but the time has come to put the true costs on the table.

THE LINCOLN STAR
Lincoln, NE, May 10, 1986

The Chernobyl nuclear plant disaster will serve as a valuable laboratory in the study of radiation effects upon human beings. That is not to diminish the tragedy of lost lives, but simply to recognize the reality of the situation.

Even if the deaths from radiation exposure are now at the low level claimed by the Soviet Union, the amount of contamination is unknown and could be far reaching.

Editorial Research Reports speculates that millions of people could suffer in the years ahead from the effects of radioactive materials deposited on the land and in the water of parts of the Soviet Union and other European countries.

The report describes the Soviet case as the most serious nuclear accident in history. It cites nuclear experts who believe radiation levels will lead to higher death rates from cancer and other diseases and probably greater problems with birth defects caused by genetic mutations.

As the human toll of Chernobyl's accident grows, perhaps the reality of all nuclear matters will sink more deeply into the world's consciousness. It is an unwanted analytical process that has been provided the world but the only thing left to do with it is to learn whatever lessons it teaches.

As is typical of people, the world has more or less resigned itself to the presence of nuclear energy. The world has come to live with something it has seemed unable to do anything about.

But before this latest Soviet nuclear accident has run its full course, the world is very likely to gain a new appreciation of the horrors of uncontrolled nuclear power. The greatest threat, of course, is that of nuclear warfare.

Should any nation ever resort to the use of nuclear weapons, the consequences would make Chernobyl look like a Sunday school picnic. Nuclear power may offer a great danger of radiation accident but nuclear weapons offer a level of human suffering of unequalled immensity.

Without a continuing awareness and appreciation of the awesome nature of such weapons, the possibility of their use is greater.

The disaster in the Soviet Union is a tragedy but it should serve as a long standing warning of the fragile hold we have on life in the nuclear environment in which we live.

SYRACUSE
HERALD-JOURNAL
Syracuse, NY, May 1, 1986

While we've been distracted this week by the nuclear plant disaster in the Soviet Union, there have been a number of significant developments in our own latest case of technology gone awry — the explosion of the space shuttle Challenger.

After months of confusion since the Jan. 28 tragedy — in which seven astronauts were killed — the U.S. space program is finally starting to return to a sense of normalcy. Cape Canaveral today was to see its first launch since Challenger — an unmanned weather satellite aboard a three-stage Delta rocket. And the National Commission on Space is about to recommend to President Reagan an ambitious plan for manned space flight well into the 21st century.

Not that the Challenger episode has passed. The ugly reminders will be with us for the forseeable future. Seven flag-draped coffins were taken to Dover Air Force Base in Delaware this week, where the remains of Challenger's crew were to be prepared for burial. And new test results show that the accident was inevitable, largely due to fundamental flaws in the design of the craft that were exacerbated by cold temperatures on the morning of launch.

▽   ▽

Parallels between the two disasters, half a world away from each other, are striking. It was not really the technology that failed. Technology is neutral — bound by the laws of science and incapable of acting outside them.

The failure, instead, lies with humans who expected too much of technology, who neglected to consider all the contingencies, who smugly discounted the risks.

Before the meltdown at the plant near Kiev, Soviet engineers insisted there was no need to enclose the reactor in elaborate and costly containment facilities. The chances of an accident were so remote, they calculated, such a precaution involved unnecessary trouble and expense. Obviously, they were wrong, and that miscalculation reportedly has cost thousands of lives so far, with incalculable long-term consequences.

So it was with Challenger. We now know that the disaster was not merely bad luck, that it was bound to happen sooner or later because the techology was inadequate to perform what was asked of it. We believed those who told us it was safe. They were wrong, and we feel betrayed.

Are there other technological disasters waiting to happen? Of course. They don't have the dramatic effect of a nuclear meltdown or a spacecraft explosion, but they're everywhere. We read about them every day — asbestos, the Dalkon Shield, PCBs, Pinto gas tanks — developments touted as improvements in our quality of life that are only later unmasked as threats.

▽   ▽

This is not to say all technology is bad, but neither is it benevolent. It is a tiger that requires a sturdy cage or it will revert to nature and bite us when our back is turned. It punishes complacency. We can remain its masters only through conscientious effort.

That effort cannot be left solely to the technologists. It is incumbent upon all of us who enjoy technology's benefits to raise questions about its safety and demand real answers — not merely reassurances — before it is allowed to go forward. We can't allow ourselves to be anesthetized by vague advice to "let the experts handle it," or intimidated by patronizing claims that "it's too complicated for the layman to understand."

Laymen bear the consequences of taking too much for granted in technology. And as has been dramatically demonstrated twice this year, those consequences can be catastrophic.

Los Angeles Times
Los Angeles, CA, May 1, 1986

The automatic response of spokesmen for the U.S. nuclear industry to the Soviet nuclear disaster is to say that it couldn't happen here. They may be right—although nobody will really know until and unless the details of the Chernobyl accident are available. However, anybody who really believes that the Soviet disaster is irrelevant to the American nuclear program is mistaken.

It is true that the ill-fated Soviet reactor was of a fundamentally different design than the water-cooled and moderated reactors that are used in commercial nuclear power plants in this country. More important, it is probably true that the catastrophic release of radioactivity from the Soviet plant wouldn't have occurred if the reactor had been enclosed in a containment structure like those that the Nuclear Regulatory Commission requires of all U.S. commercial reactors. Without such a containment structure to bottle up escaping radioactivity, the Three Mile Island accident in this country seven years ago would have had far, far worse consequences.

The fact is, however, that the U.S. government operates five reactors—at Hanford, Wash., and Savannah River, S.C.—that produce nuclear weapons material, are not subject to all the regulations that apply to commercial power reactors, and do not have containment structures. Congress should insist on an immediate review to determine if these plants should be shut down.

As for commercial reactors, the disaster in the Ukraine is a useful reminder that nuclear power is not inherently safe but inherently dangerous. When nuclear power enthusiasts tell us that there isn't a chance in a million of a catastrophic accident at a given site, that is not entirely reassuring. Any system devised by human beings can fail. What makes nuclear accidents unique is that, when they do occur, the cost in lives and public health can be so enormous and long-lasting.

It is a little unsettling, with the benefit of hindsight, to read that a Soviet official once told the governor of Pennsylvania that Soviet reactors were so safe that one could be built in Red Square without danger to the populace.

A Soviet magazine recently carried an article on the Chernobyl complex itself in which an engineer boasted that working at the plant "is safer than driving a car."

At the very least the Reagan Administration should back off from proposals to make federal regulation of nuclear power plants less stringent. But a more fundamental rethinking is also in order.

In the absence of a determined, well-funded program to develop alternative energy sources as a hedge against declining reserves of oil and gas, it may not be practical to close all U.S. nuclear power plants as demanded by Ralph Nader, Helen Caldicott and other nuclear activisits. However, the handwriting may already be on the wall—for both safety reasons and the diminishing economic feasibility of nuclear power.

Austrians voted in 1978 not to turn on a newly built reactor. The Danish parliament last year shelved plans to build nuclear plants. And Sweden, a world leader in nuclear technology, is planning to phase out its 12 reactors early in the next century. When you consider that no new construction of power reactors has been initiated in America for several years, it is obvious that we may be following a de facto phase-out policy ourselves.

It may not be a bad thing.

FORT WORTH STAR-TELEGRAM

Fort Worth, TX, May 2, 1986

Call it an awakening.

Everyone everywhere with an ounce of human compassion should lament the loss of life and the injuries associated with the nuclear tragedy that has occurred in the Ukrainian Republic of the Soviet Union.

It is in that spirit, although it may be interpreted otherwise by Soviet officialdom, that the United States has offered to assist the Soviet Union in containing the disaster.

That offer also is predicated upon the unassailable evidence that when it comes to nuclear radiation, no country, no continent, indeed, no island is an island. The radiation that has spewed from the burning Soviet nuclear reactor at Chernobyl near Kiev poses a health threat to much of the Soviet Union, to parts of Europe and perhaps even to parts of the United States.

This worst accident ever at a nuclear power plant sends a double-barreled message that cannot be ignored.

One part of that message is that the dangers associated with nuclear power plants must never be underestimated. The Soviets have paid dearly, for example, for not enclosing all of their nuclear reactors in containment buildings.

Had they done so, the dimensions of the Chernobyl accident might not have been nearly so bad. But, from their way of thinking, such an accident was not supposed to happen.

The tragedy gives added credence to the nuclear power critics in this country, whose opposition has caused prolonged delays in the construction of nuclear power plants and has driven up the cost of such facilities enormously.

They are now fully justified in saying, "We told you so," and in pointing out that the increased costs and the long delays are justifiable if they reduce the risk of a Chernobyl at, for example, Comanche Peak.

The other part of the message pertains to nuclear arms. The disaster at Chernobyl, for all the damage it has done and all the human suffering it has caused and will continue to cause, pales into insignificance when compared to what the effects would be of even a limited nuclear exchange between the superpowers.

This terrible accident, then, should be viewed by those whose decisions could determine the fate of human civilization as a sign that it is time to take serious action to reduce the nuclear peril that hovers ominously over this planet and threatens to rain ultimate destruction.

If the Chernobyl tragedy provides a spark that starts productive nuclear arms reduction negotiations at Geneva, then it may even prove to be a horribly disguised blessing.

THE DAILY OKLAHOMAN

Oklahoma, OK, May 1, 1986

WHAT we don't yet know about the extent of the Soviet nuclear accident far exceeds what we do know. But that hasn't deterred extremist speculation, aided by media sensationalism, about the disaster.

Indeed, given the xenophobic closed-door policy of the Soviets, we may never know the full story of what happened at Chernobyl — the number of casualties and the amount of resulting environmental contamination.

There was the predictable comparison by commentators with the 1979 shutdown at Three Mile Island, the only U.S. mishap in more than a quarter-century of nuclear generation. But that's the old apples and oranges game.

Nobody was injured at TMI, and the limited release of radiation did not threaten public health or safety.

If there was in fact a reactor core meltdown at Chernobyl — which some eminent nuclear experts doubt — it would truly be a calamity for the Soviet Union. Pollution of soil and water could turn the entire area into a wasteland for decades, and radiation casualties could be heavy.

Will this first major recorded accident cause a further slowdown in the already crippled U.S. nuclear power industry? Quite likely. Will it have a similar effect abroad? Probably not.

More than 370 atomic power stations are operating throughout the world. And energy-short nations like Japan, France, Germany and the Republic of China are heavily committed to uranium as their electricity source for the future.

If nothing else, the Russian accident will bring strong external and internal pressure on Gorbachev & Co. to cooperate with other nations in limiting the risks inherent in what has become an interdependent high-technology society.

The Philadelphia Inquirer

Philadelphia, PA, May 2, 1986

Nuclear safety is not a domestic issue, as the events of the past days have demonstrated. It is one of enormous international consequence. Radiation respects no borders. The most stringent standards applied in one nation are meaningless if a neighbor sacrifices safety for expediency or over-confidence. That is what the Soviets have done, jeopardizing the well-being not only of their citizens but of the residents of Europe.

Twenty-five nations around the world have nuclear power plants. By 1990, six additional countries will have operating reactors. While construction of new reactors has slowed or stopped completely in many industrialized nations, reliance on atomic energy is growing in the Third World. Ten Third World nations have reactors; by 1990 that number will grow to 15.

By all accounts, many of these nations have embraced the technology but not stringent safety controls or regulatory oversight.

According to a classified study released Wednesday by Sen. John Glenn (D., Ohio), there have been 151 "significant safety incidents" at nuclear plants around the world since 1971. That is not a comprehensive list; no reports were filed by Eastern bloc nations, including the Soviet Union.

Among the nations with the greatest commitment to boost nuclear generating capacity is the U.S.S.R. The Soviets have doubled their capacity since 1980 — they now have 45 reactors — and plan to double that number again by 1990.

The few Western experts who have been permitted to examine Soviet reactors, or profess knowledge of their program, have asserted that safety has been foresaken in the haste to expand. Approximately half of the 45 Soviet reactors are not surrounded by containment buildings which might seal in radiation in the event of an accident such as the one that occurred at the Chernobyl plant. Such a safety feature was regarded by the Soviets as "a waste of money," according to one U.S. expert on Soviet nuclear operations.

Fifty-six nations, including the Soviet Union, are members of the International Atomic Energy Agency, a 30-year-old United Nations organization that has concentrated its efforts on limiting the spread of nuclear weapons. Yet one of its mandates was to set standards and rules for the safe generation of nuclear energy and to oversee the adherence to those standards.

That mandate never has been fulfilled because there never has been an accident like Chernobyl. Now that the world has seen the potential consequences of such an incident, there can be no doubts about the need for international controls and inspections.

It won't be a simple task. The Soviets, who have failed thus far to acknowledge the magnitude of the accident, hardly can be expected to reverse their longtime policy of secrecy. The Reagan administration says it won't try to persuade the Soviets to change and won't promote any international control program under way. Both are wrong. They are only guaranteeing that sooner or later the world will be endangered by another disastrous nuclear accident.

The Detroit News

Detroit, MI, May 4, 1986

The meltdown of the Soviet reactor at Chernobyl has produced three kinds of fallout: 1) the standard-issue radioactive fallout; 2) fallout from anti-nuke groups across the globe; and 3) economic fallout within the Soviet Union. The first kind seems to have abated for the most part, although it could cause considerable damage to the Soviet Union and some of its near neighbors. The other two, however, could produce more lasting damage.

Here in the United States, a vast array of anti-nuclear and anti-technology groups have issued grave warnings that what happened in Chernobyl easily could happen here. The World Council of Churches issued a gravid letter from Geneva, hinting darkly at the dangers of nuclear energy. Closer to home, the usual band of Luddites has asked state officials to consider closing down all the nuclear plants in the state, presumably to replace them with fossil-fuel plants that offer even more immediate pollution problems.

The Safe Energy Coalition of Michigan, for instance, asked the governor to close all of Michigan's nuclear plants, pronto. Mary Johnston of the coalition argued that "Nuclear power plants . . . represent an unacceptable risk to human health and safety and are a threat to the Great Lakes, the largest body of fresh water in the world." She then cited a Sandia National Laboratories study that provided some hoary worst-case scenarios for a nuclear accident in the state: 8,000 early radiation-induced deaths, 340,000 peak-early injuries, and 13,000 cancer deaths at a cost of $136 billion, not including health care, on-site or litigation costs for the people who live within 70 miles of the Fermi 2 nuclear plant.

These are garbage statistics, as are most worst-case numbers, because they rely on a host of untenable assumptions. The equivalent worst-case assumption for deaths related to products used to unclog drains, for instance, might be that millions of people would die each year from mistakenly drinking the liquids or eating the crystals.

The real core of the anti-nuclear hysteria after Chernobyl is a deep suspicion of all new technology, especially that which relies on the atom. This is partly understandable. Scientists don't understand radiation all that well, except to know that too much can kill. But the nuclear industry in America is perhaps the safest industry of all, due in part to the strenuous efforts of environmental groups to legislate extensive safety regulations. Yet, as we argued several days ago, the American nuclear industry bears no significant relation to the Soviet nuclear industry. Our industry must withstand incredible scrutiny, and excessive review, while the Soviet system answers only to the strategic whims of the old men in the Soviet Politburo.

The real question about the future of nuclear energy in America is whether we should continue building nuclear plants. The answer is "yes." Although no technology is risk-free, the nuclear industry has struggled to become as risk-free as possible, and to a large extent has succeeded. But the larger point is that we can never have a risk-free society, and never should. American society depends on the constant expansion of knowledge. The marketplace is, in a real sense, the ultimate forum for ideas. Whoever gets an idea to build a better mousetrap can test that brainstorm in the marketplace. The same goes for everything from electric can openers to nuclear power plants.

Every innovation bears a risk; someone can misuse a product and get hurt. But ultimately, the prudent expansion of knowledge produces a society richer in possibilities, while attempts to "manage" innovation merely mire nations in backwardness and repression. The Soviets should understand this. They have tried for years to manage economic growth — through the promulgation of five-year plans and the use of the secret police — and have been rewarded with a sputtering economy and a vodka-sotted workforce.

Although anti-nuke activists are right in saying that we should not blunder recklessly into new realms of technology and think carefully about shutting down obsolete and possibly dangerous facilities, America has met both those conditions.

THE  SUN

Baltimore, MD, May 1, 1986

The worst of the fire seems to be out at Chernobyl. Soviet officials, stung by Western criticism, have invited the U.N. International Atomic Energy Agency and Western doctors to help assess the disaster. The fire in this country is just beginning.

What will happen to nuclear energy here when the full extent of the disaster is known? The Soviets acknowledge that a zone of life-threatening radiation surrounds Chernobyl's reactor, that 84,000 people were evacuated, and that four people are dead and 200 suffered radiation poisoning. Will the public fear of an insidious, killer contamination spreading through the environment put an end to the atomic age?

That cannot be allowed to happen.

This country needs nuclear power. Texas oil fields, which once made the United States a net energy exporter, now provide only 28 percent of our oil, and almost a third is imported. The Alaskan oil bounty, once the hope for energy independence, has passed its peak. Not every utility and large industrial user can burn coal, even with new pollution controls. Coal brings its own environmental hazards and some plants are too far from the fields, can't dispose of fly ash in an environmentally acceptable way, or simply require other energy sources.

France, which has little coal and no oil, gets 65 percent of its electricity from the atom. Japan, the only country to feel the devastation of nuclear weapons in war, continues to operate nuclear plants and to build new ones. In the United States, 99 commercial plants produce 13 to 15 percent of the electricity. Even if no new reactors are ordered, 30 plants already being built ensure that nuclear power will continue to have a role here.

Large industries, using complex technologies and handling substances whose toxicity our grandfathers could not have imagined, pose inherently greater dangers to public health. They also have brought the average citizen a standard of living once reserved for kings. So they will remain, requiring the best possible means to limit their hazards. Thus, safety must be re-evaluated at Department of Energy reactors not protected by containment shells, and at Tennessee Valley Authority plants not meeting commercial standards. Thus, congressional efforts to weaken safety standards and limit operators' liability for injuries caused must not succeed.

Something good can come from Chernobyl: better information-sharing among nations; increased attention to evacuation plans, safety systems and regulation everywhere, and a sober recognition that the hazards of a technological society must be weighed even while counting the benefits.

The Des Moines Register

Des Moines, IA, May 12, 1986

Nuclear power plants generate 13.5 percent of the electricity used in this country, and the nation leads the world in the number of plants. But the industry is in big trouble. Enthusiasm for it exceeded expertise, performance never lived up to promise, and industry expansion has all but ended. There hasn't been an order placed for a new plant in the United States since 1978.

"The technological and economic design of nuclear power has been the biggest failure of any civilian industry in history," is the way economists Caroline and Richard Hellman of the University of Rhode Island put it in an article in The Wall Street Journal.

The industry likes to blame its problems on government regulation that results, it says, from excessive concern for safety. And it has an ally in the Reagan administration. Reagan, says his energy secretary, John Herrington, is "irrevocably committed" to nuclear power.

Herrington told the Atomic Industrial Forum last November:

"Unwarranted public fears about the safety of nuclear power certainly add to the regulation and litigation which has hamstrung nuclear power in this country. A genuine problem — the incident at Three Mile Island, for example — is magnified and feeds the public perception of nuclear power as too risky. . . ."

The industry must share responsibility for its problems, Herrington said, although it is "tempting to lay responsibility . . . on government regulators, overzealous environmentalists and an overly fearful public. . . ."

Overly fearful?

Tell it to those living downwind of the burning Chernobyl nuclear plant near Kiev. Ask the relatives of the victims whether they wish some "overzealous environmentalists" had had a voice in establishing safety standards for Soviet reactors.

One of the virtues of a free society is that industry and government are precluded from ignoring concerns for human welfare. That's why American standards for the safety of nuclear plants exceed those in the Soviet Union.

The most rigid of standards can't provide an absolute assurance of safety. But they lengthen the odds against disaster.

St. Louis ⚜ Review

St. Louis, MO, May 9, 1986

The Soviet nuclear accident at Chernobyl has produced much more than the radioactive fallout which has contaminated USSR and neighboring territories.

The very first concern, of course, is the well-being of Soviet and other citizens affected by the nuclear accident. It is clear that the international community stands ready to provide technical and medical assistance as required. It is a mark of the overriding international spirit of cooperation in the face of disaster that an American surgeon is among those assisting the victims by performing bone-marrow transplants. Our compassion and our prayers for the victims of tragedy must know no natonal or ideological borders.

The need to fulfill responsibilities to the international community by sharing detailed information about nuclear accidents in a timely fashion is a clear conclusion from this incident. The USSR failed to live up to its clear obligations by delaying announcement of the accident for two days.

The reluctance of the USSR to provide information will undoubtedly complicate efforts to arrive at nuclear weapons treaties. The need to verify nuclear weapons reduction and the track record of credibility of the USSR will be important factors in arriving at arms reductions treaties. On the other hand, the tragic accident may impel the USSR to deal realistically with the nuclear peril which is a common danger for all nations.

In our own country as elsewhere there will be renewed studies of the benefits and hazards of nuclear power plants. At the dawn of the nuclear age, we were told that nuclear power would be generated so inexpensively that it would be too cheap to monitor. The actual cost of nuclear generators belies this rosy prediction. The question of how to dispose of the radioactive waste from nuclear generators has not as yet been resolved. The storage of these dangerous materials can hardly be maintained indefinitely. Questions of environmental impact are common problems for all the nations of the world. As the Vatican newspaper L'Osservatore Romano stated, the whole incident illustrates the need for a system of international consultation and controls on atomic energy.

ASK NOT FOR WHOM THE REACTOR TOLLS; IT TOLLS FOR THEE.

the Charleston Gazette

Charleston, WV, May 1, 1986

RADIATION spewing from the burning Kiev nuclear power plant, spreading to Poland and Scandinavia — perhaps even to America — underscores what Wendell Willkie preached four decades ago: the security of all peoples around the globe is intertwined; everyone shares one world.

At the moment it's impossible to predict the death toll in the Ukraine, Poland, anywhere — not solely because of Soviet secrecy but also because some radiation effects don't show up for years. Great Britain still is attempting to count cancer deaths attributable to a minor meltdown decades ago.

The health menace spreading through the atmosphere knows no national boundaries. If one of America's nuclear power plants were to suffer a similar disaster, peril would be greatest for nearby residents and drifting radiation could sow seeds of cancer around the world. Each nation's risk is shared by all nations.

Consequently, concealing nuclear problems affronts humanity. The Kiev crisis began late last week, yet the Soviets didn't reveal it until abnormal radioactivity was detected Monday in Scandinavia. The British likewise hid their meltdown years ago. Worse, despite the lesson that should have been learned from this catastrophe, the worldwide nuclear industry still operates in maximum secrecy.

This secrecy is justified on the ground that nuclear disclosure could help renegade societies develop thermonuclear bombs. But safety matters mustn't be hidden. All nations with nuclear plants should share knowledge of precautions and emergency methods. For example, countries could cooperate in developing robots able to enter lethal radioactivity and extinguish fires.

U.S. authorities assure us that America's 101 civilian atomic plants are safe. The Nuclear Regulatory Commission mandates 3-foot-thick concrete-and-steel containment shells around reactors. In 1979's Three Mile Island accident the shell prevented vast amounts of radiation from escaping into the countryside. Just a microscopic dose was loosed in water at the start of the mishap. If U.S. shells can hold an explosion and fire of the Kiev magnitude, that's encouraging.

Several government-owned U.S. reactors used in bomb production have no containment structures. Experts say they aren't needed, as these reactors operate at lower temperatures. Experts, alas, are correct until the impossible occurs.

West Virginia's Farmington tragedy triggered a revolution in coal mine safety. The Soviet Union's nuclear calamity ought to convince all nations to make nuclear safety a priority cooperative international venture.

WORCESTER TELEGRAM
Worcester, MA, May 9, 1986

The Chernobyl nuclear disaster arrived at a tricky time for the New England power industry.

After 13 years of controversy and stop-and-go construction, the $4.5 billion nuclear plant at Seabrook, N.H., will be completed next fall and ready for licensing. A few weeks ago, that licensing seemed likely — and with it the assurance that New England would have adequate electric power until at least 1993. Now Chernobyl has raised a new wave of concern about the safety of nuclear plants and the adequacy of plans for evacuation of nearby residents in case of an accident.

Utility executives insist that a new American plant like Seabrook is infinitely safer than the typical Soviet plant. They note that American plants rely on water, not flammable graphite, to control the reaction. What's more, Seabrook, unlike Chernobyl, has a double-walled containment building to stop the release of radiation. The first concrete wall, 4½-feet thick, is reinforced with arm-thick steel rods. It is surrounded by a second concrete wall 15 inches thick.

Even so, critics of nuclear power point out, the 1979 accident at Three Mile Island in Pennsylvania was only the most serious of a number of mishaps in American nuclear plants. They point to operator errors and equipment malfunctions at plants in Ohio, southern California and Sacramento within just the past year.

Proponents of nuclear power reply that none of those mishaps had serious consequences. They say this proves that the American back-up systems and containment can be depended upon to prevent disaster. They note that 101 nuclear plants have been in operation in the United States for periods up to 26 years and nobody has yet died because of a mishap at any one of them.

The safety issues bear sober reconsideration in light of Chernobyl. So do evacuation plans. Gov. Michael S. Dukakis is right in his cautious approach in approving the plans for Massachusetts communities near Seabrook.

The aim should be to make Seabrook safe, however, not to prevent its completion and licensing. New England needs the power Seabrook can produce. Lacking its 6-percent contribution to the regional power pool, utility executives estimate that the region will face brownouts by 1991.

About 10 percent of New England power will come from Quebec hydro facilities by then. It might be possible to bring in even more power from Canada and make up for the loss of Seabrook, but utility executives say the cost to electric customers would be formidable. On top of the cost of the extra hydro power, they would still have to pay the $4.5 billion for an inoperable Seabrook plant. There would have to be steep rate boosts.

Ironically, those rate boosts would not free New Englanders of the risks associated with nuclear power. Eight nuclear plants are already operating in New England. They generate 28 percent of the region's power. Replacing all these plants would take years. The cost would be enormous — for nuclear power generation is comparatively cheap once the huge capital investment has been made to build the plants. And the many new coal or oil plants that would have to be built to do the job would raise the level of acid rain, in the case of coal, and increase U.S. reliance on costly and uncertain imports, in the case of oil.

The Chernobyl disaster may turn out to be a blessing in a sense. It seems likely to turn the attention of the American power industry and its regulators to the need for even greater safety precautions than are now in place. That's good. But American power companies have invested $180 billion in nuclear plants — far too much to allow serious consideration of abandonment of those plants.

Now that the plants — including Seabrook — have been built, we simply can't afford to close them. There is only one sensible thing to do. We must spare no effort to make sure that these plants are managed and maintained properly and that the risks are constantly kept to an absolute minimum.

The Record
Hackensack, NJ, May 1, 1986

Core meltdown: The two words pulse with horror. We know something about it already.

Three Mile Island, where meltdown was narrowly averted in 1979, taught us what that could mean: a nuclear reactor out of control, runaway fuel-cell temperatures, radioactive particles spewed into the atmosphere — and God knows what health consequences down the road. Three Mile Island showed the vulnerability of populations downwind of a meltdown and the unyielding duty of utilities and governments to protect them.

Three Mile Island taught us other things: the critical importance of effective emergency training for power-plant employees; the value of solidly built facilities to contain tainted air, water, or steam from radioactive escape; and the clear mandate to err on the side of caution in building and operating nuclear power plants.

But Three Mile Island could not prepare us for the catastrophe in the Soviet Union and the paranoid response of the totalitarian regime. The first maps showed a broad plume laden with isotopes of cesium and iodine, spreading from Chernobyl in the Ukraine northwest across Russia's Baltic neighbors and then over the North Pole to the American West Coast. Wind changes sent the fallout back over the Soviet Union. The winds will change again, dropping their burden at random around the globe.

Scientists in the United States and Europe estimate, on the basis of incomplete information, that a few hundred miles from Chernobyl, the hazards to human health are small. The highest level of radiation reported in Finland was five times that occurring in nature. Emergency responses — staying indoors or evacuating — aren't ordered until the level reaches 50 times normal.

The danger is less frightening than the uncertainty. The striking thing is how little we have learned about the meltdown since it began — possibly a week ago. The Russians acknowledged the disaster only after Scandanavian monitors disclosed sharply elevated radiation levels — a clue to physicists everywhere that a meltdown had occurred. The rest of the world — along with the Russian people — are still in the dark, despite their compelling need to know.

The Soviets' close neighbors are properly angry that they were not warned immediately, so that they could judge whether to evacuate people in the path of the plume. We hardly dare trust what little the Soviets choose to tell us. They admit to two deaths, while rumors postulate hundreds. In our alarm, it becomes clear to us that the inhibitions and restrictions of a closed society override any sense of duty that that society has toward those on whom it has (albeit inadvertently) imposed a grave hazard. Secrecy and face saving come first, decent concern for fellow human beings second.

In trade journals, Russians have called the Chernobyl model one of their safest. But until very recently, they've shown little concern for safety. They have never built the containment structures designed, in other industrial nations, to protect neighboring populations from the fallout of nuclear accidents. Only recently has the Kremlin installed evacuation procedures in the event of radiation release.

Swedish officials called immediately for higher nuclear-safety standards in the Soviet Union — perhaps putting Russia's civilian nuclear installations under the control of the International Atomic Energy Ageny, a worldwide organization that polices nuclear plants to insure that atomic fuels are employed only for peaceful purposes. The Soviets agreed last year to permit agency inspection of two of its units. World opinion should move the Kremlin to open all nuclear generating stations to the agency at once.

Chernobyl also demands the establishment of an international hot line for instantaneous communication of nuclear-disaster details. Governments around the world need that information to decide how best to protect their citizens, in time to make such actions meaningful. The World Health Organization would be an appropriate site for such a warning system. The unloosed atom has shrunk the world to a village. The Kremlin is scurrying to hide, but there is no place to hide.

IAEA Conference Studies Chernobyl A-Plant Accident

A conference of nuclear power experts convened in Vienna Aug. 25, 1986 under the auspices of the International Atomic Energy Agency. The purpose of the symposium was a study of the causes and likely effects of the accident at the Chernobyl nuclear power plant in the Soviet Ukraine. (See pp. 52-59) The symposium was attended by 547 delegates from 45 nations.

Valery Legasov, the head of the Soviet delegation to the conference, spoke at length on the findings of a special Soviet commission that had studied the accident. While the report blamed the mishap on human error, Legasov surprised many delegates by admitting that RBMK (water-cooled graphite moderated) reactors, like the crippled Chernobyl No. 4 Unit, were vulnerable to blunders by technicians. "The defect in the system was that the designers did not foresee the awkward and silly actions by operators," Legasov told the participants. "The accident assumed catastrophic proportions. . .because all the negative aspects of the reactor design. . .were brought out by the operators."

Legasov conceded that the Soviet Union was late in recognizing the dangers inherent in the RBMK's design. That tardiness, he said, was "a great fault on our part."

Legasov revealed that over one-half of the U.S.S.R.'s 27 RBMK reactors would shut down for safety modifications. Many Western experts expressed doubts that the measures would greatly enhance the safety of the RBMKs. At a later press conference, reporters noted that Legasov had failed to address the key Western criticism of the RBMK, the lack of a containment vessel. He dismissed that point, saying "no containment can guard a system against an explosion process." Two experts, Dan Beninson of Argentina and Morris Rosen of the United States, told the conference Aug. 26 that, based on the Soviet report, as many as 24,000 people in the U.S.S.R. would die of cancer over the next 70 years as a result of the Chernobyl accident.

The Soviet Union Aug. 21 formally unveiled a 382-page report on the Chernobyl disaster. The report had been prepared by a special committee that concluded that the accident was the result of human error specifically stemming from an unauthorized test conducted by the operators of Chernobyl Unit No. 4.

THE ⟨SUN⟩ SUN
Baltimore, MD, August 25, 1986

Despite the Soviet Union's cynical attempt to turn its Chernobyl nuclear power plant disaster into a propaganda vehicle for its nuclear weapons diplomacy, some good may yet come out of catastrophe. The same Kremlin regime that first tried to suppress all information about the April 25-26 accident, even from neighbors endangered by radiation, is now advocating global early-warning systems and extolling "the fundamental necessity of deep international cooperation."

Today, in Vienna, the International Atomic Energy Agency is to hold a symposium on the Chernobyl affair in which the centerpiece will be a Soviet report that is remarkable for its openness and detail. While it places responsibility for the accident on operators who committed six egregious errors, it also describes a system whose designers completely ignored the human factor in plant breakdowns. The report's description of the past, present and future damage resulting from Chernobyl calls into question the basic technology of Soviet reactors, the training and accountability of their operators and the siting of multiple-reactor plants near population centers.

Soviet officials acknowledge that the Chernobyl accident has "hurt the nuclear program badly." But whose nuclear program? There is little evidence to date that the Soviet Union has fundamentally altered the pace or design of its nuclear energy development. But in the United States,

with its array of nuclear power critics in and out of Congress, Chernobyl already is having its effect on an industry still paralyzed by Three Mile Island. The House Energy Committee has approved a bill raising liability limits for a nuclear power accident to $6.5 billion — 10 times present limits. Utilities are pushing for a $2.5 billion limit, saying anything larger could bankrupt them.

Operator error was at fault both at Three Mile Island and at Chernobyl. But it was only at the latter facility that reactor failure and resulting explosions vented large amounts of radiation — more radiation, in fact, than was released to the atmosphere by the bombs that fell on Hiroshima and Nagasaki. Even if demonstrably better safety provisions in U.S. plants prove reassuring to the American public, the country is a long way from a new generation of nuclear power plants.

If Chernobyl leads to a much better exchange of information among nations and an early warning system, public confidence in nuclear power may gradually revive. But it will take time and perhaps a series of jolting oil shortages. In the meantime, the United States should offer the Soviet Union the help it will need as it proceeds with a post-Chernobyl clean-up that will take decades — decades that will chart the full extent of death and sickness and contamination and dislocation that Soviet authorities once tried to hide from the world — and themselves.

WORCESTER TELEGRAM
Worcester, MA
August 26, 1986

The Soviet Union now admits that the Chernobyl disaster crippled the Soviet nuclear power program and produced far more radioactive contamination in a much wider area than previously indicated and that many more people are apt to die as the result of the accident. But it is also increasingly evident that Moscow is trying to put the best possible face on this tragedy and make it serve Soviet foreign policy.

Mikhail Gorbachev and other Soviet leaders are portraying the Chernobyl disaster as a historic event and a telling lesson, not the embarrassing fiasco they at first tried to sweep aside. The point is advanced that the disaster tested the spirit of the Soviet people and the nation is emerging from the trauma stronger than ever. There are reminders that the explosion of the smallest nuclear warhead would equal three Chernobyls.

More to the point, Gorbachev has cleverly established a linkage between Chernobyl and arms control, stressing that the accident was an inkling of the dangers of nuclear war. He has repeatedly said that it would be pointless to hold a Soviet-U.S. summit meeting unless progress is made on disarmament. Should a summit materialize, the Soviets insist that it must focus on arms control only. Gorbachev is using Chernobyl to present the Soviet Union as a responsible country that, unlike the United States, is striving to rid the world of the nuclear menace.

The strategy is not without results. It has put the United States on the defensive; the Reagan administration has been responding to Soviet proposals lately, rather than the other way around. Because the world has not been accustomed to Soviet candor, the recently disclosed detailed assessment of the Chernobyl disaster has triggered another round of speculation about "openness" in Moscow.

Indeed, there is a lot to learn from Chernobyl, the worst commercial nuclear accident in history. It serves as a warning to designers and managers of nuclear power plants; it serves as a model of how not to handle a disaster. It is a reminder of how devastating even a tiny nuclear explosion can be, something scientists and arms-control negotiators know full well. But Chernobyl should not be viewed as a bargaining chip in international policy-making. That simply doesn't work.

Richmond Times-Dispatch

Richmond, VA, August 31, 1986

"A remarkable series of errors," said Kennedy Maize, a nuclear specialist with the Union for Concerned Scientists, "almost as if it were a comedy and the plant was run by the Marx Brothers." That's as good a description as any, at least for laymen, of the accident at Chernobyl. But nobody's laughing, least of all the philosophical descendants of Karl (not Groucho) Marx.

Having neglected immediately to inform the world of the worst commercial nuclear accident ever, Moscow has since been more forthcoming than usual — but more for self-serving than altruistic reasons, and hardly so forthcoming as necessary. The Soviets invited Western analysis and criticism; but as the cross-examination at the symposium convened by the International Atomic Energy Agency proceeded this past week, Moscow's receptiveness to outside scrutiny and opinion of Chernobyl specifically and its nuclear power program generally waned. Soviet scientists, rather than answer the few pointed questions presented to them, grilled Western scientists about Western programs instead. "I thought," said the U.S. permanent delegate to the IAEA, "the point was for us to find out about the Soviet program."

The details of Chernobyl the Soviets did reveal only raised more questions. Six "gross violations" of operating regulations, say the Soviets, ensured disaster. Human error compounded by haste, an "inadequate understanding" of the basics of nuclear power generation — the Soviet explanation seems understated.

To Western experts, it also seemed facile. And as the week went on, the West's kid gloves came partially off, forcing the Soviets' reluctant admission on several key points Moscow had previously denied: That flaws in the design of the reactor contributed significantly to the accident. That similar reactors elsewhere in the Soviet Union have been shut down pending design modifications Western scientists had recommended

a decade ago. That the Soviets' slowness to count design a contributing factor is "a great fault on our part."

Western experts worry still. The design of the Chernobyl reactor, and the Soviets' 18 others like it, seems inherently unstable: Modifications cannot, as a chief Soviet delegate to the conference claimed, "guarantee" no more Chernobyls. And for lack of adequate Soviet reports of the dispersal of radiation from Chernobyl, its fallout in human terms is still disputed, still unknown.

Lamenting Soviet stonewalling is not mere Soviet-bashing. The only possible plus to catastrophe is that it can be a learning experience. Learning causes and effects, divining how to avoid a repeat of this one, discovering how better to treat radiation victims and to deal with crop and other contamination — and then putting that learning to use — are in the best interests of everybody everywhere. Ignorance and arrogance are a dangerous combination; their striking presence in the Soviet delegation in Vienna is far from reassuring about Soviet handling not only of nuclear power but nuclear weapons. The world could surely do without catastrophic reminders of nuclear dangers: what it should usefully do with them is redouble its safety efforts.

The suspicion persists, from this and previous disasters, that however competent Soviet scientists, Soviet politicians will prevail. Soviet politicians, in their zeal to prove superpower capabilities, have been known to treat Soviet citizens — and, regarding Chernobyl radiation, Europeans — cavalierly. Is Chernobyl a case of political hacks overruling scientists, of financial considerations or power struggles superseding safety, of a system without channels for dissent?

Despite technical questions still unanswered, the science of Chernobyl may be more easily plumbed, and the faults corrected, than the politics.

The Kansas City Times

Kansas City, MO, August 23, 1986

The Soviet report on Chernobyl submitted to the International Atomic Energy Agency in Vienna and the news conference in Moscow on that subject are important and remarkable for two reasons. The first is the warning to other nuclear-powered societies that is implicit in the report. The second is the extent of detail and unpleasantness that is recited, however belated it may be.

The Soviets tell of a series of blunders born of ignorance, poor training and faulty guessing. The builders of the reactors, they say, could not have foreseen the "premeditated diversions of technical protection facilities." Rules were violated on purpose in stupid experimentation. Such a set of circumstances, says the report, was regarded as "impossible."

"Impossible." The word ought to send a chill through governments, private enterprises and individuals responsible for the design and maintenance of any nuclear plant anywhere in the world. The Soviets say that the very success of the Chernobyl operation had bred complacency and carelessness. Such are the universal human characteristics that make "impossible" accidents not unusual but inevitable. This "impossibility" will cause more than 6,300 premature deaths by Soviet calculations, and perhaps many, many more.

All these admissions must be painful to the Soviets beyond the imagining of Westerners accustomed to the criticism and denunciations common in democratic societies. Perhaps its significance can be exaggerated. Mikhail Gorbachev can, of course, place the blame on past regimes. He might not be so forthcoming later. But taken in the context of the ancient Russian obsession for secrecy, the report and the conference are astonishing.

Yes, the words are linked with the routine propaganda about peaceful Soviet intentions in arms control. The aberrations of individuals, not the system, are the focus of censure. But the point is not those things, or that it is happening five months after the event, but that it is happening at all. It is different. It is new. After all, this is the country of which a Scottish visitor to St. Petersburg 225 years ago wrote: "Half of Russia may be destroyed and the other half know nothing about the matter."

It means that the West, and most especially Washington, needs to be prepared for a different Soviet Union that may be emerging in the Gorbachev years. It may be superficial and it may not last. But it could mean a Soviet Union that is both more amenable to reason and more formidable as a rival.

THE CHRISTIAN SCIENCE MONITOR

Boston, MA, August 27, 1986

"WE all live in Middletown," the T-shirts said after America's closest brush with meltdown, the incident at the Three Mile Island nuclear power plant near Middletown, Pa.

Since April, we have all lived in Chernobyl.

For the West, one of the most horrifying aspects of the nuclear disaster there was the Soviets' stonewalling about it. The customary Soviet secrecy, tolerated perforce by the West much of the time, was absolutely inexcusable in a situation where the threat was of radiation and nuclear contamination, which respect no borders. Forthright communication about the dangers should have been a minimum requirement for the Soviet Union as a world citizen.

Now, to their credit, the Soviets seem to have opened up somewhat. At the meeting in Vienna of over 500 nuclear scientists from around the world to discuss the Chernobyl explosion, the Soviets have been uncharacteristically forthcoming with information.

And the Soviets have conceded that, yes, Western nuclear scientists are right in ascribing an important role in the disaster to various design flaws — flaws which British scientists had warned the Soviets of in 1977.

Before the Vienna meeting, the Soviets' line, taken in their report released Aug. 14, was that "human error" was responsible. That can be a deflecting tactic and an excuse for not making (expensive) corrections in the plant itself — or modifications in the country's nuclear energy policy.

The Soviets have announced in recent days that they are planning safety changes in Chernobyl and their other nuclear plants — but that those changes must be made within certain economic constraints. Soviet decisionmaking is of course vastly different from that of the Western countries; but it would seem that, like many Western utilities, the Soviets are having a hard time balancing safety and cost-effectiveness in their nuclear plants.

Despite the Soviets' "new openness," there remain, however, many unanswered questions; it's not clear, for instance, just what the radiation readings in the area around the Chernobyl plant were after the accident. As the Vienna meeting continues this week, and Soviet scientists are questioned by their counterparts from around the world, their "openness" will be put to the test.

The Houston Post

Houston, TX, August 28, 1986

The Soviet Union at first claimed that the Chernobyl nuclear plant disaster stemmed from operator error — managers and technicians conducting an unauthorized experiment. But now for the first time a Soviet official has conceded that safety design flaws in the reactor also contributed to the April 26 explosion and fire that spewed radiation across Europe.

However, much of the blame for the world's worst nuclear accident lies with a flawed policy of the closed Soviet system. That point, as well as the design problem, emerged this week at an International Atomic Energy Agency conference on Chernobyl.

Valery Legasov, chief Soviet delegate to the Vienna meeting, said designers of the reactor that malfunctioned, a type widely used in the Soviet Union, had not incorporated enough tamper-proof safety devices to counter operator errors. That was no surprise to some Western nuclear experts, who had warned the Russians of these deficiencies nine years ago.

The Soviets did not modify the reactors, which were designed three decades ago, when, Legasov said, automatic safety systems were not considered reliable enough to deal with emergencies. This decision became policy and apparently wasn't changed because the reactor was more economical without the safety equipment.

The Soviet leaders, who are committed to an ambitious nuclear power program, do not allow criticism of their policies. Chernobyl was the price they and the Russian people paid — and will continue to pay in years to come with a projected 24,000 or more future cancer deaths and thousands of acres of contaminated land.

The Philadelphia Inquirer

Philadelphia, PA
August 24, 1986

Although the U.S. nuclear industry from the very beginning has stressed the differences between American reactor design and that of the Soviet's Chernobyl nuclear facility — saying that a similar accident could not happen here — there is one compelling and critical similarity.

Human beings operate the plants, regardless of where they are located or how they are designed.

As Soviet officials in a remarkably candid and apparently forthright briefing noted on Thursday, it was human error — not the reactor design — that caused the world's worst nuclear accident on April 26. That also was the finding of a U.S. panel of experts who reviewed the 1979 Three Mile Island accident.

For that reason, it is impossible not to draw striking comparisons between the two events.

The operators at Chernobyl became complacent, lulled into a sense of security by the plant's past performance record and assurances from engineers that the possibilities of a major accident were remote, according to the Soviet inquiry. The same was found to be true at TMI. Chernobyl workers ignored safety procedures, overrode backup emergency systems and failed to understand that a disaster was unfolding. That also occurred at TMI.

There are, to be sure, substantive differences. The accident at TMI occurred during normal operations. At Chernobyl things got out of hand during a test to determine how long turbine generators would run by sheer momentum in case of an unforeseen reactor shutdown. Furthermore, the damage caused by Chernobyl is staggering — far worse than at TMI. Extremely high levels of radiation spread over far greater areas than originally reported. The reactor continues to emit radiation. It has experienced at least one potentially serious fire since April, and it will be many years before the danger can be mitigated.

When the government formally submits its 382-page report on the accident to the International Atomic Energy Agency in Vienna tomorrow, the Soviets also hope to solicit ideas about containing the intensely radioactive reactor. It is an unprecedented task that will require consultation with the best minds of science.

Even as they described the devastation caused by Chernobyl, the Soviets reaffirmed their commitment to nuclear energy. Thus they have refused, as have many in the United States, to heed the most basic lesson of Chernobyl and TMI.

It is that the potential for human error in a nuclear plant can't be eradicated regardless of design changes and improved operating procedures.

Los Angeles Times

Los Angeles, CA, August 27, 1986

Since its creation 30 years ago the International Atomic Energy Agency has concentrated on encouraging the development of nuclear-power generation and, within limits, trying to see that nuclear materials are not diverted from nuclear-power plants to the production of atomic weapons.

The business of trying to head off the spread of nuclear weapons is a worthwhile endeavor. But, as the Soviet nuclear accident at Chernobyl amply demonstrated, there is also a crying need for greater IAEA attention to nuclear-reactor safety.

The IAEA meeting now under way in Vienna is encouraging evidence that the agency recognizes that responsibility. It remains to be seen whether the international body is ready or able to undertake the sticky job of clamping down on nations whose nuclear programs fail to meet strict safety standards.

The purpose of the Vienna gathering is to receive a Soviet report on the Chernobyl disaster. The Kremlin originally indulged in an outrageous cover-up of the accident, which turned out to be even worse than Western experts thought at the time. In the Soviet Union itself many thousands of acres of farmland were contaminated. Food supplies may be affected for 70 years. Cancer deaths attributable to the accident could reach 45,000. In Norway it turns out that grass and other vegetation has been irradiated in large areas of the country—necessitating, among other things, a large-scale slaughter of reindeer.

The Soviet technical report to the IAEA turned out to be straightforward by usual Soviet standards. But while the Russians admitted to design problems with the Chernobyl reactor, they tried to put the blame almost entirely on human errors by the reactor operators.

Western experts at the meeting are not buying that. The British, for example, recall that they investigated the Chernobyl-type Soviet reactors in the mid-1970s and decided against using the technology because of a built-in tendency to generate sudden and hard-to-control bursts of power.

Making the reactors safe, they decided, requires an excessive dependence on control mechanisms and human operators.

The Soviet nuclear-power program is heavily dependent on graphite-moderated reactors of the Chernobyl type. What the Soviets seemed to be saying at Vienna about their next step was that they would beef up the control mechanisms at those plants. But that will be enormously expensive, and Western experts question whether they will be safe even then.

Ideally, the IAEA should develop design and operating standards that all new reactors everywhere would have to meet. Unfortunately, an international consensus does not exist for such strong medicine. But at least the agency should lean on the Soviets to move to safer reactor designs —and, meanwhile, to do their utmost to make the Chernobyl-type reactors safe. The fact that the Soviets felt it necessary to explain themselves to the IAEA member nations demonstrates that the agency has considerable moral authority. It should use that authority as leverage to nudge the Russians and everybody else into making reactors as safe as they can be.

There seems to be no question that commercial nuclear reactors in the United States and other Western countries are safer than their Soviet counterparts. But that isn't good enough. Congress should make sure that the U.S. Nuclear Regulatory Commission makes a suitably skeptical review of nuclear-reactor safety in this country. Nuclear-regulatory agencies in Western Europe and Japan should do the same.

Any thorough review of reactor safety must ultimately include military reactors—both the onshore facilities that produce the makings for nuclear weapons, and the submarines and other warships that use nuclear propulsion.

The Soviet Union isn't ready to go that far. For that matter, neither are the United States, France and Great Britain. But the IAEA meeting is at least a step in the right direction.

The Toronto Star

Toronto, Ont., August 31, 1986

Harnessing the atom for peaceful purposes — from generating power to combatting disease — poses risks as well as promising benefits for mankind. Those risks were being carefully scrutinized in Vienna this past week as 500 technical experts from 50 countries conducted a post-mortem on the devastating accident that happened at the Soviet nuclear power station in Chernobyl last April.

The accident's death toll is now 31; hundreds of people have been injured and thousands were forced from the farms and villages in Ukraine which were poisoned by what has been called the world's most deadly case of radiation contamination. At a conservative estimate, as many as 6,500 people will die from radiation-caused cancer in the next 70 years.

Nuclear generation even for peaceful purposes cannot be taken for granted

As well as hearing the stark facts of human misery caused by the accident at Chernobyl, the experts in Vienna for the meeting called by the International Atomic Energy Agency have been perusing a 300-page report on the disaster compiled by the Soviet Union. And western officials, including Canadians from Ontario Hydro and Atomic Energy of Canada Ltd., found the report remarkably candid and forthcoming, particularly when contrasted to the complete absence of candor from Moscow when the incident first occurred. Indeed, the world only learned that something dreadful had happened when the Swedes found abnormal amounts of radiation around one of their own nuclear power stations — and shut it down before they realized the problem wasn't their fault.

So the first lesson that's been learned from Chernobyl is the importance of informing the international community when an accident occurs. To that end, steps have already been taken in Vienna to get countries to agree to provide early warning and details of nuclear accidents, to provide assistance in the event of accident, and to give the international agency more money to beef up its nuclear safety activities. These proposals will be debated at a conference on Sept. 24. While it's possible that some countries may balk at giving advance warning and details about accidents involving weapons-making nuclear enterprises, there should be no hesitation at all about agreeing to provide information about nuclear power-station incidents. Worth considering, too, is a treaty providing for international compensation in the event of an accident.

The Soviets have attributed the Chernobyl tragedy to the action of employees who, while conducting an as-yet unspecified experiment, switched off important parts of the plant's safety system. A Canadian expert compared it to "cutting the engines on an aircraft to see how far it could glide." It also seems clear, however, that nuclear plants need to be surrounded by buildings or domes to contain radioactive fallout if an accident does occur. In 1979, the mishap at the nuclear power station at Three Mile Island in the United States released large amounts of radioactive material. But it didn't drift to neighboring states and countries because the plant had a containment building — as do most western plants including Canada's. At Chernobyl, there was no containment building so the fallout drifted with the prevailing winds all over Eastern Europe and Scandinavia — with effects on the health of people in those countries that may not be known for decades.

What the awful accident at Chernobyl has taught, then, is that the safety of generating nuclear energy even for peaceful purposes cannot be taken for granted. It's a lesson to be taken to heart as much here in Ontario as in far-away Ukraine because by 1992, when the Darlington station comes on stream, two-thirds of the electrical power in this province may be nuclear-generated.

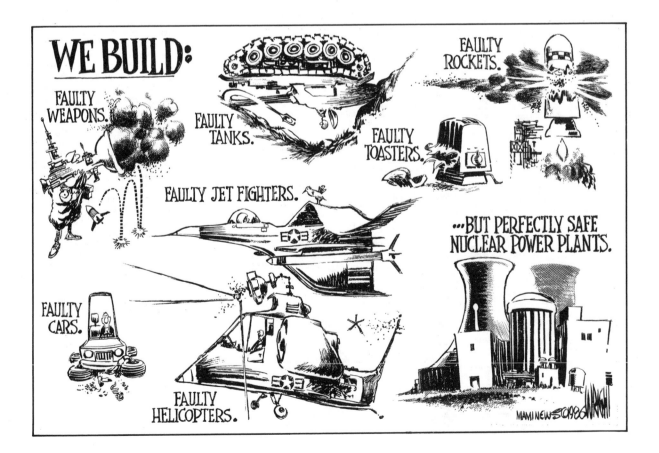

Serious Problems Revealed At U.S. Nuclear Sites

Chronic failures at the Savannah River plant in South Carolina that supplied fuel for the nation's nuclear weapons became widely known Sept. 30, 1988. The disclosure came at a joint hearing of the Senate Governmental Affairs Committee and the House Government Operations subcommittee on environment, energy and natural resources. The last active reactor at Savannah River had been shut down in August following a still unexplained power surge. Two other reactors there had been shut down previously, and the remaining two reactors at the giant, aging complex had been permanently shut down earlier for safety reasons.

A 19-page memorandum made public at the hearing listed 30 "incidents" that occurred at the five reactors at Savannah River plant from 1957 to 1985. Among them were several unexplained power surges that threatened to go out of control. One, on Jan. 12, 1960, was an increase in power at a rate more than 10 times faster than was considered safe. Another, in November 1970, was a meltdown of a radioactive rod and contamination of an adjacent room that took 900 people three months to clean up.

The U.S. Energy Department, which supervised the nuclear-weapons-fuel industry through private contractors, admitted Oct. 10 that the problems at Savannah River – lax safety precautions, poor management, inadequate training, inefficient and aging equipment – were endemic throughout the vast system of 17 major sites in 12 states. The system produces, stores and researches radioactive materials for nuclear weapons.

"The problems are there," Richard W. Starostecki, deputy assistant secretary of energy for safety, health and quality assurance, said in announcing that the department had closed down another of the sites, the Rocky Flats plant near Boulder, Colo., operated by Rockwell International Corp. The plant, which processed plutonium, had been closed Oct. 8 after three persons, one of them a department inspector, had been accidently exposed to radioactive contamination during a tour.

Pentagon officials expressed concern Oct. 8 about the cutoff of fuel for the nuclear warheads. The Savannah River plant was the only plant in the nation that manufactures tritium, a radioactive form of hydrogen that augmented the nuclear explosion, thus allowing smaller warheads.

THE PLAIN DEALER
Cleveland, OH, October 8, 1988

The belated disclosure of accidents at the Savannah River nuclear weapons plant in South Carolina has outraged members of Congress and disturbed the Reagan administration. Rightly so, for the hush-up of bad news is a glaring example of government secrecy run amok. From 1957 to 1985, there were 30 significant reactor incidents, including fires, equipment failures, melting of fuel rods, radioactive leaks and contaminations. These risks to worker safety and potentially to nearby residents were in addition to shutdowns and less serious incidents.

But fear of upsetting the public and allegedly jeopardizing the nation's nuclear weapons program kept the information from reaching top levels of government and being disclosed to the public. The secrecy was said to be engrained in practices of nearly a half-century in the nuclear industry. The Savannah River Plant is the nation's only source of plutonium and related radioactive elements used in making nuclear warheads and powering satellites.

Investigation of an unexplained power surge in August led to discovery of old reports, memos and records of other accidents. The problems were confirmed at recent hearings co-chaired by Sen. John Glenn of Ohio, whose panel uncovered yet other problems at Savannah River last year. The Energy Department has taken the blame for the mistakes and the lack of disclosure, a move that too generously took the onus off DuPont, which has operated the huge complex for the government virtually unregulated.

In response to the testimony, the Energy Department plans a comprehensive investigation of plant conditions. Four senators issued a bipartisan call for an inquiry by the department's advisory committee, established last year. These lofty-sounding announcements are hypocritical. Last year the Energy Department had sought to undercut a Glenn bill creating an independent oversight commission for nuclear facilities. But

now the department tries to sound virtuous. Two of the four senators urging an inquiry—Johnston of Louisiana and McClure of Idaho—delayed, and tried to kill, Glenn's bill. Now they are born-again safety champions. Glenn's proposal finally was attached to another bill signed by President Reagan in late September.

Several steps are essential now. Any probe must look at the obvious shortcomings in safety procedures and operator training. Glenn should pursue his goal of including certain facilities exempted from review for environmental and safety standards, including Los Alamos, N.M., the Nevada Test Site and nuclear enrichment plants in Ohio.

But a priority also must be the revamping of the long-held policy of secrecy, of keeping bad news buried in the bureaucracy to protect pay raises and promotions. The hoary argument that disclosure would be a national security risk ignores the dangers of operators of Savannah River and other facilities becoming technologically isolated and not being forced to implement lessons of Three Mile Island and other nuclear sites. Thus, the risk of an accident merely escalates. An accident would lead to public demands to shut down the entire nuclear operation—which unquestionably would jeopardize the national security that secrecy-lovers want to protect.

Glenn, as security-conscious as anyone, says that national security is not a good enough reason to withhold safety matters from the public and high officials at Energy. As a new administration takes office in a few months, it must mandate revised information policies at the Energy Department and a realistic budget that adds funds for environment, safety and health programs. There is no reason why federal installations should operate at lower standards than those demanded of civilian utility plants. As Sen. Ernest Hollings of South Carolina said, "The Savannah River Plant can and must be run in a way that protects both the nation's defense and the safety of its workers."

The Philadelphia Inquirer
*Philadelphia, PA,
October 5, 1988*

Born in secrecy, America's nuclear weapons program has zealously clung to the shroud that has kept its operations hidden from public scrutiny since the days of the Manhattan Project to build the atom bomb.

Officials at the Department of Energy — and its predecessor, the Atomic Energy Commission — have long argued that secrecy is essential to protecting national security. That may be true. But the federal government has also used the shroud to hide an environmental record that threatens the health and safety of those who live near weapons-production facilities.

Over the past few years, the extent of the unsafe operations at the Energy Department's 18 installations around the nation has begun to leak out. Vast tracts of land have been so contaminated with radioactive materials — including plutonium and strontium 90 — that the cleanup would cost an astounding $155 billion. Radioactive wastes, indiscriminately dumped at the facilities, have already spread to drinking water supplies, including the Columbia River.

Last week, another alarming facet of the problem surfaced. Documents were released in Congress describing 30 accidents that occurred between 1957 and 1985 at the department's Savannah River Plant in South Carolina. The incidents — some of which were the most severe ever recorded at a U.S. nuclear facility — included fuel meltdowns and extensive radioactive releases into the environment.

What makes these new revelations noteworthy is that nobody in the lower echelons of the Department of Energy thought them important enough to pass along to their superiors. They were noted and then forgotten.

"What happened here is at the heart of the whole problem with this agency and these plants," said Sen. John Glenn (D., Ohio), who along with U.S. Rep. Mike Synar (D., Okla.) has been investigating the safety record of federal weapons facilities. Secrecy fosters this contempt for safety, Mr. Glenn asserted.

Although a spokesman for Energy Secretary John S. Herrington said the secretary has stressed increased accountability throughout the nuclear weapons program, he added, "we're having trouble getting the message out to the field."

That explanation has a familiar ring to it: The same excuse has been used by the commercial nuclear industry. But Mr. Herrington's comment hardly provides assurances for the Americans who live near Energy Department installations.

The message that must be sent throughout the department's operations is this: Nuclear safety and public accountability cannot be foresaken in the name of national security.

WORCESTER TELEGRAM

Worcester, MA, October 13, 1988

That the country's largest nuclear weapons plant producing radioactive gas, essential to keep our warheads in operation, has been rendered idle is disturbing, to say the least. It reminds us of other alarming shortcomings within our defense industry that have been discovered from time to time.

In view of vital national security interests involved, it is hard to understand how this could be allowed to happen.

Are there still major problems of control between private manufacturers and government inspectors? Have high-level officials fallen asleep at the switch again?

One by one, all three reactors at the Savannah River Plant, owned and operated E.I. du Pont de Nemours & Co., had to be shut down for safety reasons. The plant produces tritium, a gas necessary to keep the nation's nuclear arsenal in operational readiness. Unless the reactors are restarted by next summer, the United States could be forced to start deactivating some of its nuclear warheads.

The very possibility is preposterous. Yet there are danger signs that cannot be ignored.

Three of the 15 plants that form the nation's nuclear weapons manufacturing system are out of action — two because of safety problems, a third due to a strike.

Moreover, the Energy Department has confirmed that the vast industrial network of plants and laboratories that design, manufacture and test nuclear weapons systems is aged and plagued with problems,

ranging from equipment failure to radiation leaks.

While du Pont claims the company is "getting a bum rap," there have been reports of carelessness and negligence. Operators evidently ignored incidents and unusual events and went on with a potentially disastrous manufacturing process. Thus the need for the shutdowns.

It is not clear where Energy Department and Pentagon officials have been while all that was happening. It is equally astonishing that President Reagan was briefed about the problems at Savannah River only a few days ago. The White House darkly hints of a possible cover-up.

Energy Secretary John S. Herrington has taken some steps: He appointed a special management team to correct safety failures at Savannah River and put at least one reactor back in operation in January, with all three reactors scheduled to be back in business by next summer. Some experts say that, given dilapidated conditions, the plan is less than realistic.

We hope those experts are wrong. In a nuclear age, even during a period of disarmament, the United States cannot afford to lower its defenses. Nor should it allow its adversaries to draw false conclusions based on production failures in the weapons industry.

The Savannah River Plant fiasco should serve as a warning. It needs to prompt top decision-makers to investigate the roots of the problem and examine conditions within the entire nuclear weapons industry. The safe and efficient production of all components of our nuclear arsenal is an absolute must.

FORT WORTH STAR-TELEGRAM

Fort Worth, TX, October 5, 1988

If you are not outraged about the Department of Energy's abdication of responsibility and disregard for safety in the case of the Savannah River nuclear plant in South Carolina, you ought to be.

After initially denying it, a spokesman for the department has admitted that the DOE and its predecessor, the Atomic Energy Commission, had kept from the public vital information about several serious reactor accidents occurring over a 28-year period at the plant.

The plant is operated for the government by E.I. du Pont Nemours & Co., which, by DOE admission, notified the department about the accidents, which included the melting of fuel, extensive radioactive contamination and major leaks of reactor core cooling water.

Company reports were apparently sidetracked purposely, somewhere in the bu-

reaucracy before reaching a level within the DOE where steps could have been taken to assess responsibility for the accidents, which posed a significant threat to life in the surrounding area.

Although the plant was engaged in weapon production and not energy generation, a nuclear accident is a nuclear accident, and such flagrant disregard for safety does little to enhance the industry's campaign for public acceptance.

John Harrington, the current secretary of energy, is dedicated to stricter safety standards, which is encouraging, but the fact that he has encountered resistance from some career bureaucrats is not. The potential for disaster with nuclear power is too great for hazards to be ignored. Those responsible for hiding the danger in South Carolina for 28 years should be identified and held strictly accountable.

The Chattanooga Times

Chattanooga, TN, October 10, 1988

The dimensions of the continuing unsafe operation of the government's vast Savannah River nuclear complex are breathtaking. As the story has unfolded over the past week, it has become clear that the Department of Energy's five-reactor plant, which employs 16,700 people on an isolated 192,000-acre reservation in South Carolina, has long been incredibly mismanaged. The lives of workers and nearby residents — as well as the integrity of the nation's nuclear weapons program — have been threatened over the past 28 years by no less than 30 serious nuclear "incidents," which, in turn, were apparently covered up.

Congressional hearings have revealed that both safety procedures and reporting requirements have been blatantly violated; reports of the incidents — including two serious fuel meltdowns — have "mysteriously" failed to reach top Washington officials. DOE officials' feeble response is that they intend to find out why they haven't known what's been going on.

Sorry; that's not good enough. The officials who have failed to keep up with their responsibility to oversee the plant should be removed from office, as should any "field" people guilty of failing to report mishaps.

The miserable record also demands much more in the way of regulation, oversight and attention to safety. And it raises disturbing suspicions of cover-up collusion — in the perceived interest of national security — that has, ironically, weakened a vital weapons program by hiding its flaws so long.

Given the seriousness of some of the accidents, the official version of ignorance at the top is frighteningly incredible. One fuel assembly meltdown released radiation that contaminated cooling water and processing areas. It took 900 people three months to clean up. A number of unexplained power surges threatened to go out of control: One increased power 10 times faster than the standard safe level. In all, the reactors have unexpectedly shut down 9 to 12 times a year for nearly two decades — twice the rate of civilian nuclear reactors. The physical stress on the reactors from bringing them back on line quickly after unexpected shutdowns is believed to have caused damage and produced many of the "incidents."

There is little doubt that had the plants been regulated by the Nuclear Regulatory Commission, as are private utility plants, they would have been closed long ago. Moreover, any cover-ups or deliberate evasions of safety and reporting procedures likely would have brough criminal indictments. The suspicion of broader knowledge is raised by officials' admissions that the plants have been operated on the basis of secrecy for national security since their inception. DOE officials, in fact, have already cleared the contract operator, E.I. du Pont deNemours & Co., of any blame in reporting failures. Why the reports never got up the line — or, if they did, what happened — is one of the central mysteries of the case.

Whatever the outcome, it is undeniable that public safety as well as the nation's nuclear weapon capability have been compromised. The plant, designed to produce plutonium and tritium for nuclear missiles, now has no active reactors, even though its operations account for 21 percent of the $7.75 billion the Energy Department intends to spend next year on weapons programs. Of the five reactors, two have been permanently shut down; a third was shut down last August after an unexplained accident, and other events have forced the shutdown of the other two active reactors.

Had proper safety and operating procedures been applied, both safety and the nation's weapons capacity would have been better served. It is clear that secrecy has exacted a high price.

Los Angeles, CA,
October 6, 1988

If any added proof was needed, the recent revelations from Savannah River pile it on. The next administration must clean house at the Department of Energy.

For 31 years, officials assigned to supervise the government-owned, privately run nuclear weapons factories at Savannah River covered up dozens of accidents. Some of these could have been as deadly as the 1986 Chernobyl reactor fire had they not been contained in time.

DuPont, the longtime contractor that will turn over operations to Westinghouse April 1, seems to have informed the appropriate government agencies whenever an accident occurred. But that information never made it to headquarters at the old Atomic Energy Commission or its successor, the DOE. Consequently, no corrective actions were taken.

While the government can be blamed for giving free rein to its field operators, DuPont is hardly off the hook. Why didn't it make changes on its own to improve safety? Or, failing that, at least ask federal officials what had happened to its accident reports?

The latest disclosure is no surprise to longtime observers. Years of mismanagement, lackadaisical self-regulation, arrogance and secrecy have made a disaster of the government's 13-state network of nuclear production facilities. Estimates just for containing radioactive contamination run as high as $175 billion. Nobody even dares guess what it will take to clean up the mess, including tainted water.

Appalling as the situation is, it wouldn't be so bad if it could be chalked up to the environmental ignorance that accompanied the nation's early days as a nuclear bomb-maker. However, the facilities today are plagued by the same problems as in the past: poor procedures, poor training, poor attitude. Accidents decades ago stemmed from the same mistakes that nearly caused another mishap at Savannah River in August.

Before Westinghouse takes over, before another gram of plutonium or tritium is manufactured, the White House and Congress should make sure DOE officials understand that safety is as high a priority as production. On that score, the record is persuasive that only a major turnover in personnel will do the job.

THE SACRAMENTO BEE

Sacramento, CA, October 12, 1988

Between 1957 and 1985, two congressional committees recently learned and disclosed, there were at least 30 serious accidents at the nation's nuclear weapons production facilities in Savannah River — accidents, the experts say, that were among the most severe ever experienced at any American nuclear facility. Yet they were kept secret from the public.

The Energy Department first tried to blame the DuPont Co., which operated the plants. But the company did report each accident at the time to the government agency in charge of nuclear bomb manufacture. The Energy Department now claims that it was lower-level officials who hid DuPont's information — not just from the public, but from their superiors as well.

Whether the fault was at the bottom or the top, government management of nuclear weapons production has clearly been a shambles. Everyone from the Energy Department to the White House now acknowledges as much; and all three Savannah River reactors, as well as the government's plutonium processing plant in Colorado, are now shut down because of safety concerns. But even before the latest revelations, a congressional report had described a pattern of Energy Department mismanagement that had resulted in radioactive leaks, water contamination, dangerously outmoded facilities and inadequately contained wastes at a dozen sites around the country. Where was the administration then?

Estimates are that it will cost more than $100 *billion* just to clean up that legacy of inattention — and more to build needed new facilities and bring older ones up to the same health and safety codes that private industry must meet. The administration has not yet suggested where to find that money.

Then, last month, another congressional committee discovered that it may not even be possible to begin the needed cleanup, since there may be no place to put the radioactive wastes removed from contaminated sites. After spending $700 million carving out a radioactive waste repository in the salt beds outside Carlsbad, N.M., which was supposed to have opened in early October, the Energy Department announced that it was postponing that opening indefinitely. The decision came after the House committee released internal Energy Department memos showing that the department's own investigators aren't sure that the facility is safe.

Far from learning from its past experience, the department tried to ignore these investigators' memos, until Congress got hold of them. And one has to wonder whether this month's worse revelations wouldn't also have been swept under the rug if Congress hadn't publicized them.

Congress can't allow that mode of operation to continue. And it must make sure that the overwhelming scale of the problem doesn't become the new excuse for making do with the same old policy of cut corners, sealed lips and crossed fingers. The Energy Department's mismanagement has already endangered the public's safety and the nation's weapons programs. Enough is enough.

The Washington Post

Washington, DC, October 14, 1988

ALL FIVE of this country's weapons reactors—the machines that produce the material for nuclear warheads—are now out of operation. In each case, the reasons are related to safety. Two of them will probably remain out of commission permanently. The remaining three, at the Savannah River Plant in South Carolina, are waiting for the Department of Energy to decide when and under what conditions to start them up again.

They can't be allowed to remain down indefinitely. One component of nuclear weapons, tritium, decays over time, and any prolonged interruption in production will affect the country's nuclear arsenal. The Energy Department is beginning the process of building two new reactors, but they won't be completed until the turn of the century. Any tritium produced in this country over the next decade will have to come from the Savannah River Plant.

It was built in the 1950s, and the reactors there are aging. One of them malfunctioned when it was being started up last August; that's the reason for the current shutdown. These reactors have been pushed hard throughout the 1980s for the Reagan administration's buildup of weapons, and the administration has skimped on the necessary investment to keep them up to date.

The accumulated size of that investment is daunting by any measure. The General Accounting Office has concluded that, to bring all of the Energy Department's weapons facilities up to current health and safety standards, including adequate waste disposal and environmental protection, would cost $100 billion to $130 billion.

It's not just a matter of replacing worn hardware. Ever since World War II the weapons plants have worked behind a heavy veil of secrecy that has segregated them almost entirely from the civilian world. The steady tightening of environmental and safety requirements over the past two decades never reached these facilities. The sweeping reforms of the civilian nuclear industry after the Three Mile Island accident never touched them. Old habits became entrenched, and the supervisory structure became ingrown.

Several years ago Sen. John Glenn and his Governmental Affairs Committee began to take a serious interest in the subject, and the current attention is largely owed to their work. After the Chernobyl disaster in the Soviet Union, the Energy Department commissioned a study of safety issues and, like Sen. Glenn, it concluded that independent oversight was essential. The department appointed a committee of outsiders headed by John Ahearne, a former chairman of the Nuclear Regulatory Commission.

The Energy Department now expects to restart one of the Savannah River reactors by the end of the year, after safety improvements, and the other two in 1989. It would be far better to turn those decisions over to the Ahearne committee. These machines have been severely overused by successive administrations that have consistently ducked the costs of bringing the weapons plants up to the standards on which, everywhere else, this country insists. Under these circumstances, the judgments about putting the reactors back into production are ones that this administration would be wise to leave to the outsiders.

The News and Courier
Charleston, SC, October 9, 1988

We may never know exactly who was responsible for hushing up the 30 serious accidents that have occurred over the past 31 years at the Savannah River Plant, which produces plutonium and tritium for the nation's nuclear weapons. But the exposure of SRP's troubles, described by government officials and scientists as being among the most serious in the history of the nuclear industry, reveals the answer to one mystery: why E.I. du Pont de Nemours & Co. suddenly announced that it would not renew its contract to manage the plant for the Department of Energy.

Regardless of who is to blame for keeping from the public the truth about dangerous mishaps at SRP, including the melting of a fuel rod and extensive radioactive contamination, it is now clear that Du Pont was better at managing information than it was at managing nuclear reactors. In the light of the information that has come tumbling out, like skeletons from a closet, it is obvious that Du Pont misled public opinion in South Carolina by sending up smokescreens whenever anything went wrong.

The picture that emerges, now that the truth about the operations at the plant is out, is the opposite of that cultivated by Du Pont's public relations spokesmen. A memo released at a recent House Armed Services subcommittee hearing indicates that when Westinghouse, the new contractor, takes over at SRP on April 1, 1989, oversight must be improved dramatically. The memo, written by Richard Starostecki, who is assistant secretary for safety, health and quality assurance at the Department of Energy (DOE), charges, "There are currently some senior managers within the department with an attitude toward production reactor safety which on the face seems to be similar to that which existed in the space program prior to the [shuttle] Challenger accident."

The attitude of spokesmen for the plant must also be reviewed. Du Pont's spokesmen are now claiming that they provided the Department of Energy with information about all 30 of the accidents that have recently come to light. After initially denying that it had been informed by Du Pont, DOE finally came to the conclusion that the SRP management had gone through the motions of informing the department but that the reports had never reached the higher echelons in the chain of command. Whatever the truth and whoever is to blame for the coverup, the facts are that everyone from SRP's management up to DOE's top officials, as well as members of the now defunct Atomic Energy Commission, cooperated in keeping important information from the public. A review of the statements made over the years by Du Pont spokesmen in response to public concern over safety confirms a total lack of openness.

"We cannot leave safety up to chance," said Mr. Starostecki. "We cannot sacrifice safety for national security. The two must be treated as equally important. I have often said it will do us little good to build weapons to protect ourselves from the Russians if we poison our own people in the process."

Amen to that. What is needed now is a genuine commitment to openness. At SRP we need glasnost, to avert the risk of a Chernobyl, just as much as the Russians do. With openness and the new requirements for independent oversight, which should prevent DOE or SRP from covering up accidents and hiding the truth, Westinghouse can do the job that Du Pont botched.

But safety is only one of the factors that the new management must deal with. Radioactive contamination of soil under waste basins must be cleaned up if confidence in SRP is to be restored as, we hope, Westinghouse turns over a new leaf (with, we trust, credible spokesmen or spokeswomen) at SRP six months from now.

The Seattle Times
Seattle, WA, October 9, 1988

THE deeply disturbing revelations of serious operating problems and chronic equipment failures at the federal nuclear-weapons facility at Savannah River, S.C., could have far-reaching repercussions – even in this state.

A report just made public (after an unexplained five-month delay) by the federal Department of Energy, information released by two congressional committees, and admissions by the DuPont Co., which operates the plant, reveal that:

■ Some of the five reactors at Savannah River had to be shut down up to 12 times a year between 1971 and 1987 – a shutdown rate three times that of civilian nuclear plants.

■ 25 workers were exposed accidentally to radiation, and some exposures greatly exceeded federal safety guidelines.

■ As many as 30 significant mishaps occurred over a 30-year period – but these were never reported to the government or made public by DuPont.

■ Between 1954 and 1982, DuPont admitted, the plants experienced fires, equipment failures, contaminated-water floods and a reactor-coolant leak that almost caused a spontaneous nuclear reaction.

Overall, a deplorable pattern emerges of lax oversight by the federal government and sloppy performance by DuPont that threatens the nation's continuing need for weapons-grade materials. Call it a management meltdown.

How might this affect Washington state? Last February, the DOE put the Hanford N Reactor on "cold standby" and announced that the nation's plutonium and tritium needs would be met at the South Carolina facility. But depending on what happens next at Savannah River, it's possible that the N Reactor – which underwent extensive safety improvements – could be needed again. Indeed, the Savannah River disclosures make the N Reactor's problems seem relatively trivial.

In addition, the idea of converting the mothballed WPPSS Nuclear Plant No. 1 at Hanford to defense production – which could be faster and cheaper than building a new reactor from scratch – may soon start to look more attractive.

Wherever the plutonium and tritium are produced, the nation's weapons stockpile simply must be maintained. Progress on arms control could eventually reduce the need for these materials, but that remains highly speculative.

Some members of Congress have called for full investigation by the Advisory Committee on Nuclear Facilities Safety. The sorry story of Savannah River clearly needs investigating.

Omaha World-Herald
Omaha, NE, October 13, 1988

A dump, according to our dictionary, is a rubbish pile. That's why we are always surprised when people in the anti-nuclear movement refer to a "nuclear waste dump" and few voices are raised in objection, demanding an honest description of what is being talked about.

"Nuclear waste dump" is an inaccurate and, most of all, loaded description of what is being contemplated in Nebraska. But the expression has gained such acceptance that it sometimes even creeps into television news stories and stories in some newspapers, although rarely in this one.

"Dump," sad to say, has become a political word, a point-of-view word, in the Initiative 402 debate. It serves the purposes of people who don't want a disposal facility for low-level radioactive waste in Nebraska under any circumstance. By referring to the facility as a dump, they evoke the image of what used to be called city dumps — open pits into which trash, garbage and other wastes were tossed, eventually to be covered with a thin layer of soil.

Obviously, no responsible person would advocate storing radioactive materials in a dump. "Vault" would be a more accurate word than "dump" for what the Nebraska plans envision. The regional facility would be an above-ground structure in which solid waste would be stored in sealed containers. It would be watertight and, as an added precaution, surrounded by sensors to detect any radiation leak.

Some defenders of the phrase, "nuclear dump," assert that the use of "low-level radioactive waste disposal facility" instead of "dump" might seem like a violation of the old Journalism 101 rule that favors simple, clear, descriptive words over Latinized, bureaucratic jargon.

But Journalism 101 also teaches that accuracy comes first. In this case, "dump" doesn't fit.

NRC Safety Conditions Come Under Fire

A study released Jan. 6, 1987 by the National Research Council charged that the Nuclear Regulatory Commission's (NRC) program to improve the safety of commercial nuclear reactors was "in dire need of reform." The council was an arm of the National Academy of Sciences.

The report charged that the research arm of the NRC had neglected to examine the "human factors" that could lead to a nuclear accident. The panel said that accidents at the Soviet Chernobyl reactor in 1986 and the Three Mile Island plant in the U.S. in 1979 had shown that the people who built and operated plants were as vital as the mechanical systems in the plants. (See pp. 52-59, 82-85.) Lack of research in the area "indicates that something is seriously wrong with the way the agency goes about structuring its program," the report said.

The study blamed budgetary neglect and indecisive management for the weakness in research, pointing out that the research unit's allocation had been cut each year since 1981. The indecisiveness, the study said, resulted from the "five separate philosophies" the five NRC commissioners held for the agency.

The chief inspector for the NRC said April 9 that agency documents about safety violations at a nuclear plant had been leaked to the plant's owner in 1983.

The inspector, Ben B. Hayes, told the Senate Governmental Affairs Committee that the documents had given Louisiana Power & Light Co. "a tremendous advantage" in a later inspection of its Waterford plant near New Orleans.

Hayes blamed NRC Commissioner Thomas M. Roberts for the leak, and testified that Roberts had also taken and destroyed all the relevant documents after the leak was discovered in 1985. Roberts denied that he or his staff leaked the documents, although his initials were on the copy found in Louisiana Power's files. According to Hayes, Roberts, an unwavering supporter of the nuclear industry, blamed "janitorial personnel" for the leak.

Hayes also charged that in 1986, NRC executive director Victor Stello Jr. had advised the beleaguered head of nuclear operations at the Tennessee Valley Authority (TVA), Adm. Steven A. White, on how to respond to an NRC inquiry. Hayes said that Stello told White "not to give a definite response" to questions about whether the TVA's Watts Bar facility met safety standards. White's misleading statements about Watts Bar were currently the subject of investigation ordered by Stello.

Despite mounting pressure in Congress for his resignation, Roberts June 19 refused to resign as a member of the Nuclear Regulatory Commission, calling allegations against him "ludicrous."

Omaha World-Herald
Omaha, NE, May 28, 1987

Nuclear power may not ever become entirely free of risks. Few things in life are. But the relatively substantial amount of safety research being done in the nuclear power industry raises the possibility that more progress will be made in the area of safety.

Directors of the International Atomic Energy Agency in Vienna said recently that the nuclear power industry commits more money and manpower to safety-related research than a number of other sectors of the energy industry.

One of the more promising results of the research is a new type of nuclear reactor fuel that could reduce the chance of a nuclear meltdown. Tested at a U.S. Department of Energy laboratory in Argonne, Ill., the fuel tends to swell rather than explode when reactors provide too much power. The swelling can be contained, researchers said, without leading to uncontrolled reactions that result in meltdowns.

Development of the new fuel demonstrates again the leadership that the U.S. nuclear industry has exerted over the years. A number of other nations, including England, Japan, South Korea and France, have adopted American designs for their nuclear power plants. U.S. Energy Department officials said several other nations now have expressed interest in the U.S. fuel research.

The U.S. Nuclear Regulatory Commission has put the chances at 50-50 that a serious meltdown will occur in the next 20 years. Research like that being done with reactor fuel could help reduce those odds.

THE COMMERCIAL APPEAL
Memphis, TN, April 17, 1987

THE action taken recently by the federal Nuclear Regulatory Commission against a Pennsylvania nuclear power plant seemed overly drastic.

The NRC discovered that operators were sleeping at the controls and it ordered the plant, run by Philadelphia Electric Co., shut down.

Of course it is unacceptable to have operators sleeping on the job at an installation containing radioactive material. But wouldn't it have made more sense to tell the plant owners to keep its employees awake or fire them and get new ones, instead of putting the unit out of commission?

ST. LOUIS POST-DISPATCH
St. Louis, MO, January 8, 1987

The Nuclear Regulatory Commission's safety research program is deficient. Its Office of Research is not able to attract top scientists. It has not addressed such vital areas as human factors research — an area highlighted in the wake of the Three Mile Island and Chernobyl accidents. Its management has been indecisive and neglectful of the need to push Congress for budget support. Finally, its research may have taken a back seat to politics.

Those charges are at the heart of a report made by a panel of 13 experts convened by the National Research Council of the National Academy of Sciences.

The Office of Research was intended to inform the commission when it came time to draw up regulations for nuclear plants. But the experts on the panel found little evidence it was doing that. Part of the problem is administrative anarchy: While the Office of Research is technically managed by the five members of the Nuclear Regulatory Commission, in fact "they do little policy formulation, program planning or staff guidance, and do not appear to understand the program." The research summaries the Office of Research prepares, on the other hand, "are either unread or not useful" for the NRC's work.

What may be the experts' most far-reaching recommendation is the call for the Office of Research to expand its scope. It should not hesitate "to challenge the existing wisdom of nuclear plants," they said, nor should it suppress work that might bolster critics of nuclear energy.

With 100 nuclear plants in operation, many of them nearing the end of their useful life, the demand for studies pointing to ways to enhance safety will rise in years to come. If that demand is to be met, the NRC has to begin now the urgent work of reforming its Office of Research.

THE SACRAMENTO BEE
Sacramento, CA, August 16, 1987

Congress has decided that the federal Nuclear Regulatory Commission — and not the states — should have the last word on whether a nuclear power plant is safe enough to license. It was a practical and appropriate decision, but it carries with it the burden of making sure the NRC is up to such a responsibility. And that will take some doing.

The NRC, never wholly free of charges that it was nurturing rather than regulating the nuclear power industry, is now made up only of Reagan appointees who hardly acknowledge a distinction. There is "no other regulatory or investigative agency," a Justice Department attorney recently testified in Congress, "where senior agency officials have taken as many bizarre and seemingly deliberate actions intended to hamper the investigation and prosecution of individuals and companies in the industry the agency regulates."

Symptomatic, if not typical, is the case of NRC Commissioner Thomas Roberts. His initialed copy of an internal agency memo about problems at a Louisiana utility mysteriously showed up in the office of the utility's vice president, a friend of Roberts' who, for his part, appended a note to the memo about "protect(ing) the source within the NRC." Congress can't seem to get a straight story about any of this from Roberts, who has been so uncooperative and unbelievable that seven different congressional committee heads have demanded his resignation. (He has refused.) But even more appalling than Roberts' own behavior is the NRC's response to it. As soon as they knew of it, the NRC's other top officials halted the agency's investigation of the leaked memo and turned the matter over to Roberts himself to take care of.

The Senate, in reaction, has been taking its time about confirming the president's latest appointee to the NRC, Kenneth Rogers, a nuclear physicist who in other circumstances would have been a shoo-in. But under the senators' closer than usual questioning, Rogers has been revealed to be unenthused about tightening the NRC's regulatory style or even about establishing an independent investigative branch within the agency to avoid future farces like the Roberts affair. Rogers' vague and tepid statements are just not good enough when none of the other four NRC commissioners is pushing in this direction either.

On the contrary, the other commissioners, over the Reagan years, have moved to ease regulatory burdens on the nuclear industry — as in the procedure they adopted in 1985 for considering a utility's financial situation before deciding whether it has to retrofit its nuclear power plants with new safety equipment. A federal appeals court last week ruled that approach unacceptable. By law, it said, the NRC must require whatever safety equipment is necessary to adequately protect the public, regardless of cost. But the NRC hasn't even defined what adequate protection is. Its retrofit rule, the court found, is "an exemplar of ambiguity and vagueness. Indeed, we suspect that the commission designed the rule to achieve this very result."

So far, there is no sign that the court's message has gotten through to the NRC, much less the administration that appoints its members. It is thus left to Congress to force a change of attitude on the agency. If that means holding up, or even rejecting, the Rogers nomination; if it means passing legislation that reduces the NRC's freedom of maneuver in setting and enforcing safety standards; if it means imposing a new organization on the agency, then that's what should be done. When the NRC has the last word on nuclear safety, Congress had better go to great lengths to ensure that its word is right.

The Wichita
Eagle-Beacon
Wichita, KS, April 20, 1987

THE Nuclear Regulatory Commission, organized initially to protect the health and safety of nuclear workers and the public, has strayed from its intended mission. Despite scientific evidence that the NRC's maximum allowable annual intake of radioactivity is too high, it's requesting that radioactive standards be increased, rather than decreased — by as much as 17 times the current levels, in some instances.

The propensity for contracting radiation-induced cancer is more than 10 times what it was believed to be in 1962, when the current levels were established. Numerous studies and epidemiological research reveal shocking numbers of cancer deaths among nuclear workers who stayed well within the NRC's levels.

To reduce the NRC's accepted levels for radiation intake tenfold, as the medical and scientific communities have encouraged, admittedly could have a considerable economic impact. For the government to admit publicly that its standards were too weak would imply liability, with the risk of a wave of lawsuits from citizens living near nuclear facilities and from veterans exposed to atomic test blasts.

Public outcry over the matter is expected to force the NRC to make some concessions. Standards won't be strong enough to ensure the public's safety from dangerous levels of radiation, however, until the acceptable levels are lowered dramatically.

THE KANSAS CITY STAR
Kansas City, MO, May 11, 1987

The Nuclear Regulatory Commission is now embroiled in five separate congressional and legal inquiries about how it does its job. The development is alarming. This agency should be above reproach. It is extremely important to make sure reactors are well-managed and that utilities obey the law in operating them.

As it is now set up, the NRC is supposed to promote the safe use of nuclear power in this country. The five members are not supposed to be flaks for the nuclear power industry; neither are they supposed to be card-carrying members of any anti-nuclear group.

But allegations are being made that at least one member, Thomas M. Roberts, has crossed the line and become an adamant supporter of the industry. Ohio Sen. John Glenn has been the most vociferous critic. He contends Roberts may even have broken the law in telling a Louisiana utility that a secret investigation was being made into how one of its reactors was being operated.

An internal investigation is already being made of Roberts' activities. The Justice Department is also looking into the matter. Separate congressional committees are delving into commission activities. On Thursday, Roberts announced he was taking a leave of absence from the NRC to prepare for the battles ahead.

The mere presence of yet another investigation on Capitol Hill is not the disturbing element here. More to the point, the NRC is the prime federal authority established to make sure nuclear power plants are operated safely in this country. When that mission is questioned, the usefulness of the commission should be scrutinized.

Allegations about wrongdoing would not be so worrisome if all the reactors were being operated without problems. That's simply not the case. Indeed, critics are calling for the NRC to be much tougher in punishing utilities that improperly run their facilities.

But if the commission is in reality little more than a cheerleader for nuclear power, its usefulness goes out the window. And new commissioners should be chosen. This is a case worth special attention from Congress in the coming weeks.

4/12/87 THE PHILADELPHIA INQUIRER.
UNIVERSAL PRESS SYNDICATE.

AUTH

FORT WORTH STAR-TELEGRAM

Ft. Worth, TX, January 3, 1987

The Nuclear Regulatory Commission had no choice but to take the unprecedented step of changing monitors for the Comanche Peak nuclear power plant in order to reach any credible conclusion about licensing the plant.

The report issued by NRC investigators last November criticizing the performance of the NRC's Region IV, headquartered in Arlington, in overseeing the construction of the plant severely damaged the credibility of that office for continued monitoring of the project.

That report asserted that Region IV supervisors downgraded, delayed and rewrote inspection reports critical of Comanche Peak and suggested that Region IV's reports couldn't be relied upon as evidence that the plant is safe.

If NRC investigators placed no faith in the veracity of Region IV's inspection reports, the public could not be expected to do so either. It is, therefore, in everyone's best interests that the NRC has decided to turn over the monitoring of Comanche Peak to its new special projects office, which also will oversee the Tennessee Valley Authority's nuclear projects.

The head of the special projects office summed up the move this way: "We realized that, the way things were going ... there weren't going to be timely solutions developed. ... It is going to take an extraordinary effort to bring these projects to completion."

That extraordinary effort means that the new Comanche Peak team will have twice the staff of the Arlington office. That kind of intensified effort on the part of the NRC is long overdue. The Comanche Peak plant is already 10 years behind schedule, and its cost has escalated tenfold.

A decision must be made soon on whether Comanche Peak can be licensed, and, if so, what it will take to get it to that point.

THE TENNESSEAN

Nashville, TN, March 27, 1987

AMID growing concern that the Nuclear Regulatory Commission may be dealing unfairly with the Tennessee Valley Authority, Sen. Jim Sasser is co-sponsoring legislation to put an inspector general over the NRC.

The NRC regulates all of the nation's nuclear power producers, both private and public. The inspector general would have power to determine whether the agency is doing its job correctly and fairly, or whether it favors one utility over another.

Senator Sasser is not the only one to have noticed that the NRC's treatment of TVA is suggestive of ill will and may be inspired by outside forces hostile to TVA. There has been particular concern expressed about the NRC's investigation of Mr. Steven White, who was appointed last year to straighten out TVA's lagging nuclear program.

On March 20, 1986, only a few weeks after going to work for TVA, Mr. White told the NRC in a letter that there was "no pervasive breakdown of the quality assurance program" at TVA's Watts Bar nuclear plant.

Mr. White later conceded that "significant" breakdowns had occurred, and now the NRC is investigating whether the TVA nuclear chief intentionally misled the commission. It was the type of error that could have been made by anyone on the job for such a short time. The NRC's insinuation that Mr. White may have deliberately lied about conditions at the nuclear plant, if not based on solid evidence, borders on harassment.

Representatives Marilyn Lloyd and Jim Cooper have suggested that NRC's investigation of Mr. White was being influenced by persons outside the NRC, some of whom may have a personal grudge against Mr. White.

That could well be true. TVA has plenty of enemies, both inside and outside of government, some dating from TVA's creation and some of more recent vintage. It would not be surprising to learn that some of TVA's enemies are using the nuclear regulatory agency to get at TVA.

It would be unfortunate if the NRC should be found to be making decisions based on political considerations. Its job is a very sensitive one. Safety in nuclear power production is a priority with the public, and the people need to have confidence that the NRC is doing a thorough, tough job in keeping nuclear plants safe.

That includes TVA. The NRC needs to crack down on TVA when TVA gets lax on safety matters. But there needs to be some assurance that the NRC is acting fairly and objectively. While the NRC is keeping an eye on nuclear power plants, there should be someone to keep an eye on the way the NRC is doing its job. That is a task for an inspector general. Congress should create such a post for the NRC. ■

The Philadelphia Inquirer

Philadelphia, PA, April 12, 1987

Some of the most damning testimony about the pervasive failings of the Nuclear Regulatory Commission that has come to light since the Three Mile Island accident was offered by witnesses Thursday before the Senate Governmental Affairs Committee.

They provided hauntingly familiar examples of the agency's refusal to deal with serious safety problems at nuclear reactors around the country.

"I can unequivocally state that I know of no other regulatory or investigative agency where senior agency officials have taken as many bizarre and seemingly deliberate actions intended to hamper the investigation and prosecution of individuals and companies in the industry [it] regulates," testified Julian Greenspun, who until recently was in charge of criminal prosecutions brought by the U.S. Justice Department on behalf of a number of federal agencies including the NRC.

Defensive NRC officials at the hearing attempted to portray their agency as an aggressive protector of the public, citing the decision to shut down the Peach Bottom reactor in York County after learning that control-room personnel routinely were sleeping on the job. The shutdown came one week before the hearing, and one committee member, Sen. John Heinz (R., Pa.), speculated that the NRC took its unprecedented action at Peach Bottom solely to give the commissioners ammunition to counter critical testimony at the hearing.

Among the incidents detailed by witnesses were these:

• A 1983 internal NRC memo alleging that a Louisiana utility covered up potentially serious safety defects at a reactor was leaked to the utility, apparently by NRC Commissioner Thomas M. Roberts or his staff. When the memo was discovered in utility files by an NRC investigator probing the same allegations, the investigator was ordered to report to Mr. Roberts, who allegedly attempted to destroy the evidence. The NRC did not probe the matter further.

• Victor Stello, director of operations at the NRC, was said to have personally advised a Tennessee Valley Authority official how to answer an NRC inquiry about safety problems at a TVA reactor in Tennessee. Mr. Stello allegedly told the executive to stall and not answer the NRC's questions. Although the conversation took place in front of two other NRC officials, according to testimony, there was no investigation.

Sen. John Glenn (D., Ohio), who chaired the hearing, has cosponsored a bill creating four independent inspectors general, one of whom would oversee activities of the NRC. Although the NRC has an internal watchdog bureaucracy, it is weak and ineffectual, as the witnesses, who included frustrated NRC employees, clearly demonstrated.

Sen. Glenn and others believe an independent inspector would make the NRC more responsible. Perhaps. Ultimately, however, the NRC will never fulfill its obligations to the public until an entirely new attitude pervades the agency. Underlying that attitude is a simple premise: Those in charge of regulating and providing nuclear power must regard it for what it is — a force so great as to always pose a potentially grave threat to the public's health and safety.

That attitude certainly doesn't prevail today.

The Star-Ledger

Newark, NJ, July 24, 1987

After hearing some disturbing testimony from a senior Nuclear Regulatory Commission security inspector and other witnesses, the House Interior and Insular Affairs subcommittee on general oversight has expressed concern about alcohol and drug abuse at nuclear power plants.

The finding was released at an opportune time. Key officials at the Soviet Union's Chernobyl plant are being tried for their role in the tragic accident that is the world's most serious nuclear disaster.

Last August, the NRC said it would give the nuclear industry an 18-month trial period to establish self-policing procedures to deter alcohol and drug abuse and to punish those violators caught on the job. A tipsy or turned-on employee can be a serious threat to life and safety in the vicinity of any nuclear plant.

The subcommittee is doubtful that industry can do the job, citing testimony that the companies simply are not up to the job. That conclusion, however, seems to be premature. And it is highly unlikely that any management team would knowingly tolerate or condone keeping employees with drug or alcohol problems at work, particularly if they can freely enter the inner control areas of the nuclear plants.

No one really is sure, at this time, just how widespread the abuse of alcohol and drugs is at nuclear power facilities, but the problem should be approached as though it were extensive. Strong, protective measures are necessary to safeguard the public, and this requires giving the nuclear plant operators the authority they need to weed out any employees given to drinking or drug abuse.

Lawmakers and judges, at the federal and state levels, however, have been reluctant to sanction routine or random testing on grounds that it violates constitutional rights to privacy. New Jersey court cases, including one involving schoolchildren, have ended in verdicts against officials and in favor of those who were targeted for tests.

Strong laws and a constitutional amendment, if necessary, should be put in place to permit precautionary testing—and give the public some assurance that employees with hands-on access to nuclear controls are not staggering about the premises, free to pull the levers or press the buttons.

ST. LOUIS POST-DISPATCH

St. Louis, MO, April 13, 1987

Cooperation is a good thing, but it has its limits, and the Nuclear Regulatory Commission has overstepped them by a country mile. For years, top officials at that agency have been tipping the hands of investigators. In snuggling up to the nuclear power industry, they have left conscientious lower-level agency investigators — to say nothing of the public — out in the cold.

Perhaps the most egregious incident is the Senate Governmental Affairs Committee's implication of Commissioner Thomas Roberts. In 1983, a copy of a sensitive memo alleging problems with the Waterford nuclear plant near New Orleans turned up in the files of company executives just four days after it was seen by top-level NRC people. The copy bore the initials of Mr. Roberts, one of industry's staunchest backers on the commission.

NRC staffers told of other investigations that managers have stymied. NRC Executive Director Victor Stello, the agency's most powerful staff member, was accused of running interference for the industry, once even coaching the head of the Tennessee Valley Authority on how to respond to investigators' questions.

Mr. Stello, it was alleged, also covered up evidence that the NRC knew of radioactive leaks at the Three Mile Island plant before the 1979 accident there, saying an investigation at TMI would be bad for operator morale.

Whenever regulators cozy up to the parties they're supposed to regulate, an unhealthy policy can result. When the regulated industry is nuclear power, where lax oversight holds the potential for catastrophe, that's cause for more than tongue-clucking. Violations of regulatory independence alleged at the NRC are serious enough to warrant revamping the agency's management structure.

Nuclear Reactor at Hanford Closed

The Energy Department said Feb. 16, 1988 that it was not reopening its plutonium-producing nuclear reactor, known as the N-reactor, at the Hanford nuclear site near Richland, Wash.

The reactor had been temporarily closed for saftey repairs since January 1987. The decision to mothball the reactor was not made for safety reasons, according to the department, although the plant drew close inspection after the 1986 Chernobyl nuclear disaster in the Soviet Union, because, like the Soviet reactor, it had a graphite core. (See pp. 52-59)

The N-reactor, one of four used by the U.S. government to produce weapons-grade nuclear materials, was being closed because the Defense Department's need for new plutonium for nuclear weapons had fallen off, the department said.

The safety repairs were to be finished on the N-reactor in case it was ever needed again. Meanwhile, the reactor's nuclear fuel would be removed and the plant put in "cold" standby. In that status, it would take two to three years to restart the reactor, the department said, because new personnel would have to be hired and trained.

Closure would result in layoff of about 2,600 of the plant's 3,300 employees over the next two years. The plant was operated for the government by Westinghouse Electric Corp.

The Idaho STATESMAN

Boise, ID, May 22, 1987

The Department of Energy may think it can operate the N Reactor at Hanford, Wash., safely, but it is having no luck convincing the people of the Pacific Northwest of it.

The department should keep the reactor shut down until an independent group such as the National Academy of Sciences or the National Academy of Engineering determines that the reactor can be operated safely.

The 23-year-old N Reactor, which produces plutonium for nuclear weapons, was shut down in January after safety problems were found. The Department of Energy is planning to restart the reactor in July, even though all the improvements will not be finished.

The department has held eight public hearings in the Northwest on the question of restarting the reactor. Only at Richland, Wash., the hometown of many Hanford workers, did the restart get a green light from the public.

At hearings in Spokane, Portland and on Tuesday in Lewiston, the public demanded either more assurance that the reactor is safe to operate or a permanent shutdown of the facility.

Rep. Les AuCoin, D-Ore., in a statement prepared for the Portland hearing, said it was "preposterous" that the department planned to restart the reactor even though a limited impact statement would be barely under way in July.

"The department has, in effect, chosen to examine a single rivet in the hull of a leaky ship, and ordered the ship back out to sea before doing a full examination," Rep. AuCoin said in his statement.

J.R. Wilkinson of Moscow said in Lewiston: "The DOE is a self-regulated, self-guided elephant in the democratic playpen we call America."

The people of Idaho should care about what happens with the N Reactor, which is the reactor in the United States most like the Soviet Union's troubled Chernobyl reactor. If there were an accident, it is likely that the nuclear fallout would blow across northern Idaho, over the cities of Moscow and Lewiston.

Many in the Northwest want the N Reactor shut down for good. Even two of the six members on the special panel that looked at the reactor last year said it should be permanently shut down within five years unless it is determined that national security requires the reactor's plutonium.

The N Reactor, after the safety improvements are made, may or may not be safe. But a limited environmental study by the Department of Energy is not good enough. The department should conduct a full environmental impact study.

An independent investigation should also be conducted into the safety of the reactor and the adequacy of the safety improvements before the N Reactor is restarted.

Nothing less will satisfy the people of the Pacific Northwest – nor should it.

THE KANSAS
CITY STAR
Kansas City, MO,
April 16, 1987

For more than a year, Congress has known something is dangerously amiss at the Hanford nuclear reservation. The facility is used partly to process plutonium for nuclear weapons. Defending the nation is an important task. But so is protecting the health and welfare of people in the state of Washington.

So far the Department of Energy has badly fallen down on the job. New documents indicate high doses of radiation have either leaked or been purposefully released into the air and the water over the last decade. Who's been minding the store? Negligent federal officials, that's who.

Congress is the only neutral party that can do anything about this behavior. The Department of Energy is busy making excuses for its abysmal operation. Indeed, its executives last month released a report about the need for nuclear power to fuel the nation's energy needs in the 1990s and beyond. The administration backs up the department, which comes as no surprise. President Reagan and his advisers have always had a lot of faith in the power of the atom, and in man's ability to control its harmful effects.

But the people of Hanford beg to disagree. Many trot out a host of illnesses they attribute to living close to the site. The federal government's own figures show releases of potentially harmful radiation have been tolerated for too long.

Congress has several options. One is to force the Department of Energy to give up its supervisory capacity to the Nuclear Regulatory Commission. Granted, just shifting bureaucrats around won't be totally satisfying. But at least the NRC has more knowledge about nuclear facilities and how to better handle them.

The lawmakers cannot stop there. Obviously a lot of pressure bears down on officials at Hanford to keep producing material for America's bombs. Congress, working in conjunction with the NRC and other experts, needs to clearly outline how Hanford is to be operated in the future.

The people who live near the facility have been very supportive of the jobs it has brought. It's appalling that the federal government has repaid this support with such a shoddy operation.

The Register-Guard

Eugene, OR, March 9, 1989

Washington state officials say they have negotiated a "Cadillac agreement" with the federal Department of Energy to clean up wastes at the Hanford Nuclear Reservation. But a Cadillac can't go anywhere without gas in the tank. Money — lots of it — will be needed to fuel the agreement and make it meaningful.

The pact approved late last month after a year of discussions is an important achievement for Washington state and the Northwest. The Department of Energy is now committed to a cleanup, and it has agreed to accept oversight by the state. The department also agreed to a faster timetable for the cleanup — 30 years instead of the 50 it had originally proposed.

The amount of work that needs to be done at Hanford is daunting. Material for nuclear weapons has been manufactured at the 570-square-mile reservation for nearly 45 years. An estimated 1,200 separate sites are contaminated with about 5 billion cubic yards of radioactive or toxic wastes. Some of the waste has contaminated groundwater and threatens the Columbia River. It will cost an estimated $57 billion to clean up the mess.

Under the agreement, the department has pledged to spend $2.8 billion on cleanup programs at Hanford during the next five years. That's double the current pace of cleanup efforts.

But even the first $2.8 billion installment on the cost of a cleanup won't be made unless the agreement gains the backing of the Bush administration and Congress. The federal government has many other claims on its resources.

The agreement enlists the Department of Energy as a powerful advocate for obtaining cleanup funds, which ought to be a help in persuading Congress and the administration to support appropriations. It might also help if the federal government regarded the Hanford cleanup as a cost of maintaining the nation's nuclear deterrent for more than four decades — a military expense that has been forgotten or ignored until now.

It is helpful, even vital, to have Washington state and the Department of Energy working as partners at Hanford. But a cleanup won't occur without the financial support of many congresses and administrations to come. Obtaining that support and maintaining it through future decades will be a lasting challenge.

THE SPOKESMAN-REVIEW

Spokane, WA, September 13, 1989

The U.S. Department of Energy has developed a magnificent concept for the study of nuclear and chemical waste cleanup, a concept that holds considerable importance to Eastern Washington as well as to the nation as a whole.

At a press conference on Sunday, U.S. Rep. Sid Morrison, R-Wash., said the department has asked that the federal budget for fiscal 1990 include funds for the beginning of a national hazardous waste research center to be located at the Hanford Nuclear Reservation's Pacific Northwest Laboratory in the Tri-Cities.

Because the proposal is at an early stage and has not yet won approval from the White House Office of Management and Budget, Morrison said he could not disclose such details as the amount of money or the number of jobs the proposal would involve.

No matter. The important thing is that the Department of Energy has recognized not only the need for a national center for hazardous waste research but also the ideal site for such a center.

Throughout the nation are thousands of individual cleanup chores which will require the emergence of a major new industry. Many of the country's nuclear power reactors will reach the end of their designed life spans within the next decade or two and will require decommissioning and cleanup. A whole generation of nuclear weapons plants also is wearing out and poses extremely difficult and expensive cleanup challenges. In addition, chemical waste dumps are everywhere.

In most of the communities where these problems are emerging, the technical expertise required to resolve them is in short supply, but to the scientists at Hanford, for 40 years the scene of intense environmental monitoring and management of both chemical and radioactive wastes, the challenges and the technical solutions are familiar.

Hanford contains nine shutdown nuclear reactors, one operating commercial reactor, a fast-flux test reactor, five plants that have processed both hazardous and radioactive chemicals, approximately 1,000 sites where environmental cleanup is required and laboratories filled with scientists expert in environmental monitoring, waste management and cleanup.

As such, Hanford is two things: a place in need of cleanup and also an unsurpassed laboratory for the development of cleanup technology.

A central laboratory for research on cleanup would attract the best scientists in that field. Housing the research under a single roof would save money, producing transferrable technologies at the lowest possible cost. Establishing the center where technologies can be field-tested and where the needed scientific community already exists also would minimize costs.

From Eastern Washington's point of view, the Energy Department's proposal has two additional virtues: The winding down of nuclear weapons production at Hanford creates a need for new industry in the Tri-Cities. And the government does have an obligation to dispose of Hanford's wastes safely. If Hanford becomes headquarters for the nation's cleanup industry, adequate funding for management of its wastes ought to be assured.

THE ANN ARBOR NEWS

Ann Arbor, MI, April 20, 1989

Federal legislation in 1980 made states responsible for their own radioactive nuclear waste. For Michigan, that's a significant matter of concern.

Low-level radioactive waste comes from commercial power plants, medical procedures and various industrial processes. Michigan produces about 60,000 cubic feet of low-level waste a year, and one can't just bury the stuff at any old landfill.

The federal law encouraged neighboring states to form compacts and build collective disposal sites. The Midwest compact which Michigan joined along with Indiana, Iowa, Minnesota, Missouri, Ohio and Wisconsin has chosen Michigan as the host state for the region's first low-level radioactive waste dump.

Sometime in June, three communities will be named as candidates for the dump. That announcement by state officials is sure to cause more controversy. Obviously, with nuclear waste as with prisons and group homes, the NIMBY principle (Not in My Back Yard) comes into full play.

Legitimate environmental concerns, as well as unresolved questions over liability and economic issues, are sure to dominate the state's preparations for the disposal site. A major problem is that there is so much government officials, environmentalists and scientists still don't know about waste management.

A great deal of research is needed to enlarge scientific understanding of the waste problem. And essentially no research has been done on low-level radioactive waste by universities or independent researchers, according to James Martin, a health physicist at the University of Michigan School of Public Health.

To remedy that paucity of data, U-M scientists are proposing to state officials a nuclear waste research institute as an independent technical and scientific resource center.

David Hales is commissioner of the Michigan Low-Level Radioactive Waste Authority, and was recently named director of the Michigan Department of Natural Resources. In a conversation with The News, Hales shared Martin's concern over the complexity of the radioactive waste issue and the dearth of applicable solutions.

"It's a very technical issue," Hales said, "and it's hard to understand the nature of what kind of waste we're talking about unless you have a background in nuclear physics."

That rules out nearly everybody in Michigan, but it doesn't preclude a strong effort to increase our knowledge base about waste management.

Among questions U-M researchers want to explore are how radioactive waste breaks down and changes with time, and what type of sealant at a disposal facility would best ensure against the possibility of leakage.

In addition to research, goals of the institute include training experts, providing community education and offering technical assistance. The institute as proposed would involve a consortium of U-M, Michigan State University and Michigan Technological University scientists.

The MSU team offers expertise in structural and environmental engineering, and extension service outreach programs. Michigan Tech scientists are skilled in the geological sciences and engineering. Ideally, the institute would be located in Ann Arbor since the proposal originated here and the U-M's reputation as a top-flight research institution qualifies it in many ways.

Authorization has been given by the Legislature. The need has been recognized and up to $1 million a year from waste disposal fees will go to fund institute activities. Our lead time for getting the institute off and running is short, because the regional waste site is to begin operations for a 20-year period beginning in 1993.

The institute's purpose and general goals are clearly in the best interests of a state which is shouldering an enormous responsibility in nuclear waste management.

EPA Stresses Radon Risk

The Environmental Protection Agency Sept. 12, 1988 issued a national health advisory on radon recommending testing of homesites for the presence of the cancer-causing gas. Radon, which is invisible and radioactive, is produced by the natural decay of uranium in soil. Its presence in dangerous amounts – equivalent to smoking half a pack of cigarettes a day, or having 200 to 300 chest x-rays a year – was found by a recent study in one-third of the homes in seven states surveyed. The incidence was greater than found by an earlier study in 1987 that one in five homes possibly had unsafe radon levels.

The latest study, undertaken by state health and environmental agencies, reported potentially toxic levels of radon in more than 65% of homes tested in North Dakota, 40% in Minnesota, 25% in Indiana and Pennsylvania, 20% in Massachusetts, 15% in Missouri and 10% in Arizona. The warning was accompanied by a statement from the Public Health Service that smokers living in suspect homes had a 15% greater chance of developing lung cancer than did nonsmokers. The smoke became an agent moving radon to the lungs, Assistant Surgeon General Vernon J. Houk said, enhancing the opportunity for cancer. "If your house has any detectable levels of radon," Houk said, "don't permit smoking in your house."

Radon detecting kits were relatively inexpensive, and the exposure risk could be reduced or eliminated by ventilation, which dissipated the radon, or by sealing off entry points.

The Hutchinson News
Hutchinson, KS, Sept. 19, 1988

Frankly, we really could have done without the radon problem.

The greenhouse effect is quite enough for any generation to have to worry about.

It that were not, the fact that nation-nuts like Syria, Iraq and other Third World nations are stockpiling chemical weapons will. And then there's the prospect of having President J. Danforth Quayle in arm's reach of The Button.

But radon is a problem. Radon is a gas. It's colorless and odorless. It seeps up from the natural breakdown of uranium in ground formations.

The gas was known to be a health hazard as early as 1879. It has been linked to lung cancer by the U.S. Public Health Service in the 1950s and 1960s.

The U.S. surgeon general has declared it to be the second-leading cause of lung cancer in the nation. That alone should encourage further action in Kansas, even if the earlier studies show low levels of risk in this part of Kansas.

Further action should be clear.

State government should be expected to test every home in the state. No panic is needed, because the early indications are that the dangers are not overwhelming.

But Kansas need not dither around, either. This is a public health problem. Government ought to be trusted, and expected, to find the most effective, efficient and prudent way to fix it.

THE SACRAMENTO BEE
Sacramento, CA, Sept. 15, 1988

It's been almost exactly four years since the day Stanley Watrous set off alarm bells at the Limerick Nuclear Power Plant near Pottstown, Pa., because he showed up for work radioactive. The problem, it turned out, wasn't in the plant but in Watrous' house. That's how America found out about the risks of radon gas, and the alarm bells have been ringing ever since.

Earlier this week, the Environmental Protection Agency did no one any favors by dramatically announcing that "millions of homes" were possibly contaminated with radon and urging all Americans to hire somebody to test for the cancer-causing gas. That's set off something like a nationwide panic as worried homeowners have deluged state and local health authorities with phone calls asking for information on how to ward off the presumed threat. State Health Director Ken Kizer consequently deserves a lot of credit for his efforts to put the radon problem in perspective for Californians.

Radon is serious. An estimated 20,000 Americans may die from exposure to it every year. But unlike many of the other environmental problems that agencies like the EPA have to wrestle with, it's not the sort of problem that requires a lot of governmental intervention. Radon doesn't arise from pollution, and it's not the consequence of regulatory shortcomings or inadvertent error. It's a function of soil content and weather. As a purely natural phenomenon, this color-less, odorless gas apparently poses a threat to human health only when it seeps from the soil into someone's basement and then becomes trapped inside a tightly closed house during the winter.

Those risks can be contained pretty easily with better seals at ground level and better ventilation above. And in California, even those precautions aren't often necessary. Most California homes, after all, don't have basements. Most residents of the Golden State don't live in areas where they have to keep their houses buttoned up as tightly during the winter as people in the other parts of the country do. Most important, as the state Department of Mines and Geology points out, there are very few areas in California where the kind of soils that produce radon can even be found.

Kizer's department is nonetheless conducting tests in randomly selected homes throughout California to see whether there's any risk from radon. The results will be ready next year, and should provide a rational basis for determining whether there's any need for further action by anyone in California. Kizer was right, therefore, to complain that the EPA's alarmism, in this part of the country at least, is premature. Certainly the widespread testing that the EPA suggests every homeowner should undertake would be, in Kizer's words, "a profound waste of money" in California.

THE LINCOLN STAR

Lincoln, NE, Sept. 15, 1988

Radiation.

The very word inspires a chill of fear in many folks.

Then there's radon gas — that invisible, odorless gas produced as uranium decays. It exists naturally in most soils and can enter buildings and be inhaled. And it can increase the chances of getting lung cancer.

All scary stuff.

So it's no wonder that folks started calling the local Department of Health this month after the Environmental Protection Agency advised homeowners to have their homes tested for radon. The EPA has found homes in seven states with higher-than-expected levels of the gas.

There's nothing wrong with checking your home for radon. It's fairly inexpensive; it's fairly simple.

But there is also no reason to panic.

LINCOLN IS NOT a hotbed of radon gas. Checks of 450 Lincoln homes indicated that about 36 percent had levels of radon higher than the EPA guideline. But most of those homes had radon levels at the low edge of trouble — 4 to 8 picocuries per liter of air.

It takes a very long and very intense exposure to that amount of radon before there is a health danger.

A person who spends 75 percent of her time in a house with a radon level of 4 picocuries for 70 years increases her chances of developing lung cancer by about 1.5 percent, according to EPA information. That's 18 hours a day, seven days a week, for 70 years.

Even the 4 picocuries is not an infallible number. That trigger number is based on mathematical calculations, on modeling. Another group using the same data but different modeling came up with an 8-picocuries risk level.

The purists want radon levels of 1 to 2 picocuries. Other experts feel we're safe at 20. So the danger level is debatable.

AND RADON ITSELF is a minor player in the arsenal of things that kill us.

EPA estimates that radon is responsible for 20,000 deaths a year.

A puny number compared to the 771,169 people who died in 1985 from heart disease.

Cars kill more than twice that number of people a year.

Breast cancer, a fairly treatable disease if discovered and treated early enough, kills double the number of radon victims.

Granted there's certainly a risk in radon. The EPA describes the radon risk like this: If 1,000 people are exposed to 4 picocuries of radon gas for 18 hours a day for 70 years, 13 to 50 of them will die from lung cancer.

It appears from the EPA information that there's time to handle the radon problem. In fact, it takes an entire year just to conduct a good, useful home radon test.

So while we're waiting for the radon results, we could tackle a few more mundane health risks.

We could reduce our cholesterol. A person who reduces his cholesterol count by 15 percent decreases his chances of developing coronary heart disease by 30 percent.

Or simply use seat belts. Between 12,000 to 15,000 lives a year could be saved if everyone in a passenger car used a belt. And Lancaster County adults are still not very smart about seat belts. An August study showed that only 38 percent of adults were using this life-lengthening device.

The Duluth News-Tribune

Duluth, MN, Sept. 14, 1988

So there's one more health and environment cause for Minnesotans to take up.

This week's call by two federal agencies that residential property owners across our nation test their dwellings for the presence of radon is of particular note in Minnesota, where more than two homes in five reportedly contain excessive levels of the radioactive and potentially carcinogenic gas. According to figures from Minnesota health officials, 46 percent of 919 homes tested in the state contain levels of the colorless, odorless gas at which federal officials report residents face increased health risks. About 20,000 lung cancer deaths per year in our nation are attributed to radon exposure.

Radon is a naturally occurring vapor. Relatively simple and inexpensive tests — $10 to $25 — can be administered for the gas. And remedial action to prevent the seepage and buildup of radon in homes is also relatively simple and inexpensive.

So, while this is certainly a cause for public concern in our region, it need not at this time be considered a cause for great public alarm. Public authorities — federal, state and local — should be and are formulating policies to address radon pollution.

Radon poses a public health problem. But since it is a natural, not man-made danger, prudent public policy would seem to be to require owner-financed, not public-financed, testing of all residential property for radon and remedial action to stop its buildup. This would be particularly applicable regarding rental property and at the time of sale of all other residences.

The proper government role here should be to provide public enlightment about a health problem which may be surrounding us all.

The Dallas Morning News

Dallas, TX, Sept. 18, 1988

Amid all the disturbing news about acid rain, ozone and other pollutants in the atmosphere, many people at least have had the feeling that they were somewhat safer indoors. No more, though. Environmental scientists are concluding that indoor air pollution, which still is largely unregulated, constitutes a more dangerous public health problem than outdoor air pollution.

A good case in point is radon gas, which seeps into homes from the underlying rock and soil and increases the risk of lung cancer. The Environmental Protection Agency this week found the colorless, odorless gas exceeded federal levels in nearly one in every three houses it tested in seven states. That finding should be alarming, because it means radon is far more prevalent than the agency once thought. A survey last year of 10 other states turned up excessive amounts of the gas in one in every five homes.

Texas environmental officials believe radon contamination may not be as severe here as in other regions of the country. That is because the types of rock typically associated with it are not as prevalent in this state as elsewhere and also because basements, where the highest levels of the gas normally are found, are not a common feature of Texas homes.

But until more testing can be done, the potential threat of radon should not be underestimated in the Lone Star State. Although the radioactive gas may not be as widespread as it is in the East, that is not to suggest it is safe here. Based on preliminary readings, thousands of Texas homes may have excessive levels. Homeowners concerned about the possibility should follow the EPA's advice and have their houses checked by a qualified contractor. If a problem exists, it usually can be remedied with better ventilation.

Beyond that, the EPA's latest measure of radon's prevalence should give Congress the impetus to pass legislation that authorizes $42 million over three years for federal grants to help states reduce the level of the radioactive gas in homes and schools. The measure has been making its way slowly through Congress for more than a year, and its approval is long overdue.

Since people cannot see or smell radon, they may be tempted to dismiss its danger. But that would be risky. Radon poses a far greater health threat than many other pollutants that command more public attention. It is considered by environmental scientists to be the nation's second-leading cause of lung cancer — after cigarette smoking — killing perhaps as many as 20,000 people each year. As the EPA's new findings underscore, the days when Americans could feel confident about the impenetrability of their homes clearly are over.

Radon, a radioactive gas that seeps into houses, was splashed across the front pages of America's newpapers yesterday.

The reason was the release of an Environmental Protection Agency survey of seven states which indicated that the prevalence of radon is more widespread than previously believed. In Rhode Island and Massachusetts, for example, it was projected that more than one out of every five homes has potentially dangerous levels of radon.

Radon results from the breakdown of uranium in the earth and can enter a basement through crevices in the foundation. Though harmless in open spaces, it can have long-term effects on health when not dispersed by ventilation in a house. After smoking, it is the leading cause of lung cancer deaths.

While radon is a legitimate health

The Providence Journal
Providence, RI, Sept. 14, 1988

threat, the survey's findings should not trigger an overreaction. First off, it involved an initial test only that measured homes in the location (basement) and season (winter) at which radon levels are at their highest.

So the recordings of high levels which occurred in this survey do not necessarily represent a hazard to the inhabitants. They simply suggest the need for year-long tests to discover the actual amount of radon in the homes. It is predicted that from this second test one in 10 homes will be shown to have dangerous levels — a sizable reduction from more than one in five.

There are, as well, varying degrees of high levels. The EPA standard is 4 picocuries per liter of air. Agency studies indicate that out of a hundred people, one to five would die of lung cancer af-

ter 70 years of spending 75 percent of their time in a house with this level. At 20 picocuries the number of people at risk out of a hundred increases to six to 21. Other variables come into account, most notably, smoking: radon risks are estimated to be 15 percent higher for smokers than for nonsmokers.

What all of this indicates is that there is cause for testing, but not for panic. A headstart fortunately has been made via legislation Sen. John H. Chafee and two colleagues drafted early in 1987 to provide $40 million over three years to help states develop radon detection programs. The Senate passed the bill last year and the House is expected to send it to the president shortly. Meanwhile, those wishing to move on their own for home tests can obtain names of experienced firms from the EPA or the state Department of Health.

The Pittsburgh PRESS

Pittsburgh, PA, Sept. 15, 1988

In Pennsylvania, there's better than a one in three chance that your home, besides being your castle, may also be your gas chamber.

The grisly statistics are courtesy of the Environmental Protection Agency, which found that 37 percent of 429 Pennsylvania homes it tested had unsafe concentrations of deadly radon gas.

In Allegheny County, one in four homes registered above the EPA's "action level," at which long-term tests should be taken to determine if concentrations are consistently — and dangerously — high.

Radon, formed by the natural decay of uranium in soil and rock, is a radioactive gas that causes cancer. The EPA estimates that 20,000 of the nation's 130,000 lung cancer deaths each year are the result of radon.

But despite all the gloom, radon is not apocalyptic. Usually, it can be controlled without great expense.

All home owners should purchase testing canisters, which cost between $12 and $25.

If the test results suggest action, it should be taken immediately. To reduce the levels, a homeowner may simply have to open a few windows or seal cracks in basement walls. Others may have to install comparatively expensive ventilation systems.

In either case, the expenditure is a prudent investment in the family's health.

DESERET NEWS
Salt Lake City, UT, Sept. 18, 1988

A few years back, Utah had a problem with radioactive radon gas collecting in some buildings. The invisible, odorless gas is a major contributor to lung cancer. It was a man-made problem, the result of using tailings from a uranium mill as fill under foundations.

But many other parts of the country are discovering they have radon gas problems of their own — not as a result of anything man has done, but simply from the workings of nature.

Radon gas is released in minute quantities due to the decay of trace amounts of uranium found in all rocks and soil. The gas tends to enter buildings through cracks in foundations and other openings. It gets trapped in homes and is inhaled into lungs where it leaves its own radioactive decay products.

What's the danger? The National Academy of Sciences estimates that 13,000 people die each year from radon-caused lung cancer — about 10 percent of all lung cancer deaths. EPA officials said this is 10 times worse than the hazard from outdoor air pollution.

The news is even worse for smokers who already are putting their lungs at risk. Smoking makes radon 15 times more effective in doing damage to the lungs.

The EPA has set 4 picocuries of radon per liter as its "action level." Yet 4 picocuries of radon has not been determined as harmless, either. Radon measured outdoors amounts to about one-half of 1 percent of that amount. Indoors, it builds up to heavier concentrations, particularly in today's well-insulated homes.

A survey of 10 states last year by the Environmental Protection Agen-

cy indicated that perhaps one in 10 American homes had a radon problem. But a study of 10 more states released this week showed more widespread and higher levels of radon than earlier believed.

The latest survey found 63 percent of the homes in North Dakota above the 4 picocurie level. Minnesota, 46 percent; Pennsylvania, 37 percent; Indiana, 26 percent; Massachusetts, 24 percent; Missouri, 18 percent.

So what's to be done?

The first advice is: don't panic. This is not a sudden, new problem. What's true in one state, may be entirely different in another. There is no indication that radon is a critical issue in Utah. No EPA study has been done here, but Wyoming and Arizona have not shown major radon levels.

Initial screening tests for radon can be done for $10 to $25. If they show a high amount, a followup test can be done. Fixing a house to seal it against radon can be expensive, depending on what is needed. Perhaps $1,000 would be average, but that's an uncertain figure.

A word of warning. Unscrupulous scam artists may try to frighten people into having expensive tests and even more expensive repairs. Stay calm and don't fall for pitches based on scare tactics. The safest bet is to say "no" to such approaches.

The EPA has authorized some 1,000 companies to do radon testing. The names of such companies may be obtained by writing EPA's regional headquarters in Denver, 999-18th St., Denver, Colo. 80202.

One thing is clear. A safe and healthy environment doesn't come easy. Even living in a house has its drawbacks.

When my parents have nightmares about radon, I let them sleep out here with me...

MARGULIES
©1988 HOUSTON POST

The Evening Gazette

Worcester, MA, Sept. 16, 1988

Lethal holes in the ozone layer, the greenhouse effect and toxic med tides now have been joined by a killer in your cellar: radon.

The dangers of the cancer-causing gas are doubtlessly real. Yet it is hard to imagine why the Environmental Protection Agency adopted such an alarmist tone in issuing its findings.

Radon forms as tiny amounts of uranium in soil or rock decay and can seep into houses through foundation cracks. In well-insulated houses that are not aired out regularly, the gas can accumulate, with potentially dire health consequences over years or decades.

After a 10-state survey two years ago, the EPA warned of household radon, saying it might be responsible for 5,000 to 20,000 of the nation's 140,000 lung-cancer deaths each year. The newest seven-state survey, which includes Massachusetts, supports that assessment.

Those figures may well lead prudent people who believe their homes might have a high risk to test for radon. The cost of the tests is about $25 to $30. Reducing high radon levels by sealing cracks and improving ventilation typically would cost about $1,000.

The EPA said millions of homes nationwide may exceed the federal radiation standard due to radon, but it overstated the danger when it recommended that every house, town house, rowhouse and mobile home should be tested. People who spend 75 percent of their time for 70 years in a house at the standard level will increase their risk of lung cancer by about 1 percent.

Stated that way, the increased risk is probably less than alarming to most people. The risk does go up with the concentration of radon, but the EPA's characterization of radon as "one of today's most serious public health issues" is open to debate. That tone already has caused a run on radon-testing kits — although their reliability is questionable during the warm months when doors and windows are often open.

Worse, it has prompted calls for new radon-control laws, including making a radon test compulsory whenever a home is sold. It takes little imagination to predict the flood of radon-related liability and damage suits that soon would inundate the courts.

Information about radon is available from local and state public health departments and from the EPA. People concerned about their health would be wise to check into whether their circumstances warrant radon testing. However, we hope the shrill EPA warning will not result in a spate of ill-considered laws or in unwarranted panic about a killer gas lurking in our cellars.

Portland Press Herald

Portland, ME, Sept. 19, 1988

Radon, according to the federal Environmental Protection Agency, is a far more serious problem than anyone had realized. Virtually every home in America should be tested to determine if the cancer-causing gas, caused by the decay of uranium found in most soils, is present in amounts beyond acceptable levels.

But if there is a problem, solutions are available. The problem of unhealthful amounts of radon accumulation in homes usually can be solved — by sealing basement cracks and installing vents — for $1,000 or less. Testing kits to determine the amount of radon in homes are widely available at a small cost.

True, not all test results are reliable. Because a colorless, odorless gas is involved, poor positioning of a test canister can result in misleading results. But testing is at least an indicator of the extent of the radon problem which, nationally, may cause 20,000 lung cancer deaths a year, second only to cigarette smoking.

The results of the latest round of EPA testing (Maine is among the states to be tested next year) is bound to increase pressure for implementation of a variety of suggestions made earlier this year by the Maine Commission on Radon. The commission recommended testing all schools and public buildings for radon content over the next two years (at an unspecified cost) but shied away from endorsing legislation requiring anyone selling a home to have it radon-tested first.

Where would the money come from? Sen. George J. Mitchell says the federal government should spend $30 million over a three-year period to aid states in footing the bill. He's yet to convince the House to go along. Whatever the eventual answer, the risks of radon — unlike other environmental problems — can be easily eliminated, and at relatively small cost. It's a sensible investment in both public and private dollars.

Waste Dump
Plan Restudied

Faced with lawsuits and political controversy, the U.S. Energy Department Jan. 28, 1987 announced that it would postpone until 2003 the opening of its first permanent repository for highly radioactive nuclear waste. The dump was originally scheduled to open in 1998.

The department said that until the delay was necessary because of obstacles and unanticipated problems in the process of selecting a site for the repository. In 1986, the department narrowed its choices to three sites: Yucca Mountain, Nev.; Deaf Smith County, Texas; and the Hanford Nuclear Reservation in Washington state. Fierce opposition to the department's plan and its methods had emerged in all three states, and the governors of those states promptly filed lawsuits seeking to block the selection process. Environmental groups such as the Sierra Club had argued that all three sites posed threats to critical underground water supplies.

The department in 1986 had also decided to postpone a search for a second dump site in the East. Environmentalists charged that the department, in postponing the search, had been seeking to concentrate opposition to the dump in fewer states and to avoid hurting Republican candidates in New Hampshire and South Carolina. Both states had strong antinuclear movements and had appeared on an early list of possible Eastern sites.

In its Jan. 28 announcement, the department for the first time offered a complete rationale for dropping the search for a second dump site. Its projections indicated that the first dump would not be filled until 2020, so that the search for a second site would not have to begin before the mid-1990s.

While postponing the first permanent dump, the department said it would store high-level waste from nuclear plants throughout the U.S. in a proposed "monitored retrievable storage" facility at the Clinch River site near Oak Ridge, Tenn. Congress, which in 1983 cut funding for a plutonium breeder reactor at Clinch River, had not allocated funds for the retrievable storage facility.

The process of finding and developing a dump site had been laid out in a 1982 law that set a strict timetable and, as part of a political compromise, mandated that sites in the East and West be developed simultaneously.

Several members of Congress called the department's decision to change the timetable "blatantly illegal," but those from the states involved expressed some approval of the delay.

An aide to Sen. Brock Adams (D, Wash.), for example, said that the department's action represented "a whole new approach to the Constitution," but called the decision "encouraging" because of the delay.

The delay in the program would also benefit opponents of nuclear power in other states. In California, for example, licenses of new nuclear generating facilities were banned until a permanent dump was available for waste.

The Department of Energy confirmed March 10, 1988 that a plan to bury radioactive waste in New Mexico salt beds had been sharply curtailed after reports of water leaks in the repository. Enough water had penetrated in the $700 million repository, 26 miles east of Carlsbad, for scientists to recommend further study of the project to entomb radioactive material there, material that would remain radioactive for hundreds of years.

The department decided to follow the scientists' recommendation to store only enough of the waste for experiments and further evaluation of the seepage. Less than a quarter of the 125,000 barrels of plutonium-contaminated wastes planned to be stored there were now headed for the salt beds.

The radioactive material derived from the nation's production of nuclear weapons. Much of it was now stacked above ground at the Idaho National Engineering Laboratory near Idaho Falls.

A House Energy and Commerce Committee panel was told the same day, March 10, that cleanup of the nuclear production plants across the country could cost as much as $100 billion.

FORT WORTH STAR-TELEGRAM

Fort Worth, TX,
January 14, 1989

Through his end-of-term, $81 billion proposal to clean up and modernize nuclear weapons plants, President Reagan has bounced a costly, complex ball into President-elect Bush's court.

Although belated, Reagan's action does help to assign the nuclear cleanup-modernization task the priority it must have. Leakage and waste dangers at nuclear weapons plants have raised legitimate public concerns, and failure to modernize nuclear plants has raised serious questions about the nation's continued ability to have a sufficient, reliable source of nuclear weapons for defense.

The high projected cost estimate causes difficulties for the Bush administration, because Bush is pledged to reducing government spending to balance the budget while maintaining the nation's nuclear deterrent capability and protecting the environment. Performing the nuclear cleanup-updating job in an acceptable

manner while containing costs will require innovative thinking and constant oversight by the new administration.

But the problem must be forcefully attacked. There is ample frightening evidence of severe safety deficiencies in the nuclear arms plants, including the fact that nuclear wastes are harming the environment. There also is ample frightening evidence that the nuclear plants are not capable of producing in sufficient quantity some materials essential to the production of nuclear weapons, which is a threat to national security.

Reagan should have taken aim at the problem sooner, but at least he now has presented a blueprint for corrective action. Bush and Congress no doubt must redraw it, especially to make it fit financial realities, but they must not ignore it, as too long has been done, for the problem goes to the core of survival — both in terms of a livable environment and the ability to protect ourselves.

ST. LOUIS POST-DISPATCH

St. Louis, MO, March 4, 1989

Under a complex and arcane federal law, the Missouri Legislature agreed in late 1983 to join with six other states in building a repository for so-called low-level radioactive waste, to have this repository open by 1993 and, for the next 20 years after that, to ship all low-level radioactive waste generated inside the borders of those states to that repository. But recent events show how flawed that agreement is.

The latest troubles started in late January, when Michigan Gov. James Blanchard, whose state was selected by the compact to host the first waste repository, called a halt to further work on selecting a site for the dump pending resolution of liability issues. At a recent meeting of governors in Washington, then, Missouri's John Ashcroft and his colleagues bailed him out. In a letter to Mr. Blanchard, they agreed that their states would share "responsibility and liability for those expenses not paid for by insurance or the funds established in Michigan statute." In addition, they promised that if any state withdrew from the compact, that state "shall be obliged to pay to the host state the amount that would have been paid for the waste generated (by the withdrawing state) for the life of the facility."

What it amounts to is this: The governors have committed themselves to actions that, in Missouri at least, usurp the responsibility of the Legislature. Missouri joined the interstate agreement by an act of the General Assembly, and only following prolonged public debate. With a single sweep of his pen, the governor appears to have made the agreement no more than an expression of his personal views.

In fact, the Midwest governors' letter, regrettable as it is for any number of reasons, is understandable. In the years since the federal law setting up this system of handling low-level radioactive waste was passed in 1980, its fundamental unwieldiness has become increasingly evident. The Midwest compact is not the only one troubled. In Illinois, for example, which has joined with Kentucky in its own compact, the search for a dump site has caused the state to engage in conduct unbecoming any public body — in effect, bribing local officials to agree to accept a dump, even when the sentiment of the local population is overwhelming against it.

Indeed, in nearly every compact, host states are finding local communities more and more skeptical — justifiably — of the promises of safety and prosperity that dump builders and compact officials so freely dish out. Given the difficulties of siting and building even one repository, then, Congress should reconsider the framework it set out that will require a dozen or more low-level radioactive waste burial grounds scattered across the country. Yes, provisions must be made soon for storing radioactive waste as safely as possible, but surely not at the cost of undermining democratic processes.

LAS VEGAS SUN

Las Vegas, NV, January 23, 1989

Will Nevada legislators ever learn to say NO to the nuclear dump at Yucca Mountain? We beg the 1989 Legislature to say a plain "No," not "maybe," "if" or "some day."

Sen. John Vergiels, D-Las Vegas, is sending the wrong message about the nuclear dump with his proposal for a committee to negotiate with the federal government.

Attorney General Brian McKay has already issued an opinion that any move by the Legislature or local governments that hint of striking a deal with the U.S. Department of Energy invites the dump into Southern Nevada.

That goes for Clark County's proposal to set up a similar committee with some representatives from Clark, Nye and Lincoln counties.

Remember the legislation that created Bullfrog County and the ribbing the state took? Here was an entity specifically set up to take the dump. Even former Sen. Chic Hecht, in a losing bid for re-election, pointed out during the campaign how wrong a message Bullfrog County sent to Washington.

Nevada has sued the federal government for dropping the dump into Nevada's lap in the "Screw Nevada" bill approved by Congress in the waning days of December 1987.

Some lawmakers appear to fail to understand the consequences from silence (implied consent) or from launching a negotiating committee. A 1987 survey made the point distinctly.

A national opinion survey presented at the American Association for the Advancement of Science showed Nevada residents were unconvinced their state was the safest place for the dump.

The risks of trying to keep 70,000 tons of radioactive waste safe for 10,000 years outweigh the benefits, the poll results said.

People fear that the dump could have a serious "ripple effect" on Nevada's economy, which is based on tourism. If vacationers, retirees and new businesses don't want to live with a nuclear dump in their backyard, they won't come here anymore, the survey said.

The survey's results are interesting, because the answers are the same, whether researchers talked to residents or those living outside Nevada.

Both groups — by 49 percent — said that economic benefits from jobs, growth and research on the dump will not outweigh the risks.

Only 20 percent thought Nevada was the safest place to stash nuclear garbage, while 40 percent in both groups said the Yucca Mountain site was unsafe.

Not even the Nevada Test Site justified the Silver State as a radioactive waste burial ground, respondents said.

More than 50 percent of those polled nationally and in Nevada put transportation as the greatest risk, and nearly 80 percent thought a shipping accident was a distinct possibility.

If the public can see the dangers so clearly, why can't our elected representatives act in a responsible manner and respond to the will of the people?

The best bet for Nevada lawmakers to make this year is a yes vote for the resolution by Assemblyman Myrna Williams, D-Las Vegas, to send a clear message of opposition to Congress and the federal government. She has tried in the previous two sessions to get state representatives to reject the dump, but while the Assembly passes the resolution, the Senate kills it.

Perhaps the third time is the charm for Williams' resolution to oppose the dump.

If lawmakers can't read our lips, perhaps they should read the public survey conducted in and out of Nevada, then act on the concerns of a majority of residents and visitors: No nuclear dump here.

THE KANSAS CITY STAR

Kansas City, MO, March 29, 1989

President-elect Bush supports efforts to build more nuclear power plants in the United States. Critics worry about that. They have new ammunition: The country's efforts to permanently store high-level radioactive wastes from already-operating plants are at a standstill.

This failure is a black mark on the federal Energy Department. The agency is supposed to find a good site, evaluate it as a storage area and then build a permanent repository. All indications are that the department has botched the job badly.

In 1987, through political machinations, a site was selected in Nevada. The government essentially coerced Nevada to take the repository without a detailed explanation of why the state was any better than other areas.

The site was supposed to be ready to open in 1998 to take all of the high-level radioactive wastes from commercial nuclear power plants such as Wolf Creek in Kansas. That date already has been set back to 2003. Now experts say even that is optimistic.

Geological concerns have cropped up about the Nevada site.

So have scientific questions about how well the Energy Department has studied the site and its usefulness during the next 10,000 years. The process has disappointed even supporters of nuclear power.

"We're not making much progress out there. If you look at it from a milestone standpoint, we may have gone backward rather than forward," said Karl E. Stahlkopf, an official with the Electric Power Research Institute, a group of utilities that has talked for years about how safe nuclear power is.

That claim is also frequently made closer to home by officials in charge of the Wolf Creek plant. Scientists know how to handle the wastes, goes the claim, and only lack the political decision necessary to accomplish that task.

That's not a good enough argument, as recent events indicate. The Energy Department has a lot more hard work to do before it can convince Americans that the problem of what to do with high-level radioactive waste has been solved. Until that happens, any grand plans to expand the nation's nuclear power system should be held in check.

THE COMMERCIAL APPEAL

Memphis, TN, January 18, 1989

DECADES of neglect are coming home to roost at the government's nuclear weapons plants and other installations operated by the Department of Energy.

The department estimated recently that it will cost between $91 billion and $128 billion over the next 20 years to clean up 45 contaminated facilities and to upgrade production and research plants.

The vast majority of the money would be spent at 17 major facilities used to produce nuclear warheads, some of which may have to be abandoned and new ones constructed.

These plants have been under heavy criticism for many months for inattention to health and safety problems.

Sen. John Glenn (D-Ohio), who requested the figures from the department, said the cleanup costs undoubtedly are underestimated. He said that the department has a history of underestimating the costs of its projects.

Nor do the figures include $1.8 billion a year which the department estimates will be needed for day-to-day compliance with the agency's own policies for safety and environmental protection.

The government faces this massive cleanup because it did not require its nuclear weapons facilities to meet the environmental and safety standards demanded of private nuclear power plants. Now the aging weapons plants have developed structural weaknesses that present potential safety and health hazards to workers as well as to people who live around them. In addition, soil and water on and around some plants are reported to be contaminated with toxic chemicals and radioactive wastes.

Although some environmental and anti-nuclear activists have exaggerated the conditions and dangers at the older government-owned facilities for political reasons, it is clear that a major cleanup and upgrading must be started. Coming up with the money won't be easy but the incoming administration of President-elect George Bush will have to find it somewhere.

THE CHRONICLE-HERALD

Halifax, N.S., March 3, 1989

THE GOOD PEOPLE of Root, New York, are asking themselves a question which is commonly heard in North America and Europe: "Why in my backyard?"

The area near Root, in the state's Mohawk Valley, is on a list of potential disposal sites compiled by The New York State Low-Level Radioactive Waste Siting Commission.

The commission's goal is obvious from its name, and it insists that the technology exists to store low-level radioactive waste safely, in a manner which endangers neither health nor the environment.

"Good on you," the prevailing attitude in Root seems to be. "If the method is so safe, why not store the waste in Manhattan?"

This good though skeptical question, and one which should be posed in light of the record of the nuclear industries in their disposal and handling of waste.

Contamination linked to arms production has come dramatically to light in the United States, no more so than at the Hanford Reservation nuclear weapons plant near Richmond, Washington.

Hanford, where plutonium was produced for the bomb dropped on Nagasaki, is a toxic brew of both chemical and radioative waste. A $2.8-billion agreement has been reached to clean up the site, but even this proposal has its critics.

The New York Times has reported that waste at the site is leaking from underground steel tanks. Furthermore, plutonium, cesium and other radioactive substances are leaking into reservoirs from open waste pits.

Of course, New York's low-level radioactive waste committee has a relatively minor problem on its hands — disposal of the 100,000 cubic feet of waste produced annually in the state.

Still, the fact remains that the capability of the nuclear industries to produce everything from bombs to reactors has far outstripped their capacity to handle, dispose of, or safely store radioactive waste.

The legacy of this record in North America and Europe is strong citizens' groups like the one formed in Root. The nuclear industries have helped spawn an international, grassroots protest movement with with a common slogan — "Not-In-My-Backyard".

Canada, meanwhile, may have an answer to the 12,000 tonnes of spent nuclear fuel now stored at reactor sites, though some will argue that disposal of this waste deep in the Canadian Shield will also cut deeply into the national psyche.

Nuclear technology might still yield great benefits in this world. With the exception of hydro power, nuclear reactors might yet prove to be the cleanest way of producing electricity, despite the near tragedy at Three Mile Island and the very real disaster at Chernobyl.

But making an argument on its own behalf is now the toughest job facing the nuclear industry. Finding a safe way of storing radioactive waste is a formidable challenge; convincing the public that the job can be done will be harder still.

THE BLADE

Toledo, OH, January 27, 1989

OHIO or any other state that has facilities that manufacture nuclear weapons or component parts must not be shortchanged by federal officials who now may be inclined to back away from cleaning up radioactive and toxic wastes.

According to Sen. John Glenn, that is what is happening. The Ohio Democrat, worried in particular about contamination at the Fernald uranium-processing plant near Cincinnati, is angry about proposals in the federal Energy Department's "2010 Study" released earlier this month.

The study suggests that Fernald be closed by 1994; Senator Glenn said that no cleanup funds are guaranteed for the plant. The report also says that removing accumulated toxic wastes from nuclear-weapons facilities will take only $29 billion over the next 21 years. To modernize the plants another $59 billion will be needed.

When the story of widespread contamination broke last year, one estimate for the cleanup project was $130 billion, a far cry from the $29 billion mentioned in the DOE study. Although the tab would be spread over many years, it would still be a giant headache, given the federal deficit which is approaching $3 trillion and the need for a multibillion-dollar bailout of savings and loans.

What Mr. Glenn fears is that the federal government is trying to shirk its responsibilities. He also says it would be "simply unacceptable" to spend in the 1990 fiscal year, as proposed last week in the Reagan budget, only $315 million for the cleanup and $1.4 billion for environmental, health, and safety programs at all U.S. facilities.

Given the enormity of the problem which has been unfolding in recent months, the cleanup effort should not be swept under the budgetary carpeting. The need for a full-scale effort is long overdue at a time, unfortunately, when enormous pressure is being directed toward reducing federal-government spending.

One way or another the piper should be paid — in full. It would be irresponsible for the government to do otherwise. President Bush should make certain that the program is not watered down by unwise false economies, even if that decision may move him a bit further away from the vision of no new taxes.

DEPARTMENT OF ENERGY URANIUM WASTE DUMP

BUFFALO EVENING NEWS
Buffalo, NY, January 29, 1989

THE NATIONAL problem of what to do with radioactive waste is supposed to be solved by the building of a nuclear repository at Yucca Mountain in Nevada, where the waste hopefully will remain isolated for 10,000 years. But the problems that have arisen stir nagging doubts whether it will ever be built.

Work is still in the preliminary stage to discover if the repository is feasible, and this alone is expected to cost $2 billion or more. The facility was supposed to be ready to accept radioactive waste by 1998, but the many delays have already postponed this to 2003.

The building of any kind of nuclear facility is subject to stringent inspection and possible delays, as the builders of many nuclear power plants have discovered to their sorrow. With a facility that must last for 10,000 years, the Nuclear Regulatory Commission must be especially careful to protect the health of the next 500 generations of Americans.

The NRC is responsible for licensing the facility since it would store waste from commercial, as well as military, nuclear reactors.

Another obstacle is that the Department of Energy, which is building the facility, must learn to work under a different set of rules from those by which it has been maintaining nuclear weapons plants around the country. Such plants lacked outside civilian oversight, and as a result many have critical environmental problems that will cost billions to remedy.

Last March, the NRC protested the lack of proper quality control methods in the preliminary work at Yucca Mountain. An NRC official said it was feared that "they might be building something that was not licensable."

The NRC complained that the Department of Energy was planning to collect only one-sided data, ignoring findings that might rule out use of the site for a repository. In addition, it carelessly lost track of data on geological core samples from deep in the earth where the waste would be deposited.

In the background is the potential problem created by the fact that the site was chosen mostly because there are few people there and posed the fewest political problems. No one claims it is the best site from a geological point of view. Some scientists fear an earthquake might bring the water table in contact with the radioactive waste.

It is up to the Bush administration to get this project moving by insisting on proper quality-control procedures by the Department of Energy in the preparation of the preliminary studies.

Perhaps the Yucca Mountain site is not suitable for the repository. If so, we should find out before billions of dollars are spent on it.

The Oregonian
Portland, OR, January 9, 1989

Congress should pass a bill introduced by Rep. Ron Wyden, D-Ore., that would prevent a mothballed civilian nuclear plant from being turned into a reactor to produce nuclear-weapons materials.

The U.S. Department of Energy has announced plans to build new defense-production reactors in South Carolina and Idaho, but it is still studying the possibility of converting the Washington Public Power Supply System plant at the Hanford nuclear reservation in south-central Washington state.

Over the past several months, mounting safety problems have kept the Energy Department's reactors that produce tritium for nuclear weapons shut down, and there are some concerns the nation may eventually face a tritium shortage.

The conversion idea is still alive because backers argue that converting the WPPSS plant for tritium and plutonium production could cost half of what it may cost to build a new plant from scratch, and perhaps would take half as long to complete.

The idea of converting the partially completed WPPSS project into a weapons reactor would send the wrong signal to other nations. It would be telling nations that have commercial nuclear reactors but do not have nuclear weapons that they, too, can use civilian reactors for military purposes. Such uses of the peaceful atom would violate the nation's long-standing policy of nuclear non-proliferation.

The conversion of the WPPSS plant, furthermore, could touch off a new round of WPPSS lawsuits. It also could force the Bonneville Power Administration to raise its rates, assuming that the converted WPPSS plant also would be used for power production, as some of the advocates of this idea envision.

Using the converted WPPSS plant for military and civilian purposes sounds expedient, but such arrangements, as experience with Hanford N-Reactor have demonstrated, pose conflicts in safety standards and with production schedules.

10th Anniversary of Three Mile Island Marked

March 28, 1989 marked the 10th anniversary of the Three Mile Island plant accident. A series of breakdowns in the cooling system at Pennsylvania's Three Mile Island plant March 28, 1979 resulted in the shutdown of the facility's No. 2 reactor and the release of radiation into the atmosphere. A highly flammable hydrogen gas bubble, which formed in the overhead reactor vessel, threatened to explode without warning. The force of such an explosion could have conceivably destroyed the walls of the containment building and thus released all the radioactivity inside. The containment building had the highest level of contamination recorded in commercial nuclear operations history.

The crisis eased April 2, the sixth day of the near-disaster, when nuclear experts announced that the gas bubble had shown a "dramatic drop" in size and fuel temperatures in the core continued to drop significantly.

The Three Mile Island plant was located 10 miles south of Harrisburg. About 500,000 persons lived in a 15-mile radius of the facility, a pressurized water system that supplied electricity. The plant produced steam to drive a turbine, which in turn powered a generator that produced electricity. The heat source was the energy released from the fission (splitting) of the nuclei of atomic matter – in this case uranium 235. Three Mile Island No. 2 had been only operating since December 1978. At the time of the accident, reactor No. 1, in operation since 1974, was closed for routine maintenance.

The federal Nuclear Regulatory Commission (NRC) and the Metropolitan Edison (Met Ed) Co., one of the plant's owners, were in charge of efforts to explain and cope with the facility's failure. The cause of the accident was disputed by NRC and Met Ed officials, and conflicting reports were also issued by the state of Pennsylvania and companies that had constructed elements of the reactor system. Met Ed claimed that a valve had failed in a pump in the primary core cooling system. But officials of Babcock and Wilcox, which designed and built the reactor, said there were no valves inside the pumps. The NRC believed that there had been multiple failures in the pumps and relief valves that carried heated water from the turbine to the steam generator. At a critical moment, the NRC stated, a plant operator had manually turned off the emergency core cooling system that had been automatically set off when the primary system failed to deliver adequate cooling water to the reactor's uranium fuel rods.

The gas bubble was the result of the unexpected starts and stops in the primary and emergency core cooling systems. Technical experts theorized that when the intense pressure in the reactor vessel dropped (during failure of the cooling systems) hydrogen and oxygen gas, which was formed during fission as water molecules were torn into their constituent parts, remained in the reactor.

On March 29, low levels of radiation were detected in the atmosphere as far as 20 miles from Three Mile Island. The next day, after a new burst of radioactive gas escaped, Pennsylvania Gov. Richard Thornburgh advised pregnant women and preschool children within a five-mile radius of the plant to evacuate the area. Evacuation plans for persons living 10 to 20 miles downwind of the facility were prepared for implementation when or if technicians decided to force the hydrogen gas bubble from the reactor vessel. But on April 3, officials reported that the bubble had been eliminated and that experts would continue efforts to bring the reactor to a "cold shutdown" state.

The Three Mile Island incident focused attention on the possibility of a "worst case scenerio" in which a complete meltdown of the radioactive core of a nuclear plant would release lethal radioactivity over a wide area.

THE
KANSAS CITY STAR
Kansas City, MO,
January 18, 1989

Constant critics of nuclear power are wrong to suggest that all the country's reactors should be shut down. But when the industry has turned its back on federally required safety regulations, the credibility of nuclear power suffers yet another setback.

The latest news is that nearly four out of five reactors have not fully complied with safety changes developed after the Three Mile Island accident 10 years ago. Yet the Nuclear Regulatory Commission has not fined the plants for these sins, nor has it shut any down.

This is the kind of galling behavior that makes people see the NRC as little more than a lap dog for the industry.

Granted, a high percentage of the alterations have been accomplished, at great cost to utility shareholders and ratepayers. But federal requirements for nuclear power are not sent out to be "almost fully implemented." The margin for error in running a reactor can be thin.

So why hasn't the industry complied? "Not all the requirements are absolutely necessary," says an NRC official. That argument completely ignores the fact that several "top priorities" designated by the NRC have not even been completed.

According to the NRC itself, many reactors have not installed instruments to help operators determine a plant's safety status, to tell operators about conditions inside containment vessels and to detect cooling in the reactor's core.

These are not just rules that were written down on some kind of wish list. They are regulations developed after President Carter appointed a special commission to investigate the Three Mile Island accident and suggest ways to make nuclear power safer.

The rules were announced, with fanfare. Many were implemented by law-abiding operators across the nation. Some were not, for reasons that too often stretch the imagination. The fact that a change might be "costly" is absurd when measured against the death and destruction that one accident can cause.

The entire nuclear establishment gets a failing grade for this kind of behavior.

The Record

Hackensack, NJ, March 10, 1989

Nuclear power is back. President Bush wants to make nuclear energy safer, cheaper, and more plentiful. So do Rep. Morris Udall and Sen. Timothy Wirth, both Democrats, as well as environmentalists who were once fervently anti-nuke. Good. Nuclear power plants should be a larger part of America's energy plan, but they can't take their rightful place unless they're built with a lot more brains and care than most utility companies have shown to date.

Three years ago, after an accident at the Soviet Union's Chernobyl nuclear plant killed 31 and frightened the wits out of most of western Europe, it appeared that no new nuclear plant would ever be built. An earlier accident, at Three Mile Island, had already raised serious safety questions. A thriving anti-nuke movement and Jane Fonda's movie, "The China Syndrome," brought those fears home to millions of Americans. Public opposition forced abandonment of a string of plants, and it's been 11 years since a new nuclear reactor was ordered. Long Island's Shoreham nuclear plant, built at a cost of $5.4 billion, is to be abandoned.

Now, however, people are more and more aware that oil and gas have dangers that are hard to correct. Acid rain and carbon dioxide buildup could, in the long run, be at least as hazardous as occasional leaks or small accidents at nuclear plants. Demand for electricity is rising. And promising new technology offers hope of a nuclear plant that really would be foolproof. A Westinghouse design, for instance, sets 400,000 gallons of water above the reactor. In an emergency, automatic valves would open and gravity would douse the reactor with coolant — even if the plant's operators were all asleep or dead. A new breed of gas-cooled reactors has a core that can operate, in emergencies, with no coolant at all, eliminating the possibility of a dreaded core meltdown.

President Bush and Messrs. Udall and Wirth seem to be operating on roughly the same track, which is the right one. They are interested in encouraging — possibly with help from the U.S. Department of Energy — development of a standardized, proven reactor design. Until now, utility companies have usually designed reactors from scratch. This made safety checks difficult and created problems peculiar to each plant. Thanks partly to the standardized design, it should be possible to cut the time required for plant approval from the present maximum of 15 years — a figure which makes plants uneconomical — to only a few years.

Still to be solved is the problem of how to dispose of the 1,700 tons of radioactive waste generated each year by nuclear power stations already in existence. In addition, the government and the nuclear industry will have to do a giant public information job to sell nuclear energy. Congressional hearings scheduled for this spring should help. Finally, it's important not to overestimate the benefits of electricity generated at nuclear plants. Only about a third of the energy consumed in America every year goes to producing electricity. They rest is used for cars, heating, and other purposes that will still require gas and oil.

Nuclear power can't solve all of America's energy problems, but it can help. South Korea, France, Japan, and a number of other countries use nuclear power — safely. The United States should seriously consider following their lead. A lot of people will be startled to find that nuclear energy back on the nation's agenda, but that's exactly where it belongs.

THE ☼ SUN

Baltimore, MD, March 28, 1989

With a burst of steam and a sound "like a jet taking off in the yard," Three Mile Island engraved itself on the public consciousness 10 years ago today, changing the dynamics of nuclear power. The aftermath in political turmoil and economic trauma continues for the electric-power industry and the plant's Central Pennsylvania neighbors:

☐ Although 112 licensed reactors generate 20 percent of U.S. electricity, no new plants have been ordered since 1978. Some partially built plants have been dismantled.

☐ Babcock & Wilcox, builders of TMI's two reactors, went out of the power reactor business.

☐ Besides the $1-billion cleanup cost at TMI, fixing the flaws TMI revealed is expected to cost another $150 billion, significantly hiking the cost of nuclear-generated electric power.

☐ Communities near the stricken reactor suffered disruption that continues today as frightened families and aroused activists struggle to cope with the fear of another accident.

Nuclear engineers all over the world studied the TMI reports, rethinking their own approach after the massive failure of systems thought to be "failsafe." The Soviets, confident their radically different reactors would never experience a TMI-style accident, were thus unprepared for the far-worse disaster caused by operator error at Chernobyl. For many, the two accidents have come to symbolize the impossibility of safely using nuclear power.

Today, nuclear power stands at a crossroads. Industry leaders point to a new generation of passive-shutdown reactors, smaller and inherently safer. They note that "greenhouse effect" fears have caused even the Audubon Society to re-examine nuclear alternatives, and that electric power demand is inching upward after years of flat energy use. Reports of massive air pollution, coupled with widening rush-hour auto gridlock, will only boost electric demand as communities turn to clean, electric-powered rail transit solutions.

But even an inherently safer nuclear plant generates waste, unless a Salt Lake City experiment turns out to be the hoped-for solution to cheap fusion energy. Until it does, the acrimonious debate over what to do with nuclear wastes, and the companion issue of safe transportation to repositories, will limit nuclear power's growth. It is a very different world from the one that engineers expected in the heady days of the 1950s, of nuclear generated electric power so cheap it wouldn't even be worth metering.

The Providence Journal

Providence, RI,
March 28, 1989

This week marks the 10th anniversary of Three Mile Island, the memorable incident at the Pennsylvania nuclear power plant, which caused not a single human fatality, but came perilously close to killing off the entire nuclear energy industry in this country.

There is general agreement that the lessons of TMI should be learned, but there is considerable disagreement about just what those lessons are.

Nearly all informed observers — beginning with the investigatory commission appointed by President Jimmy Carter and headed by Dartmouth University President John Kemeny — have come to roughly the same conclusions:

The incident at TMI, while provoking enormous anxiety at the time, demonstrated our ability to cope with just about the worst imaginable combination of errors, malfunctions and sheer bad luck. The TMI incident uncovered construction, management and operational flaws, but this has had the beneficial effect of encouraging measures which have eliminated, or significantly reduced, these flaws. In short, nuclear power, which was already a safe and efficient means of producing energy, emerged from the crucible of TMI safer and more efficient than ever.

That, however, is not the view propagated by those who oppose nuclear power: TMI served to harden their stance and embolden their tactics. Like the old Bourbon monarchists so scathingly characterized by Talleyrand, today's anti-nuclear zealots "have learned nothing and forgotten nothing." They choose to "remember" TMI as a disaster, when in fact it was an accident that did *not* become a disaster precisely because of the multi-layered safety measures designed into the system. And they conveniently ignore the progress made since TMI in further improving the safety of nuclear power plants.

Polls indicate that most Americans continue to harbor anxieties about the safety of nuclear power, while recognizing that it is the most plausible long-term solution to our need for abundant and non-polluting energy. It will take responsible leadership — by politicians, scientists, educators, and media commentators — to help resolve that ambivalence in favor of nuclear power. Despite TMI, and in part *because* of TMI, it is, relatively speaking, the most efficient, safest and cleanest source of vital energy for our nation's future.

SYRACUSE
HERALD-JOURNAL

Syracuse, NJ, March 30, 1989

Three Mile Island was every nuclear plant operator's worst nightmare come to life. A decade ago this week, half of TMI's radioactive core melted down, sending radioactive emissions into the air. The accident was attributed to human and mechanical error — a double curse. It meant both the equipment and the people who were supposed to operate it failed.

The fact that TMI could have been any nuclear plant anywhere in America should have made plant owners wary enough to do everything in their power to prevent a replication of the near meltdown.

But 75 percent of nuclear plants in existence today, including Niagara Mohawk's Nine Mile 1 and 2 plants on the shores of Lake Ontario, have not completed the safety requirements that were recommended by the National Regulatory Commission after TMI.

Nine Mile 1 and 2, for example, did not complete mandatory reviews of control-room designs to insure that workers had enough information on hand to help prevent or deal with an accident. Nine Mile 2 still does not have a display system that could readily determine the safety of the plant. The NRC deadline for installation of the system was Jan. 1, 1982.

Two reasons for some plant operators' laxness about the post-TMI safety recommendations may be that their plants are plagued by problems in general, among them design plans and systems. Nine Mile 1 has not been in operation since 1987 and Nine Mile 2 has been off line since October 1988. Both are considered among the worst-run nuclear plants in America.

Plant operators also may sense the NRC's own feelings about safety. Since TMI, the NRC has indicated its safety recommendations may have been too harsh. "Not all of the modifications were absolutely necessary," said an NRC spokeswoman.

It is no wonder nuclear plants have left a bad taste in so many Americans' mouths.

The government agency in charge of overseeing nuclear safety can't even decide what's really needed to make a nuclear plant safe and has been accused by consumer groups of ignoring or underreporting problems at nuclear plants.

Can we take the industry's word when it says no health-related problems, such as infant mortality rates, can be tied to the radiation produced by TMI's near meltdown? Many people in the vicinity of the plant disagree. Two thousand claims have been filed, and the plant's insurance company already has agreed to pay a $1 million settlement to a woman whose son was born with Down's Syndrome nine months after the accident.

Since it is the public who will suffer the consequences of plant errors, it is the public who must oversee the overseer (the government) and the nuclear plant operators. If it doesn't, Three Mile Island may not be the only nuclear plant with an anniversary worth noting.

The Toronto Star

Toronto, Ont., March 28, 1989

On March 28, 1979 — a decade ago today — something went terribly wrong at the Three Mile Island nuclear reactor on the Susquehanna River in Middletown, Pennsylvania.

Although no one died, Unit 2 experienced a meltdown that is still classified as the worst nuclear plant accident in U.S. history.

And after 10 long years and $1 billion (U.S.) in cleanup costs, the disaster at Three Mile Island isn't over.

Men in cumbersome protective suits still grapple painstakingly through 40 feet of water, lifting chunks of radioactive material from the ruined reactor.

Surprisingly, even though 100 nuclear projects were cancelled — most in the shadow of the Three Mile Island mishap — Americans rely more on nuclear power than they did a decade ago.

When the breakdown occurred, the U.S. had 72 nuclear plants. They accounted for 11.4 per cent of the country's power needs. Now, 111 stations generate 20 per cent of U.S. electricity.

Meanwhile, some Americans wonder if anything has been learned in 10 years, even though unexpected automatic shutdowns have declined by nearly two-thirds, to 2.7 per plant in 1987.

"It's beyond dispute that the plants are safer," says Robert D. Pollard, a technical expert from the Union of Concerned Scientists. "The question," Pollard told the *New York Times* recently, "is how much safer, and is that enough?"

And is anyone prepared to gamble that Three Mile Island can't happen again?

NUCLEAR WEAPONS PLANT

The Houston Post

Houston, TX, March 28, 1989

IT HAS BEEN 10 YEARS TODAY since the Three Mile Island accident, an artifact of history that probably is as arcane to today's high school seniors as the Yalta Conference. Yet it represents a pivotal point in the evolution of nuclear power plants in America — and, ultimately, in much of the world at large.

Even though 1979's events on Pennsylvania's Susquehanna River never became a disaster, prior to Russia's Chernobyl calamity TMI was the most-used phrase in the lexicon of nuclear power. Most of that attention, or at least the tone of it, was unfair in the sense that little radiation escaped. The containment system worked. But that cannot overshadow the fact that at TMI man and machine together failed and failed badly. A partial meltdown did take place.

The chief benefit of TMI lay in showing what *could* occur. We learned valuable lessons without having to pay with lives. True, nuclear plants completed since then have a heftier price tag, much of it attributable to more meticulous design and better training of personnel. The South Texas Project near Bay City, for instance, will probably cost half a billion dollars more over its lifetime than it would have without TMI. But the added safety is well worth it.

Did TMI price nuclear power out of the market? Probably not, unless last week's quickly-challenged reports of a successful nuclear fusion reaction prove accurate. Fossil fuels are still finite, and they will someday be supplanted by something — something pricey.

Sadly, accidents can never be ruled out. There is much still to be done in improving safety, but we have come a long way. Part of the reason is that we saw Three Mile Island's future, and it didn't work.

The Philadelphia Inquirer

Philadelphia, PA, January 14, 1989

It was called the "nuclear bandwagon" in the late 1960s and early 1970s. Electric utilities, captivated by the perceived glamour and promises of cheap power from the atom, committed themselves to building nuclear reactors.

Many lacked the expertise to engineer and operate a complicated nuclear plant, driving up the costs. Other utilities overestimated future power needs — needs that could be met without undertaking a multibillion-dollar reactor project.

Early warnings of the economic downside of nuclear power went unheeded by the utilities. They continued to build as if there were no tomorrow.

But tomorrow came in the form of an economic downturn, a drop in oil prices and the nationwide rethinking that followed the Three Mile Island accident. Soon the nation was long on half-finished reactors that could not be economically justified. U.S. utilities are carrying as much as $100 billion in unrecovered construction costs for dozens of uncompleted reactors.

So who should pay for these mistakes?

The U.S. Supreme Court ruled Wednesday that in the case of two Western Pennsylvania utilities, the stockholders, not the ratepayers, should bear the burden, which totals a relatively paltry $44 million. The ruling upheld an earlier decision by the Pennsylvania Supreme Court in a lawsuit brought by state Consumer Advocate David Barasch against Duquesne Light Co. and Pennsylvania Power Co., which had planned and then canceled four reactors.

Consumer groups have heralded the 8-1 decision as a resounding victory. A utility industry spokesman declared it "disappointing." In reality, it probably will have only limited application. The court said it ruled as it did because the financial burden to the utilities' stockholders was small and the companies could afford the cost.

The justices left open the question of how they might rule if absorbing the expense of an unfinished reactor would bankrupt a utility. That very issue is pending before the Supreme Court in a case brought by the troubled Public Service Co. of New Hampshire, which owns — but hasn't been able to start up — the controversial Seabrook nuclear plant.

In their arguments before the court, the Pennsylvania utilities maintained that their decisions to invest in the reactors were "prudent" at the time and therefore the companies should be allowed to recover the expenses from ratepayers.

While not addressing that argument directly, the high court upheld state authority to regulate utilities and bar the pass-through of such costs, which many states have done.

The significance of Wednesday's ruling will be its effect on planning by utilities in the future.

For too many years, utilities were not held accountable for their decisions to build expensive new plants when far cheaper programs — such as conservation or lower-cost forms of generation — could have met customer needs.

If the case of *Duquesne Light Co. v. Barasch* forces utilities to invest with more caution, then it will be an important victory for ratepayers.

The News Journal

Wilmington, DE, March 28, 1989

TODAY IS the tenth anniversary of the Three Mile Island nuclear plant accident.

Some folks are still shouting, as they offer not-quite-persuasive alternatives, that nuclear power can never be acceptable.

Other folks cry that nukes, far from being dead, remain viable parts of our required energy mix, now providing some 20 percent of the electricity we use. These advocates, however, must face ugly reports that the nuclear power industry still has not cleaned up its act.

Sunday, a scant two days short of a decade since the partial meltdown of one of the Pennsylvania plant's units — worst U.S. nuclear accident on record — Rep. Edward J. Markey released a damning report on the industry. The Massachusetts Democrat and critic of the Nuclear Regulatory Commission reported that only about 20 percent of operating reactors in this country have completed all changes required in the wake of the Three Mile Island mishap.

Congressman Markey sniffed at an NRC response that since TMI the plants are safer, and that in total they are 97.5 percent in compliance with all safety requirements. "Nuclear power is not horseshoes," he said. "The difference betwen coming close and getting the job done can mean the difference between safety and catastrophe."

That "close" counts only in hand grenades and horseshoes is catchy, but doesn't mean a lot. No human activity is 100 percent safe; even some adversaries concede that nuclear plants are safer since TMI, but question whether "safer" equates with "safe enough."

If nuclear power cannot be made perfectly risk free, can we do without it?

There are indications that we are nearing limits on the capacity of today's sources to meet our continually rising energy demands in environmentally acceptable ways. One observer long associated with the NRC remarked recently that people will not heed the situation that is closing in on our industrial society unless and until blackouts and brownouts in electricity supply occur frequently.

Critics answer that alternatives to fission — nuclear generation as we now know it — already are available if we have but the will to use them. Amory Lovins, a leader in the "soft energy" field, stresses the "E word" — efficiency. Efficiency in generation and use of energy says Mr. Lovins, director of the Rocky Mountain Institute, beats all other alternatives. New products and techniques, he says, can let us power our present economy with one-fourth of the electricity we now use.

Amid this and continued hopes for expanded use of "renewable" forms of energy, tantalizing hints keep emerging that fusion — a form of nuclear energy that is free of many of fission's problems — may be closer than had been hoped. Such a report came just last week from the University of Utah, where two scientists completed a modest experimental program that yielded more energy than was needed to sustain the process. Confirmation of such achievements for fusion remains our long-term hope but may not come soon enough to relieve short- and medium-range energy shortfalls.

Polls indicate that substantial numbers of Americans think nuclear power will be needed, but resist siting any new plants in their neighborhoods.

That attitude may continue until scarcities and soaring costs become serious obstacles to continuing the levels of convenience and consumption we now insist upon.

Part III:
Chemicals, Toxic Waste,
Pesticides & Asbestos

Despite a reduction in cutting back the traditional pollutants, notably visible contaminants such as smoke, the spread of toxic chemicals and metals in quantities that are hard to detect continues. Some of these pollutants are deadlier than anything we have had to face to date. DDT, dieldrin and other pesticides are suspected of causing cancer and birth defects, among other problems. Polychlorinated biphenyls (PCBs) constitute a family of chemicals with over 200 types, and are used in plastics, electrical insulators, and hydraulic fluids; they are unusually toxic and persistent, affecting vital organs and causing cancers.

In the realm of toxic waste, the improper disposal of hazardous wastes is proving an increasing problem throughout the industrialized world and the Third World.

Worldwide, some 325 million-375 million tons of hazardous waste were generated in 1984, ninety percent of it in the industrialized world. In the U.S., some 260 million tons are generated each year – the equivalent of one ton for each U.S. citizen. In 1984, the 10 nations that then made up the European Community generated an estimated 160 million tons of industrial waste a year, of which 30 million tons were classified as "toxic and dangerous."

Unless disposed of with great care, hazardous wastes pose a severe threat to public health and the environment. In particular, the use of landfills has led to the pollution of surface and groundwaters, to the contamination of land, and to the mass exposure of whole communities to the dangerous effects of highly toxic chemicals.

Numerous "problem" sites have now been unearthed, the most infamous being Love Canal in New York state. All told, the U.S. has an estimated 50,000 hazardous waste landfills, 20,000 of which are thought to pose a potential threat to human health, according to the Environmental Protection Agency (EPA). In addition, there are some 170,000 industrial compounds – used to dump liquid wastes – and 7,000 deep wells into which hazardous wastes have been injected under pressure. According to the EPA, 2,000 sites require immediate cleanup under federal "Superfund" legislation. The Office of Technology Assessment estimates that cleanup costs could total $100 billion.

If properly treated, most of today's wastes can be rendered harmless before disposal, primarily through high-temperature incineration. However, the long-term solution to the problem of hazardous wastes lies as much in reducing the production of wastes, not least through recycling, as in the use of more sophisticated disposal technology.

Bhopal was the site of a major chemical accident in central India in 1984, involving a pesticide plant belonging to Union Carbide. Any accurate measure of the number of casualties is impossible for a number of reasons. Many of the bodies were cremated, destroying crucial evidence of the cause of death. Many died some time later and in a different locality, so their deaths were not registered with the Bhopal authorities. Many are still dying today.

At a local and individual level, therefore, the Bhopal disaster is still very much a reality. Any alleviation of the pain and suffering caused by the accident is still in the distant future. At a more general level, the accident seems to have led to little in the way of making the chemical industry either more accountable or safer.

Other companies have also suffered major accidents, the most notorious being the pollution of the Rhine by a spill from the Sandoz warehouse in Basel, Switzerland. Such events suggest that more Bhopals lie in store.

Pesticides have also come into the forefront of the environmental debate. World production of pesticides in 1986 was about 2.3 million tons. In the U.S., more than 450,000 tons of pesticides are used every year, or four pounds for every American citizen. Despite various legislation enacted to curb their application, use of pesticides continues to increase. It has doubled in the U.S. since 1964, and is increasing worldwide at a rate of 12.5 percent a year.

Pesticides cause widespread pollution of the environment, seeping into rivers, killing off fish life, and contaminating groundwater, drinking water and food, most of which now contains pesticide residues.

Though levels of pesticides in the general environment are usually low, pesticides tend to concentrate as they move up the food chain, a phenomenon known as bioconcentration. The consequences for wildlife and human health are severe. Our body fats also now contain pesticides, as do ova and spermatozoa. A World Health Organization (WHO) study in 1987 warned that human breast milk is now seriously contaminated with pesticides and other chemicals that could have serious effects on the health of our children. The WHO experts even recommend that, in certain areas, breast feeding be avoided.

The pesticide industry argues that pesticides are essential for feeding the world. The standard claim, originally made by Dr. Norman Borlaug, the father of the Green Revolution, is that without pesticides, world food production would fall by 50 percent, causing starvation.

But pesticide opponents argue that since the introduction of pesticides in the 1940s, crop losses have increased rather than decreased, from an estimated 32 percent to 37 percent, due to changing farm practices, with much bigger farms, ever-greater stretches of monoculture, the cultivation of high-yielding varieties that are particularly vulnerable to pests, and a greatly reduced farm labor force. In addition, they note, problems inherent to the use of pesticides: notably, their tendency to increase pest infestations by killing off predators that previously controlled target species, and the latters' tendency to develop resistance to pesticides. This problem is particularly acute in the tropics where conditions are most favorable for pest infestation. Such factors have given rise to what has been termed the "pesticide treadmill," with farmers being forced to use ever greater amounts just to keep crop losses at a given level. What, then, would be the real cost of dispensing with pesticides?

A study undertaken by Cornell University concluded in 1978 that without pesticides financial losses would be about nine percent higher, while food crop losses, in terms of food energy, would be about four percent higher. This is a long way from the pesticide industry's 50 percent claim.

Asbestos is the generic name for a group of fibrous silicates. Once mined, the asbestos fibers are separated out from the rock in which they are embedded. They are then spun into a cloth that can be mixed with cement or resin to give it shape. Because it is highly resistant to both heat and electricity, asbestos has been used in a wide range of materials – from roofing slates to firefighting suits.

The dangers of asbestos lie in its fibers. If inhaled, the fibers lodge in the lungs and the tissues of the bronchial tubes. The result is a crippling lung disease called asbestosis. In the U.S., official statistics put the potential death toll from exposure to all forms of asbestos at two million people. According to the EPA, 65,000 Americans currently suffer from asbestosis, a further 12,000 dying every year from asbestos-related cancers.

The EPA has now proposed a total ban on the production of all asbestos products within the U.S., arguing that "there is no level of exposure without risk." The ban would phase out all asbestos products within 10 years.

EPA Bars Use of EDP as Grain Pesticide

The Environmental Protection Agency (EPA) Feb. 3, 1984 prohibited use of the pesticide ethylene dibromide, commonly known as EDP, on grain products. The controversial pesticide, under investigation by the agency since 1977, had been banned as a soil fumigant in 1983. Other uses of the pesticide, determined by laboratory tests to be a cause of cancer and birth defects in animals, included fumigation of citrus and other fruit crops and of grain-milling machinery. The 1983 ban on using EDP as a soil fumigant had been put into effect after new evidence came to light that the chemical was contaminating underground water supplies in several states, among them Florida and California. The most recent restriction on EDP use followed individual actions by several states where detectable levels of EDP had been found in certain foodstuffs on store shelves, especially in cake, muffin and pancake mixes. Florida had begun taking contaminated products off store shelves. Massachusetts banned the sale of 18 grain-based products Feb. 6. In California, high levels of EDP had been discovered in imported citrus pulp and in cake and muffin mixes, and the state had requested that the EDP ban the pesticide.

The Miami Herald
Miami, FL, February 11, 1984

THE Environmental Protection Agency's (EPA) effort to quell national panic over the presence of tiny quantities of the pesticide ethylene dibromide (EDB) in the nation's grain supply is to be welcomed.

By banning the use of EDB as a grain fumigant and by recommending responsible tolerance levels for the use of already-treated grain, the EPA has averted both a public-health emergency and an economic crisis. The destruction of $3 billion worth of grain would have wreaked havoc on the nation's agriculture for many years. Instead, the EPA has introduced a risk-management plan that reasonable people throughout the nation can support.

National standards for EDB in food products still are needed. At present EDB remains officially exempt from Federal regulation. The Food and Drug Administration (FDA) granted the exemption when it was thought, erroneously, that EDB quickly evaporated. Until the FDA lifts the exemption, EPA standards are only guidelines to be used and enforced by the states.

Florida Agriculture Commissioner Doyle Conner and Dr. Stephen King, the state director of public-health programs who triggered much of the national concern, wisely have agreed to adopt and enforce the EPA's guidelines in Florida. Without uniform national standards, the distribution and food-marketing system that makes U.S. groceries the envy of a hungry world cannot be maintained.

To be sure, there are arguments for the more-stringent state standards imposed last December. EDB undeniably is a potent carcinogen. The state's one-part-per-billion (1 ppb) standard clearly offered more protection than the EPA's 30 ppb standard for ready-to-eat foods. (Higher guidelines were set for unprocessed foods that would be cooked.) It is estimated that over a lifetime of exposure, the 30 ppb standard would result in 480 new cancers for every 100,000 persons.

But, as demonstrated by the saccharin controversy, total protection is not a practical standard. The increased risk of one to two years more of exposure to EDB at these greatly reduced levels is truly minuscule. The American people routinely, and often deliberately — witness smokers — expose themselves daily to greater risks.

What is most unfortunate is the EPA's failure to act sooner. The agency took more than seven years to develop its standards. During that time, use of EDB became widespread. To some extent the delay reflects the division of scientific opinion, but the Reagan Administration's attempt to emasculate the agency was a more-important factor. Under the leadership of William D. Ruckelshaus, the EPA is regaining credibility. Mr. Ruckelshaus's orderly, rational program to "eliminate EDB from the American diet" is one reason why.

San Francisco Chronicle
San Francisco, CA, February 2, 1984

LAST WEEKEND'S news of the discovery of EDB contamination in Duncan Hines muffin mixes has elevated an old and somewhat quiescent health protection issue to a new level of concern.

The state Department of Health Services opened the subject to public view on Thursday. By Friday, major grocery chains were busy pulling the Duncan Hines muffin mix off their shelves out of fear, more of public backlash, than of the danger of creating a public health menace.

By Monday, the manufacturer, Procter & Gamble, had yielded to the pressure of health authorities and voluntarily ended distribution of the contaminated mix within the state. The company felt that its muffins were entirely safe to eat, pointing out that baking should dissipate the carcinogenic chemical to a safe level of human tolerance. But it could not hope to withstand the uproar that EDB news was creating among California muffin lovers.

"The uproar," wrote David Perlman, The Chronicle science editor, "poses one of the many typical conflicts marking the use of chemicals that may threaten human health." And this conflict is particularly awkward, he continued, "when the actual threat is unknown and the substitutes for the chemical may also pose hazards."

EDB HAS BEEN KNOWN for a long time to be carcinogenic to test animals, but to extend this effect to humans is "only theoretical," says a leading UC biochemist. Yet health authorities, environmentalists and consumer activist lawyers are now running with the ball, demanding that something be done. The Environmental Protection Agency is being skewered for not having set a safety standard; a lobbyist for California Rural Legal Assistance says, colorfully, it's been dragging its feet "while the American people have been guinea pigs for a potent cancer-causing pesticide."

This, one can see, is not going to be an easy matter to contend with, since EDB's low-level health effects are still unclear. If the chemical's effects on humans were identified and declared harmful at a really low level, there would certainly be great trouble, because federal agencies, according to the New York Times, are now finding detectable levels of the pesticide in half the samples of grain products taken from wholesale and retail shelves.

We are bound to ask, what is government going to be able to do about this? The problem may be larger, at least for the time being, than any manageable solution.

THE CHRISTIAN SCIENCE MONITOR
Boston, MA, February 6, 1984

Prudence is important in the response of government officials to reports that trace amounts of the pesticide EDB may exist in some foodstuffs. But a calm and measured approach to the situation is of equal import. It would be counterproductive for government at any level to alarm the public through precipitous action or intemperate statement. This sometimes has been done in the past with various pesticides and other chemicals, most recently dioxin.

The Environmental Protection Agency's decision late last week to suspend nearly all use of the pesticide seems appropriate. So, too, does EPA's issuance of guidelines concerning levels of EDB in different kinds of foodstuffs.

If levels of EDB are found high in specific food products already on in supermarkets, it may be the better part of wisdom for them to be removed from the shelves. But for other foodstuffs there should be no wholesale withdrawal based on fear. The need of the moment is to alert, rather than alarm.

THE WALL STREET JOURNAL.

New York, NY, February 14, 1984

All America's worked up about ethylene dibromide, or EDB, the pesticide called a public-health menace by the Environmental Protection Agency. We wondered about all the fuss, so we made a few phone calls and then got worked up too. But not about EDB. We got mad at the public and regulatory hysteria that caused housewives around the country to throw out perfectly good Duncan Hines cake mix (as New Jersey governor Thomas Kean urged Sunday). That's the real public menace.

We don't mean to belittle the agency's work. EDB is a poison, all right, and the fact that it turned up in ground water suggests that some controls on its use are needed. But that said, the agency's near-total ban created a public hullabaloo that has exaggerated the threat posed by EDB. Worse, a few state regulators have lost their cool altogether.

In assessing these periodic cancer scares, a few facts need to be kept in mind. First, modern civilization is not killing us; it has led to spectacular and continuing increases in life expectancy. Second, we are not suffering a cancer epidemic; age-adjusted death rates from most forms of cancer have been steady or declining for 50 years. Third, the one big exception is lung cancer, which has been steadily increasing first among men and now among women. If the various environmental protection agencies and the Nader groups and the television broadcasters want to get excited about public health risks, they ought to direct their excitement at cigarettes

When these various worthies decided instead to worry about ethylene dibromide, we called a few scientists. They said there isn't all that much EDB out there. Farmers spray it on some 2% of the nation's fruit crop and perhaps 40% of its grain. Most of that is washed off or, in the case of grain, cooked away. The amount eaten by an average person turns out to be less of a cancer risk than many things that occur naturally in other foods. Take peanut butter. That's right, the average jar contains *aflatoxin*, a poison produced by mold that grows on peanuts and is 1,000 times more carcinogenic than EDB. However, since aflatoxin is a natural product rather than a food additive, it escapes the usual environmental scrutiny.

Among those quick to cite the peanut-butter analogy, by the way, is John Weisburger, director of research at the American Health Foundation in Valhalla, N.Y. Dr. Weisburger happens to be the man who discovered the link between EDB and cancer in laboratory rats. "We've had 30 years exposure to EDB," Dr. Weisburger says. "So why alarm the public with one more cancer risk, especially when according to my evidence it's not a very likely cancer risk?" Bruce N. Ames, another expert on toxic chemicals, makes a similar point elsewhere on this page.

The scientists, for one thing, recognize the limitations of their rat studies. Dr. Weisburger's researchers, for example, poured EDB down rat gullets, and the resulting stomach irritation can itself be carcinogenic. In order to detect "weak" carcinogenic properties, the idea was to stuff the rats with as much as possible short of killing them right away—12,000 times the EDB dose allowed by law, five times a week for 30 weeks. For a human to get that high a dose he'd have to chug EDB like beer.

The point isn't that we should ignore these rat studies, which are what we have to work with in making decisions about these issues. There is no point in denying that carcinogens exist, and Dr. Weisburger's tests do implicate EDB. But we need to be more careful about extrapolating any cancer-causing potential from animals to humans, and particularly in thinking about *the extent* of the risk involved. We shouldn't, as one friend puts it, panic "at the drop of a rat.'

That's especially true when the substance we decide to ban is replaced by something potentially worse. EDB again proves the point. Its best substitute for fumigating grain, methyl bromide, happens to be a gas (EDB is a liquid), so it's more volatile and more dangerous to the workers who apply it. Methyl bromide also happens to be more expensive. And, although it hasn't yet been rattested, many scientists believe methyl bromide will itself turn out to be carcinogenic.

We suppose we could live in a world that was free of pesticides. In fact, that may be exactly what some of our more rabid environmentalists want. But we doubt most people would agree, at least once they understood that the cost included higher food prices (as pests destroyed more crops), more insects in food, and more of the "natural" diseases that still bedevil the developing world.

The modern world isn't risk free. The trick for public policy is to balance the risk of using modern technologies against the risk of not using them. The EDB episode is a good example of how not to make that decision.

The Boston Herald

Boston, MA, February 7, 1984

IF THE State Public Health Council's decision to bar sales of 18 grain-based products here because they contain "high" levels of the suspected carcinogen EDB is a mistake, it is one the people of Massachusetts can live with — literally.

It's true that the ban the council imposed on cake, muffin and pancake mixes, cornmeal, flour and bread dough containing more than 10 parts per billion of the pesticide ethylene dibromide is far stiffer than the level the Environmental Protection Agency decided was "safe."

But the temporary standard the EPA settled on late last week, of 150 parts per billion of residue levels in cake mixes and 30 ppb in ready-to-eat products has also been criticized as a mistake, by State Public Health Commissioner Bailus Walker among others.

Given a choice between two supposed mistakes, it's far better to err on the side of caution.

That's pretty much what the Public Health Council did and, all things considered, the decision was a wise one.

The council's timely action was an encouraging contrast to the 30-year record of footdragging by the federal establishment to control or restrict the commercial use of a pesticide that has long been suspected of being a cancer-causing agent. The projections that a person would have to eat an inordinate amount of EDB-treated grain products daily for an extraordinary length of time to run a serious risk of cancer have a falsely-reassuring ring to them.

That's not an acceptable risk. It is, however, an avoidable one, and as the laboratory evidence against EDB mounts, the government has a responsibility to protect the public against it.

The Public Health Council has done that, but we are not at all sure the same can be said for the EPA.

The Houston Post

Houston, TX, February 5, 1984

The Environmental Protection Agency has finally decided that ethylene dibromide could be a health threat but is nothing to panic over. The agency's ban on the chemical as a grain fumigant and its guidelines on levels of EDB residues in food products seem a sensible response to growing pressure for the EPA to take action on the controversial substance.

The measures announced by the regulatory agency Friday should cause no major dislocations in the nation's food distribution system. Food manufacturers are being asked to voluntarily check their products in grocery stores and warehouses and remove any that do not meet the agency's suggested new standards on EDB residue for grain-based food products. It will be up to the states to establish their own procedures for carrying out EPA's guidelines, which may be made mandatory later.

The prohibition against the use of EDB as a fumigant for stored grain and milling machinery is largely in effect already as a result of the furor over the chemical. Measures similar to those applying to grain will be issued for citrus fruit in the next few weeks.

EDB has been used for more than three decades as a pesticide, grain and citrus fumigant, and gasoline additive. But it was not until the early 1970s that government researchers found it caused cancer, birth defects and sterilization in test animals. It was long believed that air and heat broke down EDB so rapidly that it posed no health threat. But using improved instruments, scientists have discovered it in grain, grain products and citrus in minuscule amounts measured in parts per billion.

After traces of the chemical were found in the ground water supplies of Florida and some other states, EPA Administrator William Ruckelshaus banned it as a soil fumigant. The agency's new prohibition against its use as a fumigant for stored grain and in milling had originally been scheduled to go into effect next Sept. 1, but industry protests had threatened to delay it.

The question remains: Does EDB pose a human health risk and, if so, at what level of exposure does that risk begin? Ruckelshaus has downplayed the potential health threat, estimating that less than 1 percent of wheat-based products and 7 percent of corn-based products contain EDB residues that exceed the new EPA standards. He says the poison can be bled out of the food supply within three to five years.

Some officials in Texas and other states, as well as some environmentalists, have criticized the new federal EDB control steps as too little, too late. But there is not enough evidence available now to support draconian measures that would disrupt the food distribution system and cause severe economic losses. Until a stronger case is made against the chemical as a threat to human health, the EPA's ban and guidelines seem both reasonable and prudent.

DESERET NEWS
Salt Lake City, UT,
February 8/9, 1984

For 30 years, American farmers have been using EDB or ethylene dibromide to protect grain from pests.

Though scientists became aware 10 years ago that EDB can cause cancer in laboratory animals, researchers are still divided on how much of a threat it poses to people.

Even so, Director William P. Ruckelshaus of the Environmental Protection Agency still did the right thing a few days ago when he reluctantly banned the use of EDB as a pesticide for grain.

Though the ban means some inconvenience for pesticide makers and farmers, it's better to err on the side of too much safety rather than too little when it comes to the public's health.

Besides, there are plenty of other chemicals and methods that farmers can safely use to protect their crops and increase yields. The public should not get alarmed about other pesticides just because of the ban on EDB. Government restrictions on pesticides have been progressively tightened over the years, yet many pesticides never have been shown to cause harmful side-effects.

Despite increasingly strict federal regulations, pesticide spraying has doubled over the past two decades as science has developed a burgeoning array of chemicals to protect their crops.

American farmers now apply about 700 million pounds of insecticides, herbicides, and fungicides a year, at a cost of around $2 billion. Though this trend shows the need for being alert to possible dangers, there's certainly no reason to panic.

These chemicals are responsible for much of the remarkably high productivity of the American farmer. In fact, if poorer nations were as eager to use pesticides, they would be much better able to feed themselves instead of importing so many crops, and there would be much less hunger in the world. Pests, according to a study by the National Academy of Sciences, cost the world about 35% of its potential food production.

Even so, there are no easy answers to the problems of pest control. Despite the development of more numerous and effective sprays, insect damage has nearly doubled since 1945. Eventually, pests can develop an immunity to a particular chemical, so science has to keep developing new pesticides.

As government tightens its safety standards and as science learns more about the risks posed by pesticides, older chemicals ought to be subjected to periodic re-certification.

This point has become particularly important now because the recent ban of EDB is going to sharply increase the demand for other existing pesticides. Are the replacements still considered as safe as when first approved? Let's lose no time in finding out.

The Washington Post
Washington, DC, February 15, 1984

THE CASE OF the chemical known as EDB is an unusually clear illustration of the perplexities of environmental health protection. American farmers and millers have used it widely for more than 30 years to keep bugs and mold out of grain. In 1956 the Food and Drug Administration exempted it from having to meet a standard in food products, on grounds that it was harmless. You have been eating it, in small quantities, for a long time.

Its status has now changed, not because the chemical—ethylene dibromide—or its use is any different, but because scientific testing procedures have recently developed the capacity to measure risks that previously went unnoticed. It became clear in the middle 1970s that EDB can cause cancer. It is now found in food products because, within the past five or six years, chemists have developed techniques for measuring its traces to parts per billion instead of merely parts per million.

Last year it was found in groundwater in Florida; farmers pump it into the soil as an insecticide. That's the point at which the Environmental Protection Agency began to give serious attention to the residues in other places—such as food products on grocery shelves.

First, because the contamination of water was the most imminent health threat, the EPA banned its use in soil. Next it banned EDB as a fumigant for grain. But what's to be done with the grain already treated with the chemical? It's not clear precisely how much of the American grain supply carries traces of EDB. But it's enough, if it were all condemned, to cause a severe impact on the price and availability of many common foodstuffs.

The EPA's administrator, William D. Ruckelshaus, has to weigh those considerations against the small but, unfortunately, not negligible health risks here. Earlier this month he issued advisory guidelines to the states, as an interim measure. But most states are not well equipped to attempt enforcement in this field, and should not be encouraged to get into it. The EPA says that it is proceeding toward mandatory legal rules. The sooner the better.

Beyond the EDB case, both the agency and Congress need to consider how best to accelerate the long process of re-examining, with the sophisticated procedures now available, the long list of chemicals like this one that are widely used and likely to turn up in unsuspected places. It is probable that, like EDB, none of them is very dangerous in the amounts in which you are likely to meet it in any one week. But over a lifetime, the effects can accumulate—particularly when, as you must expect, the traces of many similar chemicals in food and water reinforce each other.

THE PLAIN DEALER
Cleveland, OH, February 3, 1984

This is how agri-business works in America: Farmers spend millions of dollars buying pesticides, so they can grow more crops, so there is more food in storage than we know what to do with, and so the government can pay farmers to leave some of their land fallow.

That perverted system works a double hardship on the public. It requires billions of dollars in unnecessary tax subsidies to farmers. And the grow-more-with-chemicals-approach is hazardous to consumers.

Witness the recent controversy over ethylene dibromide (EDB), a cancer-causing pesticide found last year in Florida drinking water. It had entered water supplies through its use as a soil fumigant to control root pests. After Florida recalled food products—flour, baby food, cake mixes, etc.—containing more than 1 part per billion of EDB, the federal Environmental Protection Agency halted its use by farmers in the field. The EPA still allows the pesticide to be used to fumigate grain in storage, but is considering a ban on that application as well. Even the Soviet Union is concerned. Soviet officials have asked about the safety of the 7.1 million tons of corn and wheat they are buying from the United States this year.

EDB has been used for nearly quarter of a century in grainaries. It is a big reason you rarely find bugs or worms in your flour, cake mix or uncooked cereal. But researchers also have found that EDB can induce cancer in animals, and according to federal law, no such foreign substance can be allowed in food products if it is found, through "appropriate" tests, that the substance causes cancer.

Therein lies the old and familiar rub. Are tests that force-feed huge amounts of a substance to laboratory animals appropriate in evaluating whether small amounts of that same substance should be used in food products?

EPA officials say trace levels of EDB could result in three cancer deaths per 1,000 people exposed to them for a lifetime. That is too many deaths, and today EPA Administrator William D. Ruckelshaus is expected to recommend measures that could require 8% of the country's stored corn, 2% of the stored wheat and 13% of the grain to be destroyed.

The move will be costly and is expected to be appealed by grain processors and scientists who don't think trace levels of EDB present a threat to the public. But Ruckelshaus and others in the government appear to be convinced that the safety of consumers too often is not given the standing it deserves, despite more than a decade of efforts to weigh the harmful side effects of pest-destroying chemicals.

It was 22 years ago—three years after EDB was approved for field use—that Rachel Carson's "Silent Spring" made consumers aware that the chemical revolution in agriculture was hazardous as well as beneficial. Carson didn't advocate banning pesticides and other agricultural chemicals; she did want to ensure that chemical products would be used safely. The expected action from Ruckelshaus regarding EDB appears to take just that approach. It would sharply limit, but would not ban, EDB use on stored grain. It is action that is long overdue.

EDB Gothic

THE KANSAS CITY STAR
Kansas City, MO, February 8, 1984

The nation has avoided an overreaction to the possible effects of ethylene dibromide on public health. The chemical is potentially risky to humans, and so the Environmental Protection Agency's ban on its use in almost all of agriculture makes sense. It should not be used as a fumigant in grain storage facilities, given its track record of causing tumors, sterility and birth defects in laboratory animals. Too much is simply unknown about its effect on humans to take that risk.

EDB already had been banned last fall as a soil fumigant, and so was no longer in use in many operations by the time of the most recent EPA order. However, state officials will have to determine in what local areas it might still be used, and act accordingly.

In the great wheat-producing state of Kansas, officials do not know if any stored grain, possibly contaminated by the chemical, will have to be destroyed. After a preliminary review, officials in both Missouri and Kansas believe contamination in those states may be small, but further tests are necessary to determine if that is actually the case.

Certainly if EDB is found in high levels in certain facilities, steps must be taken to make sure that contaminated grain is not used for human consumption—at least within the EPA guidelines for levels of concentration. If that occurs, a decision will have to be made on whether to destroy grain, and whether to compensate farmers for it.

In the meantime, farmers and elevator operators will have to resort to other pesticides which may not be as effective but which are considered safer. Above all, safety must be the overriding consideration, despite the inconvenience and cost it may cause to agriculture and the consuming public.

The Birmingham News
Birmingham, AL, February 11, 1984

As rational human beings have probably already judged, the hysteria over EDB (ethylene dibromide) has been generated by those who know little, if anything, about either the chemical or cancer.

Unfortunately, politicians and the media have had a field day scaring the wits out of a large segment of the population. Fortunately, however, the two scientists-researchers who have worked longest and hardest with the chemical have come forward to put the public's fears to rest.

Dr. John Weisburger, who in 1972 was among the National Institutes of Health scientists who established the first link between EDB and animal cancer, says:

● There is no evidence that the pesticide causes human cancer;

● There is no risk from residue levels discovered so far in grain and grain products.

● EDB levels reported in grain and grain products are at least "10,000 times less" than those used in laboratories to cause cancer in rats and mice.

A large part of the blame for the hysteria must also be placed on the doorstep of the Environmental Protection Agency for failing to evaluate for the public the tests that were made on rats and to put them in a proper context as far as human beings are concerned. Where is the expertise for which taxpayers are paying and is supposed to be resident in the EPA?

The whole affair smacks of the kind of irresponsibility that surrounded the scares of a few years ago relative to the assumed effects of saccharin and cyclamates on human beings.

And New York Gov. Mario Cuomo should be chastized for his bellicose threat to ban from entering his state grain products that could not be certified as meeting New York's uninformed standards. The same can be said for Massachusetts' health and environmental agencies.

The manufactured hysteria should serve as a warning to officials everywhere that: (1) The American public has become punchy over supposed environmental threats; (2) most feared chemical holocausts never occur; (3) superstitions about the environment are far more widespread than real knowledge and (4) that there are people and groups ever ready to capitalize on such fears and superstition to advance their own agendas.

Alabamians, we are glad to say, and Gov. Wallace, especially, seemed to show a great deal more common sense about the matter than their fellow citizens in the North and West.

THE BLADE
Toledo, OH, February 11, 1984

The acronym EDB is quietly vanishing from everyday conversation, joining DDT, PBB and DDE in that alphabet soup of environmental hazards only dimly remembered by the public.

Two weeks ago America was being swept by a wave of concern as traces of EDB (ethylene dibromide) were detected in more and more grain products on supermarket shelves.

Today the EDB — a pesticide and soil fumigant — is still there, as it has been since the 1940s. But the panic has abated, and Americans have developed a more sophisticated appreciation of the actual health threat posed by environmental contaminants like ethylene dibromide.

This calmer, more rational outlook is due in large measure to the adroit way in which William Ruckelshaus, administrator of the U.S. Environmental Protection Agency, responded to concern about EDB. Mr. Ruckelshaus banned further use of the pesticide to kill insects in grain and established safety limits on the amount permitted in raw grain, flour and other grain products. These steps, he said, will result in a gradual clearing of EDB from the American food supply over the next several years.

Further, Mr. Ruckelshaus acknowledged the existence of EDB in certain citrus and other tropical fruits, primarily those imported from Caribbean and Central American countries. He promised definitive action on that problem pending the outcome of new EPA studies.

But the EPA director coupled these actions with some much-needed words of reassurance about the nature of the health threat posed by EDB. "Calm down," he urged the public. "We are not faced with a public health emergency, but an effort to eliminate a long-term public health risk."

The true threat from EDB, he said, comes from ingesting it over an entire lifespan. The pesticide has been in the food supply since its introduction in 1948. Nobody, he said, will be harmed by continuing to eat grain products containing traces of EBD. At currently detected levels, he explained, the substance is not an acute poison, but it does pose a long-term, unacceptable risk.

Scientists, he said, previously believed that EDB disappeared from grain long before products like flour and cake mixes reached consumers. But today's ultrasensitive laboratory tests show that the compound persists. Other tests with laboratory animals show the chemical to be a potent carcinogen, linking it with reproductive difficulties and other problems. Even though these tests are of questionable significance for humans, prudence required the final elimination of EDB from food.

These actions are typical of the reasoned approach to environmental problems and the candor which have guided Mr. Ruckelshaus during his stewardship of EPA.

It is a refreshing change for an agency that has seen such troubled times in the recent past. And it is a course that could do much to calm the "panic-in-the-pantry" syndrome that so frequently diverts Americans from the nation's well-established and truly massive public-health menaces.

These are cigarette smoking, high blood pressure, unhealthful diet and other easily correctable problems that kill hundreds of thousands of persons each year.

Union Carbide Plant Gas Leak in India Kills at Least 2,000

In what was described as the worst industrial accident on record, toxic gas escaped from a pesticide plant in the central Indian city of Bhopal Dec. 3, 1984, killing at least 2,000 people and injuring more than 50,000 others. The gas leak occurred at a chemical plant owned by Union Carbide India Ltd., a subsidiary of the Union Carbide Corp. based in Danbury, Conn. The gas was methyl isocyanate, a chemical compound used at the plant for its annual production of 2,500 tons of carbamate, a pesticide marketed as Sevin Carbaryl. The Indian plant was 50.9% owned by Union Carbide Co. and 49.1% owned by Indian companies and individuals.

It was not immediately certain what caused the gas leak, although Indian government officials and Union Carbide engineers believed that pressure had built up within an underground storage tank containing 15 tons of liquid methyl isocyanate, and that a "vent scrubber" system designed to neutralize the gas failed to function properly when confronted with the sudden overflow.

Union Carbide was expected to face massive damage claims. Teams of U.S. lawyers already had begun arriving in Bhopal to work with Indian colleagues in the preparation of damage suits. By Dec. 11, a total of $35 billion in claims had been filed against the company in the U.S. A Chicago, Ill. relative of six victims of the gas leak Dec. 12 filed a $50 bilion class-action lawsuit against the chemical company. The chairman of the U.S. Union Carbide Corp., Warren M. Anderson, arrived in Bhopal Dec. 7. He was immediately arrested and charged with criminal conspiracy and culpable homicide not amounting to murder. Anderson was freed six hours later and told to leave the country.

It was also uncertain what the long-term medical effects of the disaster would be. The highest number of casualties occurred among residents of two densely populated slums located immediately adjacent to the plant. A night breeze swept the gas through the area, killing many of the area's residents in their sleep and causing others to awaken with burning eyes, sore throats and shortness of breath. Most of the dead had suffered from what were described as massive asthma attacks when the air passages in their lungs were blocked by the toxic gas. Others died after fluid accumulated in their lungs. Medical experts expressed fears that thousands of victims would suffer permanent lung, kidney or liver damage, blindness or sterility. Authorities also voiced concern about a health epidemic caused by the thousands of decomposing animal and human corpses strewn throughout the city of Bhopal. Indian government officials charged that the Indian plant had not been maintained at the same safety standards as Union Carbide and other similar plants in the U.S. Assertions by Union Carbide spokesmen that the Indian plant had indeed been designed and built to the same safety standards as American plants prompted widespread fears that the U.S. plants might be unsafe to operate.

More recently, the Indian government March 24, 1986 rejected a proposed $350 million settlement by Union Carbide of claims arising from the 1984 fatal gas leak at its subsidiary in Bhopal, India in which 2,000 people died and 20,000 others were injured.

ST. LOUIS POST-DISPATCH
St. Louis, MO, December 5, 1984

To understand the horror of what happened in Bhopal, India, one does not need precise figures. It is enough to start with the knowledge that the leak of methyl isocyanate, a toxic gas used in the production of pesticides, from an underground storage tank at a Union Carbide plant caused hundreds of men, women, children and animals to die by suffocation as they slept. And, by some sad measure of misery, they might be considered the lucky ones. For others awakened as the chemical's pungent odor filled the air, death came neither so quickly nor so peacefully: Even as they sought to flee their homes, their own body fluids were filling their lungs, causing slow death by drowning. Thousands were injured, with many of them hurt badly enough to require hospitalization.

No one has suggested that the leak was anything other than an accident — but could it have been prevented? Union Carbide had taken precautions. The poisonous effects of any leaking gas were to have been neutralized by scrubbers activated when safety valves opened to relieve pressure inside the tank. Obviously, the precautions taken were not enough.

What more could have been done? To suggest that the manufacture of pesticides should be banned outright would be folly. Rather than seeing hundreds of people perish in occasional industrial accidents, we would be consigning millions of people in India to certain malnutrition and, more probably, starvation. But there is every reason to insist that plants with the potential for creating harm on an order seen in Bhopal be built or relocated far from any urban area. It might inconvenience workers, and manufacturers might have to overcome logistical problems. But if such a move will save lives — hundreds or thousands, or even just one — what objections can be reasonably sustained?

THE ARIZONA REPUBLIC
Phoenix, AZ, December 8, 1984

IN the aftermath of the tragedy in India, there is growing concern about whether a similarly disastrous accident could occur elsewhere. And people wonder if adequate precautions are being taken to prevent such a thing from happening.

On the basis of what evidence is available, the answers, unhappily, appear to be, yes, it could and, no, they aren't.

In the United States, for example, an official of the Environmental Protection Agency says that thousands of leaky storage tanks dot the nation, but the federal government doesn't know where they are and only recently received authority to regulate them.

Dr. John Skinner, director of the Office of Solid Waste, said that the government has no idea of how many Americans are threatened by tanks like the Union Carbide Corp. one that leaked in India, killing more than 1,200 people with a poison gas.

Elsewhere, the threat is even greater. Some nations, such as India, do not have zoning laws separating industrial and residential areas, with the result being that potentially hazardous facilities are scattered throughout crowded cities.

Compounding the problem is the lack of enforcement where laws do exist. In the Third World, even if there are environmental regulations, they are hard to enforce.

But the real dangers in these unregulated environments are often more insidious than explosive. They include deadly wastes from industrial plants that slowly poison the air or drinking water, and the misuse of agricultural chemicals.

The latter accounts for 370,000 cases of accidental poisoning in Third World countries annually, according to an official of the United Nations Environment Program headquartered in Nairobi, Kenya.

Some of the many thousands of man-made chemicals in use every day, especially toxic pesticides, are beginning to trickle into once-pure food supplies throughout the developing countries, with sometimes deadly consequences.

In Brazil, where the highly toxic insecticide DDT is widely used, studies show up to 10 percent of the population suffers from mild forms of toxic poisoning, mostly from the misuse of pesticides.

For years, a United Nations commission has been trying to develop an industrial "code of conduct" to encourage greater environmental safety in the Third World. To date, it has made little progress.

Pesticides are truly wonders of the modern world, providing developing nations with the means to increase crop yields and kill malaria-carrying mosquitoes. As such, they're lifesaving agents.

But without proper handling, in the tank and in the field, they become dealers of death. The United States should do everything it possibly can, through federal agencies at home and through the United Nations abroad, to further environmental safety.

It's a matter of life or death.

THE SACRAMENTO BEE

Sacramento, CA, December 6, 1984

Something went wrong. So far, that is the only certainty about the tragic episode in Bhopal, India, where upwards of 1,000 persons have died — ultimately, the total could be far greater — as the result of the escape of a poisonous gas used in making insecticides. For the moment, this enormous disaster, made more poignant by television pictures of people gasping for breath as medical personnel frantically try to help, is itself the overriding concern. A shocked world can only grieve and offer its sympathy to a community devastated by an episode whose long-term effects on survivors' health may be even worse than now imagined.

But inevitably, shock and compassion must give way to the task of finding out just what did go wrong, and trying to prevent its repetition. And inevitably, that process will result in the laying of blame, wherever it may be found. Whether the responsibility is ultimately affixed to Union Carbide, builder and operator of the pesticide plant, to bureaucratic failure to enforce safety regulations, or merely to a single act of human or mechanical error, there is a larger responsibility, and it is a global one.

It hardly seems coincidental that the most disastrous recent industrial accidents have occurred in overcrowded slum areas of Third World cities, where zoning laws are either non-existent or laxly enforced. In Bhopal, as earlier in Mexico City (where 452 persons died in the explosion of liquid petroleum tanks only weeks ago), poor people with nowhere else to live had settled immediately adjacent to potentially dangerous industrial plants, a phenomenon only rarely found in advanced industrialized countries. Nor is it disputed that — in general, if not necessarily in the case of Bhopal — safety and environmental standards in the Third World are less stringent and less rigorously enforced, both by government and by industrial firms.

Some of the blame for this can be laid to Third World governments which, understandably, are eager to develop industry as rapidly as possible in order to raise standards of living. At the same time, Western corporations, often abetted by their governments, are partly responsible. They rush to set up plants in the Third World not only to take advantage of cheap labor but to escape environmental and safety restrictions that in their own countries raise the cost of doing business.

Righting these and other wrongs will not help the victims of Bhopal, but the jarring reminder such tragedies provide offers the small hope that governments will recognize the common interest in setting and enforcing standards worldwide that at least reduce the likelihood of future calamities. Regardless of who or what is directly responsible for that lethal gas leak, the ultimate blame can be found in the collective mind-set that assumes it's all right, in the name of rapid economic development, to put poor people at greater risk than those fortunate enough to distance themselves from such perilous reality.

The Philadelphia Inquirer

Philadelphia, PA, December 6, 1984

In today's high-risk society — where it seems hazardous materials outnumber benign ones — some people persist in believing that certain things are impossible. Safety equipment will not fail. Accidents will follow a predicted course. Emergency planning will not be thrown awry by unplanned events.

Actual experience proves otherwise, of course.

The poison gas tragedy at Bhopal, India, is only the most recent — and most horrifying — case in point. There have been others. Some have taken awesome tolls in lives and injuries; some have been controlled by human intervention — or good luck.

If there is one lesson to be learned from these accidents and near-accidents, however, it is that there is no such thing as an "impossible" set of circumstances involving technology.

Shortly after the accident in Bhopal, a spokesman for Union Carbide, owner of the Indian plant, told reporters that events leading up to the release of the poison gas were totally unpredicted and unexpected. According to preliminary reports, a valve regulating pressure in an underground storage tank failed and the deadly gas spread through a densely populated residential area. A backup safety system also apparently failed.

Union Carbide is no different from any one of tens of thousands of companies that daily produce, handle or treat hazardous materials. And an accident such as the one at Bhopal could have happened at any one of them — such is the danger of the product they manufacture and the risk to those nearby.

Short of eliminating such products from modern society — a response no sensible person could advocate — what is the answer?

Many things will be proposed in the aftermath of the Bhopal disaster. The siting of such plants must be considered. Dangerous industrial processes should not take place around people. Yet the impracticality of that becomes obvious in places like Bhopal, or in Mexico City, where at least 452 died in November in an explosion at a gas plant situated in a residential neighborhood. In those cases, the plants were there first; people from rural areas followed, crowding into shantytowns in the land-starved cities. As was true in America for many years, and is true in developing nations today, the only way to get to a job is to walk and the only choice is to live near the job site, however risky. Many Americans, particularly in older, industrialized regions of the country continue to live surrounded by such hazards.

Installation of redundant safety systems must be required. But no safety system is infallible. Consider the example of nuclear reactors, built with an array of duplicative safety components. Those responsible for building, operating and regulating the reactors were so convinced the equipment was adequate and that certain types of accidents could not take place that they labeled those accidents "not credible." Ironically, the sequence of events that led up to the accident at Three Mile Island were not considered "credible" by some nuclear experts until *after* they occurred.

The message from Bhopal will be meaningless unless a fundamental change takes place among those responsible for the technology that surrounds almost every citizen of the world. That is the recognition that the impossible *is* possible, and every decision made must reflect that fact of life and death.

AKRON BEACON JOURNAL

Akron, OH, December 7, 1984

INDIA'S AGONY with the results of a terrible toxic chemical spill grows worse each day. At least 1,200 and perhaps 2,000 are dead in Bhopal, many of them children, and as many as 20,000 may ultimately be found to have been seriously affected by the poison gas.

The fact that the poisonous gas leak occurred at a plant owned by an American company, Union Carbide, adds to the sense of tragedy in this country.

Officials of that company, from the top down, are apparently doing all they can to help. Union Carbide's chairman, Warren M. Anderson, led a team of engineers, safety experts and doctors that flew to the disaster site Wednesday.

If any good is to come from this horrible tragedy it must be a realization that the world increasingly deals with technology and substances that are complex and dangerous. Such dangers may not become the reality of the Bhopal horror if industries, governments and scientists learn how to guard against such devastating toxic spills.

The Honolulu Advertiser
December 5, 1984
Honolulu, HI,

Grim statistics and superlatives still dominate the disaster scene in India where deadly gas escaped from a U.S.-owned pesticide plant and spread over nearby shanty towns.

But this is also likely to be a story with ongoing implications reaching back to this country. It should produce some lessons for the future.

THE SHOCKING death toll will keep rising for days, weeks or much longer. For this was one of the world's largest man-made tragedies, an industrial accident as awesome as war.

Hundreds died in their sleep. And it seems they were the "lucky" ones compared to some others. Of the thousands of survivors who overflowed hospitals, there was this description by a volunteer worker:

"They came choking on their own vomit and unable to open their eyes. It was horrifying, like nuclear war."

More likely, it was like chemical warfare would be, and that is a point to reflect on when that option comes up in Washington, and when we consider disarmament topics with the Soviet Union.

WHILE WE are shocked, saddened and mourn the loss of life in far-off India, it is also natural to wonder what would have happened had this massive tragedy occurred in this country.

It is not an idle question since the American firm, Union Carbide, has a plant in West Virginia, which uses the same chemical that escaped in India. The U.S. plant is now also temporarily closed.

So all sorts of questions will — and should — be asked here as well as in India about safety equipment, inside and outside alarms, the kind of gases used, the distance such plants should be from populated areas, etc.

Moreover, since Union Carbide is one of the world's largest chemical producers and has plants in more than 30 countries, such questions will be asked elsewhere as well.

NO DOUBT there will be compensation for victims in some form by the company. But the larger compensation should be that we can make sure a tragedy of this magnitude does not happen again.

The News and Courier

Charleston, SC, December 12, 1984

The tragedy that claimed the lives of some 2,000 people in Bhopal, India, when gas leaked from underground tanks at a Union Carbide pesticide plant, is being turned into a melodrama. The villain of the piece — hissed and booed at every mention of its name — is Union Carbide, the wicked multinational. Coming to the rescue of the victims of the tragedy, however, are some unlikely heroes. One of them, Melvin Belli, the flamboyant lawyer from San Francisco, who is known as the "King of Torts," has already filed a class action, claiming $15 billion in compensation and punitive damages. Mr. Belli seems to think that he knows who and what caused the accident in Bhopal: "The American businessman is concerned with profit and that's all. I think we should be more concerned with safety than the dollar."

As Mr. Belli's own incredibly profitable career testifies, American businessmen have long been aware that any lack of concern about safety can have a very high dollar cost. Even businessmen who think only of the bottom line have to think about safety. After the Bhopal disaster, perhaps the worst industrial accident every recorded, there is even less likelihood of safety factors being overlooked.

It is questionable, however, whether Union Carbide and its Indian partners, who own just under 50 percent of the plant, were ever in a position to provide a basic safety measure. The enormously high death toll can be attributed to the fact that thousands of slum dwellers lived around the plant. This was also why there was a shockingly high number of fatalities in two other recent industrial accidents. Over 400 people were burned to death when liquified gas at a storage facility outside Mexico City caught fire last month. About 500 people perished from burns sustained when a leaking gasoline pipeline ignited in southern Brazil last February. In both cases, the toll was so great because those high-risk industrial installations were located in heavily-populated areas.

In the case of the accident in Mexico City the undergound tanks, owned by a state company, were in existence before people began settling in the area in shacks. In Cubatao, in southern Brazil, the state-owned gasoline company Petrobras, refused to accept blame, arguing that society should be held responsible for allowing people to live so close to the pipelines.

The question of Union Carbide's responsibility is still open. The company has produced pesticide at a similar plant in West Virginia for the past 17 years without incident. It should be possible to establish whether safety measures within the plant in Bhopal were lax. But responsibility for the high death toll also rests with local authorities who failed to realize the danger of allowing people to live in such close proximity to a high-risk chemical plant.

The point that can be made in regard to all three tragedies is that a very low price is placed on human life in the Third World. Mr. Belli's efforts on behalf of the victims in Bhopal will not help the victims of the accidents in Brazil and Mexico. There is no nasty multinational company to sue, only two state-owned companies which have not admitted any responsibility. It is an ironic commentary on Mr. Belli's views about American businessmen that victims of industrial accidents in the Third World do not stand much chance of receiving compensation unless wicked, profit-minded American businessmen can be hauled into American courts by altruistic American lawyers like Mr. Belli.

Accidents happen to everyone. Union Carbide should be judged according to the way it handles this tragic situation, not on baseless charges about alleged greed for profits. So far, neither the company nor its chief executive, has shirked duty. Making this tragedy into a melodrama will not help make amends. That is the immediate task at hand. Then steps must be taken, with everyone accepting his share of responsibility, to make chemical plants, gasoline pipelines and inflamatory storage installations safer — throughout the world. Safety is the real bottom line that we must all scrutinize.

THE MILWAUKEE JOURNAL

Milwaukee, WI, December 6, 1984

In the streets, under the doors and through the windows of homes in the central Indian city of Bhopal, the toxic mist crept silently and remorselessly before dawn Monday like a crafty animal with a deadly purpose. More than 1,000 persons died after realizing too late that they were breathing a lethal gas, methyl isocyanate, used in the manufacture of insecticides at a nearby plant owned by a subsidiary of Union Carbide, of Danbury, Conn.

No one knows how the terrible accident occurred. Union Carbide promises to find out, and to provide emergency relief to the victims.

But why were the plant and heavy population permitted in a proximity that virtually assured the maximum consequences in any such mishap? Why weren't the victims warned of the accident so they could be evacuated? Were safety measures at the plant violated? Were they too lax to begin with? Could such an accident happen in the US?

Those and other urgent questions presumably will be addressed in the investigation. Some of the questions involve tricky issues and tough trade-offs. For instance, profit-minded companies may not be eager to build plants in countries that impose high safety standards — in some cases impoverished countries where jobs are urgently needed.

The Bhopal disaster showed that a breakdown of safety can mean a loss of lives, not merely of jobs. Thus, the same high standards that Union Carbide and other US firms are required to meet in this country ought to be extended to their foreign operations. The responsibility for safety in the workplace belongs to the employer.

The only way to extract any good at all from the accident in Bhopal is to learn from whatever mistakes allowed it to happen. If no lessons are learned, if no corrective measures taken, those dead and maimed will have suffered to no purpose.

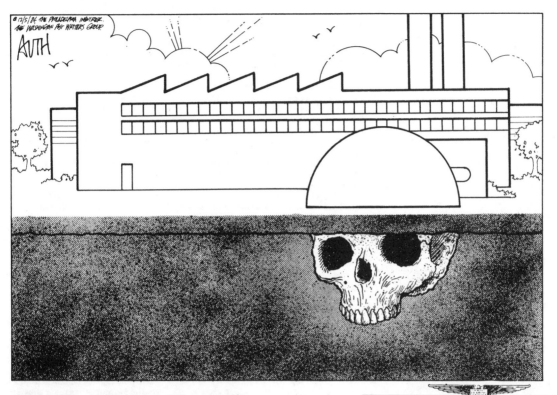

© 12/5/84 THE PHILADELPHIA INQUIRER.
THE WASHINGTON POST WRITERS GROUP

AUTH

The Providence Journal

Providence, RI, December 5, 1984

The extraordinary poison gas disaster in India on Monday was more than just a tragedy for that sorely beset nation. The 1,000 or more deaths from a toxic chemical discharge at a pesticide plant may be the worst industrial accident in world history.

As with the aftermath of any disaster, there will be investigations and proposals to prevent a recurrence. Safety standards for such processes have to be strict and strictly enforced. Such toxic chemicals, in quantity, do not belong in a metropolitan area.

Union Carbide Co., the American firm that holds a controlling interest in the Indian plant, promptly acknowledged its heavy responsibility, sent medical aid, halted shipments of the chemical around the world and as a precautionary measure stopped its production at a similar plant in West Virginia.

The disaster-struck plant is 49 percent owned by the Indian government and managed entirely by Indians. Their vast nation is a bewildering combination of the primitive and the sophisticated, but it has had heavy and light industry for more than a century.

However, in a land like this, most plants are on the edge of large metropolitan areas, to provide worker accessibility. Thus, it's usually the poor neighborhoods that suffer most from big industrial accidents. That was true of the recent liquefied petroleum gas plant explosion in Mexico City, where 452 died — and now it is true in Bhopal, a Dallas-sized Indian state capital.

The toxic substance, methyl isocyanate, is used in making carbamates, such as Union Carbide's brand-name pesticide Temik. Ironically, carbamates are in favor because they are less persistent in the environment than older pesticides. The isocyanate itself is altered in manufacture and is not present in the marketed product, but is extremely poisonous while it exists.

Many deficiencies apparently contributed to the Bhopal tragedy: a breakdown of a valve that allowed the leak; the subsequent failure of anti-pollution "scrubbers" that should have trapped most of the poison, and the reported delay in sounding alarms.

Most important, why did the leaking tank contain an astonishing 45 tons of the liquid chemical? That is a huge quantity — roughly 10,000 gallons — but some experts say methyl isocyanate is usually stored in batches of not much more than 1,000 gallons.

An excessively large concentration might explain why a cloud from the leak hung like a blanket over 25 square miles, affecting 20,000 people. This question deserves investigators' attention. If a smaller volume of the chemical had leaked, it might have harmed a few people — but not the hundreds who died in this nightmarish catastrophe.

ALBUQUERQUE JOURNAL

Albuquerque, NM, December 6, 1984

Two man-caused disasters occurring within two weeks of each other in widely separated, densely populated cities have claimed hundreds of lives, injured thousands and left the specter of disease and even more death to trouble the survivors. Both graphically illustrate the deadly forces man can unleash by accident or through carelessness.

Two weeks ago, more than 500 Mexicans living in Tlalnepantla, a Mexico City suburb, were burned to death when a liquified gas plant exploded. Hundreds more were severely injured. A trucker accidentally triggered the initial explosion. This week more than 1,000 people were killed by a poisonous gas cloud that escaped from a pesticide plant in Bhopal, India, when a valve and special filters failed.

Try as they might, governments are hard-pressed to protect their citizens completely from similar disasters. Even in the United States, where safety and zoning laws and regulations are strongly enforced, disasters of major magnitude occur.

The toll in the Bhopal disaster came despite a government regulation calling for location of plants such as the Union Carbide facility 25 kilometers from population centers. An estimated 250,000 lived nearby, thousands of whom had built shacks and huts close-by in hopes of finding jobs there. Similar desires swelled the population around the Tlalnepantla plant.

Ideally, buffer zones would isolate hazardous material production plants from large populations. Enforcing such zones where population is dense and jobs and land are scarce requires extraordinary government diligence, a diligence that is not always present when hundreds of thousands of people are poor, hungry and uneducated.

Man is the most fragile ingredient and the most susceptible to disaster when his own creations go awry. The only thing certain about both the Tlalnepantla and Bhopal disasters is similar tragedies will likely occur elsewhere when triggered by an accident, carelessness or unsafe practices. It is to be hoped that the enormity of the tragedies, determination of their causes and punishment of those found to have violated safety measures will somehow help prevent a recurrence elsewhere.

St. Petersburg Times

St. Petersburg, FL, December 6, 1984

The final dimensions of the tragedy at Bhopal, India, where thousands of people were overcome as poison gas leaked from a Union Carbide pesticide plant and crept through the city at night, may not be known for months or even years. Many of the 50,000 who survived with burned eyes, lungs and other injuries may suffer more than those who died in the streets while trying to outrun the silent, white cloud of death.

As the death toll mounts and the full horror of Monday night becomes clear, India's sorrow may sweep the world. But in West Virginia's smoky Kanawha River Valley, crowded with chemical plants that spew acrid fumes among the hills and hollows, human sympathy will mix with nagging fear. A sister Union Carbide chemical factory, larger than the one in Bhopal, sprawls along the riverbank at Institute, near Charleston.

The disaster at Bhopal raises troubling questions about governmental failures — in India, the United States and other nations — to provide better protection for workers on hazardous jobs and the people who live in industrial areas.

Even though Union Carbide has a good safety record, and the American chemical industry generally has a low accident rate, the Kanawha Valley's 225,000 residents know now that the tragedy at Bhopal might some day be their own.

That is the risk that chemical industry workers take, and the potential threat they must live with, for jobs to support their families. And along the Kanawha River, one of the largest chemical producing regions in the United States, the stinging sulfurous vapors that envelop the valley night and day are called "the smell of meat and potatoes."

It is much the same in Bhopal, only far more desperate. Most of the victims of the lethal gas that leaked from underground storage tanks were poor country people who moved to the city in central India to find jobs, building mud hovels near the pesticide plant. But their risk turned to terror Monday night as the gas cloud swept through the slums, killing hundreds as they slept and sending hundreds more into the streets with burning eyes and bursting lungs.

Whether one of the world's worst industrial accidents was caused by human error, equipment failure or Union Carbide's negligence remains unclear. But the disaster at Bhopal raises troubling questions about governmental failures — in India, the United States and other nations — to provide better protection for workers on hazardous jobs and the people who live in industrial areas.

In the world's most advanced industrial nation, the U.S. Environmental Protection Agency (EPA) has no regulations to control underground storage of chemicals such as those that leaked the death cloud at Bhopal. Recent legislation requires rules to insure that such tanks are safely managed and calls for the EPA to determine how many such tanks exist, what they contain and what their condition is. But none of that has been done yet.

And the Reagan administration, which virtually wrecked the EPA during Anne Gorsuch Burford's reign, has failed to restore the agency's strength or resolve to protect the environment or the people. "It can happen here," said an EPA official in Washington Tuesday, but the agency does not have enough staff for adequate monitoring of industry and relies on "self-policing" by chemical plants that produce pesticides and other toxic substances.

The EPA estimates that some 6,000 American plants make chemicals considered dangerous to human health.

Until Union Carbide officials determine the cause of the Bhopal disaster, the company has halted production of the poison gas, methyl isocyanate, at the West Virginia plant. That was the only responsible action the company could take. The plant at Institute is nearly identical to the one at Bhopal.

But the real test of Union Carbide's responsibility to its workers and the people of the Kanawha River Valley will be the safeguards it provides when and if the plant resumes operation in an urban area that now lives even more uneasily under a cloud of fear.

"We can have a safe chemical industry here," said David L. Grubb, executive director of the West Virginia Citizen Action Group. "We don't have to choose between jobs and the environment. But the industries have to spend more money."

So does the Reagan administration — by providing the EPA with an adequate budget and staff to protect the environment and people.

The Salt Lake Tribune

Salt Lake City, UT, December 9, 1984

The catastrophe in Bhopal, India, in which more than 2,500 persons died when chemicals leaked from a Union Carbide Co. pesticide plant, will soon be under investigation by a special government commission. But there is no need to wait for the official findings to conclude that accidents that cannot happen do happen.

Company officials say that the same safety precautions in effect at a similar plant in the United States were also followed at the facility in Bhopal. It is hard to imagine federal, state and local governments in this country permitting operation of such a potentially dangerous plant unless stringent safeguards reduced the possibility of such a failure to the vanishing point. Yet the same safety rules did not prevent the disaster in Bhopal.

The obvious but not necessarily correct explanation for the fact that the Indian plant's malfunction was not prevented or discovered in time to limit danger is that because of rapid industrialization there, the employees of Union Carbide's Indian subsidiary were not as thoroughly trained or that the government did not enforce safety restrictions as diligently as it should have.

The official investigation will undoubtedly look into that, but until it completes its work, it must be assumed that the people and government of India are no more willing to submit to dangers posed by plants manufacturing lethal products than are the people and government of this country.

In that case the Bhopal accident must be seen as one that defied technology's best effort to prevent or respond to breakdown. It becomes a tragedy that could not happen.

Nobody knows how many other impossible accidents of equal or greater magnitude are caged in world industry and, in effect, "waiting" for some human or mechanical failing that will set them off in deadly fury. At a time when little good is being said about the industrial establishment, it speaks well of it that malfunctions on the scale of the Bhopal disaster are indeed one in a million occurrences.

Even so, the Bhopal deaths are a scary and tragic reminder of the high price civilization pays for the benefits of industrialization. This spectacular accident must inspire a redoubled effort to prevent other impossible nightmares from coming true.

Arkansas Gazette.

Little Rock, AR, December 8, 1984

Unspeakable horror has descended upon the downtrodden of Bhopal, India, and lest Americans shrug off the gas poisoning of tens of thousands existing in poverty near the pesticide plant, they might consider the fact that the tragedy might have occurred in the Charleston area of West Virginia, where Union Carbide operates what is said to be an identical chemical plant.

Safety features built into the Bhopal plant, supposedly identical to those in Union Carbide's Institute, W. Va., facility, simply did not work, apparently overcome by rising pressures in an underground chemical tank. The tank contained methyl isocyanate, which is a liquid that turns into gas when it comes in contact with air.

Investigators will be sorting out the details of this gas leak, which at last accounting had taken perhaps 2,000 lives, and the principal aim should be to assure that such a leak is not repeated either in Bhopal or Institute. That the accident didn't happen at Institute may tell something about the efficacy of federal regulations that many American industries rail about and then find a sympathetic audience in the Reagan administration.

One resident of Institute concedes that he doesn't know what happened in India, but adds that "I doubt whether the plant officials over there have OSHA or the EPA looking over their shoulders all the time." The implication is that federal regulators in the United States have made a difference. Whether they actually have is not easily discerned, but the Bhopal tragedy certainly does give warning to one and all that immediate and effective steps must be taken to prevent accidents of this kind, involving toxic chemicals, not only in the United States but also across the globe.

The Seattle Times

Seattle, WA, December 4, 1984

INDUSTRIAL accidents can and do occur anywhere that machinery exists, of course. Yet there are certain striking parallels to the two massive tragedies that snuffed out hundreds of lives last month in Mexico and this week in India.

The fiery gas explosion in Mexico City and the leak of poison gas from a pesticide factory in Bhopal, India, devastated entire neighborhoods of poverty stricken people forced to live in close proximity to industrial installations.

Such conditions prevail in any number of American or European cities, too. But generally the overcrowding is far worse in the developing countries.

There are many and diverse causes for such tragedies. Yet there is one underlying reason for the scale of the disasters — over-population. The incidents, shocking though they may be, merely cast brief illumination on what is a continuing, day-by-day tragedy in the developing world of too many people and too few resources.

The Star-Ledger

Newark, NJ, December 6, 1984

Tragedies in far-off lands frequently seem as distant to many Americans as the countries in which they happen. Terrible as the consequences may be, there is a comforting aspect to human nature that sometimes leads to the belief: "It can't happen here."

No such comfort, however, can be taken from the terrible tragedy in Bhopal, India, in which inhalation of a deadly gas has already killed over 1,000 persons and injured many thousands more. The poison gas, which has a lingering effect and which may ultimately cause additional fatalities, is also manufactured and stored in the United States, in West Virginia.

There does not seem to be a great deal of difference in the manufacture and storage procedures followed by the Union Carbide Co. in India and in the United States. The gas is methyl isocyanate and its deadly qualities are considerable, so much so that workers in the United States can be legally exposed only to the smallest of amounts. The product is used in the production of a variety of pesticides.

There is no indication that the safety precautions taken by the company in India were any less than those in West Virginia. In fact, Union Carbide is unsure what was the exact cause of the gas leak in India. As a precaution, the manufacturing plant in West Virginia has been shut down, but the storage tanks of the poisonous substance naturally remain.

The entire field of pesticide manufacture and storage has been marked by a decided information gap. Scientists are only now able to state with any accuracy what is deadly and what is not—and under what circumstances. Even now, the information seems sketchy.

New Jersey had its own brush with this information gap earlier when traces of dioxin, another potentially deadly product used in the manufacture of pesticides, were found at an abandoned Newark plant site. The state moved forcefully to take appropriate action, without falling into the twin pitfalls of panic or neglect. The question remains, nevertheless, a disturbing one for the many areas in which pesticides are made—or used.

The tragedy in India points out once again the extreme peril that can result from certain chemicals. There is an obvious need for more information on this subject, as the number of confusing and conflicting statements of the past few years indicate.

It is up to the regulators—in particular the federal regulators—to have complete and up-to-date information and to have it quickly. It may be that a scientific panel should be assembled to report on a regular basis as to what additional precautions are necessary. The tragedy of Bhopal certainly could happen here—or anywhere—unless intelligent precautions are taken and strictly enforced.

WORCESTER TELEGRAM

Worcester, MA, December 7, 1984

The hideous tragedy in Bhopal, India, is almost beyond imagination. The human toll — dead and afflicted — from the deadly gas leak may number in the tens of thousands. Bhopal is one huge charnel house.

Union Carbide, builder and owner of the plant, says it does not know why the methyl isocyanate gas in the huge tank heated up and leaked out in such quantities. Until it finds out, the company has halted production of the gas at its other plants, including one in West Virginia. Company spokesmen say they had no idea that such a catastrophe was possible.

Yet they did know that there were risks. They knew that methyl isocyanate is extremely volatile. Company regulations required that it be kept chilled. The company claims that the safety precautions in India were identical to those in West Virginia. If so, it is clear that far stricter measures are called for.

Methyl isocyanate is a highly toxic chemical used in insecticides and other chemical compounds. No doubt it is a useful substance. But until it can be determined that the stuff can be produced without risk to human lives and health, it must not be produced.

There must never be another Bhopal catastrophe. Never, never, never, anywhere in the world.

Union Carbide Issues Report on Bhopal Disaster

Union Carbide Corp. March 20, 1985 issued a report on the December 1984 lethal gas leak at its Bhopal, India subsidiary that killed more than 2,000 people. (See pp. 92-99) The report blamed the "inadvertent or deliberate" introduction of a large amount of water, instead of nitrogen, into a storage tank containing methyl isocyanate gas for triggering a chemical reaction that caused the disaster.

The seven-person company team which had conducted the three-month investigation, found that conditions at the plant prior to the disaster were so unsatisfactory that the plant "shouldn't have been operating." The situation that resulted in the leak, the report said, was aggravated by the failure of several safety devices, including a pressure gauge, a refrigeration unit and a vent gas scrubber designed to neutralize any escaping gas. The refrigeration unit and gas scrubber had been turned off several months prior to the accident in direct violation of company procedures. The report declined to assign blame for the disaster, citing its lack of access to personnel at the subsidiary (Union Carbide India Ltd.) and to other key data necessary for a complete investigation (The Indian government had denied Union Carbide investigators access to local officials while it carried out its own investigation). Speaking at a press conference, however, Union Carbide Chairman Warren M. Anderson maintained: "Compliance with safety procedures is a local issue."

The Indian embassy in Washington, D.C. March 21 released a statement on behalf of its government, calling the implications of the Union Carbide report "unjustified and unacceptable." A government official said in New Delhi that India was prepared to prove in a U.S. court that the parent company was responsible for the leak. Meanwhile, the final death count from the disaster was still in dispute. The Indian government maintained that about 2,500 people died as a result of the leak, while other estimates ranged from 1,400 to more than 10,000. Thousands of other victims, according to estimates by environmental and health experts, might have suffered permanent lung damage from inhaling the gas.

The Hartford Courant
Hartford, CT, March 22, 1985

Safety conditions at Union Carbide Corp.'s chemical plant in Bhopal, India, were shockingly poor, according to the company's chief investigator of the accident that caused the loss of more than 2,000 lives.

Chairman Warren M. Anderson, who on Wednesday released the results of the investigation, said he had "no indication that the plant was operating under these conditions."

Who's to blame, then? No one at corporate headquarters in Danbury, the company's top officials insisted. "Compliance with safety procedures is a local issue," said Mr. Anderson, who maintained that Union Carbide's Indian subsidiary bears the legal responsibility for the accident.

Not so, claim officials of the Indian government. Responsibility for the accident belongs to headquarters. Union Carbide experts in Danbury should have made certain that these lapses in safety did not occur, the government argued.

The chemical reaction, which injured 200,000 people, was not an accident. It was a disaster that shook the world. Of course the local plant managers bear some responsibility, as does the Indian government for failing in its regulatory duties. But any attempt by Union Carbide in Danbury to distance itself from or disown the Bhopal facility is futile.

The Bhopal plant was built according to the specifications of Union Carbide. The plant carried the name of Union Carbide, and most of the profits went to Union Carbide.

Perhaps Mr. Anderson and other top officials in Danbury didn't know how bad the conditions were at the Bhopal facility. But ignorance is no excuse.

"You can't run a $9 billion or $10 billion corporation all out of Danbury. You can't be there day in and day out, week in and week out," said Mr. Anderson. Yes, he can't. But Mr. Anderson's subordinates can be there at least periodically to make sure that a potentially dangerous facility is being operated properly. The company's headquarters is ultimately responsible.

Mr. Anderson implicitly acknowledged that Union Carbide needed to toughen its standards. He appointed a special committee to review corporate safety and said the company would triple the frequency of its special safety audits.

The disaster in Bhopal occurred on Dec. 3, 1984. The last on-site audit conducted by corporate auditors was in mid-1982 and revealed numerous safety problems. There were no followup checks from Danbury, just assurances by mail from Bhopal that the problems would be taken care of.

Obviously, they weren't.

the Charleston Gazette
Charleston, WV, March 26, 1985

UNION Carbide's official report says slipshod operation of the Bhopal plant allowed the Indian tragedy to occur.

Although the source of water that entered the Bhopal tank and loosed lethal MIC gas remains unknown, Carbide says mass death wouldn't have happened if the plant's crucial security devices hadn't been turned off. They included a refrigerating unit to prevent a runaway reaction and a flare to burn escaping gas.

Carbide vows that a similar disaster can't arise from the Institute MIC unit, and the safety record of the Institute plant — indeed, the record of all Kanawha Valley plants — is impressive.

However, after Bhopal, people who live near chemical plants need solid assurances — such as tighter safety standards and frequent governmental inspections to see that they're followed.

An event this month was unsettling. The 5,-700-pound acetone and mesityl oxide leak at the South Charleston Carbide plant was unidentified for hours and unexplained for two days. To be sure, the chemical was not deadly MIC, but any such discharge that affects public health can't be ignored.

Chemical jeopardy is worse in New Jersey. There, 14 such leaks in three months — that's right, 14 — led the Legislature to raise the fine for serious emissions from a maximum of $2,-500 to a minimum of $10,000. For the South Charleston episode, Carbide wasn't fined, and perhaps it should have been.

But fines come after the fact. Far more important is prevention. Carbide has made changes at Institute to improve safety, acknowledging that lessons are to be learned from Bhopal.

Those changes include storing and shipping less MIC. While the chemical industry considers similar changes for plant procedures, Congress is preparing to set new national safety standards. Currently, for example, no OSHA rules govern the maintenance of storage tanks and no EPA rules cover large-scale leaks.

Although the safety changes at Institute are encouraging, can people be sure they are enough — or that every chemical plant, here and elsewhere, will do likewise? What's needed is an independent review process as part of new national standards to put communities at ease.

Union Carbide, a good citizen, surely wouldn't oppose increased outside scrutiny. Nor should any company which manufactures lethal products amid residential communities. They should put aside traditional resistance to regulation, and realize that only such regulation can restore confidence in the chemical industry and preserve both safety and jobs.

The Courier-Journal & TIMES
Louisville, KY, March 27, 1985

ENVIRONMENTALISTS and health authorities have been predicting for several years that toxic air pollution, which made dramatic headlines this week after release of a congressional survey, would be the next big-ticket item on the nation's health agenda. This tough issue has been neglected, they believe, mostly because of the U.S. Environmental Protection Agency's endless procrastination.

That's the darker side of the story presented last month when EPA boss Lee Thomas came to Louisville to help celebrate dramatic progress in cleaning up "conventional" air pollution — the hydrocarbons and the oxides of nitrogen and sulfur that are more obvious trouble sources. The public has heard very little about even deadlier substances that, in much smaller quantities, escape into the atmosphere to present more subtle dangers.

Two recent happenings have changed that. The first was the Bhopal catastrophe December 3, when more than 2,000 Indians died within hours after a large-scale release of one of the most toxic of these substances. Bodies in the street will get attention. But it has been politically safe to ignore low-level emissions that well may cause just as much harm over time by triggering cancer and other diseases.

Chemical companies surveyed

The second happening, set in motion by Bhopal, was the first systematic survey of toxic emissions, done not by the EPA but by Congress. The information comes from responses to a survey of 80 large chemical companies. The heart of the report is that thousands of tons of cancer-causing agents and other intensely hazardous materials are released by hundreds of factories with little or no regulation.

But long before Bhopal, air pollution authorities, including those in Jefferson County, were disturbed by the EPA's failure to set standards for toxic chemicals. Some states, such as Texas, California, New York and Pennsylvania, have been developing programs on their own, in the absence of badly needed national guidance. But not even the larger and richer states have the resources to deal with the scientific problems involved.

Even if they could, an undesirable patchwork already is developing. Philadelphia regulates 99 toxic air pollutants. Other cities and states regulate a few, or none. A consistent national policy is badly needed.

As matters now stand, the release of methyl isocyanate, the substance that killed so many at Bhopal and that also is made at Institute, West Virginia, wouldn't violate any U. S. environmental regulation — even in the quantity that escaped the plant in India. Similarly, there's no regulation on how much acryonitrile (a particular problem in Louisville), arsenic and perhaps thousands of other deadly substances can be released into the atmosphere.

Of course, no one can say precisely what level of emissions of these chemicals can be allowed without undue risk to health. But even the chemical industry feels that uniform standards, based on reasonable estimates of the risk, are needed. "The chemical industry has gone through a lot of soul searching since Bhopal," the president of the Chemical Manufacturers Association told *The New York Times* the other day. Only the EPA can appropriately set such standards. More prodding should not be needed.

St. Petersburg Times
St. Petersburg, FL, March 28, 1985

The chemical cloud of death that drifted through the slums of Bhopal, India, on a windy December night has long since dispersed. But the nagging fear evoked by the worst industrial accident in history has not been dispelled. Could it happen elsewhere? Might the tragedy at Bhopal some day be another city's disaster?

Such troubling questions were the impetus for the first systematic survey of toxic air pollution in this country. Henry A. Waxman, D-Calif., who is chairman of the House Subcommittee on Health and the Environment, ordered the survey and released the results Tuesday at a hearing on chemical-industry safety.

Soon after the Bhopal tragedy, it was disclosed that the United States had no regulations controlling the release of methyl isocyanate, or MIC, the poisonous gas that leaked from a Union Carbide pesticide plant, killing at least 2,000 people and injuring as many as 200,000 others. That revelation merely hinted at the extent of the government's failure to protect the public from the potential danger of airborne poisons.

THE CONGRESSIONAL survey found that at least 204 chemicals discharged into the air were considered hazardous to health and safety by the industry that makes them — including such cancer-causing chemicals as chloroform, benzene and formaldehyde. Of the 204 toxic chemicals identified in the survey, only five are now regulated under the hazardous air pollution provisions of the Clean Air Act. The consequence of this lack of regulation is predictable. Largely left to their own controls, chemical companies routinely release into the air thousands of tons of cancer-causing agents and other very hazardous materials.

The Bhopal accident was terrifying proof that a massive release of toxic gas can kill and injure thousands in a matter of hours. The congressional survey raises the concern that America's chemical companies are engaging in a slow-motion version of the disaster at Bhopal. As Waxman put it, "If you get smaller doses of some of these chemicals over a longer period of time, you die as well."

In scientific circles, there is some controversy about what levels of chemical discharges are safe and to what extent disease can be caused by cumulative chemical effects and by synergism — the action of two or more chemicals that together produce biological effects greater than might be otherwise expected. While that debate is being waged, however, several studies have shown higher incidences of cancer in areas of the country where refineries and chemical companies are concentrated.

Decisions on public policy sometimes have to be made before scientific debates are resolved. Considering what is now known or suspected about the health risks of long-term exposure to chemicals, it would seem suicidal not to adopt strict national standards to control the venting of poisonous gases into the air.

A RELATED ISSUE is the public's right to know about the risk of chemical exposure. Waxman's survey revealed that toxic gases are being released into this country's air at far higher levels and at many more locations than suspected. Another study by Congressional Research Service found that three of every four Americans live near a chemical manufacturing plant. Not every plant releases poisonous gases or has the potential for producing another Bhopal disaster. But some do. Legislation also is needed to assure the right of Americans to know what chemicals used in their communities might endanger residents' safety and health.

Furthermore, Waxman's survey found that some chemical companies have detailed plans to handle emergencies, while others have only sketchy emergency plans or none at all. Earlier this week, the Chemical Manufacturers Association encouraged the executives of chemical companies to work with local and state officials in developing better emergency response plans. The industry's call for corporate responsibility is welcome, but experience has shown that voluntary regulation often means no regulation. And the public health is to ' precious to leave to chance.

The terrible deaths and the living agonies of the Bhopal victims provide a sorrowful impetus for the adoption of much stricter controls of toxic air pollutants. The Environmental Protection Agency (EPA) now has the discretion to regulate hazardous air pollutants, but not the requirement to do so. Congress should exercise its discretion to order the EPA to regulate the emission of poisonous gases and set a deadline for doing so.

Union Carbide Plant in West Virginia Leaks Toxic Gas

A toxic gas leak Aug. 11, 1985 at Union Carbide Corp.'s pesticide plant in Institute, W. Va. injured six plant workers and sent 134 area residents to hospitals for treatment. The leaked gas, aldicarb oxime, caused eye and skin irritation and, if absorbed through the skin, "systemic illness with headaches, dizzines, nausea, vomiting and collapse," according to a Union Carbide materials safety data sheet. The plant also produced methyl isocyanate, the substance that killed more than 2,000 people and injured tens of thousands when it leaked from a Union Carbide plant in Bhopal, India in December 1984. (See pp. 92-99) The West Virginia plant had been shut down after the Bhopal disaster and had reopened in May, after safety equipment and procedures were bolstered.

The leak of aldicarb oxime apparently was caused by an accidental entry of steam between the double insulating walls of a tank containing 500 gallons of the gas. Pressure built up, blowing gaskets and opening a safety valve, which vented the system. The toxic gas then leaked into the atmosphere from a ruptured disk in the emergency system. A computerized monitoring device to detect such leaks had been installed at Institute's methyl isocyanate unit following the Bhopal disaster. No such device was installed at the nearby unit that produced aldicarb oxime.

The latest leak, despite the precautions taken by Union Carbide after the Bhopal incident, brought the company under severe criticism from public officials at all levels of government. Some of the criticism focused on a delay of approximately half an hour between the time the leak was discovered and local authorities were notified. Public concern was further aroused by a second, minor leak Aug. 13 from the Union Carbide plant in South Charleston, just five miles from the Institute site. The leak – of about 1,000 gallons of chemicals used for brake fluids – resulted in hospitalization of four residents for eye irritations and nausea.

the Charleston Gazette

Charleston, SC, August 13, 1985

AFTER THE Bhopal tragedy, Union Carbide spent $5 million to make the Institute plant a model of safety — and look what happened Sunday.

Around 400 Kanawha Valley residents suffered gas poisoning; hospitals were swamped as far away as Gallipolis, Ohio; a temporary medical center and 21 ambulance crews were required; emergency warning and traffic control operations tied up western Kanawha County; several victims remain hospitalized today.

Ironically, the leak happened in a unit established three months ago for safety purposes. After Bhopal showed the menace of methyl isocyanate, Carbide decided not to ship MIC from Institute but convert it into a more benign compound first. The conversion utilizes aldicarb oxime — the culprit in Sunday's leak.

The aldicarb unit was opened in May, after rigorous inspection. Now it has suffered a pressure buildup, safety device failure, and rupture — just like the Bhopal MIC unit. State Air Pollution Control Commission Director Carl Beard asked the key question:

"Why didn't their control equipment work and cut that stuff off the way it's supposed to do? The fact that it apparently didn't work presents a serious problem."

This incident proves that, no matter how hard chemical plants try to build infallible systems, no matter how much they spend on safety, no matter how earnest their intentions, danger will remain for people who live nearby.

Thus it's imperative that every possible step be taken to minimize the risk that can't be eliminated. Three needed reforms:

▲ The 1985 Legislature passed a hazardous chemical right-to-know law — but no disclosure warned the public that the Institute plant harbored the potential to do what it did Sunday. What's the point of disclosure laws if they don't disclose dangers? The right-to-know law must be made realistic.

▲ Carbide's own safety inspections didn't prevent Sunday's occurrence. Perhaps better results might be obtained by independent outside inspectors with power to shut down a plant, as federal and state mine inspectors can close a dangerous mine. Stricter safeguards are imperative.

▲ Neighbors say they weren't warned quickly of Sunday's leak. Mayors say they weren't told what gases would be faced by their paramedic crews. The valley's emergency warning and evacuation system needs improvement.

Already, voices are uttering the usual praise of Carbide as a Kanawha Valley benefactor and job-provider. It's true: Carbide is a boon to the region, and Carbide strives mightily to attain foolproof safety. But toxic leaks continue. Eight other Carbide episodes have happened in 1985.

Ultimately, society must answer a fundamental question: Should deadly chemicals be manufactured within breathing distance of residential neighborhoods? Perhaps just relatively safe products should be allowed at plants close to people, and the worst poisons, corrosives and explosives should be relegated to isolated factories.

Recurring leaks and danger in the Kanawha Valley make this question unavoidable.

The Miami Herald

Miami, FL, August 5, 1985

THE phrase "Better living through chemistry" is more than an old corporate motto. It's a modern reality. Farming especially benefits as chemicals boost harvests and conquer pests to help feed a hungry world.

Mankind pays a price for chemistry's wonders, however. Last December in Bhopal, India, more than 2,000 persons died when deadly methyl isocyanate gas (MIC) leaked from a Union Carbide plant there.

After Bhopal, Union Carbide shut its Institute, W.Va., plant for five months because MIC is processed there. Between 1980 and Bhopal's disaster, MIC had leaked inside the Institute plant 61 times.

The West Virginia plant finally reopened in May after being certified safe by Federal, state, and company officials. Yet on Sunday morning, hundreds of persons who live near the Institute plant were endangered by a gas leak: not MIC, but another gas — aldicarb oxime — that is derived from MIC.

Investigators do not yet know why and how the incident happened. Plant officials say a gasket on a 500-gallon tank leaked, but why it did may not be ascertained until an official probe has been completed.

Already, though, there are disturbing signs that the plant's alarm did not give nearby residents a timely and sufficient warning. Victims say they smelled the noxious fumes before they heard the alarm. More than 150 residents were treated for gas inhalation; more than two dozen were hospitalized.

Whatever the particulars or the cause, this kind of occurrence is unacceptable. Firms that profit from the use of toxic chemicals have a concomitant responsibility to ensure that such substances do no harm while they are being manufactured, transported, or used.

Union Carbide manifestly failed to meet its responsibility in Bhopal. Now the incident at Institute raises questions anew about the thoroughness of the company's safety precautions in the United States.

Moreover, because of the way chemicals are transported in this country, the matter is of concern far beyond the immediate vicinity of chemical-manufacturing plants. Unless great care is exercised, toxic substances escaping from ships, trains, trucks, and pipelines can pose as serious a threat as those from manufacturing sites. Indeed, aldicarb oxime, the gas that sickened Institute residents, is routinely shipped from West Virginia to Georgia for processing into the pesticide Temik.

Temik is the substance whose misapplication to California watermelons was linked to the illness of dozens of persons. Doctors blame those illnesses on the aldicarb in Temik. Therefore, Sunday's leak of aldicarb oxime — though by no means another Bhopal — is a serious incident that demands swift and thorough investigation.

The Chattanooga Times
Chattanooga, TN, August 13, 1985

The specter of Bhopal rose again Sunday in Institute, W. Va., when a chemical leak sent six Union Carbide employees and 125 residents to area hospitals.

Institute is the only place in the United States where Union Carbide produces the lethal methyl isocyanate which killed over 2,000 people in Bhopal last December. Thankfully, the leak from the Institute plant was not the deadly MIC, but a far less toxic derivative, aldicarb oxime. Those exposed as a result of the accident suffered gastric and respiratory distress but, apparently, were not seriously injured. Nevertheless, the accident serves as a sobering reminder of environmental dangers posed by chemical production — and the need for far more effective public health safeguards at chemical plants.

It's not as if Union Carbide hasn't tried. The MIC unit at Institute was shut down for five months after Bhopal, and the company added $5 million worth of new safety equipment. The U.S. Environmental Protection Agency gave the unit a clean bill of health before MIC production resumed, and during the shut-down period, a federal Occupational Safety and Health Administration report said chances of an MIC-related accident at Institue were "extremely remote." But at that time an MIC-related accident was only six months into the future.

Likewise the deficiencies of a new warning system installed at Institute since Bhopal were exposed on Sunday. Residents reported seeing the cloud of toxic chemicals released from the Union Carbide plant 20 minutes before the company sounded an alarm. One resident said she was awakened by the strong, irritating odor of the chemical, again before any alarm sounded. Another said he stayed in his home for at least 10 minutes after smelling the fumes because he thought there would have

been a warning siren if there was a problem. Had the leak been of a deadlier nature there could have been tragic consequences of the delay to sound the alarm.

Fortunately there were not; the inadequacy of measures taken to enhance public safety at Institute was demonstrated without loss of life. The incident can be seen as a blessing in disguise if it produces greater urgency, both among chemical companies and federal officials, in seeking solutions to the complex environmental problem presented by the production, use and storage of toxic chemicals.

There is a dearth of regulations in this area now, but we need look no farther than West Virginia's "Chemical Valley" to see the need not only for safeguards against accidental leaks but also for effective controls on routine emissions. According to Perry Bryant of the West Virginia Citizens Action Group, residents of Kanawha County (where Institute is located) experienced a respiratory cancer rate 25 percent above the national average between 1968 and 1972. From 1973 to 1977, the rate was 21 percent above normal; and in 1982 a neighborhood near one Union Carbide plant recorded a cancer rate twice the national average. "Is there anyone in this room," he asked during a congressional hearing last December, "who honestly believes that these abnormally high levels of cancer and the discharge of 737 tons of chemical pollutants each year are not related?" Surely there was not.

The public must demand effective protection from hazardous chemicals if those in authority are to summon the political will to tackle the issue of regulating toxics in the environment, Otherwise, we will continue to court disaster.

The London Free Press
London, Ont., August 15, 1985

Within 60 seconds of the discovery that deadly aldicarb oxime was leaking from a Union Carbide plant in West Virginia, the plant's warning alarm rang.

That's no comfort to thousands of area residents — 134 of whom were injured — for whom the first emergency broadcast didn't occur for three quarters of an hour when the gas was already settling over homes and burning their eyes, noses, throats and lungs.

Union Carbide employees waited for 20 minutes after the leak was found before they decided the chemical cloud might

endanger others and notified county emergency officers. It was 15 minutes before the community warning whistle on a local fire station was sounded and 10 minutes before a broadcast — in all, 45 minutes.

Somewhere along the line, the warning that a chemical as toxic as the one which killed 2,000 persons in December after it leaked from a Union Carbide plant in Bhopal, India never came in time. The West Virginia plant is the same one from which a gas leak in March injured eight persons at a nearby shopping mall.

Can there really be any question anymore that the public has perfectly good reason to shout "Not in my backyard!" when large companies soothingly propose potentially hazardous operations nearby? All the promises in the world are of no benefit when the lid blows off or when toxic wastes end up in community wells or streams.

One of the key issues is public trust, and the best way to lose that trust is to fail to send out an alarm when a fault has been detected. A different situation but a similar principle applies in London where the ministry of environment took four years to notify the public that Pottersburg Creek was contaminated with hazardous material.

West Virginia residents were reporting injuries 15 minutes before they heard an alarm. A Union Carbide official explains the wait by saying "We did not believe the emergency would affect the community because the cloud was hovering over the plant."

Can emergency response officials in Canada say with certainty that a similar travesty wouldn't occur here?

The Burlington Free Press
Burlington, VT, August 14, 1985

Laxity on the part of Union Carbide officials in warning the public of impending danger after poison gas leaked from its chemical plant in Institute, W.Va., was inexcusable in light of the fact that 2,000 persons were killed nine months ago in a similar accident in Bhopal, India.

While company spokesman at first said the gas that leaked from the Institute facility was safer than the methyl isocyanate that caused the Indian tragedy, it has since been learned that the aldicarb oxime involved in West Virginia has a similar toxic rating. Yet emergency services in Kanawha County were not notified of the leak until 20 minutes after the gas had escaped from the Institute plant. Carbide officials said the delay was due to the fact that they did not believe the gas cloud would affect the community. The

"cloud," they said, was hovering over the plant and a computer system showed that it would pass back over the plant.

Yet it would seem that steps should have been taken to alert the public in case of a shift in the direction of the cloud. A warning would have prepared the residents of Institute and surrounding communities for the events that followed. Instead, the leak caused injuries to 135 people. With the lesson of Bhopal in mind, the behavior of those in charge of the plant was inexplicable.

Angry community officials have criticized the warning procedures and their comments undoubtedly will trigger an investigation of the situation by West Virginia officials. "The system didn't work," Charleston Mayor Mike Roark said.

What must be troublesome to local offi-

cials is the fact that Carbide ostensibly spent $5 million on a warning system after the plant was closed last December following the Bhopal tragedy. Yet several residents detected the pungent odor of the chemical before emergency horns warned them of the danger. Either the alarms are inadequate or plant officials decided on their own not to sound them. In either case, the company's credibility must be called into question.

Unless the firm makes basic changes in its emergency procedures to reassure the public that there will be more timely warnings of accidents in the future, there are bound to be demands from some groups that the Institute plant be again shut down until further safety measures are taken.

THE ☁ SUN
Baltimore, MD, August 15, 1985

The injury-causing, accidental release of a mixture of acrid chemicals into the air from Union Carbide's plant in Institute, W. Va., compounds the credibility problems of the large American chemical company. Union Carbide operated a similar plant in Bhopal, India, from which a leak of deadly methyl isocyanate killed some 2,500 people and injured 177,000 others last December.

The latest accident caused no deaths, and an Environmental Protection Agency pesticide expert says the 136 injured people will suffer no permanent aftereffects. The major chemical released, Aldicarb oxime, although it is made from methyl isocyanate at Institute, is not as toxic.

After the Bhopal incident, Union Carbide revamped safety features at its methyl isocyanate unit at Institute, and the unit was inspected by EPA officials before a May reopening. "Other parts of the plant, including the part that handles Aldicarb oxime, were not included in the revamping," the EPA now has acknowledged. All parts of the plant that handled toxic substances should have been included. A faulty gasket was the immediate cause of the chemical release at Institute. Not only was the gasket faulty, so was the plant's warning system: Area residents reported that by the time they heard a warning whistle they already were breathing the chemical.

Union Carbide's difficulties in making its plants safe suggest the social cost of manufacturing and using highly toxic agricultural pesticides in large quantities may be too high. Pesticides of the kind manufactured at Bhopal and Institute have contaminated groundwater on Long Island and elsewhere. EPA officials admit that while residues of these pesticides left on fruits and vegetables are harmless in themselves, they aren't necessarily harmless in combination with other chemicals to which people are exposed. Growing numbers of experts think it is time to move quickly toward a phasedown of chemical pesticides, replacing them with safer biological controls. Chemical companies and the EPA should start putting a high priority on developing these replacements.

THE TENNESSEAN
Nashville, TN, August 15, 1985

LAST Sunday's chemical leak at the Union Carbide plant in West Virginia was a frightening reminder of how humans are often held hostage by their own technology.

Because of a series of malfunctions and mistakes — some mechanical and some clearly human — aldicarb oxime, an active pesticide ingredient, was released into the air in Institute, West Virginia. The exposure of 135 persons to the chemical was serious enough to require hospital treatment for skin, eye, throat and lung irritations.

Plant officials say that the aldicarb was stored in a vessel designed as a chemical reactor container. As such, it was fitted with an outer jacket in which fluids could be pumped to heat or cool the contents. Steam was inadvertently pumped into that jacket, thus raising the temperature of the aldecarb, and increasing the pressure inside the vessel. The container's gaskets blew off, allowing the chemical to escape.

But the problem with the storage vessel was not the most troublesome aspect of the Union Carbide accident. The company waited 20 minutes after the plant's internal alarm detected the leak to alert local officials and hospitals, and another 16 minutes to notify community residents. Rep. Bob Wise, who represents the area, said that of the 254 Institute residents his office interviewed after the leak, 144 indicated they were exposed to the gas before they heard any alarm. Company officials say that the community alarm was not sounded because a plant computer indicated that the gas would hover directly over the plant, and was no threat to area residents.

The accident will give Union Carbide a beating, both in West Virginia and on Wall Street, and that beating will be particularly harsh due to the fresh memory of the company's Bhopal, India, disaster last December which killed 2,000. The company lost no time in trying to make amends in Institute by calling for an investigation, and saying it would pay the medical expenses of the injured persons. Company officials also say they will not ask victims to waive their legal rights to futher damages.

Those steps are good for community relations, and might blunt the criticism of Union Carbide in this instance. But the real issue here is not public relations but public safety, and that issue goes far beyond Institute, W.Va., and the board room of Union Carbide.

If the Institute plant was violating federal or state safety requirements, then government inspectors should have made it correct the problems. And if the plant was in compliance with guidelines, then the guidelines are obviously too lenient to protect the public.

Malfunctioning computers and the poor judgment of company employees can take some of the blame for the Institute accident, but that blame should be shared with the government agencies that exist to assure the public's safety.

WORCESTER TELEGRAM
Worcester, MA, August 13, 1985

That leak of toxic gas at the Union Carbide plant in West Virginia sent a shudder across the land, particularly in communities that have chemical plants.

Six employees and more than 100 neighboring residents were treated for eye, throat and lung irritation Sunday after a small cloud of toxic gas leaked from the plant. The gas, aldicarb oxime, is a less dangerous derivative of MIC, the deadly pesticide ingredient that escaped from a Union Carbide plant in Bhopal, India, last December, killing 2,000 people.

The Institute, W. Va., plant is now the only one where MIC is manufactured. The plant was closed for several weeks after the disaster in India. Union Carbide said it invested $5 million to guarantee against any similar disaster in Institute. Before the plant reopened May 4, it was examined by a task force from the Federal Environmental Protection Agency, which concluded that it could be operated without endangering nearby residents.

Now both company officials and the EPA task force look incompetent. Who will believe anything they say from here on?

The company says the leak Sunday occurred when a gasket failed on a storage tank of aldicarb oxime. Perhaps the improvements completed in May dealt only with the section of the plant devoted to making and storing MIC. If so, that is simply not good enough.

First reports suggest further that the company's alarm system did not function as swiftly as it should have after the leak was detected. Neighbors say they smelled the escaped gas well before they heard the company siren that is intended to alert people to turn on radio or television to get instructions on emergency procedures.

There is very little margin for error in the manufacture of deadly chemicals. Equipment must be engineered with adequate safeguards and then must be properly maintained. Correct procedures must be carefully planned and stringently enforced. Bhopal demonstrated what can happen if all this is not done. The new accident at Institute is a further warning.

If a large, experienced chemical manufacturer like Union Carbide does not have the know-how, the resources and the concern to insure safety, and if government can do no better than that EPA task force in overseeing safety improvements, then where are we to turn? There must be a thorough and independent investigation of the whole problem at Institute before that plant is allowed to operate again.

THE LOUISVILLE TIMES
Louiville, KY, August 15, 1985

After the catastrophic leak of a poisonous gas from a pesticide plant in Bhopal, India, Union Carbide Co. presumably understood the need to devise a safety plan that would stop anything remotely similar from happening at a chemical complex that makes the same products in Institute, W. Va.

In fact, amidst assurances that West Virginians had nothing to fear, the company shut down its Institute plant and invested $5 million in improvements. Among the innovations is a computer to help in alerting employees and local residents to chemical dangers.

Yet all the purported emphasis on safety proved woefully inadequate last Sunday. First, a chemical called aldicarb oxime leaked into the atmosphere, forming a cloud that drifted over the adjoining community.

Then Carbide employees, incorrectly believing they could contain the cloud, delayed an alert. As a result, local authorities were not notified for 20 minutes and a siren did not sound for 36. Many residents learned of the leak in the worst possible way — by actual exposure to the chemical.

So what happened to "emergency preparedness"? For one thing, the computer system, which predicts the route of escaped chemicals, didn't work because it hadn't been programmed for aldicarb. The operator told the computer to assume the cloud was methyl isocyanate, which killed 2,000 in Bhopal. Since the chemicals are different, the computer's prediction was useless.

The next question is all too obvious. Why hadn't the computer, which has worked well elsewhere, been fed information about aldicarb, a chemical regarded as very toxic? It turns out the company ordered programming for 10 of hundreds of chemicals made at Institute, and aldicarb was not among them.

Why didn't someone notify local officials? Well, comes the response, if you panic every time a little poison gets away, you'll get no more attention than the boy who cried "wolf." Perhaps, but it's a safe bet folks in West Virginia, shaken by Bhopal, won't ignore the company's warnings for a long time.

The worst part of it is that Carbide's bungling merely hints at the problems in making, handling and transporting hazardous chemicals. Leaks and accidents were reported the last few days in Arizona, New Jersey and at yet another Union Carbide plant. Almost 24,000 chemical mishaps were counted by a federal response center in two years.

Yet industries and governments have have been appallingly slow in facing this menace.

From Institute comes the unsettling news that undersized pipes and valves installed at many plants are believed to increase the danger. Louisville, a chemical manufacturing center for 40 years, has just enacted a tough law requiring prompt notification of spills. Emergency planning is said to be confused in West Virginia's industrialized Kanawha Valley. Many places haven't done that well. In fact, the Environmental Protection Agency is compiling an "acute hazards list" of up to 200 dangerous chemicals to spur companies and towns to prepare for accidents.

Happily, Institute's injured are expected to recover. But a word to the wise should be sufficient. The chemical threat needs to be contained before tragedy strikes.

Washington, DC, August 15, 1985

It was supposed to be a slow Sunday in Institute, W.Va. Some sleepyheads were still in bed. Church-goers were wearing their Sunday best. Golfers were on the greens.

Then it hit them — a cloud of poisonous fumes that made 135 people sick, 28 sick enough to be hospitalized.

There was no warning. They were breathing it before they knew it. Some victims were already choking and coughing by the time Union Carbide finally sounded its siren, 36 minutes after the toxic chemical, aldicarb oxime, leaked into the air.

Chemical accidents are all too common in the USA. In just over two years, there have been at least 4,500.

This week alone, there were six: Forty-six chemical containers overturned on an Arizona railway, a tanker sprang a leak on a Virginia highway, and another West Virginia plant disgorged 1,000 gallons of brake fluid into a river. There were two other spills in New Jersey.

These mistakes poisoned air and water, sickened a few people, and forced thousands to leave their homes.

Some say the chemical industry has the skill and the staff to handle hazardous chemicals safely. They say we should not overreact to one incident.

One incident in an otherwise safe industry might be acceptable. But not six accidents in one week. Not 4,500 accidents in two years. There is too little safety in that record.

The industry has not done all that it can, or all that it must, to protect the public. There have been too many accidents, too many spills, too many injuries.

And the government hasn't done all that it must to protect public safety.

The USA's chemical industry is ensnared in a confusing web of regulations — state, local, and federal.

The Environmental Protection Agency has pollution rules. So does the Occupational Safety and Health Administration. So do state and local governments.

But no federal agency regularly monitors the manufacture, use, and storage of the most dangerous chemicals — some so toxic they can cause illness years after exposure.

What the industry and the nation need is a coordinated, well-structured set of regulations that can be enforced. Congress must give the EPA authority to lead the way.

EPA must identify hazardous chemicals and inspect the plants that make the poisons. And it must do more to help state and local officials deal with emergencies.

What happened in West Virginia this week was serious. But it could have been far worse.

Last December, another dangerous chemical spilled from another Union Carbide plant in Bhopal, India — and 2,250 people died. The survivors are still suffering.

The cloud over Institute was not deadly, but it cast a warning shadow over the chemical industry. Clouds should bring rain, not pain and death.

The Houston Post
Houston, TX, August 13, 1985

The white cloud of toxic gases that descended Sunday upon the West Virginia town of Institute brought with it disturbing questions about the safety of U.S. chemical production plants.

The noxious fumes dissipated two hours after they escaped from the Union Carbide plant. Yet the questions remain, waiting to be answered.

Institute, thankfully, did not become an American version of the disaster in Bhopal, India. About 130 people were injured in the Institute leak. Bhopal suffered more than 2,000 deaths as the result of a chemical leak from a Union Carbide facility.

Institute does indicate that we are not immune from this type of industrial accident. Aldicarb oxime, the chemical released from the West Virginia plant, is a derivative of methyl isocyanate — the toxic pesticide ingredient that left so many dead in India.

After the Bhopal tragedy, there was immediate concern about similar factories in the United States, particularly the Institute plant. Union Carbide invested in a $5 million safety system designed to prevent such an accident from happening.

Despite the safety system, Union Carbide has been criticized by the communities that surround the plant. Local officials say they were not notified of the leak until at least 15 minutes after it occurred. The company admitted a computer error caused the delay in alerting the public.

Union Carbide should be warned that it is not allowed any margin for error in the production of these toxic chemicals and that area residents deserve only the most forthright conduct by the pesticide plant.

Labor Department Seeks Fine Against Union Carbide for Violations

The Labor Department announced April 1, 1986 it was seeking a $1.4 million fine against Union Carbide Corp. for 221 alleged health violations at Union Carbide's Institute, W. Va. plant. Labor Secretary William Brock, appearing at a news conference and showing anger at times, said, "very serious problems" had been found at the Institute plant relating to safety systems, safety management and record keeping. "We were just surprised to find conscious, overt, willful violations on such a widespread basis," he said. Federal inspectors had discovered that employees without respirators had been requested "to detect the presence of deadly [phosgene] gas by sniffing the air after alarms indicated a leak," Brock said. "We used to use canaries for that."

Union Carbide President Robert Kennedy protested later that day that the Labor Department had "grossly distorted the actual safety conditions and attitudes in the plant." The company's formal response could be submitted to an administrative judge and an appeal process was available after that before recourse to the courts, if necessary. Union Carbide officials had accepted full responsibility in August 1985 for the large leak of toxic gas from the Institute, West Virginia facility. (See pp. 100-103)

THE SACRAMENTO BEE
Sacramento, CA, April 4, 1986

Labor Secretary Bill Brock, when he took office last year, promised Congress he'd strengthen the Occupational Safety and Health Administration (OSHA), which the Reagan administration had previously been working hard to defang. And Brock is trying. The just-proposed $1.4 million fine against Union Carbide — by far the largest in OSHA's history — is a sign of it.

Union Carbide says that OSHA's charges against it are grossly exaggerated. But after the disastrous industrial accident at Carbide's plant in India, followed last summer by a gas leak at the company's West Virginia facility that required the hospitalization of six workers and emergency treatment of over a hundred local residents, Brock could hardly have failed to investigate. And when a thorough study of the West Virginia plant turned up 221 alleged violations of 55 federal safety regulations, Brock had to react.

OSHA had found 130 violations it listed as "willful" and "very serious" — like Carbide's "customary" practice of having a worker check for poison gas leaks by sniffing the air. For Brock to have responded with anything less than a huge penalty would have signaled others that federal safety regulation is a shuck. He wasn't making an example of Union Carbide, Brock said, but "if others want to draw some understanding from the process, I encourage them to do so."

That's a welcome change from previous Reagan administration policy, under which OSHA staffing and investigations declined precipitously. And no doubt it's in part as a result of those cutbacks that the rate of industrial injuries and illnesses in the nation has recently begun climbing. The many serious safety violations OSHA found at Union Carbide's West Virginia plant — the human canaries, the safety valves corroded shut, the protective equipment that didn't work, the inadequate safety training for employees — suggest just how inadequate the department's previous inspection program and its policy of "voluntary safety compliance" had been.

In some cases, the mismanagement appears to have gone much further: OSHA's Philadelphia office has been accused of taking bribes to ignore safety violations, and its Manhattan office apparently looked the other way while workers were being poisoned by mercury exposure.

Brock is now investigating those charges. He has also launched close inspections of several dozen chemical facilities, owned by other corporations, although he says he doesn't expect conditions elsewhere to be anywhere near as bad as at the Carbide plant. The labor secretary is said to be making a behind-the-scenes fight for OSHA funding as well, although that's an uphill battle with the Gramm-Rudman ax poised to slice even more from OSHA's already depleted inspection forces. The proposed Union Carbide fine is of a piece with those other activities. And if Brock is as determined to change things as all that suggests, thank goodness.

THE CHRISTIAN SCIENCE MONITOR
Boston, MA, April 9, 1986

IF the $1.38 million fine the Occupational Safety and Health Administration (OSHA) has proposed to levy against Union Carbide were really an indication that the Reagan administration was serious about workplace safety, it would be something to applaud.

But there's not much indication that the proposed fine against Carbide, for alleged health and safety violations at its Institute, W.Va., plant, is really that kind of signal at all.

For one thing, Carbide is unlikely ever to have to pay $1.38 million. This is the biggest penalty ever assessed by OSHA, but its record includes fines actually paid that are a small fraction of fines originally imposed.

For another, one big fine does not an enforcement trend make.

Under the new budgetary restrictions, like any other arm of government, OSHA is having to choose its targets carefully. In the case of Union Carbide, whose Bhopal, India, plant was involved in the world's worst-ever industrial accident in December of 1984, and whose Institute plant had a gas leak last August that resulted in hospitalization of six workers and emergency-room treatment for 129 area residents, the press did much of OSHA's work for it.

Carbide's president has complained that many of the violations for which the company was cited are along the lines of failure to record an employee's social security number. But the company was also cited for allegedly using employees to "sniff out" leaks of deadly phosgene gas in the Institute plant. "They used to use canaries for that," Labor Secretary William Brock said of this charge.

There is also cause for concern that hitting Carbide with a huge fine will divert attention from other companies whose practices may need correcting.

Over the years, OSHA has been the federal agency that people who love to hate federal agencies *really* love to hate. As a presidential candidate, Ronald Reagan once proposed disbanding it. We remember the stories about toilets to be installed in the cornfields, and all the rest. The agency has not had a permanent chief since last May, and it took the White House half a year to make Secretary Brock's nominee for the spot official last month. No wonder there has been a lack of direction within the agency.

But maintaining workplace safety remains an important charge. The deregulators who feel that everyone will benefit if government gets off the back of business will end up shooting themselves in the foot if deregulation becomes identified with laxity in safety policy.

More important — and effective — than an occasional blockbuster fine is sending a consistent signal to industry that standards will be enforced.

The Hartford Courant
Hartford, CT, April 12, 1986

In recent years, the Occupational Health and Safety Administration (OSHA) has shed its reputation for being overzealous in enforcing work place safety laws. It therefore says a lot that the U.S. Labor Department, acting on a report by OSHA, has fined Union Carbide Corp. $1.37 million for health and safety violations.

Fifteen OSHA investigators combed the company's plant in Institute, W.Va., and found 221 health and safety violations, 130 of them willful violations, the most serious category. Violations are so designated when an employer either knows he is violating federal safety standards and refuses to act or fails to correct a safety hazard not covered by federal rules.

The most disturbing charge is that company officials ordered an employee to find the source of a phosgene leak — a poison gas used in World War I — by sniffing the air. At least miners at the turn of the century had the good sense to use canaries to detect the presence of deadly gases.

Although the official complaint cites only one such incident, Labor Secretary William E. Brock and Acting Assistant OSHA Secretary Patrick R. Tyson claim the practice was customary.

Most of the violations are less serious, involving failure to keep adequate records of workers with asbestosis and failing to report such injuries as broken bones, eye injuries, sprains, cuts, bruises and scrapes to federal officials.

Union Carbide President Robert D. Kennedy has vowed to fight the fines. The federal agency "grossly distorted the actual safety conditions of the plant," he said.

Perhaps, but using a human being to do a canary's work is appalling.

Investigators decided to visit the Institute plant after a gas leak in August 1985 that injured six employees and 135 area residents. A year before that, the company's plant in Bhopal, India, spewed deadly methyl isocynate, killing about 2,500 people and injuring tens of thousands.

OSHA is charged by law with ensuring work place safety. It shouldn't be attacked for taking that responsibility seriously.

Los Angeles, CA, April 3, 1986

The $1.4 million fine imposed on Union Carbide by the U.S. Occupational Safety and Health Administration would be impressive if it reflected a tougher resolve to protect workers. Unfortunately, the fine appears to be OSHA showmanship.

Carbide, which has shown a lack of concern for worker safety at many of its operations, was fined for "willful" violations of federal standards at its Institute, W. Va., chemical plant. As Labor Secretary Bill Brock said, the worst problem at Carbide was "the attitude." That criticism can be leveled at OSHA itself.

In his 1980 campaign, Ronald Reagan vowed to abolish OSHA. Finding that politically infeasible, he slashed its budget and appointed a director, Thorne Auchter, who weakened the agency's regulatory role.

Under Auchter, OSHA tried to ease exposure limits for cotton dust and lead and refused to set exposure limits for 116 other substances. It also stopped inspecting firms which had injury rates below the national average, thus exempting nearly 75 percent of American companies from inspections and creating a powerful incentive to underreport injuries to the Bureau of Labor Statistics. When the bureau proposed that OSHA investigate if employers were falsifying injury reports, Auchter vetoed the proposal.

It's still unknown how many companies understate injuries. In Union Carbide's case, OSHA investigators uncovered 128 unreported worker injuries at a single plant.

Although Auchter has left OSHA, his attitude remains. The White House cares so little for OSHA that the agency has been headed by an acting director since July. Last year, the Office of Technology Assessment reported that after 15 years OSHA hadn't had a significant impact on injury rates. Each year on-the-job accidents kill 6,000 Americans and disable tens of thousands of others. Occupational health hazards kill another 100,000.

The American work place will remain unnecessarily dangerous until the federal government makes a commitment to carry out OSHA's mandate.

THE PLAIN DEALER
Cleveland, OH, April 3, 1986

Want to know what progress is at Union Carbide? Progress is abandoning the use of canaries to detect poison gas. Progress is replacing them with humans. You can almost imagine the foreman saying: "Say, George, before the start of your shift, why don't you nose around the phosgene tank? Let us know if you smell anything." And you can almost imagine the emergency response should George actually find something amiss. "George? George? Quick, get the canaries out of here!"

You might have come to expect the worst from Union Carbide—the catastrophe at Carbide's Bhopal, India, plant, in which 2,000 died during a gas leak; a similar leak at its plant in Institute, W. Va., that forced 130 to go to hospitals; and now charges from the Occupational Safety and Health Administration that an inspection of Union Carbide found, in the words of Labor Secretary Bill Brock, "constant, willful and overt violations" of federal safety and health regulations. In at least one instance, according to OSHA, Union Carbide did not provide safety equipment to a worker who was assigned to track down phosgene leaks by smell.

That's the sort of dark and bizarre approach you might have come to expect from OSHA itself. Since the start of the Reagan administration, OSHA has been operating under a limited enforcement policy based on the presumption of "voluntary compliance" with safety regulations. Demoralized and armed with limited resources, OSHA used "record reviews" to determine which firms deserved close inspection. As a result, illness and injury logs kept by industry became the leading measures of hazard. Naturally, such a policy encouraged companies to cheat. It might not be coincidence that, according to OSHA, Union Carbide failed to record 128 injuries from 1983 to 1985.

Certainly, the record-review policy has been an abject failure. OSHA visited an Illinois plant that used cyanide extensively only six weeks before a worker there died of cyanide poisoning. During that review, it found a low rate of injury and decided against a thorough inspection. Those standards have been applied nationwide for five years, with the exact result that pro-industry administration officials desired. Overall, OSHA enforcement actions declined by as much as 90% between 1980 and 1982, according to one analyst. The number of actions has increased somewhat since then, but it has yet to reach the 1980 level.

"Voluntary compliance" did not just restrict government action based on nitpicking and overprecaution. The policy also limited federal inspections of industries using high-hazard poisons like cyanide and phosgene. The Reagan administration's cure for industries that claimed to be plagued by petty, hyperliberal whining was to cut off the arm that was attached to the hand that contained the finger that had the hangnail.

Brock's indictment of Union Carbide might signal a reversal of the doctrine of "voluntary compliance." But several questions remain. Is the change in OSHA permanent? If so, how much will Brock be allowed to do? And how much will he be given to do it with? Like the Environmental Protection Agency under Anne Burford, OSHA is plagued by low morale; good personnel have fled, resources have been reduced, inactivity has set in. At the same time, Washington's balanced budget panic squashes any hope for more personnel and money.

OSHA's experience with voluntary compliance has been dreadful and perilous, and its rejuvenation would be a welcome first step. Certainly, reviving the agency will be easier than trying to resuscitate some hapless human canary.

KVCC KALAMAZOO VALLEY COMMUNITY COLLEGE LIBRARY

The Courier-Journal & TIMES
Louisville, KY, April 4, 1986

THE FEDERAL government's startling account of safety violations found during a "wall-to-wall" inspection of a Union Carbide chemical plant in Institute, W. Va., reads like a muckraking report on industrial working conditions in the early years of this century.

Many employers back then felt little obligation to worry about protecting workers from injuries or death. But they cannot have been any more callous in their indifference than Union Carbide, which, according to Labor Secretary William Brock, used employees as human "canaries" to sniff for leaks of phosgene gas. Phosgene was known as mustard gas when used as a chemical weapon during World War I.

The Labor Department imposed almost $1.4 million in fines for 221 violations that, says Mr. Brock, constitute "a willful disregard for health and safety." Carbide officials claim the charges are untruthful and have more to do with paperwork than chemical manufacturing. An appeal is planned.

The company has every right to offer a full defense. Indeed, a public airing of the case would be instructive. But the allegations made by the Occupational Safety and Health Administration — under-reporting of injuries, defective safety equipment and the absence of monitoring devices for dangerous chemicals — suggest that the problems go way beyond red tape.

Moreover, Mr. Brock's comment that OSHA investigators found a "laissez-faire attitude" toward safety is revealing — and ominous. It harks back to that time when safety was the lowest priority for most industrialists.

An important question is whether OSHA, having given its muscles one mighty flex, will now return to the obscurity ordained by the Reagan administration. After the catastrophic leak at Carbide's pesticide factory in Bhopal, India, the Institute plant was an easy target. When a dangerous chemical escaped there last year, inspectors swarmed into West Virginia.

But legitimate doubts remain not only about safety practices in other places where toxic chemicals are used, but also about the agency's over-all effectiveness. Mr. Brock appears so shaken by the findings at Institute that he has promised to look aggressively for similar problems elsewhere.

Unfortunately, OSHA may no longer have the clout or resources to do an effective job. The agency was founded in 1970 to combat serious workplace hazards and quickly drew the wrath of business. It has languished under President Reagan, who has little sympathy for its mission and appoints politically helpful businessmen instead of health and safety experts to run it.

For the last nine months the agency has not had a permanent boss, further reducing its influence and leaving it with no clear direction. As inspections and prosecutions have declined, the number of workplace injuries and fatalities has sharply increased.

The Institute investigation is a welcome sign that OSHA has not been immobilized by the "nonadversarial" approach to enforcement ordered by Mr. Reagan. But the Carbide case will be doubly gratifying if Mr. Brock recognizes the need to revitalize an agency whose quiescence has surely left other occupational hazards undetected.

BUFFALO EVENING NEWS
Buffalo, NY, April 9, 1986

THE RECORD FINE of $1.3 million levied by the federal government against Union Carbide underscores the seriousness with which Washington regulators view alleged safety problems at Carbide's Institute, W. Va., plant, the only facility in the United States that manufactures methyl isocýanate.

That is the chemical that leaked from Carbide's Bhopel, India, plant in late 1984, killing up to 2,500 people, and from the Institute plant last August, sending more than 100 area residents and six plant workers to hospitals.

It was after the August incident that the federal Occupational Safety and Health Administration (OSHA) conducted rigorous inspections leading to the fine announced by U.S. Labor Secretary William Brock, the largest in OSHA's 15-year history.

OSHA cited 221 alleged safety and health violations. The fine was "necessary and appropriate," Brock said, "to correct a situation characterized by complacency and what we believe to be a willful disregard for health and safety."

That is harsh criticism and Carbide, which has denied any willful violations, plans to contest the ruling. But the inspections and large fine signal that OSHA, which a few years ago was repeatedly chided for petty enforcement actions, is serving a substantial public function in reviewing safety precautions in the American workplace.

OSHA can focus experienced and independent eyes on suspected instances of serious hazards in American plants, many with highly complex manufacturing processes. It can spotlight problems for the public and force corporations through fines and adverse publicity to correct those problems. Brock was right when he acknowledged that there "is no way to absolutely guarantee the safety of this or any other plant." But he was also right in stressing that "the margin of error is very small when dealing with hazardous chemicals."

That narrow margin for error alone justifies alert attention to potential hazards by everyone in the interest of the health and safety of workers in these plants and those living nearby.

The reassuring OSHA action, which emphasizes the seriousness of alleged laxity in standards of safety in the workplace, ought to produce prompt remedies of any health and safety violations at the West Virginia and other Carbide plants.

More than that, it should encourage other operators of chemical plants, along the Niagara Frontier as elsewhere, to monitor their own safety procedures with renewed diligence.

The Miami Herald
Miami, FL, April 4, 1986

CONSCIOUS, willful, and overt," says Labor Secretary William Brock of the safety violations at Union Carbide's sprawling chemical plant in Institute, W.Va. He termed the violations so severe that Labor's Occupational Safety and Health Administration (OSHA) is referring results of its six-month investigation of conditions at the Institute plant to the Justice Department.

Union Carbide President Robert Kennedy says that the company is contesting OSHA's imposition of a record $1.3-million fine. The Institute plant's "operating integrity," in Mr. Kennedy's words, was not compromised by the alleged violations, which largely involve paperwork processing.

Both OSHA and Union Carbide likely are correct. Some violations involve accidents and equipment failures reported on the wrong forms, failure to record an employee's Social Security number, and so forth. The Federal bureaucracy has created a bog of sticky rules and forms in quintuplicate that complicate industry's business day. But OSHA also found sloppy safety routines, supervisors either poorly trained in safety procedures or careless about following them, and poor maintenance of equipment that could cause leaks of deadly chemicals.

And it isn't as if Union Carbide's safety record is free of blemish. An August 1985 toxic-chemical leak injured 135 plant employees and Institute residents. That prompted OSHA to conduct its "wall-to-wall" investigation of the Institute complex. While that investigation proceeded, negotiations over OSHA's fines resulted in the agency reducing them in return for upgraded safety measures. After its initial public blustering, Union Carbide no doubt will negotiate with OSHA over the current violations. The amount of the fine, after all, is secondary to the "operating integrity" that safeguards workers and the public.

Guaranteeing this integrity in the chemical industry is an OSHA goal of late. The agency plans investigations of other U.S. chemical manufacturers — a move praised by critics of OSHA's lax attitude in recent years. The gas leak at another Union Carbide plant in Bhopal, India, which killed more than 2,500 people in December 1984, snapped a dozing world to attention. While many chemical manufacturers have excellent safety records — which is in their best interests — others put employees and the public at needless risk. OSHA's stringency toward Union Carbide is a warning to the industry that, says Secretary Brock, "the margin for error is very small when dealing with dangerous chemicals."

The Philadelphia Inquirer

Philadelphia, PA, April 4, 1986

If what the U.S. Labor Department says is true, then *Hurrah!* for its $1.3 million fine and no-holds-barred dressing down of Union Carbide Corp., the folks who brought on the chemical catastrophe in Bhopal, India, and, to the point of the department's citation, the toxic cloud that frightened the daylights out of Institute, W.Va., last August.

The charges knot the stomach: Workers — human "canaries" the department's Occupational Safety and Health Administration (OSHA) called them — were dispatched to *sniff* for deadly leaks of phosgene gas, the nerve agent called "mustard gas" during World War I. Injuries were routinely underreported. Safety equipment to guard against fires, explosions and worker exposure was defective.

According to Labor Secretary William E. Brock, OSHA investigators turned up a "laissez-faire attitude" toward worker safety and widespread "conscious, overt and willful violations."

That's the attitude and those are the reckless dangers that OSHA was born to combat. But if it is coming out swinging against Union Carbide, already on the ropes from its Bhopal performance, OSHA also is acting out of character for an agency that has been hog-tied for much of the Reagan administration.

Fines have been reduced to slaps on the wrist. And on-the-job injuries began climbing two years ago for the first time in four years.

The administration trumpeted a new era, a happy, go-easy time of "voluntary compliance." But voluntary compliance only works for volunteers, not corporate scofflaws like Union Carbide. That's where it falls apart: Good guys obey the law; bad ones see an opportunity to ignore the rules.

Result in West Virginia: 130 people hospitalized when a toxic cloud escaped from a plant Union Carbide had touted as a "model of safety."

To optimists, the OSHA penalty signifies a resurgent agency and a warning shot across the bows of other sloppy industries. Critics, on the other hand, wonder where OSHA has been all along and whether it's simply picking on a patsy with no intention of continuing the crusade.

Either way, the episode underlines the continued need not only for tough enforcement, but for putting in place new federal rules that require notice to manufacturing workers about hazardous materials on the job. It underlines also the continued need to implement Pennsylvania's 1984 Worker and Community Right to Know Act, which seeks to warn non-manufacturing workers and nearby residents about toxics in their midst.

When government eases up, as Union Carbide demonstrates, there are industries out there ready and willing to forget about the safety of their workers and neighbors. This week OSHA's own files became the best evidence for dispensing with the hands-off days of "voluntary compliance."

The News American

Baltimore, MD, April 3, 1986

"Some people in this country have the attitude that a few accidents here and there is the price of production."
— Labor Secretary William E. Brock

Does Union Carbide — of Bhopal fame — regard its employees as mere pieces of plant equipment? How can anybody believe otherwise after reading the federal government's charges that led to a record $1,377,000 fine for "willful disregard for health and safety" at the company's plant in Institute, W.Va., in connection with the gas leak that sent 130 people to the hospital last August? After the accident, Union Carbide all but shrugged its corporate shoulders; in reaction to the fine, it called most of the citations — for 221 violations of 55 federal laws — "completely unjustified. ... The allegation of complacency with respect to safety is an outrageous misrepresentation of the truth."

Secretary Brock, whose Occupational Safety and Health Administration made a "wall-to-wall" examination of the plant and its practices, believes otherwise. When it came to safety, he said, there was an "absence of motivation." Early warning devices were not installed in dangerous areas; the safety equipment was poorly designed; testing and inspection of that equipment was haphazard; supervisors got no training; when phosgene gas leaked — and one whiff of it can kill — employees assigned to find the leak were not issued gas masks. They were told to sniff. And, between 1983 and 1985, the plant management failed tp report 128 injuries, including fractures, lacerations, chemical inhalations and eye injuries. No wonder that Brock called the plant's worst problem "the general atmosphere, the attitude."

That the feds have come down so hard on this company — which will appeal the fine — is heartening, a credit to the Reagan administration. Equally heartening is Brock's announcement that OSHA will take a hard look at 80 other chemical plants, and in fact is investigating 12 of them right now. Those where safety is less important than meeting the production schedule will learn, we hope, something that we doubt that Union Carbide has learned even now: There is a heavy price to pay for not giving much of a damn whether the human beings who work for you live or die.

Rhine River Polluted by Chemical-Plant Fire

A chemical spill resulting from a Nov. 1, 1986 fire at a chemical warehouse near Basel, Switzerland seriously polluted the Rhine River. The spill was considered the gravest nonnuclear environmental disaster in Europe in a decade. One expert said that the spill had reversed 10 years of progress that had been made in cleaning up Europe's primary inland waterway. It was generally agreed, however, that the extent of the long-term damage would take some time to discern. Representatives of the four countries along the Rhine – Switzerland, West Germany, France and the Netherlands – Nov. 12 held an emergency meeting at which Switzerland admitted some responsibility for the disaster.

The environmental accident began when a fire was discovered at Sandoz AG's warehouse number 956 just after midnight Nov. 1 by a passing police patrol. The storage building, just upriver from Basel, had housed some 820 tons of insecticides plus other chemicals. Investigators were probing the cause of the fire. Claims of responsibility from callers saying they represented the Red Army terrorist group were discounted. In an attempt to prevent the blaze from spreading to a warehouse containing chemicals that could explode if exposed to water, firefighters poured an estimated 6,500 gallons of water per minute onto the burning building. The huge volume resulted in chemically contaminated water flowing into the Rhine.

A second wave of pollutants, detected Nov. 7, was reportedly caused by a leak from a container after the fire had been extinguished. An estimated 30 tons of toxic waste entered the river from the Sandoz plant, including fungicides containing highly poisonous mercury. The city of Wiesbaden, West Germany Nov. 4 shut down its water system, supplied by the Rhine. Similar actions were eventually taken in other West German and French towns and throughout the Netherlands. Pollution was even monitored in the North Sea, at the mouth of the Rhine some 400 miles downstream of Basel.

The chemical spill and the resulting miles-long slick of pollution prompted heated charges against the Swiss government and Sandoz and inspired demonstrations throughout the Rhine area. Environmental ministers of the four Rhine-side nations met in Zurich Nov. 12. They were joined by representatives of Luxembourg and the European Community. Sandoz Nov. 13 said it would honor all valid claims arising from the spill.

The Wichita
Eagle-Beacon

Wichita, KS, November 14, 1986

THE urgent need for environmental accountability is on the move again in Europe. A few months ago, it was borne on the radioactive winds wafting out of Chernobyl. Today, it flows along as a deadly toxic soup despoiling the Rhine River, following a pair of poorly handled industrial accidents in Switzerland.

The political fallout has been harsh and quick following the poisoning of the Rhine, and points to the need for more formalized environmental controls and oversight among the European community of nations — perhaps a permanent joint environmental agency with enforcement powers.

Hundreds of thousands of fish and eels already have been killed by the spillage of tons of agricultural chemicals and solvents and 440 pounds of mercury into the river. Drinking-water supplies all along the river have been put at risk. To Switzerland's credit, its pledge to pay damage claims to nations downstream from the spills shows a proper if belated sense of responsibility.

Clearly, the Swiss response to the danger was inadequate — it took five days' time to discover the first leak of 88 gallons of a potent herbicide, Atrazine, into the Rhine. Officials were unnecessarily tardy in alerting neighbors sharing the Rhine to the second, much larger spill. They may, in fact, have contributed to the contamination by spraying thousands of gallons of water into a warehouse area while attempting to control a fire — the tainted runoff gravitating into the river. Questions now logically arise as to why such materials were in such proximity to the river and why adequate containment structures weren't in place to staunch the flow of a spill.

At the flow rate of 2 mph, it's estimated it may take two years for all the contamination to filter out of the Rhine into the North Sea, where its impact remains a matter of speculation. In the meantime, the Rhine may be, for all practical purposes, ecologically barren. That is a tremendous price for so obvious a lesson as has now been taught, and there's no way simple monetary compensation can make up for the damage done.

The lesson learned must be that nations sharing such elemental resources as air and water have to work together and become much more environmentally responsible — not just for themselves, but for everyone, and not just in times of crisis, but at all times. Then, such environmental disasters as the poisoning of the Rhine could be anticipated, and avoided.

WORCESTER TELEGRAM
Worcester, MA
November 14, 1986

When the nuclear disaster at Chernobyl sent radioactive clouds over parts of Europe, the Swiss government was among the first to criticize Soviet authorities for failing to alert other countries to the danger.

The Swiss were right; Moscow's stonewalling was unforgivable. It's too bad, however, that Switzerland didn't learn from it.

When a fire devastated a chemical plant outside Basel, tons of toxic material from at least two plants were dumped into the Rhine River to hide their own illegal dumping of pollutants. It was discovered in neighboring countries before Swiss authorities sent out an alert. The toxic waste has confronted West Germany, France and the Netherlands with one of the worst ecological disasters in years.

It threatens to turn part of the Rhine into a dead river. Thousands of fish have been killed, and the first wave of pollution in the Netherlands produced mercury concentration three times the normal rate. The governments have closed water-processing plants and banned fishing. Experts say it might take two years to restore the ecological balance of the river.

Environmental laws in Europe are far less stringent than those in the United States. The air is badly polluted around large industrial centers, the supposedly "blue Danube" runs thick and grey, and the lagoons of Venice are filthy with pollution. Western European governments, particularly the Swiss, are far more tolerant of industry than U.S. authorities are.

Still, it is hard to understand how Ciba-Geigy, one of the world's largest pharmaceutical companies, was allowed to store tons of toxic waste illegally, let alone dump it into the Rhine. It took Swiss authorities several days to accept responsibility and promise to pay for the damages.

The disaster is apt to trigger calls for tighter restrictions on chemical storage and safety procedures in Europe. It will also prompt a review of cooperation among neighboring countries when an emergency arises. It's time that Europeans, often critical of American business practices, learned to protect their environment.

The Providence Journal

Providence, RI, November 13, 1986

Residents and officials of four European nations are condemning the Swiss chemical firm Sandoz for the spill of 30 tons of agricultural chemicals and solvents, plus 440 pounds of mercury, into the Rhine river at Basel. The people affected were especially angered by Switzerland's failure to warn them for 10 days after the accident. (Shades of Chernobyl!)

For comparison, imagine a similar incident on the Hudson River, where the residents knew nothing about a big spill of toxic chemicals until they started to pull thousands of dead fish out of the water. Mightn't there then be protest outbreaks in New York City as there were in Basel?

The towns and cities along the Rhine are demanding not only better communications about toxic spills, but also tighter control to prevent a recurrence. The hygenic Swiss say they thought they had tight control, although it was deadly dioxin from a Swiss plant that once made the Italian town of Severo uninhabitable.

In the Sandoz incident, a fire in its big plant at Basel resulted in the chemicals being washed into the river by the water that firefighters poured on the flames. Ironically, an 88-gallon spill of Atrazin, a weedkiller, from a Ciba-Geigy plant at Basel, polluted the Rhine a day before the big spill from Sandoz.

What conclusions can laymen draw from these incidents? For Europe, the question is even bigger perhaps than for the United States. The Rhine is Western Europe's biggest river and is heavily used, not only for fishing, recreation and drinking water supplies, but for the incredibly busy traffic of boats and barges.

So the people in the four countries through which the river passes — Switzerland, France, West Germany and the Netherlands — have a more intense concern than most of their neighbors. But a lot of American rivers serve multiple uses, including drinking water supply, and the users all have equal concern for preventing toxic spills.

Rhode Island can understand the anger of the Europeans who feel they were kept in the dark. Toxic wastes have been in the forefront of attention here because of their surreptitious disposal in dumps and landfills, many of which have come to light only recently. Serious concern is felt by public officials and numerous private organizations over the danger of such chemicals finding their way into wells and public water supplies.

The Rhine incident is one of the worst ecological disasters in recent years. As one official put it, "the whole ecosystem is destroyed...." Ecologists estimate it will take two years or more for the river to cleanse itself of the deadly chemicals.

Accidents will happen. Everyone admits this deplorable truth. Only renewed vigilance by officials and environmental groups can prevent recurrences of disaster proportions. That is the real lesson of the Sandoz incident. It applies to this country as much as to Europe and to any other state, such as India where the memory of Bhopal is still raw. There never can be too much attention given this industrial-era problem.

The Dispatch

Columbus, OH, November 12, 1986

European officials are working this week in hopes of containing the ecological damage of a chemical spill in the Rhine. They may be too late.

U.S. experts should stand ready to assist in any way possible to help the Europeans ease the threat to the river, its ecosystem, and the people who live near it.

More than 1,000 tons of chemicals — including dyes, insecticides, and substantial quantities of mercury, a highly toxic substance — poured into the river last week after a fire destroyed a storage warehouse in Basel, Switzerland. The scope of the threat to the river was not immediately realized, nor was full information about the spill communicated to other countries through which the Rhine flows. These include France, West Germany and the Netherlands.

Some experts fear that the Rhine is in danger of becoming a "dead" river as the chemicals kill fish and plant life. What's more, the river serves as a water source for people along its course and extensive efforts to provide water from alternative sources are under way.

Action must be taken quickly. Experts in the United States who have experience in dealing with chemical spills should be alerted and their expertise used if needed.

The Rhine is a natural treasure. The chemical spill must be contained and it must serve as a warning to people everywhere that the environment cannot be taken for granted.

Los Angeles Times

Los Angeles, CA, November 13, 1986

Is the Rhine dying? No one is sure. The extent of a spill of toxic chemicals from a Swiss plant into this vital European waterway may not be known for days or weeks, let alone the long-term effect on fish life or drinking-water supplies.

Could it happen on the Mississippi, the Delaware or even the Sacramento?

Absolutely, U.S. environmental experts say. In fact, the one certainty about such technological/ environmental accidents is that they are inevitable. Consider in the past two years alone: Bhopal, Chernobyl and, now, the Rhine.

Can such accidents be prevented? Possibly. Can their effects be controlled? Certainly. The Swiss spill occurred after fire struck a riverside storage building. About 30 tons of agricultural chemicals were flushed into the river by water used in fighting the fire. One report claims that the building was not equipped with fire alarms or automatic sprinklers. If so, such safety lapses can and should be corrected.

The Swiss acknowledge that a misunderstanding resulted in a delay of up to 24 hours in notifying West German, French and Dutch officials of potential disaster floating toward them. An immediate alert could have given downstream interests more time to cope with the problem, including the cutoff of water supplies from the river. Switzerland's neighbors, of course, were outraged. How many houses have burned down because the homeowner thought that he could handle the situation without calling the fire department?

Presumably such a delay would not occur in this country. Federal and state laws require an immediate alarm, allowing for activation of emergency response systems.

And the danger of a Rhine-like accident is not nearly so great in California, because the state does not have such a heavy concentration of industry along a major fresh-water stream. But a California official noted that freight trains repeatedly have derailed alongside the Sacramento River in Northern California. If the train is loaded with hay, that is one thing, the official said, but what if the train is carrying toxic chemicals? The Sacramento is a source of drinking water for millions of Californians.

The Rhine spill demonstrates again the need for constant vigilance by industrial officials and governmental authorities in preventing and containing environmental disasters. Above all, the lesson is that once an accident is out of control, someone must have the courage to sound the alarm and call for help.

St. Petersburg Times

St. Petersburg, FL
November 12, 1986

The severe pollution of Europe's great 820-mile-long Rhine River teaches some old and some new lessons about dealing with environmental disasters.

The unconscionable delay of the Swiss government in warning others of the toxic spill is an old story, one that need not have been repeated after the criticism of the Soviet Union's lag in disclosing the Chernobyl disaster.

The fire that caused the first chemical spill at the Sandoz Chemical Co. near Basel, Switzerland, occurred Nov. 1. A second release of toxic chemicals occurred at the same plant on Nov. 7. Exactly how long the Swiss government delayed warning other countries is not known, but the cleanup did not begin until seven or eight days after the fire. A state official charged Tuesday that the nearby Ciba-Geigy pharmaceutical company dumped 880 pounds of a toxic herbicide into the river shortly after the fire. The governments of other nations on the Rhine complained that Switzerland failed to provide them a timely warning of any of these incidents.

About 30 tons of toxic chemicals entered the Rhine at the time of the fire, including an estimated eight tons of mercury. The result is that hundreds of thousands of fish are dead, and all other life. All drinking water plants along the river were closed down in five countries — Switzerland, West Germany, France, the Netherlands and Luxembourg. Environmentalists say the river is dead and won't recover for at least two years.

It is heartening that the people most directly affected are not passive about this environmental outrage. More than 10,000 persons joined a protest march in Basel. When executives of the offending company called a public meeting to discuss the discharge, so many angry people showed up that the meeting was canceled.

Because we share the fresh drinking water in the great Floridan aquifer, the people of Central Florida are reminded often that neither environmental dangers nor resources respect political boundaries. The message of Basel and Chernobyl is that danger to the environment is increasingly an international problem. When more people are willing to march in anger against polluters, and to pay taxes to keep their nests clean, this fragile planet called Earth will have a far better chance of surviving.

The Birmingham News

Birmingham, AL, November 15, 1986

Switzerland has acted responsibly in the wake of an industrial disaster, agreeing to pay compensation to countries affected by a chemical spill into the Rhine River

It is not yet clear who will pay the money — the Swiss government, the regional government in the area where the warehouse fire and chemical spill occurred or the Sandoz chemical company. But at least Switzerland has made it clear that compensation will be paid.

In an era when it seems that no one is willing to take responsibility for anything that goes wrong, the Swiss pledge is reassuring. It will not bring back the estimated 50,000 fish and eels killed by the toxic slick created when about 30 tons of chemicals were washed into the Rhine by firefighters battling a blaze at the Sandoz warehouse near Basel. But it could help pay for clean-up efforts

The Soviet Union, which poisoned reindeer meat and milk in Scandinavia and other agricultural products in Northern Europe with its nuclear reactor fire at Chernobyl, should take notice.

The Swiss response to the Nov. 1 chemical spill may not have been perfect (other countries bordering the Rhine were not notified of the problem until 24 hours after they should have been), but it is certainly preferable to the Soviet Union's callous disregard for its neighbors.

Together, the Chernobyl fire and the Swiss chemical spill are graphic reminders of the need for international communication and coordination when the poisonous by-products of modern technology cross international borders. They also point to the need for tighter control of potentially dangerous industries, as the Swiss have acknowledged by agreeing to study ways to tighten their anti-pollution safeguards to bring them more into line with the stricter regulations of neighboring countries.

We cannot live without the chemical and nuclear industries, but we must watch them carefully to ensure that we can live with them.

WATCH ON THE RHINE

The Houston Post

Houston, TX, November 14, 1986

Several neighboring nations are justifiably furious at the Swiss, normally so efficient and methodical, over an environmental disaster that is being called "Chernobasel."

Just as the Russians failed to give other affected countries quick word of the Chernobyl nuclear disaster, the Swiss were slow in alerting downstream nations to a massive spill of pesticides and other chemicals into the Rhine River on Nov. 1. Thirty tons of poisons, including a large slug of highly toxic mercury, washed into the Rhine during a fire in a Basel chemical company's warehouse.

Downstream, the majestic and beautiful Rhine is a vital shipping artery, water supply source and tourist attraction for West Germany, France and the Netherlands.

The huge dose of Swiss chemicals came as the Rhine was showing the results of a 15-year campaign to reduce industrial pollution and restore the health of the long-abused river. Now there are predictions it will be a "dead river" for two years, and full recovery may take years more.

The West German, French and Dutch governments say they will seek millions of dollars in reparations from Switzerland and the careless chemical company. If ever there were a case where "the polluter should pay for his pollution," this is it.

ST. LOUIS POST-DISPATCH

St. Louis, MO, November 13, 1986

On Nov. 1, a fire at the Sandoz chemical plant in Basel, Switzerland, resulted in the dumping of thousands of pounds of toxic chemicals into the legendary Rhine River. Only now, as a 40-mile-long toxic "glob" heads out to sea, is the enormity of the accident becoming apparent.

Hundreds of thousands of people live along the Rhine, including many thousands who use its water for drinking and its fish for food. They can no longer do so safely. Environmentalists fear that all river life may be killed by the toxic soup, whose ingredients include 440 pounds of mercury and some 30 tons of dyes, insecticides, solvents, and other hazardous chemicals. Already more than half a million fish have died, and it could be up to two years before the river can sustain life again.

The spill took downstream countries by surprise. Swiss officials have reportedly admitted that they delayed an international alert for up to 24 hours after the accident. A misunderstanding was blamed, but the similarity with the Soviet Union's laxity in issuing an alert after the Chernobyl disaster can't help but be made.

Among other charges, the Swiss must answer those of the West German Greens party, which claims that insurance adjustors as early as 1981 had told Sandoz operators that "grave security deficiencies" existed at the site. If so, how could Swiss authorities have continued to allow the plant to operate?

Explanations aside, the disaster calls attention once again to the irrelevance of political boundaries to nature. If the environment is to be preserved where undamaged or restored where scarred already, it will take the will of many nations acting in concert. The Rhine disaster, should it give impetus to such a move, might yet have a redeeming moment.

THE ☁ SUN

Baltimore, MD, November 14, 1986

Americans should think long and hard about the consequences of a Nov. 1 toxic chemical spill into the Rhine River. Half a million bottom-dwelling fish and eels died after mercury-laden pesticides and herbicides washed downstream from firefighters' battle with a warehouse blaze in Basel, Switzerland. Officials said the building's lack of sprinklers and other means of containing the fire had worsened matters. Environmentalists say a billion-dollar cleanup program has been derailed, that the Rhine will be "dead" for two years. Can it happen here?

Unfortunately, it already does. But the spills are not usually so dramatic.

Agricultural chemicals, urban runoff, untreated storm water and industrial wastes sluice into American streams and rivers daily. Proponents of the Clean Water Act reauthorization, unanimously passed by Congress but vetoed by President Reagan, say runoff from farms, streets and mines accounts for half the pollution found in U.S. waterways. The vetoed bill would have, for the first time, provided money and enforcement tools to fight these releases, as well as funds for treatment plants to clean up wastewater reaching the Chesapeake Bay. Mr. Reagan, in a memo, said the $18 billion bill was just too much to pay.

But what does it cost to breathe life back into dead rivers? What is the cost to the quality of life for humans forced to survive on the banks of one, as the people in Germany, France and Holland will now be forced to do?

A story in Wednesday's *Sun* reported that pollution from herbicides and human and industrial wastes had turned the Nile poisonous, fouled India's Ganges and nearly killed the Yangtze in China. U.S. rivers such as the Hudson, the Delaware and the Potomac have begun to come back after decades of shameful misuse, but Americans cannot breathe easy yet.

Reclamation of the nation's rivers has progressed far since the Cuyahoga River caught fire in 1969, but the tragic decline of wildlife dependent on U.S. waterways underscores the dangers of pollution that persist. Members of Congress from both houses have pledged to reintroduce the Clean Water Act bill as passed, immediately upon reconvening. That cannot come soon enough. The death of the Rhine shows what can happen when controls are not there.

The Honolulu Advertiser

Honolulu, HI, November 15, 1986

Like the Chernobyl nuclear disaster, the accidental polluting of the Rhine River in Europe points up some serious lessons:

● Tight government monitoring and control over storage of toxic chemicals and wastes are sorely needed. Adequate local safety systems are vital.

● Prompt and wide public announcement of mishaps is essential and the urge to downplay or hide them must be overcome.

● Such accidents more and more have international implications that demand a multi-national response. Ten days after the Rhine accident, pollution finally reached the North Sea after flowing through Switzerland, France, West Germany, and the Netherlands.

It will take weeks to determine the full impact of 30 tons of at least 34 chemical compounds (including pesticides) flushed into the Rhine as Swiss firefighters fought a blaze in a riverside storage building in Basle. But already scientists say the river's ecosystem may be "dead" for at least two years.

An apparent misunderstanding delayed Swiss authorities for 24 hours from notifying other countries along the river's route. That cut the time for preventive action like limiting use of the Rhine for human and animal drinking water, fishing and transport.

The United States has reason to take warning from this incident, due to our many long Mainland river systems flowing past industrial areas in all parts of the country — especially the East and Midwest. Here, however, a prompt alarm to begin reponding to such an emergency is required by federal and state law.

The accident which poisoned the Rhine has already prompted a series of European Community meetings to assess the damage and lay plans to avoid repetition of what is justifiably being called a catastrophe. It is a reminder of one of the growing dangers of modern, technological life.

Several Pesticides Banned; EPA Revises Rules

The Environmental Protection Agency (EPA) banned the use of three pesticides and tightened the rules pertaining to use of a top herbicide, in a series of actions Sept. 24-Oct. 7, 1986.

On Sept. 24, the agency banned use of the insecticide diazinon on golf courses and sod farms because of evidence that it caused mass bird kills. Diazinon was used extensively in agriculture or on lawns of homes. Its use on golf courses and sod farms was prohibited because their large open spaces attracted migratory birds, which, apparently, died after ingesting diazinon pellets.

The EPA's action represented the first time a particular pesticide had been banned solely on the basis of harm to wildlife, according to an agency spokesman.

The EPA Sept. 25 banned sale and distribution of dicofol, widely used to kill mites on citrus and cotton crops. It was found to contain harmful levels of DDT, an insecticide that was banned in 1972. The DDT was an unintended byproduct of dicofol production. Before issuing the ban, the agency had been seeking to have manufacturers of dicofol reduce the DDT levels in Dicofol.

An emergency ban was ordered by the agency Oct. 7 on sale or use of dinoseb, a pesticide heavily used on a wide variety of crops, including soybeans, cotton, potatoes and peanuts. The chemical had been found to pose a "very serious risk" of birth defects and sterility among farmers and farm workers, EPA Administrator Lee M. Thomas said. The ban applied to use by farmers even of stocks on hand. Thomas said there was no apparent danger to consumers who ate food on which dinoseb had been used. Only workers exposed to the chemical in the field or when they prepared it were at risk, he said.

The agency acted Oct. 2 to tighten restrictions on alachlor, the nation's most widely used agricultural herbicide. While allowing continued use of the chemical, the agency cautioned farm workers using alachlor to take protective measures and ordered labels attached to the pesticide's containers warning of potential health hazards. Further studies of the chemical were being undertaken.

A report published by the National Academy of Sciences May 20, 1987 urged a standardization rule to reduce the risks from cancer-causing pesticide residues in food.

The report, prepared by a blue-ribbon academic panel, urged the EPA to establish a "negligible risk" standard that would permit approval of pesticides only if their tumor-causing incidence was less than one out of every million people exposed.

The panel recommended that the standard be applied across the board – including older pesticides and those applied to fresh foods. Neither of those categories was covered under current practice.

The prevailing standard currently was the Delaney provision of the 1954 Food, Drug and Cosmetic Act. The Delaney provision did not apply at all to raw agricultural products, and the EPA had not acted to enforce regulations covering pesticides registered before 1978, the year detailed health information was required.

The EPA's policy, in general, called for a ban of all pesticide residues in processed foods that became concentrated during processing, regardless of whether a risk of cancer was evident.

In its study of 28 pesticides linked by the EPA to cancer, the panel said current standards would eliminate about half the estimated cancer risk from the compounds. Under the panel's newly proposed system, it said, 98% of the cancer risk would be eliminated. At the same time, only 32% of the potential uses of the pesticides would be banned, the panel reported.

The panel found that tomatoes contained the highest potentially toxic residue of pesticides, followed by beef, potatoes, oranges, lettuce, apples and peaches. But the panel cautioned that the findings on this point were quite fallable.

As an inducement for farmers and food processors to forsake use of older, higher-risk pesticides, the EPA Oct. 12, 1988 said it would allow use of new pesticides that could cause cancer.

The Dispatch
Columbus, OH, September 18, 1986

Tighter safety controls lacking in the nation's basic pesticide law are contained in compromise amendments agreed upon by representatives of the chemical industry and a coalition of environmental, consumer and labor groups. But these constructive changes in the Federal Insecticide, Fungicide and Rodenticide Act are not immune to congressional tampering or inaction.

FIFRA was devised to protect the public from chemicals that pose a health threat. It establishes labeling requirements, what tests new products must pass before being marketed, who can use the products for what purposes and, finally, what evidence of hazard is needed to remove a product from the market.

Environmental groups for years criticized deficiencies in FIFRA, but attempts to achieve consensus among these critics, farmers and the chemical industry as to tighter standards failed. Last March, after 18 months of negotiations, a series of compromise amendments emerged.

This compromise proposal would speed up the re-registration of about 600 active pesticide ingredients consistent with modern safety standards and the process by which products shown to be hazardous could be withdrawn. It also would require the EPA to evaluate inert pesticide ingredients (some of them known toxins) currently exempt.

The agriculture committees of both the U.S. House and Senate have received the package during the summer and, though time is short, hope for passage remains.

Two possible amendments to the compromise package — one preventing states from imposing standards stronger than federal requirements and the other reducing compensation to the inventor of a product from a follow-on manufacturer who used the inventor's safety data — ought to be resisted.

The package would set national standards for tolerable pesticide levels in food and water supplies, and protect farm workers using pesticides and residents of areas where they are produced.

With the FIFRA amendments, Congress has an exceptional opportunity to pass meaningful environmental legislation that was as difficult to formulate as it may be to restart should it die during the present session. We urge its passage without further modification or delay.

The Washington Post

Washington, DC, September 25, 1986

TWO MAJOR PIECES of environmental legislation now hang in the balance in Congress. One would extend the Superfund program to clean up industrial dumps that threaten the ground-water supply. The other would speed up federal testing of pesticides. Their enactment would make this easily the most important environmental Congress of the Reagan administration. Failure would have the opposite result.

The Senate is scheduled to take up the pesticide bill today. The House has already passed it. It seeks to resolve a problem that has defied resolution for 14 years: the retesting of pesticides that were already on the market when Congress gave the Environmental Protection Agency the job of regulating these substances in 1972. The old pesticides and their first cousins make up most of the mixtures still on the market. They contain about 600 active ingredients; over the years EPA has managed to review fewer than 40.

The bill would set a timetable for reviewing the rest. It follows an extraordinary agreement reached earlier this year between the nation's major environmental groups and chemical companies. Previous disagreement between these customary adversaries had blocked legislation, and their current pact is perishable. That is why it is doubly important that Congress act now.

The problem with this bill, as with any such bill in the last days of a session, is that it can so easily be held hostage. Here the extraneous issue is who shall be liable, farmer or manufacturer, if a pesticide contaminates the ground-water supply. Some members are threatening to propose an amendment saying the companies would be liable; the companies would, of course, resist. This issue should be left for another bill. The House has already used the bill to say that states cannot exceed federal pesticide regulations by setting higher standards of their own. The provision is also in the Senate version. The bill would be much better without it, but the bill with it is better than no bill at all.

As to Superfund, the authorizing legislation has been in conference since last winter. Conferees finally reached agreement in August on the terms of the program: how many dumps EPA would have to clean up a year, what standards of cleanliness it should use, how it should seek to apportion costs. Still at issue is how to pay for it; the tax conferees have not agreed.

On Oct. 1, the clean-up program will have been without sufficient funds or clear direction for a year. If the executive branch had done this, Congress would be howling, and rightly so. The members should turn a little of that indignation on themselves.

THE KANSAS CITY STAR

Kansas City, MO, September 4, 1986

Yes, opponents do exist when it comes to strengthening this nation's pesticide laws. But Congress should resist these critics. It soon will consider one of the most important pieces of health and environmental legislation to come before the members in years.

The proposals tighten requirements on the testing, marketing and using of new pesticides. The Environmental Protection Agency would have to redetermine the safety of hundreds of older products. A new standard would be established to protect the public against chemicals that contaminate drinking water supplies. Companies finally would be required to complete thorough health and safety testing on so-called inert ingredients which are more toxic than first thought.

Pesticide reform is necessary. The effort is being led by an unlikely, and fortuitous, combination of environmental organizations and the agricultural chemicals industry. It was an incredible feat for these groups just to agree on anything, much less to spearhead a campaign in favor of new rules.

Now, a few last objections to their ideas exist.

The biggest has been erected by the Grocery Manufacturers of America. It complains that, under one version of the bill, states could set tougher regulations for pesticide use on groceries allowed across their borders. Let this happen nationwide, the association warns, and states will usurp federal power and a crazy-quilt patch of regulations with dire economic consequences will come into being.

Congress can safely ignore that argument. The states already have the right to do this and no such upheaval has been sighted. On the contrary, several cases exist in which a state—California and Florida are two—has banned certain pesticides before the EPA has done so. States properly must have this kind of power.

Proponents of reform realize they have a fragile coalition on their hands. They warn that any attempts to amend the bill could lead to its death. Which is why they properly argue against the change demanded by the grocers. The bigger goal should be kept in mind: the first rewriting of U.S. pesticide laws in 14 years.

Los Angeles Times

Los Angeles, CA, August 5, 1986

For years environmental, business and labor groups have been negotiating the terms of a new law that would tighten federal safety controls over pesticides. There are still loose threads, however— so many that the package could come unraveled on Capitol Hill if the competing forces keep pulling in their own directions instead of toward the public interest. If the package does fall apart, there may not be another chance to improve this important area of environmental law for many years.

Several key issues remain to be resolved in the Senate Agriculture Committee as it nears a vote Wednesday on changes in the Federal Insecticide, Fungicide and Rodenticide Act. Among them are the right of local and state governments to set higher standards than federal law. Committee members who want the public well protected should insist that the federal law not preempt state or local standards.

One troublesome amendment would prevent cities and counties from enacting regulations, as Mendocino County did in 1979 when it banned aerial spraying of phenoxy herbicides in a move aimed at timber companies operating locally. After Mendocino took the action, the California Legislature wrongheadedly passed a bill giving the state jurisdiction over the uses of such chemicals. The only redeeming feature of the law is that it allows local governments to write their own controls and have them adopted as state regulations.

Local governments are entitled to decide for themselves what is appropriate under special and local circumstances. And the fact that the California Legislature weakened the rights of local governments in the field of pesticides and herbicides should not be used as an argument in favor of the federal government's doing the same thing to states. Sen. Pete Wilson—who is on the Agricul-

ture Committee and may support the preemption, depending on how it is worded—should keep that point in mind.

The other preemption under debate is potentially more onerous. Many food-industry lobbyists want the legislation to preempt all state regulation of the levels of pesticides that will be tolerated in the food supply. They argue that if states are allowed to have tougher standards, they, not the Environmental Protection Agency, will be setting federal policy. Others, who saw California move more quickly than the federal agency to deal with the hazards of ethyl dibromide, want to retain that independent ability to act when circumstances warrant. We agree with them.

A spokesman for Wilson said that he might favor an approach that would require uniform standards, with no state exceptions, but apply those uniform standards only to pesticides approved in the future under the tough guidelines. That might be an avenue for compromise, but the committee should again keep the public interest uppermost in any talks of giving away any state protections.

The legislation as approved by the House Agriculture Committee and moving through the Senate would set deadlines for testing pesticides that farmers started using before tougher guidelines went into effect. It would give the public more information on where pesticides are produced. It would require the EPA to issue regulations on protecting farm workers who deal with pesticides. It might establish national standards for the amount of pesticides in groundwater. The bill is a careful piece of work, and one of the most important environmental bills to appear before Congress in many years. The painstaking work must not be undone by last-minute changes that could weaken the protection of the public.

The Kansas City Times

Kansas City, MO,
September 22, 1988

Houseowners, gardeners and farmers deserve to be protected from dangerous pesticides. For more than a decade the Environmental Protection Agency has failed to do that. Now the U.S. House has approved a bill that should spur more action by the EPA and create more safeguards for pesticide users.

The battle to reform the initial 1972 pesticide law has gone on long enough. If all the parties in this matter — chemical makers, farm groups, environmentalists — grudgingly support and at the same time attack this bill, it can't be all bad.

Indeed, it has several strong points. The EPA will be required to retest hundreds of pesticides to determine whether they are dangerous to human health. It's absurd that some chemicals already are on the market if they have been inadequately tested.

For the first time the EPA would get enough money to retest the chemicals; it would be required to finish the task in nine years. The effort had been expected to take more than 30 years thanks to the EPA's small budget for retesting.

The House-approved measure also reduces the EPA's liability for taking a product off the shelf. The current ridiculous procedure requires the government to pay a chemical maker for storage and destruction of a pesticide deemed unsafe. It also has to indemnify the company for the pesticide taken off the market; sometimes that runs into millions of dollars.

The measure is not perfect. The biggest question concerns the uncertainty of the EPA's future actions. After all the testing of a pesticide is completed, will the agency have the courage to rule that products have to be taken off the market? Chemical companies and some farm groups will maintain intense pressure and argue that the benefits of certain pesticides outweigh their risks. What risks and to whom? It will be the EPA's job to refuse to knuckle under to this kind of economic blackmail when chemicals have clear, dangerous health effects.

When that's the case, the chemical companies ought to have to come up with safer alternatives to be used by houseowners, gardeners and farmers. It's been done before. It can be done again, but only if the EPA has the money and backbone to get tough with dangerous pesticides.

BUFFALO EVENING NEWS

Buffalo, NY, October 3, 1988

AFTER YEARS of delay Congress has finally completed work on a bill that reorganizes the faltering system under which the U.S. Environmental Protection Agency determines the safety of pesticides.

Reflecting the lawmakers' desire to get something on the books at last, the bill approved by the House and Senate is a stripped-down version of more comprehensive proposals that failed to become law in previous years.

Because the bill would amend the 1972 Federal Insecticide, Fungicide and Rodenticide Act (FIFRA), disappointed supporters of more ambitious legislation were quick to dub it "FIFRA Lite."

However, while some interest groups said the legislation "does not even qualify for a bronze medal," others applauded it as a sign of progress on pesticide reform.

The legislation admittedly leaves many issues unresolved and is not all it should be. But as Rep. E. de la Garza, D-Tex., chairman of the House Agriculture Committee, said, it is a demonstration of "the art of the possible." It "will not satisfy everybody," he conceded, "but this is what we could move at this point."

Since something, in this instance, is better than nothing, the choice to move it was wise and constructive. Nothing would have been accomplished by yet another round of inconclusive haggling on pesticide control.

The legislation has several important features. Besides renewing the law barring the sale of pesticides unless they are registered with the EPA, it speeds the lagging process of testing whether hundreds of pesticides already on the market meet proper health and environmental standings. Under the bill, this testing must be completed within nine years.

The measure also requires pesticide manufacturers to pay testing fees of up to $150,000 per chemical. In addition, the EPA will no longer have to compensate manufacturers when their products are ordered withdrawn from sale, or to bear the cost of disposing of the products. This will relieve the EPA of expenses that could otherwise drain its resources and slow pesticide regulation.

Stricken from the compromise bill were provisions on whether federal regulations should pre-empt those of individual states; protection for farmers against liability for pesticide pollution; the regulation of pesticides in ground water; and federal compensation for the health data that manufacturers supply.

These matters are by no means unimportant. They can and certainly should be considered in subsequent legislation.

But for now, the measure adopted by Congress and expected to be signed by President Reagan is a welcome step forward. By ensuring faster testing of the many pesticides now on the market and those coming in the future, it can do much to protect public health and safety.

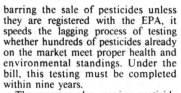

Los Angeles, CA, September 22, 1988

In federal pesticide law, even the smallest step forward is reason to cheer. Last year — in fact, for several years running — Congress was on the verge of reforming the archaic regulations that govern pesticide use when chemical companies managed to ax the legislation. Now the House has passed sensible revisions and the Senate could act soon. Americans will be safer as a result. But much remains to be done.

For 40 years, the government has tested and approved pesticides. But many of the 600 active chemicals now contained in 50,000 products passed muster at a time when testing standards were weak.

Congress recognized the problem in 1972, when it gave the Environmental Protection Agency authority to re-test and re-register pesticides, or ban them if necessary. But it also hampered the process by requiring EPA to pay makers for any leftover inventories of prohibited poisons. This pinched EPA's budget and, consequently, only a few pesticides have been re-tested. At the current rate, it'll take another 35 years to check them all out.

The House bill would appropriate more money and impose fees on pesticide makers to finish the job in eight years. During that time, EPA would evaluate each chemical to see if it is acutely toxic, causes cancer or birth defects and has pernicious effects on birds, bees and aquatic life.

All well and good. But missing from the reforms is any mention of groundwater problems. And these are growing. Two dozen cancer-causing pesticides have been found in the groundwater of 30 states. And cancer isn't the only concern. For instance, aldicarb, a highly toxic pesticide used on potatoes and citrus products, has been shown to suppress human immune systems.

Groundwater cleanups are immensely expensive when they are possible at all, so keeping pesticides out of groundwater ought to be high on the EPA's list of goals. Alternative pest-control measures should be fully explored. When only poison will work, it should be applied more cautiously, in smaller quantities, and its use should be strictly monitored. The stubborn chemical industry has proved that none of this will happen unless Congress forces the issue.

The Philadelphia Inquirer

Philadelphia, PA, September 20, 1988

Approximately 2.6 billion pounds of pesticides are used in this country each year, and most of the compounds were licensed for use before the federal government required tests to determine their safety.

Those tests were first ordered in 1972 as part of the repulsively, but explicitly, named Insecticide, Fungicide and Rodenticide Act (FIFRA). Any pesticide determined by the Environmental Protection Agency to be unsafe for humans or animals was to be withdrawn from the market.

Congress attached a caveat to that order, however. The federal government was required to reimburse the chemical manufacturer for stockpiles of pesticides taken off the market. For a widely used pesticide, that could represent a drain in the Treasury of $100 million or more.

The EPA has moved at a slug's pace in its health studies of pesticides, evaluating about 25 each year. At that rate, findings on the remaining 600 or so will not be completed for a quarter-century. Critics have argued that the EPA is in no hurry because of the potential cost of a product ban.

Congress is in no hurry to solve the pesticide problem, either.

FIFRA is up for reauthorization again this year and, as in the past, the debate has been fueled by massive lobbying by environmentalists on one side, and by the agricultural and chemical industries on the other.

Last week, the House Agriculture Committee approved legislation that gives EPA eight years to complete the health studies. It sets no penalties if the EPA fails to meet the deadline.

The bill also ends guaranteed payments to producers whose pesticides are removed from the market. EPA and the manufacturers would share the cost of storing or disposing of banned products and chemical companies would underwrite the cost of the health studies.

But some in Congress say that's not enough. They're right. The pesticide problem is far more extensive than just health studies and compensation to manufacturers.

The measure does nothing to address the growing problem of protecting ground water from pesticide contamination — and affixing liability if aquifers are polluted. It doesn't set standards for pesticide residues allowable on food products. It ignores export to other countries of pesticides that have been banned from use in the U.S. because they are too hazardous. And it is silent on exposure standards for farm workers and others.

Environmentalists find themselves in a difficult position. The present bill, which reauthorizes FIFRA for three years, represents a minor step toward wise regulation of pesticides. No one concerned about pesticide exposure in this country argues that it is adequate.

Pragmatically, however, it may be all possible from this Congress and administration.

There is growing support for amending the bill to reauthorize FIFRA for just one year and attaching to it a commitment from Congress to take up the pesticide problem in the next session when a new administration might be more receptive to tougher environmental regulation.

That seems like a sensible tack to take — if Congress can be counted on to once and for all treat pesticides for what they are: deadly chemicals.

Detroit Free Press

Detroit, MI, March 13, 1988

MORE THAN 25 years after the publication of Rachel Carson's "Silent Spring," the nation has still failed to control the indiscriminate pesticide use that she decried. Meanwhile, the reckless use of substances known to be dangerous continues.

That is why the Environmental Protection Agency and a number of environmental groups are joining to try to strengthen the licensing and control of pesticides. Under present testing schedules, some products now in use, including some that are suspect, would not be tested for as much as 40 years. In the interest of both the individuals exposed to danger and the industries supposedly regulated, the process of licensure and, where appropriate, removal from the market badly needs to be accelerated.

Some of those in Congress who purport to be friends of the farmer are fighting changes in the pesticide control law on the premise that the changes will add cost and complexity to pest control and, therefore, are not in the interest of the farmers. In fact, farm families have more interest than anyone in having good information, being protected from unsafe products, and being warned of dangers. The recurrent exposure to dangerous pesticides puts them in more jeopardy than the general population.

The broad recognition of the need for change brought Congress once before, in 1986, to the brink of passage of a revision of the pesticide control law. Bills passed both houses, but died in a conference committee. It is important that this year's effort not meet a similar fate.

Anyone who has worked on a farm can appreciate the need for simplicity and clarity in the controls. It is inherently difficult to regulate the use of pesticides in the field. The legitimate concerns of manufacturers and farmers need to be understood and, where feasible, accommodated.

But the sale in some instances and the misuse in others of inherently dangerous substances are threats to people and to wildlife. Congress badly needs to succeed at putting together a more effective package of regulations to minimize the dangers.

The Idaho STATESMAN

Boise, ID, May 25, 1988

Death by pesticide poisoning is a cruel but not unusual punishment meted out to birds of all feathers in southern Idaho. Last weekend's killing of more than 100 Canada geese on a Snake River island near Weiser was a vivid example of what happens when wildlife collides with man: Wildlife loses.

To lessen the collision, more education and training are needed in the application of agricultural chemicals. Because if wildlife keeps losing – so does man.

Farmer Ron Rollins says he didn't know geese fed in his alfalfa field when he apparently applied pesticides Furadan, Cygon and Disyston to control alfalfa weevils and other insects. An estimated 125 geese, mostly goslings unable to fly, were killed, according to state Fish and Game officials.

The kill is damaging because Fish and Game has been patiently rebuilding the flocks of geese by limiting hunters' takes. One application of pesticide can put a good-sized hole in the 1,500 to 2,000 geese estimated to live in the Snake River area.

What's more, birds of prey, including hawks and bald eagles, might feed on the poisoned geese, underlining the damage pesticides can do to the food chain.

The goose kill is only "the tiniest tip of the iceberg," according to Tracey Trent of the Fish and Game Department. Thousands of birds, including pheasants, quail and songbirds, are poisoned each year by pesticides, he said.

Mr. Rollins faces up to six months in jail or a $5,000 fine if found guilty of "unlawfully taking migratory birds by the use of a pesticide." But that won't help the geese.

Education and training, however, could.

Today's agricultural chemicals have short half-lives compared with DDT and other chemicals used in the past, state Department of Agriculture Director Dick Rush said. But they also are more deadly. For that reason, proper handling and application are even more important.

The Agricultural Department and the Idaho Farm Bureau provide some training now. But the situation demands more. A cooperative effort jointly funded by those two groups along with Fish and Game could go a lot further toward ensuring safe use of pesticides.

Farmers are hunters, too, and it's in their best interest, both in preserving game and saving money on pesticides, to use their chemicals wisely and sparingly.

Superfund Cleanup
Effort Faulted

Outlays for Superfund toxic waste cleanups would rise by $425 million to $1.2 billion in President Ronald Reagan's 1989 budget proposals, which were presented Feb. 18, 1988. The funding would cover cleanup of 30 sites during the year.

The Superfund cleanup program to detoxify toxic waste sites was condemned June 17, 1988 as "largely ineffective" because of poor management and an inadequate work force.

A report by the Office of Technology Assessment (OTA), a nonpartisan scientific agency reporting to Congress, said the Superfund program was failing because of a "lack of central management oversight and controls." This resulted in "inconsistency leading to confusion, unnecessary costs and, for some sites, ineffective cleanup," the agency said.

The agency warned that the situation was "not an academic issue," since it involved "harm to human health and the environment, loss of public confidence in government and wasting money." The Superfund program was administered by the Environmental Protection Agency (EPA).

The report focused especially on the EPA's failure to follow Congress's declared preference for "permanently effective" cleanups, such as incineration of wastes. Instead, it said, the agency continued to bury or cap and attempt to seal off wastes, remedies that had proven temporary and eventually ineffective in the past.

J. Winston Porter, the EPA's assistant administrator in charge of the Superfund program, protested the OTA report later June 17 as a "cheap shot." "We have thousands of people out there working on 850 real projects," he said. "I'll put my engineers up against them any day."

The EPA Aug. 9 ordered treatment of some hazardous wastes by companies before they dumped them on land.

The agency, in implementing the Resource Conservation and Recovery Act of 1984, allowed a two-year exemption for oil refineries in view of the industry's lack of treatment capacity.

But the rule took effect immediately for the steel and electroplating industries and certain chemical manufacturers, among others.

The rule in general required recycling or stabilization of metal in sludges. Toxic dust was to be bound into a cementlike compound. For some chemicals, including refinery wastes, toxics were to be incinerated or extracted and mixed with stabilizing compounds. The two-year delay in compliance for refineries was based on their lack of incineration capacity.

A steel industry spokesman said steel plants might have to stockpile sludge for a while to comply with the order. But disposal technology was available, Earle Young Jr., vice president for environmental affairs of the American Iron and Steel Institute, said, and "we can live with the cost."

The EPA estimated that the new rule after two years, when it would apply to the oil industry as well, would cost industry about $950 million annually.

The EPA Aug. 24 proposed minimum standards for municipal trash dumps.

The rules were designed to prevent toxic leakage from the nation's 6,000 municipal landfills. Monitoring procedures for possible leakage into groundwater supplies were to be established, and controls over odor, fires and rodents required. Specific steps to accomplish such goals would be left to states and localities.

The rules were criticized on that point by environmentalists. Jacqueline Warren of the Natural Resources Defense Council called them an "abdication" of the government's role to prevent contamination of groundwater supplies.

The council would have preferred, she said, "specific design and operating criteria instead of setting goals and allowing the states discretion on how the landfills are constructed and operated."

THE
KANSAS CITY STAR
*Kansas City, MO,
March 14, 1988*

Exporting toxic wastes to countries outside U.S. borders—and not telling them about it—has gone on for a long time. Problem is, there's little being done about it.

Rules set up by the Environmental Protection Agency are worth nothing. The companies that are bent on defying the law easily get by the EPA regulation that says American firms exporting hazardous waste must inform the federal agency and tell the receiving country what's in the casks and cargo boxes.

Good luck. There's little concern at too many companies about what Washington is going to do to them if they send a little dangerous waste out of the nation.

The environmental groups aware of the problem can do little about it. The only hope they have is publicity. They got some good coverage last year when a bargeload of garbage floated for weeks as several countries rejected it. Finally, the waste ended up back in the United States.

But the high profile given that transportation disaster is not enough to take care of the bigger problem: How can nations such as Mexico, Zimbabwe, Venezuela, Spain and others prohibit toxic garbage from being illegally and furtively dumped within their borders? It's difficult to know what's in all those containers from the United States.

We barely know what kind of problems will crop up in this country from improperly buried hazardous waste. What's worse is that no one knows what kind of future troubles are in store for other countries that receive improperly marked, and dangerous, waste from U.S. corporations.

The Hartford Courant

Hartford, CT, April 18, 1988

Sudsy foam pours from the mouth of a pipe carrying waste water from the plant of one of this region's largest firms, then drains into a potential source of drinking water in Bloomfield.

Cans, some containing more than the permitted amounts of harmful chemical residue, are dumped by the truckload into a sanitary landfill in Windsor over three months' time, and not once do landfill personnel stop the trucks to examine the trash being dumped.

Informed of these apparent violations of the law, state officials complain that regulatory agencies are understaffed and overworked. They concede that protection of the environment from chemical and other toxic-waste disposal depends largely on what one official characterized as an honor system.

That is, the state's environmental policing system for hazardous-waste disposal consists largely in hoping that potential polluters won't pollute.

Connecticut has many laws intended to prevent the sorts of abuses described above, which were revealed in stories published by The Courant last week. But unenforced laws are worthless.

Spokesmen for the Kaman Corp. of Bloomfield, the company alleged to have illegally dumped the wastes, conceded no wrongdoing on the part of the firm. When Kaman announced plans to change its disposal procedures — after The Courant's report was published — company officials maintained that the changes were undertaken at the request of Bloomfield officials, and not because Kaman had done anything wrong.

From now on, a spokesman said, Kaman will test all discharges from its plant and remove the bottoms of all cans sent to the local dump to ensure that no toxic residues remain. The company will also consider shifting all its discharges to the Bloomfield sewer system, rather than discharging wastes into local streams and brooks.

That's all well and good, but who will make sure of compliance? Will government officials follow up on the allegations?

State Attorney General Joseph I. Lieberman and officials at the state Department of Environmental Protection apparently are investigating whether Kaman violated laws. It would be reckless to wait until the end of the investigation, however, before taking preventive measures. Companies must not be allowed to take risky shortcuts in their attempts to dispose of the toxic waste. The honor system is appropriate for running a Boy Scout troop, not for monitoring a sophisticated and complex operation, like Kaman's, and for protecting the environment from damage.

If Kaman is found to have violated local, state or federal environmental laws, then the firm should be fined and punished appropriately. More important, however, is for state officials to be more aggressive as guardians of public health and the environment.

It makes no sense to spend millions touting the state's beauties, only to look the other way when they are despoiled. By all means, let Mr. Lieberman and the others pursue legal redress against Kaman or any alleged polluter, but give the DEP enough staff and resources to police, monitor and prevent such episodes.

Public health and safety are at stake. State officials have known of the hazards of improper toxic-waste disposal long enough. Connecticut's once-pioneering environmental laws need their teeth sharpened.

The Boston Globe

Boston, MA, June 14, 1988

Among the earliest targets in the battle to protect the environment were the unregulated trucking companies that, for a fee, routinely dumped hazardous wastes into any stream or open field they could find. As a result of tough laws and vigorous enforcement, the battle has moved on to more sophisticated targets.

But the dumpers may have only moved on, finding streams and open fields in countries where neither regulation nor enforcement is much of a deterrent.

Concern is now mounting that West Africa is becoming the new dumping ground – "Waste Africa," The Observer of London calls it in a report on the growing problem.

According to The Observer, 15,000 tons of toxic waste from Philadelphia has been dumped on the island of Kassa near the Guinean capital of Conakry. The wastes were brought in under an import license for an apparently fictitious brick-manufacturing project and are already poisoning plant and animal life on the island.

Benin has accepted two shiploads of nuclear waste from France. According to the London newsletter Africa Analysis, they are to be dumped at a site near one of the centers of opposition to President Mathieu Kerekou.

The financial benefits of these operations are enormous. While it may cost up to $1,000 a ton to dispose of hazardous wastes in Europe or the United States, Guinea took the waste from Philadelphia for $40 a ton, and Benin is receiving just $2.50 a ton for the nuclear wastes it is accepting. It is hard to imagine that at those prices either country is providing much in the way of environmental monitoring at the disposal sites.

The European Parliament is concerned about the problem and has called for a ban on the exporting of hazardous wastes to the Third World. With the indication that many of these waste shipments are originating in the United States, there would seem to be reason for federal environmental officials, or Congress, to investigate the matter.

The Cincinnati Post

Cincinnatti, OH, May 20, 1988

Comparatively little publicity was given the Emergency Response and Community Right-to-Know Act when it was passed two years ago in conjunction with the renewal and expansion of the Superfund waste-cleanup law.

But this sleeper legislation will have an extensive effect on nearly every community in the nation and vast numbers of businesses previously subject to few if any federal hazardous material reporting requirements.

As of March 1, hundreds of thousands of businesses were required to inform fire departments and local and state officials if they had any hazardous materials on hand during 1987.

By July 1, companies must provide information if they emit any of a number of specified chemicals into the air.

The Occupational Safety and Health Administration (OSHA) Communication Standard also has been expanded to include all businesses rather than just the manufacturers. The new communication standard states communities, as well as workers, now have a right to know about the hazardous materials a company is handling. Companies also must draw up an emergency response plan subject to community inspection.

At the same time, the Environmental Protection Agency has stiffened enforcement of another set of rules that imposed increased environmental responsibilities on small businesses. These mandates bar careless disposal of hazardous byproducts.

While all these new requirements are welcome, offering needed protection for the public, they also pose potential trouble. Specifically, many firms may be unaware that byproducts with which they have worked for years are classified as hazardous and must be reported to government officials.

At least some of these regulations extend beyond industrial operations to such businesses as auto repair shops, dry cleaners and furniture refinishers.

The Greater Cincinnati Chamber of Commerce is performing an important service by sponsoring a half-day seminar next month to provide information and advice that will help companies identify whether their wastes are hazardous and tell them how they can comply with the new federal rules.

THE SACRAMENTO BEE
Sacramento, CA, July 1, 1988

The government of Guinea has arrested the Norwegian consul general for complicity in dumping 15,000 tons of toxic wastes from the United States in that tiny African nation. Nigerian officials have seized an Italian freighter and recalled their ambassador to Rome to protest the Italian government's reluctance to pay for removing 2,000 tons of reportedly radioactive waste that Italy secretly transported to Nigeria. And another freighter laden with 10,000 tons of ash from Philadelphia's municipal incinerators is standing off the coast of West Africa, waiting for clearance to unload the hazardous cargo that no other country has been willing accept for the last 20 months.

These are only the latest incidents in the increasing furor over the way Western Europe and the United States are using the impoverished countries of Africa as dumping grounds for toxic wastes. Requirements for the treatment and disposal of these materials in most industrialized nations are now so strict that it's often cheaper to haul them overseas. For years, the most deadly materials have been taken to remote landfills in the South Pacific and the Caribbean. But those are now full, and in recent years the flow has shifted toward Africa, where unscrupulous entrepreneurs have been able to make millions in quick and dirty payoffs for helping to expedite the dumping.

Although international law currently does not restrict exports of waste materials, there's a growing recognition of the need for global cooperation on this issue. At their summit meeting in May, the 50 nations making up the Organization for African Unity called on all African states to oppose the traffic in toxics. The European Parliament in June unanimously passed a resolution against large-scale exports of toxic wastes to Third World countries. And the United Nations Environment Program recently convened representatives of 50 nations and 14 international organizations to examine ways of establishing a coordinated effort to control the problem.

Those are all steps in the right direction. The countries being victimized by these practices don't have the wherewithal to police their borders. Nor do they have either the technical or financial resources to treat, contain or dispose of the trash that's being deposited on their property. The responsibility for curbing this activity has to rest with the industrialized nations, where the wastes originate.

The Seattle Times
Seattle, WA, June 21, 1988

OF COURSE, it's only a coincidence — isn't it?

At the economic summit in Toronto, leaders of the seven largest industrialized nations agreed to help ease the massive debt of Africa's most struggling countries.

Even the United States, which had previously refused to allow any debt concessions, agreed to go along with a new plan that would benefit about 20 sub-Saharan African nations considered "the poorest of the poor."

However, just as the mucky-mucks were declaring their generosity in Toronto, news stories were surfacing about how some African countries are being used by Western powers as dumping grounds for toxic wastes.

Guinea, Gambia, Nigeria, Benin and the Congo, among others, have received thousands of tons of industrial wastes — including incinerator ash, hazardous chemicals and possibly even radioactive materials. The wastes have come from the United States, France, Italy, Belgium, Luxembourg, the Netherlands and West Germany.

The United Nations Environmental Program (UNEP), headquartered in Nairobi, said about a dozen African nations have taken or been approached to take toxic wastes, usually by private companies offering lucrative (at least in African terms) contracts. Some dumping had the approval of governments hungry for hard currency, but some was done "in the twilight," as one UNEP official put it.

"It doesn't matter what amount of money they are offered," said Omar Sey, Gambia's foreign minister. "You liberate your countries from colonialism and you talk about imperialism, apartheid. But what is more horrible than dumping nuclear and toxic waste?" Indeed, in nations with lax environmental regulations, inadequate equipment and limited knowledge of technology, what is more horrible?

The Organization of African Unity passed a resolution condemning such dumping as "a crime against Africa and the African people" — which it is. UNEP is working on a draft treaty to control international shipments of hazardous wastes, but it won't be ready until next year. Why so slow?

Meanwhile, Toronto summiteers agreed to write off some African loans, cut interest rates or stretch out payments.

Of course, it's only a coincidence — isn't it?

The News and Observer
Raleigh, NC, June 1, 1988

When, in a 1971 speech, North Carolina's Terry Sanford urged Southerners to "avoid Northern mistakes in a Southern setting," his fears sprang from seeing blighted land and polluted air and water in northern New Jersey. So it may take a while for the South to get accustomed to New Jersey as an aggressive foe of pollution.

But, belatedly or not, the New Jersey legislature is fed up with the trashing of the state's environment. Last year it enacted the first mandatory recycling law for a state. And now it has passed three bills to combat the state's growing ocean pollution problems.

Of course, Southern states haven't avoided every mistake Sanford had in mind. In North Carolina, Wake and Mecklenburg counties have failed federal air-quality tests as the auto-truck census has soared. Coastal growth and sewage runoff have fouled shellfishing waters. A number of rivers and lakes inland have stagnated with overloads of phosphorus and nitrogen.

The message from New Jersey is that procrastination will make environmental problems worse. Even with limited landfill space, that state didn't turn to mandatory composting of leaves and recycling of paper, glass, aluminum, tin and plastic until a waste-disposal crisis was at hand. Many of its 567 communities were paying premium fees for dumping in limited space, or were trying to dispose of waste out of state.

Similarly, as the legislature voted on the ocean-protection bills, the Coast Guard and police were monitoring a three-mile skein of household garbage, wood and seaweed bobbing off the New Jersey coast. Meantime, the state panel examining the fouling of state beaches last summer was recommending broader curbs on coastal development.

A bright spot in North Carolina's environmental picture is its Coastal Area Management Act. Such statutory protection for the coast, while only as effective as it is firmly and consistently applied, came too late in New Jersey to prevent many development excesses of the worst sort. But at least that state has ordered a halt to the ocean dumping of sewage sludge, and it has intensified its surveillance of illegal dumping and increased penalties.

What stands out, finally, in the New Jersey experience is how much easier it is to prevent pollution than to cure it. It's not just that pollution is unhealthy. It's also hard for citizens to take any pride in their state when its air, water and land are befouled.

The Evening Gazette

Worcester, MA, June 2, 1988

Love Canal, Three-Mile Island and Bhopal have become emblematic of the difficulties of coping with the dangerous byproducts of our industrial society — and are names we relegate to the farthest recesses of our minds. Yet it is becoming increasingly clear that disposing of hazardous waste is a problem of global scope with no simple solutions.

The latest reminder comes from the ocean-going odyssey of the Syrian frieghter Zanobia, dubbed the "ship of poison."

Until Italian authorities allowed it to enter the port of Genoa this week, the Zanobia appeared doomed to forever sail the seas, like the legendary Flying Dutchman. In February 1987, the Zanobia took on 2,200 tons of toxic chemical waste at the Italian port of Carrara.

It was refused entry to ports in the East African country of Djibouti, then Venezuela, Syria and Greece before returning to Carrera. Last weekend, Italian authorities allowed the Zanobia to offload at Genoa, the only port capable of handling and incinerating the waste safely.

As in other notable incidents involving hazardous-waste disposal, safety considerations may have taken second place to the bottom line. Reportedly, a group of Italian chemical manufacturers had paid a company in Milan to dispose of the waste at 36 cents a pound. Instead of proper treatment and incineration — which officials estimate will cost 72 cents to $1.86 a pound — the company hired the Zanobia to ship the waste out of the country.

The astronauts of the 1960s, on first viewing the planet as a peaceful globe floating in the darkness of space, dubbed it "Spaceship Earth." From their vantage point in high orbit, the similarities between races and nations could be seen manifestly to outweigh the differences.

A similarly expansive perspective is needed in confronting the growing problem of disposing of hazardous waste. Industry, governments and individuals all must resolve to prevent the Spaceship Earth itself from becoming a ship of poison.

BUFFALO EVENING NEWS

Buffalo, NY, June 21, 1988

WHEN IT COMES to hazardous waste, Americans know more than they are practicing. Technology holds promise for managing toxic compounds better, but the process of applying the technology is too slow. Government, industry and the public officially agree that disposal should be a last resort, but it is still the most common solution to getting rid of wastes.

The nation must do better at managing hazardous waste, which is still being created rapidly despite a growing consciousness of the harm it can do. Nationwide, 500 million tons of solid toxic waste are generated every year and 100 million tons of pollutants go into the air.

To make the problem easier to solve, more emphasis is needed on what Congress, the Environmental Protection Agency and industry have all agreed should be the top management priority: reducing the amount of toxic waste that is generated.

The importance of this approach is obvious, but the nation is still mainly absorbed in the difficult task of dealing with waste after the fact. The EPA spends 99 percent of its resource on managing waste after it has already been created. Industry, meanwhile, pays huge bills to treat and transport wastes that, in some cases, might be greatly reduced in volume.

A bill now before Congress would help break the predominance of after-the-fact waste management by actively encouraging new methods of cutting hazardous waste production.

Known as the Hazardous Waste Reduction Act, the proposed law has 228 sponsors in the House, though it has not yet gotten committee approval. Among them are Reps. Henry Nowak, D-Buffalo; John LaFalce, D-Town of Tonawanda; and Amory Houghton, R-Corning.

The bill would make matching grants to states for technical assistance to manufacturers that want to reduce their hazardous waste. The grants could finance modification of technology or processes, reformulation or redesign of products, substitution of raw materials or improvements in management, training or housekeeping.

It would also establish a national clearinghouse for exchange of information on limiting toxic production, and would charge the federal government with coordinating and improving collection of pertinent information.

The EPA estimates that hazardous waste production could be lowered 15 to 30 percent over the next 25 years if industry makes appropriate changes. The congressional Office of Technology Assessment is considerably more optimistic, claiming there could be a 50 percent reduction in five years if better techniques were used.

Either figure is worth some national investment. The money saved in the long run, as fewer hazardous wastes have to be dealt with, makes the reduction approach eminently desirable from both the public and the industry point of view.

THE PLAIN DEALER

Cleveland, OH, June 13, 1988

Legislative negotiators reached a reasonable compromise on a controversial hazardous-cargo transportation bill, with only one or two red flags warning of possible loopholes. Generally, the deal should accomplish the public purpose of providing notice to emergency agencies about toxic materials hauled and routes taken. The shipping and chemical industries preferred to keep all records confidential, but lost out to mounting pressures for information.

There's good reason for the bill. A 1986 train derailment in Miamisburg released deadly phosphorus gas into the air and forced the evacuation of 35,000 people. Other train and truck spills on a smaller scale are so numerous that Ohio is consistently among the nation's leaders—hardly a distinction about which the state can boast. Given society's increasing use of chemical products and Ohio's location as a transportation crossroads, the sitution is not likely to get better without legal leverage and penalties. For the safety of citizens along the routes, and for the safety and effectiveness of firefighters and other emergency crews, notification makes eminent sense.

The House version of the bill called for prior notification of shipments, while the Senate allowed later notification. The House approach offers more safeguards and, fortunately, prevailed. However, the state's Emergency Management Agency and Public Utilities Commission must be vigilant against potential abuses of the compromise language. To wit:

Under the deal reached by a House-Senate conference committee, advance notice to the EMA would be required only for cargo shipped 24 hours *after* it was ordered; first notice would be by telephone, then a written record would be sent within a week. But cargo shipped *within* 24 hours of being ordered would be exempt from prior notification; a written notice within a week would be required. Shippers could try to circumvent the prior-notice rule by insisting that the 64 super-risky items on the notice list are always shipped within 24 hours.

PUCO rules must address both the notification procedures and enforcement. The public will have to rely on official agencies to protect public interests since the compromise would shield shipping records from immediate public scrutiny. That provision is less than ideal, but the bill nonetheless addresses the primary objective of helping emergency agencies prepare for accidents. The revised bill, passed unanimously by the House on Friday, deserves the Senate's approval and the governor's signature.

THE ANN ARBOR NEWS

Ann Arbor, MI, October 5, 1988

Michigan, like other states, is threatened by a potential crisis because hazardous waste is being generated faster than it can be disposed of. It is a situation that could be prevented if state industry reduced the amount of waste it produces.

According to a News series, "Waste Woes," 4 million tons of hazardous waste is produced in Michigan each year, and the only commercial hazardous landfill, near Belleville, is expected to be filled in three to five years. There is no incinerator for such waste in the state.

Michigan, through new state laws, has the potential to establish a state network to help hazardous waste producers reduce waste. That is the long-term, desirable solution, although it doesn't completely eliminate the need for landfills or incinerators.

In the meantime, the state as well as local governments have to deal with storing these materials, and no one wants a hazardous waste dump site as a neighbor. The cost and safety of hauling these wastes as well as maintaining safe disposal sites also are parts of the overall problem.

Hazardous waste disposal is of particular interest to Washtenaw County because of the proximity of the present waste site and because a new landfill and incinerator system for such material is being proposed for Augusta Township.

While state and federal laws purport to address waste reduction, most resources and personnel still focus on management of wastes after they have been created. Even then, oversight has been uneven. And the laws are full of gray areas. Technical standards are open to interpretation, and local governments have no regulatory authority.

Close monitoring is critical. The system is dependent upon the landfill managers being good citizens. State inspectors average only four visits a year to Wayne Disposal and federal inspectors visit twice a year. Many major corporations send employees to visit hazardous landfills before using them, but even then, there's no guarantee that the waste is always satisfactorily disposed of.

Michigan's new laws, which went into effect Oct. 1, includes a four-prong strategy:

• The state has established an office of waste reduction in the Department of Natural Resources that will investigate waste reduction technologies and periodically examine state regulations to encourage waste reduction.

• A technical assistance program will be developed within the Department of Commerce that will offer education and outreach services to Michigan businesses.

• A $10-a-ton tax on landfilled hazardous waste is expected to raised about $2.5 million a year to fund to go the DNR and Commerce programs.

• The state also is setting up task force to determine by June, 1989, whether the state should support an academic institute to focus research on waste reduction.

The DNF and Commerce programs, if properly developed, can help producers of hazardous waste deal with the problem. The Commerce Department can work with the DNR in developing waste-reduction technology, and both can incorporate talent from the state's universities. Both could work in conjunction to set up a sharing program which would allow firms to exchange waste-reduction methods at reduced costs and without sharing company secrets. Similar technical assistance programs have been successful in North Carolina, Illinois, California, Minnesota, and other states.

Waste-reduction is not the only solution, but a successful program will help reduce the overall problems of hazardous waste disposal.

TULSA WORLD

Tulsa, OK, July 1, 1988

COMMON sense broke out last Wednesday at the Environmental Protection Agency. Authorities decided that oil and gas drilling wastes will not be treated as "hazardous materials" in the same category with extremely poisonous industrial pollutants.

While this obviously is good news for the petroleum industry, the real winner is the American consumer.

If taken seriously, the reclassification of oil field wastes would have increased production costs enormously. Under current anti-pollution laws, oil field salts and other wastes are usually pumped back into the ground. If treated as "hazardous wastes," much of the material would have been collected and hauled great distances for special handling and disposal. It doesn't take a mathematician to figure out what such an expense would do to the price of a gallon of gasoline.

The decision does not give producers a license to pollute. The EPA sensibly promised rigid enforcement of existing anti-pollution laws in the oil patch. In earlier times, many oil operators were reckless in their disposal of waste. They ruined streams and thousands of acres of land. With strict enforcement of existing laws, this problem has been largely corrected. Regulation and hardheaded enforcement must continue.

This can be done without breaking the consumer's back with an expensive "hazardous waste" standard.

The Houston Post

Houston, TX, July 1, 1988

The public's right to know could be well served by industry compliance with a long-overdue law governing emissions of toxic chemicals. Today is the deadline for the companies to file public reports on the amounts of any of 328 toxins released into the air, land or water in 1987 — a requirement that might help persuade them to keep a closer check on the amounts of chemicals released.

The filing deadline, a requirement of a 1986 federal law that was prompted by the Bhopal chemical plant disaster in India, was being complied with slowly by industries. For instance, one week before the deadline, only 76 of an expected 2,500 to 3,000 Texas companies had filed reports. It is hoped they will meet today's deadline.

One good aspect of the law is that it allows citizens to file lawsuits against companies that violate the reporting requirements — with penalties ranging up to $25,000 for each day of violation. That gives citizens — should the Environmental Protection Agency falter — a hand in assuring that local plants comply with the law. Perhaps this is the first step toward cleaner air, land and water in America.

AKRON BEACON JOURNAL

Akron, OH, August 26, 1988

MUCH OF the recent discussion concerning garbage landfills has focused on the scarcity of sites. Ohioans know that at current dumping rates every active landfill in the state will be full by the year 2000. Thankfully, the Legislature acted this year to limit the amount of out-of-state garbage dumped here.

But scarcity is just one issue. Another was addressed this week by U.S. Environmental Protection Agency, and the attention came none too soon. The EPA proposed federal rules to help prevent contamination of the environment from landfills.

The regulations would include the development of inspection programs, requirements for covering landfills and monitoring dangerous gases. Open burning would be prohibited, as well as the discharge of harmful wastes into surface waters.

The problem is potentially enormous. Americans produce 160 million tons of municipal waste each year, and 80 percent of the trash is dumped in landfills. Unfortunately, current measures to protect the environment fall far short. Only 15 percent of sites have liners to prevent contaminated waste from leaking into groundwater. Less than a third have some kind of groundwater monitoring system.

The EPA rules will not come without cost. It's estimated the bill will total roughly $260 million a year, or $11 a year for a household. But that's only the beginning; the tab could run as high as $900 million a year when new sites are established in the future.

The expense, however, is worth it. The EPA rules offer an important start at dealing with a critical but as yet largely ignored issue. Landfills should be required to meet stiff standards for environmental safety.

The Providence Journal

Providence, RI, June 1, 1988

According to Robert Burns, the Scottish poet, "The best laid schemes o' mice an' men/ Gang aft a-gley . . ."

Right about now, we expect, the management of Union Carbide Corp. could not fail to agree with this wise observation.

Readers will recall that when a pesticide plant in Bhopal, India, partly owned by Union Carbide, sprung a poison-gas leak in 1984, planeloads of American lawyers immediately descended on the area, making their services available to those interested in filing personal-injury claims against the company in United States courts.

Union Carbide denied culpability in the matter. But with 2,500 dead and thousands injured, the company feared the financial consequences should these cases be adjudicated in this country. Understandably so. Under our increasingly bizarre system of liability law, determining the responsibility of defendants seems to be less important than searching for "deep pockets" — that is, locating a party with sufficient financial resources to fully compensate those injured, virtually without regard to that party's actual degree of responsibility.

So the company sought to convince our federal courts that India was a more appropriate location for the trial. And it succeeded. But the change of venue backfired.

Indian jurists appear determined to prove that, when it comes to establishing "progressive" innovations in liability law, they can outdo the most imaginative American legal specialists. Last December, a district judge in Bhopal ordered Union Carbide to pay victims about $270 million — as an "advance" on any eventual award for damages — even before the company's liability, if any, has been established at a trial. And now an Indian appellate court has upheld that order (although reducing the amount to $190 million).

Fortunately for Union Carbide — but even more important, for the principle of due process under the law — the Indian courts' decrees will not be enforceable in American courts if they are found contrary to public policy here. And we expect our jurists will reaffirm that defendants still have a right to have their cases heard in court, and penalties are imposed after, not before, a finding of guilt.

WINSTON-SALEM JOURNAL

Winston-Salem, NC, September 11, 1989

Pollution, overdevelopment, greed, myopia and a sense of helplessness — all contribute to a deteriorating coastal environment. To rescue that environment will take sacrifices that people have not yet shown a willingness to make.

When asked about pollution in the chemical business many years ago, a vice president of the Du Pont Co. said pollution is a matter of attitude. At first, that sounded rather like a polluter passing the buck of blame, but the vice president elaborated:

"If you visit, say, West Germany, you will find almost no litter in the streets, and you will find fish swimming in a tank of waste water after it's been treated but before it's released back into the environment."

Well, West Germany in recent years has not escaped pollution problems of its own, but the point was one well taken: A people who won't tolerate litter won't tolerate pollution.

The deteriorating environment is a problem so vast and complex that no single solution will work. Take the situation along North Carolina's coast so poignantly described in the recent Journal series on the subject. To halt, let alone reverse, that deterioration will take focused effort from government, business and philanthropic groups working on everything from zoning waters to limiting development to regulating fishing and boating. It will take science to determine more accurately the interrelating of actions and their consequences. It will take piles of money. And it will take personal sacrifice in the interests of the public weal and the heritage of future generations.

All of which is noble enough rhetoric, but is there really anything that people in Winston-Salem can do?

Yes. There are little things and big things. Little things — like turning out the lights when you leave a room or turning off the water while you brush your teeth or finding a trash can rather than the side of the road for your litter — mean a lot. Get your family to do the same, and work on your friends and neighbors. They are part of the public attitude problem.

On another level, improve your knowledge about environmental problems in general and the coast in particular. There are organizations that need your help. Find out about them — the library can help — and offer your help to the one that seems best to fit your particular concerns and interests. Many organizations that have or can have a dramatic effect on the coastal environment have local chapters.

Make a personal sacrifice or two. Instead of spending two weeks at the beach, spend one and let someone else go the second week. If you can afford a beach house, buy one that's already built, rather than one not yet constructed. Learn seamanship before you buy a boat, and maybe you'll want a sailboat rather than something fast and dirty.

Think about how we can educate our children to the urgency of environmental deterioration and the fragility and finiteness of our ecological systems. How can we teach them their place in that environment and instill an appreciation for its natural wonders and the interconnectedness of events and things? We need to do that, desperately.

Actions have consequences. Americans' personal freedom carries with it personal responsibilities. The environment is not something you can cut up and isolate in sections. We are all responsible for all of it. If you're not part of the solution, you're part of the problem. You no longer have the luxury of thinking about that; it's action time.

THE PLAIN DEALER

Cleveland, OH, August 29, 1988

For 7½ years the Reagan administration held its nose and generally ignored the growing, smelly, risky problem of disposing of the nation's garbage and trash. The only attention seemed to be directed at cutting funds. But suddenly—less than three months before the election—the Environmental Protection Agency finally has proposed some safety rules for the monitoring and cleaning up of landfills.

The move is welcome, though insufficient and overdue. Public concern about the landfill crisis has outpaced the EPA's reaction. People know landfills can present a health threat, since liquids can be leaked into ground water. People also know landfills are filling up, though nobody wants a new one in his back yard. Potential new sites are limited, and trucks are sent across state lines to dispose of garbage. Problems will be exacerbated by a court ruling that New York City must stop dumping waste sludge 100 miles at sea.

Amazingly, the new EPA rules are the first federal regulations proposed to combat environmental contamination from the nation's 6,000 municipal landfills. The EPA wants to set minimum standards that states and localities would be required to put into law.

But how serious is this proposal when EPA wants to allow a year for public comment and revision? That's footdragging. Yet it allows only 18 months for implementation by states and municipalities? That's unrealistic. There also are problems with the EPA's lack of specifics, and uncertainty about how small communities would handle the added costs.

For once, Ohio is ahead of the federal government on an environmental issue. A state law enacted this year already covers many of the EPA's proposed rules, plus the critical issues of enforcement and planning of new sites, neither of which the EPA addressed.

The federal agency plans another announcement in a few weeks on landfill alternatives, mainly recycling and incineration. These steps are imperative. They should address incinerator hazards of air contamination and ash disposal, and Congress' role in promoting recycling through tax incentives, mandates to federal agencies, encouragement of research and development of markets for recycled products. The EPA rules may be late, but they're not too late to begin a concerted attack on an oft-ignored major problem.

EPA Issues Report On Asbestos Rules

The Environmental Protection Agency (EPA) warned Congress Feb. 29, 1988 that an estimated one in five commercial buildings could have asbestos problems. But the agency, in a report to Congress, declined to offer any immediate plan to cope with the problems.

"We've got finite resources," John Moore, head of the EPA's toxic substances division, explained, and the agency wanted to focus primarily on the asbestos problems of schools. A detoxification program was underway for schools, where, it was estimated, one-third of the buildings had asbestos problems.

The EPA estimated that it would cost $51 billion to undertake a nationwide inspection and cleanup program to rid some 3.6 million commercial buildings of asbestos. But for now, it was restricting its recommendations to a three-year program of further study and a training program for asbestos inspections and removal crews.

The EPA's report came under criticism from all sides – industry, environmentalists, unions and Congress.

"Everything in this report points to aggressive federal intervention except EPA's recommendations, which amount to nothing more than sweeping this alarming problem under the rug," Rep. James J. Florio (D, N.J.) protested. Florio sponsored the law requiring removal of asbestos in schools.

The Service Employees International Union, which represented building-service workers, rejected the report, saying it did not even require building owners to inspect for asbestos and inform workers about it.

John Welch, president of the Safe Buildings Alliance, a group of former makers of asbestos products, said the EPA should set health standards for asbestos, as it did for other contaminants, so building owners and tenants could decide whether removal was necessary or conditions safe.

In a related development the Supreme Court let stand without comment April 25, 1988 a ruling denying asbestos manufacturers the opportunity to present evidence during a pretrial hearing that they were unaware of asbestos hazards when they sold their products. The court had declined numerous appeals on asbestos-related cases.

THE SACRAMENTO BEE

Sacramento, CA, September 11, 1988

Four years ago the Legislature set aside $24 million to help school districts pay for asbestos removal. That's not nearly enough, of course, to take care of the problem in the Sacramento City Unified School District and all of the other 3,600 public schools in California that were built between 1946 and 1972, before the cancer risks of using asbestos for insulation were known. But the money could have helped make a start.

According to the state auditor general, however, the Deukmejian administration can't figure out how to get the funds to the schools that need them most. After four years of bureaucratic bungling, the Department of General Services has managed to approve applications from local districts for only about a third of that money. And that doesn't mean the cash will ever actually be delivered.

The applications that have been approved are all 3½ years old, after all. Many of them, it turns out, have been forgotten or abandoned by the schools involved. In some instances the districts simply gave up waiting for the state to come through and got the money they needed elsewhere. In other

cases, the initial surveys that the schools used to estimate how much asbestos work they had to do are now so far out of date that the original applications no longer describe the real extent of their need.

But that doesn't mean the money's going to be available for somebody else. Once it's been assigned to a district, the bureaucrats prefer to wait and see whether the district can come up with matching funds rather than go through the hassle of formally withdrawing the funds and moving it along to another district where it might do some good.

And don't bother sending in any new applications for the $16 million the department hasn't assigned yet. They've got such a big backlog of applications that they don't expect there'll be any money left by the time they get finished reviewing them.

There's a final Catch 22 involved here. The Legislature and the governor didn't bother appropriating any more money for asbestos cleanups this year. The reason? According to the state's accounts, there's still all this money lying around just waiting to be used, so why spend any more? Why indeed.

The Providence Journal

Providence, RI, June 21, 1988

The recent proposal of the Occupational Safety and Health Administration to enact stricter standards on toxic chemicals is to be applauded. If instituted, it is certain to have a beneficial effect on millions of Americans who come into contact with toxic chemicals in their work.

Indeed, according to OSHA estimates, as many as 500 deaths a year may be avoided, and as many as 50,000 incidences of disease. These would include cancer, liver and kidney ailments, and cardiovascular and respiratory diseases. Although the cost to employers is estimated to be around $900 million a year, many support the proposal — and one of the reasons they do is that they stand to benefit from an estimated 500,000 fewer workdays lost due to these illness.

Those are striking figures which, if anywhere near accurate, will have an important effect on the health of the nation's workforce. More than 3.5 million Americans are currently believed to be getting more exposure to some toxic chemicals than the new standards would permit.

The thrust of the proposal is to allow OSHA to make generalized, rather than case-by-case, assessments of chemicals, and the limits for worker exposure. The system of judging on an individual basis has delayed decisions on many chemicals; in the past three years, OSHA has established final standards for only 20. OSHA chief John Pendergrass has admitted to the agency's inability to keep up with the number of chemicals in the market.

With the new procedure, OSHA has been able to propose reductions in the exposure limits for over 200 chemicals (for which standards were last set in 1968) and, for the first time ever, propose standards for 168 chemicals.

There have been criticisms, specifically from labor, that the proposal puts too much attention on minor chemicals, and not enough on others that are more dangerous because of either greater toxicity or greater use. Yet the critics have failed to mention what these specific chemicals might be.

It seems more likely that OSHA, in using information from both the American Conference of Governmental Industrial Hygienists, and the National Institute for Occupational Safety, has carefully considered the most commonly used chemicals that pose health risks.

THE ANN ARBOR NEWS
Ann Arbor, MI, February 5, 1989

It's churlish of the federal government to mandate asbestos removal from schools and then fail to provide adequate financial support for that purpose.

It appears the feds simply have no idea of the magnitude of the problem in making available only $47.5 million in grants nationwide for asbestos removal. The cost of asbestos removal in Michigan alone could run into the "hundreds of millions of dollars," according to Richard Claflin of the state education department.

The state's Department of Public Health is sifting through hundreds of plans for asbestos removal submitted from some of the state's 1,750 local school agencies, public and private. The number of school buildings containing asbestos is nearly 6,000. Not all these buildings are unsafe, but because children are more susceptible to health damage from asbestos inhalation than adults, exposure to the substance must be minimized.

So if the carcinogenic properties of asbestos make it a genuine health hazard, why doesn't the federal government match its concern for prompt removal with the necessary dollar support to see that it's done safely and efficiently? Asbestos removal is expensive. Throwing the problem back onto the schools works a severe hardship on the smaller, less affluent school districts.

Willow Run is one of those districts. Superintendent Joe Yomtoob said removal of asbestos from the system's schools "will be very, very expensive. It will be bad news."

The irony is that school district leaders thought they were doing something good way back when in ordering their buildings protected with this fire retardant. And they *were* doing something good because no one could foresee the health risk that asbestos represented.

It's wasteful for school districts to spend a large proportion of their tax-generated revenues on asbestos removal when they ought to be spending their money on education. Isn't that the purpose of schools?

If George Bush intends to be the "education president" as he promised, here's an opportunity to show his stuff. Since the removal mandate was of federal origin, it's reasonable to expect more help from Washington than a paltry $47 million will cover.

DESERET NEWS
Salt Lake City, UT, May 19/20, 1988

Since the federal government can extend the deadlines for cities to meet clean-air standards and for Detroit to produce fewer gas guzzlers, shouldn't it also extend deadlines for school districts to inspect their facilities for asbestos?

Plenty of school administrators think so. Across the nation many local districts despair over meeting an Oct. 12 date by which they are supposed to identify buildings with crumbling asbestos and submit a maintenance or cleanup plan. They could face fines of $5,000 a day if they fail.

It's not that districts don't want to abide by federal law. There simply may not be enough qualified people around to conduct the inspections in time, let alone begin whatever cleanup may be needed. Then there is the financial wallop to consider: up to $200,000 just for an inspection and maintenance plan.

An irony is that the crisis was entirely predictable and is due in part to the intransigence of the Environmental Protection Agency.

The EPA issued its asbestos inspection rules last Oct. 20, trumpeting them at the time as a "tough" solution to the asbestos hazard. Indeed they were: tough, unrealistic, and irresponsible.

Federal officials should have known what a difficult, costly burden they were dumping on resource-strapped local districts. They also should have known that a one-year deadline virtually guaranteed hastily arranged inspections at inflated prices.

The rules failed to establish the level of airborne asbestos requiring remedial action. The EPA simply refused to set a standard. Precise measurement of airborne asbestos is required only after the cleanup, not before.

As a result, Scripps Howard News Service reports, visual inspections are the rule. School officials rely in part on the opinion of approved private contractors and other experts, whose interest may be served by exaggerating the threat and hence the scope of necessary cleanup.

As one critic noted last fall, EPA's rules could "drive schools toward unnecessary removals of asbestos-containing materials, increase exposures to building occupants, and spark a future wave of asbestos-related disease among abatement workers (whom everyone acknowledges are most at risk)."

Congress should require that the rules be revised.

AKRON BEACON JOURNAL
Akron, OH, June 2, 1988

EVERYONE agrees that flaking asbestos in a school or anywhere else is a health hazard. Once asbestos fibers are inhaled, they're in a person's lungs to stay. Ultimately, asbestos can cause cancer.

The National PTA and other groups are justified in their concern about asbestos in the schools. And they're right to push for better policies addressing the problem.

But what isn't justified is a frenzied approach to asbestos inspections and removal plans. Unfortunately, that's what could happen in districts across the country.

School boards are facing an Oct. 12 federal deadline to finish inspecting schools — for the second time — and complete their long-term plans for removing asbestos. School districts can be fined $5,000 a day for being late.

Some would argue that if districts are rushing to meet the deadline, it's their own fault. They've known about the deadline since Congress imposed it in October 1986.

While that's true, it doesn't tell the whole story: Namely, that schools already have been inspected once, as required by a 1982 law, that the total cost of the second round of inspections could approach $20 million in Ohio alone, and that schools are left to come up with the money largely on their own.

The second, more detailed inspections are meant to identify flaking asbestos missed or ignored in the earlier inspections, and identify asbestos covered by floors and ceiling tiles.

Districts that can show their buildings were inspected properly once shouldn't have to spend money on new inspections until they can correct the more serious problems found in the first inspections. Further, schools built in recent years shouldn't need inspecting at all.

In Stow, for example, the school board spent $15,000 inspecting the new Stow-Munroe Falls High School, even though school officials already knew asbestos had not been used in construction.

It seems like a lot of money is being misdirected, as if schools have money to misdirect.

Of course, the removal of any dangerous substance from a school should be a priority. And at least locally, many districts, including Akron's, have made honest efforts to find asbestos and set aside money each year to remove it, starting with worst problems. The Akron school board alone has spent $1.5 million to remove asbestos from three schools.

The government's role should be more as a helpmate. For starters, schools could use federal aid to remove dangerous asbestos already found. Further, second inspections shouldn't be required unless there is reason to believe they are needed.

It doesn't make sense at this time to rush to complete new inspections in all districts, to find, in many cases, asbestos that isn't posing any immediate threat. Congress should rethink the wisdom of the upcoming Oct. 12 deadline.

Part IV: Global Issues

The living world, or biosphere, stretches delicately around Earth. Sixty miles down beneath our feet, the globe is white hot, at 5,000 degrees Fahrenheit. Ten miles up above our heads, the air is too thin and cold for survival. In between, the green world flowers, richest around the tropical zones where the ice age glaciations have never reached. Here, in the tropical forests and the shallow sunlit seas and reefs, much of the Earth's living wealth of species is concentrated.

The Earth's green cover is a prerequisite for the rest of life. Plants alone, through the alchemy of photosynthesis, can use sunlight energy, and convert it to the chemical energy animals need for survival. It was the emergence of photosynthesizing algae in the oceans that first released free oxygen into the atmosphere – a cataclysmic event for existing life, but a precondition for present existence. The ocean microflora still supply 70% of our oxygen, and this in turn maintains the protective ozone layer in the upper atmosphere. The oceans act as a "sink" for carbon dioxide from the air.

Plant cover provides the basis of all food chains, mediates water cycles, stabilizes microclimate, and protects the living soil – the foundation of the biosphere. Legions of soil micro- organisms, and of anaerobic microbes in the shallow muds of the sea floor and swamp, work ceaselessly to recycle decaying matter back into the nutrient system.

Within this life realm, every organism is linked, however tenuously, to every other. Microbe, plant, and animal, soil dweller and ocean swimmer, all are caught up in the cycling energy and nutrients from sun, water, air and earth. This global exchange system flows through various transport mechanisms, from ocean currents to climate patterns and winds; from the travels of animals to the processes of feeding, growth and decay. Information, too, flows through the biosphere – reproduction transfers the store of genetic coding to new generations and creates new experiments; learning and communication occur between individuals. And throughout the life zone, change and diversity, specialization and intricate interdependence, are found at every level.

The "balance of nature" is a basic concept of ecology. Though the concept has been entertained by all known tribal peoples since time immemorial, in modern times it is very much part of an "organismic" or "holistic" view of the world that stresses the equilibrium and stability to be found in nature.

This section of *Our Poisoned Planet* ties together disparate elements of ecological destruction and the movement to reverse it. From ozone layer depletion, rain forest destruction, and ocean dumping to endangered animals, whaling and the Greenpeace movement, the tangible but often unseen connections between man and his fragile environment are put into sharper focus.

125

Greenpeace Moves to Forefront of Worldwide Ecology Movement

The ecological movement in the United States developed in the late 19th century. Ecologists distinguished themselves from conservationists, with whom they nevertheless had much in common. Ecologists response to the perceived ecological crisis of the times was a more fundamental one. It was man's whole attitude to our relationship with the natural world that had to change. Man was an integral part of nature, and if he destroyed nature then he destroyed himself too. (See pp. 130-133)

Today, as in the 1890s, ecologists differ from conservationists and environmentalists in that they see the ecological crisis as a fundamentally social one. Setting up national parks and adopting stringent pollution control legislation, they argue, is not enough to solve the ecological crisis; more fundamental changes are required changes in the way man views his basic relationship with the natural world, changes in the ways society is organized in its basic social and economic goals. What is required, they urge, is a new ecological world view – and a new ecological society geared to the maintenance of a stable or "steady state" relationship with the natural world. Such ideas underlie the ecological movement and are reflected in the platform of green parties in different European countries.

The environmental group Greenpeace, founded in 1971, has moved into the forefront of the ecological movement with a form of environmental protest known as direct action. It is derived from the Gandhian technique of "Satyagraha" or "non-violent passive resistance." The method's success relies on the fact that it forces an opponent to defend his position. Pacifism and clear argumentation also allow the protester to retain an advantage. Undoubtedly, too, one of the reasons for the success of direct action has lain in its ability to capture the attention of the media. Photographs of the Greenpeace inflatable rafts steering themselves in between whalers' harpoons and their targets have a great deal of appeal, and they bring seemingly remote issues directly to the public's attention. Through direct action, Greenpeace has played a major role in ending commercial whaling, nuclear dumping at sea, and the hunting of seal pups. However, use of the technique is not restricted to Greenpeace alone. Similar actions have been taken, less flamboyantly perhaps, all over the world and it would be no exaggeration to say that Satyagraha and its variants represent one of the main forms of protest in the 20th century.

The News and Courier

Charleston, SC, November 17, 1986

When a band of terrorists sponsored by France mined and sank the environmentalist "warship" Rainbow Warrior in a New Zealand harbor, a full accounting was instantly demanded and eventually received.

The environmentalists, supported by world opinion, were successful in having the terrorists put in jail.

Reaction both among environmentalists and world opinion to a terrorist attack on some Icelandic whaling vessels has been quite different — different obviously because this time it is environmentalists themselves who are the terrorists. The outrage of the government of Iceland matches the outrage of the government of New Zealand, but elsewhere it's strictly ho-hum.

Those who made the attack — a Briton and an American — are portraying it as an inevitable, acceptable consequence of what they see as indifference on the part of Icelanders to demands for an end to whale-killing.

Political terrorists should not be allowed to take refuge in self-righteousness and neither should environmental terrorists. Both will view such permissiveness as a license to extend their operations. Just as Arab terrorists are being called before the bar of justice in Europe and French terrorists have been held responsible for their actions in New Zealand, the environmentalists who call themselves "sea shepherds" must expect to be viewed as criminals.

That is the view that Prime Minister Margaret Thatcher may take, says one member of the terrorist team. If so, it should be no surprise if the United States government takes a similar view. Terrorism is terrorism. Both countries are committed to dealing harshly with it.

The continuing slaughter of whales is pushing a valuable form of life close to extinction. Those who call themselves environmentalists, as does The News and Courier, watch with abhorrence. Two wrongs never make a right, however. A world that witnesses, day in and day out, the futility of sending a terrorist to do a diplomat's job should be as quick to condemn terrorism in behalf of unfortunate whales as it is to condemn terrorism in behalf of unfortunate people.

THE SAGINAW NEWS

Saginaw, MI,
October 23, 1985

The timing, as Greenpeace members have noted, is curious. Dow Chemical Co., though, has taken the forthright, even necessary step of apologizing for spreading personal information about one of the environmentalist group's members.

With the trespassing trial of Melissa Ortquist and two other Greenpeace protesters about to begin, Dow published a full-page advertisement saying it made a "serious error" in passing on a report that Ortquist had a venereal disease.

It sure did, in several ways. The blunder cost the company the credit it had won for its quiet and restrained handling last summer of a typically provocative Greenpeace protest. The rumor was based on a jail blood test which later was proved inaccurate. The circumstances by which the company gained the information are murky. In any case, Dow had no right to it, and the Midland County Prosecutor's Office properly is investigating.

Despite the suspicions of Greenpeace, we would hope the apology is more sincere than a damage-control tactic as the protesters go to court. Probably there's an element of that; "The next few days will see substantial media exposure and publicity" during the trial, Dow President Hunter W. Henry said in the ad. But the injury against an individual was done some time ago. Why wait until now to say you're sorry?

Not often, though, do major corporations "come clean" — Greenpeace might use a different phrase — in a company town, on an internal foul-up. Henry said Dow has learned from the incident. If nothing else, that is the responsible position after an irresponsible episode.

THE SAGINAW NEWS

Saginaw, MI, June 29, 1988

The tactics of Greenpeace, whose motley crew of globetrotting environmental purists rolled through the Saginaw Valley last weekend without rocking the local boat too much, often come off as publicity stunts and little else.

Its primary targets can be ill-chosen. Midland's Dow Chemical Co., for instance, operates under stringent pollution-control regulations. In its crusade for pristine water and air, Greenpeace has not decided whether it is fish or fowl, so to speak. To eliminate all the by-products of industry is to eliminate industry, and it's dishonest for Greenpeace to pretend otherwise. Not everything people do is harmful to them and other living things.

But all that begs the issue. For years, the idealistic itinerants of Greenpeace have been saying, like environmental Chicken Littles, that the sky is falling.

Well, what about the sky? It is sending down precious little rain. The world below is more hothouse than greenhouse, its verdant hues changing to mottled shades of choking, infertile dust. Nature is telling us something. But what?

This is, on the record, no ordinary drought.

The Parchbelt now cuts a swath across the nation's midsection. The grain drain countdown in Iowa figured the losses at 4 percent for each day without significant rain.

Commodity prices have soared with the temperatures, with dire implications for the cost of feeding the family and the family pet, too.

The Mississippi River, 10 to 20 feet below normal, has stranded barge traffic. Near the delta, its flow is so sluggish that salt water is defeating the current. States along the banks want to float a loan of Great Lakes water. But lake levels, too, are falling, and the trend may accelerate through evaporation caused by climatic warming.

In Washington, scientists told Congress last week that global temperatures are at their highest level since measurements began 130 years ago. The four warmest years on record have occurred since 1980, and 1988 may be the steamiest yet.

In Toronto, at a conference of experts from 40 countries, Norwegian Prime Minister Gro Harlem Brundtland told delegates that the situation raises "crucial questions of planetary survival."

More chickens? Perhaps. Whether or not the dreaded "greenhouse effect" has taken hold, trapping in the sun's heat and suffocating the Earth, is not yet certain. Just a couple of years ago, the fear was not that the Great Lakes would dry up, but that their rising waters would wash away the shorelines. The jet stream fluctuates, as do the Pacific currents. Nature is unpredictable. Disaster is not inevitable. This drought is not necessarily permanent.

But it would be at least foolish, and could be disastrous, to ignore danger signals, what U.S. Sen. Timothy E. Wirth of Colorado termed "compelling evidence that the global climate is changing."

To stop or slow the process, Dr. James Hansen, a NASA scientst, called for a 40 to 50 percent reduction in consumption of fossil fuels. Burning coal and oil releases carbon dioxide and other gases, creating the greenhouse effect.

Another chicken? In Senate testimony, Hansen did not claim to be 100 percent certain that the global warming was unnatural — only 99 percent.

What's bad for the birds and fish so beloved of Greenpeace, then, may be even worse for people. For our own self-preservation, we need to seek new, better, cleaner ways to fuel industry and modern society. In global perspective, the crusaders and the climatologists are delivering the same message: Have a care for the earth — and the sky — before the chickens come home to roost.

DAYTON DAILY NEWS

Dayton, OH, November 21, 1986

Conservationists and environmentalists take justified pride in persuading through moral and practical argument. They don't need a bunch of saboteurs representing them.

Saboteurs is the only classification for the Sea Shepherd Conservation Society. Their members used guerrilla tactics to wreck a whale-oil plant and two whaling boats Nov. 8 in Iceland.

Their protest was against the whaling industry in Iceland, which is killing the great sea mammals despite a ban on the slaughter. The whalers are sailing through a loophole in the treaty that allows for some whaling for "research."

As objectionable as the dying industry of whaling may be, conservationists don't need destructive allies. Moral crusades are put at risk when they are waged with immoral behavior, whether it is a so-called pacifist trying to burn down a draft-registration office or anti-abortionist bombing an abortion clinic.

Greenpeace — another activist conservation group that opposes whaling — is able to protest and frustrate whalers and seal-hunters, but without committing violence or destroying property. For those with a militant bent, this is the better approach.

FORT WORTH STAR-TELEGRAM

Fort Worth, TX, November 19, 1986

Terrorist acts are terrorist acts, regardless of the perceived nobility of the cause behind their commission or the extent of damage the acts may cause.

That being the case, Iceland is fully justified in regarding as terrorists the environmental extremists who sabotaged the country's whaling industry and in seeking to have them extradited for prosecution.

Two of Iceland's four whaling vessels were sunk in Reykjavik harbor last week and an isolated station where whale byproducts are processed was wrecked.

The Sea Shepherd Conservation Society, an international organization that opposes whaling, accused Iceland of whaling illegally and claimed responsibility for both actions.

That no one was injured in the attacks is fortunate but hardly diminishes the seriousness of what occurred and certainly does not make the sabotage any less of a crime.

That is true also of the conservation organization's motives. Whales have become an endangered species, and legitimate efforts to spare them deserve both public and private support. But the sinking of ships and wanton destruction of private property do not qualify as "legitimate efforts."

Citizens of Iceland, which is largely dependent upon the fishing industry for its economic survival, were outraged by the sabotage and rightfully so.

Iceland officials have tentatively identified two members of the Sea Shepherd group as the men responsible for the crimes. If they are caught — and Iceland's friends in the family of nations should lend whatever assistance they can in that endeavor — they should be prosecuted.

To do any less only invites further terrorism.

The Boston Globe

Boston, MA, January 30, 1987

Josef Stalin once dismissed the chances for a communist revolution in Germany by saying one must trample the grass in the public parks to make a revolution, and the Germans would be too fastidious. Hitler's National Socialist revolution made Stalin's witticism a sick joke. It also made the world hypersensitive to any sign of political disorder in a nation addicted to order.

When scrutinized for portents of order, last week's West German elections appear ambiguous. In the matter of power, nothing changed. The conservative coalition of Christian Democrats and their junior partners, the business-oriented Free Democrats, received a clear, if diminished, majority.

The floundering Social Democrats, with 37.2 percent of the vote, did not come close to replacing the government of Chancellor Helmut Kohl, nor did they surmount their internecine conflicts and ideological confusion. Yet, the Social Democrats did better than polls had predicted. Their reward for avoiding disaster may merely be a protracted leadership struggle between the centrist and left-leaning factions.

The big winners were that band of environmentalists, pacifists, neutralists and vegetarians known as the Greens. Their tally rose from 5.6 percent in the last election to 8.3 percent. Their magnified voice in the Bundestag scares Bonn's allies. French Socialists interpret the neutralist credo of the Greens as a new form of a distressingly familiar German nationalism.

The Greens are as diverse as the forms of discontent with post-industrial, capitalist civilization. Some want to undertake a long march through the established institutions; others wish to avoid the compromising that comes with participation in the political process.

Though elements of this protest movement hold conflicting views about the Soviet or American threat, and though some favor and others reject an eventual alliance with the Social Democrats, they are united on certain objectives – the closing of nuclear power stations, disarming of the police and abolition of intelligence agencies.

The Greens' crusade to defend air and water against the depredations of the profit motive can be healthy for the Germans and their political system. The sure sign of a stable political order in Germany would be a demonstrated capacity to tolerate certain forms of disorder.

The Des Moines Register

Des Moines, IA, September 16, 1988

Greenpeace brought its headline-grabbing environmental show to Muscatine, staging an "environmental action" against Monsanto Co., which makes farm chemicals, among other things.

Greenpeace's action included blocking a public road and an attempt to block the discharge of wastes from the Monsanto plant into the Mississippi River. Four of their number were arrested when they refused to remove trucks blockading the plant gate.

A spokesman for Greenpeace said state and federal laws don't go far enough in protecting rivers from chemicals. If so, the answer — as another Greenpeace spokesman said — is to report problems and seek legislation.

That's advice Greenpeace should heed. Instead it exhibits no compunction in breaking existing laws. Greenpeace holds no moral or ethical license to place itself above the law. The problem poses hard enough questions without being impassioned by cheap-shot guerrilla theater.

Darrell McAllister, chief of the Surface and Groundwater Protection Bureau, Environmental Protection Division, Iowa Department of Natural Resources, said Monsanto conforms to Iowa regulations on chemical discharges.

The department has put limits on several potentially hazardous substances Monsanto dumps — from biochemicals that use oxygen to decompose, which in excess amounts could thus endanger fish, to ammonia, herbicides and chlorine. Monsanto conforms.

Meanwhile, federal guidelines governing such discharges have not been put in final form.

His department has "a good working relationship" with Monsanto, McAllister said. "They keep us informed. . . . "

Greenpeace has done good work on the environmental scene, protesting the serious overharvesting of whales and publicizing the inhumane slaughter of seal pups, which are clubbed to death in infancy when their fur is still white, making it a favorite of the over-rich and overindulged.

But when Greenpeace or any similar organization goes beyond the bounds it does a disservice to the movement it professes to champion. The environmental movement has enough probems with its enemies without being tarnished by the dramatic but ill-considered actions of those who claim to be its friends.

Lincoln Journal

Lincoln, NE, February 19, 1989

The toe bone's connected to the foot bone, the foot bone's connected to the ankle bone, and so forth, on up the joined human assembly, as we all were taught years ago, and which self-examination easily confirms.

The world's ecosystem is like that. One can concentrate on isolated bits and pieces. Virtually all fragments and subsets are fascinating and even worth lifetime careers in scientific study. Nevertheless, there are tangible connections, i.e., Pacific Ocean surface temperature variations of a few degrees cause summer droughts thousands of miles away, cause food supplies to tighten, cause animal life to diminish, etc.

It is only when the parts are put together that the environment can be viewed more in the balanced round. And in terms of political activism, environmental concerns can be cross-supported.

The idea that the whole of activism in changing public attitudes and policies might be greater than the sum of specialized parts seems to be catching.

Earlier this month, in Washington, three environmental groups announced a merger. The trio hopes to encourage still more public attention (there can never be enough) to such things as global pollution and the greenhouse effect. Coming into an alliance were Friends of the Earth, the Oceanic Society and the Environmental Policy Institute.

Roughly the same coalition impulse is alive and at work in Nebraska. Last week, eight environmental or environment-related groups announced they would associate in a coordinated, action-oriented council.

Such an approach is worthwhile. In the end, all groups are in the same boat being tossed by changing or threatening environmental winds. Shoot, everybody's in that boat, except that many passengers are foolish and refuse to recognize storm signals.

The Boston Globe

Boston, MA, August 22, 1989

There is a growing sense among environmentalists – particularly those who keep an eye on long-range trends and worldwide impacts – that this summer's unparalleled string of disasters and near disasters has finally captured the attention of both opinion leaders and the public.

If that sense is correct, there may yet be a chance – albeit a slender one – to mitigate some of the impending catastrophes, and perhaps even to reverse them.

The trick, of course, will be to keep that attention focused after the leaves turn and past the first frost.

For now, there are the vivid images of the drought-seared Midwestern fields and the waste-smeared Northeastern beaches. The phrase "greenhouse effect" has entered the common vocabulary, and most people can give a decent explanation of what happens when the ozone layer is depleted.

"All of a sudden, everyone has woken up," says a member of the World Resources Institute staff who notes that in 15 years' experience he cannot remember "a period like this – when environmental problems were so apparent to so many people."

Arguing that "the global threat is noticeable in a way it never was before," a senior scientist at the Environmental Defense Fund thinks "we are entering an era where we can make great strides to save the planet."

Talk of "saving the planet" is of course the big picture – and one that is not only worth pursuing, but must be pursued.

However, there is little likelihood that the planet will be saved if there is not a commitment to save the back yard, the neighborhood, the community, the state.

Calls for worldwide action to "do something" about the greenhouse effect will sound like a way to evade personal responsibility if there is not action to reduce the dependency on fossil fuels for energy generation and transportation.

And worries about medical wastes washing up on the beaches will be just so much hooey if there is no pressure put on local and state officials to insitute recycling programs for household waste.

The Globe and Mail

Toronto, Ont., November 12, 1988

Even when the mind accepts that there are good witches, the heart somehow isn't in it. Okay, so we're old-fashioned, but there is something far more interesting, more *authentic* in a witch cackling over a cauldron of unspeakable ingredients than one who edits a newsletter about holes in the ozone layer.

Eye of newt and toe of frog,

Wool of bat and tongue of dog.

Now *there* was a set of morsels to challenge the imaginative tastebuds, particularly when served on a blasted heath in the middle of a blasted storm. But what has happened to the *hors d'oeuvre* horrors of yesteryear? Gone. Witchcraft now comes in sanitized, sin-free containers. Give us that ole time religion, it was good enough for us. (No, sorry, the Saturday morning cartoons just don't fill the gap.)

What appears to be the wholesale abandonment of evil by contemporary witches upsets the order of a world in which good and evil strike a rough balance. Recent disquieting reports from the United States suggest that things are going from bad to better. A Wall Street Journal reporter sends this account of the goings-on at Selena Fox's coven in Brigham Township, Wis.:

"A chill wind howls through the woods here behind her farmhouse. Arms raised, she and her audience of three shake gourd rattles and chant exhortations to the elements — earth, air, fire and water. Tonight the moon will be full." Ms Fox offers a prayer to the west wind: "May humankind stop polluting the waters and may all ocean dumping stop."

Suddenly, for us, the spell is broken. We who were all set for eye of newt and toe of frog have been offered a glass of milk and a cookie.

Is there no reliable indecency left in the world? Are we doomed to live in an era when witches beat their cauldrons into woks and drop all their demons off at day-care centres before going out to fight for the beluga? Is there, in fact, any point to being a witch if you are going to behave like the woman next door? (We beg rehabilitated witches not to write us on this. These are rhetorical questions.)

To give further insight into contemporary witchcraft, we pass along the information that wiccan, as it is known to adherents, enjoys a following of more than 100,000 people in North America, male and female, and that this number includes bankers (we knew it! we knew it!) and a tugboat captain. Furthermore, and we have no explanation for this, computer company employees, at least in the United States, make up the biggest single occupational group.

We have come a long way from the days of *Malleus Maleficarum,* a fifteenth-century document sometimes known as the Witch Hammer, published by two inquisitors. They were invested with authority by the Pope to "proceed to the just correction, imprisonment and punishment of any persons . . . who have abandoned themselves to devils, incubi and succubi."

Now that's more like it. In those days they had a proper sense of good and evil. They knew tongue of dog from a gallon of font water, and rejoiced in the task of showing sinners the error of their ways, often with extreme prejudice. The other side was armed with spells, leather amulets, gruesome statues, skulls, potions and fetishes. To say nothing of incubi and succubi. How on earth could they have lost?

But nothing we say could illustrate better the deterioration of witchcraft into just another religion than the complaint of one of its leading lights: "A lot of pagans only come out on Halloween."

LAS VEGAS REVIEW-JOURNAL

Las Vegas, NV, August 22, 1988

So now the environmental terrorists have struck near the borders of Nevada.

Last week, the U.S. Forest Service announced that about 100 trees in the Tahoe National Forest, about 40 miles west of Reno, had been "spiked" by environmental extremists.

Forest Service officials said steel railroad spikes had been driven into the trees in an apparent protest against the planned sale of 202 acres of trees to lumbering concerns. The spikes not only reduce the value of the lumber, they also represent a severe danger to loggers whose power saws can break apart, hurtling metal shards that can maim or kill.

Heretofore, the spiking of trees was limited to northern California and Oregon. But the extremists have apparently branched out.

We, too, would like to see the natural environment protected, not ravaged. But there is a right way and a wrong way to go about protesting environmental policies. The extremists who spike trees known darn well they are endangering the lives of loggers. If these people are apprehended, they should be prosecuted to the law's fullest extent.

Greenpeace Ship Sunk; Inquiry Leads to French Secret Service

In early July 1985, the protest vessel of the environmental group Greenpeace, docked at Auckland, New Zealand, was rocked by two explosions. The ship sank within minutes, and a photographer for the nonviolent group was killed. Twelve other persons escaped unhurt. The *Rainbow Warrior* had been due to set sail within a week for Mururoa to protest French nuclear testing in the South Pacific. (See pp. 126-129)

A man and woman were arrested July 23 in connection with the explosion, and later found to be agents of the French secret service. The French government, as controversy mounted over "l'affaire Greenpeace," launched an official inquiry at the direction of President Francois Mitterand. The result of the inquiry was a report, issued Aug. 26, that cleared France's Socialist government and the intelligence service of involvement in the attack, although it confirmed that six French citizens held or sought by New Zealand police in connection with the ship's sinking were agents of the French intelligence service.

The 29-page report concluded that the six had been sent to New Zealand to gather information about Greenpeace and infiltrate the organization but had played no role in the sinking. The report was written by Bernard Tricot, a former adviser to President Charles De Gaulle, at the direction of Premier Laurent Fabius. Prime Minister David Lange of New Zealand immediately denounced Tricot's report as "so transparent it could not be called a whitewash."

French politicians and the press universally criticized the report as well. Lange said France should recall its New Zealand ambassador for consultations, but that New Zealand would take no action until French Premier Fabius commented publicly on the report. Fabius made a brief statement Aug. 27 indicating government acceptance of the report's conclusions but also said Tricot's report had revealed "important shortcomings" in the intelligence services that would be investigated.

THE ATLANTA CONSTITUTION
Atlanta, GA, September 24, 1985

The essential truth is finally out: Trained underwater sappers, under orders from Paris, blew up an anti-nuclear organization's vessel, killing one of its crewmembers, in another sovereign nation's waters. Seldom does the world witness a so-called secret operation as arrogant and shortsighted in its conception and as egregiously clumsy in its execution and aftermath.

At the very least, French President Mitterrand owes Greenpeace and the government of New Zealand a sincere apology. More to the point, he owes them and the citizens of France a far fuller explanation than the bare elements contained in Sunday's terse admission by Prime Minister Fabius.

Just who gave the orders to sink the Rainbow Warrior? Why were Mitterrand and his chosen investigator so easily flummoxed into thinking, so they say, that the damning evidence pointed elsewhere than France? And why are the agents who carried out the brutal deed to be absolved, as Fabius directed Sunday, of their duty to refuse what was so clearly a criminal command?

Mitterrand has an unholy mess on his hands. His government is instituting a new investigation that is colored at the outset by the stain of its first pitiful inquiry. He must establish civilian control of France's hyperactive secret services, traditionally managed by a military class suspicious of his socialist predilections. He has lost hard-to-retrieve ground in his struggle to keep his parliamentary majority in next spring's elections to a rightist opposition that seems less concerned about the evil inherent in the Rainbow Warrior bombing than about France's being caught in the act.

In addition, the affair has played into the hands of those he has labeled enemies of France, those who would dare challenge Paris' determination to continue testing nuclear weapons in its little corner of the South Pacific. Rather than being intimidated, Greenpeace is filled with new resolve and is preparing an even larger flotilla of boats to harass the tests, scheduled to resume soon on the tiny Mururua atoll. And New Zealand's Prime Minister David Lange gains new stature in the eyes of his Pacific neighbors in his campaign to create a nuclear-free zone there.

Considering the damage, Mitterrand has good reason to wonder whether the plotters behind *l'affaire* Rainbow Warrior were indeed loyal sons of France.

The Boston Globe
Boston, MA, September 25, 1985

French Prime Minister Laurent Fabius declared Sunday that intelligence agents, acting under orders from top officials in the government of President Francois Mitterrand, did indeed sabotage the Rainbow Warrior. France thus admitted guilt for what Mitterrand himself has called "an absurd crime."

The operation was a crime because an innocent civilian aboard the Greenpeace vessel lost his life, because the French state treated nonviolent protesters like wartime combatants, and because French officials authorized terrorist acts in a foreign country.

New Zealand's prime minister, David Lange, was right to condemn the mining of the Rainbow Warrior as "a sordid act of international state-backed terrorism." He might have added that the French authorities responsible for the crime were behaving like terrorist regimes such as those of Libya's Col. Khadafy or Syria's Hafez Assad.

When Khadafy orders his agents to liquidate Libyan dissidents on French soil, or when Assad orders his Palestinian foes cut down on the streets of Paris, French authorities display the same justifiable indignation Lange has expressed in response to their sabotaging of a ship in a New Zealand harbor. In all such acts, reasons of state become excuses for gangsterism.

Of course, gangster regimes in Damascus or Tripoli never denounce the crimes of their security forces, as the French have done. No Syrian or Libyan newspaper would dare try to expose those responsible. By contrast, the French press has relentlessly pursued the truth, piercing government secrecy and reminding free people everywhere of the crucial distinction between open and closed societies.

An article in the French newspaper Le Monde forced the Mitterrand government to abandon all efforts at a cover-up. The writers warned that their sources were not "disinterested." Some were tied to the conservative opposition and were seeking to have an effect upon the legislative elections next March. Others were linked to the Mitterrand government and were hoping to divulge the truth quickly in order to save the Socialists from the "snares of falsehood."

The partisan ambitions of the conservative sources, the protective motives of the Socialist sources, the skeptical impulses of independent journalists – these are the indispensable components of a pluralistic society. A crime such as the mining of the Rainbow Warrior may be committed by a democratic government, but the countervailing powers which define a genuine democracy make it hard to hide that crime.

Le Monde said the purpose of the mining was to "launch a warning to Greenpeace." It was absurd for the paranoid admirals and generals who conceived the operation to think it would silence the antinuclear movement or in any way serve French interests. It was also absurd to think they could hide the truth from a democratic society.

DAYTON DAILY NEWS

Dayton, OH, September 25, 1985

Le watergate: After months of weaving a "not us" tissue of lies over French press reports of the sinking of Greenpeace's flagship, Rainbow Warrior, in New Zealand, French Premier Laurent Faubius has admitted publicly that France was behind the bombing that killed a photographer onboard.

Laurent Fabius

The admission was an attempt to save the political hide of French President Francoise Mitterrand. There's an election next year that could strip Mr. Mitterrand of his Socialist majority in the National Assembly if this issue isn't over by then.

This admission isn't enough, however. As President Richard Nixon learned from Watergate, half-truths won't stop the whole truth from surfacing. Mr. Mitterrand should cooperate with the French assembly in a thorough investigation of the mess and let the full details air before the voters.

Premier Faubius recently said that agents should not stand trial since they were acting under orders of the French government. Oh? Does this mean official hit men are not responsible for their hits? Exactly who, then, is responsible?

When all else fails, come clean. On this matter, Mr. Mitterrand is well advised not to ask Mr. Nixon for advice.

The Hartford Courant

Hartford, CT, September 25, 1985

The Greenpeace affair, as Alice might say, grows curiouser and curiouser. But it is some distance from Wonderland, and the truth, as French Prime Minister Laurent Fabius said over the weekend, "is cruel."

Indeed it is; it is also difficult to discern.

In July, a vessel belonging to Greenpeace, the anti-nuclear environmental organization that had been protesting French military exercises in the South Pacific, was blown up in the harbor at Auckland, New Zealand, killing a crew member. Two weeks later a French couple was arrested by New Zealand police and charged with murder. The French Embassy in Wellington denied the involvement of the French government in the bombing.

However, in August, as press allegations of official French involvement multiplied, the prime minister ordered an official inquiry into the sinking. The report was issued three weeks later and absolved France of responsibility. Mr. Fabius then ordered yet another investigation to look into "shortcomings" the earlier probe had revealed about the French intelligence service.

It is now revealed that the Greenpeace ship was bombed with official sanction. Mr. Fabius admits that French intelligence agents, acting under orders, sank the boat. The defense minister has resigned and the head of the intelligence service has been dismissed.

Questions are now accumulating faster than answers. Chief among them is, what did President Francois Mitterrand know and when did he know it? We are not likely to learn anytime soon. The survival of the Mitterrand government hangs in the balance, and this affair has been as much a political gift to the center-right opposition in Paris as to New Zealand's publicity-conscious prime minister, David Lange.

Moreover, the French intelligence service is well-known for its brutal tactics and devotion to secrecy. Mr. Fabius, who has promised yet another inquiry, refuses to reveal the names of the agents who carried out the deed: "It would be unacceptable," he says, "to expose military personnel who were only obeying orders and who have at times carried out very dangerous missions for the country in the past."

Fair enough. It is incumbent on France, however, to reveal all that can be known about this extraordinary episode, and to punish those found culpable. Greenpeace has discovered that it is dangerous for private organizations to tamper with a sovereign nation's concern for its security. But France must be reminded that there are ways to respond to protests such as those conducted by Greenpeace, and murder is not one of them.

Newsday

Long Island, NY, September 25, 1985

From the moment the antinuclear protest ship Rainbow Warrior was sunk last July, there was widespread suspicion that the sabotage was the work of French agents.

The ship, operated by the environmentalist Greenpeace organization, was in New Zealand to lead a protest against a French nuclear test in the South Pacific. A Greenpeace photographer was killed in the explosion that sent the ship to the bottom.

But as quickly as suspicions about official complicity were expressed, they were vigorously denied by the Socialist government of President Francois Mitterrand. And a commission that investigated the incident exonerated the French authorities completely.

Gradually, though, details of the sinking were pried loose by journalists. French agents were implicated. The defense minister resigned and the head of France's secret intelligence agency was fired. And last Sunday, Prime Minister Laurent Fabius, confirming an article in Le Monde, confessed that the ship had been sunk by French agents acting on orders from the French government. He said the official commission that had cleared the government had been lied to.

"The truth in this affair is cruel," the French prime minister said. "But what is essential is that it be clearly and totally established, as I have committed myself to doing."

Sadly, Fabius' candor stopped short of a crucial point: identifying those in the government responsible for the sinking. If he is to fulfill his noble commitment to the truth, he has several critical questions to answer:

Who gave the orders to sink the ship? It's hard to believe that Fabius doesn't know the answer to that one by now. And presuming they were not given by Mitterrand himself, didn't the president know about them?

Or are French agents scurrying about the world engaging in what New Zealand's prime minister, David Lange, has called "state-backed terrorism" without the French president's knowledge or consent?

The truth about the sinking may be cruel, as Fabius remarked, but thus far it remains effectively obscured by official cover-ups and vanished documents.

The most perceptive observation yet made about the sinking of the Rainbow Warrior was Mitterrand's. In a rare comment on the incident, from which he has tried desperately to remain aloof, he called it "an absurd crime." It surely was that. How could responsible French officials believe that lethal violence was anything but an absurd response to a peaceful protest against atmospheric nuclear testing — something both the United States and the Soviet Union long ago renounced?

If the French government's damaged credibility — and France's reputation as a country governed by reasonable leaders — are to be repaired, Fabius and Mitterrand will have to go a good deal further than simply confirming newspaper reports that the Rainbow Warrior was sunk on orders from someone in the government. They'll have to identify those responsible and accept the political consequences that ensue.

THE TAMPA TRIBUNE

Tampa, FL, September 26, 1985

IT IS STILL unfolding but the story of the sinking of the Rainbow Warrior is setting up a classic confrontation between morality and reality.

It would be nice to believe that morality will win. It won't.

The Rainbow Warrior was the flagship of a fleet operated by the international environmental action organization, Greenpeace, best known for its colorful confrontations with such evildoers as whaling ships.

The enemy picked for the Rainbow Warrior this summer was somewhat larger. The ship was to lead a flotilla of vessels to the South Pacific atoll of Mururoa to protest a French nuclear test there.

Rather than put up with such inconvenience, on July 10 the French sank the Rainbow Warrior at anchor at Auckland, New Zealand. Two French operatives, both military officers, are charged with arson and murder. A Greenpeace staff photographer was killed in the incident.

And it was just announced Tuesday that two French intelligence agents were arrested by the French themselves for leaking information about the crime to the Paris press.

Following a few months of cover-up, French officials from the defense minister through the head of intelligence are taking a fall — not for doing wrong but for getting caught — beneath the wrath of Prime Minister Laurent Fabius. If you've never heard of the prime minister it's because he's trotted out only for such special occasions.

Hands-on President Francois Mitterrand has called the episode an "absurd crime" but displays no intention of going back to the subject if he can help it. He has sent his condolences to David Lange, New Zealand's new and actively anti-nuclear prime minister. That Mitterrand knows, will solidify Lange's recent victory.

So that Lange doesn't take his idealistic success too seriously, the French president has visited Mururoa to remind all, and especially New Zealand, that the test is part of France's *force de frappe* independent nuclear policy, and as such is vital to French national interests.

Still, New Zealand has the guilty parties. But does it? The recent truth-telling in France revealed that the pair in custody, while hardly innocent bystanders, did not actually commit the crime. That was done by mine-placing frogmen who are long gone from New Zealand. So are other French operatives in New Zealand, at least those New Zealand admits to knowing of.

Thus the pair, who posed as a Swiss tourist couple, may be accessories or conspirators, which makes for a difficult prosecution under New Zealand's Anglo-Saxon code of justice. In addition, France has not yet retaliated to expose New Zealand's intelligence operatives around the world, or even those just in the South Pacific. Such individuals might be an embarrassment to Lange. Because while it may be noble to spy on France, it may not be nearly so to spy on Australia.

If it all sounds like a bad novel that's because it's the stuff bad novels are made of: real life carried, as Mitterrand said, to the absurd.

After more posturing, the French officers will likely stand in the dock, be convicted, serve some symbolic time and then be quietly released in exchange for some unfortunate secretaries at an obscure New Zealand consulate in an African dictatorship that speaks French.

And soon we will hear France and New Zealand mutually decrying terrorism in the world.

Plus ca change, plus c'est la meme chose.

The Idaho STATESMAN

Boise, ID, September 25, 1985

The French government's admission that it was responsible for blowing up the Rainbow Warrior is at once satisfying and shocking.

French Premier Laurent Fabius admitted the "cruel truth" that French intelligence agents blew up the Greenpeace anti-nuclear protest ship July 10, an act of official terrorism that took the life of a Greenpeace photographer.

The finger had been aimed at France for 10 weeks because the Rainbow Warrior was about to lead a protest flotilla into a French nuclear-testing site. But France steadfastly denied its complicity, although admitting it had sent agents to spy on the ship.

What remains are the key questions of, "Who knew what, and when did they know it?" The government officials who ordered this heinous act, which killed a Greenpeace photographer, have not been named. Mr. Fabius proposed creation of a special parliamentary commission to investigate.

Belated honesty does not diminish the wrong done by the French government or bring back the life it took. Terrorism committed by nameless fanatics repulses civilized people. Terrorism committed by a Western democracy is unconscionable.

THE LINCOLN STAR
Lincoln, NE, September 24, 1985

France has determined that its own national security forces were responsible for the July 10 sinking of the Rainbow Warrior while it was docked in New Zealand. The ship belonged to the anti-nuclear activist group known as Greenpeace.

A Greenpeace photographer was killed in the mining that sunk the craft. Greenpeace had intended to sail the ship into South Pacific waters near French Polynesia where France had scheduled a nuclear test.

The actions of French security forces are another example of governmental justification of any means for a supposedly proper end. Beyond that, the government initially denied any connection with the clandestine sinking of the Warrior.

WERE IT NOT for the French press, that denial might have been the end of things. President Francois Mitterrand, in a letter ordering changes in security operations, said:

"It is necessary to note that the press has made known new elements whose accuracy we were unable to appreciate because of the failure of the competent authorities to obtain necessary information. This situation cannot last. The moment has come to proceed without delay to changes in the personnel and, in cases of need, in structure."

Does Mitterrand's reference to change in structure suggest that cases such as the Rainbow Warrior sinking should not again take place? There is no immediate answer to that.

Greenpeace campaign director Steve Sawyer is pressing for an admission of government responsibility in the wake of the security disclosures.

He wants the government to say not only that its own security forces were involved in the illegal sinking of the Warrior but that the action is lamented and such tactics will not be repeated.

FIRING OF the top two executives with the General Directorate for External Security is a clear government admission of its involvement but not a declaration of new direction in the future. Also, it is lame of the government to plead a lack of ability to appreciate what had happened until such was pointed out in the press.

If the press were able to so quickly establish responsibility, how could the government have failed to do so? That leaves a question that might conceivably be traced to still higher government authorities.

It can be said for the situation that France has the fundamental values and freedoms that encourage an ultimately truthful determination of matters. In nations within the Russian sphere of influence, those values would never be allowed to surface.

The Honolulu Advertiser
Honolulu, HI, September 24, 1985

There is a war of wills going on between France and New Zealand over the July sinking of the Greenpeace ship Rainbow Warrior.

After weeks of heated denials, French Prime Minister Laurent Fabius admitted over the weekend that his government ordered the bombing by its secret service officers. He did not say who gave the orders or if President Mitterrand was aware of the planning. He did say France would not send those who took part in the attack to New Zealand to stand trial.

NEW ZEALAND, which has been caustically critical of Paris from the beginning, is stepping up the pressure. Prime Minister Lange now demands reparations from France after calling the bombing an example of state-sponsored terrorism.

France, in fits and starts, appears to be moving closer to an official apology. But it is unlikely that French contrition will quiet the affair. The scandal has built enough pressure that in time it might seriously weaken, and perhaps undo, the Mitterrand government.

Whether that happens depends on what Mitterrand knew of the bombing plan. French press reports, which so far have proven accurate, say General Jean Saulnier, chief of the general staff, approved funding for the operation when he was Mitterrand's chief military aide. Saulnier and former Defense Minister Charles Henru, who resigned amid reports he was involved, are both close associates of Mitterrand.

The scandal is being called a French Watergate, and there are parallels. A relatively small event is mushrooming into a major crisis; high officials are resigning; there are charges of incriminating documents being destroyed.

IT IS not clear whether the French president stumbled into this mess or whether it is a crisis of his own doing. But if developments continue as they have for the past 10 weeks, it may not make any difference. Political realities may make it all but impossible to govern effectively.

Knickerbocker News
Albany, NY, September 30, 1985

The sinking of the Rainbow Warrior, the vessel sponsored by the anti-nuclear group called Greenpeace, raises instant parallels with America's Watergate scandal a decade ago.

Today, it's French President Mitterrand who is being asked by the press what he knew about French agents' plan to sink the ship off New Zealand, and when. In the 1970s, the Washington press corps was asking Richard Nixon what he knew about a third-rate burglary at the Democratic National Committee, and when.

The parallels are interesting but distracting. It would be wrong to conclude that the Rainbow Warrior, like Watergate, is a catch word for another coverup that might bring down a government. There's a much more important, and distressing, lesson to be learned — one involving breaks in the chain of command.

Those breaks can often lead to political disaster. In the French scandal, someone at some level of government apparently approved a mission that so far has cost one ship and the life of a crewman, and may bring down Paris' Socialist government in next year's election. Similarly, various aides at various levels in Richard Nixon's re-election campaign made unilateral decisions that forced a defensive president from office.

The cost in honor and office, however, is nothing compared with the loss of 269 innocent lives two years ago, when a Soviet plane shot down a South Korean jetliner that strayed into Russian airspace. How is that tragedy similar to Greenpeace and Watergate? Because once again, a subordinate made a crucial decision unilaterally. Moscow has acknowledged that a field commander, not the Kremlin, had given the order to fire — an order that could well have touched off a superpower conflict.

World leaders are vulnerable to their subordinates' rash judgment. But so far they haven't grasped the implications of breaks in command. Rather than face the need for urgent repairs, they opt to defend them or, worse, to cover up the gaps with lies.

Until they realize how self-defeating those tactics are, the potential for global holocaust remains chillingly real. Today an overzealous intelligence agent orders a protest ship sunk. But what happens if, in some future year, one superpower opens fire on the other's nuclear fleet — on the orders of a subordinate?

The Seattle Times
Seattle, WA, September 24, 1985

AT FIRST it seemed too easy — a gross oversimplification — to call the sinking of the Greenpeace protest ship Rainbow Warrior in New Zealand last July a "French Watergate." But consider the record, as it now stands:

■ First, an official report absolving the French government of responsibility for the crime, which claimed one life.

■ Next, high-level resignations in Paris.

■ Then, an admission, by Premier Laurent Fabius last weekend that yes, French secret-service agents, acting under orders, had in fact committed the atrocity.

■ Also, an admission by Fabius that secret-service officials had lied to the author of the earlier report absolving the government. But no names of the higher-ups who gave the orders to blow up the protest ship are given.

■ Finally, key documents in the investigation are missing — the French "gaps in the tapes."

A single question now advances inevitably to the forefront: What did President Francois Mitterrand know, and when did he know it?

Garbage Barge Travels 6,000 Miles

The barge *Mobro 4,000*, loaded with 3,168 tons of trash from Islip, N.Y., on tow behind the tugboat *Break of Dawn*, traveled 6,000 miles in search of a dump before returning in failure to Gravesend Bay off Brooklyn, N.Y. May 16, 1987. (See pp. 148-153)

During the odyssey, which became a symbol of the nation's mounting waste disposal crisis, the garbage was spurned by at least five states and three countries – Mexico, Belize and the Bahamas.

The travail began March 22 when a landfill for Islip, N.Y. refused the gigantic load. It was acquired by entrepeneur Lowell Harrelson, founder of National Waste Contractors Inc., who hoped to drop batches off at various spots for lucrative methane extraction.

First stop was Jones County, N.C., but when the noisome cargo reached Morehead City, N.C. officials ordered the barge away.

New Orleans was approached next, but Louisiana officials intervened at Venice, finding a potential health hazard. They also complained about federal indifference to the situation.

The barge wandered out into the Gulf of Mexico, tracked, eventually, by federal environmental officials aboard a Coast Guard cutter. But the *Mobro 4,000* reached the Yucatan Peninsula, where Mexico turned it away, reportedly, putting its navy on alert to ensure clean riddance. Then the vessel returned to Belize, back around to Cuba to the Florida coast and the journey back to New York.

In New York, state and city officials huddled and negotiated until July 10, when an agreement was announced by Thomas C. Jorling, commissioner of the state Department of Environmental Conservation, to have the 3,168 tons of trash burned in a Brooklyn incinerator, reduced to 400 tons of ash, trucked back to the Islip municipal landfill, and dumped.

The London Free Press

London, Ont., May 5, 1987

Could there be a more dramatic symbol of the growing garbage crisis than a barge sitting off Key West, Fla., with 2,800 tonnes of unwanted garbage from a New York state community?

The barge has been at sea six weeks, travelling 8,000 kilometres in an unsuccessful search for a place to dump. It has been rejected by at least four American states, and driven from the Mexican coast by gunboats.

In Toronto, Councillor Richard Gilbert observed that "we are already in serious trouble. By the year 1990 we'll have no place to put half of our garbage." In Middlesex County, London Township administrator Albert Bannister's estimate is slighty more cautious — five to 10 years.

It's a dual problem of collection and disposal. As more garbage is created, it becomes harder to find dump sites. Strict environmental regulations and interminable efforts to satisfy the objections of residents who don't want someone else's garbage make the search for disposal sites increasingly expensive and time consuming.

In Oxford County, it took 11 years and $2.2 million of taxpayers' money to open the landfill site at Salford; one year later, there is talk of looking for a replacement.

The best solution would seem to lie in recycling and incineration.

Recycling profits have been too modest to stimulate interest, however, and the habits of a throwaway are hard to break. Incineration in the form of energy-from-waste projects, has in turn provoked opposition because of fears of increased air pollution.

The pressures of time and space demand compromise but nobody wants to be the first to accept it.

Los Angeles Times

Los Angeles, CA, May 3, 1987

The wandering garbage scow with 3,186 tons of New York trash (actually, bound bales of industrial and business waste) is a pungent example of society's problem of disposing of its leftovers. The barge left Long Island on March 22 and has been at sea ever since in search of a place to unload. Various states and the countries of Mexico and Belize have said no. Mexico even ran the scow off with its navy.

Garbage is nothing to sniff at, but the nation has other trash that poses an even more difficult problem. The highly radioactive waste from nuclear power plants, for instance, still is piling in ponds at each plant site, waiting for the nation to come up with a solution. Also a critical problem, in large part because there is so much of it, is low-level nuclear waste. This refuse includes relatively benign material like the gloves used by radiation specialists at hospitals and tools employed by the nuclear industry. But it has to be isolated and sealed away somewhere so that, among other things, concentrated radioactive waste cannot leak into groundwater supplies.

Fortunately, California seems to be nearing a solution for the disposal of its considerable low-level nuclear stuff, which the state now sends to Washington state. A 1980 federal law requires that states work out compacts among themselves so that just a few will not become dumping grounds for all the others. After four years of deadlock, the Deukmejian Administration and Assembly Democrats have agreed on a compact with Arizona that would provide for the two states' low-level waste to be deposited in the California desert for the next 30 years and in Arizona for the ensuing three decades. The bill, sponsored by Assemblyman Steve Peace (D-Chula Vista), deserves approval by the full Legislature and the governor.

In the meantime, US Ecology Inc. of Newport Beach is proceeding under a 1985 contract with the state Department of Health Services to locate the best and most acceptable site for the low-level waste dump. After rather extensive searching, and consultation with local officials, the firm has settled on three potential sites: in Ward Valley 25 miles west of Needles and in Silurian Valley 15 miles west of Baker, both in San Bernardino County, and in Panamint Valley 30 miles north of Trona, in Inyo County. Technical studies at the three locations will take another year. US Ecology plans to choose one of the three early next year. Final approval by the state would not occur until completion of an environmental-impact report and formal hearings.

The selection of US Ecology was controversial in that the three firms preferred by the state backed out of the bidding because they were not willing to accept the financial and legal risks involved. The state had no choice but to accept US Ecology's proposal. The firm had been penalized for improper actions in several other states in past years, but an official in Kentucky said that the state also was to blame for leaking and contamination there in the 1970s, adding, "We didn't know back in the early days what we know now." William E. Prachar, president of US Ecology's parent firm, said, "You pay a price for being a pioneer."

US Ecology does have the greatest experience in this infant business of radioactive waste disposal, and the firm's painstaking work so far in California is impressive. The proper desert site should eliminate any risk of contamination of water resources. It will be up to the state, of course, to monitor the disposal program carefully.

This is a beginning, although a promising beginning, for just one of California's nagging disposal problems. But it is better than wandering aimlessly at sea for a solution.

Post-Tribune
Gary, IN, May 15, 1987

It's easy to laugh at the plight of the barge full of garbage from Islip, N.Y., that has been sailing the seas since March 22 looking for a place to call home. It has been turned away by six states and three nations during its 5,000-mile odyssey.

Now things get more curious as Islip, which set the garbage afloat because there was no more room at its dump, has decided to take it back. It seems the town has signed an agreement with the state to expand the landfill, under strict guidelines. The barge owner, however, doesn't want to give the garbage back. Even though the caper is costing him $6,000 a day, he still wants to find a place where he can bury the trash and use it to produce methane gas.

The episode isn't funny, though. The wandering barge has become a symbol of the nation's growing garbage problem.

At least 27 states are facing severe landfill problems, according to a recent Environmental Protection Agency survey. More than half the cities in the country will exhaust their current landfills by 1990, says Neil Seldman, director of waste utilization for the Institute for Local Self-Reliance, an organization that provides cities with technical assistance on waste disposal. Northwest Indiana is fast using up its landfills, plus fighting the added problems created by a massive supply of hazardous waste.

The EPA estimates that 130-160 million metric tons of municipal solid waste are generated in the U.S. each year. By 2000, that figure is expected to be 290 million tons. That's a lot of garbage.

Americans are well on the way to producing garbage faster than they can get rid of it. This is something cities and states shouldn't ignore until it reaches the crisis stage, as is the tendency with so many problems. If they do, they will end up with a lot more than a pile of garbage, including a major public health hazard.

Some cities are wisely exploring alternate disposal methods, since the fear of groundwater contamination makes sites for landfills scarce. Several are building plants to turn waste into steam or electricity. Some are having success with recycling processes. These methods have drawbacks, too, mainly involving air pollution and cost — or trying to change people's basic habits. Environmentally, recycling promises the most prudent long-term results, but convincing people to separate their garbage might take years to accomplish.

The best answer may end up being a combination of things. But it is something that all cities and states should be discussing seriously — and now.

Roanoke Times & World-News
Roanoke, VA, May 21, 1987

ISN'T IT only right that the barge laden with 3,100 tons of New York garbage has returned home with the trash? Should the refuse have been taken in by any of the six states or three countries where the barge owner sought to put his cargo ashore?

The tug Break of Dawn, which was pushing the barge, hadn't planned to wander from port to port. Had there been room in the hometown landfill, the voyage wouldn't have been necessary. The barge left the Long Island town of Islip on March 22, bound for a methane-generating waste-disposal site in Morehead City, N.C. Local officials refused to allow alien garbage on their soil, however, and the barge then began its odyssey on the high seas. Before the scow headed for home, its cargo was also rejected in Alabama, Mississippi, Louisiana, Texas and Florida, as well as in the Bahamas, Mexico and Belize. The message was the same one given to children: Don't expect anyone else to clean up your mess.

Part of the problem in getting rid of the garbage was the amount. A few hundred pounds of refuse might have been slipped into the sea when no one was looking, but 3,100 tons is a different matter. That's more than four times the amount of rubbish taken to the Roanoke Valley landfill every day. Although Environmental Protection Agency officials got some heat in Congress for not doing enough to solve the garbage barge's dilemma, EPA staffers did track its movements and did remind the owner that dumping at sea is illegal.

The political resistance wherever the barge sought to dock illustrates the severity of the space shortage for solid-waste disposal that communities are facing. The barge could only be invited back home after the town of Islip negotiated an agreement with the state to allow expansion of its landfill. And the town's charge for taking the load will be $240,000.

A recent survey conducted for the EPA found that 27 states are facing severe landfill problems. The Roanoke Valley has no immediate space shortage, but the landfill shared by Roanoke City, Roanoke County and Vinton could be filled in five years. That time may be extended, however, if a pilot recycling project involving 1,000 homes in the county is successful. Recycling materials can be expensive, but it is becoming essential in solid-waste disposal.

The garbage barge arrived in New York harbor last Saturday, but has run into more legal trouble. A plan to unload the trash in Queens and truck it to Islip was resisted by some Queens officials, who feared a health hazard. Amazingly, the barge's crew maintains that their cargo doesn't stink, and the waste has been pronounced harmless by environmental officials. However, it has been sitting in the sun for weeks, and Queens President Claire Shulman believes it probably contains tropical insects and vermin.

While the details of getting the trash ashore are being worked out, the barge has become a tourist attraction in New York harbor. Fortunately, such a sight is still rare. But if communities don't act to expand landfill space before their need is critical, barges of garbage could be seen more frequently.

There would be no point in pushing them out to sea, though. The recent voyage makes it clear that no one wants another's trash heap. The only alternative is to work on refining the disposal process — recycling a greater amount of waste and processing the rest more efficiently.

Wisconsin State Journal
Madison, WI, April 23, 1987

As we marked the 17th annual Earth Day, a 3,000-ton bargeload of rotting garbage was floating somewhere in the Gulf of Mexico on its way to . . . who knows? Perhaps to wash up on the shore of your favorite Caribbean beach.

The garbage came from Islip, N.Y., which is running out of landfill space and no longer accepts commercial solid waste. So the good folks in Islip dealt with the problem by loading their garbage on a barge and hiring someone to tow it away. Out of sight, out of mind.

But people in North Carolina, Alabama and Louisiana said they weren't interested in accepting any New York garbage, thank you, they had plenty of their own. So the barge wound up in the Mississippi River delta, where it cooked in the Cajun sun until it was finally ordered out of Louisiana waters.

Islip, N.Y., is not the only community in the country that is running out of places to put its garbage. The same thing is happening in Dane County and Madison, where a "not-in-our-back-yard" attitude toward landfills may soon have frustrated officials weighing the pros and cons of barges on Lake Mendota.

A case in point is a proposed landfill on Madison's far East Side. Everyone from Madison Mayor Joseph Sensenbrenner to Dane County Executive Jonathan Barry to the head of the Greater Madison Chamber of Commerce opposes this particular site — and for what appears to be good reason.

The landfill at the corner of Pflaum and Vondron roads is adjacent to a growing residential area and across the street from land earmarked for business development. It's close to wetlands, and the city water utility would have to rethink plans for a new well nearby. The neighborhood is virtually unanimous in its opposition.

But if not there, where? What is the difference between a community like Islip, N.Y., which puts its garbage on a barge without knowing where it might wind up, and Madison, which puts its garbage on street curbs without pausing to think we're running out of places to bury it?

By the time the next Earth Day rolls around, let's hope we have thought more as a society about recycling, producing consumer goods that are biodegradable and responsible use of landfills. "Not in my back yard" means someone else's back yard suffers.

UNIVERSAL PRESS SYNDICATE.
5/5/87 THE PHILADELPHIA INQ.

Rockford Register Star

Rockford, IL, April 24, 1987

What does the Rockton Village Board have to do with Islip, N.Y., and 3,000-ton barge load of garbage last seen wandering in the Gulf of Mexico? The answer, quite simply, is the concern — growing everywhere — for solid waste disposal.

This week, Rockton Board members heard arguments for and against joining other communities in Winnebago and Boone counties in a commitment to an incineration plant. That's the best-known present alternative to placing all solid waste in a landfill. It's going to be costly, board members heard; perhaps $37 a ton to incinerate garbage as opposed to the present $12 a ton for simply dumping it into a landfill.

But just how costly is that?

We hope the residents of Rockton, and of other communities still pondering alternatives to joining the incineration generation, were watching a national news development this week. In the Gulf of Mexico, about 17 miles off Grande Isle, La., 3,000 tons of increasingly odorous garbage originating in Islip, N.Y., still were hunting a final resting place.

Islip had a problem: There was no more landfill space available for its solid waste. So the community contracted with an Alabama firm to haul the garbage away by barge. The contractor thought he had a spot in North Carolina. No sale. Then another possible deal in Louisiana fell through.

When last heard from, the Alabama man's tugboat captain was looking for places to dump his barge load in Central America or the Caribbean.

The residents of Islip, N.Y., and an Alabama contractor now know that garbage no longer is either easy or cheap to get rid of.

The time for tough choices has come for northern Illinois and to communities like Rockford, Belvidere and Rockton. The final choice — it probably won't be barge loads of garbage down the Rock River — won't be cheap. But we no longer can afford landfilling anything more than the residue of incineration.

THE DAILY HERALD

Biloxi, MS, April 21, 1987

What's so special about 3,000 tons of garbage that it holds a spot in the daily news for days? It's not the garbage that's making the news, it's the fact that nobody wants it.

The barge carrying the stuff has become a modern Flying Dutchman, doomed to sail endless seas if landlubber politicians have their way about.

The good people of Islip, N. Y., don't want it. They're the ones who shipped it off. Folks in North Carolina, in Alabama and in Louisiana don't want it either. Lowell Harrelson, the contractor hired to get rid of the trash, doesn't want it either, unless he's still being paid by the day, a doubtful situation.

Where will the garbage finally come to rest? The latest destination seems to be somewhere in the Caribbean, in a country not so environmentally conscious or politically pressured that it can't bury one more load of garbage.

The gypsy journey of the garbage barge has served one worthwhile purpose, though. It has made everyone aware that the earth is not a landfill of infinite capacity.

Other solutions must be found for disposing of solid waste, solutions such as in Moss Point, where waste is burned to make steam and the steam is sold to an industrial plant. In New Jersey just this week, a new law requires residents to separate materials such as glass, aluminum cans and newspapers from their household trash. It is a comprehensive statewide recycling program aimed at saving dwindling landfill space, cutting garbage disposal costs and helping protect natural resources. Oregon and Rhode Island have similar recycling programs.

The day of unlimited garbage burials at sea or in landfills is fast passing. Today, recycling is in in New Jersey, Oregon and Rhode Island. Look for it soon in other states.

Edmonton Journal

Edmonton, Alta., May 16, 1987

Unlike the Flying Dutchman, the Break of Dawn will not be condemned to roam the seas forever.

Its incredible journey is almost over. Soon the barge of garbage that nobody wanted will ooze back to Islip, N.Y. — the port it left more than a month ago.

With its cargo of 3,100 tonnes of gargabe rejected by three countries and six states, the Break of Dawn seemed destined to wander the seas. But it was spared when Islip inked a deal with New York state allowing the town to expand its dump.

Islip officials promise a warm welcome. "We're probably going to put some yellow ribbons outside the gates of the landfill to welcome our garbage back," said Islip supervisor Frank Jones.

It's a fitting end to the smelly saga. While the rest of the world lets out a collective sigh of relief over the barge's fate, residents of Islip enjoy what may be their last breath of fresh air for awhile.

Honolulu Star-Bulletin

Honolulu, HI, May 7, 1987

The odyssey of the New York garbage scow that nobody wanted, reported in this newspaper yesterday, highlights a problem that affects Hawaii, too. Like most states, Hawaii has trouble finding ways to dispose of its garbage.

The National Solid Wastes Management Association figures that Americans generate about 220 million tons of garbage annually, of which 95 percent is buried in landfills. But about one-quarter of American cities have less than five years' space left in their landfills.

The problem in Hawaii, of course, centers on Oahu, which has the bulk of the islands' population but little available land. City officials have warned for years that they were running out of space for landfills.

The solution arrived at was the garbage-to-energy plant. After years of controversy over a site, Campbell Industrial Park was selected and a contract for construction of the plant negotiated.

But environmental groups are fighting the project on the ground that provisions to limit air pollution from the plant are inadequate. The city and the state respond that the additional equipment sought by the critics would make only a minimal improvement in air quality at exorbitant cost.

It's difficult to say when this dispute will be resolved. But if it gets tangled up in the courts, the delay may run into years. In the meantime, the garbage disposal problem can only get worse. And that will probably present more serious environmental problems than any the plant itself could produce.

THE ANN ARBOR NEWS

Ann Arbor, MI, May 12, 1987

The saga of the garbage scow without a home may finally be playing itself out.

Ever since March 22, a barge filled with 3,100 tons of New York garbage has been on a slow 5,000-mile odyssey which took it down the Atlantic Coast and into the Gulf of Mexico. Currently, it is heading back north toward Islip, N.Y., where this floating piece of pungency originated.

In the meantime, six states and three foreign countries — Mexico, the Bahamas and Belize — rejected the baled trash. In that connection, the story has not been without its comic elements.

Mexico, alerted by the State Department that the garbage scow was heading its way, mobilized its coast guard to forestall the invasion of Yankee trash. Not to be outdone in the popular Latin sport of Yankee-bashing, neighboring Belize did likewise, calling on its 15-plane air force.

Johnny Carson suggested sending the smelly cargo to Iran as our nation's symbol of affection for the Ayatollah. At this point, the jokes start to wear a little thin.

The garbage without a home is a symbol all right, but not of our love for Iran. The barge symbolizes "U.S. policy on disposal of municipal and hazardous waste — totally lacking in direction or purpose," according to Rep. Thomas Luken, D-Ohio, chairman of the House subcommittee on transportation, tourism and hazardous materials.

Federal environmental inspectors, who surely must have held their noses in the process, said the baled trash is non-toxic. But that really is beside the point. Even if the barge contained 3,100 tons of waste ping pong balls, the fact remains nine major jurisdictions said, in effect, return to sender.

The nation generates an astounding 160 million tons of solid waste annually. The Environmental Protection Agency predicts that up to 27 states won't have any dumping space left by 1990.

The trash originally was turned away from the landfill at Islip because that facility is running out of space and no longer accepts commercial garbage.

That is terribly unfortunate but why didn't the city fathers of Islip foresee that contingency? Now, because it was "convenient" for Islip to barge away its troubles, the American taxpayer paid to have those federal environmental agents board the scow to see what was aboard, and if there should happen to be an accident at sea, you can be sure the taxpayer would get soaked there, too.

At one point the scow passed above Florida's reef line, prompting that state's officials to worry about protecting its natural resources.

The moral to the story of the barge without a country is that alternatives such as safe-burning incinerators and recycling plants are needed to take the place of landfills. Landfills take up precious real estate, a critical factor in the heavily populated Northeast.

The industries and communities which generate garbage are also responsible for how it is disposed. That is a responsibility one cannot refuse.

So saying, Islip had better open wide its golden gates for 3,100 tons of homing garbage. No one welcomes another community's discards or as one Michigan state senator put it so colorfully some years ago, "We don't want to drink somebody else's toilet flush."

More research into waste-to-energy technology still makes the most sense. The humor and the attention which have been focused on a humble garbage scow will have served a useful purpose if a growing national problem — our shrinking space for landfills — is given the priority it deserves.

Newsday

Long Island, NY, May 21, 1987

Enough, already! Now that everyone from Phil Donahue to Queens Borough President Claire Shulman has wrung about all the publicity they can from the itinerant garbage scow in New York Harbor, it's time to put a lid on this long-running farce.

State Supreme Court Justice Angelo Graci was right Thursday when he urged officials to "get this thing resolved." Minutes earlier, he had ruled that the 3,186 tons of trash on the scow pose no health hazard and lifted an order preventing it from docking at a transfer station in Long Island City. "The thing is," Graci said, "the garbage is there. It's got to be disposed of."

If only Mayor Edward Koch and Shulman would see it that clearly. Instead they continue to troll for political points. Koch insists that no matter what Graci says, the trash won't be unloaded until arrangements are made to ship it immediately to the Islip Town dump. That understandably doesn't sit well with the barge's owner: He finds Islip's $127,000 tipping fee onerous and would like

to dump his trash for free in a city landfill.

So what to do? State environmental officials suggest that Islip should forgo its fee so the yuk can be dumped without further delay. Why doesn't the state itself pick up the tab? After all, this *is* a crisis. And not just for the garbage, but for the crew that's been stuck with it since late March. As important as it seems to all of us to get the refuse ashore, it's of considerably more importance to the crew. When the garbage hits land, they get shore leave.

Panel Warns of Global Crises

Widening pollution and depletion of natural resources were "making survival ever more difficult and uncertain," the World Commission on Environment and Development warned in a global report issued in London April 27, 1987 after three years of study.

The commission urged drastic changes on a worldwide basis in government, business and industry, agriculture, energy and population. "We are unanimous in our conviction that the security, well-being and very survival of the planet depend on such changes, now," the report asserted.

The commission was created by the United Nations. Membership, drawn from 21 countries, included 22 economic, political and environmental experts, headed by Dr. Gro Harlem Bruntdland, Norway's premier and former environmental minister.

Their report called for a "new era of economic growth," one based on "sustainable growth" that kept "within the planet's ecological means" and was focused particularly on development of the poor nations.

The economy and environment had become completely intertwined, the commission said, and development, energy, food and pollution all were facets of a global crisis. The industrial revolution was rushing at breakneck speed and pushing environmental change so fast that assessment and control by science and statesmen were not keeping pace, the panel said. The problems were so gigantic and complex by this point, it said, that "the transition to sustainable development must be managed jointly by all nations."

The commission recommended that governments make all cabinet ministers, not just environmental heads, accountable for pollution and loss of resources flowing from their decisions. "Environmental regulation must be built into taxation, approval for investment and technology and foreign trade incentives," it said.

"Urgent steps" should be taken to control populations, the panel said. Currently, the world population of five billion contained more people than ever before who were hungry, illiterate and without sound homes, safe water or fuel for heat and cooking. Some 1.7 billion people lacked clean water, it was estimated, and 1.2 billion lacked adequate sanitation. By the end of the century, it was estimated, there would be 900 million illiterates in the world.

The food supply could sustain a global population in the 7.5 billion range, the panel estimated, but population was expected to stabilize in the next century at between eight and 14 billion people. At the 10 billion level, it said, food habits would have to be changed and farming efficiency vastly approved.

The commission's report took the West to task for being self-serving and even selfish in its attitudes toward food production. On the one hand, Western farmers were jeopardizing their future with intensive growing practices that were destroying the soil and the water supply and poisoning food with an excess of pesticides. On the other hand, the West demanded specialty foods from Third World nations, which should be producing corn, wheat, rice and other staple crops but were induced to provide meat, coffee, oranges and sugar for the richer nations.

"A global economic system that takes more out of a poor continent than it puts in" was the bane of the world's food system, the panel said. "Growth in many developing countries is being stifled by depressed commodity prices, protectionism, intolerable debt burdens and declining flows of development finance."

The report stressed that the world banking system was driving the Third World deeper into poverty by exacting debts that could not be met.

"Debts that they cannot pay force African nations to overuse their fragile soils, thus turning good land to desert," the commission said. Natural resources were being spent "to meet financial obligations to creditors abroad, not for development."

The commission said the international funding agencies should consider the long-term health of developing nations rather than repayment of short-term debt.

BUFFALO EVENING NEWS
Buffalo, NY,
April 15, 1987

WHAT KIND of world will we hand over to our children? Most people would like to think it will be a better place, but a recent global environmental study by the Worldwatch Institute, a Washington research group, points to alarming trends that threaten the world's future quality of life.

The study, "State of the World 1987," concludes that the environmental state of the world is not good. Even more sobering, mankind's destruction of some of the world's delicate ecosystems threatens to go beyond "thresholds" beyond which they cannot restore themselves.

The most pressing problems, the report said, are the destruction of the ozone layer in the atmosphere that protects us from the cancer-causing rays of the sun, the climatic changes caused by the burning of coal and oil and the loss of biological diversity through the advance of "civilization." Once gone, a species is lost forever.

The degradation of the environment is not some academic issue of interest only to scientists. The report cited the effects in practical terms. For example, in Central America, high population growth, deforestation, soil erosion and high energy costs have contributed to political instability that stirs deep international concern.

Efforts to solve such nations' economic problems by stimulating growth may create new dilemmas. The report noted that poorly planned development programs "are themselves beginning to threaten the health of the global economy." Environmentalists in the past have criticized the World Bank for encouraging development that is destructive to the environment. That is self-defeating in the long run.

While the food production in the world is growing, it is declining in some areas of Africa through soil erosion. Even in the United States, a sixth of our grain production comes from eroding areas or is based on diminishing water sources.

David Attenborough, a zoologist who presented the stunning series, "The Living Planet," on public television, has noted that the tropical rain forests, a great natural resource second only to the oceans, are being plundered recklessly. Every year, an area of forest the size of Switzerland disappears.

The threats to the environment are now coming so rapidly, the Worldwatch report says, that we are the first generation faced with decisions "that will determine whether the earth our children inherit will be inhabitable."

Individual nations can do much to halt mankind's assault on the environment, but obviously it is a global problem that must be addressed, as the report said, by the world's political leaders at the highest level.

The Dispatch

Columbus, OH, May 4, 1987

A just-released study takes an all-encompassing look at environmental problems facing the planet and holds out hope that progress in solving the problems can be made. If, that is, people and leaders of the world's nations are willing to face their responsibilities.

"The next few decades are crucial. The time has come to break out of past patterns," the World Commission on Environment and Development said in a report released in London and Washington. The 383-page report is entitled *Our Common Future.*

The 21-member commission was formed by the United Nations in 1984 to examine critical environmental and developmental issues and propose strategies for dealing with them.

"Our report . . . is not a prediction of ever-increasing environmental decay, poverty and hardship in an ever-more polluted world among ever-decreasing resources," the report said. "We see instead the possibility for a new era of economic growth . . . absolutely essential to relieve the great poverty that is deepening in much of the developing world."

The panel considered population growth, energy strategies, global warming due to atmospheric changes, man-made disasters and economic conditions that cause the destruction of tropical forests.

"Poverty itself pollutes the environment," the panel said. "Those who are poor and hungry will often destroy their immediate environment in order to survive: they will cut down forests; their livestock will overgraze grasslands; they will overuse marginal land and in growing numbers they will crowd into congested cities." The report noted that some poor countries have foreign debts that lead to overexploitation of forests, croplands and mineral deposits.

It also noted that military operations, international conflict, and neglect in handling powerful technologies such as nuclear energy, all contribute to the degradation of the planet's environment.

There are no easy solutions to the problems created by the sometimes out-of-control confluence of forces that result in "pollution." But it is important to know what the factors are and that something can be done to protect the world we live in.

Studies such as the one just released help to keep our attention focused on the responsibilities we have, not only to ourselves but to every generation that follows. We must take those responsibilities seriously

The Honolulu Advertiser

Honolulu, HI, April 14, 1987

ur world is still in bad shape.

In fact, human activities are driving many natural systems beyond critical thresholds of stability. That poses serious economic consequences and direct threats to the earth's future habitability.

That is not a new conclusion, or even an especially shocking one considering past environmental warnings.

But it is a vital statement — indeed, a warning. And it is a central point of an impressive new report in an annual series put out by the Worldwatch Institute, an independent non-profit research organization based in Washington, D.C.

"State of the World 1987" is a calm but concerned interdisciplinary look at and linked analysis of key environmental problems. This is the fourth in a series that has become required reading or reference material on such matters.

It reminds us that, at a time when we are understandably concerned about national and world political and economic problems, the physical world we all live in is still being blighted in ways that will haunt mankind.

It says that future growth in gross world products might cost more than it is worth, and that the impact of humans on the global environment is still being tragically underestimated.

A central conclusion is that simultaneous efforts in the world are needed to arrest the carbon dioxide buildup, protect the ozone layer, restore forests and soils, stop population growth, boost energy efficiency, and develop renewable energy sources.

Right now ending the nuclear arms race and reducing tensions are worthy priorities for the superpowers and their allies. But this book points up both the need and the hope for cooperation to save the world in other ways.

THE ANN ARBOR NEWS

Ann Arbor, MI, November 4, 1987

Earlier generations have always been concerned about the future. But has any generation had to confront such an enormous and complex array of challenges to determine the habitability of the earth as our generation faces?

A warning was issued recently by the World Commission on Environment and Development, a United Nations group, to the effect that the global environment and economy pose interlocking crises.

The report concluded that sustainable human progress can only be achieved through a system of international cooperation that treats environmental protection and economic growth as inseparable.

The report was prepared by 21 commissioners who conducted public hearings on five continents.

The outlook is not encouraging on the environmental front. The widespread burning of fossil fuels is believed to be altering earth's atmosphere. The industrial countries spew emissions of chlorofluorocarbon chemicals that threaten earth's protective ozone layer.

Each year, as many as 60,000 square miles of tropical rain forests are mowed down to make way for new towns, agricultural fields and industry. The deforestation process is probably the single biggest injury to earth's biological support system.

Species-depletion is appalling. The accelerating extinction of plant and animal species has prompted Paul R. Ehrlich, professor of biology at Stanford, to say, "Within the next decade, we will lose one-fourth of all of the kinds of organisms in the world. It is a threat to civilization second only to that of thermonuclear war."

Ehrlich is author of "The Population Bomb" which made such a splash in the '70s with its warning of the dire consequences of overbreeding. Today world population stands at 5 billion and it is growing by 87 million annually.

More than 90 percent of demographic growth occurs in the world's poorest countries, many of them projected to double in population size within the next two to three decades. These nations must, in turn, double all of their basic services just to keep pace with their present inadequate standards of living.

In just over half the world, the Worldwatch Institute said in its December, 1986, report, "time is running out in the effort to slow population growth by reducing birth rates. Unfortunately, not all national leaders recognize the basic relationship between population growth, ecological support systems and economic trends."

Even those who understand the links aren't always consistent in their support of effective family planning programs. A case in point is the U.S., traditionally a leader in the family-planning movement, but which in 1984 withdrew its total contribution to the International Planned Parenthood Federation.

Third World peoples are most vulnerable to the ramifications of high fertility rates. These include environmental degradation, joblessness, hunger, resource depletion, economic stagnation and urban crowding.

According to the Population Institute, a Washington-based public-interest group concerned with bringing the world's population and its environment and resources into a more equitable balance, many of these conditions "have already surfaced in areas of the developing world where a preponderance of evidence demonstrates that rapid population growth erodes or cancels out development gains."

What can be done to reverse the systematic extinction of species, the toxification of air, soil and water and all the other environmental ills which are afflicting us?

The U.N. group supplies some answers but not, of course, the will and commitment to order major policies into effect, nation by nation. For example, the U.N. commission said the environmental trends can only be reversed by solving the related problems of hunger, poverty, rapid population growth and the inequitable distribution of wealth.

A transfer of resources from the wealthy industrial countries to the poorer developing nations will be resisted with might and main; the Reagan administration has said as much and it can safely be concluded that *any* succeeding administration will say pretty much the same thing. Sharing wealth is no easier for nations than it is for small children.

A starter list of major undertakings for the benefit of humanity should include: (1) Putting technology to use for constructive and not destructive purposes. An example would be research into converting waste to energy and detoxification of lakes and rivers. (2) Channeling money away from the munitions industry and into productive economic development. (3) Applying a variety of effective modern contraceptives to the global population problem while promoting responsible family planning.

The Wichita
Eagle-Beacon

Wichita, KS, February 19, 1987

IF it were a Hollywood script it would make the greatest disaster film of all time — huge floods wiping out whole countries, forests denuded of vegetation and animal life, widespread hunger around the world.

Unfortunately, that is no screenwriter's fantasy but a plausible scenario of the future of the Earth. A new study, "The State of the World 1987," says overpopulation and pollution jeopardize the Earth's natural resources and could lead to worldwide disaster.

The report by the Worldwatch Institute, an organization active on global issues, notes that since 1950 world population has doubled, food production has nearly tripled and fossil fuel use has more than quadrupled. The result has put unrelieved pressure on the Earth's ability to tolerate pollution, sustain cropland and meet energy needs.

Most of the problem is that humanity is depleting the Earth's carrying capacity, and doing little to replenish and protect land, water and air supplies. One of the most immediate dangers is that carbon dioxide and other pollutants is theatening the earth's ozone layer, which protects the globe from harmful radiation from the sun. The "greenhouse effect" could melt some of the polar icecaps, raising ocean levels and flooding coastlines.

The world also is losing millions of acres of forestland, mostly for agriculture and resource development. The loss of forests could change climatic patterns and lessen the Earth's biological diversity through the destruction of rare plant and animal forms.

Easing the global environmental threat will require an unprecedented level of international cooperation. Population-control programs need to be expanded. Anti-pollution efforts must be accelerated. Agricultural methods should become more productive, without endangering land and water quality.

Worldwatch did well in documenting the dangers faced by the Earth. Humanity must be stopped from destroying its own nest.

The London Free Press

London, Ont., April 28, 1987

In an ominous warning of looming environmental disaster because of increasing pollution, overpopulation, soil erosion and environmental mismanagement, a United Nations report calls for what seems an impossible goal: international co-operation.

The World Commission on Environment and Development offers little in the way of new information and few recommendations beyond challenging governments to work together.

African drought, the greenhouse effect, Chernobyl nuclear disaster, overpopulation and grinding poverty, the destruction of lakes and forests by acid rain and industrial catastrophes such as Bophal are, lamentably, nothing new. Nor is the puzzle of how to prevent them.

Though a global approach sounds reasonable, national self-interest invariably intrudes.

American attitudes toward acid rain have made Canadians all too aware of that reality. Its environmental consequences have been established beyond all reasonable doubt, yet the Reagan administration continues to resist attempts to reduce sulphur dioxide emissions that drift across eastern Canada from coal-fired power plants in the midwestern United States. Political expediency at home takes precedence.

Nor is Canada free of hypocrisy. While vocally criticizing U.S. intransigence on acid rain, Canada continues to drag its heels on lead pollution. While the U.S. has set a level of 0.03 grams a litre of automobile gasoline, Canada persists in postponing adoption of a similar standard until 1993.

Our resistence to American efforts to ban the use of asbestos also contains a strong element of self-interest.

The UN report calls for cleaner economic growth, but the practical difficulties remain enormous.

Nowhere are they more obvious than in the tonnes of garbage produced daily by North Americans and the problem of finding some place to put it. The common, unhelpful response is: Not in my backyard. If neighborhoods in the same county can't agree on landfill sites and incineration plants, how can individual nations be expected to find common ground?

To take just a tiny example, Middlesex County administrator Albert Bannister figures only five to 10 years remain in which to find a solution to the county's garbage disposal or there will be a crisis. Multiply that problem globally.

As long as some states remain secretive, hopes for international co-operation remain slim. When Chernobyl blew up last year, the Soviet Union's two-day delay in admitting its technology had failed prevented many steps that might have protected Europeans from the radioactivity carried across their territory. Despite Mikhail Gorbachev's highly-touted new openness, it's possible that the Soviets — or some other country — could be equally secretive again.

In the Third World, where the problems are the immense, corrupt and inefficient governments seem unable or unwilling to face up to the problems themselves, least of all accept international interference. Poverty, as well, inhibits a long-term approach.

"Our report . . . is not a prediction of ever-increasing environmental decay, poverty and hardship in an ever-more polluted world among ever-decreasing resources," the world panel wrote. "We see instead the possibility for a new era of economic growth . . . absolutely essential to relieve the great poverty that is deepening in much of the developing world."

That goal is laudable but daunting.

The Toronto Star

Toronto, Ont., April 28, 1987

When our children are grown, they will live during a time when "the planet feels the heavier effects of acid precipitation, global warming, ozone depletion or widespread desertification and species loss." This is our legacy.

And worse, according to the weighty 383-page United Nations report of the World Commission on Environment and Development, which reads like an advance obituary of the world in which we live. Unless we change.

The 22-member commission from both sides of the Iron Curtain — headed by Norwegian Prime Minister Gro Harlem Brundtland and including Canadian businessman-diplomat-environmentalist Maurice Strong — was formed almost three years ago.

In that time 1 million Africans died because of drought. Some 60 million people, most of them youngsters, died of diarrheal diseases caused by unsafe drinking water and malnutrition.

The litany goes on. The cliche that the rich get richer remains true only for a short time longer. The rich — or the industrialized nations — will also become poor as they continue to plunder the land and pollute the air and water.

The U.N. report, which deserves high praise for its global overview, says the development of new technology can slow or even stop the approach of doomsday. But as the report says: "It entails high risks, including new forms of pollution and the introduction to the planet of life forms that could change evolutionary pathways."

And what about Canada? We talk a good tune, but when the Progressive Conservatives took over in Ottawa in 1984, they cut Environment Canada's budget by $46 million. Now, federal environment minister Tom McMillan says the U.N. report "by and large, tends to reflect the over-all priorities and approach of this government in dealing with domestic, regional and global environmental issues."

But the Tories in Ottawa have given us more rhetoric than action on the environment. If the U.N. report reflects Ottawa's "over-all priorities," we look for a better balance between deeds and words in the future.

St. Petersburg Times

St. Petersburg, FL, February 23, 1987

What kind of world will the children of the 21st century inherit? Will it be a place of poisoned air, barren land, dead seas, rationed food and water, a world so overpopulated and environmentally degraded that the very survival of life on Earth will be threatened?

An urgent warning of man-made environmental dangers is the sobering theme of *State of the World 1987*, a new report by the Worldwatch Institute, a Washington-based research group.

"No generation has ever faced such a complex set of issues requiring immediate attention," said Lester R. Brown, president of the institute and director of the study. "Preceding generations have always been concerned about the future, but ours is the first to be faced with decisions that will determine whether the Earth our children inherit will be habitable."

To the World War II generation, its children and grandchildren, the awful threat of nuclear destruction has seemed the ultimate, though unpredictable, terror. The idea that the world could be just as certainly destroyed by environmental abuse and overpopulation is relatively new and has seemed minor when measured against The Bomb. Suddenly, the world is endangered by a more insidious enemy, one that would be unimaginable if the damage were not popping up all around us — in dead and dying forests, lakes and rivers, polluted or depleted water supplies, contaminated air, the spread of deserts and the disappearance of endangered plant and animal species.

Human activities that degrade the environment are driving many natural systems beyond critical thresholds of stability, warns the Worldwatch Institute. The pressures of world overpopulation and reckless economic exploitation are causing permanent environmental damage. Human use of the air, water, land, forests and other systems are pushing those natural systems over thresholds from which they cannot recover. Their ability to sustain life on Earth is being eroded.

It is not science fiction.

The trouble signs have been cited by many scientists. Last year, a team of British scientists intensified previous warnings that uncontrolled emissions of carbon dioxide, chlorofluorocarbons and other "greenhouse" gases threaten to make the Earth warmer than at any time in human history. More than a century of temperature data show the warming trend is speeding up; five of the nine warmest years since 1850 occurred during the last decade.

Besides causing a worldwide rise in sea levels, with drastic impact on places like Florida, the global warming trend and depletion of the ozone layer would cause more skin cancers, impair human immune systems and retard crop growth.

The United States, the Soviet Union and China hold the key to whether major reductions in burning fossil fuels will slow the global warmup and weather changes. They account for half of the world's carbon dioxide emissions from fossil fuel and also possess about two-thirds of the world's remaining coal reserves.

The report said that having so many natural systems become unstable within a short time could cause economic and political pressures that "could overwhelm the capacity of governments and individuals to adjust adequately."

It cited Central America as an example of an area where high population growth, deforestation, soil erosion and high energy costs have led to political and social turmoil.

"Many nations face a demographic emergency," the report warned. "Failure to check population growth will lead to continued environmental deterioration, economic decline and, eventually, social disintegration."

The worst recent failure on that front was the Reagan administration's 1986 announcement that it was withdrawing all financial support from the United Nations' agency that coordinates family planning programs in 134 Third World nations. In some countries, that will mean that population growth will be slowed by rising death rates rather than falling birth rates.

How well, or whether, the world makes any effective political response to the threat of uncontrolled population growth, environmental destruction and economic ruin will depend upon global public education and cooperation. If enough people see and understand the gravity of the threat, it will increase the chance of international action to save the world from itself.

In that fight, says the Worldwatch Institute, the most scarce resource is time.

The Burlington Free Press

Burlington, VT, April 12, 1987

Working quietly while the spotlight was turned elsewhere, the House Natural Resources Committee has endorsed a group of five environmental bills that deserve the support of everyone concerned about the future of Vermont.

Editorial

Some of the legislation addresses specific, immediate problems; some deals with long-term challenges in a thoughtful way.

Perhaps the most urgent is a bill that will close the so-called nine-acre loophole in Act 250. The loophole has allowed predatory land development companies to subdivide thousands of acres of Vermont in the name of a quick buck.

Act 250 requires review only when a subdivision contains 10 or more lots of 10 acres or more. So companies like the Patten Corp. of Stamford carve up their subdivisions into nine lots, sell the parcels to down-country buyers and pocket a big profit. The land, cut up like confetti, is lost forever for farming or productive forest use.

The Natural Resources Committee bill would discourage this process by turning on the Act 250 spotlight if a developer created more than nine lots — even if different subdivisions were involved — within the region covered by a single district environmental commission. It would also impose a stiff tax on any land bought and re-sold within three months.

If the Patten problem is clear-cut and simple, the solid waste problem is huge, complex and difficult to solve. Legislation is only part of the answer, but the Natural Resources Committee has a made a start.

The bill requires a state solid waste plan by July 1, 1988, and local plans by 1990. It would add 17 employees to the Environmental Conservation Agency to provide technical assistance to towns, and impose a new tax on trash dumping to cover the cost.

Towns or regional solid waste districts would collect 100 percent of their planning costs from the state, which would also pay 40 percent of the price of a new waste-to-energy plant or landfill.

As a backdrop, the bill uses many of the recommendations of a committee that studied the state's trash problems last year. The study concluded that within eight years Vermont's waste will outstrip landfill capacity by 40 percent. Like the study report, the House bill emphasizes the importance of such alternative disposal methods as recycling.

The other environmental bills would:

• Set up a process to protect the state's outstanding rivers and streams from gravel mining and hydro development. The House passed this measure last week. It is to be hoped the Senate will soon follow suit.

• Allow the designation of "rapid growth areas" in Vermont. In such rapid growth areas, developers of phased projects could be required to submit their master plans for review under Act 250 to measure the cumulative impact of growth.

• Establish a housing and conservation trust fund by increasing the property transfer tax. The fund would be used to make grants and loans to preserve farms and natural areas and to help provide low-income housing.

The environmental problems facing Vermont have become enormously more complicated in the decade and a half since passage of Act 250. While none of these bills will solve the dilemma of growth and the changing landscape, they will help mitigate some of the worst effects.

Recycling Ideas
Gain Ground

Every day, thousands of tons of materials are thrown away by consumers and industry – New York City alone discards 24,000 tons of domestic waste a day. Much of that "waste" could be reused – either directly or after relatively simple treatment – and as such it represents a potentially valuable resource. According to David Morris of the Washington-based Institute for Local Self-Reliance, "A city the size of San Francisco disposes of more aluminum than is produced by a small bauxite mine, more copper than a medium copper mine and more paper than a good-sized timber stand." (See pp. 148-153)

The ecological benefits of reusing waste materials extend beyond good resource management: recycling also cuts energy consumption and reduces pollution. A 1987 study by the Worldwatch Institute found that the energy equivalent of half a can of gasoline is saved every time an aluminum can is recycled. (See pp. 138-141) In addition, "One ton of remelted aluminum eliminates the need for four tons of bauxite and 1,540 pounds of petroleum coke and pitch, while reducing emissions of air polluting aluminum fluoride by 77 pounds." The report calculated that, by doubling worldwide aluminum recovery rates. "over a million tons of air pollutants – including toxic fluoride – would be eliminated."

Several countries now operate successful recycling projects. In the United States, the amount of paper collected by recycling has doubled every year between 1975 and 1980, while in Switzerland more than 40% of glass is recovered, with recycled glass now supplying the material for 60% of glass production.

Recycling has also been adopted by a number of industries. In the electroplating industry, for example, electrolysis has been used to recover gold, silver, tin, copper, zinc, solder alloy and cadmium. Equally, in the motor industry, many companies now recover the polyvinyl chloride in scraps of car-seat fabric by washing the material in a solvent. Previously, the scraps had been incinerated, causing vinyl chloride, a potent carcinogen, to be released into the atmosphere.

In both Holland and Great Britain, where waste exchange networks have been operating since the 1970s, more than 150 wastes sites were being listed for exchange. In the United States, the recycling of industrial solvents is already a $200-million-a-year business, which is expected to reach $1 billion a year by 1990.

Intertwined with the move toward recycling are soft energy paths. Soft energy is a term coined by U.S. energy consultant Amory B. Lovins and used as the title of his influential book published in 1977. It refers to a complex of industrial, commercial and political strategies designed to reduce the dependence of industrial societies on conventional sources of energy. These call for an intensive energy conservation program and for a shift from nuclear power and fossil fuel combustion to renewable sources of energy.

Lovins's argument is that conventional forms of energy production provide electricity but are uneconomic in providing heat for cooking and space-heating, for which much of the energy generated in society is required. Such "end use services," Lovins argues, "are best provided by a sophisticated energy conservation program, which would include draught-proofing, thermal insulation, window shutters and shades and coatings, greenhouses, heat-exchangers and the like."

In such an event, the cheapest and most appropriate methods of generation would be combined-heat-and-power stations, low temperature heat engines run by industrial waste heat or by solar ponds, modern wind machines and small-scale hydro power projects in good sites, and solar cells.

Increased use of Solar power is one of the primary goals environmentalists set for a future agenda. Solar collectors are devices used for the extraction of useful heat from the warmth of sunshine, to heat water or provide space heating.

THE COMMERCIAL APPEAL
Memphis, TN, October 7, 1988

HAVING recently and appropriately proposed new rules for cleaner operation of landfills, the federal Environmental Protection Agency has turned attention toward keeping some of the nation's trash from getting to the dumps in the first place.

The EPA called on state and local governments the other day to step up programs for recycling of household wastes. At present, only 10 percent of American wastes are recycled, compared to half in Japan and some West European countries. Another 10 percent is incinerated and most of the rest goes into landfills.

The federal agency has set a goal of having 25 percent of U.S. wastes recycled. Since Washington is limited in how far it can go to solve an essentially local problem, the EPA is undertaking a largely promotional campaign. It plans to establish a National Recycling Council to do research and give advice on the problems. Congress has provided $15 million for the solid-waste work in the next fiscal year, up from a current $2 million.

Solutions cannot come too soon. The nation's trash and garbage now weigh in at approximatley 160 million tons each year, about 3.5 pounds per day per person. By the end of the century, the figure is expected to reach 190 million tons.

Moreover, the nation is rapidly running out of dumping places, and the cost of disposal is skyrocketing for homeowners and municipalities.

Memphis and Shelby County officials, blessed with more and cheaper landfill space than many major cities, yet aware that it won't last forever, are studying alternative methods of waste disposal, including incineration and recycling.

Some local governments already have begun to require that homeowners separate paper, metal cans and glass from other wastes so they can be recycled. Techniques also are being developed to recycle plastics, an especially troublesome part of household trash.

Most people in America's throwaway society don't take to the idea of segregating household waste. But the growing problem of disposing of it in an environmentally sound manner soon will require that state and local governments compel them to do it. If Washington can give the recycling process a nudge, that's to the good.

The Charlotte Observer

Charlotte, NC, September 15, 1988

Local governments, which bear the responsibility for disposing of garbage, are learning that they need to reduce the amount of garbage they have to bury. Sanitary landfills are becoming scarce in some parts of the country and, to meet today's environmental protection standards, enormously expensive everywhere. Throwaway products and packaging have multiplied in recent years, helping to create a garbage crisis in some parts of the country and bringing other areas ever closer to the crisis point.

But local governments can't effectively regulate the nationally marketed products that contribute nonbiodegradable materials to the waste stream. Nor can local governments do much to expand markets for recycled products and biodegradable materials. That's why it's important to put the influence and resources — and ultimately the enforcement powers — of the federal government behind efforts to encourage recycling and eliminate, wherever possible, products and packages that aren't biodegradable.

Legislation introduced in the U.S. House of Representatives last week by Rep. George Hochbrueckner, D-N.Y., is designed to accomplish those goals. Its cosponsors include John Spratt, D-S.C., from York, and Martin Lancaster, D-N.C., from Goldsboro.

In its initial phase, H.R. 5000 would direct the Department of Commerce to make grants supporting recycling programs and to recommend to Congress ways to encourage the development of recycling technologies. The department also would be directed to recommend ways to expand the market for recycled materials and encourage development of biodegradable products.

In a second phase, the legislation would require the Department of Commerce and the Environmental Protection Agency (EPA) to identify and list consumer goods for which recycling is feasible.

Based on that research, the bill, five years after enactment, would prohibit the manufacture and sale of certain products that can't be recycled and aren't biodegradable. Rep. Spratt says, for example, that six-pack rings, shopping bags and packaging for food and drink sold for immediate consumption would have to be biodegradable.

Landfilling once was a cheap and easy way to get garbage out of sight and out of mind. But because of limited land resources, in urban areas it is no longer easy; and because of environmental concerns, it is no longer cheap. Landfills built to new, tougher state environmental standards in North Carolina, for example, can cost more than $150,000 an acre. And the cost per ton of burying garbage has quadrupled in some parts of this state.

In order to protect the environment and save the taxpayers' money, it's time for the kind of national effort represented by H.R. 5000.

The Wichita Eagle-Beacon

Wichita, KS, October 10, 1988

IF Americans truly pride themselves on their ingenuity and entrepreneurship, they should apply it more fully toward the recycling of disposable products. As never before, recycling presents economies with tremendous benefits: Natural resources are conserved, the pressure on landfills is decreased and jobs are created.

The ingenious part comes in encouraging individuals to segregate their wastes for recycling, finding new uses for discarded items, and providing incentives to business and industry for recycling their own wastes and using recycled products.

The rising costs of waste disposal — to municipalities, business and industry, and individuals — reflect the growing restrictions on space for storing it. Local officials understand that landfills are approaching capacity and demands upon them are increasing; while recycling can't eliminate all of the city or county's garbage, it certainly can decrease the volume. That's far preferable either to waste incineration or to landfill expansion.

But in order to ensure the success of a nationwide recycling effort, businesses must continue to look for more uses for recyclable materials. In Minnesota, for example, a tire recycling plant sells its materials as a substitute for virgin rubber, typically used in products as diverse as athletic mats and pickup bed liners. The company also learned to recombine recycled rubber with recycled plastic, producing laundry baskets that don't break and garbage cans that don't crack in the cold.

State and local governments should offer tax advantages to companies that process wastes or make new products out of recycled materials. Oregon, Minnesota, Pennsylvania, New Jersey and California all have initiated very progressive tax credits and investment incentives for companies that recycle plastic, tires, glass and paper. All the states have found their efforts quite successful. The same kinds of incentives just as easily could be put to use in Kansas, boosting economic development and providing waste management alternatives at the same time.

The time has come for Wichita and Sedgwick County fully to embrace recycling efforts. It's a perfect example of taking local action against the global problem of pollution and turning it into an economic gain.

THE SACRAMENTO BEE

Sacramento, CA, June 8, 1988

California's new system to promote the recycling of beverage cans and bottles is less than a year old, but already it's showing strains. The volume of returned containers, only 50 percent, is lower than both expectations and the targets set by the Legislature. As a result, some recyclers are closing "convenience centers" mandated under the law, and another company is delaying installation of automated-return machines.

The problem is that the current penny-a-can deposit is too small an incentive, either for consumers to carry their cans and bottles back to a recycling center near their grocery or for scavengers to go around to homes to retrieve them.

For the average consumer who's bought a couple of cases of soda pop and beer, it's an inconvenience to store four dozen cans and bottles for a couple of weeks, then load them into the car and drive them to a recycling location. Once at the recycling center, he or she can spend 10 minutes waiting for an attendant to count the returns and write out a chit, which has to be redeemed inside the grocery store across the street. The reward for all that is not quite four bits, plus whatever the recycler is paying for the materials.

What's needed to make the new bottle bill system work is a greater payoff for returning beverage containers to a recycler. The original bottle bill pegged the deposit at a nickel a container, a level that has worked in other states to enlist the energies of both consumers and enterprising service organizations and scavengers. That deposit was successfully opposed by brewers and soft drink companies as too high.

But now that California has real experience with the penny deposit, it's obvious it won't suffice. Assemblyman Burt Margolin, D-Los Angeles, author of the state's plan, is proposing that the redemption value be raised to a nickel for two containers. Even that may not be enough. But unless the Legislature is prepared to waste the substantial investment California has made in recycling the bottles and cans that otherwise end up as litter and trash, two for a nickel ought to be tried.

THE ANN ARBOR NEWS
Ann Arbor, MI, August 22, 1988

Michigan residents are rightfully proud of our returnable bottle law.

The 10-year-old legislation has cleaned up our roadsides and kept them clean, and it has made our state a leader in recycling of materials. The law, which has been copied by several states and some national parks, represents Michigan's commitment to environmental quality.

But it appears that these principles has been lost by Owens-Brockway Glass Containers, a Toledo-based division of Owens-Illinois, Inc.

At a level of corporate arrogance and irresponsibility more associated with the 19th century, it has declared war on Michigan's bottle law by refusing to buy colored glass from our state's recyclers or offering the recyclers only 40 percent of what it pays for used glass from states without bottle laws.

"Take the 10-cent deposit off, and we'll take all (the glass) you can give us," said an Owens-Brockway's corporate recycling manager.

It also offered to help promote voluntary recycling programs in Michigan only if state officials support the repeal of the bottle law.

Owens-Brockway, one of the biggest glass firms in the United States, controls 40 percent of the glass market. It is blaming Michigan's bottle law on reduced use of glass for beverage materials.

The firm claims that the lighter containers made of plastic and aluminum are easier to return, and thus fewer consumer choose glass. But that reason doesn't hold water. Consumers might prefer lighter containers for a lot of reasons which have nothing to do with the bottle law. These could include preferring the taste of certain beverages in cans over bottles, or the convenience of screw-on lids used on many plastic bottles and fewer glass bottles. It could also be related to the policies used by beverage makers to promote purchase of liters, which are usually plastic bottles.

Owens-Brockway says its encourages voluntary recycling, and that bottle laws hamper effective glass-recycling programs.

That's "hogwash," says Fred Clinton, a recycling specialist with the Michigan Department of Natural Resources. The returnable bottle bill, he said, complements community recycling programs.

Owens-Brockway's stubborn policy is especially unfortunate at a time when landfill space is sparse.

There are at least three ways for Michigan to let the firm know its policy is unacceptable here. One is for consumers to think twice before knowingly buying products made by Owens-Brockway.

The other is for recycling firms to do what Recycle Ann Arbor has done — it sells its glass for a lower price to another processer, Mid-Way Cullet of Detroit.

The third, and most effective, is to create through state public policy an incentive to develop more reprocessing plants in the state. The lack of such plants here are a major reasons for reusable glass ending up in landfills, according to Ann Arbor's Jim Frey, vice president of Resource Recycling Systems, Inc.

With both Republicans and Democrats making recycling a campaign priority this year, the time is right for the state to assist communities not only in setting up reprocessing plants for glass but also with creation of community recycling networks which include curbside pickup.

If Owens-Brockway is determined to show the world the bottle law doesn't work, Michigan should be even more committed to proving it does.

The Hutchinson News
Hutchinson, KS, September 23, 1988

The next time Chicken Little screams the sky is falling — take cover. The little chick just might be right.

Canadian scientist Sidney van den Bergh is warning the world that space, filled with orbiting junk, isn't safe and is becoming more hazardous as nations continue to leave their garbage behind them.

The same problem occurred with the advent of bottles. The solution, though not a completely efficient one, was to post a surcharge on bottles so the buyer would return them and regain his deposit. It sort of worked on earth. There's no reason it couldn't work in space.

In Hutchinson, aluminum is collected at a number of worthy places, but for entertainment value the place to go is the Golden Goat.

This recycling machine eats cans and pops out coins. It shudders, it bellows, and it clangs as digital numbers are displayed to show how much the goat has ingested and how much the customer is to be rewarded for recycling.

What space needs is a very hungry goat. Or a deposit system. Or both. Sounds like an entrepreneurial opportunity more than it does a problem.

LEXINGTON HERALD-LEADER
Lexington, KY, September 14, 1988

Islip, N.Y., was known in the spring of 1987 as the town that couldn't flush. The city put its garbage on a barge and sent it to the ends of the hemisphere in search of an open landfill. Nobody would let the barge land. After a five-month voyage, the 3,000 tons of trash ended up where it started.

The rest of the country got a good laugh at Islip's expense. But, as they are wont to do, the tables have turned. Islip is now a model of waste management, while much of the Midwest, Kentucky included, is scrambling to regulate the burgeoning business of for-profit landfills.

Islip and the rest of New York have cut down on their waste problem with an approach that is as simple as a Cub Scout paper drive. Islip is recycling everything from pop bottles to cardboard boxes to tuna fish cans. Over the last two years, the Long Island city has set up a system to recycle 40 percent of its garbage. By 1989, the city of 300,000 hopes to reuse half of its waste.

After the barge debacle, it was clear that Islip and the rest of New York needed a new approach to garbage disposal. Every city in the state of New York is now required to make a plan for cutting down on its waste by recycling. The state won't give out permits for new dumps unless it is presented with a plan for how the folks using the landfill will begin to recycle. The goal is to cut the amount of waste entering landfills by 40 percent by the end of the century.

Syracuse, for example, is using its landfill only as a last resort. This summer, the city began separate collections of newspapers, cardboard and mixtures of glass, plastics and metals. Private companies are processing the discarded goods and making a profit on the deal. Even the grass clippings and tree trimmings that account for 20 percent of the town's refuse are being composted and sold for mulch. Only what can't be recycled will be burned at a waste-to-energy plant.

Syracuse had the opportunity to open a huge landfill in an abandoned quarry outside of town, but chose to recycle. There was some concern that the floor of the quarry was fractured and that a dump there could pollute the ground water system. Besides, said a city official, recycling "is just a better way."

Recycling isn't just the ecological fad of the moment. Other states concerned with the mounting supply of municipal waste are now requiring each city to come up with a recycling program. Our level-headed neighbors in Ohio, for example, passed legislation this summer that will require every community in the state to formulate a recycling plan. Pennsylvania also passed a law this summer that aims at reducing the amount of garbage by 25 percent.

The lesson for Kentucky is obvious. The state has ordered a six-month moratorium on new landfill permits. During this time, the Department of Natural Resources plans to toughen its regulations for opening new landfills. At the same time, Kentucky should begin requiring communities to develop recycling plans.

People are making trash faster than we can find places to put it. It only makes sense that while we worry about properly disposing of this waste, we should also begin to cut down on the supply.

THE KANSAS CITY STAR
Kansas City, MO, September 26, 1988

A nearly worthless program has been announced by the federal Environmental Protection Agency. The plan aimed at handling the nation's household garbage crisis is a sham. The EPA is trying to make people think the government is ready to move, ready to take commendable action such as reducing household waste through recycling.

Forget it. The EPA has really only announced that such a program would be nice—yes, it would—and pretty much left it to states and cities to go from there. It's an attempt to grab positive election-year attention for Republicans, who have been no friend of the environment during the 7½ years of the Reagan era.

Look at the EPA plan more closely. The agency wants to increase recycling so it will reduce solid waste creation by 25 percent within four years. It's a laudable goal—as well as a ludicrous and unreachable one. The EPA says it's going to turn up the volume on public relations megaphones and tell people to recycle more. Has that worked before? No. Will it work this time? No.

So what will? The best approach is to incorporate the cost of dealing with solid waste into the cost of the product. Money powers the recycling engine. If people have to pay more money at the store to buy disposable diapers, they would buy fewer and create less waste. Convenience is nice; that's why 16 billion disposable diapers were bought last year.

The EPA also says the government is going to promote recycling throughout the nation. Boy, that'll get the attention of wasteful Americans. Oh, yes, and the government is going to buy more recycled goods. Fine, but that policy was adopted by forward-looking companies and governmental bodies years ago.

This administration can't follow this script if it really wants to make recycling a legitimate way to handle waste. Lee Thomas, the EPA administrator, and other officials can spout their pro-recycling speeches for months to come. But it will do little to get people to change America's throw-away society.

Only a change in the economic structure of waste disposal will do that. Companies and utilities have to charge prices for their goods that accurately reflect society's cost of handling waste produced by those goods. Until that happens, all the public relations in the world will have only a slight affect in changing attitudes toward recycling. Pretending otherwise, as the EPA is doing, is a shameless attempt to fool people.

The News and Courier
Charleston, SC, August 1, 1988

Garbage disposal remains a growing problem throughout the United States. Every American man, woman and child produces about one ton of garbage per year.

To help combat the problem, Hamilton County this week approved a $20,000 study to focus on recycling as a way to decrease the amount of county refuse and extend the life of local landfills. The study is part of a 10-year solid waste plan.

While the county commissioners are wise to study the prospects of recycling, they should be warned that it is not a quick fix to getting rid of trash in our throw away society. Recycling is an attractive idea but it has its downside.

Recycling reduces waste through the re-use of old cans, bottles and cartons and is pushed by environmentalists. Unfortunately, it has limited popular appeal because people don't like separating their garbage.

To encourage recycling, the Ohio Legislature recently passed a bill levying a 50-cents-per-ton tax on trash dumped in landfills. Trash collected out of state will be assessed $1.50 per ton. That penalty, of course, will be passed along to customers of Rumpke Containers Service, which picks up most of the garbage in Greater Cincinnati.

The fact is Rumpke already recycles many materials at its Colerain Township site that can be sold at a profit. Ferrous metals and cardboard, for instance, are reclaimed because there is a market for them. If re-cycling could be made more profitable, it undoubtedly would increase in popularity.

But neither recycling nor incineration, the other commonly mentioned method for reducing volumes of waste, will eliminate the need for landfills. Even incinerator ash has to be buried.

Waste management experts agree that it will take a combination of landfills, incineration and recycling to get rid of our trash. Garbage is a problem not easily disposed of.

The Cincinnati Post
Cincinnatti, OH, July 21, 1988

There is no "away" when you throw things away. All waste must be treated with care. It will always be with us.

These thoughts came to us as we dealt with a backlog of trash and we realized that it is becoming increasingly important to be more specific about such generic words as trash and garbage. Even in their crumpled state, there is something about aluminum cans that sets them apart from the rest of the trash. Although we haven't gotten to the point where we are willing to go to the trouble of taking them to a recycling center, we would be happy to set them aside for pick up. We also find it difficult to condemn glass containers to a journey with no return.

We wouldn't mind sorting household garbage if we knew that we were doing something to solve the increasing problem posed by garbage that has no place to go. If people thought more about their garbage. instead of simply throwing it "away," we would see more support for measures that would reduce the amount of "disposable" containers and packaging.

Non-biodegradable Styrofoam and other plastics used in packaging do not break down in landfills and, although there is no evidence that they give off toxic gases when incinerated, many of these products are made with chlorofluorocarbons, thus contributing to the breakdown of the earth's protective ozone layer.

More and more municipalities are requiring householders to separate glass, metal and clean paper from the rest of their trash. It is an obligation that many people would accept willingly, although there is a case to be made for providing some kind of incentive in order to get garbage recycling off to a good start in the Lowcountry.

THE ARIZONA REPUBLIC

Phoenix, AZ, January 3, 1989

SOMEBODY finally is doing something about those pesky plastics that plague the environment. A plant to recycle such items as foam coffee cups and food trays is scheduled to open this month in Massachusetts.

Though it is unrelated to the military, it might be called a defense plant since one of the objectives of its creators is to defend the reputation of the much-maligned material.

On that count, the two New York state backers, Mobil Chemical Co. of Rochester and Genpak Corp. of Glens Falls, have a long way to go. Plastic-foam food packages are blamed for many of the problems on and above the Earth.

The $4 million plant, called Plastics Again, is a converted warehouse equipped with machines that can turn 3 million pounds of used food containers — the amount that 1,000 schools toss into the trash yearly — into hard, pea-size pellets. The backers see a commercial use for the pellets as packing material and for making such things as wall insulation, fence posts and flower pots. The world has no shortage of recyclable material. Along with what the schools throw away, it is estimated that the nation uses 5 billion pounds of polystyrene annually, most of which ends up in dumps.

And therein lies the problem, or at least a large part of it. Environmentalists and other critics of polystyrene argue that plastic foam products — which take virtually forever to biodegrade — are straining the capacity of already overflowing landfills. Polystyrene gets another rap because the chlorofluorocarbons (CFCs) used to manufacture plastics pose a threat to the Earth's ozone layer.

The polystyrene industry has volunteered to stop using CFCs in plastic manufacture, which would help ease this threat to the environment. Even so, the matter of the sheer volume of plastic foam still has to be contended with.

That is where recycling comes in. The new plant's backers are so convinced they have found the answer to the problem that Robert Barrett, safety environmental officer at Mobil, predicts that "the plastic bashing that's going on today will stop and polystyrene will become an environmental hero."

Mr. Barrett's prediction may be a tad optimistic. Environmentalists, who get a large share of the credit for the new plant because of their insistence that something be done about the polystyrene glut, are not that easily mollified. It will take some solid results to convince them that polystyrene is not the environmental pest it has proved to be, as the plant's backers, having dealt with the issue for years, should know.

By defusing the plastic explosion, let us hope their pioneering in recycling plastic foam will lead the way to a cleaner, more durable environment.

The Register-Guard

Eugene, OR,
February 16, 1989

Less than a month after two Lane County recycling organizations announced they would begin accepting certain types of plastic, half a dozen local garbage companies agreed to add plastic to their curbside recycling programs. Other companies may soon follow, particularly if people begin doing their part to make plastic recycling a success.

Plastic recycling began locally with the discovery of Asian markets for the material. Previously, the only way to get rid of a plastic item was to throw it away. It was wasteful to fill the dump with non-biodegradable plastics, but there was little that anyone could do about it short of trying to avoid products packaged in plastic.

But last month BRING recycling and Diversified Production Services began collecting some types of plastic as well as the more familiar recyclables such as glass and paper. The material is ground up and shipped to such nations as China and Taiwan for reuse.

As with other recyclables, public participation is the weak point in the plastic recycling program. The program can't succeed unless people separate recyclable plastics from their household garbage. Garbage companies can make recycling much more convenient by collecting recycling materials as they make their rounds, thereby saving people a trip to a recycling center. Curbside recycling is available throughout the Eugene-Springfield area, and now six companies have added plastic to the list of materials they will collect.

All that's required is that plastics be separated, reasonably clean and with labels and caps removed. The garbage companies and recyclers will do the rest. Recycling can't get any easier than that, but it's up to individual people to make it work.

The Times-Picayune

New Orleans, LA, February 10, 1989

A national waste stream that sends millions of plastic containers from manufacturers through stores and households daily has resulted in one of the major environmental problems of our time. Municipal landfills simply cannot cope with the relentless stream of milk jugs and other plastic containers.

If there is an answer, it may have to be found not in reducing the stream of plastic containers at their sources but in recycling them as waste after use.

Because of their convenience and widespread application in the nation's commerce, the number of plastic containers is not likely to be reduced significantly by their producers and commercial users any time soon. This shifts attention to recycling, and fortunately, the outlook for recycling plastics is improving.

Wellman Inc. of Shrewsbury, N.J., is the nation's largest plastics recycler. According to The Wall Street Journal, new technology, much of it belonging to Wellman's, might soon make it possible to recycle 75 percent of plastic waste.

The recycled plastic is converted into such things as carpet fiber and fake wood and given another commercial life.

Today only about 100,000 tons of 10.5 million tons of plastic waste generated annually are recycled. As a result, it is estimated that hard plastic packaging takes up 30 percent of scarce municipal landfill space.

One of the biggest obstacles to recycling plastics is consumers' reluctance to sort cans, paper waste products and other trash components into separate bags for pickup. Furthermore, because of their bulkiness, collecting plastic containers is more difficult and less economical than collecting aluminum cans and newspapers.

But new technology might soon overcome much of the plastics collection problem. In Billerica, Mass., New England Recycling Inc. is building the first plant of its kind in the United States. The plant will automatically sort plastic, glass, cans and ferrous metals, eliminating that essential chore for consumers.

The recycling plant is scheduled to begin operating in about a month and is expected to process about 160 tons of recyclables a day. The company has a recycling contract with Rhode Island, one of four states with mandatory recycling programs.

In Shrewsbury, N.J., the principal business of Wellman Inc. is converting the polyethylene teraphthalate (PET) bodies of plastic soda bottles into such things as fiber for carpet, pillows and comforters. It does this at a South Carolina plant by melting the plastic and filtering out contaminants.

Wellman and several smaller companies also recycle the high-density polyethylene used to make milk jugs and the black bases of soda bottles.

If it becomes clear that plastics recycling can be profitable, the business should gather momentum nationwide. If it works, wholesale plastics recycling would be the answer to the prayers of many municipal officials and other citizens concerned about the environmental impact of the daily deluge of plastic containers.

The Union Leader

Manchester, NH, February 17, 1989

"I have one word to say to you about your future," Dustin Hoffman was told in the movie "The Graduate."

"Plastics," said the man. The future's in plastics.

The character couldn't have known just how right — and thus how wrong — were those lines.

That immediate future was made much more convenient by plastics. The problem is that those same materials will be around — piling up — long, long into the future.

That problem is now being recognized. People are beginning to question whether the tradeoff in presumed convenience is worth the hassle and cost down the road of overflowing landfills.

In many cases, the answer they're coming up with is no.

Leave it, then, to a New Hampshire congressman — Second District freshman Rep. Charles Douglas — to propose legislation designed to curb the explosion in plastics packaging.

The bill attacks the problem on several fronts. It discourages the continued use of plastics that last forever (non-biodegradable is the fancy term). It would also encourage research into recycling technology; and it encourages use of plastics that eventually do break down.

Amazingly, even as the problems with plastic packaging become more evident, more and more of it seems to be coming onto the market.

Plastic shopping bags abound. Plastic inner wrappings are now encased in — plastic.

Just what is the "convenience" in these plastic beverage carriers? Does a cardboard six-pack carrier cost that much more?

We will question Douglas on one plastic package, however. Douglas' bill includes disposable diapers.

For a guy who is supposed to be "pro-family", he isn't going to win a lot of friends with that idea!

All in all, however, his bill appears to be clever and most timely.

"As a nation, we have reached the boiling point when it comes to handling our solid waste," Douglas said. "We are a disposable society, but we have no place left to put our disposables."

The Register

Santa Ana, CA, January 4, 1989

The nation finally is getting a chance to test a sensible but too often ignored proposition: If you want to make progress against environmental degradation, figure out a way somebody can make a profit from desirable behavior like recycling rather than rely on secular sermons and government bans. That's the theory behind the nation's first plant designed to turn plastic items like foam coffee cups and fast-food trays into insulation, fence posts, flowerpots, and packing material, which opens this month in Leominster, Mass.

Plastics Again, as the new plant is called, became possible because a method was developed to wash used foam plastic as it is being crumbled. It is then reformed into plastic pellets that can serve several purposes. The plant is being financed by two chemical companies that recognize both a threat to the plastics industry from environmental concerns and an opportunity to make a few bucks.

It may well be that opposition to foam plastic, or polystyrene, cups and food servers is overblown. Contrary to popular belief, polystyrene is biodegradable (eventually) and it's a long way from being a major component of the nation's solid-waste disposal problems. But two months ago, the Laguna Beach City Council banned the purchase of foam-plastic containers for use in city buildings. Other localities, including Berkeley in California and Suffolk County in New York, have banned polystyrene.

Such moves probably have more to do with symbolism and visibility than with genuine environmental improvement, but they will have a real enough impact on polystyrene manufacturers. If a practical way can be found to recycle those old foam coffee cups, it could mean a slight reduction in environmental degradation while holding at bay other enthusiasts of an outright ban on the material.

The new plant has an agreement with 20 schools and two Wang Co. cafeterias to pick up polystyrene that is placed in special separate containers. This involves urging schoolchildren and employees to take a little extra effort, but a three-month experiment in two school districts indicates that most of them will cooperate. Getting the material to be recycled for the cost of picking it up is a key aspect of making the enterprise potentially profitable.

The new plant is an example of an approach to solving social problems that should be tried more often. When a problem is identified, instead of looking for some piece of coercive legislation that offers a (usually false) hope of making it go away by decree, we should encourage entrepreneurs to look for ways they can make money by solving the problem.

If Plastics Again is successful, it should help break down the widespread superstition that the only way to approach problems is to give government agencies more money and power.

Chicago Tribune

Chicago, IL, February 14, 1989

Barely a week goes by, or so it seems, that some suburb doesn't start a recycling program, or announce plans for a recycling program. The suburbs are catching on fast that recycling no longer is a pet cause of trendy-chic environmentalists; it is a necessity.

Barely a year goes by—or does it only seem so?—that Chicago doesn't defer, delay or generally diddle around in getting serious about recycling.

It is 15 months now since Mayor Washington, shortly before his death, announced a gargantuan recycling program to involve 10 wards by the end of 1988, and the rest of the city by the end of this year. It is 14 months since an aide to Mayor Sawyer announced the program was still on track; a year since Sawyer dumped it to ballyhoo his own plan for mandatory recycling with similar ambitious goals and timetables. It is a month since the city council rejected the notion of tying recycling quotas into an extension of the city's moratorium on landfills.

This is not progress. Chicago still does not have a program, except for the yeoman efforts of neighborhood nonprofit groups that account for most of the city's paltry 2 to 3 percent recycling total. It does have the promise of another one: Mayor Sawyer's new, scaled-down pilot effort to begin in four wards in July. That will be the first progress, assuming the city figures out how to make it work and it actually begins.

Other big cities, all over the country, make it work. Seattle, for example, recycles 24 percent of its garbage, toward an astonishing goal of 60 percent. Little cities make it work, some of them innovatively. Woodstock recycles a third of its trash, with the incentive of having residents pay for garbage pickup by the bag.

There are all kinds of ways to make it work, and experience has shown what the best ones are. It must be, if not mandatory, enticingly convenient, with regular curbside pickup of city-supplied containers to hold the different recyclables. It is done most commonly, and cheaply, by garbage hauling firms that have made it part of their business to design and run recycling programs. Whether it is done privately or—as Mayor Sawyer would have it—by adding more trucks and manpower to city crews, the goal is the same: to remove from the garbage flow those items that can most easily be reused and cause the biggest problem in landfills. By sorting out bottles, aluminum cans, plastic containers, newspapers and magazines, grass clippings and other yard waste, residents can help shrink the garbage glut and create a new source of revenue at the same time.

There are all sorts of good reasons to make recycling work, and one superior one: money. As landfills dwindle and the cost of dumping in them skyrockets, every pound of trash that goes back into use also goes to the municipal bottom line. That is the lesson the suburbs have learned, and the one that Chicago—with its current $46 million garbage budget—inevitably must heed.

It can work in Chicago, too, and somewhere in this city there is a leader who someday will see to it.

EPA Proposes City-Dump Rules

Every living organism uses energy to process raw materials and, in doing so, it often produces some form of waste. In natural systems, such wastes are soon exploited by other organisms, in a perpetual cycle of reuse. Human communities process materials on a grand scale, using enormous quantities of energy and other resources in doing so. We also produce mountains of waste, the bulk of which passes through the system just once. In many Third World countries, fortunately, a high proportion of many waste materials is reused. As for the devloped countries, although the "throwaway society" still flourishes, new recycling industries are emerging, generating new employment and boosting energy efficiency. The challenge of waste management lies not so much with technical fixes, but with our approach to the world around us.

Landfills are a method of waste disposal, used to dispose of most of the world's domestic and hazardous wastes. At their most primitive, landfills consist of no more than a hole into which waste is dumped. Modern "sanitary" landfills, however, are specially engineered, the waste being tipped into prepared cells and covered daily.

Numerous pollution incidents – notoriously Love Canal – have made the landfilling of hazardous waste the subject of bitter controversy.

Several countries have already outlawed the use of "dilute and disperse" sites for the disposal of hazardous wastes. Since such sites make no effort to prevent wastes from seeping out of the landfill, all too often the wastes simply migrate undiluted into local groundwaters. One U.S. survey found that of 50 sites studied, 40 had contaminated groundwaters. Nonetheless, dilute and disperse sites remain the most common form of landfill in the world.

The Environmental Protection Agency (EPA) Aug. 24, 1988 proposed minimum standards for municipal trash dumps.

THE ARIZONA REPUBLIC
Phoenix, AZ, September 28, 1988

THE oft-heard claim that the United States trails Japan and some West European nations in the field of technological development usually focuses on automotives. The foreign brands, it is argued, are better-made and more reliable.

The argument also might be advanced against the poor record compiled by the United States in solid-waste management. When it comes to the sensible disposal of garbage, both the Japanese and West Europeans seem to be way ahead of us.

An estimated 80 percent of all solid waste produced in the U.S. is buried in landfills, about 10 percent is burned and what remains, a paltry 10 percent, is recycled. In Japan and some West European countries, half of the municipal waste is recycled.

The United States — a nation that produces some 160 million tons of waste annually, or about 1,300 pounds per person — clearly needs to borrow a page from the Japanese and West Europeans. This, happily, is just what the U.S. Environmental Protection Agency is doing in a long-overdue move toward reducing this nation's garbage glut.

Acknowledging that the U.S. "is facing a crisis in managing the staggering amount of trash it produces," EPA administrator Lee Thomas outlined a plan under which the agency will provide national leadership in recycling along with the companion strategy of "source reduction," or generating less garbage in the first place.

A number of similar programs already are in place or on the drawing board. Ten states and about 600 communities, including Phoenix, have recycling projects in the works or are planning to implement them.

The EPA hopes to reduce the volume of trash now being dumped into the country's 6,000-plus landfills — a third of which are expected to reach capacity within five years — through recycling and reducing waste. The goal is a 25 percent reduction in garbage by 1992.

Except for spearheading the drive, the EPA is going slow. It is not playing a particularly strong role in what it calls an "Agenda for Action." That means it does not plan to spend a lot of money on the national effort and will not bare its fangs.

This could be both good and bad. Federal leadership often leaves a good deal to be desired. On the other hand, in dealing with crushing problems, states and local communities often have limited resources.

The next administration, which will be in place in less than four months, should put waste disposal high on its agenda. As the EPA says, the problem is "on top of us" and won't go away by itself.

Birmingham Post-Herald
Birmingham, AL, October 3, 1988

While garbage disposal is essentially a local problem, it has enough ramifications to justify a federal role.

With disposal sites getting scarcer, garbage often makes long treks across state lines. For example, earlier this year, garbage from New Jersey was shipped to Alabama for disposal in a private landfill.

In addition, some garbage, whether it stays close to where it was generated or is shipped away, is polluting the environment far beyond the places where it is deposited.

The result is that the U.S. Environmental Protection Agency, acting under authority granted by Congress, has proposed minimum standards for the operation of landfills, most of which are managed by municipalities and a few by private owners.

The regulations would require state and local governments to pass laws by 1991 complying with or exceeding the EPA standards. The federal government could step in and enforce its rules if states decline to act.

Approximately 6,000 landfills are in operation in the United States. They receive more than 80 percent of the 160 million tons of garbage and other household wastes produced each year. Most of the remainder is either incinerated or recycled.

Under the EPA regulations, inspection programs would have to be devised to prevent dumping of hazardous wastes in landfills, which aren't supposed to take such materials. Discharge of harmful wastes into surface waters would be prohibited.

Groundwater would have to be checked at least semi-annually to insure its safety. Explosive gases generated during waste decomposition would have to be monitored and removed. Wastes would have to be covered adequately each day to control rodents, insects, fires and odors.

It is expected that the new rules eventually will add nearly $1 billion to the current $4 billion to $5 billion cost of disposing of the nation's household wastes.

That's a substantial increase and it will pain those who have to pay it — which eventually will include all of us. But the alternative is to continue poisoning the environment, and that is indefensible and unacceptable.

The New York Times

New York, NY, October 11, 1988

Each year Americans throw away 16 billion disposable diapers, 1.6 billion pens and 2 billion razors. That's just part of an annual 1,300 pounds of household waste per person. Yet acceptable places to dump the garbage are fast disappearing because of tighter environmental standards and opposition from local communities.

The Environmental Protection Agency has now proposed a national strategy to avert the garbage crisis. Achieving it will require some painful adjustments by states and townships.

About 80 percent of household garbage is dumped in landfills, 10 percent is burned and 10 percent recycled. This cannot long continue. Of the 6,000 landfills still operating, a third will be full in five years. The E.P.A. wants the share of garbage sent to landfills to drop by a quarter by 1992, with more trash being incinerated or recycled.

Similar goals, though with considerably more recycling, have already been adopted by states like New York and New Jersey. But to attain them requires persuading households to separate reusable items, or building expensive plants to sort the trash stream. Recycling centers must then be set up, and markets created for the recycled commodities.

Legislators in Suffolk County recently decided to ban certain kinds of non-biodegradable plastic packaging, so as to decrease the volume going to landfills. Plastics can be made biodegradable, but then they can't be recycled. In any case, even biodegradable material like paper doesn't decompose much in a landfill because there isn't enough moisture to encourage decomposition. In short, quick fixes to the garbage problem are hard to find.

Incineration converts garbage to energy, and proper operation can control emissions of dioxin and acid gases to acceptably low limits. But the plants are expensive and their presence is not generally welcomed. It's one thing for the E.P.A. to set 20 percent incineration of garbage as a national goal, quite another for local authorities to find neighborhoods willing to accept incinerators.

Even if recycling and incineration of garbage can be significantly increased, there will still be a need for new landfill sites. Yet a recent survey in New York failed to identify any suitable sites within seven upstate counties, after parks, national forests, watersheds and other protected areas had been eliminated.

Other countries, which ran short of landfill space long ago, have made greater progress. Japan recycles 50 percent of its garbage, West Germany burns 30 percent. The E.P.A.'s goals are just the first cut at America's daunting trash mountain.

copyright © The New York Times 1988

The Boston Globe

Boston, MA, November 4, 1988

"We must change dramatically how we get rid of our trash. Over the next decade, Massachusetts should replace virtually all of its single-community landfills with three very different alternatives: reduction and recycling of up to one-third of our waste stream; resource recovery [incinerator] technologies that protect the quality of our air; and regional landfills."

Those words are from the introduction to a document titled "A Solid Waste Plan for Massachusetts," issued by Governor Dukakis and Environmental Affairs Secretary James S. Hoyte on May 29, 1985.

Three years and five months later, the Dukakis administration has unveiled a 10-point solid-waste program. The key item in that program is a one-year moratorium on the licensing of new incinerators – the very same "resource recovery technologies" that were hailed so recently as part of the solution to the solid-waste problem.

There are certainly good reasons to "reappraise" the state's commitment to incinerators; with the number now in operation, plus those that have been approved, there is the capacity to burn 50 percent of the state's trash.

Most environmentalists would argue that a policy that allows as much as 50 percent incineration errs on the high side. Although they generally cheered yesterday's announcement, some expressed fears that the reappraisal could end up setting a higher incineration goal – and result in the approval of even more incinerators.

There must also be a concern that the reappraisal marks just one more delay in confronting and dealing with the state's trash-disposal crisis.

And delay has been the hallmark of the Dukakis administration's approach to this problem – and the related problems of hazardous-waste disposal and low-level nuclear-waste disposal – over the past six years.

Take just one example of the effects of that policy of delay and procrastination, of study and reappraisal, an example that any state environmental bureaucrat can see just by looking out his office window.

The brisk and gusty winds of the past few days have turned the colorful fall foliage into windrows of dead leaves. Those leaves make up 15 percent of the 6.1 million tons of solid waste generated in Massachusetts each year (that figure of 915,000 tons does not include the leaves that fall in the woods far from the sight of suburban leaf-rakers and state bureaucrats).

In the 1985 Solid Waste Plan, the Dukakis administration said it would convene a Task Force on Solid Waste Reduction that would "study initiatives such as large-scale composting of leaves."

This fall, only 200,000 tons of leaves will be composted; 700,000 tons will be trucked off to incinerators and landfills because, over the past three years and five months, the state has been able to organize leaf-composting programs in no more than 85 communities. Moreover, some of those programs are not fully under way or are only pilot programs.

In the 10-point program unveiled yesterday, a goal of 100 percent composting of leaves is proposed for 1992.

Environmentalists had hoped to see that goal reached by 1990 – and have it be coupled with an absolute ban on the landfilling of leaves and yard trash – but considering the state's chronic inability to act on the solid-waste problem, rather than just study it, there will probably still be leaves being trucked off to incinerators and dumped in landfills come 1992.

Omaha World-Herald

Omaha, NE, September 30, 1988

The Environmental Protection Agency, long involved with pesticides, toxic waste and other pollutants, is focusing on garbage. Trash and garbage are an enormous problem in this country. Each person, on the average, generates about 1,300 pounds of it every year, or 3½ pounds a day.

Municipal garbage production has increased 80 percent since 1960 and is expected to rise an additional 20 percent, to 190 million tons annually, by 2000. One-third of the nation's 9,284 municipal waste landfills are expected to be full within five years.

The EPA's goal is to reduce the nation's garbage and trash glut 25 percent by 1992.

Currently, 80 percent of the nation's waste is buried, 10 percent is burned and 10 percent is recycled. In Japan and some West European nations, half is recycled; that percentage might be a realistic goal for this country, too.

The waste-to-energy plant proposed for the city of Bellevue is an example of an innovative and potentially money-saving way to deal with some solid waste problems. The city must decide whether such a plant is economically feasible, but in concept, at least, such facilities are attractive alternatives to creating more landfills.

The easiest recycling actions can be undertaken quickly, according to J. Winston Porter, the EPA's solid waste expert. He suggested increased paper recycling. Omaha's curb-side pick-up of bundled newspapers, which gives jobs to the handicapped while saving the city's landfill space, is an excellent model.

Recycling can be profitable as well as ecologically responsible. Recyclers of metal, glass, paper and other materials added an estimated $61 million to Nebraska's economy in 1987.

The EPA's involvement in waste management and recycling will be more in the area of leadership than hands-on operation of such things as dumps or glass-recovery systems. The agency plans to support national research efforts, help develop markets for recycled materials, spur changes in the design of packages and products and help state and local officials plan waste management. The public can help by learning about the various solutions and by participating in trash-reduction and recycling programs wherever possible.

THE SACRAMENTO BEE

Sacramento, CA,
September 12, 1988

Few other states have the kind of laws that California has to ensure the environmental safety of garbage dumps. Thus, the Environmental Protection Agency's new proposal to impose federal regulations on municipal landfill operations, to keep them from leaking hazardous chemicals into air and water, is unlikely to have much impact here. But it is very important to the rest of the country.

The proposed rules are not as detailed as most environmental groups had wanted, but they are the right first step, and they cover the essentials. They prohibit building garbage dumps in wetlands and on earthquake faults, and they require landfill operators to keep out toxics (which are supposed to be disposed of in special facilities) and to monitor and prevent escaping gases and seeping liquids. Enforcement and decisions about precisely what steps have to be taken to meet the federal requirements are left largely to the states. And given the diversity of circumstances at the 6,000 municipal dumps around the country, that's where the authority ought to rest — unless and until evidence develops that the states are not going to comply.

Still left to be addressed is the even more difficult problem of creating enough landfill capacity to meet the national need, a problem reaching crisis proportions in major Eastern cities. The EPA has disappointed both those who think the solution to that is legislation to overcome the NIMBY (Not In My Back Yard) syndrome and those who think the answer is recycling and other programs to reduce the amount of trash that must be landfilled.

But with this first-ever proposal for federal regulation of garbage dumps, the EPA has started where it had to. As long as the bulk of American garbage is disposed of in landfills — and there's no indication that will change any time in the foreseeable future, even with the best recycling programs — the landfills themselves have to be made safe. And until they are, it will be politically impossible to solve the NIMBY problem. The EPA may not be on the fast track, but it is certainly on the right track.

THE INDIANAPOLIS NEWS

Indianapolis, IN, September 15, 1988

The wasteful culture of America has generated unprecedented amounts of refuse, much of it extremely dangerous. The stories roll in like the ocean waves that deposit used syringes and surgical supplies on beaches from North Carolina to New England.

No one seems to know what to do with all this waste. Remember the garbage barge that floated from state to state and country to country before it finally found a home?

Some officials in West Virginia have even proposed allowing East Coast states to dump their trash in the mountain state's abandoned coal mines — for a price, of course.

Official attention has focused on where to put the ever-growing mountains of trash. You almost never hear proposals that deal with the sources of waste.

How about, for instance, encouraging Hardee's, Wendy's and others to cut back on their use of plastic, which is non-biodegradable.

Or imagine if McDonald's — the world's largest restaurant chain — announced it would use only biodegradable packaging for Big Macs, McNuggets and almost everything else they sell.

What an eye-opener it would be if Ronald McDonald used environmentalism to sell more burgers. Corporate executives around the world would be forced to sit up and take note. If they saw profits in being perceived as environmentally conscious, corporate bigwigs would do what it takes to get that edge on their competitors.

Environmentalist groups tend to devote the biggest chunks of their time, money and effort trying to change things through government regulation and enforcement. They have largely ignored the great potential the business sector holds for helping with efforts to clean up the environment.

True, some effort has been made to pressure some corporations to adopt more environmentally sound business procedures.

A few groups, for instance, called for a boycott of some restaurants because they use beef imported from Central America, where cattle farming is killing vast tracts of irreplaceable rain forest.

But the attempted boycotts, like most other such efforts, have had little impact. The food giants' business was never substantially affected, and the group that called for the boycott says there's no evidence that restaurants ever quit buying beef in Central America.

The pace at which man is fouling his own nest requires more forceful action than the obscure boycotts and timid government regulation that have thus far characterized the environmental struggle.

The powerful engines of capitalism created the affluence that has unfortunately generated so much damage to the environment. Conversely, a new breed of free enterprise — call it environmental capitalism — could unleash powerful market forces to help clean up the world.

All this, of course, is predicated on the assumption that consumers care enough to buy one brand over another because it's been advertised as more environmentally sound. That's an untested marketing strategy.

But untested selling strategies, when put into practice, have often made people rich. Environmental capitalism — two words rarely placed together — could be the wave of the future.

ST. LOUIS POST-DISPATCH

St. Louis, MO, September 10, 1988

There's little doubt that society is creating more refuse than it can safely dispose of and that conservation and the use of biodegradable materials are a must. But there are some scientific fixes that should permit us to continue to use some modern materials we prize, which until now have been difficult to handle. Common plastic and PCBs — polychlorinated biphenyls widely used for insulation — are two encouraging examples.

Plastic doesn't degrade, because its molecules are too big for microorganisms to eat. Until recently, only starch had been known to break plastic into small enough bites for germ consumption. Unfortunately, starch also weakens plastic's structure, making it possible for microorganisms to begin eating the plastic when it is still on the retailers' shelves, rather than waiting until it reaches the landfill.

Now researchers at Purdue University have found that cellulose acetate, which is derived from wood pulp, breaks down plastic molecules into the proper size for microorganisms to consume, but only after it has first interacted with the soil. Binding cellulose acetate to plastic should make that ubiquitous material completely biodegradable.

PCBs have been a problem because when burned they give off dioxin, a deadly poison. So they are stored, not always effectively, in expensive sealed containers. But researchers at Texas A&M University have found that when two oxygen atoms are added to an electron, a "superoxide ion" is produced, which breaks down PCBs into bicarbonate of soda and table salt.

Promising as these developments are, they don't imply scientific fixes are available for all our environmental problems. For instance, it would be dangerous to continue building nuclear power plants on the theory that eventually a way will be found to make their wastes harmless.

The News and Observer
Raleigh, NC, August 31, 1988

People haven't often thought of it in these terms, but it has been a luxury to live in a society in which getting rid of the garbage has been both cheap and easy. For most of us, once the lid has dropped back onto the trash can, that's been the end of it. The nominal disposal fee that has shown up on the monthly bill from City Hall has scarcely caused a nose to wrinkle.

But this is one luxury that won't be available much longer. Space in landfills is fast disappearing, and the environmental hazards of solid waste disposal have become unmistakeable. If Americans want to enjoy the true luxuries of clean water, clean beaches and clean air, they need a new trash ethic. It ought to be based on the premise that if something has to be thrown away, somebody goofed.

Not that people's throwaway habits won't die hard. After all, common sense tells that it's better to recycle, but how many of us go to the trouble? And companies that aggravate the solid waste problem with disposable products and unnecessary packaging obviously figure that's the best way to make a buck.

Government must play a bigger role if the inertia and self-interest that contribute to the waste dilemma are to be overcome. And it's a welcome sign that Washington finally is becoming involved. Last week, for example, the Environmental Protection Agency for the first time proposed federal standards for the design of landfills. Under those standards, landfills no longer would be the path of least resistance for waste disposal in many communities, and other solid waste strategies would receive an important boost.

The EPA proposes that when new landfills are built or old ones expanded, they must not leak into the groundwater or into nearby streams. Practically speaking, that means using expensive plastic liners to keep contaminated rainwater from leaking out. The cost of the liners is bound to drive up the fees many people pay for trash service. When throwing trash away begins to seem like throwing money away, other options suddenly start to look attractive.

What else can be done with trash besides burying it? There's incineration, which is useful in some respects, but which poses its own set of environmental risks. The real avenue of promise lies not in disposal, but in reuse.

That's a goal toward which governments at all levels must strive. Recycling of paper, glass and metal had its moment of faddishness when environmentalism bloomed during the early 1970s, but then fell out of favor as many people decided it wasn't worth the trouble. Local and state leaders now have a duty to convince their constituents that recycling makes economic sense — and to ensure that it really does.

Municipalities, for instance, could band together to operate resource recovery stations where economies of scale would come into play. And why should people have to cart their own trash to the recycling place? That should be a standard municipal service. In exchange, of course, people should be required to sort their trash into proper categories — newsprint, aluminum and so forth. It would be a small burden that paid large dividends.

And what about all the plastic, from bottles to packages of every description, that crowds American shopping carts? Its use ought to be restricted. Companies no longer should have an absolute privilege to compound the country's solid waste problem just because they find it convenient — just as ordinary people no longer should have the luxury of forgetting about the trash once it goes out the back door.

The Duluth News-Tribune
Duluth, MN, September 24, 1988

The federal government is falling short of what it ought to be doing in another area involving the ecosystem (above editorial) by failing to show strong leadership in the growing problem of garbage disposal.

But small progress can be noted: The feds now admit that solid waste disposal *is* a problem, but they don't go far beyond that.

The Environmental Protection Agency, which has been silent on the issue of solid waste disposal throughout the 1980s, released a report this week encouraging state and local governments to increase recycling and waste reduction by 15 percent by 1992. The key word here is "encouraging." The plan does not include any mandatory regulation, although it does appropriate $15 million next year for education about ways to dispose of solid waste other than reliance on landfills.

EPA Assistant Administrator Winston Porter called the need for changes in solid waste disposal "an urgent problem," and said recycling is the cornerstone to weaning reliance on landfills.

He's right on both counts, but the key to solving this "urgent problem" is not simply education or cajoling of state and local governments; it must be action at the federal level. National legislation — not just encouragement — is needed to help curtail the garbage binge America has been on for 40 years and to encourage the reuse of wastes through recycling.

The Wichita
Eagle-Beacon
Wichita, KS, August 17, 1988

THE industrialized nations of the western world generate more waste than they know how to properly dispose of, and the world's capacity for accepting used and unusable products and byproducts is nearing, if not exceeding, capacity. The costs of storing or treating all manner of waste materials in this country are rising dramatically, as is their quantity.

Several U.S. companies are resorting to dumping their garbage and toxic wastes in Third World countries, where the costs are significantly lower. What would cost $2,500 a ton to dispose of in the United States could cost as little as $1 a ton to dump abroad. Toxics can be dumped abroad at bargain rates, while unscrupulous haulers reap outrageous profits.

Since 1986, seven nations — Brazil, Haiti, Mexico, Guinea, Zimbabwe, Nigeria and South Africa — are known to have received U.S. waste. In Haiti and Guinea, thousands of tons of fly ash from Philadelphia incinerators, shipped under false pretenses, have been dumped on beaches and deserted islands. Yet, regulation of such shipments to Third World destinations by either the U.S. Environmental Protection Agency or the State Department is virtually non-existent.

Opposition to the United States' dumping policies is growing considerably stronger. African Unity, a coalition of African states, has called on its member states to reject such waste schemes; Latin American nations, too, are drafting measures to ban waste imports.

These nations are right to consider the exportation of hazardous and toxic wastes from the United States as another form of American exploitation. It is morally reprehensible for those nations that produce hazardous and toxic waste to endanger the lives and safety of innocent people around the globe. The United States has been dumping on the developing nations of the world too long. Enough is enough.

The Hartford Courant

Hartford, CT, March 1, 1989

Prospecting in old dumps isn't exactly a glamorous occupation, but it may pay off handsomely for Thompson, in northeastern Connecticut, and also set a good example for other towns and cities.

The idea of trying to mine the trash heap for valuables came from Donald E. Williams Jr., Thompson's first selectman, who was inspired by an experiment in Florida. He applied for a $50,000 state grant to fund about half the cost of the program.

On Feb. 14, the town became the first recipient of a grant from the Office of Policy and Management's $400,000 Innovative Recycling Technologies Program. That money is from the settlements of several national lawsuits against major oil companies that were accused of overcharging customers during the energy crisis in the 1970s.

Thompson plans to spend $117,000 during the next 22 months digging through its old dump, which was covered over long before recycling became popular. Buried under the tons of earth are salvageable materials.

The prospectors will first sort out all the valuables and take them to recyclers. Then today's trash will be buried in the old space and covered over with the reprocessed dirt fill. This will extend the life of the landfill by about three years and the town some money.

This after-the-fact recycling program is only the second such operation in the nation. The digging in a 30-year-old section of Thompson's landfill began in November and reportedly has been working well.

Another innovative program being undertaken by Thompson officials requires all town departments to use recycled paper. Wastepaper recycling firms are hurting because few people buy their products. As a result, the firms are charging more and more to haul away wastepaper.

Leaders of other towns that are running out of landfill space should visit with Mr. Williams and his landfill miners. And if all 169 towns and the state government decided to use reprocessed paper, the recycling business would get much needed boost.

The Des Moines Register

Des Moines, IA, March 1, 1989

Before he or she outgrows diapers, the baby will be changed between 6,000 and 10,000 times (it just seems like more). And with 90 percent of parents using disposables, more than 16 billion of the plastic diapers, carrying 2.8 million germ-laden tons of excrement and urine, pile up in U.S. landfills yearly. Cost to the public is estimated at $300 million.

That's the disposal cost alone. Health costs are undetermined.

Disposable diapers took hold in the early 1970s, and now amount to a $3.3 billion annual business.

According to estimates, washing cotton diapers would cost parents $300 over the child's three-year diaper phase; hiring a diaper wash-and-delivery service would cost $1,170. The disposables cost $1,716. But saving $1,400 isn't enough to induce today's parents to opt for the yucky job of washing, which safely flushes feces and viruses into the sewage-treatment cycle.

Users of disposables are supposed to dump feces down the stool, but only 1 percent do, according to the National Association of Diaper Services. Instead, rainwater falling on landfills flushes it into the groundwater.

Ads for "biodegradable" plastic diapers are surfacing, but as with other so-called degradables, they aren't. They may be held together with corn starch, but when the small fraction that is thus truly degradable has dissolved, the plastic remains — in small pieces, but just as durable.

Meanwhile, as modern medicine keeps oldsters alive beyond their ability to control their bodily functions, the market for adult diapers increases. Sales have shown a 50 percent yearly growth since 1983. Last year, sales hit $160 million.

There is some indication that cotton is scoring a comeback with parents, in part because some consider it more natural for babies and in part due to environmental concerns. It is a trend deserving significant encouragement — perhaps in the form of a tax on disposables to cover disposal costs.

Those who can afford to pay an extra $1,400 per child for the privilege of avoiding washing diapers can afford to pay a little more to help determine how great a hazard they pose.

Just ask their grandmothers.

DESERET NEWS

Salt Lake City, UT, March 7/8, 1989

Decades of conspicuous consumption, throw-away products and enormous waste are beginning to catch up to America. The coming national crisis may be one of garbage — chiefly, where to put it.

There are growing piles of radioactive nuclear waste but no agreed-upon N-dumps in which to store it. Toxic wastes present their own problem. And even ordinary garbage is becoming a threat.

Tighter environmental controls and space restrictions are making the city dump a dinosaur. Up to one-third of the nation's 6,000 garbage dumps are expected to shut within five years, forcing communities to find new ways to dispose of their garbage.

Incinerators have been touted as a way to produce energy while reducing garbage. But questions about air quality and the disposal of byproducts laced with toxins persist. Burning isn't always the best solution.

Recyling is offered as one answer. That calls for products to be reused instead of buried or burned. But recycling also requires extensive separation of garbage into different categories before it is collected.

Every American man, woman and child generates 3.5 pounds of refuse a day — adding 160 million tons to the nation's trash heap every year. Only about 10 percent is recycled — although studies suggest as much as 86 percent of household trash is recyclable.

Will recycling be the wave of the future? Only time will tell. Ten states already require — or will soon require — residents to separate newspapers, glass jars, milk cartons, tin cans or other discarded items for recycling trucks or bins. Legislators in 33 states are expected to consider plans to increase recycling this year.

Whatever the answers, it is going to cost money. Tossing out the garbage will have to be paid for. This is giving rise to new kinds of companies, and some are reaping significant profits — especially those that deal with hazardous waste.

Almost everything America consumes — from pharmaceuticals to consumer products to even decaffeinated coffee — produces hazardous waste that must be disposed of. Hazardous waste processing will be a $5 billion industry this year, and that number is likely to more than double by 1994.

The hazardous waste disposal industry already claims several millionaires. Companies specializing in infectious waste, radioactive contamination and dirty drinking water are in high demand.

So are places to dispose of the stuff, which makes the wide open spaces of Utah and other Western states such attractive targets for Easterners, many of whom tend to think of the empty areas as useful garbage dumps. It's an attitude that has to be opposed at every turn.

A high standard of living is wonderful, but it won't last if it continues to be careless, wasteful and geared to throw-away convenience. America is searching for a way of disposing of its trash, but the best answer would be not to produce so much of it.

The News Journal

Wilmington, DE, February 28, 1989

NEW York City, whose problem certainly is one of the world's greatest, finally is confronting — or beginning to confront — the need for a realistic plan to handle its solid wastes.

Its landfills are filling rapidly — as are others all over the country.

Costs of hauling trash are escalating day by day.

One estimate published recently was that by the year 2010, Gotham will need to dispose of as much as 38,000 tons of garbage daily — 33 percent more than today's already huge total — and no plans are even on the drawing boards to accommodate that need.

With these facts beginning to penetrate officialdom, moves are being made to turn to recycling of wastes. It is part of the way to go, but not the whole solution.

If the metropolis can accomplish 40 percent recycling, no mean feat, in that target year mentioned above, it still will have to dispose of almost 90 percent of the volume of wastes it is generating today. It will have to do that without landfills of its own. It will meet increasing difficulties and costs in exporting trash to foreign nations that will be ever more reluctant, for environmental reasons of their own, to accept it.

There is a practical limit, too, to recycling. It is doubtful that any jurisdiction ever will approach 100 percent. That is especially so since the market for recycled products is not infinitely expandable, witness difficulties fund-raising programs in Delaware have met recently in waste-paper collecting.

Although recycling can be and should be a very significant contributor to solving the waste disposal problem, other steps must be taken. One of the most important is reduction of the amount of waste generated in the first place. An example of this might be a program designed to impose appropriate restrictions on packaging.

We are all in this together. We don't want to wake up some day, year or decade in the near future and find ourselves drowning in garbage. Regional, national and international steps should be studied — and not studied indefinitely in the name of postponing action.

The Burlington Free Press

Burlington, VT, February 24, 1989

Burlington's voters face a simple decision on Town Meeting Day: vote for a $7.8 million bond issue for a new landfill, or start piling up garbage on the back porch.

Burlington needs a new landfill. That's not open to question. The current dump, off Manhattan Drive in the Old North End, is near capacity. It is scheduled to close by the end of the year.

Fortunately, a fund already exists to close down the old facility and develop a new public park with tennis and basketball courts, hiking and skiing trails, a pond and open space for sitting or playing.

But if the bond fails — support from two-thirds of the voters on March 7 is needed for passage — prospects for developing the park dim. The projected maximum allowable height of garbage in the landfill is 15 feet below Manhattan Drive. The landfill is less than a foot below that level now. If the garbage piles up any higher, no park. Instead, Burlington would be left with a permanent blight.

The city isn't sure where the new landfill will go. Public works officials say there are no acceptable sites for a new dump within the city's borders. But they are working on options for sites in Lamoille and Chittenden counties. The bond appropriately leaves city officials leeway in determining a new site without threatening the availability of funding.

Repayment of the bond is also well taken care of. It will be repaid through tipping fees — payments from haulers for dumping privileges — rather than through tax revenue.

Major public works projects are expensive. But Burlington officials have done an excellent job in developing a new landfill plan that has drawn wide praise. Patrick Parenteau, state environmental conservation commissioner, has said the plans promise a state of the art facility that would rank among the best in the nation.

Not only is the bond essential, it will be money well spent. Burlington's voters should endorse it enthusiastically.

RAPID CITY JOURNAL—

Rapid City, SD, March 1, 1989

Turning trash into gold?

It's possible. Although a past project to take sewage ash from Minneapolis and turn it into precious metals and useful products through high-tech alchemy failed to materialize, not all proposals to dispose of mankind's wastes are spurious. There is economic opportunity as well as environmental peril involved in disposing of the nation's refuse.

Thus, the Senate State Affairs Committee acted wisely Monday when it endorsed a summer study of the prospects for the state becoming involved in the solid waste disposal business. Unfortunately, the House State Affairs Committee weakened the possibilities and protections for the state by killing a proposal to place a one-year moratorium on applications for solid waste dumping sites.

The freeze would have allowed breathing room for the state to take an unhurried look at the potential and problems inherent in the nation's rising tide of garbage disposal problems, and the opportunities for the state that may be contained in that teeming ocean. Unfortunately, by a 7-5 vote, the House committee decided that Gov. George Mickelson's solid-waste bill contains sufficient safeguards to protect state interests. That might have been true until Tuesday, when the Senate removed a provision from Mickelson's bill that would hold out-of-state entities disposing of trash within South Dakota responsible for subsequent environmental problems. That was a mistake. Without the freeze, it is imperative to retain the stringent protections originally contained in the bill.

With adequate safeguards, the state can face the realities involved in the solid waste issue and South Dakota's proper role in resolving it. Without them, the state cannot adequately regulate companies that establish waste sites here.

The state cannot legally completely exclude solid waste disposal projects. It can and should regulate them tightly.

South Dakota may have the proper environment, suitable climate and correct geology in some areas to safely dispose of non-toxic solid wastes — if sufficient safeguards and adequate oversight are in place. The truth is that the state is remote, lightly populated and hungry for responsible development. Unfortunately, there are those who are hungry for any kind of development, and that tends to cloud the issue. In truth, the state could be well positioned to handle this type of industry if the right proposal comes along.

As Sen. Roger McKellips, D-Alcester, said, "I'm not saying we should do it, but we should at least look at it."

If stringent conditions are met by the right company or companies or the state itself, it would be foolish for the state to reject out-of-hand the positive potential of waste disposal — just as foolish as inviting any and all comers without adequate investigation and regulation.

Arctic Refuge Protection Sought

A bill designating the coastal plain of the Arctic National Wildlife Refuge as a protected wilderness was introduced in the House Jan. 6, 1987.

The Interior Department had released late in 1986 a preliminary proposal recommending that the entire coastal plain be opened for oil and gas development, with restrictions to avoid "unnecessary adverse effects."

The House bill, sponsored by Reps. Morris K. Udall (D, Ariz.) and Bill Green (R, N.Y.), would bar any development, including oil and gas drilling, from the area.

Interior Secretary Donald Hodel recommended to Congress April 20, 1987 opening the coastal plain of Alaska's Arctic National Wildlife Refuge to oil drilling.

It was vital to U.S. interests, he said, to find additional energy sources. "It's important that we look at whatever resources we do have for the future," he said.

Environmental groups had denounced the proposal when it emerged in draft form in November 1986. They cited in particular the potential damage by development to the environment and wildlife, such as the caribou and musk oxen, for which the refuge was established in 1980.

The proposed search for oil and gas resources would take place in 8% of the wildlife refuge along the coastal plain of the Beaufort Sea, east of the Prudhoe Bay oil field, which currently supplied 20% of the nation's oil production.

Hodel, at a news conference, said it was not a choice between wildlife and oil production. In his opinion, the area could be developed for oil and gas production without significant environmental damage or harm to the wildlife.

Spokesmen for the American Petroleum Institute and the National Association of Manufacturers supported the proposal as important to the nation's energy policy. National Wildlife Federation executive director Jay D. Hair accused the administration of suddenly discovering the energy crisis after having undermined conservation efforts throughout his tenure.

The geologic report on the proposal said there was one chance in five of discovering major oil reserves there. If it were found, the "mean estimate" of the quantity was 3.2 billion barrels, about one-third as large as the Prudhoe Bay field.

The U.S. Court of Appeals for the District of Columbia Dec. 30, 1988 ordered an environmental review of the the Interior Department's five-year plan for leasing offshore oil and gas.

The court said the department failed to comply with a federal environmental law requirement for a statement on the potential impact on wildlife from the leasing program. The particular wildlife involved were migratory gray whales and various birds.

The plan had been challenged by the Natural Resources Defense Council and other environmental groups and the states of California, Massachusetts, Oregon and Washington.

Leasing activities were not held in abeyance by the ruling, but the first possible lease offering that could be affected, in Alaska, was not scheduled until December 1989.

*Los Angeles, CA,
April 22, 1987*

Oil companies have long had free access to 1,100 miles of the northern Alaska coast, on shore and off. At their insistence, Secretary of Interior Donald Hodel proposed Monday to open up the remaining 100 miles, a move that could cause severe damage to a wildlife preserve, all in the name of slightly less dependence on foreign oil. It's not worth it.

Californians eager to protect the state's precious coastline have become quite familiar with the administration's two-pronged oil policy: abandoning conservation measures and energy alternatives while spurring the drilling of environmentally sensitive regions. Hodel's Alaska proposal means more of the same.

Interior's target is a 1.5 million-acre coastal slice of the Arctic National Wildlife Refuge in northeast Alaska. The area is less than 100 miles from Prudhoe Bay, site of one of North America's largest oil strikes, which now provides about 12 percent of U.S. oil but will soon decline. One study speculates that oil reserves beneath the ANWR coast may run as high as 9.2 billion barrels or as little as 600 million barrels, a 40-day supply.

To get at whatever is there, drillers would have to disrupt a delicate ecosystem, which includes the calving grounds of the largest protected caribou herd in the world.

Just how anxious Interior is to get at that oil can be seen in the department's apparent willingness to override the findings of its own biologists. For instance, in a draft report issued last November, researchers stated that the experience with the tiny but thriving caribou herd at Prudhoe Bay could not be extrapolated to predict the consequences of oil production on the larger herd. In fact, there's good reason to believe the caribou in the undeveloped site would be seriously affected. However, Interior contorted the researchers' findings.

In all the wailing about dwindling oil supplies, Interior ignores the fact that even a massive discovery wouldn't make the U.S. energy independent.

What's more, it's still cheaper to save a barrel of oil than produce one. Future energy self-sufficiency depends on conservation, efficient use of existing sources and research into alternatives. Rather than risk wrecking this continent's richest arctic wildlife region, the administration should reorder its priorities.

THE SPOKESMAN-REVIEW

Spokane, WA, June 4, 1987

U.S. Interior Secretary Donald Hodel wants to permit oil drilling in Alaska's Arctic National Wildlife Refuge because the Arabs cut oil prices and Americans abandoned the conservation ethic.

That is not, of course, the way Hodel would put it. He would say he wants oil rigs in the wildlife refuge because of a recent increase in the nation's reliance on foreign oil.

But our increasing oil imports result from two problems — lower oil prices and rising oil consumption — and Hodel's plan would solve neither one. Hodel simply would create a third problem — damage to an environmental treasure.

Since taking office, President Reagan has fought, successfully, against energy conservation. Federal outlays for conservation research and development fell from $776 million in 1980 to $375 million this year, and Reagan proposes only $86 million for next year. Meanwhile, the administration repeatedly has rolled back fuel-efficiency requirements for new automobiles, yielding to domestic automakers who lust for the fatter profits to be made from gas-guzzling cars and who would rather not invest, as the Europeans and Japanese have, in more-efficient auto designs. On top of that, Reagan drained the nation's strategic petroleum reserve.

In short, this administration has played right into the hands of foreign oil producers.

About a year ago, Saudi Arabia glutted the world market with oil, causing prices to fall from $26 to only $10 a barrel. U.S. oil producers couldn't make money at that level, so they capped wells, halted exploration and laid off thousands of workers.

Accordingly, U.S. oil production dropped last year by 800,000 barrels a day, to about 11 million barrels a day. At the same time, thanks to the abandonment of conservation plus the lower prices, U.S. oil consumption jumped by 400,000 barrels a day.

That combination of events touched off the current panic over U.S. oil imports, which rose last year from 5.1 million to 6.1 million barrels a day.

Enter the Organization of Petroleum Exporting Countries. OPEC reined in production and brought prices up to $18 a barrel — a price high enough to fatten the wallets of overseas producers who sit atop an ocean of oil that is cheap to tap, but a price that is not high enough to restore the health of devasted U.S. producers, whose reserves are more expensive to tap.

Now, Congress faces numerous proposals to rescue domestic oil firms.

Restoring the conservation ethic ought to be the first order of business. Gluttony is an unnecessary risk. And to neglect research into alternative energy sources is shortsighted.

Another goal is better health for U.S. oil producers. Their friends in Congress want an oil import fee. Then, domestic producers could raise prices to a point equal to the world price plus the import fee. Their profits, in turn, would rise, and they might be able to increase domestic production, thus reducing the need for oil imports.

But higher U.S. energy prices would push up inflation and bite into the profits of every non-oil-producing business in the country.

What does the rape of a wildlife refuge, in which the 1980 Congress voted to ban oil exploration, have to do with these knotty problems? The Interior Department's own research estimates there is only a 20 percent chance of finding enough oil in the refuge to make production profitable.

As long as U.S. oil firms cannot make a profit pumping oil from existing wells and cannot afford to seek more, Hodel's proposal is irrelevant. High-cost oil suppliers won't improve their lot, in the current environment of glut and low prices, by pouring money into more high-cost production.

ST. LOUIS POST-DISPATCH

St. Louis, MO, March 28, 1987

By hook or crook, the Interior Department seems determined to have oil wells dot the coastal plain of northern Alaska. Early this year it announced plans to open up 1.5 million acres in the Arctic National Wildlife Refuge to mineral exploration. When that generated heated opposition in Congress and from environmental groups, the department turned to more underhanded methods of getting what it wants.

Under the guise of rationalizing land management, the department is offering to give mineral rights — and the promise of profits they may bring — under the Arctic coastal plain to native Alaskan corporations, established to protect the interests of Alaskan Indians. In return, the corporations would give up their inholdings — areas inside refuges — on which subsistence hunting is permitted.

According to the Sierra Club, which, with the Trustees of Alaska and other groups has sued to stop the talks, the Interior Department hopes to be in a better position to pressure Congress to permit the oil extraction if the native Alaskan corporations agree to the deal.

Aside from the attempt to skirt Congress, the talks could harm the native Alaskans, creating a rift between the corporate managers who would trade away the inholdings and the people who actually depend on those lands for their subsistence. Says the Sierra Club's Michael Matz, "The bottom line is, the negotiations are a nefarious scheme to try and get a better foothold to open up the coastal plain to oil exploration." If the court doesn't stop this insult to Congress by the Interior Department, Congress must.

Los Angeles Times

Los Angeles, CA,
April 23, 1987

No one was shocked when Secretary of the Interior Donald P. Hodel proposed to Congress that 1.5 million acres of the Arctic National Wildlife Refuge in Alaska be leased to oil companies for oil and gas exploration and development. Hodel has been Interior secretary for two years, but he acts as if he were still running the Energy Department.

The only surprise was the extent to which his report ignored the wilderness value of the unspoiled Arctic plain and the extent to which he claimed that national security hinges on the ability to wring every last drop of oil from the refuge. The only people who may have a reasonable idea of the oil potential of the area are not telling. They are the handful of oilmen who know the results of a 14,500-foot-deep test well drilled on native land in the midst of the wildlife refuge about 100 miles east of Alaska's Prudhoe Bay field. There is said to be a definite gleam in their eyes.

The results of the test well drilled near the native village of Kaktovik fall into the realm of "proprietary information." This means that it is the oil companies' secret, not to be shared with the 250 million Americans who are custodians of the adjacent wildlife preserve. All that the oilmen will say is what Hodel mimics: The refuge may contain the nation's last big onshore oil field.

Therein lies a major flaw in the nation's current policy of leasing federal lands for oil and gas activity. It virtually always is an all-or-nothing proposition, with the oil boys deciding where to drill and when. All that the rest of us are told is that there may be a one-in-five chance that the Arctic refuge might yield anywhere from 600 million to 9.2 billion barrels of oil. There might be none, or there might be more.

Let it be said also that rhetoric from the other side of this battle often is not much more illuminating. Environmental groups claim that oil development will do grave damage to the Porcupine caribou herd that migrates into the Arctic plain to calve. They claim that the oil companies are willing to destroy one of the last great natural areas of the country for a quick buck.

So the battle is joined at high moral and emotional pitch, with Congress asked to decide between Hodel's request to open up the refuge to leasing and the environmentalists' demand that it be preserved as wilderness area.

The fight could be waged more intelligently if Hodel had not abdicated his responsibility as the nation's chief environmental officer in making this recommendation. He rejected other options including limited leasing, further exploration and taking no action—that is, to allow the area to remain as a refuge with no drilling at this time.

Environmentalists have focused on the caribou. In response, Hodel's report went to considerable lengths to argue that while oil development might have "major effects" on the caribou habitat, there would be no major *adverse* effects on the herd.

Hodel dismissed the wilderness value of the unique mountain-to-ocean ecosystem as unworthy of consideration, since there is so much wilderness in Alaska already. He carried this absurd argument to the extreme by saying that oil development "ultimately will be in the best interests of preserving the environmental values of the coastal plain." But in the same statement he said that the effects of oil production would "include widespread, long-term changes in the wilderness character of the region."

In fact, major oil production would create a new industrial complex on the Arctic plain with roads, pipelines, housing, an operations center, processing facilities, land disruption and air pollution. It would alter the environment for decades at least. The American people, acting through Congress, may ultimately decide that the oil is worth the sacrifice. But they should not be forced to make that decision on the basis of incomplete and misleading information from their own government.

THE KANSAS
CITY STAR

*Kansas City,
MO, May 16, 1988*

The debate over future oil drilling in Alaska has taken a new turn. A draft report by the U.S. Fish and Wildlife Service bluntly says problems caused by previous exploration have been far greater than expected. The news ought to slow the move in Congress to open added land in the Alaskan wilderness to drilling.

The oil companies have been claiming for years that the original development of Prudhoe Bay and the building of the Trans-Alaska Pipeline have not greatly affected wildlife or the environment. "When oil was discovered at Alaska's Prudhoe Bay, the future of the Central Arctic Caribou herd was of paramount concern," notes a recent publication by ARCO Alaska. "However, many years of study have shown that the Central Arctic herd has not been significantly displaced by oil operations at Prudhoe Bay . . . .In fact, the herd has tripled in size since development began."

Sounds good. Now for the full story. The new Fish and Wildlife report says the caribou herd has indeed grown. Why? Because wolves, bears and other predators have been killed or pushed out since oil projects began, and new roads and air fields made the area accessible to hunters.

The Fish and Wildlfie Service report contains other bombshells. It says more than 11,000 acres of vegetation used by wildlife have been lost because of development, almost twice what was predicted in the original environmental impact statement two decades ago.

The administration remains adamant about plunging ahead with exploration and drilling in Alaska. True, the country needs to do something about meeting its future energy needs. But the federal government ought to be pushing harder for development of alternative fuels and solar power. Conducting business as usual, despite the risks to the environment, is not the right way to go.

Arkansas Gazette

Little Rock, AR, May 20, 1988

Though James Watt is gone from the Interior Department, the policy he came to symbolize remains in place: exploitation over conservation.

The Interior Department and the oil and gas industry support legislation that would allow oil and gas exploration in the coastal plain of the Arctic National Wildlife Refuge in Alaska. The refuge is perhaps the grandest wilderness and wildlife complex in North America. Conservation groups want to keep it that way.

But it will not be easy. The Senate Energy Committee recently approved, by one vote, a bill to let the drillers in. Soon the bill will reach the floor of the Senate.

The justification for the bill is that it would reduce the nation's dependence on foreign oil. But even the Interior Department estimates there is only about a 20 per cent chance of finding oil in an economically recoverable quantity. The Department also has estimated that if the oil is there, there would be no more than enough to meet the nation's needs for seven months. The country could save more oil than that merely by increasing the fuel efficiency of automobiles by two miles a gallon. In 1986, the administration *rolled back* the fuel mileage requirement from 27.5 miles per gallon to 26 m.p.g. This is why opponents of the exploration, including Senator Dale Bumpers, say that the country should adopt a comprehensive energy policy before it begins to destroy irreplaceable resources.

The Interior Department has said that the experience at the Prudhoe Bay oil field in northern Alaska shows that oil development can occur without harm to the environment. That story may be harder to sell now that it has been revealed, by *The New York Times*, that an unreleased report by Fish and Wildlife Service officials says that development at Prudhoe Bay has caused far more environmental damage than the government predicted.

The Interior Department and oil and gas interests are asking the country to take a huge risk for little gain. It's not a good deal.

Los Angeles Times

Los Angeles, CA, March 15, 1988

One of the greatest scandals of the Reagan Administration is its refusal to spend more than $6 billion since 1981 in offshore oil revenue intended for federal, state and local park acquisition and recreation development. The Administration's 1989 budget proposes to use only $59 million out of a potential $900 million from the Land and Water Conservation Fund during the coming fiscal year. Most of that amount has to be spent because of court rulings and legal settlements.

The new budget would halt acquisitions for parks and wildlife refuges through 1993. Grants for state and local parks and recreation areas would be eliminated. The total of unused land-purchase authority will grow from about $6 billion now to an estimated $6.7 billion.

Since 1981 Congress at least has insisted on a modest program of the most urgently needed land acquisitions, reaching a peak of $295 million in 1983 but falling to $170.5 million this year.

The Administration's refusal to use the offshore oil revenues helps explain why the White House has shunned the 1987 report of the President's Commission on Americans Outdoors. The commission was appointed by President Reagan with considerable fanfare in 1985 to advise him on how best to provide Americans with the recreation facilities and opportunities that they would need in the next decade.

There was magnificent precedent for this. The major recommendation, and success, of the Outdoor Recreation Review Commission in the early 1960s was the creation of the Land and Water Conservation Fund in 1964. Reagan's commission came back with a remarkably similar recommendation—a new fund that would provide $1 billion a year for park and recreation land and facilities. The President has ignored the recommendation. But Democrats in Congress are moving ahead with legislation to implement it.

The Administration's excuse for holding the park funds hostage is that the nation should take care of the parks that it has before buying any more. But the longer that critical lands remain in private ownership, the more that they will cost when finally bought—if still available for park use. Most of the parcels proposed for purchase by a coalition of conservation groups are in-holdings within existing park boundaries. Most have been approved in advance by Congress. An example of such property now under intense development pressure is the private land inside the Santa Monica Mountains National Recreation Area.

There is the budget-deficit problem. By not spending the offshore oil money on lands each year, the Administration has been able to keep the deficit about $800 million less than it might have been. But the intent of Congress was that the money be spent on the land purchases as a form of long-term investment. This concept was reaffirmed by Reagan's own commission, which declared: "The nation should invest in the outdoors some of the money from the sale of non-renewable assets, such as oil." This would be done through a trust fund so that the money could not be diverted for other uses.

The Administration's moratorium does not even make economic sense. The land purchases and park development would provide an economic boost to many areas. And the spending of the federal money would put additional dollars into local economies. Of the $875 million proposed by the conservation coalition for spending this year, $200 million would go to state and local governments, which would match the funds—in some cases with assistance from private groups.

Many of the park purchases would be in urban areas that are desperately short of recreation facilities. And the President's own commission recognized the need "for a strong outdoor commitment from the nation's capital to safeguard the environment, to expand recreational opportunities on federal lands and to protect and improve the federal estate."

The United States now has all the natural wild lands that it ever will have. If they are not protected now, they may be lost forever. The nation cannot stand another year of squandered opportunity and shameful neglect of a program launched with such promise in 1964 and crippled since 1981.

The Charlotte Observer
Charlotte, NC, February 3, 1989

When candidate George Bush declared himself an environmentalist, one thing environmentalists hoped that meant was that a Bush administration would reverse the Reagan administration's support for oil and gas exploration in the Arctic National Wildlife Refuge. Apparently they're in for a disappointment. The new president has said he favors "prudent" exploration in the refuge, and that has drawn predictable but persuasive blasts from environmental groups.

Environmental activists oppose any drilling in what National Wildlife Federation President Jay Hair calls "this final vestige of untouched Alaskan arctic country." Their immediate concern is the effect of toxic byproducts and wastes on a delicate ecosystem. Beyond that, they raise the larger issue of the environmental impact of continued reliance on fossil fuels for energy.

With plenty of relatively inexpensive oil available on world markets, there's no reason for the United States to exploit and deplete its own oil reserves, particularly if that means disturbing environmentally sensitive areas. This period of world energy abundance, in fact, is a good time to emphasize research and development of alternative energy technologies that won't cause smog, acid rain and possible long-term undesirable changes in the world's climate.

Mr. Hair also raises the question of international relations in connection with drilling in the arctic refuse. He points out that the United States is urging Latin American nations to stop cutting down the tropical forests that consume carbon and may help prevent a global warming trend. It's hypocritical to do that while rushing to produce more of a fuel that is believed to contribute to that trend. And he notes that the United States has an agreement with Canada to protect a caribou herd that uses part of the refuge as a primary calving area.

The issue of oil and gas exploration in the Arctic National Wildlife Refuge is an early test of President Bush's commitment to a cleaner, more stable environment and the protection of wildlife and dwindling wilderness areas, and at this point he seems to be flunking it.

In Mr. Hair's words, "The American public is ready for the new breeze that Mr. Bush described during his inaugural address. If a dirty wind blows down from a once-pristine Arctic refuge, it is sure to leave a residue of dismay and distrust at a time when we need cooperation and commitment from a true environmental president."

The Atlanta Journal
THE ATLANTA CONSTITUTION
Atlanta, GA, March 26, 1989

It's hard to blame Alaskans for wanting to open the Arctic National Wildlife Refuge to oil exploration. Petroleum accounts for 85 percent of the state's economy, and the great price bust of the 1980s has made for hard times. While the refuge is unlikely to bring Alaskans the windfall of another Prudhoe Bay, a major oil strike there would nonetheless help fill local coffers.

The problem is, exploration offers a somewhat illusory return for the rest of us. On balance, the Senate energy committee made a bad call last week when it voted to open this region to drilling.

The refuge contains the last pristine Arctic ecosystems in North America, but the drilling would change all that. Machinery would leave permanent scars on the tundra. Musk oxen, caribou and wolverines could possibly suffer. The fragile environment would suddenly see waste pits and landfills.

But wouldn't the damage be worthwhile if it permitted the United States to weather the all-but-inevitable Energy Crisis II? It might be. In fact, though, this project will *not* allow us to weather an Energy Crisis II.

Let's say the Arctic refuge turned out to be the new West Texas. At best, it would supply less than 2 percent of all the oil Americans consume before it is depleted. The oil field would last for a few years, then it — and one of the few remaining pristine environments on Earth — would be gone. Arctic strike or no Arctic strike, we would still be dependent on imported oil.

Well, says the oil crowd, it takes years to get a field on line. The new energy crisis — like a hulking Bigfoot — is looming ever closer. Every little bit of domestic production will help. So, they ask, shouldn't we go ahead and get ready to use the deposits we have? The answer is "no," not when there are better ways to meet the crisis.

Washington could tighten gas-mileage standards for cars. It could impose an oil import fee. It could do more to subsidize public transportation. It could encourage Americans to conserve energy of all kinds. Unlike the Arctic field, these measures won't play out after a few years.

Granted, this strategy won't help Alaska solve its economic problems. Until the price of oil picks up, only diversification will do that. But it will allow the United States to face the future with confidence — and with some of its natural heritage intact.

THE DAILY OKLAHOMAN
Oklahoma City, OK, February 7, 1989

ENVIRONMENTAL activists have turned the heat on President Bush on the Arctic National Wildlife Refuge issue.

Bush had barely settled into the Oval Office before environmental groups put demands on him to review an Interior Department recommendation favoring oil exploration in the northeastern Alaska refuge. They said his actions on arctic development would be the "litmus test" on his administration's intentions toward protecting the environment.

This strongarm tactic has drawn a well-deserved rebuke from Henry Schuler of the Center for Strategic and International Studies. Schuler; a former Tulsan, is director of the Dewey F. Bartlett program in energy security studies at CSIS.

Schuler emphasized the president's reminder that national security interests are at stake in the refuge decision.

He points out that the president is faced with trade deficits, defense commitments, alliance tensions and foreign policy constraints "that can only be exacerbated by increasing our dependence upon oil imports."

Bush is following a proper course by insisting on the environmentally sound development of the arctic refuge.

Bush has a strong commitment toward the environment. For a narrowly focused lobby to attempt to push him into a corner on a single issue disregards genuine concerns about America's security.

Antarctica Imperiled by Resource Exploration

Antarctica is one of the last untouched wildernesses on Earth. The continent is the size of the United States and Mexico put together, around 5,400,000 square miles. Most of the land mass is covered with ice of an average thickness of 5,250 feet, though this can extend in some parts to a thickness of 13,000 feet.

Antarctica's environment is without doubt the world's harshest. The average temperature in the coldest months in the interior is minus-160 degrees Fahrenheit and the lowest temperature ever recorded on Earth (minus-190 degrees Fahrenheit) was recorded there. Winds from the interior can sometimes exceed speeds of 186 miles per hour.

All this does not prevent Antarctica from being regarded as a continent of tremendous resource potential. A large number of minerals have been found, though the logistics of recovering these under the extreme conditions of the continent could be prohibitively expensive. It is thought, however that oil exploration is a possibility.

Antarctica's enormous marine wealth has long been exploited. As early as 1824, British and North American sealers had almost exterminated the fur seal population and it was not until the mid-1970s that the seals recovered to any degree. Factory ships were already making a considerable impact on whales during World War I and by the 1930s catches had already started to decline.

Fin fish, such as the Antarctic cod, had been so overfished by the early 1970s that the catches declined to a fraction of their previous levels. Today, the Russian, and to a lesser extent Japanese, Polish and West German fishing fleets, are concentrating their efforts on fishing for krill, a small shrimp-like creature that exists in enormous quantities in the Antarctic seas.

There is clearly tremendous interest in Antarctica's huge mineral and marine resource potential. However, the potential for irreversible environmental damage is very high. The pesticide DDT has already been found in penguin fat and eggs, though the nearest inhabited continent is 1,100 miles away. Biological processes operate only slowly and intermittently. The terrestrial ecosystem is particularly fragile and has little capacity to withstand physical, chemical or biological changes without itself being altered. Though there are more than 500 different species of lichen, 70 species of moss, and two types of flowering plant, such vegetation is sparse and vulnerable. A human footprint in a bed of moss can remain for several years. Some damage has already occurred because of the research stations there.

In 1977, the consultative members of the treaty agreed not to proceed with any kind of commercial mineral exploitation some kind of general agreement. Such an agreement has not been reached and it will probably not be until in 1991 that any decision is made. The fate of Antarctica's marine and terrestrial environment still hangs in the balance. Conservationist interests have featured heavily in all the negotiations. However, the United States and Japan are pursuing a vigorous search for oil, in possible violation of a 1977 commercial moratorium, and that may yet tip the scales.

Scientists March 9, 1987 told Congress that there had been an alarming depletion of the protective layer of ozone in the Earth's atmosphere in the last 10 years. Ozone was a form of oxygen that absorbed harmful ultraviolet radiation. Susan Soloman, the leader of a 1986 expedition that investigated a continent-sized "hole" in the ozone layer over Antarctica, warned that "large-scale depletion of ozone at other latitudes" could be expected. "It's a question of when and by how much," she said.

In a related development, depletion of the protective ozone layer in the atmosphere over Antarctica was the worst recorded since measurements began in the 1970s, researchers reported Sept. 30, 1987.

The reduction in the ozone content of the atmosphere at 60,000 feet was 50% at its worst, surpassing the 40% depletion recorded the previous winter. Adding to the alarm was the fact that the winter mass of frigid air over Antarctica remained weeks longer than usual in 1987, according to British and U.S. scientists Dec. 18. The discovery prompted concern that the depletion of the ozone later was affecting the climate.

BUFFALO EVENING NEWS
Buffalo, NY, June 18, 1988

THE ANTARCTIC is one of the few unexplored, undeveloped spots on earth. Scientists are increasingly probing this vast continent, however, and speculating about its mineral wealth. The need for some international regulation of economic development is thus becoming increasingly apparent.

After six years of complex negotiations, 33 nations have agreed to an international convention to do just that. The United States achieved its goals in the treaty, which allows the development of Antarctic resources, but with procedures to protect the delicate ecological systems on the frigid continent. In addition, the current international cooperation on the continent will be continued.

The pact builds on the Antarctic Treaty of 1959, which barred military activities, allowed scientific projects by many nations and made no decision on the conflicting territorial claims of various countries. That treaty did not regulate economic development, but there has been an informal moratorium on mining development.

The need for more formal regulation has arisen as traces of copper, uranium, platinum, iron and coal have been discovered. Natural gas has been detected offshore. The potential could be vast, since Antarctica, which is not even shown on most maps, is much larger in area than the United States.

On the other hand, any commercial exploration for minerals, oil or gas would face formidable obstacles. The ice over most of the continent is a mile thick, and the weather on land and sea might make commercial development impractical. And special precautions would have to be taken to avoid harm to the environment.

Under the new treaty, any major geological exploration or economic development would have to be approved by a new commission created under the treaty. Other regulatory bodies would be set up to continue monitoring such developments.

Even though some countries make territorial claims, the unknown continent is thus being treated and regulated as an international area, much as whaling in the world's oceans is curbed by international agreement.

The treaty steers a sensible, middle course between uncontrolled exploration and the demands of some environmentalists that the continent be closed to exploitation and declared a world park. One can only guess at the future of the Antarctic, but the new pact will help ensure that development, if any, will take place in a responsible manner.

The Hartford Courant

Hartford, CT, August 20, 1989

Antarctica remains the most pristine place on Earth, but it might not stay that way. Year after year, visitors abuse the environment and pollute the continent's polar expanses.

According to a report released this week by an environmentalist group, the Environmental Defense Fund, one of the chief polluters is a government agency. The report says U.S. research bases dirty Antarctica's environment in violation of U.S. laws and international agreements.

It seems the National Science Foundation, which supervises U.S. scientific research in Antarctica, has for decades permitted ocean dumping of untreated sewage and toxic chemicals, burning of solid wastes in open pits and the use of diesel generators with no emission controls.

The results are apparent. McMurdo Sound, adjacent to the largest U.S. installation, is reportedly more polluted than virtually any waterway in the United States. Scrap metal piles up in landfills. Wildlife is threatened. Toxic heavy metals have been found in penguins' tissue.

Not only is the polluting bad in itself; it sets an ominous precedent. At a time when oil, gas and mineral prospectors are preparing to descend on Antarctica, the United States has failed to show it recognizes basic obligations to clean up after itself. If government-funded scientists can't follow the rules, how can developers be expected to?

The government says it is moving to improve environmental controls in Antarctica. But previously promised improvements have been slow in coming. As long ago as 1960, for example, the U.S Navy pledged to build a water-treatment plant and an incinerator with emission controls. Neither has been built.

The NSF also notes that its outposts aren't the only polluters. But the foundation's practices hardly put it in a position to press for better pollution control by less-responsible nations with Antarctica bases.

The U.S. government allows American exporters to sell, to Third World nations, pesticides that are banned in the United States. It allows firms to build plants overseas that wouldn't meet American safety standards. It allows companies to ship garbage to nations that don't share Americans' concern for proper disposal methods.

So perhaps it's not surprising that a U.S. agency has been polluting Antarctica without regard for what U.S. laws allow. This doesn't make the NSF's disdain for a wondrous continent any less outrageous.

The Chattanooga Times

Chattanooga, TN, August 24, 1989

The Environmental Defense Fund last week called public attention to a situation in Antarctica which is a disgrace to this country: The National Science Foundation, which orchestrates U.S. research efforts on the polar continent, is polluting the environment there.

In 1959, the Antarctic Treaty established the continent as a demilitarized scientific preserve. NSF operates four of 57 bases established by the 18 nations that have research teams there.

Last week's EDF report charged that "The environmental practices of the NSF ... would not be permitted anywhere in the United States." In some instances, the report said, they violate international accords on waste disposal.

It is an outrage that any agency of the U.S. government would be so environmentally irresponsible. It is particularly abominable when the agency is dedicated to scientific research and thus should understand the unacceptable dangers of failing to abide by sound environmental practices. But NSF has ignored those dangers.

Among findings of the EDF report, which is acknowledged as factual by NSF, are that NSF:

● dumps raw sewage into Antarctic waters;

● disposes of combustible waste through open burning, without pollution controls;

● dumps non-combustible waste at sea or bulldozes it into open pits;

● fails to restrict discharge of toxic chemicals from scientific research into the water;

● carries out dynamite blasting and construction near wildlife colonies, endangering animal life and habitat; and

● operates its diesel power generators without emission controls to reduce air pollution.

From this broad range of environmentally destructive practices, it must be concluded that NSF has abdicated its responsibility to protect the pristine environment of Antarctica. Or should we say the formerly pristine environment?

The EDF report said that McMurdo Sound, adjacent to the largest of four U.S. installations in Antarctica, is more polluted than virtually any U.S. waterway. It said highly toxic polychlorinated biphenyls (PCBs) and heavy metals are being found in the tissues of penguins and seals.

NSF officials say the agency is taking steps to improve its environmental record, but there is cause for skepticism. Despite a 1978 directive from Congress, NSF has failed to assess the environmental impact of its activities in Antarctica. Despite a 1980 promise to issue pollution control regulations and to mitigate environmental damage, those actions have not been taken. Current plans, NSF officials say, call for a wastewater treatment plant at the McMurdo base and, possibly, a waste-burning incinerator with pollution controls. But the lack of a timetable for those improvements inspires little confidence they will be implemented soon.

The NSF's performance in Antarctica is a source of shame for America. The Environmental Defense Fund has performed a public service in bringing the agency's abysmal record to light. And Congress must do whatever is necessary to force this reluctant agency to change its ways.

The Providence Journal

Providence, RI, June 17, 1989

Although no one asked them, the penguins of Antarctica would probably be pleased to hear of an agreement initialled recently by 33 countries.

The pact will permit private development of mineral resources throughout the frigid continent — but only under rules designed to protect the stark grandeur of its environment. As much as anything, this is a peace treaty among interests strongly divided over Antarctica's future.

The negotiations took six years, arriving at what seems to be a sensible resolution of what might have been irreconcilable differences among those few who are concerned about what happens to Antarctica. The talks were held in New Zealand, and are an outgrowth of the Antarctic Treaty of 1959. That treaty's signatories set guidelines on international activity in the land *really* down under.

The debate over how to regulate the exploitation of Antarctica's resources pitted environmentalists against developers. It also set seven nations that have staked a claim to Antarctic territory against those that have not, including the United States. The negotiators met in the middle on the first issue, and sidestepped the second.

Under the new agreement, developers will have the right to prospect for oil and metals wherever they like, so long as they use methods with minimal effects on the environment. Large-scale development would require permission from a rotating commission of 20 nations, where the United States and Soviet Union would have permanent seats.

The opinion of Greenpeace, which insisted that negotiators "have done the Antarctic a great disservice," was not shared by the representative of a consortium of 176 environmental groups who said the pact "could have been a lot worse."

That, certainly, is true — inasmuch as the previous eight years have seen a voluntary moratorium by developers, and an attempted ban on development probably would have concluded the moratorium without preventing development. Illegal mining and pumping would likely have proceeded as member nations debated about what to do.

The new mineral convention of the Antarctic Treaty should help keep the peace in Antarctica for the foreseeable future — without unduly threatening the habitat, environment, or even the lifestyle of its most famous inhabitants.

Ocean Dumping Emerges As a Major Issue

The U.S. Senate Aug. 9, 1988 passed a bill to bar dumping of sewage sludge into the ocean by January 1992. The vote was 97-0.

The measure would also make dumping of medical waste into the ocean a federal crime. (See pp. 26-27) That provision was in an amendment proposed by Sen. Christopher J. Dodd (D, Conn.). Another amendment, by Sen. Bill Bradley (D, N.J.), was accepted to impose criminal penalties for disposal of medical waste at sea of up to five years' imprisonment and fines of up to $250,000.

The legislation itself was initiated by Sens. Frank R. Lautenberg (D, N.J.) and John H. Chaffee (R, R.I.).

Any effective opposition to the measure had ended Aug. 8, when New York Sens. Daniel Patrick Moynihan (D) and Alfonse M. D'Amato (R) announced their decision to support the bill as co-sponsors.

New York City Mayor Edward I. Koch criticized the bill Aug. 9 as "simply not do-able in terms of the time requirements and the heavy fines which will be imposed."

Lautenberg said the penalties were necessary to present a deterrent to "using the ocean as a sewer." It was "time for New York City to make firm plans to get out of the ocean once and for all," he said.

Bradley, in thanking his New York colleagues for their "difficult decision" to support the legislation, said there had been a "national effort to protect the air, the land, our drinking water and even our inland waters and streams" but "no concerted ocean policy."

"We have viewed the ocean as a great sink which could absorb almost anything we threw into it," he said. "We simply cannot continue to do that any longer."

THE ARIZONA REPUBLIC
Phoenix, AZ, August 4, 1987

FOR centuries ancient mariners have used the vast expanses of the world's oceans as a convenient dumping ground for the excess baggage of everyday life at sea.

Waste, as a rule, is merely dumped over the rail to naturally decompose in the murky depths.

With the advent of modern-day, man-made materials, however, the age-old disposal solution has resulted in some unintended, and all-too tragic consequences: The indestructible garbage is becoming a denizen of the deep which is destroying ocean life.

The plastic six-pack yokes, trash bags, foam cups and polymer lines and nets left in the wakes of the thousands of ships that cross the oceans are responsible for the deaths of more than 1 million sea birds and other forms of marine life each year, according to a study prepared for two congressional panels now studying the ocean slaughter.

Scientists say the plastic garbage — an estimated 6.4 million metric tons are dumped overboard each year — ends up ensnaring or choking to death marine wildlife.

The floating plastic death is responsible for noticeable declines in the population of northern fur seals, stellar sea lions, Hawaiian monk seals and other sea species.

In an effort to halt the needless deaths of marine life, President Reagan has proposed legislation — as part of an international maritime treaty — that would ban the dumping of plastic garbage into the sea.

If the treaty is ratified by the Senate — 28 nations representing 48 percent of the world's shipping tonnage already have signed the agreement — the disposal of plastic products would be illegal in any part of the ocean, and other degradable refuse could not be discharged within 12 miles of land.

Barring immediate success in scientific efforts now under way to produce plastics that decompose, the treaty is the best hope yet to stop the irresponsible killing of sea life.

For too long, the world's maritime industry has been getting away with murder. Ratification of the agreement could come none too soon.

ST. LOUIS POST-DISPATCH
St. Louis, MO, July 13, 1987

Vast, remote and inhabited by mute creatures unable to protest, the world's oceans are rapidly becoming the last frontier for the harmful detritus of 20th century civilization. But it is wrong to regard the oceans as infinitely capable of absorbing mankind's waste — especially when that waste is plastic.

The damage wrought by ocean dumping is most visible along shores, where beachgoers are affronted by trash washed up with the tides. But beach cleanups deal only superficially with the problem, which is much more than aesthetic. What is unseen is even more worrisome: the devastating toll that plastics have on marine life.

The worst offender is the plastic drift net an expanse of sheer mesh that can be up to 30 miles long. It was intended to snare squid, salmon and albacore, although it is not very efficient at that task. According to the National Marine Fisheries Service, up to half of the young salmon and a third of the mature salmon catch will die — and thus be inedible — before being brought up. It is notoriously efficient, however, as a deadly trap for air-breathing marine life, such as porpoises, seals, whales and sea birds. Frequently, especially during storms, the huge nets become impossible to manage and are simply cut loose by fishing crews. The resulting "ghost nets" don't stop trapping marine life until the weight of dead animals causes them to drop to the sea floor — something that can take as long as two years.

The Japanese are especially careless. In the North Pacific, more marine mammals and birds are killed in their drift nets — whether hauled in or set adrift — than die from any other cause.

Other types of plastic trash also pose a hazard to marine life. Six-pack yokes are a menace to playful young seals. Odd bits of plastic are mistaken for food by sea birds and turtles. When enough is ingested to block the animals' intestines, they will die of malnutrition.

The United States is not helpless to stop the dumping, but it has so far done little, continuing to allow Japanese fleets unencumbered privileges in U.S. waters. Absent administrative action, bills are pending in the U.S. Congress that would require Japanese and other commercial fishing fleets to reduce the incidence of accidental kills as a condition for future fishing permission. Also, the Senate should ratify Annex V of the International Convention for the Prevention of Pollution from Ships, a treaty that would go far to restrict dumping of plastics at sea.

So long as nothing is done, the problem will worsen. Each year, nearly 300 million pounds of plastic fishing gear will continue to be dumped, gear that will be around for hundreds of years, cluttering beaches, killing marine life and doing harm — perhaps irreparable — to an environment that we have neglected for far too long.

The News Journal

Wilmington, DE, December 26, 1987

MAYBE, just maybe, we are being left off the hook in the matter of the dying dolphins.

The pictures of summer are still stark in the memories of those who care about the seas and their creatures. We saw bottlenose dolphins by the score lying dead along the Atlantic coast.

There have been recent deaths of whales along the Cape Cod beaches and a marine pathologist named Joseph R. Geraci said the other day that apparently these deaths can be traced to contaminated fish the great mammals ate. The contamination, he traced to a toxin which is carried by algae in the so-called red tide phenomenon. One puzzle is that although it has been known that these particular substances can kill fish, the mackerel found in the dead whales apparently carried the toxins without being affected themselves — sort of nautical Typhoid Marys.

Mr. Geraci says that right now he cannot state with certainty that there is a connection between these whale deaths and those of the dolphins, but that "we can't disregard" the possibility and will be redirecting efforts to establish the cause of the dolphin deaths.

Mankind can be blamed, and should be blamed, for a great deal of the contamination of the lands and waters of Earth.

If the red tide is the cause of these deaths, however, we can grieve the loss of the marine mammals without feeling especially guilty about it. The red tide is a seasonal thing caused by dinoflagellates. These organisms release a toxin into the water. It would be death by natural causes.

We've done plenty to feel guilty about, but as far as we know we didn't cause the red tide. Unfortunately, we can't do anything about it, either. What we can do, given enough will, is stop, or at least drastically curtail, the release of our own man-made poisons into the seas.

The Honolulu Advertiser

Honolulu, HI, October 16, 1987

The House of Representatives sent to the Senate this week a bill that would bar U.S. vessels from dumping plastic trash into the ocean. And this Saturday Hawaii and other coastal states will try to rid their beaches of tons of plastic-studded debris that's washing in and out with the tides.

More than scenic beauty is at stake. Over 100 million tons of plastic trash per year are being dumped into the world's oceans. Each day, merchant ships alone discard about 700,000 plastic containers.

Unlike marine garbage of the past, today's discards don't rot. Pieces of plastic fishing line and bleach bottle fragments are swallowed by sea birds. Green sea turtles gobble up plastic bags, mistaking them for jellyfish, and die.

An even larger problem is the entanglement of turtles, monk seals, fur seals, sea lions and sea birds in plastic nets and packing straps. Lost and abandoned "ghost nets" keep on killing fish for years.

Even the plastics industry is calling for controls, fearing a backlash against its products. It favors recycling and stricter enforcement of litter laws. The long-range solution must also include responsible disposal and development of plastics that break down quickly in the environment.

The industry predicts 28,000 plants and 1.5 million workers will be churning out $345 billion in plastics products by the year 2000, more than double today's production.

It's easier to understand in this context how worthwhile it may be for beachgoers to retrieve each and every bit of plastic litter that catches the eye. If they make it a habit, they'll be part of the solution.

Those who would like to be part of tomorrow morning's larger community campaign to "Get the Drift and Bag It!" should look for newspaper ads listing the phone numbers of the coordinators for each island.

The Star-Ledger

Newark, NJ, September 7, 1987

There are widespread, multiple investigations either underway or planned to obtain further information about the mysterious 50-mile-long garbage slick that closed beaches on the New Jersey Shore. And it is well that intensive probing is being done because the consequences of the spill are considerable and some hard answers are needed.

What must be ascertained is not only who was to blame but why it happened and whether it is likely to happen again. If laws were ignored, the offenders should be punished. If there are loopholes in the law, they should be corrected.

Even if there is no legal gap or enforcement gap, there is an obvious informational gap. Little is known about how many municipalities and others dispose of their waste.

All this has led Rep. James Howard, the Monmouth County Democrat who chairs the House Public Works and Transportation Committee, to initiate a federal probe. Rep. Howard has instructed the investigations subcommittee of his House unit to open hearings when Congress returns from vacation.

What concerns Rep. Howard is the possibility that there was a breakdown in enforcement of garbage disposal regulations contained in two federal statutes—the Clean Water Act and the Ocean Dumping Act. Since the Environmental Protection Agency (EPA) is responsible for this enforcement, it would seem a likely target of the probe. Also at stake is whether the existing laws require amendments to give enforcers more power.

In addition to the House investigation, W. Cary Edwards, New Jersey's attorney general, is leading a joint state and federal probe that includes the Coast Guard, the EPA and New Jersey's Department of Environmental Protection. Also, the state Senate has a special committee opening hearings. And, as an additional incentive to finding a solution, Gov. Thomas Kean has offered a $5,000 bounty for anyone providing evidence that convicts and jails those responsible for the Shore garbage slick.

Not long after the beaches were reopened from the effects of the first garbage slick, there was a new slick of trash that began washing up on New Jersey beaches. No beaches were closed as a result of the second spill and authorities said there were no health hazards involved. Nevertheless, the probers will probably want to probe this incident as well in making their generalized investigations.

With all these investigators at work, it is important that there be a full, coordinated exchange of information. It would be unfortunate indeed if a failure to communicate affected the results. No doubt the various probers will take precautions to make sure that all findings are exchanged.

Ocean dumping is an environmental problem that is becoming a matter of increasing concern in New Jersey life. Both our health and our economy are dependent on the probers getting the right answers and taking the appropriate action.

Newsday

Long Island, NY,
August 14, 1988

Investigators still don't know for sure where the needles, syringes and other medical waste that washed up on New York beaches last month came from. But it's evident that the rules for disposing of potentially infectious refuse — "red bag" waste — from medical facilities is full of gaps that must be plugged.

This week, New York and New Jersey announced a joint program to track red bag wastes. Good. But there's much more to be done — now, to prevent further damage, and over the longer haul, to keep it under control.

The immediate need is to extend state regulation to *all* sources of red bag waste and to further tighten the controls over it. The long-term need is for new disposal facilities, so the growing volume of hospital refuse won't have to be trucked as far away as South Carolina.

Infectious waste is a big problem. New York State generates 1.8 million *tons* of it a year. New York City hospitals, clinics and labs account for 800,000 tons; Long Island about 500,000 tons. Disposal costs are astronomical: $800 a ton, says the Long Island Hospital Council, mostly because it's shipped so far.

As the volume of waste and the cost of disposal grows, so does the likelihood that more will wind up dumped illegally in the water.

The new New York-New Jersey plan will require sources of infectious wastes to maintain a paper trail until the red bag's final incineration. A floatable ID tag will have to be packed in the red bag, so it can be traced if washed ashore. That's good — but not enough.

State law says infectious waste must be burned or sterilized. Usually it's burned, either in hospital incinerators or commercial ones. But the law covers only larger sources of infectious wastes. Doctors' offices, clinics and small labs that produce less than 220 pounds a month aren't covered (though they are by New York City law). Statewide they account for about 10 percent of red bag waste. Legislation to cover these smaller sources and stiffen penalties for violations must become law.

In addition, to assure that hospitals and other waste generators maintain the paper trail, there must be periodic state audits.

And, ultimately, the paper trail should be backed by federal law. Red bag wastes are trucked across many state lines, so the manifest system needs to be interstate, too.

But even that is not enough.

Municipal incinerators won't take red bag waste and there is only one major commercial medical-waste incinerator in the New York City-Long Island area. That's why much of it must be hauled out of state — at great cost.

This is where the state must come in.

Albany has already mandated that New York communities replace landfills with modern incinerators by 1992. Those incinerators could burn infeetious wastes with perfect safety. But incinerator workers refuse to handle it. One answer is for the state to require that municipal incinerators accept red bag waste — and help train workers to handle it.

The state also could play a role in siting a new incinerator dedicated to medical wastes, financed by public or private moneys. One obvious site is the old Pilgrim State Hospital in Suffolk County, which has land and access.

Albany has another role to play, too. City and Long Island hospitals seeking solutions to this problem could end up working at cross-purposes. The state is the only level of government that can coordinate such activity and wield the clout to mandate solutions if private or voluntary measures don't work out.

The Miami Herald

Miami, FL, August 12, 1988

WE HAVE viewed the ocean as a great sink, which could absorb almost anything we threw into it. We simply cannot continue to do that any longer," said U.S. Sen. Bill Bradley, Democrat of New Jersey, on behalf of a bill that outlaws dumping of sewage sludge in oceans. The bill, which also stiffens fines for illegal disposal of hospital waste, passed 97-0 in the Senate this week.

House approval is expected.

Mr. Bradley echoes alarms sounded for years by scientists, environmentalists, and fishermen. Dumping has killed many Atlantic fishing beds. The hospital refuse and sewage washing up on Eastern Seaboard beaches this summer provided repelling evidence of the menace and caught Congress's attention.

But the reactive legislation is really symptomatic of the overall waste-disposal problems — inland and coastal — of the country. They encompass municipal, county, and state jurisdictions as much as Federal control. Many cities — including some in South Florida — still discharge undertreated sewage into coastal waters. Recognized toxics remain unattended. The toxic sludge on the Miami River's bottom flows into Biscayne Bay. So does river-borne sewage.

Industrial chemicals continue to contaminate rivers and lakes despite Federal regulations. Government at all levels has responded by enacting toxic-waste controls — then denying regulators enough money for adequate enforcement. Thus a contractor trucks drums of toxicₜ to the nearest out-of-the-way vacant lot. In time the drums rust through, allowing toxics eventually to seep into the ground and the aquifer.

Disposal contractors aren't the only ones dumping contaminated hospital refuse illegally. The U.S. Navy is cleaning up an unexplained spill that washed up on a North Carolina beach. Meanwhile, a Federal suit has temporarily halted a plan to haul a bargeload of toxic waste out to sea and set it afire.

So while it's good that the Feds may soon address some waste dumping at sea, that's a fraction of the problem. The issue to confront is that of mounting waste — all kinds — and how best to dispose of it safely.

Laws are not enough. There has to be more enforcement, more research into safe waste disposal. It's too late to whine about the difficulties of complying with good laws. Better to redirect the energy into finding the will and the money required to encourage technology toward timely answers.

The Charlotte Observer

Charlotte, NC, August 12, 1988

The Navy has accepted blame for dumping waste — including used hypodermic needles and vials of blood-colored liquids — off the N.C. coast, but neither Navy nor state officials seem to know if any Navy or state regulations have been violated.

If ever there were a case for state action to develop clear guidelines for what can and can't be dumped off the N.C. coast, and where, this is it.

Lt Gov. Bob Jordan says it's unclear whether N.C. law prohibits such dumping. He has asked the attorney general to investigate. Federal law prohibits dumping anything in the ocean that may endanger human health. But state officials have not said absolutely whether the Navy's waste poses health risks to the public. Dr. Ron Levine, state health director, says there is little "likelihood" of any danger and that the greatest risk to people on the beaches would be stepping on a contaminated syringe, with only a "small risk" of disease transmission.

The Navy says it routinely dumps waste in the ocean and has guidelines for such dumping. Medical waste, if sterilized, can be dumped 25 miles off shore, for example. But the Navy doesn't know whether it followed its own guidelines in dumping the medical waste that fouled N.C. beaches.

Neither the Navy's nor the state's responses thus far inspire much public confidence. This much is clear: The Navy must be required to keep track of where it dumps its wastes. And North Carolina must have regulations that determine what, if anything, can be dumped near its coast.

WORCESTER TELEGRAM

Worcester, MA, August 16, 1988

As the tides carrying medical waste touch more beaches, an agonizing truth is coming to light. There are no federal laws and too few state laws to regulate the proper disposal of syringes, intravenous tubing, vials and other hospital leftovers. And little is being done to correct the situation.

What started out as a problem on Long Island beaches has now washed to the faraway shores of Lake Erie and the outer banks of North Carolina. A congressional subcommittee is looking into the problem and finding a hodgepodge of state laws that haven't done the job and an appalling absence of federal regulations.

There are differing definitions of medical waste, but two practices are evident: 1. Many incinerator operators have refused medical debris for years, leaving haulers to dispose of it in the water or land, usually unsecured. 2. Disposal companies in states where medical refuse is monitored or regulated simply haul to another state with fewer or no regulations.

New York State, where the first med-tides became evident, was embarrassed to discover that it had no recourse even if those responsible for dumping the mess in the ocean were identified. It has since hastened to impose regulation. The state cited one culprit with "filing false documents" for saying that medical waste had been burned when it had merely been dumped.

The real villain in the continuing saga of medical debris washing ashore may be the Environmental Protection Agency, which was charged 10 years ago with establishing regulations for proper disposal of this waste.

First the EPA delayed seeking a decision on the best treatment of such debris. Then, in 1985, it issued convoluted recommendations for packaging, hauling, storing and disposing of used medical items. These guidelines proved to be unenforceable.

Now the EPA claims there is little or no hazard from medical debris and/or that state regulations are strict enough — although the EPA has just begun evaluation of state laws and won't complete the job until next year. Congress was told the EPA has only one staff member assigned to the investigation of medical waste problems.

Meanwhile, the tide of trash in our oceans is rising, not receding. The environmental group Greenpeace has called for an investigation of the deaths of more than half the harbor seals in the North Sea because of chemical pollution, a problem that may require international regulation of ocean dumping.

For health and safety's sake, the EPA or some federal agency must set standards and coordinate efforts to stop careless and improper disposal of medical waste, as has been done with toxic waste and nuclear waste.

DAILY ⬛ NEWS

New York, NY, August 25, 1988

THE ARMY CORPS OF ENGINEERS numbers among its duties the dredging of ship channels, keeping the waterways open for commercial and recreational vessels. This is a good thing. The dredged material is then dumped in the ocean, provided such material meets federal standards. According to the Corps, 90% of the sediment it will dredge from New York Harbor is perfectly safe to be so dumped. But another 10% will be from the bottom of the Gowanus Canal and Newtown Creek—gunk contaminated by heavy metals and PCBs. Thus, instead of ocean disposal,

the Corps is thinking of burying it in underwater pits. Off Staten Island. Monmouth County. Coney Island. Maybe in Jamaica Bay. This is, at the very least, a controversial thing. At the very worst, a dangerous thing.

Since the Corps released its draft Environmental Impact Statement, there has been an uproar. Environmentalists, fishermen, local political leaders, average citizens are crying "Foul!" And rightly so.

The Corps sees "subaqueous borrow pits"—holes that had been dug by sand miners to obtain construction material—as the best disposal method, the alternatives being containment facilities or landfill. The sediment would be buried either in existing pits or in new pits dug by the Corps. It then would be capped with a layer of clean sand. And it supposedly will sit there safe and snug without doing any harm to the water, the fish, the people. Problem: Nobody really knows how safe and snug it would remain.

THE ENVIRONMENTAL STATEMENT notes that although the procedure is "based on reasonable assumptions and projections, it has yet to be verified in a full-scale operation." In other words, it will be an experiment. Monitored, yes. But still an experiment.

Luckily, this project will not be implemented immediately. The Corps will evaluate the public's comments. It could then issue another environmental impact statement and hold more hearings.

It is to be hoped that will not be necessary, that this proposal will be withdrawn. What it comes down to is taking a risk. The local waters are far too fragile for risk-taking. They must not be harmed any more than society has harmed them already.

The Morning News

Wilmington, DE, July 31, 1988

SOME reports circulating over the past year might have led casual observers to speculate that the medical community, unwittingly or not, was turning the Middle Atlantic beaches into a landfill.

Obviously medical folks would be disturbed by such an implication. If any group wants to be known as squeaky clean it is this one.

But refuse from various medical activities has been washing up on the sands, causing great distress both to those who enjoy the beaches and to the resort owners.

It does not do much to lessen the reaction to this beach debris to note that it is far from being as medically hazardous as the public perceives it to be. Nor does it help much to know that some members of the medical professions go to extraordinary lengths to assure proper disposal of wastes.

Whether the debris is likely to lead directly to infection of humans is almost irrelevant. Its mere presence is offensive enough to those who pay king's ransoms for the privilege of enjoying the strands. Beyond that, these objects bobbing in the surf and beyond present enough peril to marine life and shore birds to justify outrage.

One problem with medical wastes and with other messes washing our shores is its non-degradable nature. Ocean swimmers always have risked bumping up against some sort of vegetable wastes that could be expected to be here today, gone tomorrow. Today's plastics don't act that way.

In any case, it is going to be a major undertaking, perhaps doomed, to identify all of the culprits. That is to determine whether they are that minority of medical facilities that one observer last week termed "fly by night" or waste disposal firms that flout decency and the good faith of clients who themselves would not countenance wanton waste dumping.

There is some reassurance. An Environmental Protection Agency official said last week in a report on beach debris: "We would love to pin it on somebody," said the administrator. "I'd hate to be the individual we would catch."

Medical trash littering beaches is only the tip of the problem. This nation is fast being buried in garbage. We need a national commitment, by government, business and private citizens to keep at least our heads above the gunk.

We are generating more than 150 million tons of garbage per year. Each of the 240 million of us blithely tosses out 1,250 pounds of the stuff annually. If trends continue, we'll up that to 1,600 pounds by the year 2000.

J. Winston Porter, EPA's assistant administrator for solid waste, observed recently that (1) a third of our total landfill capacity will be used up within five or six years and (2) it is getting more and more difficult to obtain citizen approval to put waste facilities in their areas. Nobody wants a landfill or incinerator in the yard.

Dr. Porter notes that we may have to develop new consumer attitudes. To start, those may include a different view of the use of "disposable" merchandise.

He also urges an all-out effort to increase recycling. At present we recycle 10 percent of our waste. In some fields we do better. About half of all aluminum cans are recycled now, according to EPA, and about a third of newspapers. Only 1 percent of plastics are recycled, however. Japan long ago realized it had no place to put large amounts of trash; it now recycles 50 percent of all its waste. Dr. Porter calls for a modest initial U.S. goal of 25 percent.

Recycling is only part of the answer. Other partial solutions are a reduction of the amount of solid waste generated in the first place and incineration, where appropriate, with adequate environmental controls.

Incineration may have to include carefully monitored high-tech burns at sea. Nobody wants wastes, especially toxic wastes, barged past their waterfronts, but we may have to settle for that if the alternative tempts the careless or ruthless to toss the stuff onto the tides.

WORCESTER TELEGRAM.

Worcester, MA, July 30, 1988

Public health and environmental officials are avoiding speculation about the source of medical waste washing up on beaches from New Jersey northeastward to Massachusetts. They say the invasion of "med tide" along the East Coast may have many unrelated causes.

Maybe so, but ordinary folks have reason to suspect that the simultaneous appearance of similar kinds of trash over such a long stretch of beaches must somehow be connected. If nothing else, humanity's insensitive mistreatment of the oceans links all these incidents.

Whether it is one source or many, state and federal investigators must press their probe vigorously and prosecute where appropriate. The region's beaches are one of its most precious resources and need protection from inappropriate ocean dumping. Just as alarming, the safety of people who use the beaches is at stake.

According to the Massachusetts Department of Public Health, there have been 18 confirmed reports to date of medical trash washing up on state beaches. The refuse has appeared on beaches in Chatham and Edgartown and as far north as Plum Island and Newbury. At least one beach had been closed in Massachusetts as the result of med tide. The Department of Environmental Quality Engineering is involved in trying to determine the source of the debris.

Massachusetts beaches come under the jurisdiction of local boards of health. The state health department has issued an advisory to local boards on how to collect medical waste that washes up on shore. Authorities urge beachgoers not to touch such trash but to alert a lifeguard or other beach authority.

Health officials claim there is a "next to zero" chance of contracting AIDS or hepatitis from the syringes or vials that have washed up since the new tide began in the New York area earlier this month. But they warn that anyone cut by such debris may need to get a tetanus shot and should see a doctor.

Medical debris has been spotted on some Rhode Island beaches, too, including Misquamicut State Beach in Westerly and beaches along Narragansett Bay. The danger is real, present and widespread.

Action is needed on several fronts. The dumper, or dumpers, of this potentially dangerous refuse must be determined and held responsible. That effort should be cooperative and cross state lines. Federal agencies should also be involved.

Federal and state laws regulating the disposal of medical trash and ocean dumping must be evaluated and strengthened if they are found wanting. Here again, an effort must be coordinated to produce a set of uniform regulations from state to state.

The medical community — including hospitals, clinics and laboratories — must examine its own practices for disposing of contaminated medical waste. New voluntary guidelines would be welcome until sensible laws can be enacted.

The health and safety of beachgoers and shore dwellers are threatened by this latest, and perhaps ugliest form of pollution. It must be confronted by persistent efforts. Awareness and concern should not vanish with the tide.

St. Petersburg Times

St. Petersburg, FL, July 6, 1988

Global warming, known as the "greenhouse effect," is no longer just another grim projection by scientists and environmental doomsday prophets. It's here. So is acid rain. So are the widespread and various results of dumping toxic effluents into rivers and lakes at a rate of up to 26-million gallons a day.

For instance, a recent *Greenpeace* magazine article on how toxic pollution has affected the Great Lakes included these startling statistics:

There are 150 toxic waste dumps along one three-mile section of the Niagara River, including one dump that holds a ton of dioxin. According to one researcher, just a shovelful of dioxin released into Lake Ontario could kill all the birds living there.

Scientists have found close to 500 chemicals in the bodies of fish inhabiting the Great Lakes. As early as 1981, the U.S. Fish and Wildlife Service found DDT, PCBs, chlordane, toxaphene and dieldrin in almost all fish tested.

In Ohio, laboratory samplings suggest that 80 percent of the adult bullhead trout in the Black River have cancer or precancerous conditions. Reproductive disturbances among trout have been noted everywhere but in Lake Superior, the least polluted.

Fish-eating birds suffer similar fates. During one two-year study of Caspian terns and cormorants feeding in Lake Michigan, three-quarters of the eggs in some bird colonies failed to hatch. In Saginaw Bay, also part of Lake Michigan, half the birds had physical defects.

More than 26-million of the 40-million people who live in the Great Lakes basin depend on it for their drinking water. Some of the worst pollution is found on the St. Lawrence River at a large Native American reservation between New York State and Ontario, Canada.

The source of this pollution is not mysterious. Canada and the United States have concentrated industrial activity in the region for decades, with little attention to environmental impact. A 1978 treaty identified 350 substances that should be kept out of the Great Lakes, and called for a ban on toxic discharges. Ten years later, with fish dying of cancer and toxin-related birth defects visible in wildlife, the two nations are still squabbling over everything from jurisdiction to "acceptable" levels of pesticides in drinking water.

Sullying our own lakes and rivers is inexcusable enough, but we have cast our toxic refuse on foreign shores as well. In recent years, countries in the Caribbean, Latin America and Africa have been willing — and sometimes eager — to sell dumping rights at a fraction of the cost European and North American industries would pay to dispose of toxic garbage at home.

Philadelphia incinerator ash, which would have cost at least $1,000 a ton to dispose of locally, was shipped to Guinea for dumping at a rate of only $40 a ton. Such a deal. This ash wasn't in a class with dioxins; it wasn't even classified "hazardous." All the same, the vegetation died on the island near the Guinean capital where the ash was dumped.

Ironically, the countries with the strictest domestic regulations are often the most ruthless purveyors of toxic waste abroad. According to Jan Huismans, director of a U.N. environmental program, highly regulated countries are stepping up toxin export efforts aimed at nations "suffering economic hardship and which have large areas of land. Several of the West African countries fall into that category."

Guinea arrested the middleman in its import deal, and at least two other African countries say they have had enough as well. Nigeria has threatened to execute a group of businessmen who engineered a deal to import chemical waste from Italy, including some refuse that may have been radioactive. In the Congo, authorities foiled a plot by three government officials to pocket a staggering $4-million each for accepting a million tons of industrial waste.

The obvious sticking point in the toxic waste controversy is profit, and polluters are surprisingly candid about it. Environmental protection is a noble goal, they say, but the effort is just too expensive. Dumping waste abroad is a practical matter; it is simply cheaper and more efficient than conforming to domestic constraints.

The real issue is kept hidden, although it lurks just below the surface of every environmental debate: If animals, marine life and plants cannot thrive in the toxic environments that have bloomed during this century as never before, what is happening to the people who must drink the same water, breathe the same air?

Answers have come quickly for creatures with relatively brief life cycles. Not so where human beings are concerned. Are we really willing just to wait and see?

In Highland County, for instance, Florida Department of Agriculture officials have discovered concentrations of the herbicide bromacil in water used for drinking. One well yielded a bromacil level more than three times the 80 parts per billion considered "safe" by federal standards.

It has already been established that over-exposure to bromacil can cause thyroid damage, leading to high blood pressure and rapid heartbeat. Yet the herbicide is not classified as acutely poisonous or carcinogenic. Small comfort to those families in Hendry, Highlands and Hillsborough counties who have been drawing this toxin from the kitchen tap and feeding it to their children.

The Hartford Courant

Hartford, CT, July 28, 1988

Why are used syringes, hypodermic needles, medical tubing and vials of blood and crack washing onto shores of the Northeast, forcing the closing of beaches and fueling fears about AIDS?

The waste first surfaced on New York and New Jersey beaches last summer. More of the junk appeared last month. Similar debris has since washed ashore in Connecticut, Massachusetts and Rhode Island.

Illegal dumping of hospital waste was the obvious and first suspicion of public health investigators. But in the words of Thomas C. Jorling, commissioner of New York state's Department of Environmental Conservation, "The honest answer is, 'Nobody knows.'" Sewage overflow and drug addicts' or dealers' flushing supplies down the toilet are two possibilities.

The FBI, federal Environmental Protection Agency and state agencies have declined to comment on their inquiries. We hope they have good reason to keep quiet, such as being on the verge of solving the mystery.

Although health experts have said that contracting AIDS from the wastes is impossible, it hasn't stopped the fear from spreading. Still, there is a danger of bacterial infections. Officials prudently have closed beaches when even a few discarded syringes or vials have been found.

What's most troubling about this threat to public health and degradation of the environment is the apparent inability of authorities to trace the source. Federal regulations require that records be kept on the disposal of hazardous waste so that illegally dumped material may be traced. But no such record-keeping is required for the disposal of medical paraphernalia. Investigators should be given the regulatory help needed to find out, and to do so quickly, which hospital, manufacturer, clinic or drugstore, if any, is illegally discarding refuse.

Amazon Environmental Plan Unveiled

Brazilian President Jose Sarney Oct. 12, 1988 announced a series of measures designed to check the rapid destruction of the Amazon rain forests. The president's announcement, made in a televised speech to the nation, followed a wave of international criticism of Brazil's environment polices.

Hundreds of thousands of square miles of forest in the Amazon basin had been felled and burned during the previous two decades by Brazilians attempting to clear the region for government-sponsored and private development projects. The tropical forests were disappearing largely because of the population push for arable land and industrial exploitation of timber resources.

U.S. and Brazilian researchers, using satellites to monitor fires in the region, estimated that 77,000 square miles of rain forest had burned in 1987 alone. At least 30,000 square miles of that had been virgin woodland.

An average of 5,000 fires were burning in the area on any given day, the research team said. Many scientists believed that the huge man-made fires were contributing to worldwide pollution and buildup of carbon dioxide in the Earth's atmosphere, stimulating the so-called "greenhouse effect," or overall warming of global temperatures.

By some estimates, the Brazilian fires accounted for one-tenth of all the man-made carbon dioxide being released into the atmosphere. "Fires, deforestation, huge agricultural projects, gold mines and predatory development are destroying our flora and fauna," Sarney declared in his speech. "We must contain the predatory actions of man."

The centerpiece of the president's plan was a suspension of government subsidies – including tax cuts, loans and other incentives – for agricultural development in the rain forests. A complete ban on the export of logs was also imposed. In addition, Sarney announced that cattle-raising would be severely restricted in the Amazon region and would be outlawed in the woodland along the Atlantic coast.

The Atlantic rain forests, believed to have once covered 140,000 square miles, now covered only about 4,000 square miles, it was reported.

The action came in response to a July 3, 1987 call to action by an international group of development experts and Third World political leaders to reverse the continuing loss of the world's tropical forests. The tropical forests were diminishing by an area the size of Belgium every year, it was estimated. The experts, meeting at Bellagio, Italy, urged international support for a "tropical Forestry Action Plan" launched in 1985, funded by major development agencies. Funding for forestry assistance had risen to the $1 billion level for 1988 because of the effort.

The meeting was organized by the Rockefeller Foundation and attended by officials from several developing countries and from several United Nations agencies, the World Resources Institute and the Rockefeller Foundation.

In a related development, Francisco Mendes Filho, an internationally renowned environmentalist and labor leader, was shot to death Dec. 22, 1988 at his home in the northeastern village of Xapuri. Chico Mendes, as he was known, had been outspoken opponent of the destruction of Brazil's Amazon rain forests. He had been a recipient in 1987 of the United Nations Global 500 ecology prize, for his work to save the forests. He was also president of the Xapuri rural union workers union, an organization of itinerant rubber trappers.

Mendes was reported to have received numerous death threats from businessmen and landowners in the Xapuri region. A local cattle rancher's son, Darcy Pereira, surrendered to police Dec. 26 and confessed that he had hired a professional killer to murder Mendes. Police Dec. 27 arrested six other suspects in connection with the murder.

THE KANSAS CITY STAR

Kansas City, MO, April 21, 1986

An environmental group is taking important steps to protect rain forests and other resources in the Third World. It's a wonder—and really a shame—such logical action has not been previously achieved.

One key to this effort is the work of Bruce Rich of the Environmental Defense Fund. Mr. Rich's message, which he began spreading several years ago, is simple but effective.

The four major multilateral development banks in the world, which issue up to $22 billion to developing nations each year, must stop handing out loans for massive building programs that cause too much damage to the countries' environments. The United States, as a major donor to the organizations, should throw its weight and help shield fragile environments, Mr. Rich argues.

Consider this success story. The World Bank has been a major contributor to developers building a 1,100-mile road into an extremely large forested area in Brazil, ostensibly to use it to help in the planting and growing of rice and other crops. But the project has obvious ecological drawbacks. The soil is not rich enough to support the crops for more than a few years, especially after the trees have been cut down and no longer protect the land. Then, of course, it will be time to destroy more forests for more land to grow more crops. It's a dangerous, wasteful process.

Mr. Rich, testifying before Congress last year, pointed out these unavoidable environmental damages. The United States then vetoed one-fifth of a $73 million loan designed to continue the road. Two months later the World Bank halted over a quarter billion dollars of lending until the Brazilian government answers tough questions on environmental concerns about the road.

The multilateral aid banks are very powerful in the Third World; the less-developed countries need their help and will do almost anything to get it. Which gives the banks extra clout. They should use it properly, lending money for projects that improve nations while not overly damaging their environments.

The Register

Santa Ana, CA, November 10, 1986

The World Bank and other international development institutions are coming under fire from environmentalists. Last month a consortium of organizations, led by the Environmental Defense Fund, sent a report to Barber Conable, the Bank's new president, condemning a project in Indonesia that would force the resettlement of hundreds of thousands of people, destroy millions of acres of virgin rain forest and place emigrants in an environment that would not sustain long-term development.

This protest is another sign that individuals and organizations concerned about the long-term health of the earth's environment and ecosystems are beginning to understand that government interventions are a more pervasive and dangerous threat than private development. Perhaps more people understand that economics and ecology — two words with the same Greek root, connoting household management or stewardship — are ultimately harmonious in the world as well as in lexicography.

The World Bank and other international development organizations — though they may have some of the trappings of private insitutions — are government organizations, financed by money extracted by force from taxpayers. They are specifically set up to promote what they call development by financing projects the private market is unlikely to undertake.

It is not accidental that many projects that the private market views as economically unproductive are also environmentally destructive. While private development undertaken for private gain may sometimes result in things that others find aesthetically displeasing or disruptive of a pristine natural environment, there is little incentive in a system of private ownership for the kind of large-scale, massive disruption of the environment that often characterizes big government projects.

To an owner of property, outright destruction of that property seldom makes economic sense — though one person's "enhancement" may be another's "desecration." To a non-owner in the service of "larger social goals," as most development bureaucrats are, such destruction may be of little concern.

Thus we find, as in the Garrison Diversion project in North Dakota and in dozens of dams, that projects both economically inefficient and environmentally destructive are virtually inevitable, given the incentives built into the system of government management. This is not to say that some environmental destruction would not take place in a regime of private property rights and voluntary transactions, but it is extremely unlikely that it would occur on the scale that is routine with government projects. Such projects not only destroy wetlands and other habitats, but they lose money. That's of small concern to a bureaucrat, but of overriding concern to a private owner.

It is helpful and necessary, but not sufficient, for environmental groups to urge the World Bank and similar organizations to take more account of the environmental consequences of their development projects. Such groups would be well advised, however, to go beyond urging more environmental impact statements and sensitivity to demanding a simple standard: If a project doesn't make economic sense without subsidies, don't do it. Period.

Of course if the World Bank adopted such a standard, it might quickly discover that it had no useful role in the world — which, come to think of it, might not be such a bad development.

The TENNESSEAN

Nashville, TN, January 24, 1986

THE World Resources Institute, a private policy research group based in Washington, has called for spending $8 billion over the next five years to protect rain forests in 56 tropical countries.

Probably no project is needed more — the forests are being cut at an accelerating rate for economic gain with possibly disastrous consequences for the world — but with many countries in financial difficulty, saving the rain forests may get a low priority with them.

This could be a mistake. The rain forests are thought to have a direct influence on climate in many parts of the world. Their destruction could bring about unwanted changes in the weather. The forests are also a source of many plants, chemicals, and other natural resources that are of biologic and economic importance to the developed world.

But such matters are of little concern to people who are only a few days away from starvation — as many are in the tropical latitudes where the rain forests are located.

Thus, the cost of any effort to safe the forests would have to be borne largely by the industrialized nations. Most of these are far removed from the rain forests, and it may be hard to convince their citizens that destruction of the forests affects them.

The political leaders of some developed nations have not been in a hurry to protect their own forests from acid rain. Thus, they are not likely to be enthusiastic about spending money to protect the rain forests in South America or Africa. It seems the need to save the forests may not become apparent to many until it is too late to save them. ■

Minneapolis Star and Tribune

Manchester, ME, May 31, 1986

The U.S. Forest Service is ruining America's last great rain forest — and losing millions of dollars in the process. It is subsidizing logging in large areas of southeastern Alaska's Tongass National Forest, marring the land and selling the harvested timber at a loss. That policy is environmental and economic folly; Congress should correct it.

Home to bald eagles, grizzlies and 800-year-old spruce, the Tongass was wisely set aside as protected wilderness by the 1980 Alaska Lands Act. But one provision of that law guarantees special privileges to two pulp mills that 35 years ago secured contracts to harvest Tongass timber at a profit. The provision authorizes the companies to log 4.5 million board feet of timber over 10 years — and directs the government to underwrite road-building and to spend whatever is needed to assure the mills' success.

For its beneficiaries, that subsidy program buffers the bite of plummeting world timber prices. But it does so at great cost to the environment and to taxpayers. The logging has claimed huge stands of ancient spruce and hemlock. According to a new study by the Wilderness Society, subsidizing the

logging venture now costs more than $50 million a year. The forest service reclaims only 7 cents on every dollar it spends to prop up the two pulp mills.

The timber companies and Alaska's congressional delegation argue that the subsidies are essential to sustain the Alaskan logging industry. But the program has failed at even that mission: Since 1980, the number of logging jobs in southeastern Alaska has dropped from 3,000 to about 1,500; the current per-job subsidy is an astonishing $36,000 a year. The subsidy program actually threatens more jobs than it preserves: Soil runoff from logging jeopardizes the region's fishing industry, which provides half again as many jobs as timber.

Why should the federal government underwrite such destruction — especially when demand for Tongass timber is likely to remain low for years? That is the question before the House Interior Committee, which now is conducting a five-year review of the Alaska Lands Act. Lawmakers will find no good reason for logging the Tongass. The best course is to trim back the subsidies, phase out the logging and buy out the pulp mills. Alaska's rain forest should suffer no further indignities.

Los Angeles Times

Los Angeles, CA, June 23, 1987

The simple act of cutting down a single tree seems to be a harmless thing. There are so many trees. But the felling of one tree can trigger a series of events that reaches beyond the imagination of the tree-cutter, whose thoughts perhaps extend no further than firewood for the week's cooking. Where that tree's living roots and leaves once reached out to grasp the rainfall, the water now runs off in rivulets. The rivulets pick up soil as they swirl down a hillside. Enough rivulets quickly make a flood. Enough erosion can move entire mountainsides. Enough silt can render dams and reservoirs impotent and create new river deltas. The loss of the forest cover can alter entire ecologies, even the climate.

Naturalist John Muir had such concepts in mind when he wrote more than a century ago: "When we try to pick out anything by itself, we find it hitched to everything else in the universe." Now staff writer A. Kent MacDougall has dramatically demonstrated Muir's thesis in his four-part series, "The Vanishing Forests," which concluded in Monday's editions of The Times.

The concept of worldwide deforestation has always seemed to be one of those very remote problems that registered well down on the scale of immediate attention, behind such issues as whether to pursue that new job opening or when to pick up the dry cleaning. Deforestation was like the threat to the ozone layer. If the situation ever got that bad, it perhaps would affect some future generation or people in some far-off land. In any event, what can one individual do about such cosmic problems?

The crisis of forest devastation is most acute today in the developing countries, primarily in the tropics. Sometimes it is the result of the poorest of the poor attempting to scratch the most meager of livings from the land. Too often it is an old historic pattern: the result of powerful economic interests ravaging the land for private gain without regard for damage that may never be overcome.

The industrialized nations in temperate lands, like European countries and the United States, pursued such practices in the past and only now are beginning to realize the devastation to be caused and the ultimate price to be paid. As MacDougall wrote: "Humans owe a debt of thanks to forests." They clear the air, moderate the climate, protect soil from erosion and keep water clean. They provide lumber, fuel and food and raw material for thousands of products. In fact, the story of the forests is virtually a history of the world. Wars were won and empires lost because of the forests and lack of them. Civilizations rose and declined. Bountiful lands became deserts.

The road back begins with awareness and education about the importance of forests in the balance of nature, the need for rigorous forest management practices everywhere, and the realization that some remaining virgin tracts should be allowed to stand because, once cut, they can never be the same.

In art and literature, trees often are used as a metaphor for life itself. The allusion is appropriate. How well a civilized world respects and nurtures its forests says much about just how civilized the world is.

Wisconsin ⚓ State Journal

Madison, WI, December 9, 1987

The list of issues worthy of discussion at this week's Washington summit is almost without end. Arms control, Afghanistan, human rights, emigration freedom for Soviet Jews, self-determination for the Baltic states and Warsaw Pact nations, and reduction of Soviet conventional forces in Eastern Europe is a burdensome agenda for so short (75 hours) a meeting.

Yet there is one more issue that deserves a spot on the U.S.-Soviet agenda, if not this week, soon. That is the alarming problem of tropical deforestation around the world.

The statistics are striking: Half the world's rain forests in Latin America, Africa and Asia have disappeared since World War II. Destruction continues at the rate of 50 to 100 acres per minute, a pace that could wipe out half of what remains by the end of the century. If the tropical forests are lost, world temperatures and climates will change dramatically and harshly.

Granted, there are no "tropic" zones in the United States or the Soviet Union, but a combined effort by the world's two leading scientific and economic communities might help to blunt this terrible threat to the global environment.

The World Bank, with U.S. prodding, has announced reforms that should make it less likely that environmentally degrading development projects are carried out. Or, at least, not carried out with World Bank assistance. The same kind of leadership is needed from the Soviet Union, which has economic influence over communist states around the world.

Three U.S. senators, including Wisconsin's Robert Kasten, have urged that tropical deforestation be put on the summit agenda because they know that environmental degradation in Africa or Latin America eventually affects everyone. The world ecosystem isn't capitalist or communist. It exists for all.

The Des Moines Register

Des Moines, IA, July 20, 1987

Millions of years ago, a natural catastrophe wiped out the dinosaurs. Today, other life forms are dying by the thousands or even millions yearly, victims of a man-made catastrophe that threatens man's own well-being.

The planet's tropical moist forests, the nurturing greenhouses for biological treasures yet undiscovered, are falling to slash-and-burn developers at a rate that threatens to wipe them out in a few decades. When they go, mankind will be forever impoverished.

Scientists have studied and described 1.6 million living species of plants and animals on this globe, but more than that — possibly as many as 30 million — species have not yet been studied. Half of those are found only in the tropical forests that cover less than 10 percent of the Earth's land mass.

One-fourth of today's prescription drugs were developed from exotic species thriving in the tropical forests. Just a bit deeper into the forest may be the rare plant whose mix of chemicals includes the cure for Alzheimer's disease or the solution to the mysteries of cancer. But once an uncataloged species dies under the bulldozer treads, its secret is lost forever.

In South America, where 40 percent of the tropical forests are found (the rest are in Africa and Southeast Asia), the destruction results primarily from opening new land for farming and grazing. But the wet soil is thin. Once exposed, it soon erodes away, meaning more forests must fall to expose more land that will be rendered worthless after a few quick harvests.

Some of the forests are ravaged by loggers who destroy trees by the hundreds to harvest a handful. The trees are sold to the United States and other developed nations, which today import 15 times as much hardwood lumber as they did 30 years ago.

Last week, a non-profit U.S. organization, Conservation International, took a small but significant step toward slowing the destruction. It bought $650,000 worth of Bolivia's huge debt to foreign investors in return for an agreement that Bolivia would protect 3.7 million acres of forest.

Both bargaining chips are pitifully small: The acreage represents less than one-sixth of the annual worldwide destruction, and $650,000 represents less than one-six-thousandth of Bolivia's foreign debt.

But it's a start. The urgency of expanding on that beginning can't be overemphasized.

Omaha World-Herald

Omaha, NE, June 11, 1987

The potential damage caused by deforestation is comparable in some respects to what might happen if Earth collided with a giant asteroid. Fortunately, in the case of deforestation, mankind has the power to avert disaster.

Some geologists believe that a collision with an asteroid or comet led to climate changes that caused the extinction of thousands of plant and animal species, including dinosaurs.

A major loss of remaining plant and animal species could occur if the world's rain forests continue to be destroyed. Worldwatch Institute, a Washington-based think tank, says that if the destruction of the Amazonian rain forests of South America continues at its present rate, the Earth could lose 14 percent of its remaining plant varieties by the year 2000, along with thousands of species of birds and animals.

A rain forest is a huge, delicate ecosystem in which clouds, rain, soil and living things replenish each other in a balanced cycle of nature. Trees play a central role in the ecosystem, holding the soil against erosion, transferring water vapor from the soil to the atmosphere, providing organic material to replenish the soil and supplying food and shelter for other living things.

In parts of Africa, Asia and South America, the rain forests are being destroyed through overgrazing, wood gathering, urban development and slash-and-burn agriculture. About half the world's rain forests were destroyed between 1900 and 1980.

The loss of rain forests leads to a cycle that brings a loss of other plants and animals, proliferation of pests such as rats and roaches, disruption of rainfall patterns, depletion and erosion of the soil and, ultimately, famine.

The World Bank has begun taking environmental concerns under advisement when making loans to Third World countries. The United Nations, the United States and private international agencies are sponsoring reforestation projects. Soviet scientists have displayed an interest in joining international efforts to save the rain forests. Tree planting has received more emphasis in private and government aid programs.

The situation may not be hopeless, but time is running out. So long as the bulldozers continue to rip away at the world's rain forests, an ecological disaster remains possible.

BUFFALO EVENING NEWS

Buffalo, NY, May 31, 1987

RAIN FORESTS DISAPPEAR; deserts spread; self-supporting people are dislodged from ancestral lands to end up in urban slums; natural resources are squandered and lost in a single generation. Too often that has been the underside of development in Third World countries.

And too often, richer nations have gone along with the environmental damage or even assisted it, rather than directing their scientific expertise to help stop it.

One institution with power to direct much Third World development is the World Bank, and in the past it has paid far too little attention to the long-term consequences of projects it helped finance.

Now, however, that is about to undergo a welcome change. An environmental revolution is in the works at the World Bank, and it is coming none too soon. With its vast lending power, the bank can make a difference in the thinking of developing countries' leaders and in the effects of their efforts to better their nations.

Under its new president, Western New Yorker and former Congressman Barber Conable (and partly in response to pressure from critics), the bank now plans to give much more consideration to the long-term consequences of actions funded by its loans.

It will increase the number of environmental specialists at its Washington headquarters from 17 to between 50 and 60 and organize them in a new department. It will add to regional environmental staff. And a new policy announced by Conable will aim to make environmental awareness "integral to all the bank's activities."

Shortsighted thinking in nations trying to better themselves isn't a new phenomenon; our own country, for instance, made plenty of environmental mistakes as it "tamed the wilderness." But modern technology raises the price of ecological carelessness.

In West Africa, for instance, modern lumbering methods are leveling a forest area the size of Maine each year. The Sahara desert has advanced 219 miles in the past 20 years, partly as a result of the loss of trees.

A report by the United Nations-sponsored World Commission on Environment and Development envisions a new era when economic growth comes under environmentally sound principles, and Conable says he shares that optimism. But, as he told an environmental group recently, what has to change is not just the bank's policies but also "the customs and ingrained attitudes of hundreds of millions of individuals and their leaders."

This can hardly be easy, but the bank is planning initiatives that will help. It will make a five-year assessment of environmental threats to the most vulnerable countries, increase its lending for forestry projects and promote work to stop the damage in Africa.

And most important, it will take an environmentally sound look at everything it funds.

The Orlando Sentinel

Orlando, FL, May 18, 1987

Meanwhile, U.S. and Soviet scientists have joined to halt destruction of tropical rain forests. That's news of the best kind.

Both countries have a substantial stake in this issue. Tropical deforestation is only the first step of a vicious cycle.

First, population pressures lead to clearing forests for agriculture and fuel wood. In turn, this causes rapid erosion. The land that was meant to feed the expanding population becomes, instead, infertile desert. Haiti offers a classic example of the process and a painful lesson in the results.

If theorists of the "greenhouse effect" are on the mark, tropical deforestation also threatens the planet's environmental balance. Carbon dioxide trapped in the lush vegetation is released into the atmosphere when the forests are cleared, promoting a gradual global warming. In time, that can alter worldwide growing patterns and lead to massive coastal flooding.

The scientists propose a joint U.S.-Soviet demonstration project on the Indian Ocean island of Madagascar. The island offers a handy lab for developing alternative methods of farming and providing fuel without sacrificing forest land.

To succeed, though, both superpower governments must throw their weight behind this largely private initiative. The world offers too few opportunities for such cooperation, but the simple truth is that if the rain forests disappear, everyone loses.

Arkansas Gazette

Little Rock, AR,
March 22, 1987

Incredible as it sounds, American taxpayers are shelling out some $40 million a year to destroy a unique natural area, the country's last great rain forest.

There is some hope for ending this economic and environmental madness. Legislation to do so has been introduced in Congress, and 49 senators and representatives have signed on as sponsors. The bill is called the Tongass Timber Reform Act.

The huge Tongass National Forest in southeast Alaska is a rare old-growth rain forest that is the home for significant populations of bald eagles, grizzly bears and other wildlife. The Wilderness Society says the forest is far more valuable as an "ecological history book" than as timber. Yet a federal law requires — or so it is interpreted by the United States Forest Service, which manages the Tongass — that an average of 450 million board feet of Tongass timber be prepared and offered for sale each year, no matter what the demand is.

In fact, the demand is so low that the Tongass timber is almost worthless. But under the present interpretation of the law, the Forest Service is guaranteed an appropriation of at least $40 million annually to build the logging roads and cover all the other activities that are part of the sales process — and that do ecological damage to the forest and its wildlife.

The two big companies that get almost all of the Tongass timber at cut-rate prices are happy with the present arrangement. No one else should be.

The Hartford Courant

Hartford, CT, January 9, 1989

The murder of Francisco Mendes Filho last month has an impact far beyond the Amazonian frontier where he died.

Mr. Mendes was a labor organizer, an activist who rallied thousands of his fellow rubber tappers to fight the developers who threaten their livelihoods — and the Earth's environment. Cattle ranchers, land speculators and homesteaders, attracted by the Brazilian government's open-for-business policy in the Northwest Region, are burning and bulldozing the rain forest at an alarming rate. Almost 20 percent of the forest in the state of Rondonia may already have been destroyed.

Most important, the wholesale development robs all the people of the Earth of a precious resource: the rain forest as a giant cleansing mechanism whose chlorophyllic action rids the atmosphere of excessive pollution. The burning and bulldozing also destroys rubber, food and timber resources that could be safely harvested, and threatens a fragile ecosystem supporting an Indian culture and wildlife species that could be lost forever.

This was the environmental holocaust that Mr. Mendes sought to stop. Several weeks ago he was warned that landowners had put out a contract on his life. The police were supposed to protect him, but he was shot to death at home as his guards sat in the kitchen. The commitment of Brazilian authorities to protect him, and to bring his killers to justice, is open to question. His death symbolizes the difficulty of curbing excessive, destructive development.

Like the animal poachers in Africa, who are pushing the elephant and the rhinoceros to the edge of extinction and killing game wardens under the noses of corrupt officials, the rapists of the Amazon and the murderers of those who fight it seem to be operating at the sufferance of Brazil's government.

The exploitation of the Northwest Region began with grants of land by the government and the construction of a pan-Amazon road, financed by the World Bank. Government loans and tax credits have spurred development. The United States — and its fast-food chains — has been a ready market for cheap South American beef that can be fed on pastures growing from the ashes of rain forests.

The World Bank now places environmental conditions on its lending. Other creditors should do no less. William K. Reilly, the administrator-designate of the U.S. Environmental Protection Agency, who is especially knowledgeable about worldwide environmental problems, should help President-elect George Bush formulate an effective U.S. response to Brazil's destructive development policies.

The rest of the world cannot tolerate a climate of development that allows voices like Mr. Mendes' to be stilled, and that threatens the well-being of everyone on Earth.

Omaha World-Herald

Omaha, NE, February 7, 1989

Brazil's program of protecting the vital rain forests of the Amazon from slash-and-burn development has stalled in recent weeks. The country's new willingness to accept international help is welcome.

Brazil's rain forests are an ecological treasure, with plants and animals that constitute unknown scientific potential. They are also a key element in world ecology — the dense greenery helps cleanse and refresh the atmosphere.

When ranchers, farmers and developers cut down the forests and burn the plant matter, it is a double disaster: The loss of the trees combined with the carbon dioxide and pollution emitted by the burning contribute to the greenhouse effect.

Just four months ago, Brazilian officials announced a new program to discourage further deforestation in the Amazon Basin. Until that point, tax incentives. and government programs had encouraged development. But the Brazilians had wanted to handle their own environmental program, fearful that with outside funds would come outside interference and, some thought, outside exploitation or ownership of key portions of the basin.

But the Brazilian program was easier to announce than to implement, and natural resources officials there have been having one problem after another. The country has never had enough forest rangers or police officers to enforce the new laws. Some peasants couldn't afford to pay fines in any case. The program budget was cut and cut again. And to many Brazilians seeking economic security, there has been little alternative to the slash-and-burn cycle.

The policy change will permit international aid to flow into the Amazon project, under strict Brazilian controls. Some experts are discussing "debt-for-nature" swaps in which other nations would buy off a portion of Brazil's foreign debt, and Brazil would plow the money it saved into rain forest preservation.

The Brazilian military has opposed foreign involvement in saving the rain forests, citing security reasons. The acceptability of any type of foreign aid could be a matter for delicate diplomatic negotiations. In the meantime, other nations and financial institutions such as the Inter-American Development Bank and the World Bank should maintain the pressure on Brazil.

The rain forests are vital to the whole world; the senseless destruction that has been going on for years should end, for the good of everyone.

GUESS WHICH ONE IS CONSIDERED A CIVILIZED COUNTRY...

The Oregonian

Portland, OR, January 18, 1989

A striking pair of stories about concern in tropical countries for the preservation of forest land appeared in the news last week.

In Brazil there has been a widespread outcry at the murder of a rubber tapper, Francisco "Chico" Mendes Jr. A cattle ranching family is suspected of having him shot because he had been leading a campaign to preserve a reserve of rubber trees on land they wanted to clear for grazing.

On the opposite side of the globe the government of Thailand decreed that it would close the country's forests to logging. Floods that killed 350 people in northern Thailand in November had been blamed mainly on illegal tree cutting that had removed the land's cover. "We have almost no forests left," Prime Minister Chatichai Choonhavan said, in a country that was 70 percent wooded as recently as the end of World War II.

These were dramatic reactions to the deforestation of the globe. A study published last year by Worldwatch Institute reported that Europe is the only continent where forests are spreading rather than shrinking. In the tropical regions the devastation has been running at the rate of 10 acres of trees destroyed for every acre planted.

Scientists may describe the loss in terms of the disappearance of plant and animal colonies dependent on the forests, and of the greenhouse effect of heat-retaining carbon dioxide when the trees no longer are there to recycle it out of the air.

For the people in the denuded countries, or downstream, deforestation means loss of firewood and charcoal, of shelter, food and timber for export, the spread of deserts, and the dangers of flood and landslide.

It may sound sanctimonious for people in the prosperous West to preach forest conservation to people in poor countries where alternatives seem to be few. Especially is this true when most of those Western countries went through similar deforestation earlier in their histories.

Worldwatch reported an estimate that by 1920 the United States had lost one-third of the forest cover it had when the Pilgrims landed, and that its forested acreage was about 7 percent lower in 1982 than in 1920.

But there are examples of successful reforestation efforts in Third World countries. The news from Brazil and Thailand suggests that alarm about the rate of tree-clearing exists or can be aroused in such places.

There could be no better indicator of the health of the planet than the extent of its tree cover, and no better goal for international cooperation than to make that cover increase.

Pittsburgh Post-Gazette

Pittsburgh, PA, February 16, 1989

Brazil, in a major policy switch, has decided to accept international funds to protect the rain forests of the Amazon.

In the past, the Brazilian government has refused outside assistance out of fear that it could erode Brazil's sovereignty. But it now apparently is recognizing the growing international outcry over the continued destruction of forests by farmers and developers.

The concern has been not just with the effect in Brazil but with fears that wiping out the forests could unbalance the global weather environment, including furthering the so-called "Greenhouse Effect" of continually heightened temperatures.

Already, the World Bank and the Inter-American Development Bank have postponed a number of loans Brazil had sought for highways and energy production in the Amazon.

In October, President Jose Sarney ordered a temporary freeze on any new subsidies and tax breaks for ranchers, mining and lumber industries in that vast region.

A five-member congressional delegation, including Sen. John Heinz of Pennsylvania, has just returned from visiting the Amazon Basin to discuss with Brazilians the depletion of forests that once covered an area the size of the continental United States. Upon returning, Sen. Heinz said he has "a new sense of urgency" about protecting the forests, contending, "It's like having a bulldozer driven through the Garden of Eden."

The human dimensions of curbing the deforestation became excruciatingly clear in December with the assassination of Francisco "Chico" Mendes, leader of the Brazilian rubber-tappers union and a leading conservation advocate. That murder was seen as part and parcel of activities by ranchers and speculators not only in setting huge fires to clear the land but in the killing in recent years of an estimated 1,000 rubber-tappers and Indians native to the forests.

International pressure on Brazil recently has focused on persuading it to make debt-for-nature swaps in which foreign governments or institutions would buy off a portion of Brazil's $115 billion foreign debt and channel those funds toward environmental-protection measures. (Brazil has argued that it had to exploit the Amazon for export goods to earn foreign exchange to pay its external debt.)

Even with its altered posture, the Foreign Ministry has made it clear that it will retain all decisions over its own territory, with funds preferably channeled through international organizations, and will reject "any solution where outsiders think they can take over a piece of the Amazon." But if the Brazilian government now has the means to set a forest-saving policy and make it stick, despite the opposition of settlers and speculators, there is a chance yet to save what remains of one of the globe's most priceless assets.

The Chattanooga Times

*Chattanooga, TN,
February 10, 1989*

Rain forests play a vital role in the ecological balance that sustains life on Earth. Preserving them is essential to combating global warming from the "greenhouse effect" and protecting countless species of plant and animal life from extinction. But the industrialized world's understanding of the need to save the rain forests is late in coming; those which remain exist primarily in developing countries, where they are being rapidly destroyed.

Curtailing that destruction will require broad cooperation between rich and poor nations. And establishing that cooperation will require sensitivity to the economic and nationalistic concerns of countries where the forests are located. For the most part, these countries are burdened by widespread poverty, overpopulation and massive international debt. Those problems have created a desperate need for economic development, which fuels the damaging exploitation of the rain forests.

In an effort to link economic relief and rain forest protection, so-called "debt for nature" swaps have been tried on a limited basis in Bolivia and Costa Rica. They involve complex financial arrangements under which an outside entity purchases a portion of the country's foreign debt on the condition that the funds will be used for environmental protection.

But in Brazil, with its great Amazonian rain forest, there has been official suspicion of such deals. The fear is that foreigners interested in protecting the rain forests are trying to impede economic development in Brazil and threaten an erosion of Brazilian sovereignty by seeking control of the rich mineral and biological resources of the Amazon for themselves.

"Every time someone in the U.S. says the Amazon belongs to mankind," explained one Brazilian official, "it becomes more difficult here to have a rational discussion." Others suggest, with an understandable albeit unhelpful resentment, that since the industrialized nations have destroyed so much of their own environment and are largely responsible for the global pollution problems of today, they have no business trying to tell Brazil what to do with its natural resources.

When a delegation of U.S. senators and representatives visited Brazil in January, President Jose Sarney rebuffed talk of links between reducing Brazil's massive foreign debt and protecting the Amazonian rain forest. Now, however, officials in Brazil suggest a softening of President Sarney's objections. They say he is willing to support debt-for-nature programs, so long as Brazilian sovereignty is protected by retention of authority over its own territory. His change of position bodes well for the future.

Debt-for-nature swaps will be only one part of the solution to the problem of global deforestation, but they are based on a concept which should guide the full range of efforts to reach the needed solution. That concept is that the forest-protection programs must serve the interests of all: giving impoverished nations economic help (whether through debt relief or assistance with environmentally responsible development) in return for their commitment to preserve natural resources which exist within their borders but which provide ecological benefits to the entire world.

Whaling Comes Under Fire

The first records of commercial whaling date from the 10th century, when the Basques started hunting in the Bay of Biscay. By the 16th century, the Basques had decimated the Biscayan right whales and had moved north to Greenland, Iceland and Newfoundland in pursuit of the bowhead whale. They were joined by Dutch and English whalers. Together the whalers hunted the bowhead to commercial extinction by 1680. The 18th and 19th centuries marked the period of the great American whalers. The sperm whale was their target, and at the peak period betwen 1835 and 1846, 600 ships were hunting them in the Atlantic. By the 1920s the whale stocks were practically exhausted in the Pacific; the gray whale in Baja California was decimated within 45 years of the first kill.

By the turn of the century, interest had shifted to the Antarctic. There, the killing was aided by the invention of the explosive harpoon and the development of steam vessels, which enabled the pursuit of faster whales. In 1904, the British established a whaling station on South Georgia, where thousands of blue whales were processed each year. In 1914, the Norwegians, in competition with the British, developed the first factory ship. Within 10 years, such ships had stern slipways, allowing a whale to be hauled on board and processed within an hour.

As a result of these technological improvements, species after species has been hunted to the brink of extinction. In the 1930s as the blue whale was getting rarer, attention was turned to the smaller fin whale. By 1960, the fin whale stocks had been commercially depleted and whalers concentrated on the minke whale, which until then had been left in peace.

The International Convention for the Regulation of Whaling, ratified in 1946, marked the first attempt to regulate the hunting of whales on an international basis. The International Whaling Commission (IWC), set up by the convention, voted in 1982 to impose a five-year moratorium on commercial whaling, starting in October 1985. But the IWC has no power to enforce its decisions and, by the end of the 1985-1986 season, 4,989 minke whales had been killed. Several countries, notably the Soviet Union, Japan, South Korea, Norway and Iceland, have exploited loopholes in the IWC rules, which allows whales to be killed for scientific research. In 1987, the IWC passed a U.S. resolution calling for governments not to issue licences for "scientific" whaling. None of the IWC nations has to abide by the decision but any nation that fails to do so will face stringent U.S. sanctions on imports and will be barred from fishing in U.S. waters. Nonetheless, Iceland, South Korea and Japan have all said they intend to continue scientific whaling.

THE PLAIN DEALER
Cleveland, OH, April 12, 1988

What Japan needs is a quick course in how to win friends and influence people. First it walloped American and European industry by manufacturing quality products at low prices. When markets softened, it began dumping products at far below cost. Then, when barriers began to spring up, Japanese businesses began channeling dumped products into restricted markets via third countries. And now, just when public and political sentiment is getting *really* rabid, Japan announces that it will resume whaling.

In feudal Japan, whale meat was an important source of protein. In modern Japan, however, it is only an expensive delicacy. Still, Japanese whalers stalk the seas, supported by a government policy that implies that whaling is an important way of Japanese life. We've seen that "way of life" argument before, and it looks no more relevant this time around. "Ways of life" come and go. If samurais can change, so can fishermen.

Progress or no, Japan continued hunting despite a moratorium worked out by the International Whaling Convention. Tokyo agreed to halt commercial whaling only after Congress threatened to banish Japanese fishing fleets from American waters. At that time, Japan also withdrew its formal objection to the international moratorium. Then, following in the steps of Iceland and Korea, it invoked a particularly nasty loophole.

The international moratorium allows nations to grant themselves "research" permits for "scientific" whaling. Through that catch, Japan will subsidize a commercial fleet to take almost 900 whales next season. It says it wants to prove its longstanding contention that some whale populations are not endangered. Of course, this is spurious. Many species have been decimated by whalers. Ironically, only the decimated species that have restricted habitats—the northern right whale, for instance—can be counted. Even then, population estimates range tremendously. Other whales travel throughout the world's oceans and are impossible to count. For that reason, dissecting 900 minke and sperm whales will prove nothing. Why do the Japanese bother? Because after the hunt, the carcasses will be returned to Japan, processed and sold to consumers.

As have its trade practices, Japan's stubbornness about whaling has created a dilemma for the Reagan administration. Congress can complain all it wants about commercial whaling, but very little can be done about hunting in the name of science. At least until this coming June, when the IWC will meet in England. At that time, the United States plans to introduce a resolution to limit the practice of scientific whaling. Short of closing the loophole entirely, new restrictions are the best that can be hoped for.

In the meantime, Tokyo needs to realize that its popular image in countries like the United States continues to decline. Unless it changes its rapacious ways, Japan is liable to discover that efforts to invoke punitive measures against it—in trade, in fishing, in defense—have gained unstoppable momentum. If Tokyo is going to insist that Americans respect its concerns, it must start showing a little respect in return.

FORT WORTH STAR-TELEGRAM
Ft. Worth, TX, June 28, 1988

Five years ago, an international commission voted for a moratorium on commercial hunting of whales — starting in 1986 — to save the magnificent, once-plentiful creatures from extinction. Unfortunately, the first year of the moratorium only slowed the whale killing, instead of stopping it.

How big is the problem? Before the advent of modern commercial whaling, there were an estimated 250,000 blue whales. Twenty years ago, such whales were declared protected against whaling because their numbers had dwindled to about 10,000. But an official count in recent years could only find 1,000 blue whales.

Other species of whales also are becoming more scarce. Exact figures are lacking, but some heretofore common whale populations appear to be getting dangerously low.

Despite the ban by the 45-nation International Whaling Commission, a number of countries that traditionally hunt whales have kept right on doing so because of loopholes in the treaty.

Japan, Norway, and the Soviet Union all protested the moratorium. That means they are not bound by its rules. Japan and the Soviet Union took a total of more than 6,000 whales in the 1986-87 Antarctic season. All three nations are now starting the summer hunt.

In addition, the moratorium allows whaling for "scientific purposes," but the phrase is poorly defined. Each country can issue permits for scientific whaling and simply set its own limits. Some observers have called such activities merely a cover for commercial whaling.

At the commission's annual meeting this week in Great Britain, the United States has made the sensible suggestion that those nations that allow whaling for "scientific" purposes be checked to see exactly what research is being done.

That such "research" is only a cover for commercial purposes can be seen from the protest the proposal has raised from Japan, Norway, Iceland, South Korea, and the Soviet Union — all whaling nations.

But unless the international body gets tough, the magnificent sea-going mammals — the world's biggest creatures — may disappear forever from the oceans. That would be a terrible price to pay for the sake of a little short-term profit.

BUFFALO EVENING NEWS
Buffalo, NY, June 1, 1988

THE CAMPAIGN to "save the whales" over the past 15 years has at times faced an uphill fight against custom and entrenched economic interests. Now, with the Soviet decision to end all commercial whaling, victory is in sight.

The International Whaling Commission called for a five-year moratorium on all whaling, beginning last year, as a means of allowing the many tragically depleted species of whales to make a comeback. The Soviet whaling fleet, now on the way home from the Antarctic, has been taking about 3,000 whales a year, half of the entire worldwide catch.

Japan, once the major whaling nation, has already agreed to end commercial whaling next spring, but it is still planning considerable whaling under the guise of "research." The other remaining whaling nations, Norway, Iceland, South Korea and the Philippines, all are using the same loophole in the international moratorium, claiming their whaling expeditions are for scientific purposes.

There is thus still considerable scattered whaling going on, but the total catch is now quite small compared with the 1970s, when some 50,000 of these majestic, intelligent creatures were relentlessly slaughtered each year by highly efficient "factory" ships. This indiscrimate hunting decimated the whale population, and some species are now threatened with extinction.

One such species is the blue whale, which is up to 100 feet in length and is the largest animal that has ever existed on earth. The huge sperm whale is also an endangered species. With most whaling halted, the whales should make a comeback over the next few years. In 1990, the Whaling Commission will reassess the situation and decide whether more whaling is advisable.

The United States has taken a leading role in the fight for the whales, and it deserves credit for bringing pressure on the whaling nations. The Soviet Union objected to the IWC moratorium, saying that not all species were endangered, but it has now gone along with the ban because of U.S. economic incentives.

Fishing in American coastal waters is highly lucrative, but under a 1978 law these waters are closed to any nation that defies the IWC moratorium. The Reagan administration has been alert in demanding compliance with this law and in 1985 it cut the Soviet fishing catch in half as a warning measure. Last year, Soviet trawlers were barred from American waters completely.

The United States also put pressure on Japan to curb the purchase of Soviet whale meat. With its markets thus closing and its fishing in U.S. waters barred, the Soviet Union had great economic incentives to comply with the international moratorium on whaling. The same incentives should be used to reduce whaling to the vanishing point.

It is disconcerting to think that the slaughter of the whales may be resumed in the 1990s after their numbers are adequately replenished. Whaling nations refer to the "harvesting" of whales, as if they were wheat or corn, but, apart from conservation, whaling is distasteful because of the cruelty involved. There is no humane way to kill whales.

The main concern of the IWC, however, is to ensure the preservation of the endangered species of whale, and the moratorium is well on the way to achieving this goal. For a while at least, these magnificent creatures will be left in peace, free from their only predator — mankind.

ST. LOUIS POST-DISPATCH
St. Louis, MO, April 10, 1988

A cynical, cruel and senseless fraud is being perpetrated by Japan. It has announced its intention to kill more than 1,600 minke and sperm whales over the next two years, despite its having signed a treaty calling for a phased-in worldwide moratorium on whale hunting. The kills, Japan says, are permissible under the treaty, which allows some animals to be slaughtered for purposes of research.

The treaty, it is true, permits whales to be hunted for research purposes. Yet of all the signatory nations, only Iceland and Japan — the two longest holdouts against the whaling moratorium — have developed research programs calling for whale kills in numbers approaching what they had been allowed while commercial whaling was permitted. Japan's first-year "research" target of 825 minke whales, for example, amounts to nearly half the number of minke whales it was allowed to kill in the year that ended March 31, when the international agreement called for the Japanese to stop commercial whaling.

What makes Japan's stated scientific interest so suspect is its disposition of the carcasses. Said Kazuo Shima, a spokesman for Japan's Fisheries Agency: "The carcasses of the samples will be consumed in Japan after the research."

What scientific purpose is served? With straight face, a scientist at the Japanese Whaling Association says the kills are needed to make precise estimates on whether the whales are actually dying out.

Even if the loophole in the treaty permitting these kills cannot be closed, other nations should insist that the carcasses of whales slaughtered for research be destroyed rather than consumed. This, we suggest, will ensure that Japan's research is motivated entirely by its appetite for science and not its taste for whale meat.

THE BLADE
Toledo, OH, July 3, 1988

ALTHOUGH it falls outside the realm of traditional efforts to promote peace, the Soviet Union's announcement of a permanent end to all commercial whaling by its merchant fleet amounts to a historic act of disarmament on behalf of some of the most majestic and intelligent creatures on earth.

The immediate result will be a reduction by half of commercial whaling in the world's oceans. On a more long-term basis, the scuttling of the world's largest whaling fleet probably also foreshadows the day when the giant, gentle cetaceans will be able to swim freely in all waters of the globe.

The Soviet decision to turn harpoons into fish nets by converting its whaling vessels into trawlers also marks a success for conservationists like the environmental group Greenpeace. Such groups have lobbied aggressively for an end to whale killing, even to the point of directly interfering on the high seas with the Soviet fleet as it attempted to slaughter the whales.

No less effective than the high drama of the opposition, however, has been the steadily harder line against whaling drawn by the United States and other member nations of the International Whaling Commission, a group that for most of its history supervised the slaughter of the vast herds of whales that once populated the oceans.

In the last decade the IWC has had a substantial conversion to the cause of whale conservation, but it has still been the political pressure of individual members, particularly the United States, that forced the issue. Particularly potent was an American law restricting nations from fishing in U.S. territorial waters when they fail to support the increasingly conservation-oriented policies of the IWC. This restriction proved particularly onerous to the Soviet fleet, which over time would lose more from being denied access to commercial fishing in U.S. waters than it could hope to gain from the sale of its whaling catch to one primary customer — Japan.

As for Japan, Norway, Iceland, South Korea, and the Philippines, which continue to hunt the whales through a loophole in IWC rules that allows whaling for "scientific research," the end of Soviet whaling marks the loss of their greatest ally in a world where their whale killing is regarded with increasing political hostility.

The Soviet Union should now join other nations in the campaign to stop all whaling once and for all.

THE ⚓ SUN

Baltimore, MD, June 30, 1988

Scientists aboard the oceanographic ship Albatross IV put the hopes and fears of environmentalists all over the world to the test yesterday when they hauled three pilot whales out to sea and released them. The three, nicknamed Notch, Baby and Big Brute, were among 50 whales that beached themselves on Cape Cod in December. Volunteers rushed to the site and pushed half of the animals back out into the tides, but the rest stayed put. For a whale, that means agony: whales need the buoyancy of the sea; without it their own body weight can crush internal organs; they also need the water's cooling flow, or they suffer overheating; exposed to the open air, their skin cracks and intense sunlight causes burns.

Notch, Baby and Big Brute were too young to make it on their own. Researchers at the New England Aquarium nursed the young males until they seemed strong enough to stand up to life in the open ocean, and yesterday's unusual experiment was launched. No one, other than a whale, knows exactly how strong is strong enough, though these specimens seem to be surviving just now. Soon comes the hard part: getting the whales reintroduced to the society of their peers.

Three "pods" of whales were spotted near George's Bank in the mid-Atlantic. National Oceanographic and Atmospheric Administration planes are watching the animals, and the three cetaceans, tagged with radios and a satellite transmitter, are apparently having a good time nearby. They joined a group of dolphins at play right away, delighting the scientists. But the big test comes when they try to move into the whale herd.

Whales keep in touch with sonar, transmitting complex audio signals for long distances. The three ex-strandees surely can hear the herd cavorting nearby and the herd can surely hear them. But what do whales think of strange newcomers? Will the three smell bad, and get chased off by herd bulls? Will females accept and nurture the youngsters? The answers can settle a long-standing debate. Whales probably have been stranding themselves on beaches since there were whales. Only in the last decade or so has anyone cared enough to push them back. So far, no one has proven that such intervention saves the whales longer than a few days. This time, with a little help from the world of high technology, mankind may learn nature's answer.

The Dispatch

Columbus, OH, April 25, 1987

When *The Nisshin Maru No. 3* sailed into Tokyo Harbor with more than 10,000 tons of meat and oil from Japan's last commercial haul of minke whales recently, it also carried a banner reading, "With whales so abundant, why must we stop whaling?"

When Japan agreed to comply with an International Whaling Commission moratorium on commercial whaling late last year, many in the country — where whale meat is eaten as a delicacy and the non-edible parts are used for items ranging from tennis rackets to cosmetics — were outraged.

As protests mounted, the government later announced plans to hunt 875 whales for "research purposes" next year. Conservationists contend the decision was an attempt to sidestep the moratorium and preserve Japan's 400-year-old industry.

Commercial whaling comes to a complete halt next March, with the end of sperm whale hunting. Japan's $77.2 million commercial whale-hunting industry, the world's largest, employs 1,200 people.

When the International Whaling Commission called for the whaling ban in 1982, Japan and several other countries initially rejected it, maintaining the mammals were not facing extinction.

The Japanese government later agreed to comply with the ban after it concluded a treaty to maintain its fishing quota in U.S. coastal waters.

The moratorium is due to be reviewed in 1990, by which time Japan hopes to produce evidence that commercial hunting does not threaten whales with extinction.

The commission, however, says scientific evidence clearly shows that whales will face extinction soon if hunting continues.

Beyond the statistics is another issue that reflects cultural differences.

"Japanese people love whale meat and now they're being told they can't eat it because it's cruel to kill whales," a Japanese Whaling Association spokesman said. "Can you imagine how Americans would act if we told them they couldn't eat turkey? My guess is they'd be pretty upset. That's how we Japanese feel now."

But most Americans, and the citizens of most other nations, see whales as being on a quite different plane than turkeys. They see whales as an extremely intelligent mammal from which there is too much to learn to risk extinction. They also see them as too majestic and gentle to be brutally hunted down and killed.

During the upcoming moratorium, we hope the Japanese will come to agree. Risking the extinction of the whale, to the chagrin of many, is a more important concern than the provision of a delicacy for a relative few.

THE INDIANAPOLIS STAR

Indianapolis, IN, May 1, 1988

There's more than one way to harpoon a whale, and Japan knows two of them.

A country can launch an outright commercial whale hunt, or it can fish them out for "scientific" purposes. Either way, the whales die and the hunters sell the meat and oil.

Whaling was a normal, everyday experience in Japan until the International Whaling Commission declared a worldwide moratorium on whaling until 1990.

At first, Japan would not agree to the plan. But after the United States threatened to cut Japan's U.S. waters fish quota by half, Japan decided to stop its commercial whaling.

Consequently, Japanese whalers finished their last commercial expedition to the Antarctic this month; and next April, a total commercial ban takes effect.

Unfortunately, Japan does not intend to stop whaling. Instead of whaling commercially, the Japanese will resort to the "scientific" method, sheltering its hunts under the guise of research. Using a $2.5 million government subsidy, the Japanese plan to catch 825 minke whales and 50 sperm whales for research purposes during the next season. The 875 whales represent 45 percent of the 1,941 whales that can be taken during the final commercial season.

Why do the Japanese need to bring in 875 whales? To determine life spans, male-female ratios and pregnancy rates, they say. And they want to prove that the whale population really isn't in danger.

According to recent estimates, 250,000 minke whales populate the Antarctic. This number is low, say the Japanese, who insist that even at 250,000, the whales can survive their hunts.

Those who disagree have the upper hand, in this case. Even Japan's prime minister, Yasuhiro Nakasone, has said that 875 whales are too many to hunt for scientific research. Perhaps in preparation for his trip to the United States this week, Nakasone asked Japan's Fisheries Agency to add up its numbers again and see if it can't get by with fewer whales.

Call it commercial or call it scientific, Japanese whaling must be trimmed to come into compliance with international standards.

the Charleston Gazette

Charleston, WV, April 20, 1988

THOUGH COMMERCIAL whaling is scheduled for a temporary halt after this year, several countries have indicated they still plan to carry out comparatively widescale hunting for "scientific research." The International Whaling Convention's 1946 pact allows as much. Last week Japan, world's leader in whale hunting, announced its total for proposed 1988 "research" harvesting: 875.

Imagine it: Japan kills 875 whales. And Iceland, South Korea, and Norway knock off a hundred or so more, each. All supposedly in the interest of seeing whether endangered whale stocks in the Antarctic Ocean are increasing sufficiently to justify a return to full-scale operations in the 1990s.

The irony there is as thick as a roll of blubber. To see if they can justify resumption of commercial hunting later on, whaling nations anticipate killing nearly half the total taken during the final Antarctic season just ended. It is true, as "research" whalers contend, that killing is unavoidable. Observation alone cannot reveal information such as life span, pregnancy rates and male-female ratios.

But 875 kills by one nation's whaling fleet alone? Surely, it is a veiled attempt to carry out whale hunting under a different name.

The only greater irony is the United States' part in sustaining Japan's ancient whale-killing habit. At the end of World War II, Gen. Douglas MacArthur, head of the occupation forces, virtually ordered the Japanese to begin ocean-going whaling and consume whale meat. Naturally, meat from the 875 whales taken by Japan next year will go for the nation's meat industry. Iceland's whale meat will go to Japan, too (though whale meat no longer is a dinnertime staple there).

How to head off Japan's whale "research" binge? Uncle Sam must move cautiously. Japan acceded to the phaseout only after the U.S. threatened to deny fishing rights to Japanese fleets seeking to operate in U.S. waters. An overly tough stance on whaling, coupled with the recent restrictions on Japanese electronics imports, would make us seem a bully.

But to relent would be to risk depletion of several whale species. The global whaling saga's next chapter begins in late June, when the International Whaling Commission meets. The United States had better drive a hard bargain.

THE TENNESSEAN

Nashville, TN, June 4, 1988

TWO years ago the Soviet Union promised that it would temporarily halt its commercial whaling operations this year.

Last month Moscow announced that its whaling fleet was headed home from its final hunting season in the Antarctic. The announcement said the flagship of the fleet would be converted to a fisheries ship, indicating the halt may be permanent.

There is some suspicion of the Russians' announcement. But environmentalists familiar with the Soviet response to their demands over the years tend to believe the promise is genuine. They cite declining economic benefits from whaling and sanctions that have been taken against the Soviets by other nations in recent years.

Under a congressional act tied to International Whaling Commission rules, the United States in 1985 cut in half the allocation of fish the Soviet Union could take in U.S. territorial waters. It seems this has been a terrific loss to the Soviets, possibly more than the benefits from whaling.

Environmentalists say the Soviets take the world's largest catch of whales, about 3,000 whales a year for the last few years, or about half the worldwide total. An end to that take would be a tremendous boost to environmentalists' efforts to protect a threatened species.

Several other nations have whaling fleets, including Japan, Iceland, Norway, South Korea and the Philippines. Japan has been promising to phase out its commercial whaling, but progress there is slow. If the Soviets do give up whaling, it would permit the application of strong pressure on other whaling nations to do likewise. ∎

The Philadelphia Inquirer

Philadelphia, PA, May 30, 1988

Last week, the Soviet Union announced its intention to cease commercial hunts for whales immediately, having just concluded its annual hunt. Only a handful of nations continue to pursue the giant mammals.

The decision is significant. The U.S.S.R. led the world in the commercial catch of whales — taking half of the annual kill. The Soviets based their decision to end the hunt on economic grounds. Their whaling fleet is old, and international sanctions to discourage the sale of whale meat and byproducts had rendered the operation unprofitable. But Soviet officials said they also opted out of whaling for scientific reasons — a rare and encouraging recognition of environmental consciousness in the U.S.S.R.

With the Soviets out, attention now will focus on Norway, Iceland, South Korea and Japan. They must be pressured to end their hunts. Provisions of the International Convention for the Regulation of Whaling, which discourage commercial hunting but allow the killing of whales for "research," also must be changed.

Most of that research amounts to nothing more than a hunt by another name, according to Dean Wilkinson of the environmental group Greenpeace. Many of the "research" programs have no scientific value yet entail killing large numbers of whales. The Japanese, according to Mr. Wilkinson, recently announced they were ending commercial whaling in the Antarctic, but also declared they planned to kill 50 rare sperm whales and 825 minke whales — a catch that should help meet some of the large popular demand for whale products in Japan. Under current limits on its authority, the convention has no choice but to approve such projects.

Iceland and South Korea show no signs of following the Soviet Union's example. Norway claims it will end commercial hunts, but reserves the right to conduct research hunts.

Until the loophole in the international convention is closed and a moratorium on hunting is put in place, many whale species will remain in jeopardy. Several of those species are severely endangered because of overhunting. Once decimated, it takes a very long time for whale populations to recover due to their slow rate of reproduction. Some species such as the East Coast's population of right whales, overhunted 50 years ago, still have not recovered.

With the Soviets no longer hunting, worldwide losses will be stemmed. Until all nations give up the killing of whales, the world runs the risk of destroying mammal species that predate human life by eons.

Awareness of Endangered Animals Grows Worldwide

The giant panda of China was one of the animals put on the latest endangered species list issued by the Interior Department's Fish and Wildlife Service Jan. 12, 1985. The list, drawn up under the Endangered Species Act, called for special protective measures, such as safeguarding of habitat, for the animals and plants designated as endangered.

In addition to the giant panda, the woodstork and the woodland caribou of the United States were new additions to the list.

Several species were removed from the endangered list. One was the snail darter, the tiny fish that had held up construction of the Tellico Dam in Tennessee. Since then, small groups of snail darters had been discovered in several rivers other than the one at the dam site, and the snail darter's classification was upgraded from "endangered" to "threatened." Also, the brown pelican was proposed for removal from the endangered list because its population was showing recovery. The Fish and Wildlife Service, however, still had a backlog of over 1,000 "candidates" for protection on its endangered list.

Of all the endangered species, the California condor has probably garnered the most notice. Once a common sight in the mountains of California during the 19th century, the California condor has since suffered a rapid decline. In the 1930s only 100 birds remained, and by 1930 there were fewer than half that number. In January 1986 five remained in the wild and by April of the following year the last wild condor, a male, was captured and sent to join a captive breeding program.

The demise of the condor has been blamed principally on hunting, their position at the top of the food chain and their lengthy reproductive cycle. Size and lethargy made them tempting targets for the hunter's bullet and a significant number also died from ingesting lead bullets in animal carcasses. Agricultural poisons, known to cause fragile eggshells and deformed young, adversely affected reproduction. Because condors cover up to 150 miles a day in search of carrion and man's inexorable expansion has encroached on the bird's hunting grounds.

Approximately 30 birds are now in captivity, of which about half are female. The captive breeding program aroused bitter controversy, though at their rate of decline, it seems to have been the only option available. No birds have yet been raised in captivity, but there is room for optimism.

The Senate, by a 93-2 vote, July 28, 1988 passed a bill to renew the Endangered Species Act. The bill was sent to conference with the House, which had approved a similar bill seven months earlier by a 399-16 vote. Opposition to the bill by western mountain-state senators collapsed in the face of an election-year enthusiasm for the environmental measure, which was designed to protect animals and marine life. The only opponents left voting against the bill were Sens. Steve Symms (R, Idaho) and Jake Garn (R, Utah).

The Washington Post

Washington, DC, April 23, 1988

IT'S THE CARIBOU versus the motorist, again. Secretary of the Interior Donald P. Hodel has recommended opening part of the Arctic National Wildlife Refuge in Alaska to oil drilling. That was what the oil companies hoped he might do. A predictable shriek has gone up from the defenders of the refuge. The decision is up to Congress.

Environmental quarrels always seem to generate billowing exaggeration. Another major oil discovery in Alaska would certainly be convenient, postponing the effects of the decline in Prudhoe Bay production that the government expects within the next year or so. But it's not quite so vital as Secretary Hodel suggests. With or without more Alaskan wells, oil production in this country is likely to stay on a downward trend.

As for the caribou, however, oil drilling seems very unlikely to be the dire threat to them that their friends here in Washington claim. While the two cases are not entirely comparable, the Interior Department points out that the number of caribou around Prudhoe Bay, 60 miles west of the refuge, has tripled in the 19 years since oil operations began there. The aesthetic objections to oil drilling may be substantial, but the caribou do not s em to share tnem.

Preservation of wilderness is important, but much of Alaska is already under the strictest of preservation laws. The area that Mr. Hodel would open to drilling is 1.5 million acres, running about 100 miles along the state's north coast near the Canadian border. He points out that adjacent to it is an area five times as large that remains legally designated as wilderness, putting it off limits to any development whatever.

Human intrusion on the scale of oil exploration always makes a difference in a landscape. But that part of the arctic coast is one of the bleakest, most remote places on this continent, and there is hardly any other where drilling would have less impact on the surrounding life.

Drilling in the Arctic Refuge is not crucial to the country's future. But there is a respectable chance—about one in five, the department's geologists say—that exploration will find enough oil to be worth producing commercially. That oil could help ease the country's transition to lower oil supplies and, by a small but useful amount, reduce its dependence on uncertain imports. Congress would be right to go ahead and, with all the conditions and environmental precautions that apply to Prudhoe Bay, se what's under the refuge's tundra.

BUFFALO EVENING NEWS

Buffalo, NY, April 14, 1987

EVERYONE IS theoretically in favor of preserving endangered species, but we as a nation could do more — not only for endangered whales or American eagles but for the thousands of obscure species that disappear every year.

A recent study by the congressional Office of Technology Assessment cited the increasing loss of plant and animal species and urged Congress to make the preservation of the world's biological diversity a declared national policy.

Thousands of species die out each year even before scientists can identify them. Does this matter? The congressional study makes clear that it does.

For example, genetic cross-breeding of wild and domestic plants has brought productivity gains of $1 billion a year to American agriculture. A quarter of our prescription drugs are derived from plants. But species are dying out even before we know whether they might have some value either for civilization or for the balance of nature.

The congressional report cited the diminution of the world's tropical rain forests with their "extraordinary diversity of species" as a matter of special concern.

The study proposed stronger action to link environmental protection to foreign aid funds for development in Third World countries. And it seeks more funds for the implementation of the Endangered Species Act. Funds are so short that many species become extinct while they are waiting in line to get formal protection under the act.

Human beings constitute only one of the many millions of species on this earth, but they have, through the development of "civilization," done more than any other species to degrade the world's environment. We must do what we can to pass on the biological legacy we inherited to future generations.

San Francisco Chronicle

San Francisco, CA, April 16, 1987

ON THE FACE of it, the chief of the Seminole Indian tribe who was charged with shooting and eating a rare Florida panther — thereby violating the Endangered Species Act — has irrefutable logic on his side.

James E. Billie has claimed the right to shoot panthers on his reservation is in accordance with a treaty between the United States and the Seminole nation and that eating same is a part of his tribe's religious and cultural traditions, protected under the First Amendment to the Constitution. What's more, Chief Billie found it ironic that the panther has become endangered by the white man's commercial development of the Everglades and yet Chief Billie is the first person ever to be prosecuted for this offense.

But his most telling shot, a legal landmark of sound reasoning, was that "if the white man had the same commitment to preserving wildlife as the Indians, there would be no endangered species."

NO SOLOMON is needed to judge that case

THE WALL STREET JOURNAL

New York, NY, April 22, 1987

No serious subject attracts more nonsense than energy. It happened in the 1970s when the government panicked itself into an "energy crisis," and it is happening again. Ronald Reagan's top energy officials are crying about "America's dependence on unstable sources of foreign oil" and "national security." The small saving grace of this phenomenon, however, is that it usually generates unintended comedy. This time it is Secretary of the Interior Don Hodel's fight with the caribou lobby.

On Monday Secretary Hodel recommended that Congress open to oil exploration 1.5 million acres along 104 miles of Alaska's coast on the Beaufort Sea (the only thing north of there is Santa Claus's home, the North Pole). The Interior Department estimates at least 600 million barrels and possibly as much as 9.2 billion barrels could be recovered. But environmental groups are asking, What about the threat to the Porcupine caribou herd? A representative of the Wilderness Society charged yesterday that "Hodel is simply ignoring and reversing the findings of the top 13 caribou researchers in North America, who came together and affirmed the importance of the core-calving area."

Perhaps only in Washington would you find people with the inclination or time to argue at length about holding up exploration for 600 million barrels of oil to save a "core-calving area." Not that everyone outside Washington can escape this nonsense. Environmentalism's left wing imposed 55-miles-per-hour speed limits and teensy-weensy cars on the nation. We take little comfort, then, in now seeing a conservative administration pushing its own nutty energy ideas as a way to obtain tax breaks for oil firms.

Opening up potential domestic U.S. oil reserves to exploration makes obvious sense. But why are Mr. Hodel and Secretary of Energy John Herrington trying to resurrect another "energy crisis"? Mr. Hodel has warned of lines at the gas pumps in "two to five years." Mr. Herrington recently warned that the U.S. could be importing half of its oil by the 1990s (up from 33% at present). This poses a "clear risk" for national security. So Mr. Herrington asked the White House to propose a 27.5% annual depletion allowance for new oil wells and wells using "enhanced-recovery" methods.

What's in fact happening is that since President Reagan fully decontrolled oil in January 1981, the price mechanism has functioned efficiently—but not in a way that pleases some U.S. oil producers and their Washington allies. Prices fell from nearly $40 a barrel. Prices have rebounded to about $18 a barrel, but oil lobbyists claim that prices aren't high enough to encourage new domestic exploration and development. So they want the federal government to intervene again—in the name of "national security."

The security warnings are a red herring. Given the amount of fuel available from Mexico, Canada and other nearby sources, it would be hard to imagine any oil threat that would put U.S. security at risk. It is indeed cheaper at this point to buy oil in the Middle East than it is to find it and pump it in the U.S. But that has been true for years. What we have learned in the 1980s is that oil-producing nations have a greater stake in selling their oil than the U.S. has in being able to buy it.

Messrs. Hodel and Herrington have advocated energy deregulation policies that are our best guarantee of plentiful energy. They should continue to do so, using whatever energy is left over to solve the caribou crisis.

Richmond Times-Dispatch

Richmond, VA, December 26, 1987

Hunting for sport or for food remains a legitimate activity when basic guidelines of moderation and conservation are followed. Quail, duck, geese, wild turkey, deer, rabbit, squirrel and other game animals and birds are plentiful in many areas of the United States, and may be fair game, in season.

But gunning down whooping cranes on the wing? Any hunting regulation that permits such a thing has to be sadly out of focus.

That's not what the United States Fish and Wildlife Service and the New Mexico State Wildlife Agency permitted when they opened a hunting season out West on migrating sandhill cranes. But dead whoopers could be the result just the same.

The reason is that sandhill cranes are used as foster parents in a long-range, government-supported campaign to bring back whooping cranes from the brink of extinction. Spare eggs from whoopers' nesting areas have been placed in the nests of the sandhills, a close relative. This strategy has borne fruit: From the "loneliest winter" that the last 15 cranes spent at a Gulf of Mexico refuge in 1941-42, the whooper population has increased to about 130. It went up 20 percent in the past year alone.

The problem is that about 20 young whoopers are mixed in with a sandhill population at Gray Lake National Wildlife Refuge in Idaho that migrates south for the winter to Bosque del Apache National Wildlife Refuge south of Albuquerque. When the sandhills take wing, so do their whooper charges, right over the hunting areas. In an article for The Washington Times, Oberlin College biology professor Michael Zimmerman noted that "young whooping cranes are exceedingly difficult to distinguish on the wing from their more numerous foster siblings, so even conscientious hunters will mistake the two."

No whooping cranes were killed in last year's hunt, Mr. Zimmerman concedes. But he contends the risk for the endangered young birds is growing, because federal and state officials are expanding the hunt this year.

The situation is not quite as shocking as it might appear in Eastern environmentalist eyes. From talking with U.S. Fish and Wildlife Service officials in Washington, we elicited the following responses: (1) The impact of hunting migratory sandhills had been studied for several years. (2) Should a whooping crane be killed, the season will immediately be closed. (3) There is a "harvestable surplus " of sandhills. (4) In the West, sandhills have been legally hunted for many years, as opposed to the East, where they are protected. (5) Far from being as digestible as a Piper Cub, these big birds have "excellent table value."

Nevertheless, there does seem to be an inconsistency between government efforts to protect and nurture the endangered whooping cranes on the one hand and to allow them to be imperiled by hunting of related cranes on the other. The whooping crane, standing almost 5 feet tall and with an average wingspan exceeding 7 feet, is one of the most magnificent wild creatures left in North America. The government ought to rethink a policy that might threaten the whoopers' comeback.

The State

*Columbia, SC,
August 23, 1988*

ALONG the shores of the North and Baltic seas, dead harbor seals wash up by the thousands, tiny seal pups nuzzle their dying mothers and workers patrol the water's edge to pick up the rotting carcasses. Scientists now believe this tragic scene is the direct result of industrial pollution.

So far, 7,000 seals, almost half of the population in the two seas, have died. Researchers suspect two deadly viruses, which are thriving in the heavily polluted waters, and they estimate that 80 percent of the seals are doomed.

At a recent conference organized by the environmental group Greenpeace, scientists from six northern European countries urged their governments to introduce immediate, stringent measures to reduce the dumping of toxic wastes in the North and Baltic seas. "Time is running out for these oceans," said Andy Booth, Greenpeace International's North Sea coordinator.

The kill should come as no surprise. Every year, millions of tons of liquid industrial waste, dredged materials and sewage are discharged into the two seas. Indeed, man is polluting all oceans at a terrifying rate. In this country, for instance, the dumping of medical garbage, sewage and industrial chemicals has caused the closure of a number of Atlantic beaches and fishing areas this summer.

Recent photographs and television footage of orphaned seal pups, discarded vials of blood and floating sewage are graphic testament to the growing problem. It is time for all countries, not just those bordering the North and Baltic seas, to support research and more restrictive dumping laws to prevent irreversible damage to our oceans and the rich variety of life they support.

THE CALIFORMERLY CONDOR

The Washington Times

Washington, DC, August 4, 1988

Thanks to the efforts of the Congress, endangered species in the United States are about to become a little more imperiled. The reauthorization bill for the 15-year-old Endangered Species Act, which prohibits owning or trading in species listed by the Fish and Wildlife Service as threatened or endangered, passed in the Senate on July 28 and is now in conference.

The bill will provide additional funding — $56 million next year and increasing to $66 million by 1992 — a new conservation fund, a list of endangered species, protections for declining and recovering species and heavier penalties for violators. It also will place endangered plant species under more explicit protection, thus broadening the law's scope enormously. The Senate added provisions to require public comment on recovery efforts and a cost breakdown of such efforts for each species.

The bills in conference employ methods that in the past have helped send endangered species to their eternal rewards. They prohibit ownership of the flora and fauna in question and prevent their sale and any other actions that would kill or remove them from the wild. They also deny federal permits to projects that would threaten them and generally try to turn portions of the United States into a living zoo.

It is noteworthy that the conservation efforts depend wholly on coercion, not on incentives, to protect species at risk. This creates a perverse incentive for landowners not to report the existence of rare plants or animals on their land, since that discovery could destroy the value of their property. The "protection" provisions also create hazards to the endangered life forms, since hordes of naturalists and spectators, hoping to drive others away, may be expected to descend upon a spot inhabited by the rare plants and beasts.

In the past this strategy has helped destroy such creatures as the passenger pigeon, the ownership or sale of which was prohibited in an attempt to save it. Ironically, animals that legally could be domesticated and used — chickens, cattle, etc. — have thrived.

In the long run, with the huge U.S. population and expanding land development, species that cannot somehow interact with man are doomed to die out. There are simply too many species for the government to declare every single species habitat a national park. If stopping land development while a species exists is the only conservation measure, an incentive is created to send the species the way of the dinosaurs, not to save it.

Unfortunately, Congress seems more concerned with passing a bill that purports to save endangered species than with considering policies that really would guarantee that result. The only result of this year's reauthorization will be more endangered species — and more cries for even further regulation.

THE TAMPA TRIBUNE
Tampa, FL, February 14, 1989

"The growing concern about the planet's future had become the year's most important story," Time magazine declared in naming Earth the Planet of the Year instead of selecting a man or woman of the year in its Jan. 2 issue.

The writers review the most publicized environmental troubles: a possible warming trend, destruction of South American rain forests, starvation in undeveloped nations, extinction of plants and animals, and pollution of air and water.

The conclusion: "Both the causes and effects of the problems that threaten the earth are global, and they must be attacked globally." Boldly stated and mostly correct. So why, despite convincing evidence, does this urgent call for action fall a bit flat?

Because it overlooks the grassroots front lines of the environmental-protection war where the bills are paid.

Time magazine suggests charging a household for the pounds of garbage it produces. Weighing curb-side trash will seem outlandish to the politicians who set garbage rates. The reality in Florida is that even basic recycling is still experimental and many areas of the state don't even offer garbage pickup, much less pickup on scales.

The magazine suggests raising the federal gasoline tax by 50 cents a gallon to remind motorists to conserve fuel. But urban planners in cities choking on ozone and exhaust fumes understand that the price of gasoline is insignificant alongside the costs of buying, insuring, parking, and maintaining an automobile. Adding 50 cents to the price of a gallon of gasoline won't keep cars and trucks out of downtown. When the wind doesn't blow, the city air will continue to be heavy with poisonous particles.

How poisonous? The question suggests the hard, essential task — putting accurate price tags on vanishing resources and deciding how to deal with the irreplaceable, priceless ones.

The problems connected with such decisions are at the heart of many local news stories. Nor are the solutions as simple as making despoilers pay and pay until they stop despoiling. Battles are being won while the war is slowly being lost.

A development company recently was fined $20,000 in Tampa for tearing down an eagle's nest. The nest had to go so a multimillion-dollar project could continue.

Who won? The developer would say the eagle. The eagle would disagree. And the Planet of the Year would concur with the national bird that arguing over price is meaningless as long as the damage goes unrepaired.

Concern about the planet's future is admirable. But people won't save the Earth until they begin to care about where the waters from their own yards drain and where the birds displaced by development will nest next year.

AKRON BEACON JOURNAL
Akron, OH, January 23, 1989

THE GENERAL Accounting Office has issued a disturbing report on the state of endangered species in the United States. In spite of measures to protect the 500 plants and animals on the list, one-third continue toward extinction; only 16 percent are showing improvement.

Worldwide, the GAO fears a wave of extinction "unequaled since that of the age of dinosaurs." The danger is not just to aesthetics. Wild plants and animals contribute to the gene pools that strenghen domestic crops and livestock; and plants are becoming extinct before they can be cataloged for medicinal or commercial uses.

Washington should restore endangered species protection as a priority and encourage other nations to do the same. Mankind's neglect has caused this problem; only better management of the Earth's resources can correct it.

THE SACRAMENTO BEE
Sacramento, CA, January 23, 1989

Conservationists charge that Rolf Wallenstrom has been fired as Northwest regional director of the U.S. Fish and Wildlife Service because he was doing a better job of protecting the environment than the Reagan administration wanted. But what's worse, Wallenstrom may be just the latest in a growing list of federal fish and wildlife officials who have been similarly victimized.

There's no doubt that Wallenstrom often was a thorn in Interior Secretary Donald Hodel's side. Among other things, he pushed for detailed investigations of selenium poisoning at the Kesterson National Wildlife Refuge in California and elsewhere at a time when the federal Bureau of Reclamation was still insisting that there wasn't any problem. And he upset the administration's plans for offshore oil development along the Northern California coast by pointing out that the Interior Department had seriously understated the damage that could be done to marine life.

But Wallenstrom's dismissal raises a larger question of whether honest bureaucrats are themselves becoming an endangered species, at least in the environmental fields.

He is the third Northwestern regional director in a row who's been forced out as a result of policy disputes. And five other regional directors elsewhere in the country have been dismissed under similar circumstances in just the last three years.

In most administrations, people aren't punished just because they disagree. But as one federal wildlife official told the San Jose Mercury News, "In this outfit, you don't disagree because they're vindictive. They come after you."

That kind of administrative terrorism doesn't just damage the integrity of the agencies involved; it also undermines the whole process of governmental decision-making by suppressing in advance any information that the decision-makers don't want to hear. Congress has asked the General Accounting Office to investigate the dismissals at the Fish and Wildlife Service. And while that's a good start, President Bush could send a signal of his own commitment to honesty in the civil service by reinstating Wallenstrom immediately.

THE KANSAS CITY STAR
Kansas City, MO, February 10, 1989

Add the loss of Missouri wildlife to the disastrous consequences of a Shell Oil Co. pipeline spill more than a month ago along the Gasconade River in Missouri. Now the toll is beginning to become evident, as conservation specialists have walked the river bank in search of signs of death and life.

Muskrats are the biggest losers in the mishap by man, many of them apparently having lost their water-resistant coat from the oil as they swam through it. Beaver and mink also are counted among the dead. It is too early to tell what the total effect will be, but there is little doubt that this gigantic spill has taken its toll in loss of wildlife which is important to the ecological balance of things.

Of course, if the oil spill didn't get the animals, the trappers would try. There is much trapping along the river. The trapping is a little more discriminate than a giant coating of oil which covers everything in its path. But neither is a happy way to go for an animal. And both cause unnecessary loss of animal life.

Drought Disaster Affects 50% of U.S. Farm Counties

The U.S. Agriculture Department June 23, 1988 said that half of the nation's agricultural counties had been designated as drought disaster areas after the driest spring since the dust bowl year of 1934. Adding 159 new counties to the new drought disaster list, Secretary of Agriculture Richard E. Lyng said that 1,390 counties in 30 states stretching from New Mexico to Pennsylvania and from Idaho to South Carolina were afflicted by the drought.

In testimony before a joint 18-member congressional panel monitoring the drought and the Agriculture Department's response, Lyng warned that much of the Midwest and the South were nearing a crop disaster unless the unusually dry, hot weather changed for the better. "This could be, if the weather continues, such a catastrophic thing," Lyng said.

At the hearing, the panel agreed to seek administrative remedies and to consider new legislation to protect consumers, farmers and rural communities from the effects of the drought.

By its third month, the drought gripping the Midwest and South had desiccated pastures and crops, sending commodity prices on the Chicago futures markets soaring, while threatening to block the recovery of the U.S. agriculture sector from a seven-year-long depression.

The Agriculture Department said that the drought had been caused largely by a splitting of the jet stream – the high altitude wind that guided the rain-producing low pressure systems. The splitting had forced cooler, stormy weather north and south of what became the drought-afflicted areas, leaving the Midwest and the South to bake dry under an abnormal high-pressure zone. According to Agriculture Department chief meteorologist Norton Strommen, the buildup of carbon dioxide in the atmosphere – the so-called Greenhouse effect – was not been responsible for the drought, as had been suggested.

The State

Columbia, SC, June 20, 1988

FORCES of nature assume awesome, often diabolical, forms. Tornadoes strike with destructive, capricious suddenness. Hurricanes gather killer force over long periods of time, moving inexorably forward as they lay waste to land and property and threaten lives.

And in their cumulative way droughts can be just as damaging. At one time or another, South Carolinians have suffered the consequences of all these natural phenomena.

Weeks of hot, arid weather have taken their toll on the Upcountry and areas of the Midwest, where so much of the nation's farm crops are raised. Last week, three South Carolina counties — Oconee, Pickens and Anderson — were placed on a "drought" alert after rainfall had dropped less than 60 percent of the average for the January-June period.

As might be expected, tinder-dry weather conditions have their critical impact on both the economy and the environment, inflating food prices, triggering forest and brush fires and drying up water supplies.

In response to the seriousness of the situation in the Midwest, President Reagan created an interagency committee to study the effectiveness of existing federal drought programs.

Two years ago, a drought created a summer-long emergency in South Carolina. It was a bitter, gruelling experience for many who have tried to make a go of it in the financially risky business of agriculture. Farmers in the Midwest and elsewhere responded in generous, heartwarming fashion, shipping truck and train loads of hay to livestock owners in the Palmetto State.

The summer solstice doesn't occur until Wednesday, but for many of the nation's farmers the long, hot summer is already a stressful reality.

THE SACRAMENTO BEE
Sacramento, CA, June 24, 1988

The extent of the drought disaster currently sweeping the American heartland may go beyond anything the nation has experienced before. While conditions in the Midwest and Plains rival those during the worst of the dust-bowl years in the 1930s, the scope of the crisis goes much farther. The impact in the Southeast is worse than anything that has occurred since detailed records began to be kept at the beginning of this century. Meanwhile, California is suffering shortages of its own. And for all of these regions, constituting by far the greatest part of America's most productive farmlands, to be stricken at the same time is virtually without precedent.

The full range of consequences for the national economy and indeed for the world is impossible to predict. So far, the losses in American wheat, barley, oat and soybean production are already prompting fears of an international grain shortage. And the leeway for averting truly calamitous losses has now been reduced by now to a matter of days — 10 more days without rain in the Midwest, for example, means devastation for the corn crop.

At this stage in the progression of disaster, even the arrival of some long-overdue rain won't be sufficient to provide more than temporary relief. A few crops might be saved that way, and that's vitally important. But meteorologists predict that there is absolutely no prospect of breaking the current eight-year cycle of drought in the next six months.

As a result, there's little that government can do other than try to minimize the financial effects for the agricultural community with short-term aid. There's growing concern in Congress as well that widespread predictions of rising commodity prices as a consequence of the crop losses will lead to profiteering among food manufacturers, a danger that deserves to be monitored closely.

But it's the long-term effects of the current crisis that ought to be prompting the most concern. For when the drought cycle finally ends, the soils and groundwater reservoirs of middle America will need years to recover. In the interim, many small- and medium-size farming operations as well as the communities that depend upon the income they generate may not be able to hold on. And as a result, there's a very big question of how drastically the nation's farm economy itself will have changed, and will have to change, by the time the rains return.

THE ATLANTA CONSTITUTION
Atlanta, GA, June 24, 1988

Already, the great Midwestern drought has begun to wither crops, raise grocery prices and send the Washington aid brigade scrambling. The government will shell out less money for subsidies this year and more for disaster assistance. And in the sort of devilish twist that drives farm strategists to despair, the big dilemma now appears to be underproduction, not overproduction.

The 1985 farm act doesn't help. It sets broad acreage reduction requirements for wheat and feed grains, among other crops. The tactic made sense in years past, and will probably make sense in years to come. Without nature's interference, America has the capacity to produce far more than it can consume or sell abroad. But this year — working in tandem with a relentless sun over the Great Plains — the policy likely will mean a shortage of basic commodities.

We have one consolation: Things might have been worse. Other proposals in recent years, by people like Rep. Richard Gephardt (D-Mo.), have put even stronger emphasis on crop limitations. Slash production, they said, and prices for farm products will rise as subsidies fall. True enough — but even if harvests were abundant — consumers would wind up paying more while many Americans in agribusiness would find themselves out of work.

One U.S. Department of Agriculture study found that if farm production were slashed by 30 percent, the nation would lose 2.1 million farm-related jobs, see its gross national product drop by $64 billion and sustain a 5 percent to 7 percent increase in retail food prices. That's without a drought.

Fortunately, Congress opted for a plan that would keep production high enough to feed Americans easily and simultaneously regain lost export markets. With help from a falling dollar, the scheme was working.

Then came the drought. Now foreign competitors may once again snatch away our export markets, and grocery bills are sure to keep on rising. But what if Congress had gone whole-hog for crop limitations?

Not only would parched farmers be hurting, every American who likes to eat would be left high and dry.

Arkansas Gazette.
Little Rock, AR, June 21, 1988

The threat of natural disasters hovers over all regions. Some sectors fear earthquakes and volcanoes; others dread hurricanes or floods; for the United States as a whole, the most pervasive menace may be a drouth.

Prolonged dry periods are not dramatic disasters. Instead, in the absence of adequate rainfall, corn leaves roll into tight tubes and turn from green to yellow, wheat withers, and meadows are seared under the summer sun. Dejected farmers watch their dreams dry up and blow away like wisps of dust skimming acoss their barren fields.

City dwellers cannot shrug off the disaster as "just another farm problem," nor can they escape the consequences of restricted production, disrupted marketing patterns and the incipient poverty that creeps into the towns from the rural regions.

For half a century, farmers — and, for that matter, banks and just about all other types of businesses — have been trained to look to the government for assistance when a crisis develops. The massive accumulation of farm legislation makes few provisions for dealing with drouths. The primary objective of marketing programs is to raise prices. A drouth generates its own version of support for markets but the farmer who "goes to town with an empty truck" derives no benefits from a soybean price of $9.30 a bushel.

Senator David Pryor of Arkansas is leading a congressional exploration of ways to help agriculture survive the growing disaster. His two initial remedies would provide limited assistance to livestock producers. One would open conservation land to grazing or hay harvests and the other would provide farmers with emergency feed rations from stocks stored under the farm marketing program.

These and the other emergency programs that are certain to be implemented will help some limited number of farmers but will not deflect the disaster. The market through which the commodities move is geared to anticipate even the threat of shortages. Companies that process food are under "aggressive" management that will miss no opportunity to raise prices and recapture higher raw material costs — and then some. Government economists have estimated that food prices would increase 4 per cent this year but if the drouth continues the rise could be considerably faster.

Inventories of major grains at the beginning of the planting season were moderately below the year-earlier levels. The situation was regarded as favorable. Agriculture had been wallowing through the worst depression since the 1930 decade but improvement in the supply-demand balance promised better times.

With the drouth cutting into yields, the country may experience a grain drain that will reduce stocks, raise prices and lead another round of inflation. Moreover, the government could be forced to redesign its farm program. Instead of trying to manage surpluses, the experts may be called upon to stabilize an economy wherein limited supplies bring farm prices up to the parity level but leave producers with little to sell.

In due course, the country may have an opportunity to decide which is preferable: Surpluses with the government supporting prices or a grain drain with the resulting rise in the CPI.

The Oregonian
Portland, OR, June 19, 1988

When disaster strikes, emergency resources should be marshaled to limit the toll on victims, and every effort should be made to learn from the experience for better preparation in the future.

This country is in the throes of a disaster. Drought conditions grip most of its food-producing regions from one coast to the other and are particularly harsh through the breadbasket of its midsection.

Never in the postwar era has the nation faced such a test of its preparedness in stockpiling food for immediate needs or banking land to respond in ensuing growing seasons.

The drought coincides with a determined program to reduce food stocks. Wheat supplies, for instance, have been so successfully drawn down that they have dropped below the 1 billion-bushel goal.

Will whatever wheat survives the weather replenish the stocks enough to meet this country's needs at home and commitments abroad? If not, the amount that constitutes prudent reserves will have to be re-evaluated.

That is the learning phase of this disaster, and the federal government must not fail to take advantage of it. Conditions this year come as close to a worst-case scenario as the nation ever may confront.

Many individual growers and the small communities relying on them are still recovering from the recession. The drought is particularly severe for them. They are in a weak economic position to ride out a crop failure. Their problems should become the domain of the newly named Emergency Drought Policy Committee, formed to rally resources for the emergency posed by this particular natural disaster.

Assistance may range from low-interest loans and debt restructuring to allowing widespread use for livestock of land set aside from production or placed in the conservation reserve.

Oregon wheat, fortunately, is in much better shape than it looked a few months ago. Still, the crop has been damaged somewhat. Much of Washington's wheat land is in worse condition.

From here through the Great Plains, the Corn Belt and the Southeast, grain production is in jeopardy. The last threat was financial. This one is climatic. Either way, the country cannot afford to let its agricultural industry be destroyed. It also must not miss the opportunity to assess whether it has been pursuing the proper food strategy.

The Burlington Free Press

Burlington, VT, June 29, 1988

As the worst drought since the Dust Bowl of the 1930s sears crops and livelihoods from Montana to Georgia, let us finally — forever — dispel the notion that the "farm problem" is the farmers' problem.

Just as farmers live lives of chance, so do we as a nation.

We are nearly as vulnerable as the farmer standing in a withered North Dakota wheat field looking up to a cloudless sky for rain.

A drought emergency has been declared in 40 percent of the nation's counties. Estimates are that half the wheat, barley and oats crops in the northern Great Plains will be lost.

Anticipating that feed will be increasingly costly and hard to find, farmers are rushing their livestock to slaughter, gifting us with a temporary drop in prices, but undermining the long term viability of the nation's meat supply.

Commodities dealers, grain companies and warehouse operators have been purchasing grain and soybeans from government stockpiles at record rates. At the current pace, the government's supply of soybeans could be exhausted in July. The wheat supply could bottom out at 147 million bushels — the emergency reserve mandated by Congress — come August.

Agriculture Department officials, however, remain optimistic about consumer food prices. Last week they estimated that the retail price of food will likely rise only 1 percent on account of the drought. History tells us, however, that the last two times government stockpiles were so depleted, in 1949 and the mid-1970s, prices soared.

It is still not clear exactly who is buying up all these commodities and why. It is also not clear whether Secretary of Agriculture Richard Lyng's policy of helping to contain soybean and grain prices by continuing to allow unrestricted sales of government stockpiles is a wise one. Some farm advocates fear major food processors and the nation's trading partners may be buying up grain with the hope of hoarding it.

If the drought does persist, we would feel a lot more comfortable having the Department of Agriculture, not Kellogg's, the Soviet Union, or some grain traders, sitting on the dwindling reserves.

Our own Sen. Patrick Leahy has promised to buy himself a pair of hobnail boots and come down hard on speculators at congressional hearings should profiteering become apparent.

The experience of the 1972-73 wheat sales to the Soviet Union, which caused a doubling and tripling of grain prices in this country, and of the so-called Oil Crisis of the 1970s make us question, however, our ability to detect profiteering and call it to task in short order.

The drought crisis has forged a remarkable bi-partisan consensus in Washington that is agreed on helping farmers by building on the patchwork of existing farm legislation. But the drought and its implications extend far beyond the farm bills we seem to be forever discussing.

After Washington helps farmers weather this catastrophe, it needs to muster the same political adrenaline to address ominous findings about the "greenhouse effect" that were presented to Congress last week.

James E. Hansen of the National Aeronautics and Space Administration testified that the first five months of 1988 were warmer than any other comparable period since measurements began 130 years ago, and that four of the hottest years on record occurred in the 1980s.

He also said he was "99 percent certain" that this warming trend is not due to natural variations, but to a buildup of carbon dioxide and other gases because of pollution. Hansen predicted that much of the United States will be subject to frequent episodes of very high temperatures and droughts in the next decade and beyond.

We agree with Hansen that "it is time to stop waffling so much and say that the evidence is pretty strong that the greenhouse is here," and that the farmers are not the only ones baking in it.

San Francisco Chronicle

San Francisco, CA, June 24, 1988

WITHOUT QUICK administrative and congressional remedies, a vast stretch of the nation's farm belt is facing crippling financial losses in one of the most devastating droughts since the Dust Bowl era of the 1930's. And more hot, dry weather is forecast for major crop producing areas.

The drought disaster that grips more than 1200 counties in 30 states is a catastrophic emergency for farmers and rural communities and may make a significant impact on consumers as the full effects of the abnormally dry spring are translated into higher food prices.

In just four states, the Dakotas and Montana and Minnesota, the crop losses are already estimated at more than $1.8 billion and are growing daily. Agricultural economists are predicting increased prices in the fall for bakery products, pasta, beer and poultry.

ALTHOUGH HEAVY agricultural subsidies are generally inadvisable, in this emergency situation drought relief proposals could include the continuation of income support payments to farmers; freeing conservation lands for hay harvesting and cattle grazing; an emergency loan program for drought-stricken farmers; even the cutting of grass alongside interstate highways for use as forage.

If federal aid is lacking, desperate farmers have the one recourse that President Reagan suggested the other day: Pray for rain.

Rockford Register Star

Rockford, IL, June 29, 1988

If there is any great public benefit to be derived from the recent plague of hot and dry weather across much of the nation, perhaps it is in the sudden attention being paid to a decades-old theory on the climatological effect of air pollution — the so-called greenhouse effect. Perhaps, too, the current warning signs will prompt us Earthlings to make reforms that might avoid the catastrophe that could result from the greenhouse effect.

The theory, as described last week in unsettling congressional testimony by a space agency scientist, is that increasingly warmer weather of recent years is due to heat trapped by a cover of waste gases in the atmosphere. Indeed, temperatures worldwide during the first five months of this year were the warmest on record.

Climatologist Dr. James E. Hansen, of the National Aeronautics and Space Administration, told a committee of Congress that he is 99 percent certain that current weather patterns signal the start of the greenhouse effect.

The potential consequences of this trend just a few decades down the line are horrific — social, economic, agricultural and environmental chaos, not unlike the effects of global war, according to one expert.

There is time, but perhaps not much, to begin taking steps that will diminish the greenhouse effect and spare the world the worst of its consequences. These would include: curbs on chemicals that damage the ozone layer that protects Earth from the more damaging heat and rays of the sun; conservation of energy and development of safe alternatives to such fuels as gasoline, oil and coal; and protection of tropical rain forests, which absorb carbon dioxide and play a vital role in maintaining a delicate ecological balance.

The current drought across mid-America may not be attributable to the greenhouse effect, but its attendant heat wave is suspect. At any rate, this weather crisis should give us all cause to ponder the fragility of our planet and to resolve to prevent its environmental suicide.

Telegraph Herald

Dubuque, IA, June 19, 1988

Telegraph Herald editorial

The orange disc rises through the few scattered morning clouds, turning a gray tri-state morning into yet another sunny and rainless day.

With each passing arid day America's drought continues. What Agriculture Secretary Richard Lyng terms "a potential disaster" comes closer to reality.

Our Corn Belt, the world's most reliable farming area, is being threatened. Many Dakota farmers have already lost their crops. Livestock farmers across the Midwest are culling their herds, the dried-up pastures forcing them to sell before they run out of feed. The dominant crops of the Midwest — corn and soybeans — are still in a position to recover, but officials and farmers are all too painfully aware that another week without rain means a cropless year may very well come to bear.

It is the last hit the American farmer needs.

Mother Nature can be so cruel. Just when it appears as if farmers are finally pulling through five years of decline along comes the worst possible problem. No rain.

In Iowa, farmland prices have risen as much as 35 percent in some counties. As a whole, farmers have enjoyed a 15-20 percent increase in their land value. While not forgotten, the days of massive foreclosures have abated.

Better times were, at long last, at hand.

But the drought of 1988 is rapidly having a major impact. It may not be of disaster proportion yet, but each passing day without rain can only be counted as another step in the wrong direction.

Farmland values in the state have already retreated $100 per acre because of the drought. The selling off of livestock has sent those markets downward.

The impact on the consumer will undoubtedly come. Prices for products such as bread, cereal, margarine, mayonnaise and vegetable oil will rise. Some economists predict a 6 to 8 percent increase in grocery prices. A full-scale drought could also fuel inflation for all Americans.

But playing the role of point man in the impending disaster is the farmer.

It takes a special breed of a person to risk large sums of money to stick seeds into the dirt, not knowing for certain there will be a reward for his or her labors at harvest time.

It is an occupation that takes great portions of faith.

Undoubtedly, the most helpful move we tri-staters can make right now is to get down on our knees and pray for rain.

Forest Fires Burn
In Eight States

At least 30 separate forest fires, some of which were three months old, were burning out of control in seven Western states and Alaska, it was reported Sept. 9, 1988. Forest officials said the fires were the worst to hit in the West since the 1950s.

The current series of blazes had destroyed 1,611,735 acres in California, Colorado, Idaho, Montana, Utah, Washington and Wyoming, the Boise Interagency Fire Center reported Sept. 9. The center coordinated firefighting efforts in the West. Several other huge fires burning in uninhabited areas of Alaska brought the total number of charred acres to 3,674,307 in 1988.

The largest fires in the Western states were concentrated in and around Wyoming's Yellowstone National Park. More than 800,000 acres of the 2.2 million-acre park had been destroyed, officials said. Including fires in the woodlands immediately surrounding Yellowstone, a total of more than 1.2 million acres burned. Approximately 9,000 civilian and military firefighters had been brought in to battle the Yellowstone fires.

U.S. Interior Secretary Donald P. Hodel and Agriculture Secretary Richard Lyng visited the national park Sept. 10 to survey the damage. After a tour of the area, Hodel declared: "It's a disaster."

The widespread fires throughout the West had sparked criticism of the National Park Service's policy, dating from 1972, of letting wildfires burn naturally unless they threatened lives or property. The policy had been abandoned in late July, when the current series, fanned by high winds, began to spread rapidly through areas left dry by the summer's drought.

Los Angeles Times

Los Angeles, CA, Sept. 1, 1988

National park and forest officials have taken a lot of heat, so to speak, over their management —or the lack of it—of fires that have swept across hundreds of thousands of acres of Western lands this summer. Some of the flap is justified in view of the drought conditions this year. In retrospect, it seems that to have let nature take its course in such volatile fire conditions was asking for trouble. Once the popular tourist centers were threatened and the public mood became inflamed, the managers had to struggle to control the fires, particularly in Yellowstone National Park.

The danger now is that federal officials may overreact to public controversy, or to pressure from Western members of Congress, and become too timid about following the wisdom of a long-range policy of permitting most natural fires to burn themselves out. One major reason that so many fires in Yellowstone burned out of control for so long this summer is the dry condition caused by the lack of moisture. But the fires never would have covered such vast amounts of acreage if it had not been for the massive amounts of fuel that collected in the forests over the years in which National Park Service policy was to extinguish every fire as quickly as possible.

Most of the complaints have come from a handful of landowners who have felt threatened by the raging fires and from business owners on the periphery of Yellowstone who have suffered economic losses because of the fall-off of tourism. But such complaints can fuel a Bambi syndrome among members of the public who see dramatic fire walls and smoke clouds on television news.

They can envision helpless creatures of the forest fleeing the firestorms. They read of massive acreages "destroyed" without understanding that fire is a necessary cog in the life cycle of a healthy forest, or that not every tree in every acre has been scorched.

Yellowstone Supt. Robert Barbee says that fire is a stimulant that is as important to the ecosystem as are sunshine and rain. Without the clearing action of fire, dead timber builds up on the forest floor so that when fire finally does come it rages out of control. The accumulation of downed wood inhibits new growth by preventing plants from taking root in the soil. The heavy old growth, both on the forest floor and above, blocks out the sunlight that plants must have. Fire aids the spread of seeds, and the ash helps fertilize the infant plants. Most wildlife moves out of danger well in advance of the flames. And burned-over areas rapidly sprout anew into lush habitat for wild animals. Much of the Yellowstone area that was burned, in remote sections of the park, never would be seen by the average tourist.

This summer's experience in Yellowstone Park might help the Park Service further refine its fire-management policy to account for extremely dry conditions and the volatility of public opinion—even if the criticism comes from a very small public and is based to a great degree on misinformation or misunderstanding. But the Park Service should not be bullied into retreating from a scientifically sound policy that allows the forest to thrive over generations through periodic biological renewal and diversification.

The
Philadelphia Inquirer

Philadelphia, PA.
Sept. 13, 1988

The restorative powers of nature are awesome. Even as fires burn on in Yellowstone National Park, seedlings are beginning to peek through the ashes, and wildlife is grazing beneath still-smoldering pines. Nearly half of the 2.2 million-acre park — the nation's oldest — has been burned since forest fires began raging in July.

Yet, contrary to some descriptions, Yellowstone has not been "destroyed." It has merely entered into a new — natural — phase. Asked what Yellowstone will be like next year as a result of the fires, ranger Bruce Blair explained: "It will be different, that's all. There is no better or worse in this park; there is just change."

Yellowstone truly *will* be different. Interestingly enough, it's not the conservation community that's worried about that change, however. Forestry and wildlife experts know that fire is nature's way of cleaning house and is thus to be welcomed.

The loudest alarms are being sounded by those who live off Yellowstone's familiar scenic beauties: the thriving tourist industry that sells hotel rooms, food, fishing equipment, wilderness trips and souvenirs, as well as property owners who have crowded the park's boundaries to claim a piece of its beauty for themselves.

It is they who are challenging the federal government's policy that allows some forest fires to burn. The policy, which dates back to 1970, calls for human intervention in a naturally occurring fire only when it's necessary to protect human lives and property.

Critics of the "let burn" policy, who fear their livelihoods may be diminished or their aesthetic tranquility disturbed, have demanded the removal of National Park Service director William Penn Mott Jr. While Mr. Mott's job appears, for the moment at least, to be secure, his boss, Interior Secretary Donald P. Hodel, has agreed to review the policy.

He should find it perfectly compatible with the underlying purpose of national parks: to minimize man's interference with wilderness so nature can do its own thing. That's what's occurring right now at Yellowstone.

THE ☀ SUN

Baltimore, MD, Sept. 3, 1988

Yellowstone is burning. By the time winter snows snuff out the largest wildfires America's favorite national park has seen in this century, more than one-fourth of its 2.2 million acres will have been scorched. But the heat won't end then. The Senate public land subcommittee plans hearings on Yellowstone's controversial fire policy.

At issue is whether a so-called natural disaster, such as a lightning-caused conflagration, should be fought by "unnatural" counter-measures such as bulldozed fire breaks and backfires.

Back in May and June, when tinder-dry conditions set off the fires now flaring throughout the West, the National Park Service held to its post-1972 policy of non-intervention. As the blazes sent tourists fleeing, threatened park facilities and nearby towns, and broke all records for devastation, the Army was called in and volunteers were enlisted in a huge fire fight that is not over yet.

Was action taken too late? Is the 1972 fire policy realistic? How "natural" can Yellowstone be?

These questions pit environmental purists against the forces of modern civilization. The environmentalists correctly contend that forest fires are nature's way of regenerating the land. They look at acres of gray-black tree hulks as areas of natural renewal. They blame the severity of this year's fires on underbrush that grew in the interventionist years before the 1972 policy reversal.

"Burn, baby, burn," research biologist Don Despain told the Denver *Post*. One of the authors of the 1972 policy, he said, "I don't like suppression efforts (now going on)." Mr. Despain exulted that 400,000 of Yellowstone's acres have been scorched. The last "good year," he said, was 1981 when only 20,000 acres were swept by wildfires.

A contrasting view is offered by a Bozeman, Mont., researcher, Donald R. Leal, who told the *Wall Street Journal* that this year's Yellowstone conflagration destroyed "more than all the acreage burned by lightning fires in all the national parks between 1968 and 1982."

Said the Denver *Post*: "For the first time in a century at Yellowstone, the wild forces of nature controlled the park."

The Interior Department needs to chart a middle course between doctrinaire non-intervention and the kind of suppression that would turn Yellowstone into a strictly controlled tourist attraction. Lightning fires produce valid ecological benefits. When meteorological conditions indicate that forest fires will get out of control, counter-measures should be taken early rather than late.

Yellowstone, let's face it, cannot exist in the pristine conditions that prevailed before the West was settled. To think otherwise is an exercise in fantasy that ignores the yearly presence of 2 million visitors. We are counting on Congress and the Interior Department to map a new policy that will reflect reality and common sense.

The Oregonian

Portland, OR, Sept. 9, 1988

Northwesterners, of all people, can deeply emphathize with the frustrated neighbors of Yellowstone National Park, where devastating forest fires have charred more than a million acres and altered the natural landscape for generations to come.

Certainly, as trees and buildings burn, it is little comfort that fire is a natural and expectable feature of Western forests, causing in a sense the old order to give way to new. That Yellowstone's burned forests will be renewed and reinvigorated in a few generations is easy to overlook in the vista of burned acres.

But it is a point that shouldn't be lost in the inevitable and necessary post-mortem examination after the fires are out on the firefighting policies of the National Park Service and U.S. Forest Service. Leaping past the informed review that is merited, however, Wyoming's senators have called for the resignation of William Penn Mott, director of the National Park Service.

The critics have focused on a Park Service policy of letting natural fires burn rather than quickly extinguishing them. It is premature, however, to say that policy is what led to the Yellowstone area's devastation any more than the previous non-burning approach did, especially since heroic attempts were made to control the most damaging fire.

It is even more premature to assume the Park Service judgment was a bad one. In recent years, it has become recognized that putting out all forest fires as quickly as possible can be counterproductive. The resulting buildup of debris makes a fire that eventually hits an area much hotter and much more destructive to living trees than periodic blazes would have been.

Before Oregon's forests were formally managed by federal policy, for instance, mature trees routinely survived ground-hugging fires, including those both caused by lightning and deliberately set by Indians to improve hunting and foraging. More recently, planned burning has become a forest-management tool, replacing natural fires.

That doesn't mean that all forest fires — or even most of them — should be allowed to burn uncontrollably. Even without human help, nature is quite capable of a conflagration on an unacceptable scale in view of our limited remaining forest resources. But it does mean that informed policies should recognize that there is more to forest management than assuming that if we just put out the fires the forests will stay the same forever.

Regarding national parks in particular, policies must be based on the knowledge that parks are more than tourist attractions, that they are places where humans and nature should encounter each other in mutually beneficial ways — a challenge that requires sophisticated understanding of both, not quick calls for somebody's resignation.

Omaha World-Herald

Omaha, NE, Sept. 10, 1988

A million acres in and around Yellowstone National Park are in ashes, strengthening the case for the government to review its policy of not extinguishing lightning-sparked forest fires. A contained fire in a year of normal rainfall is one thing, but the policy should make allowances for a year of extreme drought, when keeping a fire from spreading is next to impossible.

Fire is undeniably part of the balance of nature. It eliminates dead and diseased vegetation, releases nutrients into the soil and restarts the natural process of reforestation. In effect, it allows old, unhealthy forests to be replaced by younger, healthier ones.

But 1988 is far from a normal year, and what is happening in Yellowstone bears little resemblance to a controlled, natural burn. Lightning-started fires appeared early in the summer and were allowed to burn, as the policy called for. Before long they raged out of control, whipped by unusually high winds through acre after acre of tinder-dry vegetation. Fewer thunderstorms than normal materialized to put out the flames. Eventually the government was forced to concede that it had an emergency on its hands.

Now much of the park lies in ruin. Homes and businesses have been destroyed. Park facilities and nearby towns have been evacuated. Thousands of firefighters, including Army units that were given emergency training in firefighting, are putting their lives on the line to contain the blazes. Smoke and ashes have drifted into the Midwest.

Public opinion is a strange thing. A suggestion to permit more logging on federal lands typically brings a storm of outrage. Clean air activists go bonkers if someone lights a cigarette on the other side of a large room. But a federal policy goes out of control, destroying millions of trees, leaving much of a major national park in ruin and fouling the air for hundreds of miles, and relatively few voices are raised. The defenders of the let-'em-burn policy have done their work effectively.

The policy need not be totally scrapped. Letting nature take its course makes sense in some circumstances. But a review is certainly in order to determine the circumstances under which the risks are too great.

THE BILLINGS GAZETTE

Billings, MT, August 28, 1988

The front-page picture on The Billings Gazette Wednesday looked like ground zero after a nuclear attack.

National Park Service photographer Jeff Henry walked over earth burned to ash, stepping over charred bones of a once beautiful forest lying like an indictment on the land.

The scene stretched the imagination, and the sky was gray with smoke.

Reports have come as from a battlefield. Yellowstone National Park has come under fire, and tourists and park workers have been evacuated as soldiers were evacuated from Saigon, fleeing a tide they cannot turn.

And in Billings, the sky is gray day after day, gray with soot, gray as the chances of stopping the fires that rage across the park.

The Gazette picture seems to reveal all. But there is something hidden in those ashes, in the charred bones of those century-old trees.

And that is an explanation from Park Superintendent Robert Barbee about how all this could have happened.

We know the standard response: The park has a free burn policy to ensure the area grows and develops as it would have in a pristine state. If man interferes with the natural process, the park is no longer a park.

Under normal circumstances that policy makes good sense. But conditions at the park this year are anything but normal, and the policy comes up as dry as Montana. Barbee and company should have seen that. The fact that they didn't is a matter of grave concern.

We are in the midst of record drought. Pine needles are brittle as glass and drip like gasoline from trees.

One match, one flash of lightning, a park policy that says burn, baby, burn, and the park was aflame.

In response, the Park Service did nothing but spray policy at the blaze until it was too late. Then, when the war was lost, an army of firefighers was called in.

This fiasco is riddled with questions, and it's not too late for Congress to demand to know why Barbee blindly rode a dead policy into hell.

HOMELESS IN AMERICA

Pittsburgh Post-Gazette

Pittsburgh, PA, Sept. 10, 1988

While the summer heat wave has ended over most of the nation, the worst wild fires of this century continue to rage through Yellowstone National Park and other large expanses of the western United States, with the Yellowstone fires alone consuming more than a million acres of timber and brushland. This year's wildland furnaces have dwarfed uncontrolled burning during other fire seasons when damage was more typically counted in tens of thousands of acres. Altogether, an area about the size of Connecticut has been destroyed.

Rains and snow predicted in the next few days will help to extinguish the fires. But it is a measure of the ferocity of this fire season that some fires may simply burn themselves out for lack of fresh fuel in devastated forests. That seems unlikely to be the case with the debate over National Park Service and U.S. Forest Service fire-control practices.

For even as fire crews were making valiant efforts to save historic buildings in Yellowstone Park and the fight continues against major fires in Montana and Washington state, Western senators were calling for the firing of the head of the National Park Service for failure to respond quickly when fires first erupted. The debate, however, reflects issues more fundamental than the alleged failure of the Forest Service to stem the burning tide.

After decades when every effort was made to extinguish every forest fire, forestry officials more recently have followed a tolerant policy toward the natural combustion of forests and rangelands, where fire plays a central role in nature's management of its own cycles of growth. By weeding out the weakest plants in the forest, natural fires strengthen the hold of the strongest on the land and contribute to the introduction of new growth by clearing away the dead wood.

At least that is the theory guiding Forest Service decisions to allow fires to run the course where possible. However, because of this year's drought, the Western forests have been as dry as gunpowder — and almost as explosive under fire. As a consequence, the theory of allowing forests to manage their own fires has appeared to test the limits of safety and public tolerance.

Given the fact that the loss of life in these raging fires has been so limited (and apparently no worse than in other fire seasons), there are sound reasons why the test need not be judged a failure. Members of Congress looking for a bureaucrat to blame should consider other factors and let the political embers cool along with those in the forest.

The drought played a stronger hand in setting the stage for these fires than any national policy. Perhaps more important for the future, the extent of the fires has reduced greatly the likelihood of such extensive conflagrations in the near future — at least in Yellowstone Park and other places where the fires were concentrated this summer.

THE SACRAMENTO BEE

Sacramento, CA, Sept. 13, 1988

The fires that have swept Yellowstone National Park this summer are a national tragedy, especially for the millions of Americans who love the park and whose most cherished spots within it have now been lost or irreparably altered. But fire in nature is a means of rebuilding and renewal as well. And there's a growing risk that the potential benefits of this summer's conflagration for the forest and for forest policy could be lost in the firestorm of political reaction that now seems to be gaining force.

The scientists tell us that what's happening in the park this year is part of the natural course of things and that the parklands and its wildlife will be more bountiful and productive in the years to come than ever before. The fires this time have been so devastating in large part because of the decades of fire suppression in the past, which allowed so much scrub brush and other natural tinder to build up.

The suggestion that Yellowstone isn't being destroyed, only changed, however, doesn't offer much comfort to those who are complaining that it may take 20 years or more for the park to grow back the way it was. The politicians in Wyoming and Montana and many of their constituents want some blood. A national treasure has been damaged, they point out, the local economy around Yellowstone has been disrupted and no one can be too sure what the park will be like in the years to come. But in fact, Yellowstone will never look the way it did last summer; nor should it, since the park in its former condition was both unnatural and dangerous.

Certainly every decision that has been made this year by the Park Service will be minutely reviewed by investigating committees of Congress and the Department of the Interior. Should so many lightning-caused fires have been allowed to burn unchecked initially given the drought conditions that prevailed throughout the area? Were there more effective fire-fighting techniques that could have been used? Once the fires are finally out, should the government continue to let nature take its course or should the Park Service intervene with reforestation and other erosion controls to limit the extent of the damage?

The answers to these and all the hundreds of other questions that are being raised about Yellowstone will help forest managers learn more about how to do a better job of handling similar fires in the future. That process of inquiry is itself one of the benefits of this summer's conflagration. But the important questions all have to do with the management of forest fires, not the policy underlying those management practices. The desire to find someone to blame that seems to be rampant at the moment in the Yellowstone area as well as in some parts of the Department of the Interior is perhaps understandable. But it should not be allowed to run so far as to undermine the scientific basis for the government's policy of allowing natural fires to burn so long as they do not threaten lives or property.

The Kansas City Times

Kansas City, MO, Sept. 10, 1988

The near-destruction of the Old Faithful complex brought home to many Americans the severity of the forest fires which have ravaged the 2.2-million-acre park and surrounding areas.

About 1 million acres of the Yellowstone area have burned, but the North Fork fire which caused the loss of 17 buildings in the Old Faithful complex brought to mind for many a former tourist the historic Old Faithful Inn with its tall gables and the geyser itself nearby.

The fires are not the only battle the National Park Service has had to wage in Yellowstone. Residents of surrounding communities, who had to be evacuated when the fires got too close, are downright mad at the park department's policy of "let them burn." Complaints prompted President Reagan to dispatch the secretary of agriculture and the secretary of interior to Yellowstone to determine what can be done about fighting the fires that won't go away.

The North Fork fire which threatened the Old Faithful area from the beginning has been tackled by firefighters because it was manmade, caused by a logger using a chainsaw in a forest just west of Yellowstone. The National Park Service may be guilty of recognizing too late that the volatile conditions of this drought-stricken year required unusual efforts to keep other fires from spreading and destroying all of the park.

The park service did not deviate from its "let it burn" policy on these natural fires until late July, when it reversed itself. Hindsight shows that things got out of control as a result.

There has been friction between the forest service and the park service over the latter's burn policy. But both the laws creating Yellowstone and the park department specified that park lands were to be left in their "natural state."

Environmentalists generally have backed the National Park Service in its policy of letting nature take its course except in fires caused by man.

The destruction does not mean the burn policy should be abandoned for all time. When man interferes with nature, there will be dues to pay later. Stopping some fires eventually can cause greater fire destruction because of the buildup of dry timber and underbrush.

But there needs to be an accounting as to the decision to wait for so long, in this dry year, before starting to fight the fires which threaten one of America's natural jewels.

The State

Columbia, SC, Sept. 8, 1988

THE WILDFIRES that have ravaged a million acres in and around Yellowstone National Park were originally allowed to burn unrestrained on the theory that it was a good idea to eliminate stands of aging, diseased trees and promote new growth. But in a summer of unprecedented dry, hot weather, that policy has proved a disaster.

This week, the U.S. Forest Service and firefighters from several Western states are belatedly waging an all-out battle to save towns, such as Silver Gate and Cooke City — its road sign has been altered to read Cooked City — and landmarks, such as Old Faithful, from the raging blazes. Odds are that hundreds of homes and vacation cabins also will be destroyed.

When the Yellowstone fires began, the U.S. Department of the Interior and the Forest Service claimed that they were nature's way of renewing the woodlands and should be allowed to burn. New trees and undergrowth would replace the gutted forests, they said, and ultimately provide a healthier environment for flora and fauna.

Under normal conditions that might have been true. But the recent devastating drought, searing heat and high winds were anything but normal. Certainly, these conditions should have alerted federal officials to the dangers of a laissez faire attitude toward the spreading fires.

A better policy, according to some experts, would be to put out all forest fires during dangerous weather conditions and, instead, engage in "controlled burning" during safer periods. Such controlled burning, whereby small fires are deliberately set and contained by firebreaks, permits reforestation without devastation.

Unfortunately, it may be too late to save the towns and historic sites in and near this country's oldest national park. But the Yellowstone disaster should force federal agencies to establish more realistic policies to protect our national forests and parks.

London Conference Urges Ozone Action

An international conference in London ended March 7, 1989 with a call for speeding up plans to phase out the chemicals believed to be destroying the ozone layer in the Earth's upper atmosphere. (See pp. 192-195.)

The ozone layer shielded the Earth's surface from harmful ultraviolet rays of the sun. Scientists and environmentalists had become alarmed over the past two years by evidence that it was being depleted by pollutants, principally a class of industrial compounds called chlorofluorocarbons (CFCs). CFCs were also implicated in the so-called greenhouse effect, in which a global warming would be triggered by the buildup of atmospheric pollutants.

Participants in the three-day, 123-nation London conference called for accelerating the timetable set by an existing international agreement for scaling back CFC production. That agreement, signed in Montreal in 1987 and since ratified by more than 30 countries, had called for a 50% cut in CFC production by the end of the century.

On the eve of the London conference, however, the 12 members of the European Community had concluded a surprise agreement to advance the Montreal timetable by banning all CFC production in their countries by the year 2000. The Bush administration in the U.S. expressed its willingness to follow suit.

Nicholas Ridley, the British environment secretary, March 7 said about 20 more nations at the London conference had now agreed to join in the Montreal agreement. They included at least two major Third World countries – Brazil and Nigeria – but not India or China. The conference pointed up a divide between the industrialized nations and those of the Third World, which were wary of being denied the technological benefits of CFCs just as they were launching into industrial development.

Kenyan President Daniel arap Moi, in a keynote speech March 5, called on the West to compensate the Third World for the sacrifices involved: "The world community, especially the industrialized nations, must help these nations make the right choice and order their priorities properly. . .They, too, must make sacrifices commensurate in magnitude with those expected from the Third World nations that must forgo the use of these ozone-depleting chemicals."

The Register-Guard

Eugene, OR, March 8, 1989

Meeting the challenge posed by deterioration of the Earth's ozone layer requires a level of international commitment and cooperation seldom seen on this fractious planet. There are encouraging signs that the world can pass the test.

Scientists have known for more than a decade that man-made chemicals — chlorofluorocarbons, or CFCs — damage the atmospheric ozone layer that shields the Earth's surface from the sun's ultraviolet rays. Two years ago, 31 nations agreed to cut their production of CFCs in half by the year 2000.

New information keeps increasing the magnitude of the threat. Holes in the ozone over both polar regions have been reported. Satellite surveys show that the ozone layer is deteriorating faster than previously believed. CFCs have been identified as one of the gases that contribute to the global warming phenomenon known as the greenhouse effect.

The nations of the European Economic Community reacted last week by agreeing to a complete ban on CFCs by the year 2000. President George Bush said a day later that the United States would do the same. The 13 nations produce two-thirds of the world's CFCs, which are used in refrigeration, aerosols and manufacturing.

Not a single death has yet been attributed to a thinning of the ozone layer. But when human activity can have global environmental consequences, the key to survival is to anticipate danger and act to forestall it. That's what the world is attempting to do with CFCs now. Still more drastic action may be required, but it's good to see that many of the world's nations can respond decisively to a common threat.

Winnipeg Free Press

Winnipeg, Man., March 8, 1989

Canada and other advanced industrial states seemed to be falling over each other this week to make bigger and better promises to cut use of chlorofluorocarbons because of the effect that scientists say they have on the earth's protective ozone layer.

Canada told a conference of 120 countries in London that its goal is to reduce the use of so-called CFCs by 85 per cent over the coming ten years. This was trumped by the United States and the 12-state European Economic Community, who say they will attempt a 100-per-cent CFC reduction in the next ten years.

It seems to be accepted by most scientists that CFCs are the probable cause of what they called a hole in the ozone layer above the Antarctic. British, Norwegian and U.S. scientists recently found, after a six-week study, that there is potential for major destruction of the ozone layer over the Arctic. Canadian scientists say the Arctic ozone layer became very thin in February.

There are differing opinions. Vladimir Zhakarov, leader of the Soviet delegation to the conference, quoted preliminary Soviet studies suggesting that cyclones, not chemical compounds, were responsible for a reduction of 25 per cent in the ozone layer stretching from Europe to Siberia. This depletion, he said, happened in winter, moving every 10 to 15 days from west to east and coinciding with the movement of cyclones.

Nevertheless, the Soviet Union is a signatory of the 1987 Montreal Protocol, like Canada and 29 other states, undertaking to halve production of CFCs by 1999.

Canada has unilaterally declared intent to ban packaging and cups made from CFCs from next January. Sale of pressurized spray cans and portable fire extinguishers using CFCs also will be banned from then. This is part of the 85 per cent in ten years promise.

Many are exercized about CFCs because a pierced or thinned ozone layer exposes the earth to cancer-causing solar radiation. CFCs are widely used. They appear in the manufacture of lightweight beverage cups, computer chips and in other electronics applications. They are used in refrigeration, such as in home fridges and automobile air conditioners.

In this state, they do not harm humans or the atmosphere we breathe. Scientists say that when CFCs rise to the stratosphere, up to 25 miles high, they disintegrate. Their chlorine atoms then attack and destroy the ozone layer, letting through harmful ultraviolet sunrays. This process apparently can take between ten and 100 years to occur.

CFCs also have been pronounced guilty of causing the notorious greenhouse effect, by trapping heat and raising general temperatures on the earth.

The gloomiest prognosis at the conference came from Sherry Rowland of the University of California. She said that even if all CFC emissions on earth ceased tomorrow morning, it would take until the 23rd century to restore the stratospheric conditions we enjoyed in 1960.

A glance at the items producing CFCs should convince anyone that an immediate ban would require great changes in industrial methods and current ways of living, especially in countries like Canada. Since technology has produced this claimed mess, technology should be harnessed to get us out of it.

Replacement chemicals for refrigeration, a major source of CFCs, are not yet commercially available. The Canadian government should give all the help it can to universities and industry to come up with replacements. Meanwhile, the Canadian government should move quickly to make available in Canada the new invention called the "vampire" that can capture CFCs released when auto air conditioners are serviced.

DESERET NEWS
Salt Lake City, UT, March 11, 1989

Twelve member nations of the European Economic Community have taken decisive action to reduce the use of synthetic compounds that destroy the Earth's ozone layer.

Chlorofluorocarbons, CFC for short, are used in aerosol sprays, refrigeration coolants, cleaning agents and several other products, and are blamed for depletion of the ozone layer that protects the Earth from the sun's harmful ultraviolet rays and for an increase in skin cancer.

By voting to decrease production of CFC by 85 percent and to seek a total ban on production by the year 2000, the market countries acted wisely.

Several other countries, including the United States, which has already banned use of the compounds in aerosol propellants, would be smart to follow the Common Market's lead.

Common Market states are responsible for about 50 percent of the world's annual CFC production of 1 million tons.

Other nations have joined the Montreal Protocol, an international accord aimed at reducing and eventually licking the problem, but they could do more.

In 1974, scientists forecast a 7 to 13 percent decline in ozone if the use of chlorofluorocarbons continued. A year later a federal task force agreed with the studies, recommending a nationwide ban on the use of such chemicals in aerosols.

Since that time, Du Pont, the world's largest CFC producer, and some other companies have taken steps to produce substitute chemicals that help to reduce the problem but which cause no serious problems for consumers. But much more can and must be accomplished.

The potential for making continued progress in combatting the ozone problem is evidenced by the fact that Du Pont recently announced the discovery of a chemical blend for existing refrigeration and air-conditioning equipment that is 97 percent less harmful than traditional CFC.

Despite cries from the CFS-producing industry, such discoveries have cost the consumer little. Scientists and companies have learned that products that provide the public with comfort and satisfaction can be made in many ways.

Omaha World-Herald
Omaha, NE, March 2, 1989

Twelve European nations unexpectedly agreed to go farther than ever before to protect the Earth's vital ozone shield, a move that carries a lot of hope for the environment.

A little over a year ago, 46 nations met in Montreal and drew up an agreement to limit the production of chlorofluorocarbons, a class of gaseous chemicals that erode the ozone layer of the upper atmosphere. The ozone layer helps protect the Earth's surface from the sun's damaging ultraviolet rays. Skin cancers are among the effects of exposure to such rays.

The Montreal agreement was signed by the United States and other nations representing about 90 percent of the world's chlorofluorocarbon use, including most of the nations of Western Europe. They agreed to a 50 percent cut in production of the ozone-attacking chemicals by the end of the century.

Now, in a new initiative, the European countries have gone far beyond the Montreal agreement. They have agreed to eliminate production and use of the chemicals in the next decade, beginning with an 85 percent reduction as soon as that can be arranged.

Chlorofluorocarbons are used as coolants in refrigerators and air conditioners, as aerosol spray propellants, as solvents and as an ingredient in foam insulation. Both Du Pont, this country's largest producer of chlorofluorocarbons, and Imperial Chemicals Inc., Europe's largest producer, have announced that they are phasing out production of the substances.

The World Resources Institute, an environmental group in the United States, has estimated that Common Market nations produce about 35 percent of the chlorofluorocarbons on the market; U.S. companies produce 30 to 34 percent. The action of the 12 European Community nations should have a significant impact on chlorofluorocarbon production and, thus, on the ozone layer problem.

Their unilateral action posed a challenge to the United States. But President Bush didn't hesitate after William K. Reilly, head of the Environmental Protection Agency, urged that America go along with the proposal. Bush endorsed the cutback and instructed Reilly to pledge U.S. support during a 100-nation conference that began during the weekend in London.

Conditions seem favorable to accelerate the schedule and eliminate production by the turn of the century. The management of Du Pont and Imperial are phasing out their production faster than the Montreal agreement would require. The heads of the major chlorofluorocarbon-producing nations are moving toward a solution.

The ozone layer is crucial to life on Earth. Banning chlorofluorocarbons might not be the entire solution to preserving this stratospheric shield, but it is an essential step. Using the international bonds of mutual cooperation and commitment that are being formed to address this issue, perhaps other environmental challenges can be faced, too.

The Kansas City Times
Kansas City, MO, March 7, 1989

Major European nations have taken a bold, correct move to ban chemicals that harm the ozone by the year 2000. The United States should follow right behind; President Bush seems intent on doing so. This is the kind of dramatic action needed to help prevent further environmental damage.

More evidence seems to crop up every day to indicate that the ozone layer is being eroded. That's bad news because the layer helps protect people, crops and wildlife from the sun's rays. Critics say more studies are needed. But this kind of approach doesn't make sense when substitutes for the current, harmful chemicals can be found.

The European agreement would mean that industries would have to replace certain chlorofluorocarbons with something less dangerous to the environment. Chlorofluorocarbons are used as coolants in air conditioners and refrigerators, as well as in foam insulation and aerosol spray cans in Europe.

Environmental Protection Administrator William Reilly indicated the United States might take the same action as the 12 European nations. Bush said he wanted Reilly to pursue that goal, as long as less harmful options are available. Reilly made a good point: "We need to be sure that any (chlorofluorocarbon) substitutes that might be developed do not pose new and unforeseen environmental risks, such as exacerbating global warming."

That's where private industries come in. They are working on substitutes now, getting ready for the day when governments phase out chlorofluorocarbons. But won't the cost go up? It depends on how one measures "cost." It will probably cost more money to buy and use replacements. But if the new chemicals can help save the ozone layer, reduce skin cancer and reduce environmental problems, then their real cost is much more palatable.

That's one aspect of the argument the United States and other nations have to keep in mind as they make any decision affecting the environment. In this case, the 12 European nations have decided that action to ban chlorofluorcarbon use — instead of more studies — is the path to be followed.

St. Paul Pioneer Press & Dispatch
St. Paul, MN, March 4, 1989

Public policy machinery often moves in delayed reaction to reality. The European Community has provided a welcome exception with its pledge to eliminate ozone-ravaging chemicals by the turn of the century. The United States should join the Europeans in getting rid of chlorofluorocarbons as soon as possible.

President Bush on Friday indicated American willingness, if adequate substitutes can be found.

The timing couldn't be better, with an international conference on the ozone crisis set to begin Sunday in London.

The rapid progression of damage to the atmosphere's ozone layer by CFCs is startling. The environmental group Greenpeace estimates that if all countries stopped producing CFCs by next year, the levels of ozone-destroying chlorine would not revert to 1985 levels until 2050. The ultraviolet rays that come through the thinning and broken ozone layer are bombarding our climate and increasing skin cancer at an explosive rate.

Now, just months after the multi-national Montreal Protocol agreed to cut CFCs in half by the year 1998, the EC countries have seen the urgency of the ozone crisis and taken more effective action. If the United States were to follow, more than two-thirds of the CFC production in the world would cease. The other producers would have strong incentive to go along.

There has been progress against CFCs. In the United States, CFCs have virtually disappeared from aerosol cans. They have been curtailed in packaging. And the Du Pont Co., primary manufacturer of CFCs, says next year it will start manufacturing a substitute compound for refrigeration needs.

Efforts to find and market safe products as industrial solvents, refrigerants and packaging should get strong, wide-ranging government assistance.

With a commitment to ozone-protection and developing CFC replacements, the United States can make a substantial contribution toward doing the right thing for the global village.

The Toronto Star
Toronto, Ont., March 6, 1989

It may get worse before it gets better. But an important step to stop at least one poison from destroying the planet's atmosphere has been taken.

Now 12 European nations have joined Canada in pushing up the deadline to ban the production and consumption of gases that threaten to destroy the ozone layer that protects earth from the sun's harmful ultraviolet rays.

Last year in Montreal, 40 countries agreed to cut chlorofluorocarbon (CFC) production in half by 1998. But the Europeans want all CFCs used in fridges and spray cans cut by 85 per cent as soon as possible and banned by 2000.

Europe's action has real muscle. While Canada is responsible for about 2 per cent of the world's CFCs, the European nations produce 400,000 tonnes of CFCs out of the world's total output of 1.1 million tonnes a year.

Holes in the ozone layer have been reported in the Arctic and Antarctic and scientists predict it will take decades for it to recover.

The next step, of course, is a worldwide ban. But that will only happen with leadership and technological help from the countries, many of which are already committed to the ban.

For Canada, the news is even better. Word is that the administration of U.S. President George Bush is drafting proposals to meet Canada's demand for a 50 per cent cut in cross-border acid rain emissions.

Is the universe unfolding as it should? In some small way, perhaps.

PORTLAND EVENING EXPRESS
Portland, ME, March 8, 1989

OZONE I
The bad stuff

There are 96 areas of the country where ozone pollution — caused largely by motor vehicle and factory emissions — exceed allowable federal standards. Six of them are in Maine. We've got to start cleaning it up. But we can't do it alone; much of the contaminated air we breathe is generated by our neighbors.

Ozone pollution — primarily hydrocarbons and nitrogen oxides that change chemically during hot sunny weather — exceeded acceptable levels last summer in Portland and in the counties of York, Lincoln, Kennebec, Knox and Hancock.

Although ozone smog was once thought to be dangerous only to persons already suffering from respiratory diseases, many scientists now believe it be a cause of lung diseases, particularly in children.

Sadly, as with acid rain, Maine is also at the end of the ozone pollution trail. State environmental officials believe that most of the ozone smog in York County and Portland is blown here from other states. Similarly, they say, much of the air pollution elsewhere in Maine is generated out of state.

Maine has already adopted several rules, including the sale of low-evaporation gasoline during the spring and summer months, designed to reduce ozone pollution. They'll be phased in over the next three years. But those rules alone probably won't reduce pollution to acceptable federal standards.

What is necessary is a regional approach that will likely require adoption of California's more stringent auto emission standards. That will assure that new vehicles pollute less. Maine may also need to adopt annual tail-pipe emission inspection tests to make certain cars and trucks don't start polluting more as they get older.

But the key here is a regional approach. Unless all states act in concert, Maine's ozone pollution problems won't get appreciably better, no matter how hard we try.

OZONE II
The good stuff

Unlike ozone at ground level, ozone suspended about 15 miles up in the Earth's atmosphere is something we can't live without. It provides the vital shield that protects the planet and its inhabitants from the sun's harmful — fatal even — ultraviolet rays.

It's also breaking down. Man-made chlorofluorocarbons (shorten that mouthful to CFCs) escaping into the atmosphere are punching holes in the ozone shield, scientists say. Considering it's a fragile shield, only about 2 inches thick, Earthlings ought to be wary.

Ultraviolet rays bombarding Earth cause skin cancer, eye damage and limit the body's ability to ward off disease. The rays also destroy plankton in the sea and, on land, attack plant life and food crops.

CFCs, which are used as coolants in refrigerators and air conditioners, in spray cans and in insulation are the culprits. President Bush and the 12-nation European Economic Community have called for a total ban on the production and use of CFCs by the end of the century provided adequate substitutes can be found.

The president and the EEC are on the right track. A current global treaty calling for a 40 per cent reduction in the use of CFCs over the next dozen years may be inadequate. Scientists say the ozone layer is coming apart two or three time faster than was earlier thought.

The Soviet Union, China and India are balking at a rapid end to CFCs, saying they want to see more hard evidence. That's too bad but it shouldn't dampen U.S. and EEC resolve. Today those nations manufacture the bulk of all CFCs. The sooner we switch to substitutes, the better off we'll all be.

THE CHRISTIAN SCIENCE MONITOR
Boston, MA, March 3, 1989

THERE'S been a tinge of unreality to the concern about climatic warming and the ozone layer. The threats are global. The pollution that causes the threats is also global. But discussions of what to do about it have been parochial and dominated by Western industrialized countries.

It's increasingly obvious that this pollution won't be curbed until a global consensus exists as to what needs to be done.

China made this point bluntly when it blew a hole in the Montreal Protocol to limit ozone-destroying chlorofluorocarbons (CFCs). Prof. Cheng Zheng-Kang of Beijing University told a University of Colorado conference that China plans to boost its CFC production tenfold. Within a decade, that should equal current United States output, negating the US plan to cut its output in half under the protocol's terms.

The Chinese want refrigerators for which CFCs are the working fluids. They can't afford the more costly substitutes now being developed. They don't see why they should do without refrigeration because of a problem caused by Western nations. They also resent protocol provisions that allow industrialized nations higher CFC production levels than third-world countries.

What's true of the ozone treaty will also be true of efforts to deal with climatic warming. The recent congressional hearing on the subject understandably focused on what the US might do to cut carbon dioxide pollution from fossil fuels. The plain fact is that industrialized nations can't do much single-handed. Their efforts could be negated by rising third-world energy use.

Thus, first priority must be to achieve global consensus on the scope of the problem and how to cope with it. There has to be give-and-take all around. Third-world nations must be willing to plan their development in environmentally safe ways, and industrialized nations must provide technical and financial aid to do it.

It will take decades of sustained effort to protect the global environment. Now is the time to build the consensus that must precede action.

MILWAUKEE SENTINEL
Milwaukee, WI, March 9, 1989

The 123-nation conference to save the ozone layer just concluded in London provided some extremely encouraging dialog on this subject.

Now it is up to the world leaders involved to act before the critical protective layer that protects our planet from the sun's cancer-producing rays is stripped away.

As Great Britain's Prince Charles told the group: "Countless numbers of people are looking toward their leaders and representatives to take bold decisions now, decisions which our descendants, yet unborn, will thank us for."

Not to do so, Charles said in a remark that could be prophetic, 'will cause our grandchildren to curse us."

These are heartfelt words from a young man who is a husband and father of small children and destined someday to take his place as the titular head of one of the greatest nations on Earth.

Some 31 nations already have agreed, in a Montreal compact two years ago, to halve the use of chlorofluorocarbons by 1998, and 20 others joined them at the London meeting.

But President Bush, breaking with the Reagan administration, commendably called for an outright end to the use of CFCs by 1999, and the 12 countries of the European Community upped their commitment to an 85% reduction.

Exceptions to the global crusade included the Soviet Union, China, India and other Third World countries.

They believe that the phase-out of CFCs — which are used as refrigerants, cleaning agents for computer chips and, still in Europe, as aerosol propellants — would adversely affect efforts to improve the lifestyles of the people of their nations and slow their economic growth.

And, as Britain's Prime Minister Margaret Thatcher said, a "two-speed" system to accommodate the slower pace of modernization might be a fair compromise with the developing nations, but only if it were part of an overall plan to eliminate CFCs in those countries sooner than some would like.

Ultimately, the CFCs capacity to trap the heat of the globe and cause major climate changes could turn the sky into a microwave oven, as the prince put it.

And because the people of this planet are not Phoenixes that can rise again from their own ashes, their survival demands that action to meet this threat be taken promptly.

Times~Colonist
Victoria, B.C., March 12, 1989

At last, there are significant international moves to ban the chemicals destroying the Earth's ozone shield. But the pledges made at a conference in London last week — working toward end-of-the-century goals — fall far short of drastic action. They appear to be based on the dubious premise that there is still plenty of time to phase out the use of chlorofluorocarbons (CFCs), the synthetic chemicals used as solvents, refrigerants, aerosol propellants and blowing agents for plastic foams.

Some of these compounds can endure in the atmosphere for a century or more. When released they are stable and non-toxic, but over many years they work their insidious damage to the fragile ozone shield. Which allows more of the sun's ultraviolet rays to reach Earth. Which brings more skin cancers, eye cataracts and suppression of human immune systems.

As if all that weren't enough, CFCs are also a major contributor to the so-called greenhouse effect, the global warming phenomenon which many experts predict will lead to severe climate changes, destruction of agricultural areas and flooding of coastal cities.

An international scientific assessment sponsored by several major bodies including the World Meteorological Association has warned that "we are conducting one giant experiment on a glocal scale by increasing the concentration of trace gases in the atmosphere without knowing the environmental consequences."

Against this scenario, the inability of some nations to grasp the life-and-death importance of swift action is downright baffling.

The Soviet delegate at the 123-nation London conference said Moscow needs more scientific evidence that CFCs destroy the ozone layer before speeding up its phase-out of such chemicals.

That evokes not-so-fond memories of former president Ronald Reagan's approach to the acid rain problem — let's study it some more before doing anything. The Soviet stance is also at odds with Mikhail Gorbachev's repeated warnings that environmental degradation is a greater threat to human survival than nuclear war.

As for the developing countries, it is easy to understand their resentment of urgent pleas from the West to join in CFC elimination. Many of them are only now embarking on the mass production of consumer goods containing those substances (China, for example, with refrigerators) and their logic is persuasive: since the West invented CFCs and produces most of them, it should also pay to replace them.

The developing nations know that such Western help is a remote possibility, and meanwhile they may allow CFC production to proceed unchecked. Of what benefit is a nice fridge today for an ordinary Chinese peasant family, if the children or their children are doomed to suffer cancer and other horrors in years to come?

DAILY NEWS
New York, NY, March 4, 1989

The European Community has taken an unexpected and welcome step. The 12 nations have agreed to phase out, by the end of the century, use of the chemicals that are blowing great holes in the Earth's ozone layer. The action was taken in light of new evidence that the ozone layer is being destroyed even faster than previously thought. And that the eventual consequences would be catastrophic: Ultraviolet rays bombarding the globe would increase skin cancer, destroy crops, kill forests.

The U.S. has led the way in ozone-saving steps. Now President Bush is acting to match the European Community's advance. The President yesterday endorsed a ban on the offending chemicals. That's more good news.

U.S. Relents on 'Greenhouse' Treaty

The Bush administration May 12, 1989 reversed itself and said it would work toward an international treaty to curb global warming.

Negotiators at a United Nations-sponsored meeting in Geneva, Switzerland were currently seeking to draft a treaty to deal with the so-called greenhouse effect, a global warming triggered by a buildup of pollutants in the atmosphere. Many scientists now believed that a greenhouse warming had begun. (See pp. 188-191)

As recently as a week earlier, the U.S. administration had held that a greenhouse treaty would be premature because too little was known about the economic consequences of actions necessary to curb the warming. Those actions might include fundamental changes in both industry and agriculture. The administration was reportedly split on the issue of a treaty, with both the Environmental Protection Agency and the State Department wanting the U.S. to take a leading role, while others, including White House chief of staff John H. Sununu, opposed it.

The administration drew harsh criticism after a top government scientist May 8 revealed that he had been ordered by the White House to alter his written congressional testimony to tone down a warning about the greenhouse effect.

The scientist was James E. Hansen, director of the National Aeronautics and Space Administration's Goddard Institute for Space Studies. He told the Senate Commerce subcommittee on science, technology and space that the Office of Management and Budget had ordered him to insert into his testimony a statement that it "remains scientifically unknown" whether man-made gases contributed more to the problem than did natural causes.

Subcommittee Chairman Albert Gore Jr. (D, Tenn.) accused the administration of "scientific fraud."

The White House May 8 confirmed the order to Hansen and said it was OMB policy to review all prospective testimony by government officials.

The administration's stance against a treaty angered environmentalists, who recalled that Bush had made campaign pledges to seek global action on the problem. Sen. John H. Chaffee (R, R.I.) May 9 sent Bush a letter saying it was "not too late" to "bolster your reputation as an environmental president."

The Evening Gazette

Worcester, MA,
May 12, 1989

When George Bush ran for the White House, he promised to be an "environmental president." In a campaign speech last summer, he declared: "Those who think we are powerless to do anything about the greenhouse effect forget about the White House effect. We will talk about global warning, and we will act."

That was then, and this is now. Even though the United States is chairing an international conference on the greenhouse effect, the American delegates will not contribute much.

Why? Because various government bureaucracies have failed to agree on a uniform policy.

In fact, the "whitehouse effect" is having an adverse impact. James Hansen, a government climatologist testifying before a Senate committee, complained that his assessment of the danger presented by global warming due to pollutant gases had been softened by the Office and Management and Budget.

While the OMB's responsibility is to coordinate government policy, particularly in fiscal matters, the agency was way out of line. Worse yet, its action raises questions about Bush's commitment to solving major environmental problems.

Evidently, the greenhouse effect as a threat to global climate is being taken very seriously by a growing number of governments. While experts disagree on how immediate the danger is, they agree that such pollutant gases as carbon monoxide do trap the sun's heat and could seriously warm the earth's climate. There is even talk about a ban on burning coal in the future.

Encouraged by Bush's pro-environment statements, the world community expects the United States to take a major role in addressing the problem. The president must make good on his promise. He should start by ending the bickering within the federal bureaucracy and formulating a forward-looking U.S. policy.

The San Diego Union

San Diego, CA, May 13, 1989

Presidential candidate George Bush proclaimed: "Those who think we are powerless to do anything about the greenhouse effect forget about the White House effect." But as President, Mr. Bush is not only dragging his feet in dealing with this clear and present danger to the Earth's life-protecting ozone layer, the White House Office of Management and Budget prefers to censor the alarming realities of the problem, as though that would make it go away.

How else explain the heavy handed manner in which the OMB forced a prominent scientist to tone down his testimony about the greenhouse effect before a Senate subcommittee?

Dr. James E. Hansen, director of the National Aeronautics and Space Administration's Goddard Institute for Space Studies, was about to warn the committee of an increasing global warming trend that could produce prolonged droughts during the next few years and other dangerous global disasters. Instead, OMB insisted that he add a contradictory sentence to his conclusion, which was clearly designed to justify the President's reluctance to act.

Never mind that Secretary of State James Baker and Environmental Protection Agency chief William Reilly have repeatedly urged the President to address the global-warming trend. Mr. Bush has not even managed to convene his own policy makers on the greenhouse effect.

Small wonder Dr. Hansen's warnings were viewed with alarm by the bean counters at OMB. They routinely review testimony to be given before congressional committees to ensure that federal policy conforms to the President's budget. These consummate bureaucrats care little if scientific data are distorted to dovetail with policy.

Dr. Hansen, it seems, is not so cavalier about such duplicity. Refusing to be muzzled, he exposed this charade to the Senate subcommittee. This, in turn, prompted even more doublespeak from the administration. White House Press Secretary Marlin Fitzwater mumbled something about the need to base decisions on sound scientific data.

Last Monday, British Prime Minister Margaret Thatcher called for an international convention to deal with the dangers of global warming. Her call, combined with mounting criticism of the administration, prompted the White House to announce last Thursday that the United States is willing to host a global workshop on the greenhouse effect later this year. Such vacillation doesn't speak well for the would-be environmental President.

BUFFALO EVENING NEWS
Buffalo, NY, May 13, 1989

AN UGLY GLIMPSE into the workings of government was provided the other day by revelations that a government scientist had been forced to alter his testimony before Congress in order to conform with the administration's policy.

This was no minor scientific official, either, but Dr. James T. Hansen, director of the Goddard Institute for Space Studies of the National Aeronautics and Space Administration. He testified on the problem of global warming caused by the "greenhouse" effect.

The text of Hansen's original testimony had said that global warming could cause drought and other upheavals in the Earth's climate. The changes he was forced to make, he said, "negated" his whole point.

In his original testimony, Hansen also said gases causing the greenhouse effect are "primarily" of human origin. This was changed to say that the relative contribution of human and natural processes "remain scientifically unknown," thus playing down any sense of urgency that might make governmental action seem necessary.

"It distresses me that they put words in my mouth; they even put it in the first person," Hansen said in an interview. At one point in his prepared testimony, he was supposed to say, "Again, I stress ... " and go on to parrot the words written for him by some government bureaucrat.

Fortunately, he didn't do it. He went to Sen. Albert Gore, D-Tenn., chairman of the subcommittee before which he was to testify, and told him what he had been told to do. Gore called the alterations "unbelievable" and said the government was trying to change science to make it conform to its policy, instead of basing its policy on the truth. "They're scared of the truth," he said.

The alterations were made by the Office of Management and Budget, which routinely reviews testimony to be presented to Congress to be sure it conforms with government policy. Policy, of course, is one thing, and scientific facts are something else. As Hansen put it, "I can understand changing policy, but not science."

This censoring and twisting of scientific reports is reminiscent of what used to go on in the Soviet Union in Stalin's time, when the pseudo-scientific genetic theories of Lysenko were given official Communist Party approval. In this country, scientists are supposedly hired for their scientific expertise, not to be mouthpieces to justify some already established policy.

This was not an isolated incident. Hansen said this was not the first time his testimony had been altered, and another government scientist revealed that the OMB had tried to amend his testimony on scientific issues.

Dr. Jerry Mahlman, of the National Oceanic and Atmospheric Administration, said that the OMB had proposed changes in his testimony that were "unscientific" and would have embarrassed him with his fellow scientists. He refused to make the changes, and the OMB backed down.

At a time when Britain and other countries are seeking international action on the greenhouse effect, the Bush administration appears to be dragging its feet. That is deplorable enough, but it is even worse when bureaucrats attempt to pressure government scientists to twist the truth. It is frightening to guess at how often scientists in such situations, with their jobs at stake, might be tempted to shade the truth.

Gore was understandably disturbed by what he called "an exercise in science fraud" and an attempt to mislead Congress. At future hearings on scientific subjects, regrettably, congressmen will be fully entitled to ask witnesses whether they are expressing their own views or those of some unknown bureaucrat.

The Honolulu Advertiser
Honolulu, HI, May 13, 1989

President Bush's proclaimed desire to be "the environmental president" suffered another wound with the altering of a government scientist's testimony on the dangers of global warming or the "greenhouse effect."

Somebody in the Office of Management and Budget edited and watered down the intended testimony before a Senate subcommittee of James Houston, director of NASA's Goddard Institute for Space Studies. The result made it appear he had doubts about the reality of the greenhouse effect. Actually, he thinks the situation is worse than can be shown by present computer technology. So do many other experts.

This goes beyond the usual editing an administration does to speak with one voice on policy issues. This was altering a scientific judgment, seemingly because some in the Bush administration don't think the situation is as serious as others do.

The White House says this was done at a lower level at OMB without top authorization. But it became known and backfired against Bush, who promised in the last campaign that his efforts on the environment would be better than those of the Reagan administration.

In a move to look better, the White House yesterday dropped its opposition to a formal treaty-negotiating process on global warming. That's a small plus. But Bush still should worry that he's starting to look like Reagan on acid rain, calling for more research on increasingly obvious environmental problems where action is needed.

THE ⚓ SUN
Baltimore, MD, May 11, 1989

George Bush, take notes: Censoring what respected scientists tell Congress and the American people is not a mark of responsible leadership. The people of these United States will suffer the ill effects of air pollution long after you leave office. They elected you to solve such problems, not to permit your minions to cover them up.

In presidential year 1988, candidate Bush said that such threats as the one affecting the earth's protective ozone layer were serious. Solving them was not exactly No. 1 on his presidential to-do list, but important enough that a man proclaiming himself an environmentalist would take notice. Now it appears that Mr. Bush is less concerned than he seemed.

At a time when world angst over atmospheric pollution is at a peak, Mr. Bush is pedaling backward. The United States, alone of the industrialized West, balks at joining efforts to hammer out an international agreement cutting harmful emissions expected to cause "greenhouse effect" warming over the next several decades. Marlin Fitzwater, the president's spokesman, told a recent White House briefing that Mr. Bush "hasn't made a judgment about scientific assessments."

It's a little difficult to make such a judgment if your chief subordinates are watering down the very assessments needed for your decision.

Mr. Fitzwater admitted an Office of Management and Budget official "five levels down from the top" had altered the testimony to be given to Congress by one of the chief climatologists, NASA's James T. Hansen. Dr. Hansen, director of the Goddard Institute for Space Studies, thinks pollution caused by human activity will soon cause upheavals in the earth's climate. He based his projections on computer studies of satellite data, ground-based observations and the principles of meteorology, but OMB put in new language to the effect that, "there are many points of view on global warming and many of them conflict" with Dr. Hansen's opinions.

It would have been wise, then, to find those scientists who don't agree, and to offer them up for a different perspective. Instead, the White House elected to overrule the judgments of the man whose job it is to give his best understanding of the conditions prevailing. That leads to questions about the judgment of the man at the top. Ducking the issue, when it so drastically concerns every American, will not suffice, no matter how earnestly Mr. Bush's White House wishes it would. If there is really an environmentalist in the Oval Office, it's time for him to stand up.

Wisconsin ⬕ State Journal

Madison, WI, May 11, 1989

You don't have to be a rocket scientist to figure out President Bush is not getting top-quality scientific advice. It's past time he rectified that situation by appointing a national science adviser and selecting a committee to help him make wise decisions on science-related issues.

Those issues seem to be proliferating faster than interest on the national debt. In his first four months in office, Bush has been faced with a disastrous oil spill; conflicting reports from the arena of cold fusion, and pressure for an international treaty banning chlorofluorocarbons to delay or head off global warming. In each case, Bush could have benefited from immediate, informed, knowledgeable counsel from scientists whose specialty it is to know about such matters. Other issues with scientific import — as mundane as the landfill crisis, as esoteric as superconducting supercolliders — have also risen: Abortion. Acid rain. Biotechnology and genetic engineering. Supermagnetic electrical storage.

New evidence that Bush is not getting the best advice possible on scientific questions came Monday, when James Hansen, director of the National Aeronautics and Space Administration's Goddard Institute of Space Studies, told Congress that White House aides altered his testimony.

Hansen was asked to testify last November on global warming, the so-called greenhouse effect caused by air pollution that destroys the earth's protective ozone layer. He told a Senate subcommittee this week that bureaucrats from the White House's Office of Management and Budget tried to water down his scientific conclusions.

The tradition of designating a presidential science adviser dates to the Truman administration. The world has become vastly more complex since then, partly because of advances made by scientists. It seems only logical, as 'Star Trek' science officer Mr. Spock would say, for the top leader in the free world to have top scientists aid him in his decision-making.

There is no need for a Cabinet-level science department; no need for more bureaucracy. The brains, and the research, are out there. Bush needs to quickly appoint a panel of top scientists from diverse fields, and select a knowledgeable and articulate person to convey the panel's recommendations.

The Burlington Free Press

Burlington, VT, May 13, 1989

The Bush administration has again put the president's insincerity as an environmentalist on display.

At an appearance early this week before the Senate Subcommittee on Science, Technology and Space, Dr. James T. Hansen said the Office of Management and Budget altered conclusions in his testimony about global warming trends.

Hansen, director of NASA's Goddard Institute for Space Studies, told the panel that computer studies he conducted showed air pollution would dramatically alter the earth's climate. He predicted that emissions of carbon dioxide and other man-made pollutants would cause temperature increases, droughts and severe storms.

OMB wanted Hansen's testimony to reflect the administration's view that not all scientists agreed with his conclusions. To some extent, that is true. It is not, however, Hansen's responsibility to present the findings of others. They can speak for themselves.

Scientists disagree on the pace of global warming, and some feel that natural events like volcanic eruptions contribute to the greenhouse effect more than man's excesses. There is virtually no dispute, however, that automobile emissions and burning coal and oil add devastatingly to the coating of pollutants in the upper atmosphere. The toxic layer traps the sun's heat; on Earth, the thermometer inches upward. That was the point of Hansen's testimony that the OMB wanted to dilute.

Bush's campaign promises to bolster education and improve the welfare of poor Americans have quickly run into an intractable budget deficit. Slowing or reversing destruction of the earth's atmosphere will also require federal spending. Acknowledging the problem and providing leadership to confront it, however, is no more costly than campaign rhetoric. Letting scientists tell the unfettered truth as they see it is the first step to providing that leadership.

The Seattle Times

Seattle, WA, May 11, 1989

SEN. Albert Gore Jr., D-Tenn., cried foul the other day when he learned that Office of Management and Budget officials had altered the statement of a top scientist with the National Aeronautics and Space Administration on the "greenhouse effect."

Granted, the OMB bureaucrats' action was questionable. They added language to Dr. James T. Hansen's testimony before Gore's subcommittee on science, technology and space that indicated scientists were divided on the subject of global warming.

That happens to be true. Scientists ARE divided.

But Hansen stressed that his scientific conclusions were his own, and he should have been allowed to declare them freely.

"I don't think the science should be altered," Gore **Sen. Albert Gore Jr.** *Taylor Jones* righteously declared. He's right. It shouldn't.

However, when it comes to scientific objectivity, Gore's laboratory coat is not exactly spotless.

Earlier this year, he declared flatly that it was "no longer a matter of any dispute worthy of recognition" that the greenhouse effect was an unprecedented ecological crisis. Those who, "for the purpose of maintaining balance in the debate, take the contrarian view that there is significant uncertainty," were hurting our ability to respond, he added.

In other words: Ignore science; play politics. Bad idea.

Scientific theories should be allowed to stand or fall on their own merits. OMB was wrong to change Hansen's testimony, but Gore was wrong to declare scientific debate irrelevant.

LAS VEGAS REVIEW-JOURNAL

Las Vegas, NV, May 9, 1989

Sen. Albert Gore, D-Tenn., was incensed when he learned that Bush administration officials censored the remarks of one prominent scientist who testified about the greenhouse effect before Gore's Senate subcommittee.

The New York Times broke the story that the federal Office of Management and Budget had rewritten the testimony of Dr. James Hansen, director of the National Aeronautics and Space Administration's Goddard Institute for Space Studies.

Hansen told the newspaper that officials of the OMB changed the text of his testimony to soften his conclusions about the potential environmental damage linked to the greenhouse effect, or global warming caused by pollutants in the atmosphere.

Hansen planned to report to Gore's subcommittee on science and technology that computer analyses pointed to the probability that carbon dioxide and other gases in the atmosphere would cause substantial increases in temperature, drought, severe storms and other stresses that will affect the Earth's biological systems.

But OMB altered the text of his remarks beforehand, and the subcommittee was presented with a watered-down version that made the prospects for these major changes in the global environment appear less certain.

Gore was justifiably upset.

It is true that scientists differ on the potential impact of the greenhouse effect; some even dismiss the concern about global warming as speculative.

Nevertheless — whether we are dealing with a passing scare or a potential ecological disaster — the task falls to Congress to sort out the varying scientific opinions and establish a sound national policy in response to global warming phenomena.

Congress cannot fulfill this duty properly unless it has access to the broad spectrum of informed scientific opinion — and that precludes the censorship of opinions functionaries in the Bush administration don't like.

THE WHITEHOUSE EFFECT

REVISED REPORT

WARNING ON THE GREENHOUSE EFFECT

©1989 HERBLOCK

FORT WORTH STAR-TELEGRAM

Fort Worth, TX, May 9, 1989

Sen. Albert Gore of Tennesse reacted with totally justified outrage at learning that officials in the White House had censored testimony on the greenhouse effect prepared by a government scientist for presentation to a congressional subcommittee.

Gore, chairman of the Senate Subcommittee on Science, Technology and Space, described the high-handed action by the Office of Management and Budget as "unbelievable" and said that the alterations of testimony by Dr. James E. Hansen represented an attempt by some members of the Bush administration to change science to make it conform to their budget policy.

Hansen, director of the National Aeronautics and Space Administration's Goddard Institute for Space Studies, said that the OMB edited his testimony to make prospects appear less certain for severe changes in climate caused by release of carbon dioxide and other gases into the atmosphere.

That editing, Hansen said, went to the extent of making changes over his objections and presenting the altered testimony as his "first person" assertions. That is unconscionable. In censoring scientific opinion, the OMB exceeded both its authority and its competence.

Although the scientific community has voiced some challenges to Hansen's contention that the greenhouse effect has already begun, there is a broad consensus that the danger is real.

The State Department, the Environmental Protection Agency and several foreign leaders have urged the United States to assume a leadership role in a concerted effort to curb the causes of the problem.

George Bush campaigned as a champion of the environment — even proclaiming that he sought to be the "environmental president" — but some members of his administration, who appear to have the president's ear, have sought to downplay the peril for fear of the economic costs of the measures that would be required to control such dangerous emissions.

Although concern about costs is appropriate for the OMB bureaucrats, that does not give them a license to tailor scientific findings to fit their preferred policy options. Such censorship poses a threat to intellectual freedom in this country that in its own way is at least as worrisome as the greenhouse effect.

The Washington Post

Washington, DC, May 9, 1989

THE SCIENTIFIC research establishment in this country enjoys a huge measure of independence and decentralization, and rightly so; its freedom from government interference despite a generous supply of government funding has been a major source of its strength. In the past two years, however, concern has risen within the government over a different kind of oversight—the ways in which scientists themselves respond to allegations of fraud, bad practice or deliberate misconduct within their ranks. That concern was reflected in dramatic hearings last week before a House subcommittee chaired by Rep. John Dingell (D-Mich.), hearings that continue today.

As the main source of research support in an era of tight budgets, government has a reasonable interest in knowing whether its money is safe from flagrant abuses; the problem is to make sure of that safety without inhibiting scientific enterprise. Can scientists police themselves? How good are they at it, and can they become better? These are the questions at issue in the Dingell hearings. They have drawn attention because they involve allegations of misconduct within the laboratory of a Nobel laureate, Dr. David Baltimore, and because those allegations had already been investigated at length last year by a review committee within the National Institutes of Health, which found "misstatement and omission" but no fraud. Rep. Dingell's committee has reopened the review of that case in great depth, even calling on the Secret Service to analyze the chronology of lab notebooks. But the seemingly picayune details of the Baltimore case do not go to the heart of the problem, which is the general reluctance of scientists to admit internal problems of this sort and to engage in self-scrutiny.

Those broader problems emerged clearly in similar hearings a year ago, which examined some flagrant cases of past misconduct and the difficulties that others have faced in bringing them to light. Those committees also heard allegations of widespread carelessness and fudging—both of which are distinct from plain, unavoidable scientific error. In the wake of those inquiries new safeguards were installed within the agencies that distribute grant money—the National Science Foundation and the National Institutes of Health—to increase the size and clout of the offices charged with investigating allegations of this type. A number of universities took similar steps.

The effectiveness of these changes has yet to be tested. Rep. Dingell's stated goal in pressing further investigations now, rather than waiting for that evidence, is to increase the level of awareness within the profession. The danger is that congressional chivvying of this kind, far from raising that awareness, will put scientists on the defensive and cause them to dig in their heels. That danger was in some evidence at the hearings, which have produced a certain amount of backlash and dismay. To the degree Rep. Dingell comes to appear to scientists to be persecuting Dr. Baltimore for no purpose, his ability to bring about changes in their outlook will necessarily be impaired.

Largest U.S. Oil Spill
Fouls Alaska Marine Habitat

The largest oil spill in U.S. history began at 12:04 a.m. Alaskan time (5:04 a.m. Eastern Standard Time) March 24, 1989 when the *Exxon Valdez*, loaded with 1,260,000 barrels of crude oil, ran aground on a reef in the Gulf of Alaska's Prince William Sound, 25 miles from Valdez, the southern terminal of the Alyeska pipeline.

The reef, Bligh Reef, was clearly marked, and the 987-foot tanker was off course, with the third mate, and not the captain, at the helm. The whereabouts of the captain, Joseph Hazelwood, at the time of the accident was not immediately explained. The third mate, Gregory Cousins, was not certified to pilot the tanker in those waters, Prince William Sound, a channeled crossing studded with icebergs.

A Coast Guard investigator found "probable cause" to have the blood of the captain, the third mate and the helmsman tested for alcohol, it was announced March 25. The results, announced March 30, were that the captain had unacceptably high levels of alcohol in his blood even nine hours after the accident.

Efforts to contain the spill lagged from the start. "The initial response was inadequate and didn't match the planned, outlined response measures to be taken in a spill," Dennis Kelso, commissioner of the Alaska Department of Environmental Conservation, said March 25. "As of 24 hours into the spill, we still haven't seen adequate containment."

Frank Iarossi, president of Exxon Shipping Co., which owned the *Exxon Valdez*, said March 25 that Exxon accepted full responsibility for the spill.

Estimates of the spill put it at 240,000 barrels. Another million barrels or so remained on the *Exxon Valdez* and were siphoned off into a companion ship. But in the first two days, when calm seas prevailed, little was done to contain the spill, which quickly covered a 12-square-mile mass inside a 100-square-mile area containing smaller slicks.

Winds of up to 70 miles an hour hit the area March 27. Containment booms were ripped apart, and attempts to use a chemical cleaning agent on the oil were abandoned. The *Exxon Valdez* itself shifted 12 degrees overnight, causing fears of a breakup and loss of the rest of the oil into the sound.

President George Bush March 28 dispatched a delegation of federal officials to the scene of the spill to survey the damage. "There is a sense that nobody is in charge there," a senior White House official remarked at the time. The slick, by then, had grown into a 40-mile-long patch, split into numerous fingers reaching out for the estuaries that harbored a multitude of marine life. The spill soiled islands and threatened the sound's $100 million-a-year fishing industry. (See pp. 202-205)

At the White House March 28, President Bush, announcing his team for an on-site inspection, was asked if the spill changed his position in support of exploratory drilling in the Alaska National Wildlife Refuge. Ten environmental groups, at a joint news conference the same day, urged the president to order an independent study on the possibility of developing the refuge without harm to the wildlife there. Bush said he saw "no connection" on that point. "They've been shipping oil out of there for a long, long time and never had anything of this magnitude or this concern," he said. "So the big thing is to correct it." (See pp. 154-157)

When the White House team reported back March 30, Bush called the oil spill "a major tragedy." But the administration decided against taking over the cleanup. Although it got off to a slow start, officials said, the cleanup was now proceeding well and a federal takeover would be "counterproductive."

Exxon official Iarossi was asked March 27 if the oil companies had been deceptive in their prior assurances of cleanup plans. When the pipeline and oil-port project was being debated, oil company officials had given assurances that action to contain a major spill would be underway within five hours of an accident, but it was two or three days after the *Exxon Valdez* ran aground before Exxon's part of the effort took shape. Iarossi said nobody had anticipated a spill of the magnitude that occurred.

Alaska state officials announced March 29 that they were beginning a criminal investigation of the accident.

Arkansas Gazette

Little Rock, AR, March 29, 1989

Big Oil's Big Spill in Alaska has happened, as many concerned about the environment had dreaded would be the case even before now Exxon's shipping people are busy trying to clean up the 100-square-mile slick after a slow start, and no doubt its public relations people are scrambling full speed ahead to control the political damage.

Even though the odds have favored a major environmental disaster since the opening of the North Slope fields, there is no reason this particular accident should have happened. So far, the investigation is concentrating on crew error as a possible cause, but the National Transportation Safety Board should not ignore the possibility that some blame could rest with those much higher in the petroleum giant, even those with policy responsibilities.

The 987-foot tanker, the Exxon Valdez, left the shipping lanes last Friday to avoid ice but ran aground on a charted reef in Prince William Sound after leaving the port of Valdez with 1.2 million barrels of oil from the North Slope. About 240,000 barrels of the crude were released into the sound. Grave threat is posed to wildlife and fish. Even if the spill is quickly contained the damaging effects will be felt for many years.

Monetary damages will be in the tens of millions of dollars, and unfortunately these costs will be widely shared. Already gasoline consumers throughout the rest of the country have seen prices rise simply because sellers jump in anticipation, or on the fiction, of an oil shortage. It is true that 20 percent of domestic production is from the North Slope, but shipments through Valdez have been resumed after only three or four days.

Big Oil has been getting a relatively smooth ride on environmental issues in recent years, but it — or Exxon — will have a lot of explaining to do after this incident. Congress simply must take a closer look at the proposal to allow exploration in the Arctic National Wildlife Refuge on a coastal plain east of the North Slope oil fields. President Bush already has given his approval — if the drilling can be done within environmental guidelines.

Sen. Max Baucus of Montana, chairman of the Senate environmental protection subcommittee, has raised a welcome and proper flag of caution:

"Unfortunately the oil spill . . . is the latest and most tragic evidence of the gap that exists between past industry assurances and actual industry performance in preventing environmental damage."

A heavy burden of proof showing there will be no environmental damage rests on the shoulders of Big Oil before the nation dare allow intrusions in the Arctic National Wildlife Refuge.

The Seattle Times

Seattle, WA, March 28, 1989

LEGISLATION to open the Arctic National Wildlife Refuge to oil exploration is coated with same 10-million gallons of North Slope oil that foul Alaska's Prince William Sound.

Jagged Bligh Reef shredded years of industry propaganda as it ripped open 11 of the 13 oil compartments on an Exxon supertanker. Technology, training and planning were supposed to prevent spills, or mitigate the damage, in the unlikely event they occurred. That has been the official line; it was wrong, but it may not matter. After all, the subject is oil.

A colossal failure of the triad resulted in a gloppy sea of crude oil threatening birds, marine animals and fisheries.

Also endangered is expanded oil drilling in other environmentally sensitive areas, especially the 1.5 million acres of coastal plain in the arctic refuge.

Editorial Research Reports

Again the industry's soothing mantra has been technology, training and planning. Nothing will happen, but if it does...

After a rash of tanker accidents a dozen years ago, investigators said improvements in navigation aids and ship construction were the key to preventing oil spills by supertankers. Number two was crew competency.

Improved technology was no help last Friday as a tanker crew ran its three-year-old ship aground on a reef outside normal shipping lanes.

Eighty percent of supertanker spills can be traced to human error, according to studies by the Coast Guard, National Academy of Sciences, the Office of Technology Assessment and the National Research Council, among others.

Once an accident happens, then what? Alaskan Gov. Steve Cowper and others are bitter about the delays in attacking Friday's record spill. Available crews and equipment were inadequate for the job. Planning was a joke.

Opening the 'arctic refuge is important to the oil companies to keep oil flowing through the port at Valdez as North Slope production drops.

For the future, questions must center on what will happen when spills occur the next time. Experience, newer technology and reams of contingency plans offer no protection.

How many 10-million-gallon spills can Prince William Sound absorb? The question is really an idle one, because the world has already said that keeping the petroleum flowing is more important than Alaska's environmental soundness.

Turning the pipeline flow at Valdez down to a trickle helped bump up the world price of oil a couple of dollars a barrel.

If that is the short-term effect, the ultimate decision about the coastal plain has been made. Drilling will occur eventually. How will everyone react when the catastrophe happens?

The Burlington Free Press

Burlington, VT, March 31, 1989

No penalities can compensate for the spread of 240,000 barrels of Alaskan crude oil into the pristine waters of Prince William Sound from the grounded supertanker Exxon Valdez.

Damage to a fishing industry that thrived on the sound until last week could easily exceed $100 million a year well into the 1990s. Birds are already dying. Sea Lions are trapped on islands surrounded by oil. Beaches are black with heavy crude.

The cleanup effort — if it can be called that — has been pathetic. Nearly a week after the ship struck a reef, less than 10,000 barrels of oil had been recovered. Attempts to mop up more have been abandoned. Only nature can do much about the damage now — and that could take 10 years or more.

The spill could not have come at a worse time for the oil industry. Heavily contested legislation is pending in Congress to permit oil exploration in Alaska's unspoiled Arctic National Wildlife Refuge. The Exxon Valdez accident supplies environmentalists with strong ammunition to refute standing oil industry claims that a major spill would not happen.

It did happen. It can happen again.

President Bush seems to see no relation between oil exploration and dangers to the environment. Sitting with a map of Alaska open on the Oval Office floor in front of him, the oil man turned politician said he saw "no connection" between the spill on the south coast and the pending authorization for more exploration in the north.

Congress has to resist that conclusion.

Instead, America needs to cure its oil dependence. Between now and 2000, U.S. energy consumption can be reduced by 20 percent through expanded use of existing technologies. Light bulbs that require less electricity and put off less heat — thus diminishing demands on air conditioning — are available now. More efficient industrial motors are also available now, and automobile fuel efficiency can be realized if Detroit's big car builders and the American people will accept smaller cars with less power.

For beyond the turn of the century, federal resources are needed now to expand research into renewable energy sources rather than increased oil exploration. Solar energy enjoyed a boom in the 1970s and fell from grace. But technologies have advanced that lessen solar's dependence on constant sunlight and expand the capacity for storing energy gathered from the sun. Recent advances in superconductivity also increase the capacity to get more power from less energy.

The oil industry ignores these advances and the potential for even greater advances. Instead, it has an easy answer to our future energy needs: exploit the Arctic National Wildlife Refuge. Easy answers, however, too often lead to difficult disasters.

Few of us will ever see the North Slope of Alaska. Yet its preservation should be as important to Vermonters as protection of the Green Mountains. Sens. Patrick Leahy and James Jeffords, and Rep. Peter Smith all mark themselves as environmentalists. They should work to prohibit oil exploration in the Arctic National Wildlife Refuge, and they should then push for expanded research into alternative means of satisfying America's energy needs in the next century.

That would be some compensation for the damage to Prince William Sound.

Newsday

Long Island, NY, March 29, 1989

Apart from handwringing, cleaning up the mess and demanding that those guilty of negligence be punished, what can be done about the devastating oil spill off the coast of Alaska?

Two things, it seems to us:

First, make sure that the potential for grave environmental damage isn't expanded in that fragile and unforgiving part of the world.

Second, create an international system for responding to environmental disasters such as major oil and chemical spills, no matter where in the world they happen.

Exxon's sorry response doesn't speak well for an industry that, when the Alaskan pipeline and the sea route linking it to the Lower 48 were approved, insisted something of this magnitude could never happen and that any spill could be contained within hours. The damage to wildlife, fisheries, tourism and to the entire region is incalculable at this point; the cleanup is likely to take months and not be very effective because of the remoteness of the area and its harsh natural environment.

The spill — the largest in U.S. history — has dimmed the outlook for Congress' approving oil exploration in the pristine Arctic National Wildlife Refuge. In light of what happened, why should we believe the assurances of the oil industry and the Bush administration that oil can be extracted and transported from the refuge without environmental harm?

The answer is: We shouldn't — and neither should Congress.

As for responding once something goes terribly wrong, how about an international clearinghouse, perhaps modeled after the one set up by a United Nations agency for the nuclear industry after the accident at Chernobyl? Notification of a nuclear accident anywhere sets in motion a system of information and direct assistance to the affected plant.

In the case of the Exxon spill, for instance, it's quite possible that help could have arrived sooner from the Soviet Union.

It's worth a try.

The Washington Times

Washington, DC,
March 29, 1989

Friday's mammoth oil spill off Alaska's south coast was not just an ecological disaster. It was also a shot in the arm for the environmental lobby and its congressional friends. Their goal is to sabotage Bush administration efforts to permit oil and gas exploration in a small portion of the Arctic National Wildlife Refuge, located in Alaska's North Slope — more than 900 miles away from the accident scene. Their success would harm the nation as a whole as well as Alaskan Eskimos who stand to benefit from energy development in ANWR and who strongly support the project.

Until Friday morning, environmentalists had provided no real evidence that 20 years of drilling and exploration in other parts of the state have hurt the environment. In nearby Prudhoe Bay, often cited by environmentalists as an apocalyptic example of what could happen if exploration is allowed in the ANWR area, the caribou herd has tripled in size since oil activities began in 1968.

"The fact that billions of barrels of oil have been produced and transported from Prudhoe Bay while the area's fish and wildlife resources continue to thrive" bodes well for such activities in the 19 million-acre ANWR, according to the Interior Department. Drilling in the area would occur in only 12,650 acres, less than one percent of the region. Even under the administration's plan, roughly 18 million acres would be managed as wilderness, meaning virtually all human activity would be banned.

Eskimos in the region are among the strongest supporters of ANWR exploration. One is Oliver Leavitt, vice president of the Arctic Slope Regional Corporation of some 3,700 Eskimos. He says that as a result of energy exploration activities in his area, natives "for the first time in history" have schools, jobs, decent housing, electricity, fire protection and, in some villages, running water and sewer systems. He adds that his people have those benefits because the area's oil development creates jobs and a solid tax base for local government.

America also needs ANWR's energy resources to offset creeping dependency on foreign oil. The Interior Department estimates that as many as 9.2 billion barrels of oil — equivalent to 20 percent of total U.S. production — are available in the area. U.S. imports jumped from 1.8 billion barrels per year in 1982 to an annual rate of 2.9 billion last month, an increase of nearly 60 percent.

While the administration is pushing a bill to allow oil exploration in ANWR, groups such as the Wilderness Society are fighting to stop it in Congress. The Senate Energy Committee approved the measure last week, with two lousy amendments included. One authored by Sen. Mark Hatfield calls for a "national energy plan." Sen. Bennett Johnston wants to use ANWR royalties to help Washington acquire new public lands.

Exxon is certain to pay through the nose for the spill, and it ought to. But its errors offer no sound reason to cut off energy exploration in ANWR. The Senate should kill the Johnston and Hatfield provisos and pass the administration's ANWR bill. And the oil companies ought to be put on notice: One more spill like this, and you'll do more to damage energy exploration than the Luddites have ever accomplished.

The Providence Journal

Providence, RI, March 29, 1989

As the pictures of oil-blackened birds come in from Alaska's Prince William Sound, two questions need to be asked about the accident of the tanker Exxon Valdez: Why did it happen? Why did it take so long for a response?

Investigations and blood test results will be forthcoming: As of now we know that the ship captain, Joseph J. Hazelwood, was not in command of the 987-foot supertanker when it ran aground. In his place was the third mate, a man uncertified for commanding the vessel in those waters.

So it is already clear that some negligence was involved: the third mate's commanding of the ship was a clear violation of both company and federal regulations. Adding some suspense to this violation are the reports that Captain Hazelwood has a history of drinking and driving.

The fault at sea was compounded by grievous inaction on land. According to contingency plans, a response is to be launched within five hours of an accident. Containment and removal equipment did not arrive until ten hours after the spill, apparently because the barge for transporting them was undergoing repairs. The president of the Exxon Shipping Co., Frank Iarossi, has been unable to give any valid explanation as to why there was no backup plan.

The failure to respond immediately is lamentable for two reasons. One, it undermines public confidence in Exxon and — by extension — the other shippers of Alaskan oil who have consistently offset environmental concerns with assurances that they have plans to contain spills within an adequate time frame. If such a plan does indeed exist, why was it not promptly and efficiently executed? Clearly two investigations are needed: one into the cause of the accident, the other into the reasons for the delayed response.

The other regrettable aspect is that the scope of the spill (at 240,000 barrels, it is the largest ever in North American waters) demanded speedy attention. Heightening the concern were both the location and the time of year of the accident. Prince William Sound is exquisitely rich with marine life, some of which is especially active now: herring are spawning and a number of seabirds are in the middle of their spring migrations.

The damage to these and other forms of wildlife, as well as to such staples for Alaska as the fishing and tourism industries, will take some time to be mended. In the meantime, increased attention must be focused on ship safety and preparedness for spills. For it is these two items — and not, as some environmentalists and members of Congress have suggested, oil drilling — that are at fault and should be in question. We do not blame the cow when a milk truck hits a guard rail. Likewise, it is not the production of oil but its proper transport that needs to be addressed.

FORT WORTH STAR-TELEGRAM

Fort Worth, TX, March 30, 1989

Spills happen. A truck attempts to negotiate a curve at too fast a speed, and it overturns, spilling some hazardous cargo. A train's crew makes a mistake, and some of its cars derail, sending toxic chemicals onto the ground. A tanker runs aground, spilling millions of gallons of oil into the water.

Spills happen. When they do, lives are put in jeopardy, fish and wildlife and their habitats are put at risk, shorelines are contaminated and damage caused by them — to the extent that such damage can be calculated — can require decades to assess.

Yet the spills go on and happen so often that there is some acceptance that they are inevitable, as if they cannot be stopped or sharply reduced, as if the environment — and those who depend upon it — somehow will recover and survive their effect, no matter how devastating.

This less-than-diligent attitude, this lack of due care must stop. The Exxon Valdez, with its Alaskan oil spill, should rally people's concern and outrage to the point that they shout: Enough!

The ship's owners can assume blame and survey the damage and scrub the beaches and employ every oil spill cleanup technique in the book, and may-be add some new ones. The U.S. government can rush in to help. But that will not correct a basic fault at work in these spills: insufficient concern and oversight — spurred by the threat of sufficient penalty — to keep them from happening.

Whether spills result from an overturned truck moving through a city, a wrecked railroad car moving through a town or a ship ripping its hull as it moves through ocean waters, sterner measures must be taken to command the constant, undivided attention of those who own and operate the transports. It is blatantly obvious that whatever rules and penalties are now in place are insufficient to the task.

Penalties for such spills must be as harsh, deep and long-lasting as the damage they inflict upon the environment. The penalties must hurt to the quick and convey a clear, unmistakable message that those who send these vehicles up and down the land and across the waters stand to lose much of what they claim as their own unless they constantly make sure that both the equipment and its operators are in sound condition and that prudent rules are in place and rigidly enforced.

Let the word go out: The irresponsible are dispensable; the environment and those in it are not.

The Salt Lake Tribune

Salt Lake City, UT, March 29, 1989

It might control any tendency toward hysteria, when considering last week's Alaskan oil spill, to put the dumping of those 262,000 barrels of crude oil into some sort of perspective.

When the Ixtoc I oil well, located in the Southern Gulf of Mexico, blew out on June 3, 1979, some 4.4 million barrels of crude oil were spilled. That's nearly 17 times the amount of oil dumped into Prince Williams Sound when the tanker Exxon Valdez ran aground.

While the Prince Williams Sound spill is the largest ever in the United States, it ranks only 12th on a list of 20 large oil spills around the world over the past 20 years compiled by Reuters News Agency. In other words, the Alaskan oil spill might well be classed as a middle-class sort of disaster.

It is also worth remembering that these large oil spills, while causing extensive environmental damage and considerable economic havoc, tend to be largely self-limiting. In a few years, initial devastation is generally mitigated.

A typical example is the Torrey Canyon disaster of March 18, 1967, when that tanker ran aground off Lands End, England, and 919,000 barrels of oil were spilled, making it 6th on the Reuter's list. Widespread damage to marine life was reported. But within three years, most traces of the spilled crude had disappeared and biological studies showed the affected area's marine life was again abundant.

This isn't to say that the situation in Prince Williams Sound doesn't portend immediate and severe environmental and economic impacts.

The local fishery will suffer as large numbers of fish and shellfish are destroyed by the Exxon Valdez' spilled cargo.

There, too, are going to be sizable numbers of ducks and other waterfowl killed when they become covered by the floating crude. And it has yet to be determined what kind of damage will result to shoreline vegetation and wildlife when some of the crude washes ashore.

These and other damages, triggered by the running aground of the Exxon Valdez, tend to be confirming evidence of the dire predictions of environmentalists opposed to construction of the Aleyeska Pipeline, exploitation of the North Slope oil fields and use of Valdez as the southern terminus of the pipeline.

What gets lost in this tumult is a very significant fact: thousands of tankers, including the Exxon Valdez, have repeatedly transited Prince Williams Sound without incident. Since Aug. 1, 1977, when the tanker Arco Juneau weighed anchor with the first load of North Slope crude, more than 6 billion barrels of oil have been safely shipped out of Valdez.

This praiseworthy record was compiled because oil and tanker companies have adhered strictly to some exacting operating rules when sailing to and from Valdez. That is, they did until the Exxon Valdez ran aground on March 24.

It has become abundantly clear, as acknowledged by executives of Exxon Shipping Co., the tanker subsidiary of the parent Exxon, that an inexperienced third mate, instead of the properly licensed skipper, commanded the Exxon Valdez when she ran aground, splitting her hull and loosing those 262,000 barrels of crude.

Already Exxon Shipping has assumed liability for damages resulting from the grounding of its tanker. This assures that fishermen will be appropriately compensated for their lost catches, as will be other people damaged by the disaster. Exxon will also pay all cleanup costs.

Television pictures of that 100-square-mile oil slick, photos of crude-covered ducks and the instinctive protests and laments of Alaskans directly affected by the oil spill trigger a lot of hand-wringing about the future of Prince Williams Sound.

Experience indicates such doomsaying is misplaced.

Areas damaged by oil spills have a consistent record of recovering on their own, as nature works her healing. Also the record of those 6 billion safely shipped barrels of crude resoundingly rebut the frantic demands of the hysterical that the port of Valdez should be closed to future oil shipments.

In a few years the damage done to Prince Williams Sound will have largely been repaired, provided there are no future oil spills. When Exxon tabulates the final cost of the Exxon Valdez accident, it is a safe bet that other oil companies are going to be especially diligent in making sure their tankers are properly mastered, at all times by licensed skippers, on voyages in and out of the port of Valdez.

The Birmingham News

Birmingham, AL, March 15, 1989

The Senate Energy Committee is once again expected to approve a bill that would open an Alaskan wildlife refuge to oil drilling, but it may suffer the same fate as a similar bill the committee backed last year.

Last year's bill never made it to the Senate floor. This year, Sen. Dale Bumpers, D-Ark., says he intends to "hold this bill hostage in exchange for a national energy policy."

The Senate should move forward to allow limited drilling in the Arctic National Wildlife Refuge. With proper controls on oil and gas operations, technology and nature can coexist on Alaska's North Slope.

Supporters of drilling in ANWR point to the growth of caribou herds in neighboring Prudhoe Bay as evidence that wildlife can be protected. Environmentalists, however, want the wilderness area permanently off limits to drilling.

Opponents of the drilling legislation believe their case is bolstered by a leaked draft report from the Environmental Protection Agency that cites several cases of toxic and oily drilling fluids being discharged onto the tundra. But the EPA itself has disavowed that report as "not an objective portrayal," and operations on the North Slope have improved.

That report and other anecdotes about mishaps in Alaskan oil and gas exploration underscore the obvious truth that no exploitation of natural resources occurs without some potential for harm to the environment. But the legislation proposed in the Senate keeps the risk to a minimum, and the trade-off in energy potential is well worth the risk.

As for the insistence on a national energy policy, that could delay drilling in the icy ANWR until hell freezes over. No consensus on energy policy appears likely, and the prospect of letting a government policy dictate energy decisions is far from comforting anyway.

The delay in winning congressional approval for oil and gas leasing in ANWR may have had the good effect of causing environmental standards to be refined and strengthened. But now it is time to approve this step toward energy independence for the good of all Americans.

St. Paul Pioneer Press & Dispatch

St. Paul, MN, March 29, 1989

The oil-spill catastrophe in Alaska's Prince William Sound confronts President Bush with a pivotal test of environmental intentions.

Five days after the Exxon Valdez ran aground, it had gushed 11 million barrels of oil into the waters and it was still leaking into a fouled and angry sea. This disaster to the windy, marine-life-rich place, where the mountains drop off the craggy water's edge, follows the oil industry's longstanding assurance that its cleanup plan could contain a major spill in five hours. With that pipeline dream turned to a worst-case nightmare, the president has sent top lieutenants to make a reliable accounting of what went so terribly wrong just out of the port of Valdez.

The immediate job facing Transportation Secretary Samuel Skinner, Environmental Protection Agency Administrator William Reilly and Coast Guard Commandant Paul Yost is to evaluate the situation at Valdez and decide the federal government's role in damage control. After the urgent tasks are attended to, Mr. Bush's men will recommend whether to seek sanctions and fines against Exxon, which assumed responsibility for cleaning up its own mess but has been unable to do so. Some piercingly pointed questions are in order from the federal government.

Why couldn't Exxon or the Alyeska Pipeline Service Co., the consortium that runs the Alaska pipeline, make good on the claims of five-hour disaster control? What must be done to prevent the nightmare from recurring? And is the environmental risk worth the payoff in this source of domestic energy?

In simplest terms, the wreck of the Exxon Valdez was caused by human error. A man not licensed to run the hulking monster was in charge. There are other tangles to the tale, but a person or persons aboard the ship caused the accident.

Yet, there are wider causes: the genuine demands of economic development, the national amnesia about the perils of cheap oil, the failure to confront energy policy comprehensively. It is these issues that will fall to President Bush if he wants to make a meaningful evaluation of environmental risks in relation to energy needs.

If wasted fishing waters and frozen, oil-soaked birds on Prince William Sound bring any constructive message, it is to strive for a national energy policy that transcends Exxon's excuses or the I-told-you-so's of environmental purists. There is only one skipper who can steer Supertanker America to a better place.

St. Petersburg Times

St. Petersburg, FL, March 31, 1989

Back in the mid-1980s, top executives of Exxon Corp. decided that they could save some money by reducing their staff of experts on oil spills. When other Exxon employees, including the company's highest ranking environmental officer, complained about the cutbacks, they were invited to leave, too.

This week, confronted with the monumental task of cleaning up the disastrous *Exxon Valdez* oil spill in Prince William Sound — a task for which they clearly understood themselves to be legally obligated — Exxon officials suddenly discovered that they couldn't even pretend to muster the manpower and equipment required for an adequate response. That admission flew in the face of Exxon's arrogant refusal to accept previous offers from the city of Valdez, as well as local fishermen and other concerned residents, to help stockpile the supplies needed to deal with a major spill.

Exxon wasn't simply unprepared to deal with an oil spill once it occurred. Other corporate actions, or inaction, helped to make a spill all but inevitable. After having lobbied aggressively for years to overcome widespread opposition to the Alaska Pipeline project, Exxon officials proved themselves unwilling to take the steps required to allay the legitimate environmental fears of the pipeline's opponents. Instead, they created the lax transportation system in which an unqualified, unsupervised third mate could find himself placed in the position of navigating more than a million barrels of oil through one of the world's most delicate channels.

Workers for other companies in the area are now telling anyone who will listen that they often witnessed open, mass drunkenness among crew members boarding the *Exxon Valdez*. Exxon officials either never managed to gather that same evidence for themselves, or they never bothered to act to correct obvious safety violations on and around the *Exxon Valdez* once they were aware of them.

In short, these and other corporate decisions made by top executives of Exxon had the effect of increasing the risk of a catastrophic oil spill — and decreasing the chances that a spill could be controlled once it occurred.

These were human decisions, although the humans who made them typically hide behind the armor of their corporate identity. Exxon executives are every bit as responsible for their actions as the officers of the *Exxon Valdez* are responsible for theirs. Yet, predictably, those beginning to ascribe blame for this disaster have focused almost exclusively on the possible drunkenness of the ship's master, or the possible negligence of its third mate. Lowly ship's officers find their names on the front pages; lordly Exxon executives who worked to make the pipeline a reality, and who helped to make the transportation of oil from Alaska even more dangerous than it had to be, remain comfortably anonymous.

Throughout the misguided search for this accident's lowest common denominator, attention has been diverted from the human beings who created, and profit most handsomely from, this multibillion-dollar network in which a single miscalculation by its weakest link — a frightened 25-year-old, or an inebriated 45-year-old — can cause an environmental disaster of historic proportions.

The buck hardly stops at Exxon's corporate offices. The decision to go forward with the Alaska Pipeline project was made in Washington, and the federal government bears ultimate responsibility for protecting our nation's environmental resources. Yet the Bush administration refuses to assume control of a life-or-death clean-up effort for which Exxon has proved itself deficient. Attempting to justify his office's inaction, Transportation Secretary Samuel Skinner announced that the clean-up "is going at full speed," even though it is retrieving only about 1,000 barrels a day of the 240,000 barrels spilled into the water. And President Bush himself insists that he perceives "no connection" between this worst oil spill in our history and the continuing debate over the possible exploration and development of Alaska's Arctic National Wildlife Refuge.

The Bush administration's almost blithe response to this environmental tragedy leaves little hope that the ruin of Prince William Sound will lead to a tough and honest re-evaluation of our corporate and governmental obligations to our shorelines. If recent history is any indication, a few low-level functionaries — perhaps even an inanimate piece of machinery — will be held accountable for this case of widespread irresponsibility. At worst, Exxon will pay a fine that can be passed on to its customers as the corporate officials in charge of the Valdez operation return to business as usual. President Bush probably won't even suffer any serious political damage as a result of his administration's ineffectual reaction. Only the rest of us — most tragically, the people and ocean life dependent upon the purity of America's last frontier — will suffer the real consequences of a man-made disaster born of corporate greed and governmental cowardice.

Chicago Tribune

Chicago, IL, March 28, 1989

Alaska runs to extremes. From its size to its climate to its natural and human resources, almost nothing about the 49th state is small-scale. So, too, with its calamities, now including the nation's biggest oil spill.

But that dubious achievement in consistency is no comfort in the aftermath of the Exxon Valdez's disgorging of 250,000 barrels of North Slope crude into Prince William Sound very early on Good Friday morning. The tanker was 25 miles out of Valdez, southern end of the 800-mile Alaska pipeline, and was outside normal shipping lanes to avoid ice when it struck an undersea reef.

At that point the damage was done; all else is anti-climax, to be settled to varying degrees of satisfaction by the National Transportation Safety Board investigation; by efforts to confine or disperse the oil, which the Coast Guard estimated affected 100 square miles; and by assessing the damage to mammals and fish, especially herring and salmon.

Gov. Steve Cowper has declared the wildlife-rich sound a disaster area, saying, "This oil spill may well be the greatest disaster to hit Alaska since the Good Friday earthquake 25 years ago."

Why was the uncertified third mate in command of the tanker when it ran aground? Were crew members under the influence of alcohol or other drugs? Did cleanup efforts begin soon enough? (Environmentalists, the governor and other state officials say no.) How much compensation will Exxon Shipping Co. pay fishermen for lost income? These are among the questions sure to be addressed, but another set might prove more difficult.

When the tanker was breached, so was the delicate energy-environment balance that seemed to be holding in Alaska. For all the dire warnings that preceded construction of the Alaskan pipeline, the exploitation of North Slope oil has not meant serious environmental degradation. Until now. Can amicable coexistence be restored? And how is the I-told-you-so crowd to be refuted? Or is it?

Answers, if any, will be imperfect, like the human factor present in cases such as this oil spill. Those involved in restoring balance need to go to extremes in environmental recovery, not recriminations, and in future precautions, not excess caution—all in the knowledge that no system is fail-safe.

The Des Moines Register

Des Moines, IA, March 28, 1989

The lumps in the blackness are the bodies of waterfowl trapped in the worst oil spill ever in the United States, a dismal chapter in ecological history bought to you courtesy of Exxon.

Loss of the birds is only the start of the impact of the disaster that big oil promised America would never happen — could never happen. Now the oil giant's response — predictably — is to try to shift the focus of the nation's outrage onto the drinking habits of a couple of its employees.

Big oil, which now all but admits it can't control or dissolve the 10-million-gallon-plus spill, would like nothing better than to dissolve instead the public's attention. But it matters little whether the pilot was qualified to guide the huge tanker — longer by 258 feet than the fabled Edmund Fitzgerald — through the hazardous waters off Valdez on Alaska's south coast. Nor will it help much to learn whether someone in charge was drinking.

Fear of just such a spill was one of the major objections in the 1970s to piping oil from the North Slope of Alaska to the sea at Valdez. The oil industry said it couldn't happen. It did. In the unlikely event that such a thing could happen, Exxon promised, it would respond within five hours. It didn't.

Far more than a beautiful bay has been blackened. If nature can someday restore the pristine nature of Prince William Sound, after sacrificing its sea and air creatures to man's stupidity, it will take far longer to restore credibility to the oil industry.

Exxon Shipping Company President Frank Iarossi has said repeatedly that his firm will compensate fishermen and others for their losses. Like most ecological disasters, this is one that money can't undo. There are some injuries that expensive medicine can't heal.

The grounding of the Exxon Valdez gives a new perspective to the Alaskan oil debate — particularly the current question of opening new fields in the Arctic National Wildlife Refuge.

Bush Pledges Help in Alaska Oil Spill

President George Bush April 7, 1989 pledged federal assistance to clean up the massive oil spill in Alaska flowing from the grounding of the tanker *Exxon Valdez* on March 24. (See pp. 196-201)

At a news conference, the president said he would send troops, military equipment and other federal assistance to help in the cleanup. The spill, of some 240,000 barrels of crude oil, extended over thousands of square miles in Prince William Sound, off the port of Valdez, and into the Gulf of Alaska proper.

"Exxon's efforts, standing alone, are not enough," Bush said in reference to the owner of the stricken vessel. He predicted that a cleanup would be "massive, prolonged and frustrating."

More than two weeks after the accident, only a small percentage of the spill had been recovered, largely because of a lack of equipment, such as booms, skimmers and pumps.

"There's not much more equipment here now than there was after the spill," Larry Dietrick, Alaska director of environmental quality, remarked shortly after Bush's announcement of help. Reports from fishermen on the scene April 5 were that the cleanup effort was chaotic at best. By April 12, the cleanup remained "a slow, chaotic effort," according to the *New York Times*. The federal role remained "a minor one" in the field, the report said, and the U.S. armed forces promised by Bush were "nowhere to be seen."

The main federal contribution reportedly was an airlift bringing Exxon's equipment to Alaska. The Coast Guard, on the scene from the beginning, also had seven cutters providing support services to the cleanup operation.

Adm. Paul A. Yost, Jr., commandant of the Coast Guard, who was assigned by Bush to oversee the cleanup effort personally, arrived in Valdez April 13. "We are going to be at this thing not for days, not for weeks but probably for months," Yost said on his arrival.

Rear Adm. Edward Nelson, commander of the Coast Guard forces in Alaska, had told a town meeting in Valdez April 11 that "we will not be bringing in massive numbers of troops." The remark was greeted with some applause from local residents who were assisting Exxon in cleanup tasks for high wages.

As of April 12, only 18,000 of the 240,000 barrels of oil spilled had been recovered, and it was estimated that at least a third of the spill had traveled into the Gulf of Alaska.

A storm, rather than containment booms or other cleanup efforts, was credited with keeping the spill from invading rich fishing grounds near Kenai Peninsula and Kodiak Island, although the same weather threatened to drive the oil past booms set up to protect Sawmill Bay, site of one of the three Prince William Sound salmon hatcheries.

At the outset of congressional hearings on the disaster April 6, Transportation Secretary Samuel K. Skinner told the House Merchant Marine and Fisheries Committee that "the contingency plan in place, and approved by the various state and federal offices, was not nearly adequate to deal with the problem."

"We have to do better," he said.

L.G. Rawl, chairman of Exxon Corp., apologized for the spill and assured the panel that "Exxon takes full responsibility and has done so from the beginning."

The Honolulu Advertiser
Honolulu, HI, April 8, 1989

Many people are in mourning over the catastrophic oil spill killing fish and wildlife along Alaska's coastline. So they might want to know that "ghost nets" and floating plastic debris take a much larger toll, each and every year.

In northern waters alone, some 30,000 fur seals and at least 250,000 birds die each year in these encounters, according to one paper given at the Second International Conference on marine debris held here this week.

Significant amounts of plastic debris have been found on all Pacific islands visited, even the uninhabited ones. It washes in and out again with the currents. Abandoned nets, line fragments and packing straps go on entangling marine life and, occasionally, damaging vessels. Plastic bags and plastic bits are fatally swallowed.

The International Convention for the Prevention of Pollution by Ships now prohibits the sea discharge of plastics and requires all ports to have disposal facilities. The U.S. implementing legislation is the Marine Plastic Pollution Research and Control Act of 1987. Up for approval in the Hawaii Legislature is a bill to ban plastic six-pack yokes and other non-biodegradable holders.

But the effectiveness of these measures obviously depends on voluntary compliance. The search is on for ways to reduce waste and encourage recycling and the substitution of biodegradable materials. National coastal cleanups also have taken tons of debris out of circulation. Hawaii has participated.

We can support these efforts by lobbying and by proper trash disposal. And next time you see plastic containers, rope and net fragments on the beach, don't think of them as harmless. Do your bit for some bird, turtle, fish or sea mammal by picking some of that stuff up.

THE SACRAMENTO BEE
Sacramento, CA, April 7, 1989

Will the damage from the Alaskan oil disaster spread from Prince William Sound to cripple the federal government's hopes for expanded domestic oil production? Interior Secretary Manuel Lujan warns that it could if a popular image of the oil industry as "uncareful and uncaring" takes root. But from Exxon's terrible example, it is possible to discern the outlines of a prescription for making sure this kind of accident doesn't happen again and for restoring public confidence in the process.

The Environmental Protection Agency is already reviewing the entire system of Alaskan oil regulation. But while that's certainly desirable, the record in Valdez suggests that there may not be a need for more regulations so much as for stricter enforcement of the rules already on the books. If the state of Alaska and the Coast Guard had been enforcing the standards and using the authority that the law already gives them, no disaster of this magnitude might ever have occurred. Now that the spill has shocked state and federal regulators into renewed diligence, perhaps the work will at last begin on detailed contingency plans for handling the kind of major accident that the oil companies have always insisted couldn't happen.

A lot now depends on Exxon's performance in the cleanup to come. The damage that this one company's bumbling has already done to the industry will grow even worse if Exxon is seen to be dragging its feet when it begins trying to live up to its promises to mitigate the impact of the spill and provide compensation where the damage has already been done. At the same time all of the oil companies operating in Alaska should begin picking up the other piles of rubbish and hazardous waste that they've left to fester on the landscape — a problem they've neglected for more than a decade already.

Clearly there's a need as well to overhaul the laws on liability for oil spills. The current limit of $100 million for cleanup costs and undefined economic losses is so low that some experts fear that it may actually encourage companies to cut costs on safety on the theory that it would be cheaper in the long run to pay for the damage from a major accident than try to prevent it. A ceiling on potential liability is appropriate in order to encourage continued exploration — but the costs that a company should have to bear need to be set high enough to ensure that, in effect, they'll never have to be assessed.

Finally, the federal government needs to take a much closer look at the rules governing tanker shipments from the end of the pipeline at Valdez. This has always been recognized as the most vulnerable element in Alaskan oil development, and the one posing the greatest risk of long-term environmental damage.

When construction of the pipeline was first proposed, then Interior Secretary Rogers C.B. Morton promised that all of the ships at Valdez would be built with double hulls to minimize the risk of leakage in a collision. But double-hulled tankers can't carry as much oil and cost about 10 percent more to build, and the Coast Guard, under pressure from the oil companies and their maritime affiliates, backed down from fulfilling Morton's promise. Establishing such a requirement now may not be the only thing that can be done to make shipping safer, but it's the right place to start.

DESERET NEWS
Salt Lake City, UT, April 7, 1989

Utah motorists are shocked and angered by gasoline prices that have jumped 20 to 25 cents a gallon in just the past two weeks. Given the facts in this instance, they have every right to be upset.

The price hikes are supposedly linked to the oil spill in Alaska, but that is the flimsiest of excuses. There are no real shortages despite a brief interruption in the Alaska oil flow.

It's true there was speculation about oil shortages in the wake of the Exxon tanker disaster off the Alaskan coast. And it's true that two oil companies have limited gasoline deliveries to distributors in Western states this week.

But that doesn't add up to justification for large price hikes.

The oil companies put limits on gasoline deliveries, not because there is any shortage, but because some Western wholesalers began "excessive" purchases of gasoline last week. The lid was put on to stop hoarding.

Shell Oil Co. spokesmen officially denied that the rationing was imposed because of shortages. Chevron Corp. said its limits were imposed in anticipation of panic buying, not because of a lack of normal supplies.

How strict is the rationing? Not very. Wholesalers who purchase from Chevron are limited this month to the same amount they bought in April a year ago. Shell buyers are being held to 90 percent of their April 1988 purchases.

Major West Coast refineries rely heavily on Alaska oil to make gasoline. After the tanker oil spill, the pipeline flow from Alaska's North Slope to the shipping port at Valdez was cut from 2 million barrels a day to 800,000 barrels because the spill limited tanker loadings.

However, the pipeline flow has since returned to normal.

So how can wholesalers justify major price hikes to retailers? The oil industry is in danger of compounding its reputation for environmental ineptitude with one for price gouging.

Portland Press Herald
Portland, ME, April 11, 1989

Senate Majority Leader George J. Mitchell has added his voice to those critical of the Bush administration's delay in taking over the massive Alaskan oil spill cleanup.

To assure rapid action, Mitchell proposes that presidents be squarely responsible for initiating major oil spill cleanups. Only when a president carefully determines private industry can do the job would the federal government fail to step in.

That approach shows promise. For one thing, it makes the line of responsibility clear. Cleanups can be started while lawyers hassle over an oil shipper's financial liability or lack of it.

For another, it recognizes the unique power of presidents to rapidly mobilize manpower and equipment far beyond those available to any private company.

Since President Bush called for the military to join the cleanup late last week, military experts have been pouring into Prince William Sound with skimmers, booms and other equipment. They represent men and equipment badly needed during the first crucial days after the tanker Exxon Valdez went aground March 24 and began spilling 10 million gallons of oil into a fertile fishing ground.

Finally, presidential leadership would force both the public and private sectors to face up to the catastrophic environmental damage a single giant oil tanker can cause. That too was missing this time in Alaska. A contingency plan developed last year by the oil company consortium that owns the Trans-Alaska Pipeline dismissed planning for such a catastrophic spill as "not useful in long-term response planning."

A president knows better.

4/6/89. THE PHILADELPHIA INQUIRER.
UNIVERSAL PRESS SYNDICATE.
AUTH

EXXON

"COVERS THE EARTH"

ALBUQUERQUE JOURNAL

Albuquerque, NM, April 8, 1989

It has been more than two weeks since the supertanker Exxon Valdez did the unimaginable, striking a clearly marked reef and spilling 10 million gallons of crude oil into Alaskan waters. For most of that time, the Bush administration appeared unable to imagine the full scope of what happened, or what needed to be done.

Finally, President Bush has stopped acting as if the national emergency in Prince William Sound requires a cautious response.

At a news conference Friday, Bush announced that military personnel will assist Exxon in its agonizingly slow cleanup efforts. More important, the president agreed to have the Coast Guard take over direction of the cleanup in the field. Exxon will remain in charge of contracts and purchases.

Alaska Gov. Steve Cowper pleaded with the Bush administration earlier in the week to put the Coast Guard in charge of the oil cleanup, but Bush dragged his feet. As the slick spread and the winds shifted towards shore, officials in Washington labored over a compromise that would allow the Coast Guard to play a larger role, but still not take complete charge of the cleanup. Precious days were lost.

Bush's concern, which he repeated at the news conference Friday, was that he did not want to "federalize" the cleanup operation. Why not? Who is better equipped than the federal government to take charge in a national emergency? Certainly not a private company — Exxon has demonstrated that. Despite its best efforts, Exxon has only managed to clean up 7 percent of the oil it spilled.

If the unimaginable happens again, few Americans will want the crisis to be handled the way the Alaska oil spill has been. A national emergency requires a swift, federally coordinated response.

Chicago Tribune

Chicago, IL, April 11, 1989

It may seem like more of too little, too late, but it is welcome nevertheless that President Bush has ordered U.S. military personnel and equipment into the mission to clean up the Alaskan oil spill. At this point, the priority must be minimizing further damage from the disaster, and the military will be invaluable in helping the citizen volunteers trying to salvage the shoreline and marine life victimized by the spill.

It is welcome, too, that the President has put Transportation Secretary Samuel Skinner and his Coast Guard in charge of coordinating the cleanup operation, without actually taking it over. It is acknowledgment that the federal government shares Alaska's distress over the oil industry's response to the spill, and firm notice that the Exxon Corp. will not be relieved of its responsibility and liability for the calamity.

Skinner's first job will be to insure that the cleanup proceeds more effectively. He already has outlined the more fundamental, future job: that from the disaster, the goverment and the oil industry forge a more realistic, reliable contingency plan for dealing with spills of this type.

The industry, Skinner noted, was complacent about anticipating a disaster of this magnitude and being ready with the means to deal with it.

That is understatement. Of the 240,000 barrels of oil that gushed into Prince William Sound when the Exxon Valdez crashed onto a reef, only 18,000 have been recovered. The rest oozes inexorably onward into the Gulf of Alaska, now covering some 2,600 square miles and threatening the Kenai Fjords National Park.

The battle to halt it seems lost, and probably was lost in the early hours of the spill when Exxon and the Alyeska Pipeline Service Co., the oil company consortium, did not move quickly enough or with enough equipment to contain it. Whatever the reason, it was insufficient response to an inexcusable incident.

Exxon has been appropriately contrite about the disaster and the tarnish it has put on an industry already viewed with skepticism by the public. Its job now, besides bearing the burden of the cleanup, is to help restore trust by leading the industry to the guarantees that will insure that this will not happen again.

The Hartford Courant

Hartford, CT, April 6, 1989

The worst oil spill in U.S. history has set up a battle between George Bush the West Texas oilman and George Bush the environmentalist.

So far, the oilman seems to be winning.

That's disappointing, because Mr. Bush sounded good, and scored points, on the campaign trail last fall, when he lamented polluted harbors and littered beaches and promised to be "the environmental president."

The 11-million-gallon spill from an Exxon Corp. tanker in Alaska's Prince William Sound put Mr. Bush to the test.

As the oil slick spread, the president sent three administration officials, including the head of the Environmental Protection Agency, for a firsthand look. What followed, however, indicates a president remarkably detached in the face of an environmental disaster of unprecedented magnitude.

The administration decided not to assume command of the cleanup even though everybody except Exxon officials say the oil company was slow to start and has not done the containment job that should have been done.

Mr. Bush seemed to make light of possible measures to prevent future oil spills. "Here you have a ship that runs up on a reef at 12 knots and driven by somebody, or under the command of someone, who had been under the influence. I'm not sure you can ever design a policy anywhere to guard against that," the president said.

The president also said he would not reassess his approval of plans to drill for oil in the Arctic National Wildlife Refuge. Because the United States is becoming increasingly dependent on foreign oil, he said, placing new restrictions on exploration and the transport of domestic oil "isn't acceptable."

A proper balance can be struck between the protection of the environment and the nation's energy needs, but Mr. Bush doesn't seem to be balancing interests.

An environmental president would not throw up his hands and say no policy can be devised to prevent such oil spills. A Coast Guard officer said a child could have piloted the Exxon Valdez through the several-miles-wide channel without running aground on a well-marked reef.

The president should have demanded to know why Exxon didn't have a crew sober enough or competent enough to do the job, and why Exxon was so woefully unprepared for the cleanup job. Mr. Bush should have insisted that federal or state authorities begin monitoring tanker crews more closely and called for stiffer penalties for negligence. He could have used his office's powers of persuasion to demand that the state of Alaska and the oil companies henceforth have emergency equipment available to begin cleanups immediately in the event of another accident.

Mr. Bush should have called for an assessment of the environmental impact of oil production, not just exploration, in the Arctic wildlife refuge. In the wake of the Exxon Valdez accident, Congress is almost certain to delay action on the bill permitting drilling.

The point is that the president should have sent a message that he was angry about the accident and concerned about the damage the oil spill has caused to the livelihood of Alaskans and to the environment. The people of Valdez and surrounding communities deserve no less. But Mr. Bush seemed more interested in sending the message that domestic oil producers have nothing to fear from his administration no matter what lessons are learned in Prince William Sound.

On the campaign trail, Mr. Bush sounded like Teddy Roosevelt. As president, he sounds like James G. Watt. That may be overstating the case, but the burden is on the president to prove that it's not so.

The Boston Globe

Boston, MA, April 7, 1989

By all the laws of man and the sea, the skipper of the Exxon Valdez must be held responsible for whichever of his actions, and inactions, were the proximate cause of the ecological disaster in Prince William Sound.

But by no stretch of the imagination can Capt. Joseph Hazelwood be considered, as a New York state prosecutor has put it, the "architect of an American tragedy."

Tragedy it has become, and its architects are many, but none of them were on board the Valdez two weeks ago this morning, and they have not been charged, hauled into a court and held overnight in jail.

Those architects include:

● The Exxon executives who decided to build the Valdez without a double bottom.

● The US officials who thwarted congressional intentions that tankers be required to have double bottoms.

● The Coast Guard officials who approved a radar system that could not track the Valdez as it swerved toward Bligh Reef.

● The Alyeska Pipeline Service Co. executives who disbanded a round-the-clock emergency oil-spill team.

● The Alaska officials who acquiesed in that Alyeska decision.

● The oil industry officials who have refused to step up research into oil-spill technology and have failed to establish oil-spill-response teams.

● The underlings in the Coast Guard and at Exxon and Alyeska who failed to take decisive action in the first hours after the Valdez went aground.

Judge Kenneth K. Rohl of New York's State Supreme Court is described as an ardent environmentalist whose courtroom is decorated with duck decoys he carved. In setting $1 million bail for Captain Hazelwood, he said (with inappropriate hyperbole) that there had been "a level of destruction" in Prince William Sound "we've not seen since Hiroshima."

It might be instructive to get the real architects of that destruction into his courtroom.

The Oregonian

Portland, OR, April 9, 1989

Oil companies have stomped down on the accelerator, pushing gasoline prices up 12 cents in eight days. That may justifiably outrage Portland-area consumers. But that also could be a blessing in disguise if those consumers apply the brakes — a reawakened energy conservation ethic.

Texaco, Shell, Arco and Mobil all began to increase wholesale prices to dealers here almost immediately after the tanker Exxon Valdez grounded March 24, spilling 240,000 barrels of crude in Alaskan waters. Yet, it is weeks before the summer, high-consumption price hike ordinarily begins. And, the oil now being delivered to pumps has been in transition from the wells and through the refineries for months. It isn't directly related to the accident.

Wholesalers' actions should jog consumer memories of even higher prices and the long lines at pumps in the early 1970s during the oil embargo by the Organization of Petroleum Exporting Countries.

Did we learn anything? Apparently little, for today the United States is even more dependent on overseas oil than it was then.

Moreover, Congress and the White House have let Detroit automakers drag their collective feet on increased fuel efficiency for Americans' great love, the autombile. That may be changing with the Bush administration. Transportation Secretary Samuel K. Skinner last week expressed alarm at both the nation's growing dependency on foreign oil and pollution impacts.

Increasing auto fuel efficiency standards by one mile per gallon for two model years would reduce carbon dioxide emissions by 18 million tons over the lifetime of the cars, according to Transportation Department figures. Skinner wants to end Detroit's complacent cruising and increase fleet requirements from today's average of 26.5 miles per gallon to 27.5. Some Democrats in Congress would go further, demanding 30 mpg by the mid-1990s and 45 mpg by the turn of the century.

The preview of coming unattractions in the aftermath of one tanker spill should renew support for requiring increased fuel efficiency of automobiles. It should make the Portland City Council rethink Mayor Bud Clark's proposed cuts in the city's energy conservation commitment. And it surely should generate legislative support for financial help for transit.

Three Major Oil Spills Foul U.S. Waters

Three major oil spills occurred within 12 hours June 23-24 in Rhode Island, Delaware and Texas. The incidents, coming only 12 weeks after the U.S.'s worst ever oil spill in March in Alaska's Prince William Sound, heightened public concern over environmental damage from oil-laden vessels. (See pp. 196-201)

The spills aroused doubts anew about the oil industry's ability to deal with such major accidents, despite the industry's unveiling June 20 of a program created to prevent spills and to contain and clean up those that did happen.

The latest disasters started at 4:40 p.m. June 23 when a Greek tanker, *World Prodigy*, ran aground on a reef in Narragansett Bay near Newport, R.I., spilling 420,000 gallons of fuel oil, a refined, light oil that was toxic but evaporated quickly. Oil containment booms were deployed around the ship within four hours after the accident, but the heating oil was difficult to contain. The area included rich fishing and shellfish grounds.

A harbor pilot, Capt. David Leonard, reported June 26 that he was on his way to guide the tanker when he saw the vessel running outside the marked channel and heading into dangerous waters, where she struck the reef. The oil dispersed quickly and large amounts had evaporated by June 26, officials said. The tanker was refloated and secured June 25.

At 6:20 p.m. June 23, a Panamanian-registered freighter, *Rachel B.*, collided with an oil-carrying barge in the Houston Ship Channel, spewing 250,000 gallons of heavy crude oil into Galveston Bay. Wind and waves forced the spill largely into a smaller channel, however, and much of the oil was suctioned up by huge vacuums. About two-thirds of the spill had been recaptured by June 26, according to a Coast Guard spokesman.

Early June 24, at about 4:00 a.m., a Uruguayan tanker left the shipping lane and hit a rock in the Delaware River near Claymont, Del., dumping 310,000 gallons of heating oil that stretched rapidly into a 20-mile slick. The ship, the *Presidente Rivera*, was refloated early the next day. Delaware Secretary of the Environment Edwin Clark said June 25 that "the standard response failed" in attempting to contain the spill. But no widespread damage to fish or wildlife was immediately detected. Members of the Delaware National Guard pitched in to help in the cleanup.

The industry's plan to cope with spills was announced at a news conference June 20 by Allen E. Murray, chief executive of Mobil Corp. and chairman of an industry study group formed after the Alaska spill.

Murray conceded, in the aftermath of the Alaska accident, that "the industry has neither the equipment nor the response personnel in place and ready to deal with catastrophic tanker spills."

He promised that the new program "will provide new environmental protection wherever tankers operate in U.S. waters."

The program called for the establishment of five regional "response centers" sited on the East and West coasts and the Gulf of Mexico, plus 15 "staging areas" for storage of containment and cleanup equipment.

Efforts were to be undertaken to improve tanker safety and navigation in ecologically sensitive waters. Research would be done on safer tankers and more effective equipment and procedures for cleaning up spills. The program was expected to cost the industry $250 million in its first five years of operation. The industry looked to the U.S. Coast Guard to assume overall responsibility for coordinating the cleanup operation on major spills.

The Evening Gazette

Worcester, MA,
June 27, 1989

The oil industry is quick to rush forward with fine-sounding plans to prevent spills and to clean them up should they occur. But actions speak louder than words, and the actions we have witnessed the past few months lead to the conclusion that all of the plans in the world are for naught when tanker crews decide to take shortcuts.

On the heels of the Exxon Valdez disaster in Alaska comes the recent grounding of the World Prodigy on Brenton Reef off Newport, R.I. Two other serious spills occurred last weekend in Delaware and Texas.

The bottom line? Personal responsibility.

Had tanker captains followed the rules, there would be no oil slime on some of the beaches of Prince William Sound or Narragansett Bay.

The Rhode Island spill never should have happened. There is no excuse for the irresponsible actions of the tanker captain who did not wait for the required coastal pilot before entering the shipping lanes off Newport. He should be punished.

Ballard Shipping Co., owner of the tanker, should foot the bill for the cleanup, which already stands at $300,000.

The spill could have been worse, although that is small comfort. The tanker spilled 420,000 gallons of heating oil, which is lighter than crude oil and evaporates quickly. Environmental damage is being reported, with dead lobsters, lobster larvae and fish eggs, oil-fouled beaches and floating slicks. But the damage is expected to be minor compared with the devastation to Prince William Sound.

What is most incredible is that the disastrous Alaska spill seems to have failed to awaken a sense of responsibility and caution among those most involved with the delivery of this vital commodity. Even more important, the oil and shipping industries must set and adhere to strict standards. Negligent crew members must be made to answer for their actions.

By the same token, port officials and other maritime authorities must act decisively and consistently against irresponsible companies and crew members. Those who flout safety laws must be made to pay — and not just when they leave environmental disaster in their wake.

Herald News
Fall River, MA, June 28, 1989

Three significant oil spills occurred over the past weekend, in Delaware, Texas and Newport. Newport's, at first, seemed the worst. On Friday afternoon, the Greek tanker World Prodigy, with a full load of No. 2 home heating oil from Bulgaria, ran aground on Brenton Point, ripping two giant gashes, 200 and 150 feet long, in the steel hull.

The spill quickly extended about 20 miles northward into Narragansett Bay, threatening fish and waterfowl, and posing a special danger to small lobsters and fish fry, as well as to the workers who spent hours trying to clean up the slick. The lobster larvae and new-hatched fish bob on the surface of the water and can't swim fast enough to escape the spreading poisonous film. Heating oil is more volatile that crude oil; it can penetrate human skin and damage the liver.

Rhode Island Gov. Edward DiPrete mobilized the National Guard. At first, the spill was estimated at a million and a half gallons, but, by Monday, the estimate had dropped to some 420,000 gallons. Nature gave unexpected help with an unusual north wind, which drove the slick back toward the mouth of Narragansett Bay. Key saltmarsh areas, like Round Swamp on Conanicut Island, escaped major damage. Containment booms were installed near the mouth of the Narrow River. Salt marshes are nurseries of marine life. Once the oil permeates such delicate ecosystems, it can kill and contaminate for years.

South County beaches were closed Saturday, but all except the sands of Point Judith were reopened Tuesday. Much credit goes to the prompt action of the cleanup team. Federal officials, including Manuel Lujan Jr., Secretary of the Interior, Environmental Protection Agency administrator William K. Reilly, and Richard Breedon, assistant to President Bush, arrived on the scene, bringing pledges of help from "every resource of the federal government."

As it turned out, the impact on Newport waters was far less disastrous than the Exxon Valdez spill that clobbered Alaska in March. But much of Narragansett Bay's escape from long-term damage was a matter of luck — boom containment, the lighter nature of the fuel, and prompt off-loading of the tanker's remaining cargo. Reilly observed the available technology would not have been adequate to deal with an ocean spill of really major proportions.

Three significant coastal spills within two days give the oil industry a bad name, despite its world-wide scope and blue chip financial clout. The Ballard Shipping Co. of Athens has enough insurance to pay for the cleanup, but why didn't Capt. Iakovos Georgoudis hire a licensed Rhode Island harbor pilot, as required by law? Was it economy — or a touch of what the ancients called "hubris" — that made the helmsman steer doggedly into the wrong side of the channel? "That's my mistake," he gallantly admitted.

But how many such 'mistakes' can our coastal environment afford?

Despite the American Petroleum Industry's claims and promises, the actual record of spill cleanup is getting worse and worse. Neither the industry nor government seem committed to preventive measures.

Ed Tennyson, research scientist for the federal Minerals Management Service, evaluates Big Oil's current cleanup technology in terms of "having a quarter-inch lawnmower working on a 40-acre field."

Arkansas Gazette
Little Rock, AR, June 28, 1989

The Exxon Valdez disaster remains the granddaddy of oil spills in United States waters, but three separate spills in these waters last weekend were hardly minor events. Luck as much as effort kept the trio of accidents from getting out of control.

Luck was especially in evidence in Narragansett Bay off Newport in Rhode Island. The Greek tanker that rammed a reef and ripped its hull released 420,000 gallons of lightweight fuel oil, much of which evaporated. Some of it reached shore, where crews quickly cleaned the mess, and lucky winds carried the remainder out to sea. Long-term effects should be minimal.

Near Houston, a collision released 252,000 gallons of thicker oil into waters that some wags already contend are so polluted they will ignite should someone toss a lighted cigarette into them. Quick action there sucked up most of the oil, despite heavy winds and rain.

The most damaging spill, involving 800,000 gallons of heavy oil, was in the Delaware River above Wilmington. Crews are still busy gathering large blobs of oil that have threatened wildlife and fisheries.

The response by the Coast Guard and others was fairly prompt on these spills, but in the aftermath the governors of New Jersey, Delaware and Pennsylvania called for tougher laws on industry liability for damage from spills. Congress has such legislation before it. Every delay in enactment just puts the country more environmentally at risk.

The Duluth News-Tribune
Duluth, MN, June 22, 1989

The nation's oil companies have announced welcome plans to create a network that can respond to a major oil spill in five hours or less.

The plan would establish five regional "response centers" staffed by specialists able to react to spills as large as 200,000 barrels. There will also be 15 "staging areas" where clean-up equipment would be stored and maintained.

The Coast Guard would be given authority for clean-up responsibility and for drug and alcohol testing of tankers' crew members.

The industry intends to spend $250 million on the network.

Environmentalists called the plan "a step in the right direction" but weren't entirely satisfied. The initiative, however, should be applauded and given time to prove itself. The network of sites appears to be well-balanced and the Coast Guard is the logical government arm to hold the reins it would be given.

It's unfortunate that it took a major disaster to prompt this plan, but any preventive action is welcome.

The Exxon Valdez, recall, ran aground in March, spilling millions of gallons of oil that fouled Alaskan beaches and extracted a heavy toll in clean-up costs and wildlife loss. The oil industry was criticized for its inability to respond quickly to such a disaster.

The announcement coincided with several actions this week on Capitol Hill relating to the oil industry, including a Senate committee's approval of a bill to establish tough contingency plans in the event of a spill and a bill that would make oil firms bear full cost for a clean-up.

An American Petroleum Institute spokeswoman said the timing of its announcement was coincidental to House and Senate action.

We share environmentalists' skepticism on that; legislative — and public — pressure can be a strong motivator for an industry lax in self-governing responsibility.

We're skeptical, too, of the petroleum industry's stated intent to absorb the entire $250 million cost of the plan. Spokesman Allen Murray said those costs would not be passed on to consumers. Tell that to the driver weary of continually rising pump prices.

AKRON BEACON JOURNAL
Akron, OH, June 29, 1989

FOUR OIL SPILLS in a matter of weeks, three within a day and one the worst ever in the United States, have alerted Americans to the deceptions practiced by the oil industry.

For years, oil executives have claimed that technological advances make it possible to clean up most oil spilled in offshore accidents. The recent record, however, suggests otherwise. Weather can wreak havoc on recovery plans; the wind can blow in the wrong direction; the seas can be too high. But even in the best conditions, on average, about 10 percent of the spilled oil is retrieved.

Most independent experts agree that the current technology can cope with spills of 100,000 gallons or less. The four recent accidents have all involved at least 350,000 gallons of oil; the Exxon Valdez spilled 11 million gallons off Alaska. Containment booms and oil-skimming boats haven't been up to the task. Off Rhode Island last week, the booms were in place within four hours, but the crews couldn't contain the slick.

Chemical dispersants have been ineffective, failing, according to one study, 94 percent of the time. Moreover, they can be more toxic to the surrounding environment than the oil. Still, even if the technology was effective, many would question the industry's commitment. Too often equipment isn't on the scene in the first critical hours.

The oil industry has announced a $250 million program to improve its response time and support research into spill control. The effort should include better training and oversight. Crew carelessness, it seems, played a part in the four recent accidents.

Washington also has a responsibility. The federal government's spill-research lab has been drastically reduced. Congress has already begun to consider stiffer financial penalties for oil spillers, which would provide a greater incentive for safety. Double hulls on tankers, in the words of one government expert, "can make the system just a little more idiot-proof."

Perhaps most controversial is the future of offshore drilling. The country has become increasingly dependent on foreign oil. Still, until significant improvements in safety and recovery are made, it simply isn't worth the risk of damaging ecologically fragile areas. The amount of oil that could be tapped at these sites is a small fraction of the total Americans use. Indeed, effective conservation would save far more oil than will likely ever be found offshore.

The recent oil spills have served a warning. The country must look carefully at how it transports oil at sea and how much it uses.

THE SUN
Baltimore, MD, June 27, 1989

In a postscript to the Exxon Valdez disaster, the waters of the Delaware River, Narragansett Bay and the Houston ship channel were befouled this past weekend by three major oil spills. If Congress and the White House needed added proof that aggressive action is required to retrain tanker crews, put them in stronger ships and beef up oil spill response capabilities, this is it. Maryland legislators should be in the forefront of this campaign — there is no body of water more vulnerable to an ecological catastrophe than the Chesapeake Bay.

The latest accidents, like the Valdez crackup, were probably the result of human bungling. This should underscore the warning issued only a week ago by Capt. Jerry A. Aspland, president of the huge Arco Marine tanker fleet, that "we need a complete reexamination of how the human being becomes a master or an officer" of an oil tanker.

Agreed. Long years of experience do not compensate for an alcohol habit. Centuries of maritime tradition are no substitute for the high-tech know-how needed for operating modern ships carrying toxic cargo. Yet however important the human factor may be, this is far from a complete answer to the menace at hand.

President Bush's spokesman said yesterday that the petroleum industry should give much higher priority to the development of chemical dispersants capable of dissolving spilled oil safely. This, too, is only a partial answer. Contrary to earlier industry claims, dispersants have been of only marginal effectiveness in dealing with this year's disasters. Moreover, the chemicals now in use often damage the environment.

Only days before the latest spate of accidents, Senate and House committees were finishing up various bills to require double-hulling of oil tankers, a huge expansion in liability funds to compensate for damages and costs of clean-up, a sharp increase in the amount of equipment available for fighting oil spills and mandatory testing of tanker officers and crew for drug and alcohol abuse. All this is laudable, as is the industry's own new program to fight a problem it once downplayed.

As the nation reacts to these oil spills, it should not go on a rampage against domestic oil drilling and exploration. The fuel spilled in Narragansett Bay and the Delaware River this past weekend was imported stuff. It had to be brought to these shores to power our modern industrial system. The issue, therefore, is not so much the dangers of oil production as the need to make oil transport as accident-free as possible. The airline industry does a pretty good job flying people safely. There's no reason why the oil and maritime industries can't do a better job moving petroleum safely.

The Wichita
Eagle-Beacon
Wichita, KS, June 24, 1989

THE 11-million-gallon Alaska oil spill on March 24 showed the whole world that the U.S. oil industry knew next to nothing about responding to massive oil spills rapidly and effectively.

While the Exxon Corp. was trying to figure out an effective way to fight it, the spill spread throughout Prince William Sound, coating hundreds of miles of shoreline, contaminating all manner of wildlife and ruining the livelihoods of thousands of people. This created a terrible public relations problem for the industry — fueled, in part, by the accompanying gasoline price hikes.

Now, the industry has announced a promising three-part program to limit the environmental damage done by future U.S. oil spills. But any good the announcement does the industry's image may be offset by its insistence, before the Senate Finance Committee, that oil companies should get tax write-offs for oil-spill cleanup costs. This would be whether the cleanups were effective or not.

The program, unveiled Tuesday by an industry task force set up two weeks after the Alaska spill, has to be taken seriously: It would sink $130-170 million of the oil industry's own money into preventing, containing and cleaning up U.S. oil spills. It would put the Coast Guard, not the oil industry, in charge of future cleanups. Once the program's centerpiece — a Petroleum Industry Response Organization with five well-equipped and staffed regional response centers — is in place, it's unlikely another massive spill would catch the industry napping, as it was caught at Valdez.

But in opposing a bill that would prevent Exxon from taking tax deductions for the cost of the Alaska cleanup until it meets federal clean-water standards, the oil industry insults people's intelligence. As the bill's sponsor, Sen. Harry Reid, D-Nev., notes, the industry effectively is claiming that ordinary taxpayers "owe millions of dollars in a tax rebate in return for destroying the environment."

Corporate tax deductions, after all, cover ordinary and necessary business expenses. The Alaska spill certainly wasn't ordinary or necessary: It's impossible to justify Exxon's cleanup costs — which could reach $500 million — any other way. Mr. Reid rightly proposes that Exxon — and, by implication, companies responsible for future catastrophic spills — be allowed to deduct spill costs only after the Environmental Protection Agency and the Coast Guard certify that the Prince William Sound cleanup meets federal environmental standards.

In any case, if the new oil-spill program works as advertised, massive spills will become less common, and whatever cleanups are necessary should have little trouble meeting environmental standards. If the oil industry truly wants to win the public's goodwill, it should drop its quest for tax breaks for sloppy cleanups.

Bill Day — Detroit Free Press / Tribune Media Services

Endangered Sea Creatures...

San Francisco Chronicle

San Francisco, CA, June 27, 1989

THE EXXON VALDEZ produced the nation's worst oil disaster, but three new spills provide evidence that the nation's shorelines are still in peril. After more than 10 years of debate, Congress has not reached an agreement on a federal cleanup program.

It would be handy if the problem of oil spills could be solved by simply blaming the whole thing on the Valdez, which was finally towed out of Prince William Sound three months after fouling Alaskan waters. But in a two-day span nearly 1.5 million gallons were spilled when the Greek tanker World Prodigy struck a well-marked reef near Newport, R.I.; the Uruguayan Presidente Rivera strayed from a clearly defined shipping channel south of Clayton, Del., and the Panamanian Rachel-B struck a barge in the Houston Ship Channel.

As Carl T. Hall of The Chronicle's Washington Bureau reported, the House Merchant Marine and Fisheries Committee has approved legislation to impose a tax of 1.3 cents per barrel of oil to finance a federal cleanup fund. The bill is criticized because it would limit the ability of states to impose penalties and place a $60 million ceiling on the amount oil companies would have to pay for most spills.

But as Representative Doug Bosco, D-Sebastopol, said, it is better to accept "the politics of the possible" than hold out for an ideal bill which has no chance of passage.

THE LONGER CONGRESS lingers, the greater will be the economic damage. The protection is especially important for San Francisco Bay, which has experienced many serious oil spills and which can expect more in the future.

THE DENVER POST

Denver, CO, June 27, 1989

OIL SLICKS are polluting U.S. shores — a repugnant sight that should anger all Americans, not just residents of coastal states. Despite industry claims that tanker spills are rare, four such disasters recently fouled waters off Alaska, Texas, Delaware and Rhode Island. Three of these spills occurred last weekend — within 24 hours of each other.

The causes of these accidents are under investigation. However, it appears sloppy industry practices and lax regulatory enforcement contributed to all of them.

Investigators have raised questions about drug and alcohol abuse by crewmen and officers. Two of the accidents might have been avoided if an experienced harbor pilot had been aboard to help navigate the giant vessels.

Shipping companies may be deliberately understaffing the tankers to save money. There also has been confusion over whether unqualified personnel are performing critical duties.

The U.S. Coast Guard, too, has closed marine traffic control systems to trim its budget.

A shipping industry group has proposed setting up five emergency response centers around the country to speed the cleanup of future spills. But those response centers would do nothing to prevent an accident from happening in the first place.

Congress, the Coast Guard and other regulators must implement — and enforce — new rules to prevent spills.

Traffic control centers should be expanded, upgraded and given the authority to issue direct commands to ships' captains. All tankers should be required to have a qualified pilot aboard before approaching or leaving any port. Shipping companies should be required to maintain an adequate crew size before being allowed to sail in U.S. waters.

The Coast Guard should be given the manpower, facilities and authority to enforce these new rules. That means, of course, that Congress would have to shore up the Coast Guard's budget.

But investing some funds now could prevent future oil spills, and, in the long run, prove much less expensive in protecting America's beaches and waters.

The Chattanooga Times

Chattanooga, TN, June 27, 1989

Nothing will undo the disastrous oil spill of the Exxon Valdez and the widespread environmental damage it caused. The effects will be felt for years to come. Still, the plan proposed by the oil industry last week to contain future spills is both a welcome and necessary response.

It came too late, of course, to be of assistance in responding to three major oil spills last week. These new spills occurred in just two days and reminded us that many areas of our nation are vulnerable. They fouled waters and beaches and threatened marine life in Rhode Island, Delaware and Texas.

Moreover, no one should be lulled into complacency by the industry plan proposed. It was offered not out of altruism, but rather in propitiation and to blunt pending restrictions being considered by Congress. It cannot be allowed to substitute for the aggressive regulation needed to limit the potential for future such catastrophes.

The oil industry has not had a change of heart; merely a change of perception. Just a few years ago, when profits slumped and the Alaska pipeline had flowed over the initial humps, oil companies cut costs by whacking spill containment programs — personnel, training and equipment.

Had the safety valve been in place when the Exxon Valdez ran aground, much of the spill of 260,000 barrels of oil might have been prevented or contained. Instead, hundreds of miles of shoreline and hundreds of square miles of open water were ruinously fouled, poisoning fishing areas and killing mountains of animal, fowl and sea life.

Now the oil industry is weighing its responsibilities against the cost of public hostility and restrictive legislation. A congressional subcommittee, for example, is working on a plan to delay for at least a year all oil and gas leasing off the entire California coast and parts of the coasts of Florida, Alaska and New England. And 59 congressmen have signed a letter urging the government to sue Exxon for the full costs of environmental damage and cleanup in federal areas. Rep. Robert G. Torrecilli, D-N.J., is advocating broad liability exposure for all spill damage.

It is in that context that the plan must be weighed. Still, the industry plan would establish a containment program that even the Natural Resources Defense Council, a national environmental lobby, concedes would make some long-needed improvements. It would establish a national response organization and regional centers manned to handle spills the size of the one at Valdez, staging areas at 19 sites to store response equipment and a $30 million research program on cleanup technology.

While the industry group would supply equipment and labor, the plan asks that the Coast Guard coordinate the response in event of a spill. This could have been a confidence-building measure, but for the Coast Guard's own ineptness in its Valdez role. Nevertheless, it is a clear delineation of who is in charge.

All this is necessary, but it doesn't quite go far enough. Still needed is tough regulation that mandates — as is required for nuclear-energy plants — regular, graded, full-response drills and rules that ensure adequate training, equipment and team deployment and funding. This is the crucial element of effective risk management.

Unless and until the government mandates and oversees such a program, the cost of the industry's "voluntary" containment program will eventually become too attractive a target for some future budget-cutter lulled to complacency by the absence of disaster. It is human nature. It happened before, and we shouldn't let it happen again.

PORTLAND EVENING EXPRESS

Portland, OR, June 22, 1989

Finally, one good result from the Alaska oil spill: The big oil companies are collectively organizing equipment and men into a rapid reaction force to deal with major spills. They plan to spend $250 million on it over the next five years and will not — they say — pass the cost on to consumers.

With Portland listed as one of 19 national "staging areas" for booms, skimmers, chemicals and other cleanup gear, our region gains additional protection against spills — and we need it. Portland transships 50 million to 60 million barrels of oil a year.

By contrast, the Exxon Valdez spill was 260,000 barrels.

The oil companies, including Exxon, say they'll place the oil equipment and response teams under the overall direction of the U.S. Coast Guard, which has its own additional teams and equipment.

The staging areas will be supplemented by six regional response centers, the closest being New York. They'll be staffed to handle spills up to 200,000 barrels.

The oil companies also propose to spend more on better navigational control for tankers in coastal waters and develop safer tankers and better spill-control equipment.

Critics say the firms are taking these steps to deflect lawmakers from cracking down on liability requirements.

They also worry that future spills could swamp even this plan, because the Exxon Valdez spill, though the biggest in American history, was only a small portion of that tanker's cargo.

Still, these proposals would increase the nation's ability to handle spills both in terms of equipment and the leadership to use it well.

The oil companies may be being forced to demonstrate a responsible concern for the environment and the national good. But as long as they are, let's be grateful.

DESERET NEWS

Salt Lake City, UT, June 28/29, 1989

If Americans seriously thought more evidence besides the Exxon Valdez disaster was needed to justify tougher laws to prevent and clean up oil spills, they now have it.

It comes in the form of no less than three major oil spills the past weekend involving Delaware, Rhode Island and Texas.

But the additional evidence should not have been needed. Last year alone, the Coast Guard reports, there were some 7,500 oil spills in the ocean, of which 250 were serious enough to require federal intervention.

In any event, let's hope these latest unhappy episodes breathe new life into congressional efforts to replace a hodgepodge of widely varying laws in 24 states plus four underfinanced federal laws with a uniform, tougher, better-funded new national law on liability and compensation for oil spills.

But there's still no justification for the proposed moratorium on petroleum drilling in various offshore and other environmentally sensitive areas. The moratorium would merely make America more dependent on foreign oil, which would require more shipping of oil and thus increase the risk of oil spills. Two of the three spills this past weekend involved imported oil.

Even more helpful than a new federal law would be stepped up research to develop more effective methods of dealing with oil spills.

Although such methods have been somewhat improved, experts agree that the basic technology of dealing with oil spills has not fundamentally advanced in two decades.

The White House thinks the petroleum industry should give a higher priority to the development of chemical dispersants capable of dissolving spilled oil. But there are limits to what science can accomplish. Present dispersants are only marginally helpful. More effective dispersants could harm the environment as much as spilled oil. No wonder that decisions to use dispersants are often delayed.

Instead, how about routing tankers away from ecologically fragile shorelines even though the longer routes involved would add to the price of oil and gasoline? How about requiring double hulls on oil tankers to make these ships less prone to spills? How about getting tougher in enforcing the rules on how oil tankers are to be handled? And how about building more oil pipelines in an effort to eliminate some of the tankers?

FORT WORTH STAR-TELEGRAM

Fort Worth, TX, June 23, 1989

The oil industry's proposal for preventing, containing and cleaning up major oil spills was a quick response to the catastrophic Exxon Valdez Alaskan spill and offers a commendable starting point for corrective action. It is, however, only a starting point.

Congress, which ultimately is responsible for deciding how best to proceed, must exercise stringent oversight both in mapping an anti-oil spill strategy and in supervising its implementation and operation. That effort must include sufficient potential punitive damages against oil companies to ensure that they pay attention, follow the rules and do not harm the environment.

Congress has been lax in that regard, and the Exxon Valdez incident bears that out. The ship's pilot has been accused of being intoxicated, and serious questions have been raised about qualifications of crew members and enforcement of ship operating standards.

The petroleum industry's proposal takes aim at many of these shortcomings. It recommends such steps to improve tanker operations as higher qualifications and better standards for harbor pilots; an expansion of Coast Guard authority to permit effective drug and alcohol testing and treatment of crew members; and the addition of automatic-pilot alarm systems aboard tankers.

A major component of the plan includes an industry response organization that would establish five regional centers — staffed around the clock and fully equipped — which would be prepared to act quickly in the event of major oil spills and which would follow the leadership of the Coast Guard and the Secretary of Transportation.

Also, a new research and development program would be set up to control and mitigate spills.

Congress should commence with the proposal but be prepared to go far beyond it if necessary to make sure that the chance of oil spills is greatly diminished or, if they do occur, that they are more quickly, more expertly and more completely cleaned up.

Congress also must make sure that the oil company responsible is held more accountable, including liability not only for actual damages but also severe punitive damages for environmental harm arising from its negligence.

THE SACRAMENTO BEE

Sacramento, CA, June 23, 1989

The oil companies' joint proposal to set up five new response centers around the country to coordinate supplies for a major offshore oil spill certainly marks a welcome and long-overdue change of heart from an industry that has been trimming back on its commitments to public safety and environmental protection for many years. But it's only a start. In light of the Exxon disaster in Alaska, this proposal by itself is hardly enough to restore confidence in the industry's competence or clear the way for expanded offshore development.

What was perhaps more important than the details of the new plan at the industry's press conference the other day was the admission by a spokesman for the American Petroleum Institute that the problems aren't limited to Alaska or to Exxon — that no one is currently prepared to deal with one of these disasters anywhere in the United States. According to Allen E. Murray, president of Mobil, "The industry has neither the equipment nor the response personnel in place and ready to deal with catastrophic tanker spills."

That kind of candor makes a refreshing change. And the oil companies are making some other important concessions in this proposal. Among other things, the report acknowledges that there have to be improvements in shipboard technology, and it calls for new studies on the need for double-hulled tankers, a significant retreat from the bitter opposition the oil companies have raised to any such improvements in structural design until now.

But critics are right that the industry proposal falls short when, for example, it suggests that the new coordinating centers should plan for a spill no larger than 200,000 barrels. The Exxon Valdez dumped 260,000 barrels and that ship was lucky enough to be able to hold onto 80 percent of its cargo. Still, as a measure of how far the companies have to go to achieve a significant measure of public safety, their proposal to plan for 200,000 barrel spills is certainly a big improvement over their current disaster planning, which imagines nothing worse than a spill of only 2,000 barrels.

Any voluntary effort by the oil companies to improve their readiness to deal with the predictable consequences of the next inevitable oil spill certainly has to be counted as an advance. But California Rep. George Miller, a leader in Congress' investigation of the Exxon disaster, is right when he points out that the safety standards the industry should be required to meet in the future, and the other lessons that have been learned from what happened in Prince William Sound, need to be nailed down in law, not left to trust and the good faith of an industry that has failed tragically to live up to its promises before now.

THE CHRISTIAN SCIENCE MONITOR

Boston, MA, June 28, 1989

THE tanker spills in Rhode Island's Narrangansett Bay, the Houston ship channel, and the Delaware River are small puddles compared to the Exxon Valdez disaster. But they underscore, in triplicate, the safety and preparedness issues raised by the Alaska spill.

Prince William Sound's mucked-up beaches and dead wildlife exposed the emptiness of oil-industry claims that its spill-containment capabilities were adequate. The acquiescence of state and federal governments, in allowing less than stringent cleanup readiness, was brought to the surface too.

Experts doubt that the equipment and techniques available today can effectively deal with much smaller spills, much less something on the order of the 11 million gallons of crude drained from the Exxon Valdez. An oil recovery rate of only 2 to 10 percent is usual for spills.

Environmental damage from the more recent accidents is still being assessed, but valuable sea life such as young lobsters and fish will certainly be affected.

Just as certainly, Congress is going to push even harder for measures to avoid future oil-spill tragedies. Expanded oil drilling in sensitive areas like the northern California coast and Alaska's Bristol Bay will be resisted. Government-funded research on oil-spill technology, which has rapidly dwindled in recent years, will find advocates. Safety precautions like double hulls on tankers will be championed.

The Senate Commerce Committee last week approved an oil-tanker safety bill mandating double hulls on new ships. Industry protests about the cost of such improvements have swayed government decisions in the past, but they are less likely to prevail now.

The oil industry, in fact, has come up with its own proposals for dealing with spills. It plans to spend $250 million over the next five years creating five regional response centers and boosting spill research.

In prior years, the sense of urgency in these matters has tended to fade with the headlines. Financial incentives to go easy on safety can quickly reemerge and dominate. That shouldn't be allowed to happen now.

Index